T0318577

Internet and Digital Economics
Principles, Methods and Applications

How are our societies being transformed by Internet and digital economics? This book provides an accessible introduction to the economics of the Internet and a comprehensive account of the mechanisms of the digital economy. Leading scholars examine the original economic and business models being developed as a result of the Internet system, and explore their impact on our economies and societies. Key issues are analyzed, including the development of open source software and online communities, peer-to-peer and online sharing of cultural goods, electronic markets and the rise of new information intermediaries, e-retailing and e-banking. The volume examines how Internet and digital economics have transformed the organization of firms, industries, markets, commerce, modes of distribution, money, finance, and innovation processes, and provides the analytical tools to understand both these recent transformations and the likely future directions of the "New Economy."

ERIC BROUSSEAU is Professor of Economics at the University of Paris X.

NICOLAS CURIEN serves as Commissioner for the French Regulation Commission for Electronic Communications and Postal Services (ARCEP). He is also Professor of Economics at the Conservatoire National des Arts et Métiers, Paris.

Internet and Digital Economics

edited by

Eric Brousseau and Nicolas Curien

CAMBRIDGE
UNIVERSITY PRESS

CAMBRIDGE
UNIVERSITY PRESS

University Printing House, Cambridge CB2 8BS, United Kingdom

One Liberty Plaza, 20th Floor, New York, NY 10006, USA

477 Williamstown Road, Port Melbourne, VIC 3207, Australia

4843/24, 2nd Floor, Ansari Road, Daryaganj, Delhi - 110002, India

79 Anson Road, #06-04/06, Singapore 079906

Cambridge University Press is part of the University of Cambridge.

It furthers the University's mission by disseminating knowledge in the pursuit of education, learning and research at the highest international levels of excellence.

www.cambridge.org
Information on this title: www.cambridge.org/9780521671842

© Cambridge University Press 2007

First published 2007
First paperback edition 2008

A catalogue record for this publication is available from the British Library

Library of Congress Cataloging in Publication data
Internet and digital economics / edited by Eric Brousseau and Nicolas Curien.
    p. cm.
    Includes bibliographical references and index.
    ISBN-13: 978-0-521-85591-4 (hardback : alk. paper)
    ISBN-10: 0-521-85591-8 (hardback : alk. paper)
1. Internet–Economic aspects. 2. Information technology–Economic aspects. I. Brousseau, Eric. II. Curien, Nicolas. III. Title.
    HC79.I55I587   2006
    384.3–dc22
2006010015

ISBN 978-0-521-85591-4 Hardback
ISBN 978-0-521-67184-2 Paperback

To Delphine

Contents

Figures

Tables

Notes on contributors

PATRICK BAJARI is Professor at the University of Minnesota. He received his PhD from the University of Minnesota in 1997. He teaches in the areas of industrial organization and applied econometrics. His current research includes the econometrics of strategic interactions, demand estimation in differentiated product markets, and the empirical analysis of asymmetric information. He is Managing Editor of the *International Journal of Industrial Organization* and Associate Editor for the *Journal of Business and Economic Statistics*.

YANNIS BAKOS is Associate Professor of Management at the Leonard N. Stern School of Business at New York University where he teaches courses on the economic and business implications of information technology, the Internet, and online media. Professor Bakos pioneered research on the impact of information technology on markets, and in particular on how Internet-based electronic marketplaces will affect pricing and competition. He holds PhD, MBA, Masters and Bachelors degrees from MIT.

PIERRE-JEAN BENGHOZI is presently Reseach Director at the National Center for Scientific Research (CNRS) and is directing the Pole for Research in Economics and Management at Ecole Polytechnique (Paris). He developed a research group on information technology, telecomunications, media, and culture. His current projects draw attention to adoption and uses of ITC in large organizations, structuring of e-commerce and ITC-supported markets and supply chains. Pierre-Jean Benghozi publishes on these topics in French and English. He teaches regularly at Paris University.

DAVID BOUNIE is Assistant Professor of Economics at Télécom Paris. He completed his graduate work at the University of Paris 1 Panthéon-Sorbonne in public economics and received his PhD in economics from ENST. His research interests include economics of payment systems and Internet economics. He is currently working on economics of payment and econometrics of consumer payment behavior. Prior to this affiliation with Télécom Paris, he served for three years as an economist with the Groupement des Cartes Bancaires (CB), the leading interbank payment and cash withdrawal system in France.

MARC BOURREAU is Assistant Professor at Ecole Nationale Supérieure des Télécommunications (ENST, Paris) and member of the Laboratory of Industrial Economics (LEI) of the Center for Research in Economics and Statistics (CREST). His main research interests are economic and policy issues relating to broadcasting, telecommunications, and the Internet.

ERIC BROUSSEAU is Professor of Economics at the University of Paris X, and Director of EconomiX, a joint research center between the CNRS (French National Science Foundation) and the University of Paris X. He is also Co-Director of the GDR TICS (Research Consortium "Information Technologies and the Society") of the CNRS. His research agenda focuses on the economics of institutions and the economics of contracts, with two main applied fields: the economics of intellectual property rights and the economics of the Internet and digital activities. On this last issue he works both on digital business models and on the governance of the Internet and of the information society.

ERIK BRYNJOLFSSON is Director of the MIT Center for Digital Business, the Schussel Professor of Management at the MIT Sloan School, and director or advisor of several technology-intensive firms. His research focuses on the economics of information and information technology, including productivity, organizational change, and the pricing of digital goods. Professor Brynjolfsson previously taught at Stanford Business School and Harvard Business School. He holds Bachelors and Masters degrees from Harvard University and a PhD from MIT.

NICOLAS CURIEN serves as Commissioner for the French Regulation Commission for Electronic Communications and Postal Services (ARCEP). He held several positions as an economist in the Administration (France Telecom, Ministry of Defence, Institute of Statistics and Economic Studies) and as an academic (Professor of Economics at the Conservatoire National des Arts et Métiers and at the Ecole Polytechnique). He is also a member of the French Academy of Technology and a member of the International Telecommunications Society (ITS). He has published several books and many scientific articles in the field of telecommunications and Internet economics.

JEAN-MICHEL DALLE is Professor with University Pierre et Marie Curie and an associate researcher with IMRI-Dauphine (Paris, France). He works on the economics of innovation and has notably focused since 1998 on the economics of software and open source software. He is an alumnus from Ecole Polytechnique and ENSAE, and holds a PhD in economics from Ecole Polytechnique. He is also the Managing Director of Agoranov, a major non-profit science-based incubator located in Paris.

GODEFROY DANG NGUYEN is Deputy Scientific Director at ENST Bretagne, an engineer's school in France, and Professor at the College of Europe in Bruges. His research focuses on Internet and telecommunications economics, on which he has written two books, and on institutional issues related to ICT. He is the scientific director of a network of seven universities and institutions located in Brittany. This network carries out statistical and case studies on adoption and usage of ICT. Professor Dang Nguyen has been an expert with the European Commission since 1983, and has been consultant for many institutions including the World Bank and ITU.

PAUL A. DAVID is known internationally for contributions to economic history, economic and historical demography, and the economics of science and technology. He divides his working life equally between Stanford University in California, where he is Professor of Economics and Senior Fellow of the Stanford Institute for Economic Policy Research, and the University of Oxford, where he is Senior Fellow of the Oxford Internet Institute and Emeritus Fellow of All Souls College. In 2003 he edited (with M. Thomas) *The Economic Future in Historical Perspective*.

JASON DEDRICK is Co-Director of the Personal Computing Industry Center and Senior Research Fellow at the Center for Research on Information Technology and Organizations (CRITO), at the University of California, Irvine. His research is focused on the globalization of information technology production and use, and the economic impacts of IT at the firm, industry, and national levels. He is co-author of *Global E-Commerce: Impacts of National Environment and Policy*, Cambridge University Press, 2006.

BRUNO DEFFAINS is Professor of Economics at University of Nancy, France. For the past few years, he has been Vice-President for research activities there and he developed a new program in law and economics which is now associated to the CNRS. He is the author of articles and books in law and economics. His research has focused on economics of accidents law, conflicts resolution, internet regulation, comparison of legal systems, as well as the question of the extent to which law constrains economic growth.

NICHOLAS ECONOMIDES is Professor of Economics at the Stern School of Business of New York University and Executive Director of the NET Institute. His fields of specialization and research include the economics of networks, especially of telecommunications, computers, and information, the economics of technical compatibility and standardization, industrial organization, the structure and organization of financial markets, application of public policy to network industries, and strategic analysis of markets. He has published widely in the areas of networks, telecommunications, oligopoly, antitrust, product positioning, and on liquidity and the organization of financial markets and exchanges. His website on the economics of networks at http://www.stern.nyu.edu/networks/ has been ranked by *The Economist* as one of the top four economics sites worldwide.

EMMANUELLE FAUCHART is Assistant Professor of Economics at the Laboratory of Econometrics at CNAM, France. Her interest in research is the field of industrial organization, and more particularly information-sharing patterns, industrial dynamics, firm demography, and the economics of online communities.

PHILIPPE FENOGLIO is Assistant Professor of Economics at University of Nancy (France). His research interests include industrial organization (oligopolistic competition, product differentiation) and economics of innovation and new technology. He is also working on the economics of alcohol, tobacco, and illegal drugs and is the co-author of several reports on this topic for public organizations.

PATRICE FLICHY is Professor of Sociology at Marne la Vallée University, LATTS. His main research topics include online computerization movements and technological utopianism.

DOMINIQUE FORAY holds the Chair of Economics and Management of Innovation at the Swiss Federal Institute of Technology in Lausanne (EPFL). He is also Director of the Collège du Management at EPFL. His research interests include all topics and issues related to economic policy in the context of the new knowledge-based economy. This broad field covers the economics of science, technology, and innovation. Intellectual property and competition policy, information technology and the new economy, capital market and entrepreneurships, national systems of innovation, education, and training policy are fields of high relevance in his research. In 2004 he published *The Economics of Knowledge*.

YANNICK GABUTHY is Assistant Professor of Economics at the University of Nancy and member of the BETA research laboratory (CNRS) since 2005. He received his PhD in economics from the University of Lyon in 2003 and was a visitor at the University of Essex in 2001. His main area of research is law and economics, with special interest in dispute resolution (bargaining and arbitration). He conducts experimental research on these topics.

ALEX GAUDEUL is a lecturer at the School of Economics, University of East Anglia and a faculty member at the Centre for Competition Policy. He holds a PhD from the University of Toulouse, France and is an industrial economist with an interest in the Internet, open source software and media industries. Current work examines the open source software production model in order to evaluate its impact on traditional methods of software production. He is also working on how intermediaries regulate competition on the Internet between the firms they intermediate.

PIERRE GAZÉ is Assistant Professor of Economics at the University of Orléans since 1999. He received his PhD in economics from the University of Orléans. His research interests are in economics of banking and industrial organization. His recent works include bundling and tying practices in the banking industry and retail payments innovations.

MICHEL GENSOLLEN was trained as an economist and an engineer in telecommunications. From 1990 to 2000 he was Chief Economist at France Telecom, in charge of the Economic and Strategic Studies department. He is currently working at the SES (Economics and Social Sciences) department at Télécom Paris. His recent publications focus on electronic commerce, network-based firms, information economy, and the new business models triggered by the development of the Internet and ICT.

ULRICH HEGE is Associate Professor in Finance at HEC School of Management in Paris. He has previously taught at Tilburg University and ESSEC and holds a PhD from Princeton University. His research interests are in corporate finance, on questions related to venture capital, corporate governance, joint ventures, bankruptcy, credit risk and credit structure, and internal capital markets.

ALI HORTAÇSU is Assistant Professor of Economics at the University of Chicago. He is interested in the theory and econometrics of auction and matching markets, product markets with search frictions and information asymmetries, and the vertical arrangement of industries. He conducts empirical research on Internet auctions and matchmaking sites, government securities markets, electricity markets, the mutual fund industry, and the cement/concrete industry.

MAARTEN JANSSEN is Professor of Microeconomics at Erasmus University Rotterdam and Director of the Tinbergen Institute. He has published numerous articles in internationally refereed journals such as the *Review of Economic Studies, International Economic Review, Journal of Economic Theory and Games*, and *Economic Behavior*. His current research interests are in incomplete information in markets and auctions.

BRUNO JULLIEN is Director of Research at CNRS and a senior member at IDEI. He graduated from Ecole Polytechnique and ENSAE, and holds a PhD in economics from Harvard University. His contributions cover a wide range of topics, with a particular strength in industrial organization, contract theory, network economics, competition policy and regulation, and the economics of risk.

KENNETH L. KRAEMER is Professor of Management and Computer Science and Director of the Center for Research on IT and Organizations, University of California, Irvine. His research includes the socio-economic implications of IT, national policies for IT production and use, and the contribution of IT to productivity and economic development. His most recent book, co-authored with Jason Dedrick, is *Asia's Computer Challenge* (1998). He recently published a book based on a five-year study of the global diffusion of the Internet and e-commerce (Cambridge University Press, 2006) and is starting a new study of the offshoring of knowledge work.

GILBERT LAFFOND is Professor of Economics and Statistics at the Conservatoire National des Arts et Métiers (Paris) and Head of the Laboratory of Econometrics. His main research concerns are in game theory, public choice, and evolutionary economics, fields where he has published several major theoretical contributions. He is also interested in industrial organization and has worked more specifically on applications to the telecommunications industry and to the Internet.

JACQUES LAYE has a PhD in economics from the Laboratory of Econometrics (Ecole Polytechnique) and is a researcher at the Laboratory of Forestal Economics (LEF, Inra Nancy, France) where he works on industrial organization and computational economics (oligopolistic competition, vertical relationships, product differentiation, coalition theory) applied to sectors like the wine industry, the wood industry, or Internet retailing. Other fields of research concern operations research (stochastic control) applied to the management of renewable ressources, and computational economics.

WILLIAM LAZONICK is University Professor at the University of Massachusetts Lowell and Distinguished Research Professor at INSEAD. Previously he was Assistant and Associate Professor of Economics at Harvard University (1975–1984) and Professor of Economics at Barnard College of Columbia University (1985–1993). He specializes in the analysis of industrial development and international competition.

VIRGINIE LETHIAIS is a lecturer in economics at the ENST-Bretagne, a French graduate engineering school in telecommunications. She is a member of the CREM, the CNRS Research Laboratory on Economics and Management of the Universities of Rennes and Caen. She uses industrial economics and applied econometrics to study pricing on the Internet and to analyze diffusion and uses of information and communication technologies.

CHRISTIAN LICOPPE, PhD, trained in the history of science and technology, is developing a research program on the uses of information and communication technologies and the ways they are embedded in various forms of activity, such as commerce and service relationships, mobility and displacements, and forms of interpersonal communication. He is currently Professor of Sociology of Technology at the Social Science department of the Ecole Nationale Supérieure des Télécommunications in Paris.

GARY MADDEN is Director of the Communication Economics and Electronic Markets Research Centre and Professor at the Department of Economics of the Curtin University of Technology, Australia. He is editor of the *International Handbook of Telecommunications Economics* series, and serves on the board of management of the International Telecommunications Society. He is also a member of the editorial board of the *Journal of Media Economics*.

SÉBASTIEN MICHENAUD is a PhD candidate in finance at HEC School of Management, in Paris, and is affiliated with GREGHEC. He has previously worked at Bankers Trust International in mergers and acquisitions and as a consultant at Arkwright Enterprises where he was an active observer of the Internet development. His research interests are in corporate finance and behavioral finance.

JOSÉ LUIS MORAGA-GONZÁLEZ is Professor of Industrial Organization at the University of Groningen. He obtained a PhD in Economics from University Carlos III Madrid. His research focuses mainly on information economics and R&D. His work has been published in journals including the *Review of Economic Studies*, *Rand Journal of Economics*, *European Economic Review* and *International Journal of Industrial Organization*.

FRANÇOIS MOREAU is Associate Professor in Economics at the Conservatoire National des Arts et Métiers in Paris, France. His main current fields of research are the economics of the Internet and media economics.

THOMAS PARIS is Affiliated Professor at HEC School of Management, Paris, and Associate Researcher at CRG Ecole Polytechnique. His research focuses on the management, the economics, and the regulation of creative and immaterial industries. He has written a book on the system of author's rights (*Le Droit d'auteur – L'idéologie et le système*, PUF, Paris, 2002) and has edited one about the challenges of the television industry (*La Libération audiovisuelle – Enjeux technologiques, économiques et réglementaires*, Dalloz, Paris, 2004).

THIERRY PÉNARD is Professor of Economics at the University of Rennes 1 and is Director of the Industrial Organization department at the Center for Research in Economics and Management (CREM). His main fields of interest are the economics of networks (Internet, telecommunication), the economics of contract (franchising), game theory, and antitrust policy.

ALAIN RALLET is Full Professor of Economics at the University of Paris South and researcher at ADIS, research center in economics there. His fields of interest are Internet economics (e-commerce, emergence of online multimedia markets on the Internet, the impact of ICTs on organizations) and regional and urban economics (ICTs and localization of economic activities, network infrastructure, and local development).

FABRICE ROCHELANDET holds a PhD from the University of Paris Panthéon-Sorbonne. His dissertation addressed the question of copyright in the digital economy. He is currently Assistant Professor of Economics at the University of Paris 11. His research focuses on the economic impact of digital technologies through topics such as electronic delivery of cultural good, broadcasting, intellectual property, and digital divide. He has published several papers on the digital protection of contents, the efficiency of copyright collecting societies, and the European copyright harmonisation.

DELPHINE SABOURIN was a PhD student at CEREMADE, Paris Dauphine University, Research Fellow at CREST, and teaching assistant at Paris Dauphine University. Her research interests included the microstructure of securities markets, with emphasis on the competition between alternative trading mechanisms and corporate finance.

MICHAEL SCHIPP is Research Associate at the Communication Economics and Electronic Markets research centre (CEEM) at the Curtin University of Technology. His research focus is network economics. This interest led Michael to empirically measure the magnitude of the Internet network effect. Michael is currently developing his expertise in e-market competition modelling. An early outcome of this research program is a model of network investment contained in a competitive game between an incumbent firm and a virtual entrant.

THOMAS SERVAL is a graduate from Ecole Normale Supérieure in Paris and Ecole Nationale de la Statistique et de l'Administration Economique. He focused his PhD work on Internet economics with a special interest in transformation of electronic capital market (ECN), law and economics (software patent), and value creation in cyberspace. Thomas is the President and CEO of Baracoda and Vice President of the French chapter of the Internet Society.

JOACHIM TAN is Research Associate at the Communication Economics and Electronic Markets Research Center (CEEM) at the Curtin University of Technology. His research orientation is in the empirical modelling of aspects of electronic, information, and communications markets in the search for dynamic regularities. Data examined include circuit- and packet-switched traffic, product adoption, and telecommunications company share price data. He is currently working on developing methods to enable reliable long-horizon forecasts based on short time series.

HERVÉ TANGUY is Director of Research at INRA/LORIA and at the Laboratory of Econometry of Ecole Polytechnique. He performs research in industrial economy applied to problems of strategy, finance, and business organization. He has participated in the conception and realization of new business software systems in several organizations (multinational firms, public companies, wine industry, etc.).

SYLVIE THORON is a maître de conférences at the University of Toulon and a researcher at the GREQAM, a CNRS research group in economics in Marseille. Her research fields are public economics and the formation of coalitions and agreements in economics. In the framework of cooperative and non-cooperative game theory, she studies the incentives and behavior of individuals and groups of individuals when deciding whether to contribute to public goods.

MATTHIJS WILDENBEEST is a PhD student at the Tinbergen Institute and the Erasmus School of Economics. His major field of interest is industrial organization. His current research interests include consumer search and the structural estimation of equilibrium models.

JEAN-BENOÎT ZIMMERMANN is CNRS Research Director at GREQAM (Groupement de Recherche en Economie Quantitative d'Aix-Marseille) and IDEP (Institut d'Economie Publique) in Marseille. His main topics of interest are economics of interactions and networks, proximity dynamics, innovation, and intellectual property economics (open source software).

Acknowledgements

This work draws from a process of interactions among the contributors, which led to a consistent set of chapters that have been written interactively. This book is therefore really a collective one, and the editors would like to warmly thank the authors who accepted the discipline needed to produce such an outcome. These interactions were initiated in a seminar held in 1999–2000 which led to the edition of a special issue of the *Revue Economique* entitled "L'Economie de l'Internet" in 2001. This publication set the basis of the contributions to this entirely new book that was elaborated in the frame of a working group of the CNRS Research Consortium "Information Technologies and the Society" (GDR TICS) in 2003–2004. This working group organized in particular two workshops held in 2004 at GREQAM (a joint research center from the French CNRS, the Universities of Marseille and EHESS) and at the Laboratory of Econometrics of the CNAM (Paris).

The editors are grateful to the organizers of these events, and in particular to Jean-Benoît Zimmermann (GREQAM) and to François Moreau (CNAM), as well as to the CNRS for its financial support. They would also like to thank the President of the *Revue Economique*, Jean-Paul Polin (University of Orléans), for his support to the project.

The editors are also indebted to Marie-Line Priot (EconomiX, CNRS-University of Paris X) for secretarial support.

While this book was being published, Delphine Sabourin passed away. Delphine was the youngest contributor to this book, but she was far from being the least brilliant scientist on the team. All of us will miss her brightness and kindness, and we are all so sad that she has been deprived of such a promising future.

Since this book aims at providing the reader with an up-to-date synthesis of what is essential in digital and Internet economics, some of the contributors decided it would be preferable to reprint (Chapters 11 and 15) or publish a revised version (Chapter 8) of papers they had already published in journals. The editors and the publishers would like to thank the American Economic Association (Chapter 15), Elsevier

(Chapter 8), and the Institute for Operation Research and Management Sciences (Chapter 11) for permissions to reprint papers that were originally published respectively, in the *Journal of Economic Literature* (vol. 42, pp. 457–486, 2004), in *Marketing Science* (vol. 19, pp. 63–82, 2000), and in the *International Journal of Industrial Organization* (vol. 14, no. 6, pp. 673–699, 1996).

1 Internet economics, digital economics

Eric Brousseau and Nicolas Curien

1.1 Introduction

Since the "privatization" of the Internet in the United States in the mid-1990s, the network of networks has developed rapidly. This has been matched by a wave of innovation in information technology, as well as in many areas of its application, giving rise to a multitude of on-line services and new "business models". In the same period, the United States experienced unprecedented non-inflationist growth. As a result of this conjunction, certain commentators considered the Internet as the heart of a new growth regime, qualified as the "new economy". This contributed to the creation and then amplification of a speculative bubble around businesses involved in the Internet.

As these unfounded hopes necessarily met with disappointment, the euphoria disappeared at the turn of the 21st century. At the same time, the forecasts of a certain number of economists were confirmed a posteriori. These forecasts had highlighted, firstly, that the use of information and communication technologies (ICTs) does not lead *ipso facto* to an improvement in microeconomic performances (Brousseau and Rallet [1999]); secondly, that information goods and services do not escape from the fundamental rules of economics (Shapiro and Varian [1999]); and thirdly that American growth in the 1990s was not necessarily founded on the innovations linked to the use of ICTs exclusively (Gordon [2000], Cohen and Debonneuil [2000], Artus [2001]). However, these analyses do not claim that nothing changes with the large-scale dissemination of these digital networks and their associated practices. By extending earlier theories (e.g. Machlup [1962], Bell [1973], Lamberton [1974], Porat [1977], Jonscher [1983, 1994]), they simply pointed out that the changes are slower and more complex than is generally admitted,

We would like to thank Michel Gensollen, Thierry Pénard and Alain Rallet for their helpful remarks on this text. However, should any inaccuracies or errors subsist, they are to be entirely attributed to the signatories.

precisely because they have a fundamental character. David (1990, 2000b) refers to digital technology as *general purpose technology* whose impact on economic performance is linked to transformations in practices in all dimensions of economic and social life: norms of consumption, modes of production, organizational forms, and so on. In the same way as the great inventions at the end of the 19th century, this technology will radically change economics, spark growth and transform the face of society, but only in the long run.

In this long-term perspective, the Internet is situated at the confluence of two older economic evolutions: on the one hand, that of telecommunications networks, created in the 19th century and becoming electronic in the second half of the 20th century; on the other, that of computers, beginning during the Second World War. The transformation of societies, under the influence of these technologies, had been set in motion well before the sudden emergence of the network of networks that therefore does not mark the beginning of ICT-related transformations. Conversely, it is premature to consider it as the culmination of this technology. Given that the majority of the trajectories of change have barely begun, it is difficult to pronounce judgment on the final result of movements which are still emerging and unstable. However, the Internet, and more generally speaking digital networks, possess specific properties which leave their mark on a number of phenomena for which they become the basis: information processing and circulation, commercial transactions, organizational coordination, network management, and so on.

The ambition of this book and of this chapter is to highlight the aspects of the Internet and digital technologies that appear to be truly innovative, in terms of both economic practices and analytical concepts. Since the 1980s, telecommunications networks have constituted a melting pot producing, on the one hand, new practices in the management of "public facilities", the regulation of competition, the design of network services, etc., and, on the other, new analytical concepts such as the notions of "contestable" market, "yardstick" competition, "incentive" pricing, etc., which were then applied to all industries. Similarly, the Internet is today giving rise to innovative practices that call for renewed conceptualization.

There are three principal reasons explaining the Internet's double role as a catalyst of practices and theories. First of all, the Internet is a planetary federation of digital networks, whose technical potential, notably the ability to act as a medium for very differentiated modalities of information management, induces a growing "digitization" of activities: access to these interconnected and flexible networks incites economic actors to increase the informational intensity of their services and to multiply their informational exchanges. Secondly, the logic of this modular and decentralized network, serving as a platform for the provision of services founded on information and innovation, deployed in a global space, makes it an archetype of contemporary economies, where industry tends to be organized according to a flexible assembly model thanks to standardized interfaces; where competitiveness is strongly associated with the ability to innovate; where products and services are undergoing an increase in informational intensity; where the economic space is more and more transnational, etc. Finally, the organizational innovations induced by the digital networks federated by the Internet are gradually spreading to the entire economy.

We shall highlight the fact that one of the Internet's central characteristics is the ability it grants economic agents to very finely control the information they exchange in accordance with the individual preferences of the issuing and receiving parties. Moreover, this control can be totally decentralized through the use of standardized interfaces. This double characteristic founds both the specificity of the Internet as a network and that of the digital economy it serves. Other frequently mentioned characteristics such as the global and multimedia nature of the Internet or its impact on information costs are certainly important factors, but they probably do not alone justify giving such marked attention to Internet economics.

This chapter is divided into three parts. In the first part, we will recall some of the factual principles and elements clarifying the nature of the Internet network as well as the issues it raises for economic activities. In the second part, we will seek to specify the link between the "internal" morphology and economics of the Internet network and the new types of relations and exchanges which accompany the development of this network, which we will refer to using the term "digital economics". We will show that this link has more to do with engendering than with causality. To put it in other terms, rather than simply considering the Internet as a technological tool, a determining factor in a new type of economic development, it is more productive to analyze Internet economics *stricto sensu* as the seed or the incubator of a future digital economy where the ability to manage information in a decentralized and customized way is massively exploited. In the final part, we will seek to draw up a research program covering the issues raised by the multifaceted development of the Internet and the concomitant emergence of digital economics. We will explain how the different chapters of this book, as a contribution to the flourishing corpus of publications devoted to Internet economics, constitute the pieces of a puzzle which is yet to be completed, and whose final form is just beginning to emerge.

1.2   Internet economics: some principles and facts

1.2.1   The "end-to-end" principle

The Internet is not a network *per se* but a network of networks that relies on common standards allowing machines that process information digitally to "interoperate". More precisely, Internet standards enable the totally decentralized interconnection of computerized networks. On the Internet there is no technical discrimination between the resources dedicated to the administration of the network and the terminals that process the information carried, as is usual in a traditional telecommunication network such as the telephone network, where terminals process information while the administrative equipment of the network – switches – connects information flow and transmission (Curien and Gensollen [1992]). On the Internet, information-processing devices (IPDs) connected to the network are simultaneously terminals and routers. In addition, the use of a standard interface and a generic addressing system creates a sort of "meta-network" presenting itself as a homogenous and seamless system to the user.

The devices interconnected by the Internet, essentially computers, process information digitally. The network organizes communication between these machines on the basis of the "client–server" model. The "client" sends requests to the "server", which processes them and then sends a response. Any device connected to the Internet can be both a client and a server. This is notably the case for the most common applications on the Internet, e-mail and the Web. Sending an e-mail involves asking the server (recipient) whether he agrees to receive information. If he does, the client (sender) sends the information. In practice, e-mail servers carry out these operations. Unlike user terminals, the servers are permanently connected to facilitate data flows. Similarly, when consulting a website, the visitor sends a request to a computer in which information is stocked. The information server sends back HyperText Markup Language (HTML) codes to the client that enable the computer to re-build pages on the client's screen. Generally speaking, independently of the application being considered, requests and responses are broken down into data packets, which their senders and recipients identify and which circulate within the network where they are relayed by routers. After the packets are transmitted and received, the receiving terminal reconstitutes the original programming lines containing an informational content or instructions to the machine that pilots it from a distance. The following elements must be in place for everything to function correctly:

- All IPDs connected to the network must be clearly identified so that the data packets actually reach the addressee; this identifier is the Internet protocol (IP) number.
- An addressing language has to allow users to formulate their request with a suitable server: domain names (www.identifier.com) make up the visible part of this addressing system; servers known as domain name systems (DNS) transform these addresses close to "human" language into machine addresses (IP addresses).
- Common communication protocols are required for communication and routing between IPDs; the Internet protocol is at the center of a vast group of technical standards responsible for communication and interoperability among network components.
- The machines must use compatible programming languages in order to code and decode requests and responses transmitted between clients and servers; in this respect, HTML language is the foundation stone of the Web, enabling different kinds of IPDs to exchange texts, images, data and sounds.

Thus the very existence of the Internet stems from the use of a generic addressing system (IP numbers and domain names) and standards (Internet protocol and HTML). These form the basis of interoperability between various sub-networks. The technical regulation of the Internet therefore is essentially based on the management of these resources with the goal of guaranteeing interoperability. Three main organizations carry out this regulation:

- ICANN (Internet Corporation for Assigned Names and Numbers), set up in 1998, is a non-profit organization based in the US. Under a delegation contract with the US government (Department of Commerce), ICANN is responsible for organizing the distribution of IP numbers and domain names. In both cases, the addressing system is a hierarchical one in which a limited number of roots (e.g. .com, .org or .net) enables the creation of addresses. This hierarchy makes it possible to delegate the practical distribution of addresses among entities that manage portfolios of addresses according to their own rules. ICANN therefore supervises two distinct functions: the distribution of IP numbers that is ensured by the administrators of the subscriber networks (the Internet service providers – ISPs) and the distribution of domain names, by setting the features of the available roots (first-order domains, or suffixes, such as .com, .fr, etc.) and by selecting and supervising the organizations in charge of collecting and registering users' claims.

ICANN's importance derives from its power over the private company Verisign (formerly Network Solution Inc. – NSI), the entity responsible for the technical management of the domain names' *root computer*. This server contains the source file able to translate the domain names into IP addresses. ICANN can therefore "erase" addresses or entities that do not comply with the rules it sets out and thus exclude them from the Web. This is why ICANN is one of the possible sources of a non-technical governance system of the Internet.

- The IETF (Internet Engineering Task Force) is de facto the entity responsible for the standardization of the communication protocols: the Internet protocol system. It has no legal status and is only a working group of the Internet Society (ISOC). The latter is a not-for-profit organization, founded by some of the "inventors" of the Internet, that constitutes a forum of reflection and a tool of influence aimed, notably, at promoting the development of an open and efficient network, which would benefit the greatest number.

- The W3C (World Wide Web Consortium) is responsible for the standardization of the multimedia languages used on the Internet. It is a kind of club where access is reserved to those organizations that can afford the relatively high membership fee.

These three organizations are, however, not really regulating bodies.

- They do not combine the three faculties of setting rules, supervising operators and users, and imposing sanctions for lack of compliance or for practices going against the principles which they stand for, such as fair competition, public freedom and secure operations. Indeed, the IETF and the W3C constitute mechanisms for sharing technical developments in a manner similar to that with open source software. Their standards are not mandatory for Net users and operators; however, they do facilitate interoperability. ICANN certainly has formal powers but it does not have sufficient means to supervise the Web, which would make the exercise of its prerogatives efficient and independent.

- Furthermore, the legal status of each of these organizations is unclear, or even non-existent in the case of the IETF. In principle, they are responsible for the traditional regulation of the World Wide Web. However, they are subject to American law and operate under contract with the United States government. Their functioning and membership principles do not guarantee their independence, which weakens their authority and casts doubt on the legitimacy of their decisions. The credibility of the norms they set and the decisions that they make is affected as a result because their enforceability is not guaranteed.

- Finally, the scope of these organizations' jurisdiction is unclear. In principle, they are responsible only for the technical regulation of the

Internet, the IETF and the WC3 in particular. However, for technical and historical reasons, the regulation of the network and its modalities of use are closely linked. Indeed, the regulatory bodies decide for or against authorizing the development of particular categories of services depending on the way in which the interoperability standards, the security mechanisms and the mechanisms for managing priorities are defined. Moreover, as Leiner et al. (2000) point out, there is a strong tradition in the Internet community to set ethical, social and economic norms in addition to technical rules. For example, until 1995, *Netiquette*, Net ethics, prohibited any commercial use of the Net.

1.2.2   Competition and complementarities among regulation frameworks

The regulatory bodies of the Net appear very different from the traditional mechanisms for regulation and international standardization, such as, notably, the International Telecommunication Union (ITU), the International Standard Organization (ISO) or the International Electrotechnical Commission (IEC). When the Internet was "invented", it was decided not to go through these different authorities for four principal reasons: firstly, they are known for being slow in elaborating standards, which seemed incompatible with the high rate of innovation in technologies linked to the Internet; secondly, these bodies did not immediately grasp the originality and the power of Internet standards and, moreover, certain aspects of the Internet put it into competition with the areas these bodies govern; thirdly, the Internet was limited to the North American continent until 1998 and even today the network is still predominantly American, despite a clear trend of internationalization; finally, the technicians and the entrepreneurs of the Internet, marked by a libertarian or liberal ideology, from the very beginning expressed an almost visceral suspicion with regard to State or international bureaucracies.

Despite their limits, the combined efforts of ICANN, IETF and W3C play an essential role in the technical governance of the Internet. However, this governance conditions in part the socio-economic regulation of activities for which the network is the basis. In fact, on a network of the Internet type, each participant has the possibility of influencing the way in which the flow of communication is administered. This possibility exists in relation to digital technologies' ability to encrypt information: in a digital system, all information is coded in the form of a digital sequence, which is then easy to encrypt. The encryption thus constitutes the key to a filtering of information use: according to the settings, one can authorize access to all or to a part of the information potentially available, depending on the identity of the user or other criteria. The combination of encryption abilities and the decentralized administration of communication therefore enables all Internet users to regulate the use of information which they make available on the network, because they can lay down "norms" of use for this information which the technology will enforce. This opens practically infinite margins for maneuver to economic agents who wish to define informational services, as well as to social actors desiring to implement specific rules of informational interaction. However, interoperability imposes one notable constraint: in order for the actors to be able to implement such specific rules, these must be compatible with the interoperability standards defined by the IETF or the W3C. This gives these bodies a notable influence on the uses that are likely or not to develop on the Internet. Moreover, the way in which the addressing system is managed also influences uses. The modalities for the management of domain names – that is to say the recognition, or non-recognition, of brand rights, the question of creating categories allowing service providers to be classified and therefore "labeled", as well as the definition of rules of inclusion for these categories – have an influence on the conditions of competition between the operators. Therefore, in the long term, they influence the nature of the services and the uses made of them.

Given these factors, and because the technical mechanisms for the governance and regulation of the Internet are neither totally legitimate nor perfectly complete, States have progressively become more involved with the socio-economic regulation of the network. More exactly, as long as the Internet affected only a coherent and closed community – that of scientists – the American State had little interest (and other States even less so) in intervening in a network which functioned according to rules that were specific to this community, and which in any case was ultimately monitored by the State. Yet with the diversification of uses and actors, the need to complement the technical regulation in order to organize competition, to enable the development of commercial activities, to protect citizens, and so on, made itself felt strongly. This resulted in intense legislative activity in the American Congress from 1995 onwards (Benkler [2000]). Other States, notably the members of the Organization for Economic Cooperation and Development (OECD) and those of the European Union, were soon to follow, from 1997/1998. The World Summit on the Information Society is the symbol of the globalization of this process, and of the attempts to harmonize the various national developments.

The first reflex in most countries was to extend the field of application for the existing regulations, as well as the jurisdiction of the authorities responsible for enforcing them. However, this movement ran into two major obstacles:

- The re-evaluation of borders between industries inherited from the pre-digital era needs time and cannot take place without conflict and inconsistencies. The Internet is a platform integrating all communication and information-processing technologies, which inevitably tends to blur the borders traditionally established between the respective areas of voice, image and data; that is to say, in industrial terms, between the computer, telecommunications, audiovisual and publishing industries. For this reason, Internet activities have been subject to multiple regulations which are sometimes contradictory and sometimes simply costly and complex to combine. This leads to a "patchwork" of legislative and regulatory environments which is consequently very sensitive to the interpretation of administrative or judiciary authorities, which more often than not appear to be unprepared for the Internet's originality and technical complexity.

- The Internet's global and open character is not very favorable for establishing national regulations. The Yahoo! case in France in 2000 showed that it is a complicated matter to enforce a judge's ruling obliging a portal to deny its clients access to certain content. Furthermore, this case, arising from complaints lodged by anti-racist associations, raises questions concerning legal disputes. In the name of the "Gayssot" law condemning the justification of the Holocaust and revisionism, the French judge obliged Yahoo!, the provider of a portal and search engine, to deny French surfers access through its site to an American auction site selling Nazi objects, failing which Yahoo! would be subject to periodic fines. However, a decision of this kind imposes technical problems: how is it possible to effectively recognize the nationality of the surfers and, above all, to deny access, since it is sufficient merely to know the URL to access the "proscribed" content? There is also a legal problem: what standard should be established between the French conception of the regulation of certain content and American ethical standards defending total freedom of expression? The world legal system is organized on a territorial basis. However, the Internet is aterritorial, to the extent that its architecture ignores the geographical localization of information-processing operations: the data carried by the network uses pathways that cannot be regulated and the information bases consulted or used can be fragmented or duplicated in several places, in such a way that it is totally invisible to the user, or even for the administrators of the network. Given that operations carried out on the network lack a geographical base, to a great extent legal norms turn out to be inefficient.

The pre-existence of regulation mechanisms for the Internet and their incompleteness, the limits of traditional State approaches, their lack of legitimacy in the eyes of the liberal and libertarian ideology that presided over the development of the Net, are all factors which explain why a so-called "co-regulation" approach imposed itself progressively, notably at the instigation of the US, the OECD and the European Union.

In fact, from the beginning of the 1990s, the United States tried to impose a model of self-regulation, which the creators of the Internet and industry had been lobbying for. However, it rapidly turned out to be impossible to maintain this logic, given the Internet's effects on intellectual property, national security, public freedoms, and so on. Moreover, it was also necessary to adapt the existing legislative framework in cryptography, evidentiary law and so on in order to allow for the development of economic activities on the Internet, notably electronic commerce. Thus, the idea of implementing cooperation between the State and non-governmental organizations (NGOs) for the regulation of the Internet progressively emerged. There were two aspects to this cooperation: on the one hand, to informally delimitate areas of responsibility between the State and involved NGOs, notably by applying the principle of subsidiarity, and on the other, to allow the parties involved in the Internet to fully participate in the elaboration of State standards, generally using the means of the network. The Europeans adopted an approach of this type straight away. However, they sought to use existing democratic institutions more than in the American approach.

1.2.3   Complementarity and competition between operators

The self-organization of the Internet is therefore not synonymous with a total lack of an institutional framework: it is "framed" self-organization. Moreover, even if, technically speaking, it would be theoretically possible, the network does not function in a perfectly homogenous and undifferentiated mode in which all the actors play the same symmetric roles. There are "network operators" which serve the purpose of supplying a range of telecommunication services – essentially access to the Web and management of communication services – making them an interface between users and the transport providers, that is to say the cable operators, the telephone companies, the owners of transmission infrastructure, etc. These Internet operators implement the standards and addressing systems described above and they perform the interconnection between networks. For reasons of efficiency, the different access networks are not systematically directly connected to each other. The network hierarchy is organized on two levels (Crémer et al. [2000]). At the bottom, the ISPs connect the final users' machines (or local networks) to the Internet using various local distribution networks: telephone and cable television networks for private customers, specialized networks of all kinds for professionals. On top, *backbone* administrators interconnect the ISP through high-speed continental and intercontinental networks. Although ISPs and backbones are competitors, they are nonetheless interconnected in order to ensure the general connectivity of the network.

The conditions for interconnection between operators of Internet services are complex, due to the convergence of two dimensions:

- Firstly, they are based on vertical agreements with elements of competition, to the extent that the operators are both complementary and rivals. On the one hand, each provides a generalized connectivity service, since the users wish to have access to correspondents or to content hosted on the other networks. On the other hand, each seeks to attract the greatest possible number of users on its own network because the production function is characterized by high fixed cost.
- Secondly, strong externalities mark relations between operators, due to the decentralization of the network administration. Once two networks are interconnected, their respective operators no longer directly control the use made of them. The logic of the Internet protocol is such that the packets of information themselves choose the most efficient path to reach their target by selecting the unsaturated parts of the network. In these conditions, the available capacity of a given operator is "automatically" used, which may degrade the quality of the services offered to its own users.

These elements combine to cause original problems where industrial organization is concerned. In particular, relations between operators must overcome a cooperation–competition dilemma that takes on an even more brutal form given the wide scope for the opportunistic manipulation of interconnection conditions. This results in a great variety of modes of governance, going from the institution of modalities for free interconnection through *peering* agreements intended to minimize transaction costs, to vertical integration internalizing the externalities, as well as various pricing formulae and organizational arrangements. These are all strategies that question competition policies, as they are situated in a context where the logic of fixed costs encourages concentration.

Finally, it should be noted that these characteristics are not unique to relationships between Internet operators: they can also be found in many relationships between providers of informational services as well as in relations between informational providers and providers of network services.

1.2.4   The universalization of the network

Originating in the American military and scientific community, the networks which became the Internet were progressively transferred to private initiatives. It was these private initiatives that were responsible for the universal success of the open standards and the addressing system that characterize the Internet. However, the process leading to the emergence of the Internet was far from spontaneous.

The Internet and its precursors were developed and administered thanks to research fellowships and licensing contracts from the American government. Until 1985, it was essentially made up of diverse, closed and, to a great extent, experimental networks, elaborated within the framework of large American research programs: ARPANet in Defense, SPAN in space technology, CSNet in computers, etc. ARPANet, the precursor launched in 1969, constituted the principal laboratory for the future Internet. This was the program in which the concepts and techniques structuring the network today were invented (Leiner et al. [2001]).

In 1985, when the National Science Foundation (NSF) decided to favor the development of a network open to the entire scientific community, the ARPANet network logically became the principal basis for NSFNet. The latter was itself rapidly transformed into the Internet when, in 1988, the NSF adopted an interconnection policy with private networks (however this was not to lead to an opening up to commercial applications until much later).

The NSF's will to open up was not limited to a simple interconnection policy. From 1985 the principal technical component of the Internet underwent an active transfer to industry. For successive administrations, opening up to private investment and to cooperation with industry effectively constituted the best way of developing the network and its associated technologies. This served a double purpose: on the one hand, to give the United States a more efficient information infrastructure, and on the other, to reinforce the advance of the American computer industry in digital technologies. This policy was finalized in 1998 when responsibility for the development of the Internet was transferred from the NSF to the Department of Commerce.

The US government therefore played a determining role in the emergence and promotion of the Internet and the policy of industry transfer, initiated in 1985, gave rise to a specialized industrial base. The authorization for industrial and commercial applications that followed in 1995 then strongly incited the private sector to invest in the Internet. This accounts for the explosion of on-line services observed from this date.

Furthermore, the head start taken by the United States stimulated the opening up of the network. Since the US government controlled the key resource – the addressing system – and since the American firms and universities were the principal providers of services and standards, the opening up of this American network to foreign actors – whether users or service providers – was considered an opportunity rather than a threat. By offering its open and decentralized standards and network to the rest of the world, the United States enabled the Internet to impose itself over other options for digital networks which were (at least theoretically) possible.

The rapid spread of the Internet therefore has nothing to do with chance or spontaneity. To a great extent, it stems from a strategy implemented by the US government and American industry. However, that is not to say that the Internet's success is not due to certain of its technical–economic characteristics.

- An initial key characteristic relates to the very essence of the Internet. Given that the Internet is a standard of interoperability between heterogeneous networks, establishing, moreover, a radical distinction between the management of network services and that of physical networks, it draws its strength from the installed base. It suffices to create links between existing networks and the Internet, or preferentially to implement the Internet's standards in existing networks so that they become a part of the Internet.
- Another essential factor of the Internet's success is its decentralized administration. Since it is possible to use Internet standards to create network and informational services whose characteristics and access are controlled, the Internet is an eminently flexible network technology. On the one hand, it grants generalized connectivity, in the same way as universal networks like the telephone, and on the other, it allows for closed "clubs", whether intraorganizational (Intranets) or interorganizational (Extranets) – similarly to the previous generation of tele-computerized networks, although these did not have the same interconnection abilities.
- A final reason for the Internet's success is the impact of open standards on innovation and prices. Internet standards in fact take the form of open source software. As standards, they are themselves dynamic and they integrate advances in communication technologies (IP protocols) and multimedia (HTML language) while making them immediately accessible to all users. Moreover, these standards are themselves

interfacing standards capable of integrating all specific technology into the Internet system provided it conforms to these standards. The nature of the Internet standards has thus facilitated the integration of innovations in the domain of the digital processing of information, or in the services based on these technologies. As a result of a snow-balling effect, the size of the market engendered by the universal and open standards stimulated these innovations. Finally, the convergence towards a global network increased the degree of competition and forced prices down, further accelerating the spread of innovations.

1.2.5   A new infrastructure for the economy

The policy of the American government, industry appropriation and the characteristics inherent to the network all largely explain why the Internet globalized so rapidly. Once it became a universal media linking all economic agents, it naturally came to be used for many economic activities and as a result the phenomenon of "electronic commerce" evolved.

The definition of this notion remains particularly vague, however. The idea of electronic commerce varies according to circumstances, between a very wide definition, covering all economic activities borne by the networks, and a very restrictive definition, limited solely to on-line transactions on the Internet. Three fundamental observations must be made at this point (Brousseau [2000], Rallet [2001]).

In the first place, the development of economic activities on the net-works, including on digital networks, started well before the Internet and continues to take place through a great number of media. While these media will probably converge towards the Internet in the long term, today they remain distinct from it. Without going back as far as the telegraph or the telephone, which nonetheless played an essential role in the integration of a certain number of markets, major systems of on-line transactions founded on digital networks started appearing in the 1970s, notably in finance, air transport and energy markets. During the 1980s a large number of inter-firm information-sharing systems emerged, notably in commerce, logistics and assembly industries such as car manufacturing and aeronautics. All of these systems still function today. As for intraorganizational computers in networks, the first were introduced in the 1960s.

Consequently, electronic commerce, in both the wide and the narrow sense, does not exclusively follow from the Internet. It is therefore possible to benefit from past experiences when analyzing the role of ICTs in the evolution of the modalities of economic coordination (Brousseau and Rallet [1999]). One of the principal conclusions that can be drawn from past experiences is that the technology in itself does not determine any optimal organizational model: although it removes certain constraints in economic agents' organizational choices, these choices remain fundamentally contingent on the way in which coordination problems appear in relation to activities and institutional frameworks. There is therefore great diversity in concrete forms of markets and electronic hierarchies – and also cases where the electronic media appear of little use.

Secondly, although the digitization of the economy is undeniable, it has not followed the path that seemed likely when reading certain growth forecasts popularized by the press in the late 1990s. It is difficult to measure in a precise and relevant manner the share of activities borne by the digital networks and an overly naive approach can lead to misconceptions. In particular, there is often an over-emphasis on evaluating the weight of operations carried out entirely on-line, whereas daily observation shows that in commercial transactions as in all other dimensions of social life, certain elementary parts of a single operation lend themselves to digitization and on-line use, while other parts escape from this "virtualization". As the "virtual" is complementary and inseparable from the "real", there is little point in trying to measure the economic weight of the purely virtual. And it is hardly surprising that the weight of the purely *on-line* appears as marginal in the economy. Taking this point of method as granted, it is necessary to re-examine the idea that the digitization of the economy is necessarily an exponential dynamic. It is true that at the end of the 1990s impressive growth rates were recorded in many areas linked to the Internet: this concerned the size and the activities of the network itself, such as the volume of the economic transactions it carried. The combination of three factors explains this very fast take-off. Firstly, the level was initially very low since, before 1995, the Internet was still just a confidential network, confined to non-commercial applications. Secondly, the speculative bubble contributed to maintaining artificial growth, since many services were provided at prices that were much lower than their cost. Finally, certain services and activities were transferred from specialized networks to the Internet.

The only really reliable figures available on electronic commerce – those of the Department of Commerce (http://www.census.gov) – illustrate the reality of a rapid take-off. In the United States, on-line retail trade did indeed grow in volume, from when it was first monitored (0.63% at the end of 1999) until the second quarter 2005, where it reached almost 2.2% of retail sales. However, objectively recorded levels of activity and pace of growth are considerably lower than the estimates the consultancy firms made, figures that many decision makers and observers nonetheless took as granted. Figures simply confirm that a part of the economic models developed at the time of the speculative bubble was not valid, that the pace of the digitization of the economy is slow because deep-reaching transformations are necessary in many areas. We are not evolving towards the complete digitization of activities and exchanges because, for the greater part, "material" goods and services make up consumption norms, and because the resulting economic and technical constraints require recourse to traditional forms of organization of production and exchanges. However, the systematic use of digital networks and technologies to manage these activities contributes to the reshaping of many activities in the long run.

Thirdly, when applied to markets and to retail, digital technologies do not always have the effects one might expect. Too much trust is placed in an insufficiently thought-out intuition.

- Firstly, it is not easy to exchange many goods and services on-line. This is not solely due to logistical constraints inherent in products with a material component. It also has to do with the difficulty in perfecting systems of description and certification to avoid problems of adverse selection and moral hazard while carrying out transactions. It follows that the electronization of commerce is often only partial. From this point onwards, certain of the effects expected of digital networks, such as the globalization of competition, remain confined to particular activities: essentially, cultural goods and services, tourism and consumer electronics. The spread of digital networks may certainly affect markets where electronization is only partial; however, the impact can only be different from that expected in an integrated and global market.
- Secondly, digital networks are not mechanisms that substitute traditional commercial intermediaries in order to carry out the fiction of the Walrassian market. The existence of networks linking supply to demand does not *ipso facto* resolve the coordination problems brought about by the interaction of millions of agents (Brousseau [2002]). Commercial intermediaries remain indispensable to perform certain economic functions which are not purely informational, such as the guarantee of transactions and logistical management, as well as ensuring the liquidity of the markets. In addition, informational intermediaries appear, because even when the intermediation is purely informational, digital networks do not immediately carry it out. Considerable resources have to be dedicated to the formatting, certification, selection and connection of supply and demand. "Infomediaries", such as eBay, develop specific skills in this respect and benefit from economies of scale to lower these costs.

- Finally, markets are not necessarily more transparent on the Internet. The available studies concur that prices vary among e-retailers, which casts considerable doubt on the idea that research costs tend towards zero. This is essentially due to providers' capacity for strategic maneuver. The latter seek to differentiate their supply, to block the functioning of comparative search engines, and to perfect strategies of attracting customers.

In a context such as this, what is the specificity of the Internet when it becomes the medium of economic coordination? One can distinguish three principal aspects.

- Firstly, its universal character makes the Internet an electronic medium capable of integrating and coordinating all levels of trade: from the producer of raw materials up to the final consumer. In the past, digital coordination was the reserve of large firms, due to the cost and the complexity of the technologies. This gave rise to trans-shipment, for which there is no longer any call. In fact, it is possible to carry out coordination and produce informational services by having all interdependent actors interact in real time, with the full power of digital technologies. In concrete terms, this has potentially three effects. The first is the *re-engineering* of entire sectors, enabling a more efficient response to final consumers by more clearly identifying their specific needs in relation to more flexible coordination. The second is an extension of the economic agents' capacities to interact, alternatively as providers and demanders, given that each can enter into contact with a great number of partners more easily than before. The third is a reorganization of intermediations.
- Secondly, the multimedia character of the Internet makes it the medium of supply for informational services with multiple functionalities. The integration of data, sound and image processing, coupled with the custom management of communication flow, enables providers – whatever their products – to supply informational services enriching their commodity or service. This results in a great variety of communication, differentiation and discrimination strategies.
- Thirdly, precision in the control of information exchanges on the digital networks federated by the Internet makes it possible to establish new modalities of interaction between economic agents. These modalities are based on using hybrid procedures to share information, combining charge-free access and paid access, market and hierarchical coordination, etc. This gives rise to the emergence of new business models, but also to "communities" within which the sharing of information is organized in compliance with specific rules, intended to preclude occasional free-riding and to ensure the recovery of the fixed costs.

1.3   From the Internet to the digital economy

1.3.1   A misleading view

The above outline of the relationship between the Internet and modes of economic coordination invites us to revisit the properties of the network and redefine them in functional rather than morphological terms. Its universal structure – end to end, multimedia, decentralized, etc. – in fact gives the Internet three essential functionalities, which make it the vector of economic transformations.

- Firstly, *plasticity*: the ability to link up new participants to the network, to insert a wealth of content of all kinds and to open or to close informational spaces. All of these actions are possible with exceptional dynamic flexibility, extreme in comparison with what was possible with network technology before the digital era.
- Secondly, *transversality*: the ability to have "seamless" interaction over geographical, political, economic or social borders. The Internet is thus trans-national, trans-industry and trans-user all at the same time, linking large firms, small professionals and the public thanks to its generic and inexpensive standard.
- Finally, *selectivity*: the ability to modulate information exchanges very subtly according to the nature of the senders and receivers and to the type of "channel", from one-to-one as in ordinary e-mail to one-to-many as in newsletters or many-to-many as in forums. For economic agents, this selectivity enhances accessibility to relevant information pertaining to their needs and strategic actions, notably facilitating the search for the most suitable partners and products for mutually beneficial exchanges.

One might imagine that the advent of this technology, the driving force of the "digital economy", ought naturally to lead both to more fluid markets and to less bureaucratic hierarchies. However, this vision, grounded in the "common sense" belief that greater technological performance will necessarily induce greater economic performance, is already weakened in part by the facts, and is misleading in its reductive simplification. It assumes that the cogs of the traditional economy remain fundamentally the same, and that ICTs produce the miracle "lubricant" serving to remove all friction, thus progressively giving reality to the double project of the perfect market and the transparent hierarchy. Such an argument is too hasty, for it disregards the fact that the profound changes affecting the availability and transmission of information not only improve the "infostructure" of the economy but also generate "mutations" in the "selection" of economic mechanisms.

Any reasoning which postulates the dynamic stability of those mechanisms and their natural convergence towards an "ideal" steady state is condemned to logical error, because existing routines are challenged and hybridized by new ones in a Schumpeterian "destructive creation" process. Indeed, the digital revolution might very well produce rather unexpected effects: markets tending to greater segmentation rather than greater fluidity; hierarchies tending towards greater malleability rather than greater efficiency; and most of all, information becoming a free input rather than a valuable output – a serious drawback when trying to build an "information society", as it was naively thought in the times of the "new economy" just before the Internet bubble, but certainly a winning card in the construction of a "knowledge society" in which the value does not originate in information for itself but in its appropriation by agents through learning processes.

1.3.2   The second paradox of the digital economy

What are the underlying processes by which ICTs and the Internet contribute to a profound change of regime in the economy? Two key drivers seem to be at work.

Firstly, the historical process of the "dematerialization" of information, i.e. the dissociation between information and its physical "marker", is now taken to its ultimate stage. Before writing, information was indistinguishable from the spoken word, alone capable of bearing it; before the invention of printing, scriptural information was strictly linked to the support on which it was inscribed, and was communicable only if the latter was transferred from one party to another. Since Gutenberg, the composed book has enabled the copying of information at lower cost, and therefore its wider distribution, while maintaining a physical link between the information and an underlying commodity; the same goes for the record, the CD, the DVD, etc. Today, this link has been broken as the Internet allows for the circulation of information content – texts, sounds and images – free of any physical packaging. Some goods such as software and video games are now pure information goods at their very native stage and all cultural goods such as books, photographs, music or movies can be formatted as digital files (MP3, jpeg, Divix, etc.).

Secondly, an increasingly large share of goods has become "information intensive", either directly because they include electronics and software or are connected to networks and databases (such as cars), or because information is needed in order to buy and to consume them efficiently – such is the case of experience or attention goods (such as cultural goods), the quality or even the existence of which is poorly known to potential buyers but may be revealed by information provided by former consumers; such is also the case of complex goods (such as computers), which require consumer guidance before purchase and consumer assistance afterwards. Experience and attention goods tend to proliferate in a world of rapid innovation where the consumption space is changing faster and faster, whereas growing "servicization" generates complex bundles, made of material goods (again such as cars) packaged with related services (such as maintenance, insurance or leasing). Consequently, the value chain is being stretched in a double movement: upstream, the "commoditization" of basic products, with no distinguishing features and bearing low informational content; downstream, the "tailoring" of differentiated retail products fitted to the specific needs of various segments of final consumers, by adding value to commodities through information-intensive processes.

Those two major evolutions in the coupling of economic goods and information bear two important economic consequences.

The result of information "dematerialization" is the emergence of an "informational commons". ICTs make information a "non-rival" good: indeed, an agent who yields information does not forego the use of it, or at least grants a very low opportunity cost in relation to the utility transferred to the receiver; moreover, a great number of agents can, within the limits of saturation effects, consume the same information good simultaneously and in its totality, as the success of peer-to-peer demonstrates. However, non-rivalry does not preclude some degree of excludability. Legal or technical means, such as enforcing the traditional copyright legislation by suing and condemning "pirates" responsible for illicit copies, or controlling access to contents through digital rights management (DRM), may be utilized to restrict the scope of the "commons". The strength of such counter-reactive forces should not be under-estimated. What technology has done, technology can undo. Although ICTs do separate information from commodities, it is possible to invert the movement in order to destroy the effects. If the trade of cultural goods is threatened by the dematerialization of information, why not use ICTs to re-establish a link between a specific content and a dedicated channel giving access to it? This is the solution currently recommended and partly implemented by major companies in the media and entertainment industry. The hope is that those attempts to go back to the "golden age" of the captive information will moderate, as the industries of contents will adapt their business models to accommodate the economics of digital technologies. The Sheriff of Nottingham may very well wish to hunt down Robin Hood, for obvious reasons, but history seems to show that behavior of this kind can turn out to be extremely inefficient and lasts for only a temporary period anyway. Eventually, the informational commons will spread and generate a considerable "club" effect, thus giving rise to the emergence of a public good within a market economy.

The second driver, i.e. "information intensiveness", increases the economic agents' need to acquire and develop higher "competencies". Information, as it is conveyed today through markets and hierarchies by traditional media or through social networks, no longer appears sufficient to innovate, to supply or to produce efficiently. More and more "off market" and "off hierarchy" information is becoming necessary. This may be produced and shared on the Web, especially within on-line communities such as open source, consumer practice or professional communities. Such communities instill cooperative mechanisms within the competitive framework of a market economy. The traditional model of competition is not only challenged by the breakthrough of a cooperative and collective processing of information; it is also questioned by a shift in the shape of the overall production function in the economy. Upstream, the mass production of commodities, as well as the research and development (R&D) necessary for the design of final products, generates high fixed costs, whereas further down the line the assembly of tailored consumption packages fitted to differentiated needs may be carried out at a low marginal cost through flexible exchanges of information between consumers and producers. This results in strong economies of scale, which favor industrial concentration, a long way from the usual characteristics of a perfect market economy.

Thus, if Solow's paradox – which stated in the 1980s that computers can be seen everywhere but in productivity and growth statistics – is today overcome, a second paradox of the digital economy can be stated: while ICTs seem to provide the technical support which should favor the efficient performance of an ultra-competitive market economy, they make information a public good, thus sowing the seeds of a cooperative economy. In other words, if they were a pure technological "neutral" platform, ICTs would certainly reinforce worldwide competition by enhancing the transparency, the ubiquity and the flexibility of transactions. However, as ICTs are also the vector of the digitization of information contents, they bring about some typical market failures, such as club effects and economies of scale, which in turn encourage market concentration or even monopolization (as in the case of Microsoft) as well as inter-firm cooperation for sharing R&D efforts or grouping purchases on commodity markets (business-to-business marketplaces) rather than unrestricted competition. The dialectics of competition and cooperation should eventually give rise to a hybrid model of "coopetition" relying upon original mechanisms, some of which may be observed on the Internet at the "laboratory stage".

The collective invention of innovative economic relationships overcoming the "second paradox" should notably respond to two major issues: on the one hand, how can increasing fixed costs be recovered, and on the other, how can it be ensured that supply meets demand when the price signal does not operate properly, either because richer information than just price is necessary (information-intensive goods) or because marginal price is close to zero (pure information goods)?

The recovery of fixed costs can be performed by a range of complementary solutions and the developments currently observed in ICTs and the Internet offer several examples of these. Firstly, there can be income trade-offs within a monopolistic market: pricing of final services above their marginal cost – practically nil – covering the fixed costs of investment and R&D, however at the price of a certain rationing of demand; the commercialization of Microsoft software pertains to this model. An alternative method consists in not billing usage, thus in a certain way selling the service at its marginal cost, while practicing subscription or fixed rates, with the risk of excluding small consumers; this is known as Coase pricing, which the Internet's flat rates typically correspond to. A third method is to call upon the State and the territorial collectivities to partly finance infrastructure; this is notably the case in France for the completion of GSM coverage, through a burden sharing between operators and administration. Finally, it is possible to cover fixed costs without limiting usage further down the line by shifting revenue towards advertising, in keeping with the traditional media model, but also towards derived products, in keeping with an already existing movement that the Internet strongly amplifies: a portal site, for example, offers free hosting and e-mail and receives commission from commercial sites it directs surfers to. This growing gap between the place where the value is generated, through the constitution of an audience, and the place where this value is collected, through the sale of advertising space, of derived products, or through an intermediation commission, seems to definitely be one of the major characteristics of the digital economy: an economy in which the fixed costs upstream are increasingly financed downstream at the end of a value chain in constant extension.

The second question, that of demand's piloting of supply, as it is raised by the increasing informational requests of economic agents, finds its natural solution in resources provided by the ICTs. As it happens, the free supply of tools and content on the Internet facilitates economic exchange, allowing for the formation of self-organized consumer communities homogenous with respect to demand profiles, as well as the realization of a tuned coupling between demand and supply characteristics. The discussion spaces, the forums, the chat rooms, or even simply the links between personal sites are all places where surfer–consumer "ecosystems" are formed and segmented. These are coherent but evolving systems, allowing providers to target and differentiate their products when they can access this information on the structure of demand. One thus observes the emergence of a function of electronic intermediation on the Internet, "infomediation", situated on the supply–demand interface. This can be institutionalized when organized by commercial sites, portals or media sites seeking to develop their audience; it can also be informal, when individuals interact directly, without an explicit mediator, to exchange information on products, "pioneers" letting "followers" know about the goods or services which are most likely to give them satisfaction.

1.3.3   From "coopetition" to an economy of knowledge

The model of infomediation is probably a key to the future of electronic commerce, faced with the difficulties and the failures initially brought about by the naive transposition of traditional functions of the commercial relationship to the Internet universe. Today the commercial sites, whose organization is based on the triptych of on-line referencing and presentation of products, on-line ordering, billing and payment, and the retail logistics of the correspondence sales type, barely break even, or generate losses. This is due to misperceptions in the assessment of constraints and advantages specific to going on-line, to over-estimation of advertising income, or to the under-estimation of logistical costs. It now appears that, given that it circumvents the constraints of physical distribution and benefits from advertising income or commercial commission, the most promising model is not to sell products but to connect sellers and purchasers. In short, the eBay archetype, as opposed to the Amazon archetype. Nonetheless, when the goods subject to infomediation are purely informational, a single site can carry out the two functions of infomediation and exchange conjointly (as on peer-to-peer sites). In this way, infomediation intervenes not only to structure the business-to-consumers (B-to-C) and business-to-business (B-to-B) markets but also to develop secondary markets of the consumer-to-consumer (C-to-C) type. Because it relies on a governance mode based on community spirit and cooperation, infomediation can give rise to practices violating or bypassing current law on intellectual or industrial property. In this respect, it is threatened by attempts to "renormalize" emanating from industry or States.

However, infomediation is essential because it plays a necessary role in bringing about the co-evolution of supply and demand, indispensable for the creation of adapted and differentiated economic exchange. Once coupled with a "meta-market" providing infomediation tools, a market operates much more as in Hayeck's view than as in Arrow–Debreu's: suppliers not knowing precisely *ex ante* what to supply meet with consumers not knowing what precisely to buy in order to "co-invent" the terms of their trade. Moreover, in the long run, consumers' preferences are transformed by the confrontation of the information collected on the meta-market and the actual experience of consumption on the market.

The digital economy should become in the long run a "coopetition" economy, with assemblers cooperating upstream, sharing high fixed costs in R&D and grouping their purchases of commodities, and opening themselves up to competition further down the line on the retail markets. To organize the interface between assemblers of final goods and producers of commodities, B-to-B marketplaces appear as an appropriate instrument: these electronic marketplaces operate as monopsonies, benefiting from scale effects generated by mass purchases. However, one should not under-estimate the impact of *antitrust* legislation, which tends to limit possibilities of concentration. As for the competition down the line, it is subject to two factors of moderation. On the one hand, the differentiation of baskets of goods and services tends to reduce the degree of competition in prices by creating niche markets. On the other, because it presents more interproduct economies of scope than economies of scale in relation to the size of the audience, infomediation should eventually lead to the coexistence of several ecosystems rather than a merciless struggle of the winner-takes-all type. Such a reconstruction of the value chain is a process that is greatly "path dependent" and many uncertainties remain as to implementation. In particular, the outcome of two opposite movements is unclear at this stage: assemblers seeking to control infomediation, in order to have as close an access as possible to the final client, are going in one direction, while infomediaries seeking to come closer to the assembling, in order to develop their client base, are going in the other. Moreover, how will the vertical relations between the actors all along the value chain be reorganized? How will firms make alliances to share grouped activities and what will their contractual relations be?

In spite of these various uncertainties, it is likely that new forms of reticular coordination will be created, lying between market and hierarchy, reconciling flexibility and stability. Indeed, they allow the creation of adaptable relations rather than hierarchical subordination; network interactions guarantee both flexibility and a certain degree of stability by favoring cooperation that is initially spontaneous and then maintained as a repeated game equilibrium. Two particular examples merit attention:

- In the management of innovation, a dilemma classically opposes the vertical integration by each firm of its own research unit, and the sharing of common research capabilities by several firms whose production units are competing among each other. The dilemma is expressed by an arbitrage between a latent risk of uncreative research which is overly oriented towards short-term commercial ends, incurred in the first case, and a risk of rupture between fundamental research, applied research and development, borne in the second. What is observed in particular in the Silicon Valley is the possibility of a hybrid structure with research taking place in a breeding ground of start-ups which disappear in the case of failure, or grow if successful, and stay independent or are integrated into large companies. This model avoids disadvantages and combines the respective advantages of the two above opposed structures. On the one hand, the decentralized and "biological" functioning of the breeding ground, in osmosis with its industrial environment, guarantees the social utility of the research and the continuity of the R&D chain. On the other, the mobilization of venture capital provides a way of mutualizing the fixed costs of the fundamental research, an alternative to what would be accomplished by the creation of a common center, and similarly enables the realization of radically innovative projects.
- Where the production of software is concerned, the open source phenomenon constitutes an exemplary case of flexible cooperation between several types of actors through the Internet. First of all, there are "developers", who appear to be operating spontaneously, openly and benevolently, but who in fact are obeying strategies motivated by the perspective of future derived revenues or enhanced ability to innovate. Then there are "testers", experimented users on the lookout for bugs, detecting faults and insufficiencies, formulating requests for improvement, and benefiting as such from free use of the software. Finally, there are commercializing firms, responsible for packaging pieces of software and delivering an installation (paying) service among the mass of "ordinary" users.

These different modes of economic coupling, successively mentioned in relation to firm–client relationships and inter-firm relationships, also take place in intra-firm relationships. In the same way that vertical or horizontal relations between firms leave room for network relations, work relations between agents within the firm are transformed. In this regard, aside from the management of information, the management of knowledge is likely to be profoundly modified by networked ICTs.

The rupture between, on the one hand, traditional computer-aided management, of which enterprise resource planning (ERP) is the most evolved form, and on the other, ICT-based management, working through the medium of Intranets and application service providers (ASPs), lies in the latter's ability to accept evolving management routines dynamically constructed around the creation and exchange of knowledge in relation to the realization of projects. Whereas the classical tools of computerized management are designed with the objective of improving efficiency by formalizing pre-established procedures, the purpose of tools provided in a network corresponds more to a notion of flexibility where knowledge is not an exogenous construct but is elaborated endogenously and adaptively, following the temporary and changing needs of users. *Groupware* software based on neuro-mimetic algorithms, bringing to the users, in the *push* mode, the data which seems most relevant with respect to the contents they are exchanging, provides an illustration of this type of tool. The development of instruments of this kind within organizations could not only assist and structure *workflow* but contribute to the formalization of tacit knowledge, the transformation of *know-how* into knowledge, and the accumulation of an immaterial knowledge capital which, in the digital economy, tends to become an essential asset for firms.

The above analyses give some clues characterizing what could be an economy of knowledge (K-economy) supported by ICTs. Three main features emerge.

- Firstly, the K-economy complies to an "open model" (in the sense of the open model of science) in which the producers and consumers participate in the same "social algorithm", the latter playing an active role as testers or even as co-producers. In this model, infomediation substitutes, at least partly, the traditional direct hierarchy/market interface, leading to a better matching between the "rational" production side and the "hedonic" consumption side, in a world of fast-moving innovation.
- Secondly, there exist strong informational spillovers across agents, each benefiting from the expertise of others: such is the case of infomediation where consumers help other consumers, either *ex ante* when deciding what to buy or *ex post* when learning how to use sophisticated goods; such is also the case of open source software where users and innovators interact in a positive feedback loop.
- Last but not least, information is a "circulating asset", the value of which is increased and not destroyed when it is transferred from one agent to another. The free circulation of information thus benefits the collectivity and constitutes by itself a non-rival good, even if some

of the circulating information goods are individually rivals or could be made excludable. In this view, infomediation, which takes place on the Web and facilitates consumption decisions, may very well be compared to the transmission of ritual objects (laces and braces) from one island to another within papouasian tribes, as a preliminary and necessary condition to efficient commercial trade (Michel Gensollen).

In an economy of knowledge, any codified information, as it may be digitalized at zero marginal cost, becomes a free input for economic processes. It can no longer be considered as a valuable output that consumers would be willing to pay for. At the same time as it creates value by generating productivity gains on the supply side, digitization also displaces value on the usage side: the value of information does not stand in its digital encoding but in the interactive processes through which codified information and ICTs are utilized in order to build up a corpus of knowledge, i.e. a complex and organized mix of "tacit" and codified information that agents mobilize when making decisions in any economic or social circumstance. The transformation of codified information – as an input – into knowledge – as an output – is important both at the individual level (learning process) and at the supra-individual level (generation of management or social routines). Even at the individual level, interaction with others proves to be essential in the learning process as both examples of open source communities and consumer communities clearly demonstrate. Indeed, on-line communities are at the core of the digital K-economy and deserve particular attention.

1.3.4 On-line communities

On-line communities (OCs) are endogenous, spontaneous and informal "economic institutions" generating a new model of inter-individual interaction, both complements and substitutes to the traditional models of infomediation, namely social networks (SNs) and mass media (MM). OCs are of very various types: "practice" OCs, devoted to *ex post* consumer assistance in final markets or to information sharing among adepts of a same hobby or activity; "experience" OCs, where future consumers of a good take advice from pioneers before purchase; "epistemic" OCs, such as open source communities, devoted to innovation or scientific research; horizontal "professional" or interfirm OCs; intrafirm "corporate" OCs, etc. But despite their diversity, OCs share some common features that confer them original characteristics compared with those of SNs and MM. To show this, we shall examine three aspects, respectively related to the infomediation structure, the social link and the role of information.

Where the infomediation structure is concerned, OCs differ from both the extreme models of SNs and MM. Within an SN, word-of-mouth information circulates both ways along a meshed graph of the "small world" type, made of preferential vicinity links complemented by some distant and weaker links (Granovetter [1973]); and the structure may be densified by creating selective or even secret social groups such as civil servant corporations in France or free masonry. In contrast, MM exhibit a "one-to-many" tree-structured graph where the information flow proceeds one way from top to bottom with almost no feedback, except for statistical information collected about audience; a two-step flow may occur when the MM channel penetrates an SN by reaching a leader of opinion; messages conveyed by MM are very simple (advertisements) and poorly differentiated, focusing attention on a narrow selection of items or products. In OCs, contrary to the case of SNs, there are almost no direct inter-individual relationships across participants, but contrary to the case of MM, a specific type of interactivity prevails: interactions proceed indirectly by posting and/or retrieving electronic messages, according to the so-called "blackboard" model; as the opportunity cost of "reading" the relevant information on the blackboard proves to be greater than that of "writing", the system is not threatened by "free-riding" as a public good classically is, but rather by an overabundance of messages which must be controlled by quality-rating procedures.

Now, where the social link is concerned, SNs are characterized by the symmetric roles of agents, the presence of long-term intimacy (links in the graph surviving to temporary inactivity), tacit reciprocal obligations (i.e. not requiring formal explanation) and the coexistence of separate networks depending on the context (for instance, personal network versus business network). In contrast, MM assign strongly asymmetric roles to the source and to the audience, intimacy is absent or "virtual" (as in a fan-to-star relationship) and the communication system is based on the principle of the "transfer of attention": broadcasting programs serve to attract audience and make it available for receiving advertising messages. In OCs, several kinds of agents are active, with dedicated and complementary roles, including authors and innovators, experts and novices, all writing and reading in turn on the blackboard. Intimacy exists – a certain degree of "personalization" is necessary for the recognition of relevant messages – but it is an "instrumental intimacy" which is both ephemeral and "problem oriented", the main question here being to maintain the permanence of the fragile link of participants to the blackboard. If the two dimensions of time horizon (ephemeral versus durable) and degree of personalization (anonymous versus personalized) were crossed in a table, the OCs would lie in the ephemeral–personalized cell, the market in the ephemeral–anonymous one, the hierarchy in the durable–anonymous one, and the family (or the sect!) in the durable–personalized one.

Finally, concerning the role of information, in both cases of SNs and MM, information may be considered as a "signal", the content of which is generally clear and unambiguous but which nevertheless needs "decoding", as the "true" meaning of the message may be biased: trust is at stake. In the case of OCs, the opposite situation prevails as trust in the veracity and authenticity of information is generally not a major issue, for it may be solved endogenously through rating procedures, whereas just understanding the content of messages posted on the blackboard is painful and costly. The reason is that formulations are fuzzy and of the symbolic type (referring to links between objects rather than to objects themselves – as C. Lévi-Strauss stresses when analyzing "savage thought") so that not only representations but also meta-representations – especially representations of others' ignorance – are essential inputs of sense construction through an interactive and collaborative process. Thus, in OCs, information does not operate as a signaling code; rather it constitutes the semantic dimension of a language. From signaling codes, on the one hand, and the semantics of language, on the other, the processing of information by agents drastically changes in nature. Firstly, unlike signaling, which is a "natural" and innate phenomenon, language is an "artificial" and acquired construct. Secondly, whereas information considered as a signal – in a Shanonnian view – may be apprehended through the economic theory of incentives (principal/agent model), based itself on game theory concepts (such as perfect Bayesian equilibrium), information considered as a language requires the building up of original models inspired by the concepts of linguistics.

The impact of OCs on economic efficiency remains to be assessed. As far as hierarchies are concerned, it can be expected that OCs will favor the decentralization of decisions by allowing for a better circulation of information at the lower levels. It is also likely that coupling across hierarchies should be reinforced and the respective roles of SNs and OCs in this regard should be examined. On final markets, which tend more and more to behave as intermediary markets, as consumers "produce" their own utility from the characteristics of the goods they purchase (according to the Lancaster model), OCs will undoubtedly play a significant informational role in the consumption of experience goods (such as cultural goods), in the learning processes facilitating the usage of complex goods (such as computers or hi-fis), or in the interaction of experts and users necessary for the elaboration of innovative and flexible goods (such as video games or software). A key issue here is the impact of OCs on competition and product differentiation: taking the spatial competition model of Hoteling as a reference, the guess is that, through providing a richer and more personalized information than both the SNs and the MM, OCs should bring up a higher horizontal differentiation for a given level of producers active in the market. While much remains to be studied and understood about OCs, one can already be sure that they constitute an indispensable "infostructure", at the core of the knowledge economy, complementing and renewing the traditional roles of SNs and MM: in a knowledge economy, markets are "OC-assisted" and hierarchies are challenged by internal and transversal OCs which tend to blur the firms' boundaries and question the control of proprietary corporate information.

The preceding analyses show to what extent the idea that the Internet and ICTs make markets more fluid and hierarchies more efficient is erroneous, due to the fact that it is naively inspired by a mechanistic and cybernetic representation of the network. In reality, the markets do not become more fluid: the final markets tend to greater segmentation, based on a marketing of the one-to-one type, and even "on request" production; as for intermediary markets, they reorganize around assemblers taking up positions as monopsonies in relation to producers of "commodities". The hierarchies do not become less bureaucratic with unchanged organization and objectives, but shift from the search for efficiency towards the search for adaptability, from the automation of procedures towards the generation of adaptive routines, from the implementation of a system of information towards the accumulation of knowledge capital. "Ecosystems" of consumers, "breeding grounds" of firms maintaining semi-competitive and semi-cooperative relations, adaptive "selection" of routines and knowledge, all are features which suggest that the most relevant metaphor to evoke the role of networks in the digital economy is that of the living being rather than that of machines.

1.3.5   The network as an institutional form

Continuing in this train of thought, the network may be considered as an institution, to the same extent as the market or hierarchy, inviting a broad parallel between three types of economic organization: hierarchy, market and network.

- A hierarchy-based economy, in the mold of the planned economies of the past, is made up of peripheral units coordinated by a central power. Causality is oriented from the collective towards the individual, the center fixing a global finality, defining the necessary tasks and means, then allocating these means and delegating these tasks to different units, each specialized in the execution of a particular task. Transversal relations between units are weak; vertical relations between units and the center are strong and based on plan contracts, acting coercively more than as incentives. The machine serves as a natural metaphor: the parts are predefined and differentiated according to the finality of the whole. This hierarchical model is viable for an economic system of modest size – such as the feudal town – and operates under a regime of increasing returns to scale. It becomes unsuitable for a large-scale economic system, due to problems originating in the transmission of information between center and periphery, thus entailing strongly decreasing organizational returns.

- A market-based economy is made up of atomized and autonomous agents, within the limits imposed by a general regulatory framework. Here, causality is from the individual to the collective, agents "freely" deciding their actions of production and consumption, in accordance with their budget constraints and individual preferences. Vertical relations between agents and the State are reduced to the strict minimum, whereas transversal relations between agents dominate and take the form of commercial transactions on markets where anonymity and a lack of differentiation prevail. A perfect gas serves as a natural metaphor: a great number of microscopic and disordered particles, colliding into each other in conformity with the laws of mechanics, produces a macroscopically stable thermodynamic equilibrium. This market model is efficient for a large-scale economic system and characterized by decreasing returns to scale. It has to make way for hierarchical organizations when they turn out to be less costly (Coase [1937]) or when the presence of increasing returns to scale, externalities or public good justifies a concentrated and regulated industrial structure.

- A network-based economy, such as the future digital K-economy, appears as a meta-system, interconnecting individual agents, hierarchies and markets. Here causality takes place in two directions: from the individual to the collective, contents on Internet sites being accessible to all and enabling the formation of communities as well as the performance of cooperative tasks; and from the collective to the individual, it being possible to reach an overall finality – such as a major research program – by mobilizing memory capacity and calculation resources dispersed among individual computers. Contrary to the hierarchical model, in which the agents are pre-specialized, and contrary to the market model, where they are undifferentiated, the network model allows a variable and adaptive personalization of each individual role, depending on the particular interaction. In addition, cooperative exchanges, which are non-commercial and more flexible than the hierarchical couplings, complete – and partially replace – the transactions inherent to markets and the subordination contracts inherent to hierarchies. Animal biology serves here as a natural metaphor: the organization and evolution of a species stems from adaptive selection and interactive behavior among the individuals that compose it. The network model adapts to both increasing and decreasing returns to scale, since it combines hierarchies and markets. It therefore has greater resilience to changes of scale: its fundamental quality is precisely its *scalability* – a firm's Intranet network or the World Wide Web operating according to similar technical protocols and giving rise to exchanges of the same nature between network nodes.

In the light of the preceding developments, it clearly appears that the Internet is not only the technical medium conveying digitalized information but also the incubator of the K-economy. In other words, the economy of the Internet system is a laboratory prefiguring phenomena that will rule many economic activities in the long run. The probable emergence of a new economic order is notably revealed by the unsuccessful attempts at directly transposing traditional market economy practices onto the Internet, the failure of a certain type of electronic commerce, soon followed by an original form of intermediation, namely infomediation. Similarly, the sites offering free access, which are significantly present on the Internet, are not just the symptoms of unsettled behavior of a medium still in its childhood, later to disappear in adulthood, but fundamental dynamics of the future digital economy.

The naive and vague idea that the Internet is supposed to bring economics closer to the double fiction of perfect markets and transparent hierarchies is based on the insufficiently precise contention that this technology will lower or even erase the costs of information. In reality, one must distinguish the costs of elaborating the information, the costs linked to its manipulation and transmission and, finally, the costs generated by its assimilation and use. The Internet, by its very nature, tends to generate costs of the first and third types, at the same time as it tends to reduce costs of the second type. In consequence, the digital K-economy will certainly not be free of information costs, but on the contrary will be an economy where value will be created and accumulated in the costly transformation of information into knowledge, a knowledge that can be put to use by actors for making better choices and decisions. This transformation is a collective process, requiring the establishment of a global network of economic agents, which would be impossible if the Internet did not offer precisely such an interconnection at a low cost and with very great flexibility.

1.4   Research perspectives

We have endeavored to show how the original characteristics of the Internet and the activities that it bears make this network a laboratory for new organizational forms in economic activities. Naturally, these organizational innovations also derive from more general trends and the emergence and growth of the Internet in fact result from major economic and social transformations, which took place in the second half of the 20th century. Nevertheless, the Internet indeed caused an inflexion in these transformations. Its plasticity, its transversality and its selectivity in information management relaxed a number of constraints in the definition and coordination of informational – and more generally economic and social – activities. Moreover, the extensive promotion around the diffusion of this technology gave many agents a strong incentive to use it for innovating in various areas of social and economic life. This resulted in an accelerated pace of innovation in usage and in the generation of new hybrid processes, for instance in the matching of supply and demand.

This is why the Internet undoubtedly deserves the attention of economists, social scientists, decision makers and citizens and not just that of specialists in network economics. Although it does not overturn the fundamental laws of economics, the Internet gives rise to transformations in the underlying mechanisms and thus leads to revisiting many issues, because some constraints disappear, because the extension of the network generates new practices, because more efficient modalities of supply and usage of informational infrastructures and resources have to be invented. In such a context, several research fields must be investigated.

1.4.1   Toward a new economy?

To better understand both the specificity of the Internet bubble and burst and the true revolution behind the rapid diffusion of Internet and digital technologies, it is useful to come back to the long-term transformations and short-term mechanisms that sustained the euphoria behind the "new economy" tale. Of course, the belief in a "new economy" – meaning a combination of a new growth regime based on knowledge and innovation and the development of new-business models outdating traditional ways of producing value and of competing – was a partly unwished for by-product of several factors: politicians' need to sell a "new frontier", the mass media's discovery of the promises of digital technologies, financial firms' need to raise money to fund new ventures, the ICT industry's desire to sell its product and services, etc. At the same time, many of the phenomena highlighted during "new economy" hysteria were illustrative of long-term evolutions of society and the economy. They changed the minds of many individuals, boosting the innovation wave by generating millions of experiments. The first section of the book is therefore dedicated to the understanding of what is actual in the virtual concept of a new economy.

William Lazonick shows in particular that at the root of the "new economy" there is an innovative vision of what firms are. This vision emerged in the late 1960s in the US ICT industry, and in particular in California, and spread globally across countries and industries. In short, firms transformed their organization to become more agile in a competitive race based on innovation. The new model – whose properties are also analyzed by Aoki (2001) – has been characterized by highly mobile labor and capital available for permanently reallocating production factors to the most successful ideas and/or on the most innovative combination of assets. As clearly shown by the in-depth case study of the US computer industry, the adoption of more agile ways of combining factors by some firms has viral properties. Its adoption by some players in an industry reinforces the innovation intensiveness of competition and leads all competitors to adopt the new model. Since most talented workers and capital owners are incited to invest their means in these new types of firms, potential reallocation of means across industries leads to the generalized adoption of the model in all countries and industries. This movement had major social impacts since it eroded the commitment of shareholders to corporations and of companies to their employees, and vice versa, and therefore did away with the model on which societal regulation was based in the post-Second World War era.

The diffusion of the new model provided some firms with major opportunities to make money and to succeed in the global market at a dizzying rate. This was clearly one of the real phenomena sustaining a transformation of the beliefs of many individuals that made the adoption of the Internet and related economics practices so rapid and radical. Patrice Flichy highlights for its part how the ideology that mobilized so many decision makers and economic agents in the late 1990s was concocted. Indeed, the few bright commercial successes based on the Internet – like those of Amazon, eBay and Google – cannot explain by themselves the huge number of resources mobilized to develop and adopt the Internet and related technologies, and the resulting impressive wave of innovation. Developers, investors, adopters were all driven by an ideology that can be characterized by the famous slogan of 1968 student protestors: "Let's be reasonable, let's call for the impossible." At the height of the turmoil, the common wisdom among those most involved was that the technology was going to do away with all the past rules of the economy, society and even physics. Free of any constraint, it was possible to reinvent everything and to envisage changes in all domains. This belief – and beliefs are the root of radical social and economic transformation, as Douglass North (2005) points out – came from the complex interpenetration of three ideologies that at the same time were partly fighting against each other, namely the "common-ism" of the academic involved in the development of the Internet, the "community-ism" of the 1968 generation, and the "free-market-ism" of digital entre-preneurs. On the one hand, all these communities shared the idea that the characteristics of information and of digital technologies were calling for the destruction of the order inherited from the prior industrial revolutions. On the other hand, they all developed contradictory visions of what the new order should be, leading to the idea that the new situation was characterized by the absence of rules. This released ener-gies and at the same time contributed to the diffusion of many erroneous visions that partially explain the bubble and its bursting.

Ulrich Hege and Sébastien Michenaud dedicate their chapter to this very subject: understanding the transformations in the financing of innovative companies that emerged with the advent of the Internet and the "Internet bubble". Their goal is precisely to explain the mechanisms that enabled the new beliefs to turn into actual investments and innov-ations because the finance industry developed new tools to fund activ-ities which were based on very mobile human capital and characterized by all kinds of network effects. The bubble was not "irrational"; rather, it is characteristic of a wave of innovations – that write off part of the stock of knowledge on sustainable business models – and of an industry characterized by winner-takes-all competition in which path dependency matters. Leading firms rationally over-invested and the bubble burst was in a sense the price to be paid for the benefits brought about by the Internet: the almost immediate availability of a global information infra-structure and the leveraging of the deep movement of organizational innovation that is reshaping so many human activities and societies.

This first set of contributions aims at understanding the roots of the digital and Internet "revolution" and to place it in the broader picture of the macro-evolutions of the global economy, and especially of the most advanced economies. Certainly, the current evolutions are not deter-mined by an exogenous technology produced by research labs and an academia following its own logic. The technology is produced to address the economic and social challenges raised by the success of the two industrial revolutions; and especially the need to realize major productivity gains in coordination activities (Jonscher, 1983, 1994). However, the technology opens new perspectives and it is one essential goal of this book to propose a reading of them and to present some of the analytical tools needed to understand the current evolutions.

1.4.2   On-line communities

As pointed out above, one of the essential innovations behind the Internet is the end-to-end principle that allows information flows to be managed decentrally and the creation of information spaces that are the core of the on-line community phenomenon. These communities are in a sense a radical innovation because, compared with communities before digital networks, they are set among individuals who are not strongly linked by territorial proximity, family and ethnic ties, or by an organization that groups them in a common entity. Not only do these individuals belonging to virtual communities not know each other since their exchanges are mediated by a technology that allows them to hide their identity or to reveal only part of it, but they are also often lightly involved in several communities, which therefore overlap in complex ways. In any case, digital technologies allow grouping by affinities, even if these affinities are weak, temporary and partial.

These communities are aimed at building and sharing common resources that can be either information and knowledge or coordination platforms. First, the technology provides solutions to effectively aggregate and make available modular goods made of dozens, sometimes millions, of contributions. Technology is the key to building and distributing these public goods. Second, the technology allows the implementation of rules to control the behavior of the various members, providing them with the right incentives to contribute, to exchange and to manage access. On-line communities give rise to innovative economic models because they blur the usual distinction between production and consumption and because exchange and reciprocity are no longer based on private property and markets (nor on hierarchy and public ownership), but on innovative ways to manage individual incentives and common rights to access and use. Three chapters explore these issues by pointing out that there are very different types of communities, which contrasted economics has still to explore. Various types of communities are based on contrasted modes of adhesion, by different types of members, resulting in different solutions to align incentives and organize the common construction/use of the common good.

In his chapter, Michel Gensollen highlights the fact that despite their heterogeneity and their contrasted aims, on-line or virtual communities share some common characteristics. In particular, virtual communities are very different from real ones because members do not really know each other. By contrast with actual communities based on interpersonal relationships and on the involvement of members in the maintenance of the collective order (well analyzed by Elinor Ostrom in her various essays, e.g. Ostrom and Walker [1997]), the technology is the sole mediator between anonymous members in virtual communities. The information corpus – the blackboard – at the centre of the community is the link among the participants. It is both the collective output, access to which incites them to be members of the community, and the tool implementing common rules of behavior. By organizing contribution to the corpus and access to it, the tools that manage the corpus allow participants that do not need to be altruistic to produce commons. What is new with virtual communities appears therefore to be this ability to hybridize the anonymity of market exchanges (and therefore potentially the wide scale), with the ability to avoid the tragedy of the commons allowed by the capability to self-organize efficiently in groups sharing common interests. It is important to point out that this hybridization is essential since it makes it possible to surpass the limits of both the public provision of common goods and market failures. Communities are self-organized on the basis of users' actual needs. They do not rely on the hypothetical capability of a third party to identify needs and to efficiently produce and distribute access to the related goods in a world where incentives to lie (on actual needs) and shirk (to access without paying) are high. They also enable the bypassing of market failures that can be of two types. Either the market does not develop because it is impossible to design a property rights system ("tragedy of the commons" – see Heller and Eisenberg [1998]; Heller [1998]) or the market is too costly because the "tragedy of the anti-commons" applies: the fragmentation of property rights leads to the explosion of transaction costs. On-line communities clearly bypass these various markets and bureaucratic failures.

In addition, Michel Gensollen highlights the fact that various types of communities emerge in various contexts. Indeed, communities can be aimed either at sharing an existing stock of information goods (e.g. file sharing) or at producing knowledge about goods (experience-sharing communities) or at producing knowledge that will result in a good (epistemic communities). Nicolas Curien, Emmanuelle Fauchart, Gilbert Laffond, and François Moreau, whose contribution focuses on consumer communities, deepen this line of analysis. They point out the incentives and dynamic constraints impacting on the building of communities. Members' objectives can vary greatly in relation to the nature of the information that is exchanged (e.g. about competitive supplies or how to use products). The result is contrasting incentives to contribute to a community (depending on whether the game is repeated or not) which impact on its likelihood to emerge and to survive as an information provider. In addition, the value of use of a community, and adhesion, are strongly linked to the quality and credibility of the information provided. This qualifies or disqualifies producers from playing a role in the organization of consumer communities. It also impacts on their interests and therefore on their ability to manipulate communities. This contribution points out the two "barriers" to the development of communities: the difficulties of self-organization on the one hand, the difficulties for a third party to extract or use information on the other. Dynamic network analysis is therefore essential to understanding the abilities of various types of communities to emerge, and explains their design and therefore the type of information service they are able to provide.

Godefroy Dang Nguyen and Thierry Pénard complement this analysis by showing how incentive systems have to be designed in on-line communities to guarantee a minimal level of contribution. They show in fact two important results. First, the coexistence of contributors and free-riders is a stable situation. Because of the characteristic of information as a good, the tragedy of the commons does not systematically apply because a small share of contributors is necessary to guarantee the long-term sustainability of the information-sharing system. However, the rules of the community – and they are especially easy to implement with digital networks since the technology can automatically manage the quality of the access to the information commons (e.g. priority) – can be manipulated to enhance the incentives to contribute and therefore reinforce the viability and the dynamism of the community.

While these three contributions focus on specific categories of communities, their findings are of general interest. Because many communities are based on individual extrinsic motivations,[1] communities do not systematically emerge. Those which do emerge have to be designed so as to align members' incentives, and communities differ because they can be driven by very different aims, given their context. This leads to a "biological" world where self-organization leads to the emergence of multiple patterns of evolving and interacting organisms.

1.4.3   Network externalities and market microstructures

The characteristics of the digital world are not only linked to the growing ability to coordinate and to self-organize, they are also due to the

---

[1] Of course, we agree that there are also intrinsic motivations in the performance of many on-line communities.

intrinsic characteristics of networks and information goods. Carl Shapiro and Hal Varian clearly explained in their 1998 book why the combination of network effects and information characteristics shapes the nature of competition and market structures in the digital era. In short, the combination of an economy of pure fixed costs and of (positive) network externalities makes monopoly stable. When a market structure is competitive, it is difficult to sell information at a positive cost because competitors are always incited to decrease prices to marginal costs, which tend to zero. However, when a monopoly is established, it can implement various strategies to extract consumer surplus (customization, versioning, bundling, etc.). There is therefore a dynamic race to attain a monopoly position. The latter pretty much depends on gaining a dominant position in the early stages of the competitive process. Indeed, positive network externalities turn in dynamics in increasing return of adoption. Competitors are therefore strongly incited to subsidize consumers in the early stages of the "winners-take-all" competitive process. These factors explain both the logic of the Internet bubble and the marketing strategies of information and network service providers.

However, the nature of information as a good and the existence of network externalities have other consequences that are developed in the two following sections. The next section will highlight some of the consequences of the fixed-cost nature of information. This section focuses on network effects.

Nicholas Economides provides us with a chapter in which the essential characteristics of network effects and their consequences are highlighted. He surveys the origin of network externalities and points out the consequences of network effects on competitors. One of the essential consequences is that, while competition is harsh because of its "winners-take-all" character, network service providers are always producing complementary goods. They therefore need to cooperate and compete at the same time, since in practice interconnection and compatibility are required, either because of (regulations driven by) consumers' needs or because of service providers' needs to combine their complementary commercial supply. At the same time, since competition is constant, the parties always strategically manipulate pricing and technological design to foreclose markets. There is therefore an intrinsic tension between cooperation and competition in the provision of any network services. These factors are therefore inherent to the digital and information industries and explain the richness and the subtleties of strategies in this permanent attempt to win the race, which is never-ending because of the permanent entry of new providers driven by technological innovation. Such a game is also highly complex because it is based on the interactions of hundreds of components/markets (i.e. the various components of physical networks, the competing physical infrastructures, the world of network services provision, the proliferation of information services, interacting software, etc.), leading to the expansion of the competition arena and the need to manage interconnections.

The latter aspect has been highlighted recently by the development of literature on two-sided markets. Jean-Charles Rochet and Jean Tirole (2004) point out that a central agent – an intermediary – could be useful when externalities occur between the two sides of a market and when it is difficult to internalize them because of transaction costs. This agent, hereafter qualified as a platform, can enhance the quality of the matching by playing on the distribution of transaction costs between the two sides of this market. This occurs when there are crossed network effects because, for instance, suppliers value the number (or the quality) of the users, and the users value the number (or the quality) of the suppliers. In such a case, an intermediary can organize cross-subsidization between the two sides of the market if they have a contrasted propensity to pay for an efficient matching. This ability to cross-subsidize and in addition to control for adverse selection or regulate competition on each side of the market can result in a better matching that is of value for market users. Alexandre Gaudeul and Bruno Jullien rely on this framework to more closely analyze the strategy of market intermediaries and the impact of their profit-seeking behavior. While these intermediaries are necessary, they are incited to expel some potential users (because they have to charge a positive price for their service). Moreover, they have incentives to strategically manipulate and conceal information to extract the surplus from trade in the market they intermediate. Generally speaking, we are in a second-best world where interacting agents need intermediaries who are more efficient when they are in a monopoly position (and are therefore stable), although it leads them to extract rent and provide their services with distortions.

Developing the idea that digital networks are giving rise to a new category of intermediaries – infomediaries – that play an essential role in markets aimed at exchanging information goods, Pierre-Jean Benghozi and Thomas Paris highlight the role of prescription on such markets. Information goods being experience goods, consumers value the services designed to help them select the products/services corresponding to their needs. On many information markets there is therefore a three-way relationship between the buyer, the seller and the prescriptor. The latter can be directly remunerated – either by the buyer or the user – for the service he provides or he can bundle his prescription service with additional services, such as information good delivery. This way of analyzing the functions of infomediaries makes it easier to understand the economics of several alternative on-line business models that combine different sources of revenues. It is also a way to envisage the business models that are emerging with the convergence between the TV and entertainment industries and digital networks and services, since prescription is an essential role for broadcasters and programmers in the mass-media system.

Understanding the complex problems linked to the management of externalities requires a diversity of approaches since by definition externalities lead to stepping outside of the market rationale.

1.4.4 *Producing, distributing, and sharing information goods*

In the digital era, network effects combine with the public-good nature of information and knowledge. Indeed, with digital technologies, information goods tend to become pure public and pure fixed-costs goods because of the almost perfect quality of digital copies and their cost tending to zero. As Carl Shapiro and Hal Varian point out, among others, this characteristic opens up new perspectives in the way information goods, and to a certain extent knowledge, can be distributed and produced. Knowledge has indeed to be contrasted with information goods since it is a "good" that magnifies some of the characteristics of information goods – e.g. knowledge generates new knowledge, leading to spillover effects – and since some of its characteristics are different from the average information goods. For instance, common wisdom states that it is rather cheap to consume information (although this is questionable since it assumes that the consumer is "equipped" with knowledge and technologies to decode, to interpret and to use or to enjoy the received signal), while using knowledge requires not only being "equipped" with the cognitive capacities to understand the new knowledge but also being able to absorb the knowledge, i.e. to understand it and combine it with the mastered stock of knowledge. That said, a lot of what can be drawn from the analysis of information production and distribution can be adapted to the economics of knowledge, and vice versa (see Foray [2004] for an analysis of the main differences).

Being oriented towards the analysis of exchange rather than production, economists have been devoting a lot of attention to the marketing and pricing of information goods over recent years. To put it as simply as possible, due to marginal costs tending to zero and to the ability to copy information at a low price (and to crack code when it is encrypted), price competition is impossible to sustain in the digital world. Optimal strategies for information producers are to try to attain a monopoly position – either by cost domination or by differentiation, or by manipulating switching costs, or by relying on intellectual property – and then to implement an "optimal" pricing scheme which depends upon other characteristics of information goods that are experience goods and non-rival, which might generate consumption externalities and lead to them being incorporated in complex goods, etc. This leads to a world of possible discrimination based on bundling and customization, on free or partly free information goods (the producer selling complementary goods or selling by-products of the consumption of information goods, like audience), of non-linear pricing in relation to the propensity to consume (the most motivated users paying fees for unlimited access, the less motivated ones paying on a per-consumption basis – see Sundararajan [2004]), and so on and so forth.

This is the direction of Yannis Bakos and Erik Brynjolfsson's chapter. They show that bundling can create "economies of aggregation" for information goods if their marginal costs are very low, even in the absence of network externalities or economies of scale or scope. Their key results are based on the "predictive value of bundling", the fact that it is easier for a seller to predict how a consumer will value a collection of goods than it is to value any good individually. As a result, a seller can extract more value from each information good when it is part of a bundle than when it is sold separately. In turn, more consumers find the bundle worth buying than would have bought the same goods sold separately. Bakos and Brynjolfsson's contribution explains why concentration is to be expected on the information market and analyzes its consequences.

Marc Bourreau and Virginie Lethiais explore the incentives of an online content provider to introduce both free content and pay content when consumers are uncertain about quality. Free content acts as a partially informative signal; the more free content is available, the higher the probability for a consumer to discover the true quality of content. However, as the total amount of content is fixed, the higher the proportion of free content, the lower the quantity of pay content, hence the lower willingness to pay for it. As a result, sellers of low-quality information offer only pay content, whereas sellers of high-quality information offer free content to signal its quality, which leads to setting prices lower than they would be in a world of perfect information.

Both contributions provide insights into the optimal strategies for selling information goods in cyberspace and their consequences on market structure. They forge links with the proliferating literature on information pricing and marketing strategies, whose main lines of analysis were recalled above. The book also focuses on the economics of production. Indeed, digital technologies make a deep impact on the economics of production of information goods and knowledge. First, the combination of digital networks and capabilities to store and retrieve information in a very flexible way allows participants in a production process to share information and knowledge on a scale that was not reachable before. It boosts spillover within a given community and maximizes the likelihood of innovation. Second, the ability provided by digital technologies to control access to digitized information and to implement systems that organize differentiated rights of use or right of access to information commons is a tool to implement new types of incentives to guarantee efficiency and participation in the production of information goods and knowledge.

So far, the open source software movement has generated a lot of attention as well as controversy among economists, who explore whether it is an efficient and universal new model of production for information goods and more generally knowledge. First, there is controversy concerning the driving forces of the movement. Some claim that it is sustainable only because indirect incentives (such as signaling on the job market) and subsidization by government (that allows publicly funded researchers to contribute to the development of open platforms) and by firms (in fact competitors of Microsoft such as IBM) guarantee participation. They therefore conclude more or less implicitly that the resulting biased competition between software editors and open source communities is inefficient. Their opponents develop the idea that many participants to copyleft movements (in open source software [OSS] communities, but also in artistic production, production of content such as blogs and encyclopedias, etc.) are driven by intrinsic motivations to share and to develop non-commercial means to produce and share informational resources and knowledge. The technology simply makes it possible to implement self-sustainable means to do so efficiently and on a large scale, which can result in an efficient allocation of means since free contents and open contents maximize diffusion (the incentives problem being solved).

Second, there is also controversy over the efficiency of the principle of open access to information and knowledge resources. On the one hand, several economists claim that the lack of validation by the demand side can result in a false allocation of inventive capacities. In addition the uncoordinated development of components can lead to a fragmentation of information resources (and technological incompatibilities), which reduces the value of use and leads users to bear the costs of incompatibilities and integration. On the other hand, defenders of OSS and copyleft point out that the voluntary contribution of hundreds or millions of developers, beta-testers, and writers results in high-quality products because they can be designed and tested thanks to wide-scale competition among talents. In addition, free access avoids the "tragedy of the anticommons" (Heller and Eisenberg [1998]; Heller [1998]), i.e. the non-completion of many transactions when transaction costs are positive due to the dedication of resources to the protection of property rights when knowledge is privatized and when exchanges occur throughout the market. The tragedy is especially damaging when it concerns knowledge since it deprives the community from many potentially productive spillovers.

These issues of incentives and efficiency are more extensively discussed in the contribution by Dominique Foray, Sylvie Thoron and Jean-Benoît Zimmermann who point out how an appropriate institutional framework (i.e. set of rules, whether they are legal or of a self-regulation nature), combined with the nature of knowledge, which can generate intrinsic motivations to innovate, disclose, and share – because it impacts on the ability to learn – generates and maintains in the long run individual incentives to contribute and the collective benefits of knowledge sharing (which combine open access to the public good and maximization of its development because innovation is boosted by the sharing of knowledge). This is not, however, incompatible with analysis in terms of extrinsic motivations. Indeed, developers can value their ability to contribute on a service/training market by selling services aimed at accessing and using the OSS efficiently. The authors show that such a "business model" is compatible with efficient incentives provided to the best developers.

The aforementioned contribution shows clearly that the understanding of the economics of open source and copyleft should not be based on a strong dichotomy – schizophrenia? – between analyses in terms of intrinsic and extrinsic motivation or in terms of community vs. market-based economy. The new modes of production (and distribution) that are invented today around information goods are hybrids between the individual incentives provided by the market system and the aim to maximize spillovers provided by governmental patronage of public science. The development of OSS and copyleft licensing creates a regime where agents can voluntarily choose to revert from the private-property/market regime to a regime which is neither purely public nor mandatory nor uniform since the inventor can choose what is open and what remains closed in its licensing policy.

The choice of the "openness" of the property right regime does not impact only on the level of spillovers or on the individual incentives to contribute, it impacts on the transmission of signals from the final users to the developers as well. Indeed, the strong advantage of market is that developers are incited to reply to the demand of consumers. The strong advantage of hierarchies, and therefore of the "Republic of Science", when it is well managed, is to efficiently divide works among contributors, essentially by avoiding duplications and by inciting inventors to invade the unexplored territories. Jean-Michel Dalle and Paul A. David analyze the mechanisms by which open source software developers' code-writing efforts are allocated. On the basis of original simulation tools aimed at describing the dynamic of OSS development, they show that developers incited by the views of their peers are likely to concentrate their efforts on "hot spots", i.e. on problems and modules that are already widely explored. This concentration of contributions is therefore not conducive to producing self-organized software code that yields high utility to end-users who want a large and diverse range of applications. This therefore calls for the design of a governance mechanism and rules that would incite developers to more efficiently allocate their efforts in order to increase the social utility of the resulting software.

In addition to enlarging the vision of the elements to be taken into account when analyzing the economics of alternative institutional arrangements to study the production of information and knowledge, the contribution by Jean-Michel Dalle and Paul A. David shows that new analytical tools are sometimes required. Here simulations are used. In other cases, as in the chapter by Nicolas Curien et al., other methods are required. The phenomena to be dealt with in the digital economy require the implementation of new analytical tools in economics.

1.4.5   How e-markets perform

At the dawn of the Internet era, there were many misleading perceptions of the impact of the Internet on markets and these played an essential role in the expansion of the bubble. The development of a pervasive and global network able to support wide-scale exchange of information and to process it at the same time as transmitting it was seen as a way to realize the dream of a Walrasian market. The technology was supposed to replace the auctioneer and allow any agent to gather data on potential supply on a wide scale (if he was a consumer) or on demand (if he was a supplier) and to easily select the best quality/price counterpart. This would have resulted in quasi-competitive markets that would have eliminated rents and unnecessary intermediaries, closely resembling the quasi-perfect market organized by the computer reservation systems in the airline industry. Since these assumptions were based on the unjustified extrapolation of the impact of ICTs on research costs – especially because they ignored strategic behavior at play on electronic networks – and since they also ignored that a market is generally the result of long and complex processes of collective learning and institution building – to generate standards of quality, tools and rules to exchange information, governance mechanisms to monitor the market and the competition process, etc. – these misleading perceptions were also at the origin of the burst of the bubble, when investors realized that the actual implementation did not match expectations.

That said, while information technologies did not stir up the organization and performance of all markets, especially because there were barriers to their implementation in many markets, giving rise to the failure of many commercial platforms and of many pure players, they significantly impacted the ability of market designers to implement sophisticated procedures to ensure the meeting of demand and supply as well as the ability of players to develop sophisticated strategies.

While implementing auctions is costly since it requires a sophisticated infrastructure to collect and select bids, an appropriate auction mechanism avoids collusion among bidders and allows the various participants' reservation prices to be revealed. This enables the seller or the vendor to benefit from the best option. Thus auctions certainly constitute one of the most sophisticated tools invented to implement efficient markets. Aimed at destroying information rents, auctions are used as widely as possible when it is feasible for a seller or a vendor to implement auctioning. From this perspective, the Internet has considerably extended the ability to implement auctions since the technology allows information flows to be controlled (so that anonymity and privacy can be guaranteed) at the global level. This enables the gathering together in the same virtual space of a large number of bidders that cannot collude – at a very low price – leading to the development of auctions for items of little value. While the most current auction systems that are implemented are far from being the most sophisticated and efficient ones (because efficient auction mechanisms can be hard for users to understand), the Internet has been multiplying the use of auction mechanisms in markets. In turn, thanks to the tracking capabilities of digital technologies, the development of these systems has provided the research community with a unique set of observations about the strategies of users, enabling a better assessment of their actual behavior and performances. Digital technologies have also made it possible to develop tools to help or even replace bidders, fully automating the auction mechanism in certain circumstances. In their chapter, Patrick Bajari and Ali Hortaçsu survey recent studies on Internet auctions and draw our attention to what we can learn both about the way on-line auctions perform and about auction design in general.

In contrast to the conventional and naive wisdom that the Internet reduces search costs to zero, the other chapters in this section show that search costs are superior to zero on the Web and can be strategically manipulated by the supply side. Maarten C.W. Janssen, José Luis Moraga-González and Matthijs R. Wildenbeest try to better understand the impact of the Internet on consumer search costs because there is mixed empirical evidence on the matter. On the one hand, it is expected and sometimes observed that the Internet will promote competition, thereby lowering prices and price dispersion. On the other hand, the actual facts show persisting price dispersion and the aforementioned manipulating strategies. According to the authors, the impact of the use of the Internet on prices should be analyzed both in a differentiated way, especially in relation to the category of goods, and in the dynamic effect because learning and adoption play a role.

Indeed, a product's value relative to search costs as well as the search engine rate of adoption impacts on consumers' search incentives. In addition, the impact of improved search technology can lower unit search costs, or can increase the search engine rate of adoption. In other words, it impacts on each individual consumer's search strategy, or on the efficiency of consumers' search activities in general, resulting in contrasted effects on price level and dispersion. Their chapter therefore suggests that the long-run impact of Internet usage on commodity markets will be sensitive to the extent to which search engines are adopted and become central places of information exchange. Future empirical studies assessing the impact of Internet usage on market efficiency should therefore take into consideration market characteristics such as product value and the search engine rate of adoption more explicitly in order to provide a more accurate vision of what should be expected in the long run. The following chapters draw some of the consequences of this persisting imperfect transparency of markets.

Jacques Laye and Hervé Tanguy address the issue of proximity. Indeed, one of the vivid features of off-line markets is their embodiment in the physical space. As the broad literature on monopolistic competition and spatial economics points out, space and geography explain a lot of actual market structures and microstructures as well as firms' strategies and pricing. What happens, then, in a market that is supposed to be freed of any localization constraint because it is global, virtual and pervasive? On the basis of a simplified model based on the idea that merchant sites can form coalitions to reduce consumers' search costs (by developing mutual electronic linkages or specialized search engines), the authors show that firms have incentives to coalesce – to gain market share from non-coalesced sites – especially with highly differentiated partners, for better exploitation of the search process of consumers against the non-coalesced sites. Thus, in a world where search costs are not equal to zero, even if they tend to be lower than in the past and even if geography no longer matters – which is obviously a strong assumption for non-pure information goods – proximity still matters. It does not come only from the user/demand side, as pointed out by the literature on communities described above, it comes from the strategies developed by the supply side of markets. While some players like Google or some collective phenomena like Wikipedia contribute to the reduction of search costs and of distances, forces are at play to maintain them, both to avoid the advent of unbridled competition and to benefit from positive externalities resulting from proximities, even if these proximities are clearly endogenously generated by the players themselves that manipulate the technology and the digital space to avoid total transparency.

Marc Bourreau and Christian Licoppe provide another example of manipulation of market mechanisms on the Internet. On the basis of a case study of a site that sells the same standardized commodity in two different ways – catalog and auction – at two different prices, it shows how e-merchants can play on the cognitive abilities of consumers and on their own ability to manipulate at a low-price interface with the market. They strategically discriminate consumers thanks to an "apparent" differentiation. However, the case study shows that this type of strategy, which is apparently simple and cheap, is demanding in terms of organization and management. Indeed, consumers also play among the alternative interfaces provided by the merchant. In particular, they try to exploit the information they extract on one marketing channel to benefit from lower prices on another. Moreover, even if they do not play intentionally, they do play. Market exchanges are embedded in social norms, customs and beliefs. The necessity to "play fair" in a world where repeated exchange is potential and not totally disembodied can lead the e-merchant to not fully extract the consumer surplus. Indeed, in the studied case, consumers who get rebates through the auction system call the on-line agents to get the same advantages on the goods sold at posted prices, because they consider they should benefit from the same "fair conditions" on the whole basket they buy.

The complex relationships between the abilities provided by digital tools to manipulate the information space so as to capture consumer surplus (often in the exchange of an added-value and customized service) and the potential reaction of users and citizens concerned by fairness, preference for equality and other moral values are certainly a broad research domain that should be more deeply investigated. Indeed, the latter provided essential conditions for the sustainability of business models. It prevented, for instance, Amazon from implementing discriminatory pricing some years ago. The understanding of the future characteristic of the digital economy should therefore combine the current analysis of what is possible in terms of business models with the analysis of what is acceptable from the users'/consumers'/citizens' point of view.

1.4.6 Evolving institutional infrastructures

The Internet and digital technologies do not impact only upon market microstructures, they also impact on the institutions that frame economic activities and in particular markets. As pointed out above, the Internet empowers agents to design and implement collective coordination rules that fit their needs better. This raises issues about the interactions between self-regulations and public regulations, because one of the consequences of this empowerment of agents is the proliferation of self-regulatory initiatives. There is also a growing supply of institutions developed by entrepreneurs on a competitive basis. Digital networks gave rise to a number of initiatives aimed at developing a commercial supply of services, whose combination resulted in institutional infrastructures for markets, generally provided by public administrations or by regulated firms, such as courts, money, marketplaces, property rights systems. The Internet stimulated the growth of new players that were able to innovate because traditional regulations were not applicable to them. Up to now, many of these new players have been unable to supplant the providers of the former order. In some cases, it is simply because they have been forced in the end to comply with traditional public regulations. In many cases, it is simply because the type of services they propose, while competing against the services provided by incumbents, are more complements to than substitutes for them. New market infrastructure providers are more efficient only in certain circumstances.

The four following chapters address the issue of the co-opetition between private instances and public regulation in the provision of dispute resolution, of money and means of payment, of financial market infrastructure and of property rights systems. The first three chapters focus on competition among alternative providers of solutions. The last chapter, which can also be linked to the section on communities, insists on the idea that co-opetition does not occur only among entrepreneurs seeking to provide coordination solutions; it occurs among all types of communities seeking to self-regulate their use of information resources and coordination platforms. The interactions among these self-regulatory efforts that concern on-line communities and also localized ones (that therefore refer to traditional public institutional frameworks) have to be better analyzed to understand how interdependences should be managed to improve the efficiency of the institutional frameworks that de facto frame the performance of the information and knowledge economy and society.

Bruno Deffains, Yannick Gabuthy and Philippe Fenoglio, provide us with a stimulating case study about conflict resolution in cyberspace that teaches us a lot about the relative efficiency of commercial solutions provided on a commercial basis by new "e-mediaries". They indeed show the success of a private commercial solution in solving disputes on-line: Cybersettle. This service has been widely adopted, not only to solve conflicts related to Internet-based transactions but also to solve conflicts related to off-line transactions, namely conflicts among insurance companies. This is the case because, thanks to an algorithm available on-line, Cybersettle provides a service aimed at automatically solving simple disputes (concerning the amount of damages), which is quick and cheap. At the same time, the authors point out that the Cybersettle algorithm is suboptimal or at least dominated by an obvious mechanism (Chatterjee and Samuelson [1983]). Since it is not obvious for the "man of art" it is patentable however, whereas the Chatterjee mechanism is not. Because Cybersettle developed its services on a commercial basis, it had to choose a conflict resolution procedure that is not optimal in terms of conflict resolution, while it provides the users with fully automated solutions that save costs and time, and which relies on intellectual property protection and on a consistent technical infrastructure. Network externalities and increasing returns of adoption ensured its commercial success. In addition, since users are mostly professional with a high volume of transactions and (standardized) disputes, they can expect that the "errors" generated by the system are compensated in the end.

This type of case study enables a better understanding of the concrete aspects of competition among organizations that deliver "institutional services" on-line. In fact, this competition is at the fringe. Clearly, the conflict resolution service provided by Cybersettle can apply only to very specific conflicts (based on divergences in the assessment of damages, in a context of repeated game, etc.) and is more a complement than an alternative to judicial conflict resolution or arbitration. Indeed, as opposed to the arbitration of online dispute resolution, it is not of the "last resort" type. Courts are there in the last resort or to solve complex cases. In a sense, the analysis developed by David Bounie and Pierre Gazé on the development of on-line payment systems and on the growth of electronic money leads to similar conclusions. In the late 1990s, the conventional wisdom was that unregulated and highly competitive entities would be able to develop a new monetary system due to their ability to de facto issue money thanks to the payment systems they were developing on-line. Through an in-depth analysis of the various payment systems that exist today, their history and their evolution through time, the authors show that in opposition to the aforementioned theory, on-line payment systems do not compete with the banking system in its role of creating money. However, the development of new payment technologies has allowed many non-banks to play an increasing role in all payment domains: payment orders, clearing and settlement, collection of resources on private accounts and issuing of private liabilities. This challenges the business models of banks, since their control of the payment system allows them to benefit from significant revenues and to extract information that is useful to efficiently play their role of financial intermediaries. Thus, digital technologies are sustaining evolutions of the institutions that frame market activities – hereby providing payment mechanisms and financial intermediation – not because new players and new institutions are substituting the old world but rather because they empower new entrants that compete with incumbents – whether they are commercial firms or public agencies – in specific niches. Doing so they often destabilize the business models of the incumbents and can potentially bring about radical changes in the way the infrastructure of markets is built and governed.

Delphine Sabourin and Thomas Serval perfectly illustrate this in analyzing the consequences of a decision made by the Securities and Exchange Commission (SEC) in 1997 concerning the organization of Nasdaq. The SEC favored the emergence of new market participants known as electronic communication networks (ECNs). These computer-trading systems bypass the market makers on the stock markets and allow investors to directly compensate and execute their orders with more discretion. Due to the electronization of Nasdaq and increasing efficiency of the alternative trading systems, the structure of the market has changed dramatically. The Nasdaq is no longer a pure dealer market and is evolving towards an order-driven market. However, the end of the story is still unknown and the authors rely on market microstructure analysis to study the possible paths of evolution. Indeed, under various conditions there are several possible equilibriums in preventing competition between market makers and ECNs, leading to their coexistence in the long run or to the dominance of one category.

These three chapters clearly show that as organizational changes within firms, information and digital technologies do not impose any specific model. Rather they empower the many actors that influence the organization of economic activities, either by designing collective coordination mechanisms or by providing coordination services. While there are huge changes, they cannot be described and understood as a radical shift from one model to another. There is complex competition and hybridization among many potential models, and the results of these complex evolutions pretty much depend on the evolutions which various industries have entered into. Specific events and players' strategic reactions to evolving conditions are changing market structures and competitors' initiatives. In-depth case studies are therefore required to understand towards which world we are evolving.

The complex question of the evolution of institutional frameworks framing information and knowledge activities, and more generally economics activities partly performed on-line, leads to the analysis of the economics of multi-type and multi-level governance. As the three previous chapters and those in the section on on-line communities point out, digital technologies make it possible to decentrally set systems of rules that lead to a multitude of movements of self-regulation. This proliferation raises the issue of coordination among these decentrally set-up regulations. Indeed, the self-regulation of all kind of communities – which interplay with all sorts of governmental regulations about property rights, privacy, security, free speech, etc. – designs rights of access and use on information goods and coordination spaces. While becoming subject to exclusion thanks to the capability of the technology to control access to any information space, information and coordination platforms remain non-divisible goods. Moreover, individual and group interests could succeed in taking a non-contestable control over "privatized" information spaces. The world of communities and self-regulation therefore has to be organized. Eric Brousseau's contribution shows that, while necessary, the regulation/governance of the proliferating norm setters is complex to implement and could lead to failures that could be worse than self-regulation failures. Again, biological and evolutionary approaches are necessary both to understand the occurring phenomena and to address the need for an efficient governance of the digital world. Instead of trying to design "optimal" regulatory and institutional frameworks, it is better to implement strategies and authorities aimed at governing the processes of evolutions, in particular by guaranteeing minimal cooperation among all kinds of norm setters and by providing solutions to solve conflicts.

1.4.7   *The impacts of the Internet at the macro level*

While the digital revolution is under way, it is essential to grasp some of its macro-impacts and the trends of its evolutions. Indeed, most of the contributions in this book focus on the specific microeconomics of the digital economy. As the famous Solow's paradox demonstrates, the remaining issue is to better understand how these microeconomic changes and performances result in macro-trends and macro-economic performance. Since many questions regarding these micro-evolutions are still open and many phenomena are just emerging, it is certainly not possible today to assess the impact of the digital revolution. It is possible, however, to begin to analyze the elements that have contributed to establishing links between micro and macro phenomena. The last three chapters of this book are attempts to do so.

As the many chapters in this book and many scholars in general point out, and in particular Carl Shapiro and Hal Varian, network externalities are at the core of many of the specific features of the on-line and digital economy. There are only few measures of these externalities, however. Measuring them is essential nevertheless since we know that their magnitude can differ in relation to the adoption/diffusion of a network or of a technology, since they can interfere with diseconomies of scale, producing congestion effects and decreasing adaptation (and therefore value of use) to the specific needs of marginal users, etc. Network externalities are therefore featured by complex dynamic, contrasted patterns given the technology, differentiated magnitude and characteristics of the population of users, and so on. It is essential to get a better idea of these specificities to more efficiently make decisions, whether they are marketing decisions made by technology providers or promotional policies aimed at stimulating the adoption and use of digital technologies and services. Gary Madden, Michael Schipp and Joachim Tan's contribution seeks to measure the change in consumer welfare as networks increase.

Alongside the problem of measure, however, it is essential to better understand the actual dynamics of the digital revolution worldwide, since various nations and regions adopting ICTs in various contexts may well follow contrasted paths of evolution. This is the line of analysis behind the last two chapters.

The main danger when analyzing the digital technology revolution is to focus only on what is changing, in particular by essentially analyzing evolutions occurring on digital networks or in IT industries in general, or in specific countries – and essentially the United States – with the risk of over-emphasizing newness and change and performing irrelevant extrapolations. This came to light in the 1980s when some scholars pointed out that the rise of the information society highlighted by some others (essentially Bell [1973], Lamberton [1974], Porat [1977], Jonscher [1983, 1994]) was mainly an American phenomenon, with Europe and the rest of the world lying far behind in terms of the share of the workforce and the economy oriented towards the production and consumption of information and related technologies. Yet, with the Internet boom, things seemed to have evolved from that perspective in the late 1990s. The Internet seemed to support the development of a truly global movement of the informationization of commerce, the economy and society. Kenneth L. Kraemer and Jason Dedrick question this vision by analyzing the convergence and divergence across countries in the development of Internet-based economic activities. They show that the globalization of e-business has first to be put in perspective with other global forces, such as the liberalization of trade, and that national environments and firm-level business imperatives led to very contrasted adoption of use. Up to now, the technology has been used more for coordination than for market transactions over markets, whereas e-market volumes have been growing steadily. The impact of e-business so far has been more incremental than revolutionary. The impact has been to support rather than transform existing patterns of business activity, and to reinforce the advantages of more global firms, particularly in B2B commerce, while allowing local firms greater opportunities in the B2C domain. The picture they draw confirms the idea that technology is adopted and used according to contrasted and specific ways in various environments and that the understanding of the future of our economies and societies should be grounded in in-depth studies of the impact of the (social, economic and institutional) context in which these technologies are implemented and of the dynamic of adoption (since, clearly, initial conditions can lead to contrasted paths and patterns of e-commerce development). In any case, this confirms the fact that digital technologies should be understood as enabling technologies rather than as technologies imposing an organizational and societal model. They are compatible with many types of economic and social interactions. It is the way and the context in which they are used that leads to homogenization or, on the contrary, to diversity being maintained or even to the generation of new diversity – the question being then to match technological and organizational changes to specific social preferences and economic imperatives to optimally leverage the potential of these technologies.

The vision developed all through this book could however be considered as Western-centric, and even as Valley-centric. While the Internet is probably the technology, and certainly the infrastructure, that has gone through the most impressive rate of development in history – thirty-five years after its invention and ten years after it left the research labs, almost 15% of the global population accesses and uses it – most users are concentrated in the large cities of the most developed countries. In this environment, network effects are fully at work. In less developed countries, in rural areas and among the poorest, however, the digital revolution, and the associated new collective practices and economy, are still a distant dream. Alain Rallet and Fabrice Rochelandet in their chapter point out that while the notion of "digital divide" has been intensively used in the rhetoric of policy making to sell all kinds of public policies, the inequalities raised by the unequal diffusion and unequal abilities to use ICTs are a major concern across and within societies because the unequal and incomplete diffusion of the Internet and, more importantly, of the associated usage, hinders the fulfillment of part of the expected benefits of this open and global information infrastructure. As a result, they identify directions for research and public policy issues which should be respectively explored and addressed to favor the rise of a renewed economic infrastructure for the benefit of all. They highlight, in particular, the complexity of the question due to the fact that the roots of the digital divide do not lie in the lack of digital infrastructure but in underdevelopment and inequalities, the risk being for a deepening of these inequalities to occur due to the increasing return of adoption benefiting those who "have".

This last contribution points out the necessity of putting the innovation wave borne by digital technology into a wider perspective to really grasp and understand the many and complex impacts of information and communication technologies on individual and collective practices, leading to all kinds of new dynamics, anchored, however, in the structures and the paths of development inherited from the past. It is precisely these innovations and this complexity which justify this book, both to contribute to their analysis and to point out the true importance of the Internet and digital economics and the issues it raises.

Part I

Toward a New Economy?

2 Evolution of the New Economy business model

William Lazonick

2.1 What is new about the "New Economy"?

The Internet boom of the last half of the 1990s seemed to herald the arrival of a "New Economy" with its promise that, after the stagnation of the early 1990s, innovation in information and communication technologies (ICT) would regenerate economic prosperity. The subsequent collapse of the Internet boom at the beginning of the 2000s called into question the New Economy's ability to deliver on this promise – and even raised questions about whether there had really been anything "new" about the economy of the late 1990s after all. Perhaps the journalist John Cassidy (2002) was correct to entitle his well-documented book on the Internet boom "dot.con: the greatest story ever sold". If the "New Economy" was just all smoke and mirrors, one would expect that, once the debris left behind by the storm of speculation and corruption had been cleared away, economic life would return to what it had been before the boom took place.

It is now clear that there was plenty of e-con in the New Economy. At the same time, however, there was something new, important, and permanent about the New Economy that transformed the economic lives of many from what they had been before. The core of that something new and important is what I call the "New Economy business model" (NEBM), a mode of organizing business enterprises that has changed, perhaps dramatically, the ways in which, and terms on which, people are employed. These changes in employment relations emanated from Silicon Valley and spread primarily to other regions of the United States. They also affected to a lesser extent various other parts of the

The research for this paper has been funded by the W. E. Upjohn Institute for Employment Research, the Work Foundation, and the European Commission. I have benefited from discussions with and comments from Mary O'Sullivan. Ben Hopkins, Sarah Johnson, and Yue Zhang have provided research assistance. I am also grateful to Mellon Consulting for access to its equity practices surveys and those formerly done by iQuantic and iQuantic-Buck.

world, especially in Europe and Asia, as US-based ICT companies extended their global reach and as high-tech companies based outside the United States sought to adopt elements of NEBM. By the 2000s the ICT labor force had become vastly more globalized than it had been before the Internet revolution.

Since the end of the Internet boom, NEBM has by no means disappeared. Rather its characteristic features have become more widespread and entrenched in the US ICT industries. With its startup firms, vertical specialists, venture capital, and highly mobile labor, it is a business model that remains dominant in the United States and that many national policy-makers around the world seek to emulate. At the same time, within the United States, it is a business model that has been associated with volatile stock markets, unequal incomes, and unstable employment, including most recently, even in a period of economic growth, the insecurity associated with the "offshoring" of high-skill ICT jobs. There is a need to understand the organizational and industrial dynamics of NEBM if only to determine how the tapping of its innovative capability might be rendered compatible with socially desirable outcomes.

The "Old Economy business model" (OEBM) is best described as one based on the "organization man". Popularized in the United States in the 1950s (Whyte 1956), the stereotypical "organization man" obtained a college education, got a well-paying job with an established company early in his career, and then worked his way up and around the corporate hierarchy over decades of employment, with a substantial "defined benefit" pension, complete with highly subsidized medical coverage, awaiting him on retirement. The employment stability offered by an established corporation was highly valued, while interfirm labor mobility was shunned.

Ironically, in the 1980s, when formidable Japanese competitors confronted US-based Old Economy companies, many US observers of Japan's "lifetime employment" system viewed it as a mode of economic organization that was quite alien to the American way of life. Yet in the post-World War II decades US business corporations had their own versions of lifetime employment, complete with what the Japanese call "salarymen". US corporations had over the course of the 20th century transformed the salaried professional, technical, and administrative employees who peopled the managerial structure into organization men. By the 1950s and 1960s, moreover, the term could even be applied to those "hourly" production workers whose long-term relations with the companies for which they worked were mediated by industrial unions and collective bargaining.

From this historical perspective, NEBM can best be described as "the end of organization man". It is not that New Economy companies have ceased to rely on the integration of the hierarchical and functional divisions of labor that seek to transform large numbers of individuals into a productive organization. Indeed, one might argue that, given heightened technological complexity and market competition in the world of ICT, the building of unique organizational capabilities has become more, not less, critical to the success of the enterprise than before. Nor is it necessarily the case that employees who spend their entire careers with one company have become an endangered species. Rather what is new is the lack of commitment on the part of US high-tech companies to providing employees with stable employment, skill formation, and rewarding careers. When an employee begins to work for a high-tech company in the New Economy, he or she has no expectation of a career with that particular enterprise. Interfirm labor mobility can, however, bring other benefits to an employee, including working for a smaller company, choice of geographical location in which to work, and employee stock options as a potential source of income. The New Economy business model represents dramatically diminished organizational commitment on both sides of the employment relation relative to its Old Economy predecessor.

A corollary of this diminution in organizational commitment in NEBM has been an increased globalization of the types of labor that US-based ICT firms employ. This globalization of labor has occurred through the international mobility of high-tech labor and the offshoring of high-tech work, both of which have intensified over the past decade or so. The employment relations of major US-based ICT companies have become thoroughly globalized, based on corporate strategies that benefit from not only lower wages but also the enhancement of ICT skill levels in non-US locations such as India, China, and Russia.

While the extent of these impacts of NEBM on ICT employment has become evident only within the last few years, NEBM itself has taken almost a half-century to unfold. Indeed, its origins can be found in the mid-1950s at precisely the time when the Old Economy US industrial corporation was at the pinnacle of its power. The development of computer chips from the late 1950s provided the technological foundation for the microcomputer revolution from the late 1970s, which in turn created the technological infrastructure for the commercialization of the Internet in the 1990s. While the US government and the research laboratories of established Old Economy corporations played major, and indeed indispensable, roles in supporting these developments, each wave of innovation generated opportunities for the emergence of startup companies that were to become central to the commercialization of the new technologies.

The regional concentration of these new ventures in what became known as Silicon Valley reinforced the emergence of a distinctive business model. From the late 1960s venture capitalists backed so many high-tech startups in the vicinity of Stanford University that they created a whole new industry for financing the entry and initial growth of technology firms. These startups lured "talent" from established companies by offering them compensation in the form of stock options, typically as a partial substitute for salaries, with the potential payoff being the high market value of the stock after an initial public offering (IPO) or the private sale of the young firm to an established corporation. As these young companies grew, annual grants of stock options to a broad base of potentially highly mobile people became an important tool for retaining existing employees as well as for attracting new ones. Moreover, these companies grew not only through investing more capital in new facilities and hiring more people but also through acquiring even newer high-tech companies, almost invariably using their own stock rather than cash as the acquisition currency. In addition, wherever and whenever possible, ICT companies that, as systems integrators, designed, tested, and marketed final products outsourced manufacturing of components so that they could focus on higher value-added work. This outsourcing strategy became both more economical and more efficient over time as contract manufacturers developed their capabilities, including global organizations and highly automated production processes, for a larger extent of the market.

These features of the new ICT business model were already evident to industry observers in the late 1980s. It was only during the Internet boom of the last half of the 1990s, however, that this ICT business model had a sufficient impact on product market competition and resource allocation, including interfirm labor mobility, to give popular definition to a "New Economy". In this chapter I outline the evolution of NEBM over the past half-century as a foundation for understanding the origins and implications of the globalization of ICT employment in the 2000s. Section Two of this chapter identifies the differences in terms of products, processes, capital, and labor between the Old Economy and New Economy business models in the ICT industries. It also provides an overview of the ICT industries, their importance to the US economy, and the major Old Economy and New Economy corporations that hold dominant positions in them. Sections Three, Four, and Five then survey the evolution of the characteristic features of NEBM from the 1960s, focusing respectively on a) products and processes, b) capital, and c) labor. Section Six analyzes the relation between NEBM and the end of "organization man", focusing on the case of IBM, the most important Old Economy company in the evolution of NEBM. Section Seven concludes with some (unanswered) questions about the future of NEBM from a societal point of view.

2.2 Business models and the ICT industries

A business model can be characterized by a) the types of product markets for which a company competes, b) the types of production processes through which it generates goods and services for these markets, c) the ways in which it finances investments in processes and products, and d) the ways in which it organizes its labor force to add value to these investments. As captured in the writings of Schumpeter (1942), Penrose (1959), Chandler (1962), and Galbraith (1967), the power of OEBM coming into the second half of the 20th century lay in the ability of already successful firms to routinize innovation, and thereby build on their superior capabilities in existing product markets to move into new product markets. In contrast, a characteristic feature of NEBM since the 1950s has been the prominence, and even dominance, of new firms as innovators in the ICT industries. R&D is important in both OEBM and NEBM, but whereas investments in *research* drove product innovation in OEBM, investments in *development* are much more important in NEBM. In the New Economy, firms that can focus on developing products for specialized new markets within a rapid time-frame have an advantage that has favored highly focused new entrants over diversified going concerns.

In the transformation of inputs into outputs, one of the strengths of OEBM was vertical integration (Chandler 1977 and 1990). To ensure the quality and quantity of critical raw materials and intermediate goods that firms needed for final products, firms took direct control over upstream activities in the value chain. In contrast, a characteristic feature of NEBM has been the vertical specialization of the value chain on the basis of a highly structured set of standards that enables the systemic integration into complex products of components produced by firms in the various vertical layers of an industry. By narrowing the range of processes in which a firm invests, vertical specialization of production processes enhances the ability of a firm to mobilize its resources to compete for specialized product markets. In terms of both products and processes, therefore, NEBM entails a much higher degree of strategic focus than OEBM.

How do these new firms come into existence? In the Old Economy there were no identifiable financial institutions devoted to the financing of startups; finance for new ventures came informally from personal savings of the entrepreneurs themselves, family members, and business associates. If and when these new ventures transformed themselves into going concerns with a record of sustained profitability, they tended to go public on the New York Stock Exchange (NYSE), with its stringent listing requirements. Once listed, these companies tended to pay regular dividends to shareholders. In contrast, in the New Economy a specialized set of venture-capital institutions arose from the 1960s to finance the startup of high-tech firms so that by the beginning of the 1970s "venture capital" had emerged as an industry in its own right.[1] The creation in 1971 of the National Association of Securities Dealers Automated Quotation system (Nasdaq) out of the existing over-the-counter markets made it possible for firms to go public on a nationally traded and hence highly liquid stock market that had far less stringent listing requirements than NYSE. The existence of Nasdaq enabled venture capitalists to exit from their investments much more quickly than if the new firms had listed on NYSE. And unlike the allocation of profits under OEBM, New Economy companies have tended not to pay dividends, thus increasing the amount of internal sources available to fund their growth while rendering the returns to shareholders wholly dependent on the appreciation of a company's stock price.

Finally, as already indicated, OEBM was known for its reliance on the capabilities and commitment of the "organization man" who tended to spend his career moving up and around one corporate hierarchy. The label attached to professional, technical, and administrative employees who generally had a bachelor's degree or higher and were paid on a salaried basis. Yet even through the 1970s blue-collar workers, who were classified as "hourly" employees (which meant that they were "non-exempt" from the labor law that obligates an employer to pay an employee 150 percent of the hourly rate when he or she works overtime), could realistically expect to spend their entire work lives with one company and that they would retire with good incomes and medical coverage based on defined-benefit pension plans. Within the United States, NEBM employees have been predominantly highly educated professional, technical, and administrative personnel remunerated on a salaried basis. New Economy firms have tended to offshore routine manufacturing operations to low-wage areas of the world and/or outsource such operations in the United States to highly automated companies.

---

[1] For the origins of organized venture capital in the United States, see Wilson 1986, ch. 2; Hsu and Kenney 2004.

Moreover, these professional, technical, and managerial employees are no longer "organization men". Rather they tend to be highly mobile on the labor market, with interfirm mobility taken as the norm. While many employees of New Economy firms may in fact stay with one company over the course of their careers, such commitment of the company to the employee and vice versa is not expected from the employment relation. To induce mobility to, and reduce mobility from, the firm, New Economy companies have offered stock options to a broad base of employees – not just to top executives, as was the practice in OEBM. In NEBM, employees have "defined contribution" 401(k) pensions that, as private accounts, are portable from one firm to another. The employer contributions to these pensions are often minimal, and their ultimate value is dependent on the performance of securities markets. In NEBM, it has also been assumed that gains from the exercise of stock options (which are of course dependent on the increase of the company's stock price) will help to provide the employee with a "nest egg" that can fund income and benefits when the employee retires from the labor force.

For each of these characteristics of NEBM, there were discernible historical breaks in the organization of the ICT industries that make the distinction between the Old Economy and New Economy a meaningful one. At the same time, Old Economy and New Economy companies still compete with one another, with, in recent years, many Old Economy corporations adopting elements of NEBM (see Carpenter et al. 2003). One needs to understand the historical origins of NEBM, I would argue, to comprehend the organizational dynamics of the US-based ICT industries and their implications for the evolution of ICT employment opportunities.

The evolution of NEBM has been intimately related to the development of the ICT industries in the United States since the 1960s. The US Department of Commerce (2003) defines the ICT industries as those engaged in producing a) computer hardware, b) computer software and services, c) communications equipment, and d) communications services.[2] ICT industries are high-productivity industries. In 2002 gross domestic product (GDP) from ICT industries was 8.0 percent of US GDP, almost two and a half times ICT's share of employment in the US civilian labor force (US Census Bureau 2003, 385). In that year

---

[2] The US Department of Commerce describes these industries as IT. I use the term ICT to describe the same set of industries in order to highlight the organizational separation of information and communication technologies in OEBM and the ongoing convergence of information and communication technologies that characterizes NEBM.

ICT accounted for 5.5 percent of US exports of goods and services, 7.2 percent of imports, and 11.3 percent of the trade deficit.[3] The fact that the 2002 ICT trade deficit was $47.3 billion was to some degree the result of the globalization of investment and employment in ICT value chains, with US-based companies playing leading roles; it cannot be assumed that the trade deficit measures US lack of competitiveness in ICT industries. US-based ICT firms spend substantial amounts on innovation, accounting for 26 percent of all company-funded R&D in the United States in 2000, and 31.2 percent in 2001. Employees in ICT industries earn, on average, much more than those in most other sectors of the economy. Even in 2002, with earnings in ICT industries somewhat depressed relative to earnings in the US economy as a whole, the average annual income of an employee in ICT industries was $67,440 – ranging from $99,440 in software publishing to $37,750 in electronic capacitor manufacturing – compared with $36,250 in all private-sector industries (US Department of Commerce 2003, Appendix Table 2.3).

From 1993 to 2000 employment in US ICT industries increased by 51.9 percent, compared with a 20.8 percent increase for all private-sector industries. In 2000 these industries employed a total of 5.38 million people, representing 4.8 percent of employment by all US private-sector industries. While ICT employment declined by 0.6 percent in 2001 and 10.7 percent in 2002, at the end of 2002 the ICT industries employed 4.78 million people, or 4.4 percent of employment in the US private sector (Cooke 2003, 21–22). ICT is very important to the growth and prosperity of the US economy.

Within ICT it is possible, with some reservations, to classify major companies as "Old Economy" and "New Economy" according to when the companies were founded (see Tables 2.1 and 2.2).[4] For inclusion in Table 2.2, a company had a) to be founded in 1955 or later, b) to not have been established by the spin-off of an existing division from an Old Economy company, and c) to not have grown through acquisition of, or merger with, an Old Economy company. I have chosen 1955 as the earliest date for inclusion in the list because that was the year that Shockley Semiconductor Laboratories was established in Mountain View, California by William Shockley, the co-inventor of the transistor. As is well known, the Shockley startup sparked a chain reaction that resulted in the emergence of Silicon Valley as a center for the

---

[3] http://www.census.gov/foreign-trade/statistics/product/atp/2003/12/atpctry/atpg04.html; http://www.census.gov/foreign-trade/statistics/historical/gands.pdf.

[4] In 2003 the 103 ICT companies in the Fortune 1000 list had 10.6 percent of the revenues of all companies in the list.

Table 2.1. *Employment, 1996–2003, at the top 20 "Old Economy" companies by 2003 sales*

In parenthesis: a) year of founding (of parent company, where applicable); b) rank in 2004 Fortune 500 list; c) State in which headquartered Old Economy companies	Sales $bn 2003	Employees						2003 sales/ employee
		1996	2000	2001	2002	2003	
IBM (1911; 9; NY)	89.1	240,615	316,309	319,876	315,889	319,273	$279,072
Hewlett-Packard (1939; 11; CA)	73.1	112,000	88,500	86,200	141,000	142,000	$514,789
Verizon Communications (1885; 12; NY)	67.6	62,600	260,000	247,000	229,500	203,100	$332,841
SBC Communications (1885; 33; TX)	40.8	61,450	204,530	215,088	175,400	168,000	$242,857
AT&T (1877; 40; NJ)	34.5	130,000	166,000	117,800	71,000	61,600	$560,065
Motorola (1928; 61; IL)	27.1	139,000	147,000	111,000	97,000	88,000	$307,955
Sprint (1899; 65; KS)	26.2	48,024	84,100	83,700	72,200	66,900	$391,629
Bellsouth (1885; 80; GA)	22.6	81,200	103,900	87,875	77,000	76,000	$297,368
Electronic Data Systems (1962; 87; TX)	21.6	100,000	122,000	143,000	137,000	132,000	$163,636
Comcast (1963; 89; PA)	21.3	16,400	35,000	38,000	82,000	68,000	$313,235
AT&T Wireless Services (1885; 120; WA)	16.7	na	29,000	33,000	31,000	31,000	$538,710
Xerox (1906; 130; CT)	15.7	86,700	92,500	78,900	67,800	61,100	$256,956
Qwest Communications (1885; 136; CO)	14.9	720	67,000	61,000	47,000	47,000	$317,021
Texas Instruments (1930; 197; TX)	9.8	59,927	42,400	34,724	34,589	34,154	$286,936
First Data (1871; 242; CO)	8.5	40,000	27,000	29,000	29,000	29,000	$293,103
Lucent Technologies (1869; 243; NJ)	8.5	124,000	126,000	77,000	47,000	34,500	$246,377
Alltel (1943; 251; AR)	8.2	16,307	27,257	23,955	25,348	19,986	$410,287
Unisys (1873; 312; PA)	5.9	32,900	36,900	38,900	36,400	37,300	$158,177
Cox Communications (1898; 318; GA)	5.8	7,200	19,000	20,700	21,600	22,150	$261,851
NCR (1884; 322; OH)	5.6	38,600	32,960	30,445	29,700	29,000	$193,103
Averages (per firm)	26.2	73,560	101,368	93,858	88,371	83,503	$318,298

Source: Fortune, April 5, 2004: F32–F67; www.hoovers.com.

Table 2.2. *Employment, 1996–2003, at the top 20 "New Economy" companies by 2003 sales*

In parenthesis: a) year of founding; b) rank in 2004 Fortune 500 list; c) State in which headquartered New Economy companies	Sales $bn 2003	Employees						2003 sales/ employee
		1996	2000	2001	2002	2003		
Dell Computer (1984; 31; TX)	41.4	8,400	36,500	40,000	34,600	39,100		$1,196,532
Microsoft (1975; 46; WA)	32.2	20,561	39,100	47,600	50,500	55,000		$637,624
Intel (1968; 53; CA)	30.1	48,500	86,100	83,400	78,700	79,700		$382,465
Cisco Systems (1984; 100; CA)	18.9	8,782	34,000	38,000	36,000	34,000		$525,000
Solectron (1977; 167; CA)	11.7	10,781	65,273	60,000	73,000	66,000		$160,274
Sun Microsystems (1982; 173; CA)	11.4	17,400	38,900	43,700	39,400	36,100		$289,340
Computer Sciences (1959; 175; CA)	11.3	33,850	58,000	68,000	67,000	90,000		$168,657
Nextel Communications (1987; 183; VA)	10.8	3,600	19,500	17,000	14,900	17,000		$724,832
Sanmina-SCI (1980; 188; CA)	10.4	1,726	24,000	48,774	46,030	45,008		$225,940
Oracle (1977; 208; CA)	9.5	23,111	41,320	42,297	42,006	40,650		$226,158
Science Applications Int. (1969; 289; CA)	6.5	21,100	39,078	41,500	40,400	38,700		$160,891
EMC (1979; 299; MA)	6.2	4,800	24,100	20,100	17,400	20,000		$356,322
Apple Computer (1977; 307; CA)	6.2	10,896	8,568	9,603	10,211	10,912		$607,188
EchoStar Communications (1993; 327; CO)	5.6	1,200	11,000	11,000	15,000	15,000		$373,333
Charter Communications (1992; 358; MO)	4.8	2,000	13,505	17,900	18,600	15,500		$258,065
Jabil Circuit (1966; 367; FL)	4.7	2,649	19,115	17,097	20,000	26,000		$235,000
Applied Materials (1967; 392; CA)	4.5	11,403	19,220	17,365	16,077	12,050		$279,903
Maxtor (1982; 423; CA)	4.1	8,940	8,551	9,811	12,449	13,554		$329,344
Affiliated Computer Serv. (1988; 445; TX)	3.8	5,850	18,500	21,000	36,200	40,000		$104,972
Gateway (1985; 484; CA)	3.4	9,700	24,600	14,000	11,500	7,407		$295,652
Averages (per firm)	11.9	12,762	31,447	33,407	33,999	35,084		$349,279

Source: Fortune, April 5, 2004: F32–F67; www.hoovers.com.

development of computer electronics. Note the predominance in Table 2.2 of California-based companies as well as information technology (as distinct from communication technology) companies. While a number of important NEBM companies, most notably Microsoft, are located outside Silicon Valley, I would argue that, in the absence of Silicon Valley, NEBM would not have emerged as a durable, much less dominant, business model.

Table 2.1 lists the largest Old Economy ICT companies by 2003 sales that were founded prior to 1955 or that, as in the cases of Electronic Data Systems (EDS) and Comcast, combined with Old Economy firms at some point in their history. Half of the Old Economy companies are communications companies, with most having their roots in the old Bell System. EDS would be a candidate for the New Economy list but for the fact that between 1984 and 1996 it was a division of General Motors; the automobile maker's failure to integrate EDS into its organization was directly related to the conflicting organizational characteristics of OEBM and NEBM. Comcast became a major player in 2000–2001 by acquiring AT&T Broadband.

Comparing Tables 2.1 and 2.2, the 2003 revenues of the top 20 Old Economy (OE) firms were 59.7 percent of the revenues of all 99 ICT companies that made the Fortune 1000 list, while those of the top 20 New Economy (NE) firms were 26.6 percent; the ratio of the 2003 revenues of the top 20 OE firms to the top 20 NE firms was 2.2. The OE:NE employment ratio declined from 5.8 in 1996 to 2.4 in 2003, reflecting both the faster employment growth of NE firms in the boom and the contraction of employment at OE firms from 2000. The average revenues per employee of OE firms were only 91 percent of those of the NE firms, indicative of a greater concentration of many NE firms on higher value-added activities.

Into the early 1980s two companies – AT&T and IBM – dominated the US ICT industries, AT&T in communications and IBM in information technology. While they were by no means the only important ICT companies in the Old Economy, their histories exemplify the evolution of OEBM, and the centrality of the "organization man" to that business model. At the same time, AT&T and IBM had very different employment relations that in effect made them two distinct versions of OEBM with implications for the ways in which, during the 1990s, these companies responded to the competitive challenge from NEBM. Let me, therefore, briefly summarize OEBM as it could be found at AT&T and IBM coming into the 1990s.

In 1881 the American Bell Telephone, the successor to the Bell Telephone Company that had been founded four years earlier, secured a controlling interest of the Western Electric Manufacturing Company, itself founded in 1872, as its exclusive manufacturer of telephones in the United States. In 1885 American Bell created American Telephone & Telegraph (AT&T) as its subsidiary to build and operate the long-distance telephone network, and in an 1899 reorganization AT&T became the parent company of what had become known as the Bell System. From the outset, salaried managers, not shareholders, ran the Bell System. The most important manager was Theodore Vail, who quit as the company's president in 1887 only to return again as a board member of AT&T from 1900 and as its CEO from 1907 to 1919 (Galambos 1992). When Vail re-entered the company, it was subject to intense competition, the Bell patents having expired in 1894. Vail's most lasting achievement was to transform the company into a regulated monopoly – a status AT&T assumed from 1913 – that was committed to delivering interconnected telephone service to every locality in the United States, no matter how isolated.

Through Bell Telephone Laboratories, established in 1925 as a joint R&D subsidiary of AT&T and Western Electric, the Bell System used its regulated monopoly status to generate knowledge that would eventually change the face of ICT. In 1984 the monopoly came to an end as a result of a US antitrust decree, after carriers such as MCI and Sprint had won the legal right to tap into the Bell System to deliver competitive long-distance service. The "breakup" of the Bell System separated the regional operating companies from AT&T as the long-distance carrier, while the wholly owned manufacturing subsidiary, Western Electric, became AT&T Technologies, an internal division of AT&T. In 1996 AT&T spun off AT&T Technologies into the independent telecommunications equipment company Lucent Technologies, which included Bell Labs within its corporate structure.

In 1947 John Bardeen, Walter Brattain, and William Shockley invented the transistor at Bell Labs, an achievement that was the foundation of solid-state electronics and for which the three men would receive the Nobel Prize in Physics in 1956. Bell Labs ran seminars on the transistor for US-based companies in 1951 and for foreign companies as well in 1952, and then licensed the technology on terms that resulted in its rapid diffusion to ICT firms (Riordan and Hoddeson 1997, ch. 10). A US government antitrust suit, launched in 1949, that had sought to sever the exclusive relationship between AT&T and Western Electric resulted in a 1956 consent decree that allowed AT&T to maintain control over its manufacturing arm but barred the company from competing in industries other than telecommunications. In addition, AT&T and Western had to license their patents to other companies at reasonable fees (Lewis

1956). As a result Bell Labs' R&D supported the development of ICT while the communications and computer industries remained organizationally distinct.

During the 1950s and 1960s IBM came to dominate the computer industry to almost the same extent that AT&T dominated communications, even though IBM was not a regulated monopoly. The company had its origins in the Hollerith punch-card tabulating machine invented and patented in 1884. Henry Hollerith gained fame through the highly successful use of his machine for the 1890 US Census (Black 2001, 25–31; Chandler 2001, 87). In 1911 the Tabulator Machine Company, founded by Hollerith in 1896, was involved in a merger that resulted in the Computing-Tabulating-Recording Company (CTR), based in New York City with 1,300 employees. Thomas Watson, Sr., previously a salesman at National Cash Register (NCR), became president of CTR in 1915. Nine years later, when CTR built a major manufacturing facility in Europe, it changed its name to International Business Machines. IBM's main business was punch-card accounting machines. In 1935 it held 85 percent of the world market, and gained the lucrative government contract for the US Social Security Administration.[5] The company also profited from its operations in Europe, including those in Nazi Germany and Nazi-occupied territories (Black 2001, 118–120). In 1929 IBM had $18 million in revenues and 5,999 employees. In 1939, the Great Depression notwithstanding, the company had $38 million in revenues and 11,315 employees. Over the course of the 1930s the company had profits of $74 million on sales of $240 million.[6]

In 1952 IBM introduced its first computer and, under Thomas Watson, Jr., who took over the CEO position from his father in 1956, became the leader in the computer industry. By 1963 IBM's dominance was such that its US revenues of $1.244 billion from data-processing computers were well over eight times those of its nearest competitor, Sperry Rand (the result of the 1955 merger of Remington Rand and Sperry Corporation). Indeed, the eight companies that followed IBM had combined US revenues of $539 million, or only 43 percent of IBM's (Chandler 2001, 86). IBM grew from $166 million in revenues in 1950 to $1.8 billion in 1960, $7.5 billion in 1970, and $26.2 billion in 1980. Table 2.3 (derived from Chandler 2001, 118–119) shows the extent to which IBM dominated the various sectors of the computer hardware industry in 1984, when the company had total worldwide revenues of

---

[5] http://www-03.ibm.com/ibm/history/history/decade_1930.html.
[6] IBM highlights, 1885–1969 at http://www-03.ibm.com/ibm/history/documents/index.html.

Table 2.3. *Top five companies by worldwide sales in computer hardware sectors, 1984 ($ millions)*

	Mainframes		Minicomputers		Microcomputers		Peripherals	
Sales rank	Firm	Sales	Firm	Sales	Firm	Sales	Firm	Sales
1	IBM	13,131	IBM	3,000	IBM	5,500	IBM	11,652
2	Fujitsu	1,536	DEC	1,527	Apple	1,747	DEC	2,500
3	Sperry Rand	1,451	Wang	971	Commodore	1,000	Burroughs	1,412
4	NEC	1,077	HP	950	Tandy	574	Control Data	1,314
5	Control Data	813	Data General	840	Sperry Rand	503	Xerox	1,180

Source: Chandler 2001, 118–119.

$46 billion, earnings of $5.5 billion, and 394,930 employees (the following year IBM's employment would reach what turned out to be its all-time high of over 405,000 employees).[7]

Both AT&T and IBM were vertically integrated companies, controlling the manufacture of components, equipment, and assembly with R&D and marketing activities. In the case of AT&T, its manufacturing arm was its wholly owned subsidiary, Western Electric, which produced exclusively for AT&T. With the breakup of the Bell System in 1984, there was no substantial change in the relation between AT&T and Western Electric when the latter was, overnight, transformed into AT&T Technologies, an internal division of the parent company. Given their dominance of the product markets on which they focused, during the 1980s AT&T and IBM remained classic "Chandlerian" corporations (Chandler 1977 and 1990).

Like all major corporations in the Old Economy, both AT&T and IBM are listed on the NYSE.[8] An important role of the stock market for both companies has been the separation of ownership from control. The number of AT&T shareholders increased from 8,000 in 1901 when it listed on the NYSE to almost 250,000 two decades later (Stehman 1925, 201, 327), and throughout most of the 20th century the company was the most widely held stock in the United States. IBM had 770

---

[7] IBM highlights, 1885–1969, 1970–1984, and 1985–1989 at http://www-03.ibm.com/ibm/history/documents/index.html.

[8] In 1996 AT&T did the largest IPO in US history up to that time when it spun off Lucent Technologies as an independent company, issuing shares valued at $3 billion. In 2000 AT&T once again did the largest IPO in US history when it listed AT&T Wireless as a tracking stock, issuing $10.3 billion in shares.

stockholders in 1914, the year before, as CTR, the company went public on the NYSE. From 1925 through the 1950s IBM regularly issued stock dividends, and also did frequent stock splits. In 1959 the company had almost 109,000 shareholders and ten years later over 549,000. Notwithstanding the fact that Thomas Watson, Sr. ruled IBM for over four decades and was able to hand over the leadership of the company to his son, he was not a founder of the company and never owned more than 5 percent of IBM's outstanding stock (Watson and Petre 1990, 267).

Both AT&T and IBM paid regular cash dividends to their shareholders. Indeed, in Old Economy fashion, AT&T has paid dividends for every quarter of every year since the first quarter of 1893.[9] Like most Old Economy companies up until the 1990s both AT&T and IBM awarded stock options almost exclusively to executive officers (AT&T *1996 Proxy Statement*, 37; IBM *1996 10-K*).

Until the early 1990s IBM was known as a company that offered both managerial and production personnel "lifelong employment", with defined contribution pension plans that provided medical coverage. In 1934, IBM gave all of its 7,600 employees access to group life insurance, with survivor benefits added in 1935, and two years later it was one of the first among major US corporations to give employees paid vacations, in this case six days per year. In 1952, when IBM employed almost 41,500 people, it was claimed that the company had not laid off an employee since 1921, and that it had never experienced a slowdown or strike (Potter 1953). In early 1958, with 60,000 employees, IBM was the first major company to place all hourly workers on salary. During 1971 and 1972 IBM reduced its headcount from 269,292 to 262,152 by offering its employees with 25 years of service the option of early retirement, five years ahead of schedule (*Wall Street Journal* [*WSJ*], September 1, 1971), a program that was repeated in 1975 when 1,900 people took up the offer (*WSJ*, January 14, 1975; April 14, 1975). The institution of lifelong employment at IBM met its demise in the early 1990s as the company cut it payroll from 373,816 at the end of 1990 to 219,839 at the end of 1994. At first IBM downsized by means of voluntary retirement schemes, but by 1992, several months before Louis Gerstner's arrival from RJR Nabisco to take over as IBM's CEO, it was clear that the tradition of lifelong employment was no more (*New York Times News Service*, December 16, 1992; Hays 1994; Gerstner 2002, 101–102).

---

[9] http://www.att.com/ir/cgi/divhistory.cgi.

If a commitment to lifelong salaried employment for all personnel characterized IBM in the post-World War decades, a distinction between salaried managers and unionized workers characterized employment in the Bell System during this period. In 1971 AT&T employed 1,015,000 people, of whom about 700,000 were union members (500,000 Communications Workers of America [CWA], 150,000 International Brotherhood of Electrical Workers [IBEW], and 50,000 independent unions) (*WSJ*, July 15, 1971). In the same year, Western Electric employed another 207,000 people, of whom almost 151,000 were union members (65,000 CWA, 71,500 IBEW, and 14,400 other unions) (*WSJ*, May 1, 1971; Adams and Butler 1999, 223). At the time Bell Labs employed 17,000 scientists and engineers (Rensberger 1972).

The salaried employees at AT&T, Western Electric, and Bell Labs had virtual lifetime employment, and were fully pensionable after 30 years of service. Collective bargaining got hourly workers the same benefits. While AT&T and Western Electric were by no means strike free, labor–management relations benefited from the market power and financial stability of these companies. When workers did get laid off in a slump, it was the practice to hire them back when economic conditions improved. As a regulated monopoly, AT&T could look to rate increases to fund rising wage costs (see *New York Times* [*NYT*], April 22, 1952). In 1956 Western Electric instituted a plan to pay the tuition of any employee who engaged in undergraduate or graduate study on his or her own time (*NYT*, November 29, 1956). In 1969 the CWA staged the first national strike against AT&T since 1947, winning a 20 percent pay increase over three years to offset rises in the cost of living and payment by the company of the full premium for the health care plan rather than only one-quarter as had previously been the case. In 1971 500,000 CWA members struck at AT&T over the erosion of their wages by inflation, and won for the first time a cost of living adjustment (COLA) and big city allowances (*WSJ*, July 20, 1971). In 1983, a 22-day CWA strike on the eve of the breakup of the Bell System – and hence the last time the union would be able to negotiate with the AT&T of old – successfully won better wages as well as improvements in employment security, the pension plan, and health insurance.[10] As was generally the case in union–management relations at major corporate industrial corporations in this era, union members enjoyed not only good pay but also attractive health and pension benefits, and their jobs were protected by seniority.

---

[10] http://local1051.tripod.com/history/hist1.htm

2.3   Evolution of NEBM: products and processes

During the late 1990s employment at the New Economy firms listed in Table 2.2 expanded rapidly, and, on average, they sustained their employment growth in the early 2000s. The top 20 companies in Table 2.2 are spread across the different ICT industrial classifications that *Fortune* uses in compiling its annual lists of the largest US corporations in terms of sales: three are in computer and data services, four in computer office equipment, two in computer software, one in networking, five in semiconductors and other electronic components, and three in telecommunications. Of the five in semiconductors and other electronic components, three are contract manufacturers, one is a semiconductor equipment company, and just one is a semiconductor manufacturing company. That last one, however, is Intel, whose growth from its founding in 1968 to dominance of the microprocessor market has been central to the evolution of NEBM.

Two of the founders of Intel, Robert Noyce and Gordon Moore, were among the eight scientists and engineers who, in September 1957, left Shockley Semiconductor Laboratories to form Fairchild Semiconductor as a manufacturer of diffused silicon transistors in a nearby location in Mountain View, California. Over the following decades the interfirm mobility of talented people to found or join startups became the defining characteristic of the dynamic regional economy that Fairchild, inadvertently, helped to create. From 1959 through 1970, 42 new semiconductor firms – 21 in 1968 and 1969 alone – were launched in the vicinity of Fairchild in what, as a result, became known by the beginning of the 1970s as Silicon Valley.[11] By 1985 the number of Silicon Valley semiconductor startups since the founding of Fairchild totaled 125. Of these, 32 were founded by at least one person who had left employment at Fairchild for that purpose, while another 35 companies were offspring from these "Fairchildren" (especially from National Semiconductor, Intel, Signetics, and Synertek).[12] These semiconductor firms lay the foundation for NEBM.

There were three distinct waves of Silicon Valley semiconductor startups from 1959 through 1985. The first wave, 1959–1964, consisted of ten semiconductor firms oriented toward military markets. It is plausible to contend that without US Department of Defense spending on

---

[11] The first public use of the term "Silicon Valley" is credited to the journalist Don C. Hoefler in a series of articles that he wrote for *Electronic News* in 1971.

[12] Silicon Valley Genealogy Chart, available from SEMI (Semiconductor Equipment and Materials International) at http://dom.semi.org.

corporate research and contracts, the US semiconductor industry would not have gotten off the ground. Between 1955 and 1963, while the value of total US semiconductor production rose from $40 million to $610 million, the proportion of this value that was for the US military varied between 35 percent and 48 percent. In 1968, when the value of US semiconductor production stood at $1.159 billion, the value of military production was still 25 percent of the total. By that time, integrated circuits (ICs) accounted for 27 percent of the value of all US semiconductor production, up from less than 3 percent five years earlier. Military demand was critical to the growth of this important sector, accounting for 94 percent of IC production in 1963 and 37 percent in 1968 (Tilton 1971, 90–91).

Meanwhile, the price per IC declined from $31.60 in 1963 to $2.33 in 1968, thus dramatically increasing the economic viability of using ICs for cost-conscious civilian markets (Tilton 1971, 90–91). The realization of these commercial opportunities precipitated a second wave of Silicon Valley startups from 1968 through 1972, a period that saw 40 startups, 13 of which were "Fairchildren", and another eight companies their offspring. Over half of the startups during this period, therefore, were direct and indirect Fairchild "spin-offs".

Through the interfirm mobility of personnel, and notwithstanding frequent lawsuits for the infringement of intellectual property, the startups were able to develop new products without engaging in expensive and time-consuming research. Fairchild was so important to the emergence of Silicon Valley precisely because, even as it drew people and knowledge from the established R&D labs of the electronic tube companies such as GE, RCA, Westinghouse, and Sylvania, it invested heavily in research, especially for processes for the mass production of diffused silicon transistors (Tilton 1971, 4). Fairchild in effect brought all this research to Silicon Valley and, largely supported by government contracts, developed the knowledge and the people who by the late 1960s could take advantage of the vast opportunities for using chips in commercial products. As Gordon Moore (1996, 171), who had been head of R&D at Fairchild when he left in 1968 to co-found Intel, wrote for a 1993 conference on the decline of corporate research laboratories in the United States:

The large, central research laboratories of the premier semiconductor firms probably have contributed more to the common good than to their corporations . . . Why do spin-offs and the community at large tend to reap so much from large research organizations and the firms that own them so little? . . . Running with the ideas that big companies can only lope along with has come to be the acknowledged role of the spin-off or start-up. Note, however, that it is important to distinguish here between exploitation and creation. It is often said that start-ups are better at creating new things. They are not; they are better at *exploiting* them.

When Moore, with Noyce, founded Intel to produce memory chips that could replace the magnetic coil memories then in use, they specifically declined to create a separate R&D lab and refused to accept government contracts for research (Bassett 2002, ch. 6). The two other most successful Silicon Valley semiconductor companies that emerged out of the second wave were National Semiconductor and Advanced Micro Devices (AMD), companies whose founders, as in the case of Intel, came from high executive positions at Fairchild and adopted similar commercialization strategies. As late as 1984 National Semiconductor had greater revenues than Intel ($1.263 billion versus $1.201 billion), while AMD had settled on being largely a "second source" for Intel products.

The third wave of Silicon Valley semiconductor startups began in 1978, peaked in 1983, and continued to 1985. During these years there were 58 new firms, of which seven were Fairchildren and another 26 offspring. In contrast to the dynamic random access memory (DRAM) and erasable programmable read-only memory (EPROM) chips that had underpinned the growth of the second-wave companies such as Intel, National, and AMD, third-wave firms such as VLSI Technology (1979), LSI Logic (1981), Cypress Semiconductors (1983), Cirrus Logic (1984), and Chips & Technologies (1985) focused on logic chips – microprocessors and application specific integrated circuits (ASICs) – for which value-added lay in chip design rather than high-yield, low-defect mass production. In pursuing this design-oriented strategy, the founders of these startups and their backers were taking advantage of the new commercial opportunities opened up by the growth of consumer and business electronic product markets. Meanwhile, during this third wave, integrated Japanese producers such as NEC, Hitachi, Toshiba, and Fujitsu that sold only a portion of the memory chips that they produced were taking command of the markets that second-wave companies such as Intel and National served (see Patterson 1981 and 1982; Chase 1983). By 1985 DRAMs and EPROMS had become known as "commodity chips", mainly because of the formidable Japanese challenge based on superior manufacturing methods that resulted in fewer defects and higher yields (see Okimoto and Nishi 1994; Burgelman 1994).

Around 1985 this Japanese challenge undermined the profitability of all the major memory producers, Intel included. So great was the Japanese threat in commodity chips that the most powerful US semiconductor companies banded together to form SEMATECH, with partial funding from the US government, in an attempt to ensure that the United States would not lose indigenous capability in the production of semiconductor fabrication equipment as well (see Browning and Shetler

2000). By the beginning of the 1990s, however, Intel re-emerged as the dominant US competitor on the global semiconductor market, its revenues surpassing Texas Instruments' starting in 1990 and Motorola's starting in 1991. The foundation of Intel's success was the microprocessor, the revolutionary device that it had invented in 1971 and that became the major source of revenues for the company with the IBM-led PC revolution of the 1980s.

In 1981 IBM announced its PC, with the operating system supplied by Microsoft and the microprocessor by Intel. Both Microsoft and Intel retained the right to sell these products to other companies. In 1982 IBM accounted for almost 14 percent of Intel's revenues (Chase 1983). At the end of 1982, IBM paid $250 million for a 12 percent equity interest in Intel that subsequently rose to 20 percent. The move was designed both to ensure that Intel had financing commensurate with IBM's reliance on the semiconductor company and to send a signal that, in competing in the PC industry that it was in the process of creating, IBM would support its suppliers (*Business Week* [*BW*], January 10, 1983; Smith 1986). The $250 million infusion of cash was over nine times Intel's 1981 earnings, and just $10 million less than Intel's capital expenditures plus R&D spending for 1982.

Some observers saw the equity purchase as the first step toward IBM taking control of Intel. While IBM did get one seat on Intel's board, it agreed not to become involved in Intel's day-to-day operations and not to increase its holdings of Intel stock beyond 30 percent. Moreover, as *Business Week* (January 10, 1983) noted, the exercise of direct control by established corporations over previously independent semiconductor companies might not yield the best results:

In 1978, Honeywell bought Synertek; a year later Schlumberger grabbed Fairchild Camera & Instrument, while United Technologies took Mostek. The trend appears to have crested in 1981, when Gould acquired American Microsystems and Westinghouse bought into Siliconix. But, notes [Intel president, Andrew] Grove, those linkups "are anything but wildly successful," so a new spirit of cooperation is emerging.

Underpinning that new spirit of cooperation, including Intel's own growth, was the phenomenal success of the IBM PC in the first half of the 1980s. In 1982 its PC sales were $500 million and just two years later 11 times that amount, more than triple the 1984 revenues of its nearest competitor, Apple, and about equal to the revenues of its top eight rivals. Subsequently, the very success of the IBM PC combined with open access to the Microsoft operating system and Intel microprocessor meant that in the last half of the 1980s and beyond IBM lost market share to PC clones such as Compaq, Gateway, and Dell (Chandler 2001, 118–199, 142–143).

But IBM's strategy for entering the microcomputer market had consolidated and reinforced the vertically specialized structure of the industry in line with what can be viewed as the Silicon Valley model (Grove 1996; Best 2001, 124). While defining the "open access" standards for the computer industry, the subsequent domination by Intel and Microsoft of the product markets for microprocessors and operating software respectively created an immense barrier to entry to actual and potential competitors who would directly confront the New Economy giants while at the same time opening up countless opportunities for new entrants to develop specialized niche products that conformed to the "Wintel" architecture (Borrus and Zysman 1997).

For the major Silicon Valley semiconductor companies in the 1970s, vertical specialization in chips had been an outcome, not a strategic choice. As part of its strategy to integrate forward into consumer products, National Semiconductor and Fairchild started producing and marketing calculators (Sporck 2001, 228–230). In 1972 Intel acquired a Silicon Valley digital watchmaker, Microma, which pioneered liquid crystal display watches. National Semiconductor and Fairchild Camera and Instrument (the parent company of Fairchild Semiconductor and by this time based in Silicon Valley) were also producing digital watches, as was Texas Instruments (*BW*, April 19, 1976). Indeed, price competition from its semiconductor rivals led Intel to exit the watch business in 1978, taking a loss of $15 million on the venture (Wharton 1990; *Computerworld*, July 1, 1996; Manners 1997; Sporck 2001, 185–187).

As Charles Sporck of National was to recognize in 1979: "The gap between our basic business and the consumer business was enormous. The semiconductor industry is a professional price/performance business, while the consumer is only distantly related to that concept. This was something the semiconductor industry didn't understand" (Schuyten 1979). Capital goods, however, were another matter. During the 1970s National manufactured checkout scanners and made money in that business before being outcompeted by IBM and NCR (Sporck 2001, 230–231). In the same 1979 *New York Times* article that quoted Sporck on consumer goods, the journalist stated: "It is almost axiomatic in the electronics industry that companies in the semiconductor business want to go into end-user businesses, in other words to vertically integrate into finished products and systems" (Schuyten 1979). Entitled "To Clone a Computer", the article described how National, following the lead of Silicon Valley-based Amdahl, had successfully entered the plug-compatible mainframe (PCM) market, producing clones of IBM's machines. By the early 1980s, however, all of National's PCMs were manufactured by Hitachi (*BW*, February 21, 1983), and in 1989 Hitachi and Electronic Data Systems bought National's mainframe business (Molloy 1989).

In addition, leading Silicon Valley semiconductor companies, including Intel, National, and Intel spin-off Zilog, entered the minicomputer industry in the late 1970s and early 1980s, but were outcompeted by not only the Japanese but also Route 128 firms such as Digital Equipment Corporation (DEC) and Data General as well as IBM and Hewlett-Packard. In 1981 Intel entered the microcomputer industry, one in which National was already engaged using Intel's 8086 microprocessor. Intel's director of corporate planning, Les Vadasz, argued that Intel's forward integration into microcomputers was strategic: "We develop products because they fit into our overall architecture of things" (*BW*, November 16, 1981). But 1981 was also the year that IBM launched its personal computer, using Intel's microprocessor. IBM's success pushed Intel out of the microcomputer business, and helped to ensure that the leading producer of microprocessors would grow to world dominance as a specialized semiconductor company.

The semiconductor companies, therefore, had tried to integrate forward into final products, but competition from integrated Japanese and US rivals forced them to specialize in chips. Vertical specialization did not stop there, however. A number of Silicon Valley design-oriented chip companies that entered the industry in the 1980s, and even more so in the 1990s, did so without investing in the manufacture of semiconductors. The pioneer in fabless chip design was LSI Logic. Wilf Corrigan, former CEO of Fairchild, launched LSI Logic in 1981 with $6 million and military orders, and with all production outsourced. By 1983, however, the complexity of the ASICs that LSI was designing compelled the company to integrate backward into manufacturing, opening its first plant in 1983 in Santa Clara, California, and as the company grew it expanded its manufacturing capacity (Hoffman 1999). Nevertheless, from the last half of the 1980s, as the demand for ASICs grew, many producers of programmable logic devices and graphics processors such as Altera, NVIDIA, and Xilinx turned to foundries to manufacture their chips. The Taiwanese in particular took advantage of the opportunity, as Taiwan Semiconductor Manufacturing Company (TSMC) and United Microelectronics Corporation (UMC) became the largest semiconductor contract manufacturers in the world. In the 2000s even IBM has entered the foundry business, with its Microelectronics division generating $2 billion in revenues in 2003 by manufacturing chips for other semiconductor firms (www.hoovers.com; Zerega 1999; Shelton 2004).

If a layer of vertical specialization has emerged in the manufacture of chips, so too has it emerged in the assembly of chip sets, printed circuit boards, and, increasingly, even finished products (Sturgeon 2002). In the 1980s and early 1990s contract manufacturers (CMs) operated as job shops that took on extra work from integrated original equipment manufacturers (OEMs) in periods of peak demand. Then during the mid-1990s a few Old Economy companies – in particular IBM, Hewlett-Packard, and Ericsson – took the lead in selling existing plants to CMs. Meanwhile, the newest New Economy companies engaged in Internet working such as Cisco and 3Com outsourced all of their manufacturing from the outset.

During the Internet boom of the late 1990s the demand for CM capacity soared. New Economy companies that did no manufacturing relied on CMs for not only assembly but also an increasing array of services including testing, design, documentation, and shipping (Curran 1997). Old Economy telecommunications equipment companies such as Motorola, Lucent, Nortel, and Alcatel also undertook major outsourcing programs to CMs; by 2000 these companies were rushing to offload manufacturing plants. Growth and consolidation among CMs that could offer the requisite scale and range of services resulted in the emergence of five dominant firms: Celestica, Flextronics, Jabil Circuit, Solectron, and Sanmina-SCI (Carbone 2000, 2002, 2004). From 1993 to 2003, the largest CM, Flextronics, increased its revenues from $93 million to $13.4 billion and its number of employees from 2,000 to 95,000, while the second largest CM, Solectron, increased its revenues from $836 million to $11.0 billion and its employees from 4,500 to 66,000 (www.hoovers.com).

2.4   Evolution of NEBM: capital

Funding the entry of firms into these specialized layers of ICT industries were technology-oriented venture capital firms that by the 1980s had become integral to both Silicon Valley and NEBM. These firms were organized as general partnerships of venture capitalists who a) raised funds, largely from institutional investors such as pension funds, universities, and banks; b) reviewed and selected the particular portfolio of industrial ventures in which to invest; c) maintained control over resource allocation *to* these ventures, including the staging of funding as the venture evolved; d) maintained control over resource allocation *by* these ventures, including the hiring and firing of executive personnel; and e) sought to realize returns to the venture capital fund through either an initial public offering of the stock of the venture-backed industrial firms or a private sale of these firms to already established corporations.

It was Silicon Valley practice, which by the 1980s became the standard for US venture capital, for the general partners of the venture capital firm to receive a "carried interest" of at least 20 percent of the returns of a particular venture capital fund that they raised, distributing the remainder to the institutions or individuals who, as limited partners, provided the general partners with the capital for the fund (see Sahlman 1990).

While by the 1980s Silicon Valley had become the epicenter of venture capital in the United States, both the concept and practice of venture capital were of East Coast origin. In the late 1930s established industrial leaders argued that by funding innovative new companies, "venture capital" could help deliver the US economy from an economy that had failed to recover from depression (*WSJ*, Jan. 13, 1938; *WSJ*, Feb 4 1939; Hsu and Kenney 2004). While the unemployment rate in the US economy never fell below 14.9 percent over the course of the 1930s, the decade was nevertheless an important one for the development of the research capabilities of Old Economy industrial corporations. The number of scientists and research engineers in the research labs of American companies increased from 6,320 in 1927 to 10,927 in 1933, a year in which the unemployment rate for the economy as a whole peaked at 25 percent. Notwithstanding the persistence of depressed economic conditions, in 1940 the number of research personnel had climbed to 27,777, over two and a half times the number just seven years earlier. The war effort, which (rather than entrepreneurship) did succeed in finally bringing the US economy out of depression, helped to increase this number to 45,941 in 1946 (Mowery and Rosenberg 1989, 64–71).[13] By the end of World War II there was an immense accumulation of technological knowledge waiting to be commercialized.

The US system of higher education had played an important role in industrial research from the late 19th century (Ferleger and Lazonick 1993; Rosenberg and Nelson 1994), and during the first decades of the 20th century the Massachusetts Institute of Technology (MIT) became the nation's most important academic institution for high-technology research and teaching (Noble 1977). In 1946 Karl Compton, the president of MIT, presided over the creation of American Research & Development (ARD), the first formal venture-capital organization (Hsu and Kenney 2004, 9–10). Along with Compton, another one of ARD's prime movers, Harvard Business School professor Georges Doriot, had been involved in pre-World War II discussions of the potential for venture

---

[13] These employment levels translated into ratios of research personnel per 1,000 wage earners of 0.83 in 1927, 1.93 in 1933, 3.67 in 1940, and 3.98 in 1946 (Mowery and Rosenberg 1989, 64–71).

capital to reinvigorate the New England economy. The expressed purpose of ARD was to support entrepreneurs in the founding of new firms in order to commercialize the accumulation of advanced scientific and technological capability that, as a result of military spending, MIT in particular had accumulated through World War II.

In the post-World War II decades both MIT and ARD played important roles in the growth of the Route 128 high-tech corridor to the north and west of Boston (Rosegrant and Lampe 1992, chs. 2–4; Hsu and Kenney 2004). In the aftermath of World War II, Frederick Terman, dean of Stanford's School of Engineering, was seeking to implement a similar vision of a high-tech industrial district, anchored by a major research university, in the area surrounding Stanford's location in Palo Alto, California (Leslie 1993; Saxenian 1994; Leslie and Kargon 1996; Berlin 2001). During the late 1940s and 1950s, in the context of Cold War military spending, many startups were spun off from Stanford and many established industrial corporations set up operations in the area, transforming Palo Alto and its environs into a major center for microwave and aerospace technology (Leslie 1993). Semiconductors came to the region in 1955 when, after an aborted attempt to work with Raytheon, a leading military contractor in the Boston area with close ties to MIT, William Shockley secured the backing of Los Angeles-based Beckman Instruments to set up shop close to Stanford.

In 1957, a little more than a year after being hired by Shockley, eight scientists and engineers – Julius Blank, Victor Grinich, Jean Hoerni, Eugene Kleiner, Jay Last, Gordon Moore, Robert Noyce, and Sheldon Roberts – left Shockley Labs in search of funding from "a corporation interested in getting into the advanced semiconductor device business" in the lower San Francisco Peninsula (letter from Eugene Kleiner to Hayden Stone, quoted in Lécuyer 2000, 163). In 1957 there were some individuals involved in venture finance working for certain San Francisco financial institutions, most notably Reid Dennis of the Fireman's Fund and an informal circle of friends he called "The Group" (Dennis 2000, 182–183). There were, however, no firms on the West Coast specifically organized for the purpose of providing venture capital.[14]

---

[14] The first firm in the region devoted to venture capital, Draper, Gaither, and Anderson, would be started a year later. In 1957, Georges Doriot and his Boston-based venture-capital firm American Research & Development backed the founding of Digital Equipment Corporation, taking 78 percent of the ownership for a $70,000 investment (Wilson 1986, 19). When the "Traitorous Eight" (as Shockley dubbed them) did get funding to start Fairchild Semiconductor, Fairchild Camera's investment was $1.38 million. It is, therefore, unlikely that, even if the Eight had been willing to relocate to Route 128, they would have been able to raise that kind of money through ARD.

In a stroke of good fortune, a letter that Eugene Kleiner wrote to his father's broker at the New York investment bank Hayden Stone inquiring about where the "well-trained technical group" of Shockley defectors might get funding that "could get a company into the semiconductor business within three months" came to the attention of Arthur Rock, a young Hayden Stone employee with a Harvard MBA. Rock had already been involved in the venture financing, IPO, and then sale of an East Coast semiconductor company, General Transistor (Lécuyer 2000, 163–164).[15] Rock quickly responded, and after considerable time and effort convinced the Long Island, New York firm Fairchild Camera and Instrument to fund Fairchild Semiconductor. The eight Shockley defectors each received a 7.5 percent equity stake in Fairchild Semiconductor, with Hayden Stone holding 17 percent and the other 23 percent reserved for allocation in hiring new managers. The deal was structured so that, at its option, Fairchild Camera could buy out the shareholders for $3 million at any time before the company had three successive years of net earnings greater than $300,000, or for $5 million if the option was exercised between three years and eight years (Lécuyer 2000, 166; Berlin 2001, 76).

Fairchild Semiconductor experienced almost immediate success. In early 1958 the new enterprise landed a subcontract with IBM for semiconductors for the Minuteman missile. In 1958 Hoerni drew on Bell Labs research to perfect the planar process for the manufacture of silicon chips. Building on this breakthrough, the following year Noyce invented the integrated circuit (Berlin 2001, 64). In two years, the semiconductor company had grown from 13 to 700 employees, and was highly profitable.[16] Its revenues for its second year through September 1959 were $6.5 million, 80 percent of which were military sales (*WSJ*, Oct. 9, 1959, 20; Berlin 2001, 81). In October 1959, just two years after the launch of Fairchild Semiconductor, Fairchild Camera exercised its option to buy back the company for $3 million. The eight scientists and engineers who had founded Fairchild Semiconductor received publicly traded shares of Fairchild Camera and became employees of the company – now a division of the East Coast parent – that they once had owned (*WSJ*, Oct. 9, 1959, 20).

---

[15] See Rock 2000, 141: "The reason I got so excited about Fairchild Semiconductor was because I'd already been in the semiconductor business through General Transistor."

[16] In announcing that his company would exchange Fairchild Camera shares for all of the Fairchild Semiconductor shares, president John Carter said the expansion of Fairchild Semiconductor's sales and profits would allow the company to grow without additional equity financing (*WSJ*, Oct. 9, 1959, 20).

As for Arthur Rock, he was by no means finished with West Coast semiconductor startups or with the eight Fairchild Semiconductor founders. In 1960, while still a Hayden Stone employee, Rock arranged financing for two former executives of the West Coast conglomerate Litton Industries to launch Teledyne, a Los Angeles-based electronics firm. Rock remained actively involved in Teledyne's affairs, and in 1961 Hoerni, Kleiner, Last, and Roberts left Fairchild Semiconductor to found Amelco as a semiconductor division of Teledyne. In the same year Rock left Hayden Stone and relocated to the San Francisco area, where he quickly teamed up with Tommy Davis, a local financier with a legal background and links with Stanford's Terman, to establish a venture capital firm, Davis and Rock. As the general partners, Davis and Rock received a carried interest of 20 percent of the returns of the venture fund.[17] Among the limited partners of Davis and Rock were the eight Fairchild Semiconductor founders. When two of them, Moore and Noyce, decided to leave Fairchild in 1968 to found their own company, Intel, they turned to Rock for financing, and within days he had raised $2.5 million (Wilson 1986, 38; Perkins 1994).

Rock was, therefore, a leading venture capitalist in both the first and second waves of Silicon Valley semiconductor startups. There was a co-evolution between the venture-capital firm entrants in the Silicon Valley region and semiconductor startups. As with the founding of semiconductor firms, the pattern of venture-capital firm entrants exhibits three waves of growing amplitude, the first around 1958–1962, the second around 1968–1972, and the third around 1978–1983. With the exception of Rock, there was little involvement of San Francisco Peninsula venture capital with semiconductor startups until the second wave. That involvement picked up slowly in the middle of the second wave, and toward the end of the period the semiconductor industry began contributing some of its well-known executives to the venture-capital

---

[17] The prime advantage of a limited partnership as an organizational form was that the general partners, who as the active venture capitalists performed the critical roles of selecting, monitoring, and exiting the portfolio of new ventures, were able to share in the gains of the venture fund by means of both the carried interest and investments made on their own account. Under the Investment Company Act of 1940, the active venture capitalists in a venture-capital firm that raised its funds through public share issues, as was the case with ARD, were prohibited from receiving a share of the profits or taking their own equity positions. It was argued that, lacking such arrangements for venture capitalists to gain from venture capital, it was difficult to employ people who would have the incentives and abilities to make the types of inherently uncertain decisions and exert the level of necessarily intense effort that venture investing demanded (see Hsu and Kenney 2004, 33). During the 1960s the limited partnership arrangement became the norm in Silicon Valley, and subsequently for independent (non-corporate) venture-capital firms throughout the United States as a whole (Sahlman 1990).

industry. In 1972 Donald Valentine, an engineer who had been head of marketing at Fairchild before joining National Semiconductor in 1967, founded Sequoia Capital, which became one of Silicon Valley's most successful venture-capital firms. Also in 1972 Eugene Kleiner joined with a Hewlett-Packard executive, Thomas Perkins, to found a venture-capital firm that, as Kleiner Perkins Caufield & Byers, is commonly considered to be the exemplar of Silicon Valley venture capital. In 1972 Kleiner Perkins located its offices in a still largely vacant new complex at 3000 Sand Hill Road in Menlo Park, adjacent to Stanford and with easy access to the San Jose and San Francisco airports (Lane 1994). Sequoia also located there, as did many other Silicon Valley venture-capital firms. So too did the Western Association of Venture Capitalists, the trade association that had been founded in 1967 and out of which grew the National Venture Capital Association (NVCA), started in 1973. The second wave of semiconductor startups, therefore, not only gave Silicon Valley its name but also laid the foundation for an organized venture-capital industry.

It was the innovative capabilities of the companies in which venture capitalists invested that created the value from which money could be made. By the 1970s the semiconductor revolution had laid the technological foundation for a multiplying range of business and household product applications, and, coming out of the semiconductor revolution, the Silicon Valley venture capitalists had become part of the regional institutional environment. What was needed now was an adequate supply of capital for the investments in new ventures that could take advantage of the plethora of technological and market opportunities. Over the course of the 1970s a number of changes in US financial institutions encouraged the flow of capital into venture-capital funds, thus favoring the growth of Silicon Valley and NEBM.

The launch of Nasdaq in 1971 made it much easier for a young company to go public, thus enhancing the ability of venture capitalists to use this mode of exit from their investments. In that year, for example, less than three years after being founded, Intel did its IPO on Nasdaq, with a loss before extraordinary items of $513,000, offset by a gain of $1,427,000 for "sale of manufacturing know-how", for a net income of $914,000 (Intel *1972 Annual Report*). Thirteen of the 20 New Economy firms in Table 2.2 are listed on Nasdaq, including Applied Materials (IPO in 1972), Apple Computer (1980), Microsoft (1986), Sun Microsystems (1986), Oracle (1986), Dell Computer (1988), and Cisco Systems (1990).

In 1975 the Securities and Exchange Commission (SEC) barred stock exchanges from charging fixed commissions on stock-trading transactions, ending a practice that had prevailed on Wall Street since 1796 (*WSJ*,

Oct. 25, 1974, 4). This change made it less costly for portfolio investors to move in and out of stock to realize capital gains as an alternative to holding stock for the sake of dividends. This type of investment behavior facilitated both an early IPO (because the public was often willing to absorb a new share issue of a firm without a record of profitability) and the subsequent growth of the firm (because these companies could forego paying dividends, using the funds instead for internal investment).

In 1978, in response to intensive lobbying led by the American Electronics Association (itself dominated by Silicon Valley), the US Congress reduced the capital gains tax from 49 percent to 28 percent, thus reversing a 36-year trend toward higher capital gains taxes (Pierson 1978; *BW*, May 18, 1981). Venture capitalists saw lower capital gains taxes as encouraging both entrepreneurial investment in new companies and portfolio investment by individuals in the publicly traded stocks of young, potentially high-growth companies.

During the 1970s, however, venture capitalists still faced constraints on the amount of money they could raise for venture funds, mainly because they could not gain access to the vast accumulation of household savings held by pension funds. That constraint was transformed almost overnight when on July 23, 1979 the US Department of Labor clarified restrictions on the portfolios of pension funds imposed by the "prudent man" rule of the Employee Retirement Income Security Act (ERISA) of 1974 (see Niland 1976). The lackluster performance of the stock market in the early 1970s had combined with inflation to create a massive underfunding of defined benefit corporate pension funds. ERISA, which a *Business Week* editorial described as "one of the most complex pieces of legislation ever passed by Congress" (*BW*, Jan. 12, 1976), made corporations responsible for underfunded pensions while at the same time making pension fund managers personally liable for breaches of their fiduciary duty to use the "prudent man" rule when making investments. Under these circumstances, pension fund managers, who controlled the allocation of an ever-increasing share of US household savings, avoided investment in venture capital funds. In July 1979 the Department of Labor decreed that pension fund money could be invested not only in listed stocks and high-grade bonds but also in more speculative assets, including new ventures, without transgressing the "prudent man" rule (*BW*, Aug. 13, 1979).

As a result pension fund money poured into venture-capital funds. Funds raised (in 1997 dollars) by independent venture partnerships (the type that prevailed in Silicon Valley) from pension funds were $69 million in 1978 (15 percent of all funds raised), $160 million in 1979 (31 percent), $400 million in 1980 (30 percent), and $421 million in 1981 (23 percent). By 1983 pension fund investment in independent venture partnerships had reached $1.808 billion in 1997 dollars, of which private pension funds alone accounted for $1.516 billion and public pensions $292 million. Throughout the 1980s and 1990s pension funds provided anywhere from 31 percent to 59 percent of the funds raised by independent venture-capital partnerships, which in turn increased their share of all venture funds raised from 40 percent in 1980 to 80 percent a decade later (Gompers and Lerner 2002, 8).

The massive infusion of capital into venture funds from the pension savings of US households underpinned the third wave of entry of Silicon Valley venture-capital firms. These venture capitalists in turn became much more active than previously in funding semiconductor startups as well as those producing the array of electronic products that silicon chips made possible. Semiconductor firms were supplying microprocessors and ASICs to a growing range of computer applications, which created a multitude of new opportunities in computer hardware and software that venture capitalists could fund, extending from video games and disk drives in the early 1980s to e-commerce and optical networking gear in the late 1990s. Apple Computer's highly successful IPO in December 1980 is generally credited with setting off the startup and IPO boom of the early 1980s. After achieving spectacular returns on its investments, averaging about 35 percent, between 1978 and 1983, the venture-capital industry was punished for over-investing, with returns averaging less than 10 percent in the last half of the 1980s. After 1990 returns moved up once again, soaring to almost 150 percent at the peak of the dotcom boom of 2000 before turning negative in the not-unrelated crash of 2001 and 2002 (Lerner 2002).

The Silicon Valley venture-capital model spread to other parts of the United States, especially during the 1990s, with investments being made in many different locations and across a wide range of industries. The main geographic center of US venture capital, however, has continued to be California, with Silicon Valley remaining by far the most important location (Gompers and Lerner 2002, 14; Green 2004). Over time there have been shifts in the leading sectors for venture financing (Gompers and Lerner 2002, 12–13; Green 2004). Office and computer machinery was the leading sector from the last half of the 1960s through the first half of the 1980s, before being barely surpassed by the communications and electronics sectors in the last half of that decade. In the first half of the 1990s biotech became important. Subsequently, from 1995 through 2002, ICT accounted for 57 percent of the value of all venture-capital investments, of which more than four-fifths were in software, telecommunications, and networking (Green 2004).

The importance of telecommunications and networking as recipients of venture capital in the 1990s and beyond reflects the evolution of converged information and communication technologies out of what had been, in the absence of networking, just information technologies. The origins of this convergence go back to the early 1970s when, at Xerox PARC, the Palo Alto-based research arm of the Old Economy copier company, Robert Metcalfe led a team that developed Ethernet, a technology that enabled computers to communicate with one another (Hiltzik 2000, ch. 13). When Xerox declined to commercialize this technology, Metcalfe sought to do so by co-founding 3Com – standing for "computer, communication, and compatibility" – in 1979. With the widespread adoption of the IBM PC from 1982 3Com was well positioned to be a leader in providing the hardware and software for local area networks (LANs).

After 3Com acquired another Silicon Valley company, Bridge Communications, in 1987, it became the largest supplier of LAN equipment, followed by Novell, based in Provo, Utah (Mulqueen 1989a). By this time, however, business, government, and non-profit organizations that had installed LANs in geographically dispersed locations wanted bridges or routers that would link their LANs into wide area networks (WANs). The company that by the beginning of the 1990s was most successful in developing this internetworking technology was Cisco Systems.

In 1984 Leonard Bosack and Sandy Lerner, a husband and wife team, founded Cisco,[18] running it initially from their living room. While working in computing in different parts of Stanford University, Bosack and Lerner had been involved in the development of the university's LANs and then had taken up the challenge of internetworking them. At the end of 1987 Cisco received an infusion of $2.5 million in venture funds from Sequoia Capital (*San Francisco Chronicle*, January 27, 1988, B3; Bellinger 1989; Mulqueen 1989b). Yet with $10 million in revenues in the 1987–1988 fiscal year, venture finance was probably the least important of Sequoia's contributions to the growth of the firm. The case of Cisco exemplifies the *non-financial* role of Silicon Valley venture capitalists in developing a promising startup into a going concern. The Sequoia partner most actively involved with the young company was Donald Valentine, who became a member of Cisco's board of directors. During 1988 Valentine directed the hiring of professional managers at Cisco, including John Morgridge, who had run Grid Computer in

---

[18] The company's name, short for San Francisco, was actually spelt cisco, with a lower-case initial "c" until it went public in 1990.

nearby Fremont, as Cisco president and CEO. More generally, with over a quarter-century of experience as a manager and financier in Silicon Valley, Valentine provided Cisco with business expertise that was based on an intimate understanding of the industrial environment in which the firm was trying to compete.

In 2004 Morgridge was chairman of the board of Cisco while Valentine remained a member of the board. Beyond the initial professionalization of the company in the late 1980s, Morgridge and Valentine oversaw the phenomenal growth of Cisco from less than $28 million in sales in the year ending July 1989 to over $22 billion in sales in the year ending July 2001. The way in which Cisco financed this growth as a publicly traded company exemplifies NEBM.

The IPO itself in February 1990 netted the company $48 million that was used for working capital and cash reserves. Funds from operations easily covered the company's capital expenditures, not only in 1990 but also for every subsequent year. In fact, 1990 was the only time that Cisco raised funds on financial markets; the company has done no further public stock offerings and has never incurred debt. At the same time, typifying NEBM, Cisco has never paid any dividends. Of the 20 New Economy companies listed in Table 2.2, the only ones that have paid cash dividends are Microsoft in 2003 and 2004, Intel since 1992, EMC in 1996, and Apple from 1987 through 1995.

While Cisco has not raised any funds on securities markets since going public in 1990, the company has taken in $7.4 billion from the sale of stock, with just over half of this amount in the fiscal years 1999–2001 (Carpenter et al. 2003, 993). The buyers have been its employees when they have exercised their stock options; these were not issues to the public. In addition, Cisco has been able to claim a total of $7.5 billion in tax credits for income taxes paid by its employees when they have exercised stock options.[19] Of this total in tax credits, $5.9 billion, or 76 percent, came in fiscal 1999–2001.

The practice of extending stock options to a broad base of employees means that a substantial proportion of the shares outstanding of a company like Cisco are committed to stock option programs. As shown in Figure 2.1, the proportion of stock options outstanding to common shares outstanding at Cisco rose from 7.4 percent in 1994 to 20 percent in 2004, with the increase in this proportion since 2000 largely due to the fact that, with Cisco's stock price down from its high levels in the late

---

[19] Under the Economic Recovery Tax Act of 1981, a company is permitted to take a tax credit equal to the amount of taxes that employees pay on the gains that they make from exercising stock options that are taxable as ordinary income (Hubbard 1982).

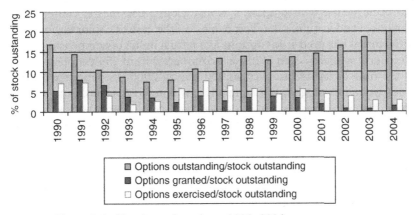

Figure 2.1. Cisco's stock options, 1990–2004.

Source: Cisco Systems Annual Reports.

Note: Options outstanding/stock outstanding based on end of fiscal year data; options granted/stock outstanding and options exercised/stock outstanding based on an average of stock outstanding at the beginning and end of the fiscal year.

1990s, a significant proportion of the options outstanding – 48 percent of options exercisable as of July 30, 2004 – has been "under water" (Cisco Systems *2004 Annual Report*, 60). To support the company's stock price, and put more of these stock options "in-the-money", Cisco repurchased its own stock in the amount $16.9 billion for 2002–2004, of which $9.1 billion was in 2004 alone.

As the case of Cisco illustrates, NEBM places a heavy emphasis on maintaining high stock prices. In pursuing this corporate objective, a need to raise funds on the stock or convertible bond markets has *not* been the main driver in NEBM. Nor has a desire to avoid a hostile takeover; such bids have rarely happened with high-tech companies because of the ease with which a firm's most valuable assets can walk out the door – although the recent hostile takeover of PeopleSoft by Oracle, carried out in a period of relatively weak ICT labor markets, may signal a new trend.[20] The main impetus to maintaining a high stock price

[20] Both Oracle (with 2003 revenues of $9.5 billion and 40,650 employees) and PeopleSoft (with 2003 revenues of $2.3 billion and 12,163 employees) are Silicon Valley-based providers of enterprise software. From the outset of the hostile bid, launched in June 2003, Oracle made it clear that it was after PeopleSoft's 13,000-strong customer base and that it intended to lay off about half of PeopleSoft's employees, making however a special effort to retain its core of developers, application designers, and quality-assurance specialists, undoubtedly through stock option awards (Bank, 2004; Pallatto, 2004).

has been the use of a company's own stock as a currency to compensate personnel and acquire other companies. In the case of Cisco, throughout its history it has used stock options as a partial mode of compensation for all of its employees, even as its headcount grew from 254 people in 1990 at the time of its IPO to over 40,000 during 2000. In periods when its stock price has sagged, the company has entered the market to repurchase its own shares – at times, as we have seen, on a massive scale.

In addition, again exemplifying a mode of finance that became a feature of NEBM in the 1990s, Cisco has used its stock rather than cash to acquire other companies (see Table 2.4). From 1993 through 2004 Cisco made 94 acquisitions valued in nominal terms at almost $39 billion, over 96 percent of which was paid in the company's stock rather than cash. In 1999 and 2000, years in which Cisco expended 69 percent of the total value (in nominal dollars) of its acquisitions, over 99 percent took the form of stock.

Cisco's practice of an almost complete reliance on stock as an acquisition currency changed, however, starting with the acquisition of Latitude Communications, based in Santa Clara, California, for $86 million in cash in November 2003, and continuing with the 12 acquisitions that Cisco made, all with cash, in 2004. There could be a number of reasons why Cisco reversed its practice of using stock as an acquisition currency. Since July 2001 the Financial Accounting Standards Board (FASB) has outlawed pooling-of-interests accounting, a practice that enabled a company that did an all-stock acquisition to put the book value rather than the market value of the acquisition on its balance sheet, thus reducing future amortization charges and increasing future reported earnings. Cisco was known for its use of this accounting device, one that by inflating the company's reported earnings presumably boosted its stock price (see Donlan 2000). This explanation, however, is clearly only a partial one since Cisco made ten all-stock acquisitions between July 2001 and March 2003 when the new FASB ruling was in place. At best the ruling made Cisco indifferent from an accounting point of view between the use of cash and stock in acquisitions. In fact, Cisco's stock price was generally higher from November 2003 to December 2004 than it had been from July 2001 to October 2003, which, all other things being equal, should have encouraged the use of stock rather than cash for acquisitions – just the opposite of what Cisco actually did.

What probably tilted Cisco toward the use of cash were the facts that it had current assets of over $14 billion on its balance sheet throughout fiscal 2004, and, given its massive stock repurchase program, the use of stock to acquire companies would have simply increased the number of shares it would then have had to repurchase to reduce dilution to a

Table 2.4. *Cisco Systems acquisitions, by value, employees, and mode of payment, 1993–2004*

Calendar year	No. of firms acquired	Total value paid ($ millions)	Average value per acquisition ($ millions)	Percent of acquisition value paid in shares	No. of employees at acquired firm	Value per employee ($ millions)	"Acquired" employees/Cisco employees percent[a]
1993	1	89	89	100.00	60	1.48	4.1
1994	3	423	141	71.63	320	1.32	13.1
1995	4	702	176	100.00	205	3.42	5.0
1996[b]	7	5,618	803	97.67	1,547	3.63	17.6
1997[c]	6	614	102	72.13	210	2.92	1.9
1998	9	1,144	127	99.85	722	1.58	4.8
1999	18	14,435	802	99.83	2,363	6.11	11.3
2000	23	12,254	533	98.80	2,045	5.99	6.0
2001	2	331	166	100.00	91	3.64	0.2
2002	5	1,789	358	100.00	418	4.28	1.2
2003	4	754	189	88.59	550	1.37	1.6
2004	12	793	66	0.00	886	0.90	2.7
Totals	94	38,945	414	96.21	9,417	4.14	

Notes:

[a] Calculated as proportion of total number of people employed by target companies at the time that they were acquired by Cisco divided by the number of Cisco employees at the end of its fiscal year (last week in July). It is not known what proportion of these target-company employees actually became Cisco employees.

[b] Acquisition cost of Metaplex, with 19 employees, not disclosed. For the purpose of this table Metaplex is valued at the average value per employee of other acquisitions in 1996.

[c] Acquisition cost of Telesend, with 10 employees, not disclosed. For the purpose of this table Telesend is valued at the average value per employee of other acquisitions in 1997.

Source: Updated from Carpenter et al. 2003, p. 982. Compiled from press releases on www.cisco.com and news reports.

desired level (see Domis 2003). It is also the case that Cisco paid much less on a per-employee basis for its recent cash acquisitions than it had paid for its stock-based acquisitions, reflecting perhaps a preference by the owners of the acquired firms for hard cash rather than volatile stock. With 183 employees, the cost per employee of the Latitude acquisition in November 2003 was $470,000, the lowest sum in Cisco's 82 acquisitions up to that point. And, at $860,000, the average cost per employee of Cisco's 2004 acquisitions was only 21 percent of the average of $4,160,000 for all its 93 acquisitions, and would be much less if one were to correct for consumer or producer price inflation. But then perhaps one would also want to "correct" for the stock-price inflation of the Internet boom that made it possible for Cisco to pay an average of over $6 million per employee for its acquisitions in 1999–2000.

2.5   Evolution of NEBM: labor

The distinctive characteristic of employment in NEBM is the interfirm mobility of labor. Especially within Silicon Valley, but even on a national and international scale, high-tech employees tend to move from one company to another over the course of their careers (see Saxenian 1994; Hyde 2003). Encouraging this interfirm movement of people have been opportunities provided by startups; a large influx of new highly educated foreigners, on both immigrant and non-immigrant visas, into the United States; an intensity of work that often results in employee "burn out"; and the use of broad-based stock option plans as an inducement for employees to leave one firm for another (see Cohen and Fields 1999).

The prevalence of stock options as a mode of compensation manifests the importance of interfirm labor mobility in NEBM. Stock options are granted to an employee as part of a compensation package that generally includes a salary based on one's hierarchical and functional position, medical and pension benefits, as well as, in some cases, variable remuneration such as bonuses, performance awards, and (for an executive) restricted stock. A stock option gives the employee the non-transferable right to purchase a certain number of shares of the company for which he or she works at a pre-set "exercise" price between the date the option "vests" and the date it "expires". Typically in US option grants, the exercise price is the market price of the stock at the date the option is granted; the vesting period is spread over one to four years from the date of the grant; and the expiration date is ten years from the date of the grant. Unvested options usually lapse 90 days after termination of employment with the company.

While broad-based stock option plans that extend to non-executive personnel are a quintessentially Silicon Valley phenomenon, stock options as a mode of compensation have their origins in the Old Economy (Lazonick 2003). From the late 1930s, in the wake of the New Deal, high-level executives of major corporations, in search of a way to avoid paying marginal tax rates of as much as 91 percent on their personal incomes, seized on the possibility that income from exercising stock options could be subject to capital gains taxation at a rate of 25 percent. The Revenue Act of 1950 transformed this possibility into reality, and over the course of the 1950s, top managers of US corporations saw income from options become an important component of their total income. In the late 1950s and early 1960s, however, a backlash of public sentiment against this enrichment of top managers led the US Congress to place restrictions on the use of stock options as a mode of compensation. In 1969 and 1976, moreover, Congress raised the capital gains rate and lowered the personal income rate, thus mitigating the original purpose of options. In 1978 Graef Crystal (1978, 145), a compensation consultant who would later become a vocal critic of excessive executive pay (Crystal 1991), stated that qualified stock options, "once the most popular of all executive compensation devices . . . have been given the last rites by Congress".

That was not the end of executive stock options, however. Congress subsequently lowered *both* the personal income and capital gains rates, and relaxed the rules on the granting and exercising of stock options, thus resuscitating them. The 1980s and 1990s witnessed an explosion in executive pay, driven by stock options. Between 1980 and 1994 the mean value of stock option grants to CEOs of large US corporations rose from $155,037 to $1,213,180, or by 683 percent, while the mean value of their salary and bonus compensation rose from $654,935 to $1,292,290 million, or by 95 percent. As a result, stock options accounted for 19 percent of CEO compensation in 1980, but 48 percent in 1994 (Hall and Leibman 1998, 661). In 2000 the average CEO compensation of the largest 200 US corporations by sales was $11.3 million, of which stock options generated 60 percent, restricted stock 11 percent, bonuses 18 percent, and salary 9 percent (Pearl Meyer & Partners 2001). Stock option income as a proportion of executive pay was highest in ICT firms (Anderson et al. 2000).

But the growing use of stock options during the 1980s and 1990s cannot be understood simply in terms of *executive* pay. The vast majority of option grants now go to non-executive personnel, especially in ICT (iQuantic-Buck 2002). In the 200 largest US companies by sales in 2000 and 2001, 15.5 percent of all options went to the five highest paid executives whose compensation companies report in the proxy statements issued in advance of the annual general meeting of shareholders. Therefore, other corporate employees, some of whom were executives but most of whom were not, received, on average, almost 85 percent of options granted. Because they compete disproportionately for technology personnel, ICT companies grant a lower proportion of options to the top five executives than firms in other industries. Cisco's five highest paid executives, for example, received 2.4 percent of all options granted in 2000 and 2.8 percent in 2001. These low proportions, however, did not prevent Cisco's CEO, John Chambers, from making $120.8 million from exercising stock options in 1999, and another $156.0 million in 2002, nor the other four highest paid Cisco executives from averaging $24.9 million from stock options in 1999 and $36.7 million in 2000 (Carpenter et al. 2003, 990).

During the New Economy boom, broad-based stock option programs diffused to many more companies, with top executives getting more of them and increasing numbers of non-executive employees getting them for the first time. In a "near-constant" sample of 350 US-based companies, the proportion that made provision for broad-based plans rose from 17.4 percent in 1993 to 54.0 percent in 2000, while the proportion that made grants under these plans rose from 5.7 percent to 22.0 percent (Sabow and Milligan 2000, 100; Mercer 2001). The use of stock options for non-executive personnel had its origins in Silicon Valley, beginning in the 1960s, and became omnipresent by the late 1990s as startups from semiconductors to microcomputers to internetworking sought to attract talent. For startups, options could also be a way of conserving cash and hence financing growth; around 1990, in Silicon Valley, established firms paid $65,000 for an electrical engineer with ten years of experience, whereas startups paid $40,000 plus stock options (Uchitelle 1990). For the employee, the hope was that the options, which had exercise prices in the pennies when the grants were made in the startup phase, would be worth a small fortune if and when the new venture did an IPO or a private sale to a publicly traded corporation.

That the growth of non-executive stock options is a Silicon Valley phenomenon, there is no doubt. A Factiva search was done on December 10, 2004 to compare the importance of stock options as a mode of compensation in Silicon Valley and Route 128. A search on "stock options" and "compensation" and "Silicon Valley" generated 2,496 hits (representing 3.5 percent of all hits on "stock options" and "compensation", with the earliest hit on September 12, 1983 and 95 percent of the hits from January 1, 1995). A Factiva search on "stock options" and "compensation" and "Route 128" yielded only 34 hits (earliest September 9,

1984, and 85 percent from January 1, 1995), a ratio of Silicon Valley hits to Route 128 hits of 73:1. Moreover, 31 of the 34 "Route 128" items also included "Silicon Valley". As a control, single-phrase searches on "Silicon Valley" and "Route 128" produced 277,389 and 12,981 hits respectively, for a leading high-tech district hit ratio of 21:1.

There is no adequate documentation of the evolution of non-executive stock options as a mode of compensation in Silicon Valley firms from the 1960s through the 1980s. Beyond the data in proxy statements on the percentage of stock options allocated to the CEO and other four highest paid executives, company filings provide no systematic evidence on the distribution of options among employees. Even though since 1994 US corporations have been obliged to publish information on their stock option programs in their 10-K filings, the evidence on who gets what remains fragmentary.[21] Intel extended stock options to all of its professional personnel (but not its clerical and production employees) from its founding in 1968, and by 1984 5,000, or about one-fifth of its worldwide employees, were receiving them (Jackson 1997, 112, 318). Coming into 1997 Intel offered stock options to the 25 percent of its labor force deemed to be "key employees". In February 1997, however, Intel announced that it would henceforth be offering stock options to all of its 50,000 regular employees (DeBare 1997), thus following a practice that had become common among younger Silicon Valley companies. It was subsequently revealed in April 1997 that in 1996 Intel CEO Andrew Grove had made $96.4 million from exercising stock options, the highest of any corporate executive in that year and over 50 percent greater than the second highest. Within the corporation, it is easier to legitimize such high returns to top executives when a broad base of employees in the organization can also gain from rising stock prices.

For NEBM employees, stock options are not only a potential form of remuneration for work but also, hopefully, a source of retirement savings. New Economy companies almost invariably have defined-contribution rather than defined-benefit pension schemes, often with a low level of contribution by the company. The expectation is that the accumulation of wealth through the exercise of stock options will form a much more significant financial foundation for retirement than the company pension plan *per se*.

---

[21] For a case study of a non-US-based company that provided the researchers with full access to information, see Glimstedt and Lazonick 2005. Annual surveys done since 1996 by iQuantic and (now) Mellon Consulting also provide option distribution information for groups of ICT firms by industry and size.

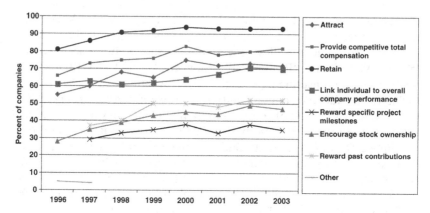

Figure 2.2. Relative importance of objectives of ongoing stock option programs, ICT companies operating in the United States, 1996–2003.

Source: 1996–1997: iQuantic High-Tech Equity Practices Survey; 1998–2000: iQuantic Equity Practices Survey for High Technology Industries; 2001–2002: iQuantic-Buck Information Services Equity Practices Survey for the High Technology Industries; 2003: Mellon Equity Practices Survey for the High Technology Industries (April 2004). Notes: The identities of the ICT companies included in the survey shift from year to year. The number of companies surveyed were: 1996, 68; 1997, 68; 1998, 82; 1999, 81; 2000, 180; 2001, 166; 2002, 174; 2003, 136. In 1996, "Rewarding past contributions" was a frequent response in the "Other" category.

Note: index of importance of objectives is 0–100, with 100 as 'most important'.

There is a widespread consensus among ICT firms that the prime function of stock options is to manage interfirm mobility on the labor market, as shown by the relative importance ascribed to different functions of stock options by ICT compensation executives who responded to iQuantic's annual survey (see Figure 2.2). Note the stability of the relative rankings between 1996 and 2003 as well as the upward movement in the importance ascribed to the "attract" function to 2000.

The practice of allocating stock options to a broad base of employees is made easier in NEBM by the fact that New Economy companies increasingly employ predominantly highly educated professional, technical, and administrative personnel; some New Economy firms employ few if any production workers. One result is that ICT has not been fertile territory for union organization. It is difficult to organize workers who have the option of "exit" via the labor market instead of "voice" via union representation, which in good times a district like Silicon Valley can provide, or who are working for companies that, to counter the threat of unionization, can outsource work or offer the relatively small number of non-salaried workers that they still employ higher pay or even stock options.

In 1985, when the Silicon Valley semiconductor industry was beset by Japanese competition, Gordon Moore of Intel was quoted as saying: "Our industry changes so rapidly, and the nature of the jobs changes continuously. I think [the lack of unionization] has served the industry well" (Malone 1985). Similarly, in his book, *Spinoff*, Charles Sporck (2001, 271), the CEO of National Semiconductor and a major figure in the semiconductor industry, contends that "unions have a way of evolving into extremely stubborn obstacles to innovation. We were constantly changing assignments around to make best use of individual talents and skills. It would have been impossible to move ahead with the rapidly developing technology of semiconductors in an organization hampered by union formalities."

Whether or not one accepts these judgments by Silicon Valley's top executives on the incompatibility of unions with NEBM, the fact is, as Sporck (2001, 271) put it, "no semiconductor facility in Silicon Valley was ever unionized". In the mid-1970s the United Auto Workers had gotten as far as a representation ballot at one of Intel's plants, but four out of five eligible employees rejected the union (Jackson 1997, ch. 16). Attempts by US unions to organize Silicon Valley employees in the mid-1980s came to naught (Miller 1984; Sawyer 1984). Indeed, the only successful union organizing in Silicon Valley has been of the janitorial labor force; in 1992 Hewlett-Packard agreed to employ a janitorial contractor whose employees were represented by the Service Employees International Union (SEIU) (*US Newswire*, August 6, 1992), and by 1996 an SEIU official announced that "every major high-tech company is cleaned by a union janitorial company except for Intel" (Holmes 1996). By the end of the decade, amidst the affluence of the high-tech boom, there was a general acceptance among Silicon Valley's high-tech employers that the people (most of them Hispanic immigrants) who cleaned their facilities needed collective bargaining to bolster their meager pay. Even Intel, which remained adamantly nonunion, paid its janitors at the union rate (Kirby 2000).

As for Silicon Valley employees who were the beneficiaries of stock options, their relatively high base salaries and the extra incomes that they reaped from the exercise of options at the peak of the Internet boom lured them into believing that "the market" would bring them ample rewards. Figures 2.3–2.6 show the changes in regular employment and real wages

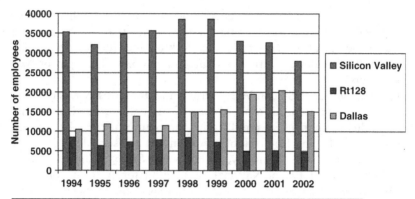

Year	Silicon Valley		Route 128		Dallas		USA
	Number	% of	Number	% of	Number	% of	
1994	35314	20.6	8489	4.9	10460	6.1	171766
1999	38635	18.8	7264	3.5	15533	7.6	205296
2000	33045	15.9	4829	2.3	19506	9.4	207211
2001	32656	14.5	5154	2.3	20444	9.1	225078
2002	28004	16.4	4731	2.8	15144	8.9	170775

SIC 3674; NAICS 334413

Figure 2.3. Semiconductor employees (full-time) Silicon Valley, Route 128, Dallas, USA 1994–2002.

Source: US Bureau of the Census.

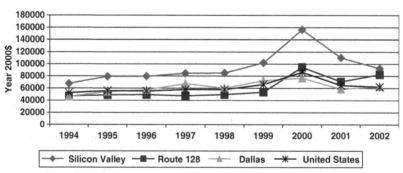

SIC 3674; NAICS 334413

Figure 2.4. Average real annual earnings, full-time employees, semiconductors, Silicon Valley, Route 128, Dallas, USA 1994–2002.

Source: US Bureau of the Census.

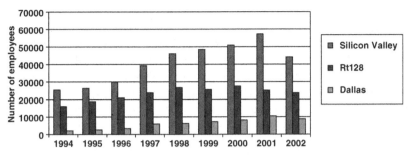

Year	Silicon Valley		Route 128		Dallas		USA
	Number	% of	Number	% of	Number	% of	
1994	25429	17.0	15949	10.6	2201	1.5	149911
1999	48427	15.9	25613	8.4	7289	2.4	304663
2000	50941	15.4	27500	8.3	8152	2.5	331485
2001	57231	16.2	25173	7.1	10508	3.0	353344
2002	44213	14.2	23674	7.6	8827	2.8	312102

SIC 7372; NAICS 511210

Figure 2.5. Software publisher employees (full-time), Silicon Valley, Route 128, Dallas, USA 1994–2002.

Source: US Bureau of the Census.

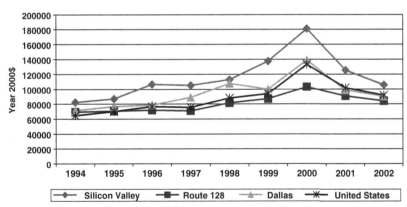

SIC 3674; NAICS 334413

Figure 2.6. Average real annual earnings, full-time employees, software publishers, Silicon Valley, Route 128, Dallas, USA 1994–2002.

Source: US Bureau of the Census.

for two ICT sectors – semiconductors and software publishing – from 1994 through 2002 for three districts in the United States that have a high concentration of ICT workers. ICT incomes were higher in Silicon Valley than in Route 128, the Dallas area, and the United States as a whole with the sharp increases in pay of 1999 and 2000 reflecting the exercising of options at the stock market's peak. Subsequently in 2001 and 2002 wages moved sharply downward (with the exception of the relatively small Route 128 semiconductor sector where wages increased somewhat from 2001 to 2002). Both semiconductors and software publishing saw significant growth of employment into 2001 but then sharp declines in 2002, with employment in semiconductors falling below its level of 1994. While the patterns of change in employment and earnings showed some variation across industries and districts over time, the overall picture is that, as one would expect, what went up in the boom of the late 1990s came down in the bust of the early 2000s.

The decline in GDP that accompanied the end of the Internet boom lasted from March to November 2001. Subsequently, however, with the resumption of growth, there was a contraction in employment in the US economy as a whole until the fourth quarter of 2003. In this jobless recovery, certain ICT occupational categories were hit particularly hard. Fourth-quarter surveys by the Bureau of Labor Statistics show employment of computer programmers in the United States falling from 530,730 in 2000 to 501,580 in 2001 to 457,320 in 2002 to 403,220 in 2003, with average real annual wages declining from a peak of $65,517 in 2001 to $65,170 in 2003. Fourth-quarter employment of electrical and electronic engineering technicians fell from 244,570 in 2000 to 220,810 in 2001 to 194,960 in 2002 to 181,550 in 2003, although the average real annual wages of those who remained employed rose from $33,155 in 2000 to $46,190 in 2003.[22] The Institute of Electrical and Electronics Engineers (IEEE) estimated an unemployment rate for computer programmers of 6.4 percent on average in 2003 and 7.6 percent on average in the first half of 2004.[23] The problem, it was widely argued, was a marked acceleration in the 2000s of the "offshoring", especially to India, of what had been well-paid ICT jobs in the United States. Even in recovery, it seemed, the New Economy was failing to deliver on the promise of prosperity even to many of the better educated groups in the US labor force.

[22] http://www.bls.gov/oes/home.htm.
[23] http://ewh.ieee.org/r5/central_texas/employment.html.

2.6   IBM and the end of "organization man"

That by the 2000s NEBM had become the dominant mode of business organization in the ICT industries, there is little doubt. During the 1990s leading Old Economy ICT companies sought to adopt elements of NEBM. Lucent Technologies, spun off from AT&T in 1996, made the attempt in the last half of the 1990s to become a New Economy company, but, as has been detailed elsewhere (Carpenter et al. 2003), in the process came close to destroying itself as a viable business organization. Not so with IBM. In the 1980s the IBM PC had consolidated the vertical structure of the microcomputer industry. In the 1990s IBM's own organizational transformation ensured the dominance of NEBM in the US ICT industries.

Between 1991 and 1993 IBM's annual revenues dropped for three successive years. Average revenues during these three years was $64 billion, just over 7 percent less than 1990 revenues of $69 billion, but greater than the company's average revenues for the years 1988–1990. Especially given that the US economy was going through a major recession, IBM's problem was not in its ability to generate sales. Yet not since 1946 had IBM experienced a year-to-year decline in revenues, and with shrinking gross profit margins from 1991 and 1991–1993 deficits totaling $15.9 billion, it appeared that IBM had lost its way.

From 1994 through 2003, however, IBM came back, its revenues rising from $64.1 billion to $89.1 billion, notwithstanding revenue declines in 2001 and 2002. The company increased its employment level from 220,000 in 1994, the lowest since 1966, to 320,000 in 2001, a level that it almost matched in 2003. Moreover, in 2003 US dollars, IBM's sales per employee increased from an annual average of $220,000 in 1981–1990 to $320,000 in 1994–2003, although that figure fell over the latter period as IBM's employment level was restored. Over the 1994–2003 decade IBM's net income averaged $5.8 billion, 7.4 percent of revenues. The fact that this profit rate was well below the 10.4 percent profit rate that IBM recorded during 1981–1990, and the rate of 13.2 percent in the first half of that decade, reflects the much more competitive New Economy environment that IBM faced (IBM *Annual Reports*, various years).

During the 1990s IBM pursued a strategy of shifting its business out of hardware into services (Garr 1999; Gerstner 2002; Lohr 2004). Continuing a trend that began in the late 1980s, the share of revenues from hardware declined from 48 percent in 1996 to 32 percent in 2003, while the services share increased from 29 percent to 48 percent.

Hardware margins (gross profits as a percent of gross revenues) trended downward from about 37 percent in the mid-1990s to 28 percent in the early 2000s, while services margins stayed relatively stable at 25–28 percent. Software's share of revenues remained at 15–16 percent from 1996 to 2003, but the segment's already high profit margins increased fairly steadily from 74 percent in 1996 to almost 87 percent in 2003. As a result the software segment accounted for 38 percent of gross revenues in 2003, compared with 33 percent for services and 24 percent for hardware (IBM *Annual Reports*, various years). In December 2004 IBM's strategy of shifting out of hardware continued with its sale of its PC business to Lenovo, an indigenous Chinese computer electronics company formerly known as Legend (see Lu 2000; Lohr 2004).

These changes in product market strategy have been accompanied by significant reductions in IBM's R&D expenditure as a percentage of sales. A clear-cut break in IBM's R&D expenditure occurred between 1992 and 1994 (see Figure 2.7) as it adjusted to its losses and as Gerstner arrived on the scene. The company's R&D expenditure averaged 9.84 percent of sales for the decade 1983–1992 compared with 6.09 percent for the decade 1994–2003. In 2003 IBM's total expenditure of $5.1 billion on R&D placed it ninth among all R&D spenders globally. But its R&D expenditure of $16,000 per employee was lower than all but seven other companies in the list of top 50 R&D spenders, far lower than 14th-place Intel's $55,000, 29th-place Cisco's $92,000, and 1st-place Microsoft's $141,000 (Goldstein and Hira 2004).

This change reflects IBM's much greater orientation toward product development rather than basic research. As the company stated in its *2003 Annual Report* (49): "A key transformation that has been taking place over the past decade and that continues today is the change in the focus and the culture of IBM's R&D organization to be more closely linked to and be primarily driven by industry-specific and client-specific needs." A major element of this strategy is extensive patenting for the purposes of cross-licensing and intellectual property (IP) revenue generation (Grindley and Teece 1997; DiCarlo 1999). Cross-licensing has enabled IBM to gain access to technology developed by other companies rather than generating that technology through its in-house R&D. IBM sees its IP revenues, which averaged $1.352 billion per year in 2000–2003, as a direct return on its R&D expenditure, which averaged $5.154 billion over the same period (IBM *2002 Annual Report*, 52; IBM *2003 Annual Report*, 54, 82).

Since 1993 IBM has emerged as far and away the leader in US patent awards. During the 1990s, as IBM scaled back its rate of R&D

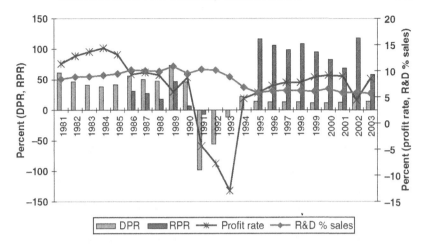

Figure 2.7. IBM's profit rate, rate of R&D spending, and payout behavior, 1981–2003.

Source: IBM Annual Reports.

Note: A negative DPR or RPR shows the relation between the level of dividends or repurchases and negative net income.

expenditure, it ramped up its patenting activity. In 1989 and 1990 IBM was ninth in number of US patents awarded, in 1991 eighth, and in 1992 sixth. With a 29 percent increase in patents awarded in 1993 over the previous year, however, IBM moved into the number one spot, and maintained that position for 12 years through 2004. As Figure 2.8 shows, IBM's level of patenting activity has created a growing gap between IBM and its rivals.

During the last half of the 1990s, while IBM was using its IP as the basis for multi-billion-dollar OEBM partnerships with other ICT companies such as 3Com, Acer, Cisco, Dell, and EMC (DiCarlo 1999), it was also taking the lead among Old Economy companies in outsourcing routine production to contract manufacturers. For example, in 1999, IBM outsourced its printed circuit board assembly for motherboards used in its mobile products to Solectron in a deal that was the second largest in the contract manufacturer's history and that included the transfer of 1,300 production workers based in Austin, Texas from IBM to Solectron (*PR Newswire*, January 6, 1999). IBM also had major supply agreements with Celestica, one of the top five

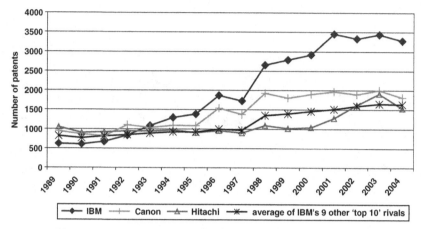

Figure 2.8. US patenting, IBM, leading Japanese electronics companies, and other top 10 patenters, 1989–2004.
Source: http://www.ificlaims.com.

CMs, which had originally been IBM Canada, the parent company's manufacturing arm.

IBM had spun off IBM Canada in 1994 as part of the restructuring process that saw IBM downsize its labor force from 374,000 in 1990 to 220,000 in 1994, in the process making history of the company's commitment to offering employment for one's working life. Much of IBM's restructuring in the early 1990s had been accomplished by making it attractive for IBM employees to take early retirement at age 55, a move that was largely responsible for IBM's $16 billion in losses in 1991–1993. In 1995 IBM rescinded this early-retirement provision not only because it had accomplished its purpose but also because, in its efforts to compete for younger talent in the New Economy labor market, the company no longer wanted to encourage all employees to stick around until the age of 55 (Schultz 2000). IBM's new emphasis on cross-licensing and technology partnerships, for example, made it much more desirable and possible for the company to make use of a fluid and flexible high-tech labor force.

That labor market logic was taken a major step further in 1999 when IBM announced that it was shifting from its traditional pension plan that gave older workers retirement benefits based on their pre-retirement salary levels to a "cash-balance" pension plan that paid annually into an account for each employee an amount equal to 5 percent of the employee's salary for that year plus annual interest (based on market rates) on accumulated balances. IBM also moved to a similar type of cash-balance plan for retiree health benefits (Geisel 1999). The cash-balance pension was defined-benefit but also portable should the employee leave the company. IBM designed it to attract younger employees who, in the New Economy, did not expect to spend their whole careers with one company. Of 141,000 people in IBM's US labor force in 1999, 60,000 had joined the company since 1993. In a communication to employees announcing the change in the pension plan, IBM's management wrote: "The fact that significantly fewer people are staying with one company their full careers means that, more and more, people are looking for opportunities to contribute and be rewarded sooner in their careers" (Lewis 1999). IBM employees were also told that "competition in our industry for skilled, talented employees has never been more fierce than it is today" (Frey 1999). IBM did permit some 30,000 employees who were within five years of the 30 years of service required for retirement to remain on the traditional plan.

While the company also provided extra contributions to the cash-balance plans of other employees aged 45 or older, it was estimated that these mid-career employees could lose 30–50 percent of their expected pensions (Lewis 1999; Lynn 1999). They did not accept the change quietly. Suddenly some IBM employees became receptive to union organizing efforts, and three years later 5,000 of them had joined *Alliance@IBM*, an affiliate of the Communication Workers of America (CWA) (Pimentel 2002). Moreover, federal legislators got involved. IBM was the biggest employer in Vermont, and Bernard Sanders, the state's lone member of the US House of Representatives, charged that IBM's cash-balance plan violated federal laws against age discrimination (Anand 1999). Vermont Senator James Jeffords, also the chairman of the Senate Health, Education, Labor and Pensions Committee, convinced IBM CEO Gerstner to permit IBM employees aged 40 with at least ten years of service – some 65,000 people – to remain in the traditional plan (*Dow Jones Business News*, September 17, 1999; Affleck 2000). The SEC blocked IBM management's attempt to disallow a vote on the cash-balance plan at the annual shareholders' meeting, thus rejecting IBM's claim that the pension plan was a matter of ordinary business that did not require shareholder approval (Burns 2000).

Shareholder proposals to permit employees to choose among pension plans failed at five successive annual meetings from 2000 through 2004, but nevertheless received unusual levels of support that reflected the animosity of employee-oriented shareholders to the cash-balance plans (Affleck 2000; Fuscaldo 2001; Freund 2002; Krishnan 2003; Arditi 2004). Meanwhile, a class action lawsuit, covering anyone who worked for IBM after December 31, 1994, was brought against the company on the grounds that changes in IBM pensions discriminated against older employees, and hence violated ERISA (Tumulty 2003a). In September 2004 IBM agreed to a settlement consisting of $320 million that was not subject to appeal plus another $1.4 billion should it lose its appeals of a lower court's decision (Dale 2004a and 2004b; Wells 2004). As of December 2004 the appeal process had not yet been completed, but IBM had announced that new employees would not be eligible for the cash-balance pension fund. Instead the company would offer them a defined-contribution 401(k) (*AFX International*, December 9, 2004).

When IBM had instituted the cash-balance plan in 1999, management had stated that it would redirect the $200 million per year that it would save on the new plan into stock options for 23,000 "key" employees (Tumulty 2003b). As, under Gerstner, the company discarded lifelong employment, it implemented a broad-based stock option program. In 1992, 1,300 executives, or less than half of 1 percent of IBM's total labor force, had received stock options, whereas in 2001 options went to 72,500 people, or almost 23 percent of the labor force (Gerstner 2002, 97). IBM's increased reliance on options over the past decade is evident in Figure 2.9; since 1997 the "burn rate" (options granted/stock outstanding) has been 2.51 percent, and the "overhang" (options outstanding/stock outstanding) has soared from 6.3 percent to 13.6 percent.

While IBM employees no longer had the promise of lifelong employment with the company, and while the prospective pension returns of many of them were being eroded, much larger numbers benefited from the 600 percent increase of the company's stock price during the last half of the 1990s. Foremost among the beneficiaries was CEO Lou Gerstner, who during his decade at IBM made $311 million (75 percent of his total IBM income) by exercising 38 percent of the options he had been granted, with 95 percent of the value of exercised options being realized between 1998 and 2001 (*IBM Proxy Statements*, various years).

In line with the transformation of IBM's employment relations to conform to NEBM practice, the company also changed its financial behavior (see Figure 2.7). In 1991 and 1992, as IBM was incurring a two-year total $7.8 billion in losses, it paid $2.8 billion in dividends per year, thus maintaining its dividend payments at the same amount that it had paid in each of the previous two years when it had a total of $9.8 billion in profits. Then, in 1993, with its losses at $8.1 billion, IBM cut its dividend payments to $0.9 billion, just 35 percent of its average payment level over the previous decade. Subsequently, as profitability

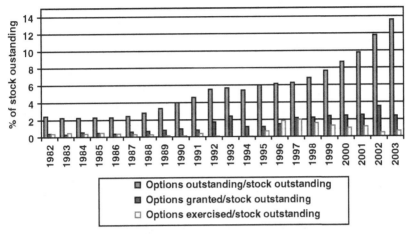

Figure 2.9. IBM's stock options, 1982–2003.
Source: IBM Annual Reports.

returned, IBM cut its dividend payments further before, from 1995, gradually increasing them, but to a lower level than prior to the cut. Whereas IBM had paid out 48.4 percent of its net income in dividends over the decade 1981–1990, it reduced this payout rate to only 14.1 percent over the decade 1994–2003, thus moving the company much closer to the practice of its New Economy competitors, which, as we have seen, tend to pay few, if any, dividends.

This dramatic reduction in IBM's dividend payout rate (DPR) does not mean, however, that IBM has been distributing less cash to shareholders, as can be seen in Figure 2.7. In 1995, when IBM reduced its dividends to a low of $591 million, it did stock repurchases of over eight times that amount. While its DPR was only 14.1 percent in that year, the repurchase payout rate (RPR) was 116.4 percent. IBM had previously done large-scale stock repurchases in 1986–1989, but the RPR for those years was 29.4 percent while the DPR was 55.5 percent. By contrast, for the period 1995–2003, the DPR was 13.7 percent while RPR was 92.6 percent, with repurchases totaling $52.5 billion, ranging from $4.2 billion in 2002 to $7.3 billion in 1999.

Driving this repurchasing policy was IBM's employment policy, focused as it was on using stock options to compete for mobile labor and making top managers (very) rich. IBM's massive and persistent stock repurchases since 1995 undoubtedly helped to sustain its stock price. As can be seen in Figure 2.10, IBM's stock price took off in the last

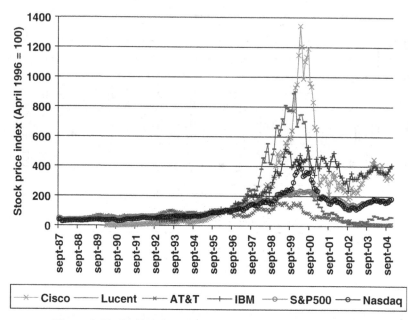

Figure 2.10. Stock price movements, Cisco, Lucent, AT&T, and IBM compared with the S&P500 and Nasdaq indices.

Source: Yahoo! Finance.

half of 1998. Although its stock price increase did not compare with that of Lucent or Cisco, it nevertheless outperformed the Nasdaq Index and, unlike Lucent and Cisco, has remained relatively stable since the peak of the Internet boom.

IBM, therefore, has made the transformation to NEBM, and indeed has helped to redefine the way in which firms innovate and compete on the basis of this model. Strategically, IBM became much more focused on development rather than research – on commercializing its existing capabilities rather than on accumulating new capabilities. It began to move down that strategic path when at the beginning of the 1980s it launched the PC by capitalizing on its brand name and marketing organization while relying on other technology companies to supply it with critical hardware and software. Organizationally, IBM has dramatically changed the terms on which it employs people, a transformation that began in the early 1990s as it slashed its huge workforce by more than 40 percent in the space of four years, incurring huge restructuring charges as the cost of bringing the tradition of lifelong employment to an end. Then, as we have seen, it even aligned its retirement system with its

New Economy employment relations based on highly mobile labor. Financially, IBM has substantially changed the way in which it distributes returns to shareholders, moving away from dividend-based returns toward price-based returns, because of its reliance on stock options as a mode of compensation. The result is that between 1995 and 2003 the company spent $52.5 billion on stock repurchases, almost $8 billion more than it spent on R&D.

Observing the relation between the trends in the rate of R&D expenditure and the value of stock repurchases displayed in Figure 2.7, one might conclude that the rise in the latter is the reason for the decline in the former. Such is not the case; IBM could and would spend more on R&D if it fit its business model. The trend in R&D expenditure as a percent of sales reflects the new way in which IBM transforms technological capabilities into revenues, while the rationale that underlies the stock repurchase program has been the need to sustain its stock price to attract and retain the high-tech personnel to carry out that transformation. Both trends reflect IBM's version of NEBM.

2.7   Some questions about the future of NEBM

IBM has clearly been successful in adopting its version of NEBM. But how sustainable is this business model both at IBM and in the ICT industries more generally? How will NEBM affect the globalization of the ICT industries? What are the implications of NEBM for ICT employment opportunities in the US economy? The purpose of my ongoing research is to generate answers to these questions; I will not try to answer them here. Let me simply conclude by highlighting three interrelated areas of concern in what might be called the economics of NEBM.

Firstly, NEBM may more fully exploit existing knowledge but it may also under-invest in new knowledge. In historical perspective, as I have indicated in this survey, NEBM would not have come into existence without the decades of investments in basic research that were undertaken by the US government and corporate labs in the Old Economy. What is the New Economy equivalent of this knowledge-creation process? And why are not more of the returns to those investments in basic research being reallocated to the source from whence they came? From a national perspective, how should the allocation of returns from long-term developmental investments be governed?

Secondly, NEBM now has access to a truly global labor supply of educated and experienced ICT labor. NEBM draws upon a highly developed system of ICT education and training. While the United

States has been the world leader in the provision of high-tech education, the high-tech labor advantage has been shifting to Asia and Europe (both East and West) as those areas of the world have upgraded the quality of the primary, secondary, and university education that they provide to growing numbers of their populations. Indeed, it would appear that these well-educated foreign nationals have become better prepared to benefit from US ICT educational offerings than the US population itself. Moreover, largely as a result of large-scale US non-immigrant visa programs – specifically the H-1B visa program for highly educated scientific and technical personnel purportedly in short supply in the United States and the L-1 visa program for employees of multi-national corporations – hundreds of thousands of foreign nationals, most notably from India, have been able over the past decade or so to accumulate years of valuable on-the-job high-tech experience in the United States. Some have subsequently become US nationals while many have returned to their homelands where they are employed by indigenous high-tech companies or by the offshore operations of multinational corporations. The result has been a globalization of the potential benefits of ICT development. However, the workers involved in this global labor market compete for jobs at dramatically varying rates of pay and conditions of work. Should this global labor supply be subject to global regulation? If so, how and by whom?

Thirdly, and finally, ICT workers in the United States face a very uncertain future. In the evolution of NEBM, the lure of working for a smaller technology company with the potential of stock-based gains led many professional, administrative, and technical workers to choose relatively insecure employment in the New Economy rather than secure employment in the Old Economy. In the 1980s and 1990s technological opportunity, venture creation, and the longest bull run in US stock market history helped to deliver the promise of the New Economy to these workers. The extent of their income gains in the Internet boom is clear in Figures 2.4 and 2.6. In the 2000s, however, the world of employment for these ICT workers has changed. They cannot necessarily choose between working in the Old Economy and New Economy; among US ICT companies at least, OEBM no longer exists. The successful New Economy companies have grown much bigger, and, as shown in Figures 2.1 and 2.9, their employee stock option "overhang" has grown much larger, creating more potential dilution. Few companies can afford to support their stock prices through stock repurchases on the scale of IBM and Cisco. At the same time, however, it is not at all clear that in the current labor market environment, ICT companies will have to rely on stock options to attract and retain a broad base of employees to the extent that they have in the past. There now exists a global surplus of educated and experienced ICT labor accessible to US ICT firms at much lower wages than those that prevail in the United States. In the last decades of the twentieth century, the evolution of NEBM was driven by the interfirm mobility of labor. In the first decades of the twenty-first century the evolution of NEBM may well be driven by the international mobility of capital.

3   Discourse on the New Economy – passing fad or mobilizing ideology?

Patrice Flichy

Economists often refer to the impact of technological innovation on business, questioning changes in the balance between capital and labor, and the effects on growth. But until now no one had imagined that a new technology could radically change the very principles of economic activity. In this respect discourse on the new economy is a departure from traditional reflection on new technologies.

To understand the beginnings of this new economic discourse we need to remember that for a long time the Internet was free; it lay outside the market economy. For nearly two decades this free access was taken for granted. Since the network was an academic research project, it stood to reason that its products would be freely available. In the 1980s those computer scientists who were immersed in the academic tradition of free access and sharing were the first to theorize the principles of cooperation and sharing in which the Internet is grounded. Their reflection constituted the underpinnings of the open-source software utopia.

In the early 1990s an important change was witnessed when the Internet progressively became a commercial network. New Internauts, unlike the founding fathers of the Internet, had the idea of doing business on the network. They considered the Internet to be a medium like any other and saw no reason not to use it for advertising and trade. A head-on collision thus appeared between the two points of view: free access and even free sharing versus payment and commerce. It was this debate that spawned the idea of the Internet as the bedrock of new commercial relations and thus of a new economy. The two conflicting perspectives were poles apart: Internet pioneers and hackers defended a model close to that of open-source, free software, while the newcomers wanted a business model based on that of the mass media, with financing via advertising and e-commerce. Discourse on the new economy was inspired by these contradictory perspectives. The outcome is, in a sense, a hybrid of the two.

I will successively present the perspectives of free software, of a media-based economic model of the Internet and of the new economy. My aim is not to analyze the birth of the new economy linked to the information society but to examine an ideology that accompanied the creation and development of the Internet and that proclaimed itself a new economy. The debates studied in this chapter are therefore very different to those that mobilized the community of economists. They took place essentially among non-economists, and concerned not macro-economy and the issue of growth but the Internet business model. It is important to study this new economy ideology since it was to play an essential part in the mobilization of a number of economic actors (entrepreneurs, consumers, public authorities, etc.).

My study and presentation of these currents of thinking draw on a number of sources, the most important of which is the magazine *Wired* that appeared in the mid-1990s as the leading US publication on reflection and debate on the Internet and digital technologies. I analyzed articles and interviews in *Wired* as well as texts published elsewhere by the same authors. As a means of comparison, I also selected articles on digital technologies in the general press and especially in *Business Week*.[1]

3.1   Who are the thinkers of the new economy?

Before studying the new economy and these two founding currents, let us first examine the intellectual origin of these discourses. Unlike many intellectual currents that adopted the "new" label, the new economy was not a product of professional economists. In fact, "new economists" were not economists at all but journalists or essayists, often from the Californian counter-culture and thoroughly familiar with computer technology.

Many of the editorial staff of *Wired*, for instance, were members of the digerati (the intellectuals of the digital generation) or cyber-elite. Some were ex-hippie intellectuals. Kelvin Kelly, former editor-in-chief of the *World Earth Review* (the well-known Californian counter-culture magazine in the 1970s), occupied the same position at *Wired*. Stewart Brand, founder of *World Earth Review*, was also on the editorial committee, as was Howard Rheingold, the great ideologist of virtual communities.

We also find journalists from other backgrounds – Steven Levy, editorialist with *Newsweek*, Joshua Quittner, journalist with *Time*, and John Markoff, correspondent for the *New York Times* in Silicon Valley – and consultants specialized in forecasting – Esther Dyson and Paul Saffo. In fact forecasting had a place of honor in the magazine to which such well-known essayists as Alvin Toffler and Georges Gilder also contributed.

---

[1] For a comprehensive study of Internet utopias and ideologies, see Flichy, 2007.

All these people tried to make the Digital Revolution a self-fulfilling prophecy. As Paul Keegan noted, the genius of *Wired* "is both illuminating this new sub-culture and promoting it – thus creating new demand for digital tools, digital toys, digital attitudes" (Keegan, 1995).

Whereas in 1993 when it was created many people thought that *Wired* had no future, it immediately found a vast readership: 110,000 digerati (digital generation) after the first year (Kantrowitz, 1994), 230,000 after two years (Keegan, 1995) and 450,000 after four, that is, nearly half the readership of the first popularized technical magazines such as *PC World*. These readers were people with a passion for the Internet and other digital media. They included many professionals of these new technologies: computer scientists, multimedia designers, artists, etc.[2]

3.1.1   A lasting trend in public opinion

Many of the digerati who wrote in *Wired* participated in other forums of reflection or debate on the digital world. The forecasting club Global Business Network (GBN) had members such as Stewart Brand and specialists in forecasting who had worked at Shell, like Peter Schwartz. This institute sold its services to firms and government administrations. Apart from a small core of permanent members, it used a network of experts, including academics (management scientists Michael Porter and Thomas Malone, economist Brian Arthur, sociologist Sherry Turkle, cognitician Francisco Varela), science-fiction authors (William Gibson and Bruce Sterling), journalists, consultants and others. *Wired* developed close ties with the GBN and the magazine's forecasts owed a lot to the institute. About ten members of GBN were on the magazine's editorial committee.

While the GBN developed prospective thinking on the information society and formed a link with corporate thinking, another forum of reflection, more political this time, was created with the Electronic Frontier Foundation (EFF). This was an organization to protect freedom in cyberspace, founded by former hippie John Barlow (lyric writer for the rock group Grateful Dead), along with computing journalist and co-founder of the computer company Lotus Mitchell Kapor and a hacker who had got rich from computing, John Gilmore.[3]

---

[2] The average reader was 37 years old and had an annual income of US$122,000 (source: *San Francisco Weekly*, 1996).

[3] John Gilmore was one of the first employees of the computer company Sun Microsystem, and was paid mostly in stock options. A few years later he sold his shares and was able to live off the interest.

The EFF was complementary to *Wired*. It provided the magazine with one of its main topics and *Wired*, in turn, was an excellent tribune for the association. Two of the three founders, half the board of directors and the legal adviser (Mike Godwin) wrote in the magazine.

3.2   From free software to a new public good

Let us revert to the reflection at the origin of the new economy ideology. Consider, first, the free software movement. What appeared above all as a utopia gradually materialized in concrete achievements not only in the world of computing but also in that of media content.

The designers of the Internet and especially hackers, on the fringes of the academic world, believed that information ought to be free and shared by all. In 1983 one of these hackers, Richard Stallman, sent a message to a Usenet newsgroup, headed "Free Unix: I am going to write a complete Unix-compatible software system, called GNU (for Gnu's Not Unix), and give it away free to everyone who can use it . . . I consider that the golden rule requires that if I like a program I must share it with other people who like it . . . If I get donations of money, I may be able to hire a few people full or part time. The salary won't be high, but I'm looking for people for whom knowing they are helping humanity is as important as money" (Stallman, 1983). This founding statement contained some of the essential features of the freeware movement:

- First, the ambition to build a complete computing system with an operating system similar to Unix and a full range of application software such as a text editor and graphic interface. Although Unix, the most widely used operating system in the research community, was easily accessible in the academic world, its user license prohibited changes to the software. Moreover, after its breakup AT&T had obtained the right to develop computer-related activities and had started to extract value from its rights on Unix.
- Second, the notion of freedom, which is often confusing. It relates to the absence not of payment but rather of secrecy and thus to the possibility of sharing. The word free in this sense comes from the tradition of civil rights movements in the 1960s and 1970s. In the world of computing, it means the opposite of ownership. Thus, freeware is a computer program whose sources (i.e. complete set of instructions) are accessible. The freeware movement was there-fore clearly opposed to computer companies which it saw in the following light: "The rule made by the owners of proprietary software was, 'If you share with your neighbor, you are a pirate. If you want any

changes, beg us to make them'" (Stallman, 1998). By contrast, it proposed the following: "You have the freedom to run the program, for any purpose . . . to modify the program to suit your needs . . . to redistribute copies, either gratis or for a fee . . . to distribute modified versions of the program, so that the community can benefit from your improvements" (Stallman, 1998). These principles of freedom were codified in a system called "copyleft" in which copyright legislation was used for a diametrically opposed purpose. "Copyleft", defined in a license (General Public License) attached to every piece of free software (GPL, 1991), specified the rights of program users to use, copy and disseminate the software. They could also change it but under no circumstances could they protect the changes they made. These were to circulate freely, like the original software. "If you distribute copies of such a program, whether gratis or for a fee, you must give the recipients all the rights that you have" (GPL, 1991).

- Finally, the third feature of the freeware movement was the wish to mobilize hackers wanting to participate in the project. Stallman defined this type of hacker not as a pirate but as "someone who loves to program and enjoys being clever about it" (Stallman, 1998). Thus, computer specialists wrote freeware above all for the pleasure of programming freely and being judged primarily by their peers. Here is a model very similar to that of the Internet. In order to pay computer specialists not financed by a university, Stallman created a fundraising foundation in 1985, the Free Software Foundation, although financial gain derived from business creation was not the prime motive. Stallman's project was above all societal; he wanted to build a public good. In an interview in *Byte*, he noted: "The principle of capitalism is the idea that people manage to make money by producing things . . . But that doesn't work when it comes to owning knowledge. They are encouraged to do not really what's useful, and what really is useful is not encouraged. I think it is important to say that information is different from material objects like cars and loaves of bread because people can copy it and share it on their own and, if nobody attempts to stop them, they can change it and make it better for themselves." He therefore considered that "the law should recognize a class of works that are owned by the public" (Betz & Edwards, 1986). This Stallman model, well known to freeware specialists, is the same as the model of production of science, academic work and the Internet.

To define these public goods, Stallman took the example of a space station (Stallman, 1985) where the cost of producing air is so high that it may seem fair to charge for its consumption. This would make it necessary to supply each consumer with a gas mask and to check that nobody cheated. To avoid such a breach of individual freedom, Stallman considered it preferable to finance the production of air by means of a tax. In a more recent interview, he repeated his idea of a public good, comparing the freeware movement to protection of the environment: "The goal is to end a certain kind of pollution. But in this case, it's not pollution of the air or the water, it's pollution of our social relationships . . . the willingness to cooperate with other people" (Barr, 1999).

In the early 1990s GNU consisted of many programs but still lacked a core operating system. *Wired*, which devoted an article to Stallman in its first issue (Moglen, 1999), suggested that the project was stalling and would fail to meet its goal. However, during the same period Linus Torvalds, a student at Helsinki University, wrote the core of an operating system similar to that of Unix. Unlike the Unix tradition, he used not a mainframe computer but a PC. Linux was soon fleshed out owing to the collaboration of hundreds, then thousands and finally tens of thousands of voluntary computer specialists (Moglen, 1999) who readily became involved because they needed only a PC to do so. The original 10,000-line code had swelled to 1 million lines six years later. Linux, articulated to GNU, offered a real alternative to commercial software and by 1997 had about 5 million users (Moody, 1997). In the words of the *Wired* journalist who studied the project: "The Linux approach is deceptively simple. All hackers are free to work on any additional features or improvements. Even in the earliest stages, new code is freely download-able for users to try out and to criticize: beta-testing is not a last-minute attempt to catch the worst flaws, but an integral part of the process. When several people work on the same area, they may compete or combine; if they compete, the best code wins through raw Darwinian selection" (Moody, 1997). With the participation of tens of thousands of hackers, Linux constituted a very large-scale cooperative project that combined coordination and anarchy. It was necessary to allow the expression of each hacker's creativity while maintaining sound coordination. What bound the partners together was shared understanding of the software. Meetings between a large number of designers and the participation of users throughout the process also helped to detect errors more easily. That is what Eric Raymond, the movement's philosopher – according to *Wired* (Freund & Bayers, 1998) – called the Linux Law: "Given enough eyeballs, all bugs are shallow" (Raymond, 1998a).

Like the designers of GNU or the Internet, those of Linux strove above all to obtain peer recognition: "For most hackers, the goal is to create neat routines, tight chunks of code, or cool apps that earn the respect of their peers" (Moody, 1997). In more economic terms, we could consider, like

Raymond, that Linux constituted a market in which hackers tried to maximize a function of particular utility: their own intellectual satisfaction and their reputation within the community. Open coordination, far more effective than a centralized plan, was thus established.

This community nevertheless needed a coordination tool. The Internet was the obvious answer. Debates took place on Usenet and bits of software circulated on the Web: "Anybody anywhere on the Net could obtain the basic Linux files. Email enabled them to comment and offer improvements, while Usenet provided a forum for discussion. Beginning as the product of one mind, Linux was turning into a tapestry, a movement of like-minded hackers" (Raymond, 1998a). But the link between Linux and the Internet was even deeper since much Internet support software was freeware.

In the late 1990s the freeware principle was no longer just a utopia, it was embodied in concrete achievements. But was freeware, for all that, a feasible economic solution? The allegory of the commons was often used, especially by economists (Hardin, 1968), to show that collective exploitation was an impossible resource. Rational behavior of farmers who share such ground is to let their cattle graze intensely, so as to extract the maximum value from the resource before everyone else. The pasture inevitably turns into a dam of mud. To avoid such an outcome, there are only two alternatives: either the collectivist model where an authority imposes shared exploitation, or the field is divided into private allotments. But for freeware advocates such as Raymond, computing was a case where the allegory did not apply (Raymond, 1999). The value of software did not decline with its exploitation; on the contrary, it increased. The more people used freeware, the more advantageous its use became. At the same time producers derived prestige and reputation for their skills which could enable them to obtain higher salaries in the job market. GNU and Linux thus showed, in the Internet tradition, that cooperation could be rational and effective. New economic behaviors were unquestionably at play. This observation was made not only by hackers but also by Thomas Malone, professor at the Sloan School of Management, who wrote in the *Harvard Business Review*: "The Linux community, a temporary self-managed gathering of diverse individuals engaged in a common task, is a model for a new kind of business organization that could form the basis for a new kind of economy" (Malone & Laubacher, 1998). After 2000 *Wired* continued to support free sharing (Goetz, 2003).

It likewise defended peer-to-peer. On the occasion of one of the first court rulings against Napster, the leading firm in this field, the magazine devoted its main section to peer-to-peer and published an article by

Napster's lawyer (Heilemann, 2000). John Barlow also vigorously defended this new social practice, commenting that this "decree transformed an evolving economy into a cause, and turned millions of politically apathetic youngsters into electronic Hezbollah . . . No law can be successfully imposed on a huge population that does not morally support it and possesses easy means for its invisible evasion" (Barlow, 2000). These opinions were part of his more general views on intellectual creation. "The free proliferation of expression does not decrease its commercial value. Free access increases it, and should be encouraged rather than stymied." Barlow considered that "there is a relationship between familiarity and value. For ideas, fame is fortune. And nothing makes you famous faster than an audience willing to distribute your work for free." While this type of reasoning was often held by artists or scientists, it was clearly not the view of media firms. Yet Barlow believed that it did not necessarily run counter to publishers' interests. He noted that VCRs had not harmed Hollywood, far from it, because it was easier to rent a video than to copy a movie. It followed that peer-to-peer was not going to kill the record or movie industries.

3.3 Finding a business model for the Internet

Hackers and Internauts in general who subscribed to the cooperative principles of freeware in the early 1990s were also reluctant to see the Internet used for commercial purposes. At the time, the network of networks was used essentially by the academic world, and Nsfnet, which constituted the heart of the system, precluded any commercial use. Yet the idea of commercialization was starting to take shape. Initially, reflection focused on payment of access to the network – the theme of a seminar at Harvard in 1990 (Kahin, 1990). Two years later three private regional networks created the Commercial Internet Exchange enabling them to bypass Nsfnet. Gradually Internet infrastructures were privatized and the commercial sector showed an interest in the network. In 1994 and 1997 successive proposals for business models were witnessed: mass advertising, the Internet as a marketplace, the push media, one-to-one marketing and virtual communities. We will now examine these different models.

3.3.1 *Advertisers invade the Net*

Although the idea was thus to open up to the business world, the concept of using the Internet for purely commercial purposes was so foreign to

Net culture that few actors even considered it. A trial run in April 1994, which caused a lot of fuss in the Internaut community, clearly illustrates attitudes at the time. Two Phoenix lawyers and Internet users, L. Canter and M. Siegel, offered their services to people wishing to obtain residence in the US. When they posted their messages on Usenet to several thousand newsgroups, Internauts were outraged. The two lawyers' email boxes were immediately saturated with complaints. One computer specialist wrote a short program that automatically erased copies of the advert in machines on the network. In the final analysis, it was less the fact that Usenet was used for advertising that caused the outcry than this general dissemination. As one commentator remarked: "Usenet is not a common carrier such as television or the radio . . . What Canter and Siegel did was only a violation of community values, abusing the cooperation of others. But cooperation, helping others to speak and exercising some restraint in one's own speech, is the only thing holding the Usenet community together, and the only law it really has. If mass advertising is allowed to continue, and others join in (as they already have), this fragile structure may well dissolve, and Usenet as we know it will cease to exist" (Wessen, 1994).

On the strength of this highly controversial experiment, Canter and Siegel founded a company called Cybersell, specializing in advertising consultancy on the Internet. A few months later they published a book, *How to Make a Fortune on the Information Superhighway*, which gave a number of practical tips on how to advertise on the network of networks. It was a weapon in their struggle to get commercial activities onto the Internet and to impose their model of functioning, irrespective of Internauts' traditions. They often used the frontier metaphor. Cybersellers were said to be new pioneers who had to set up businesses in "under-developed" countries of cyberspace. They were opposed to "natives", those academics who had raised voluntarism and the gift economy to the status of behavioral norms. Canter and Siegel considered it necessary, in the interests of business, to discipline that group that was so quick to flame people.

Naturally the pioneers held the natives' culture in contempt and saw no reason to adopt it. The two blatantly provocative authors wrote: "Some starry-eyed individuals who access the Net think of cyberspace as a community, with rules, regulations and codes of behavior. Don't you believe it! There is no community . . . Along your way, someone may try to tell you that in order to be a good Net 'citizen', you must follow the rules of the cyberspace community. Don't listen" (Canter & Siegel, 1994). Behind the colonial metaphor lay the idea that the Internet was a medium like any other and as such could be used for advertising.

3.3.2 A new marketplace

Several e-commerce guides were published in the same year. The idea that one just had to open a cyber-shop to make money was widespread. As the title of one chapter so neatly put it: "If you build it they will come" (Ellsworth, 1994). The same position can be found in the few rare news magazine articles published at the time on business on the Internet.[4] *Time*, which cited the Canter and Siegel affair at length, also published the views of an advertiser: "I think the market is huge . . . there's a place for advertising on the network" (Elmer-Dewitt, 1994). In *Business Week* John Verity wrote: "Today, after two decades of use by engineers, scientists and, lately, by adventurous PC owners, the Internet is at a turning point. Although some old-timers object, the network is going commercial – if only because it's there, it works, and it's essentially free for businesses to use" (Verity, 1994). A few months later he interviewed one of the actors of these new projects: "With the Internet, the whole globe is one marketplace . . . it also will create all kinds of opportunities to save money. By linking buyers and sellers and eliminating paperwork, the cost per transaction will go through the floor" (Verity & Hof, 1994). We thus see a new theme emerging: the electronic marketplace in which buyers and sellers could get together at very little cost.

The question was how to organize this marketplace so that buyers could find their bearings. The answer was to group businesses together. Canter and Siegel, for example, noted that "the most popular marketing idea in cyberspace today is the virtual mall". In early 1995 *Time* wrote that "online shopping centers are springing up everywhere, inviting customers to use their credit cards to buy on impulse, without even leaving their chairs" (Castro, 1995).

3.3.3 Push media

Another commercial Internet model, the push media system, appeared two years later. Instead of fetching data off a website, users received information corresponding to their profile of interests, directly on their computers. For *The Wall Street Journal*, the Internet "has been a medium in search of a viable business model. Now it has found one: television" (Kelly & Wolf, 1997). As one observer remarked: "It makes the Web relevant to the masses" (Cortese, 1997). For *Business Week*, "that ability

---

[4] In 1994 and 1995 *Time*, *Newsweek* and *Business Week* published two, two and four articles on the subject, respectively.

to 'narrowcast' is transforming the Net into a personal broadcast system" (Cortese, 1997). Thus, even if push invented a small channel, it pointed the way back to a regular media paradigm.

The authors of the first books on e-commerce, like the first press articles on the subject, believed that the Internet was a new medium which had particular characteristics but could nevertheless be used for advertising and commerce, like preceding media. They thought that, as with radio in the 1920s, professionals in these two business lines would gradually oust the first Internauts along with their anarchic and non-commercial practices. But with the failure of early attempts to commercialize the Internet through advertising, on-line selling and later push media, observers started to seriously doubt the future of e-commerce. Steven Levy, in the 1995 end-of-year issue of *Newsweek*, summed up the situation as follows: "Businesses salivate at the prospect of reaching customers worldwide from a virtual storefront. But the Net economy will force every company to change its ways" (Levy, 1995). Some digerati, like Howard Rheingold, commented that "Publishers never understood that people didn't want their content, they wanted a global jam session" (Bayers, 1996).

3.3.4   One-to-one advertising

Debate on e-commerce was not limited to early Internauts versus cyberspace colonists. Marketing specialists were wondering about the low returns from mass advertising. They were particularly interested in interactive media that were more topical than the Internet in the early 1980s. In 1993 Don Peppers and Martha Rogers published *The One to One Future: Building Relationships One Customer at a Time*. In an article in *Wired* a few months later they explained that tomorrow's marketing would be individualized. Advertising would become a dialogue between potential buyers and sellers. It could also come in the form of useful information, similar to the yellow pages. Businesses could thus develop long-term relations with consumers.

In the same issue Michael Schrage reflected on the connection between the Internet and advertising. "Is advertising finally dead?" he asked. For him, unlike Canter and Siegel, there was no doubt that "tomorrow's soft-ads are going to reflect the values of the Net more than tomorrow's Net will evolve into a digital regurgitation of today's advertising" (Schrage, 1994). Was this encounter of two cultures likely to trigger conflict? Schrage took up the cyber-punk novelist David Brin's idea of advertising viruses: "No doubt, some netcrawlers will be virulently anti-advirus. They'll want Lysol-like software to scour and disinfect adviruses from any program before it can be displayed. We'll see an epidemiological battle between the forces of digital commercialism and purists who think commerce has no place on the Net. Of course, we all know who'll win that battle, don't we?" In the final analysis, it seems that "the Net becomes the key medium for both community and commerce" (Schrage, 1994).

In early 1996 Evan Schwartz drew conclusions in *Wired* from the first Internet advertising experiments. He described the characteristics of a very specific Web economy, webonomics ("You just have to forget everything you ever learned about business" – Schwartz, 1996), and highlighted three key principles:

- "The quantity of people visiting your site is less important than the quality of their experience": loyal and regular Internauts were therefore to be given priority.
- "Marketers are not on the Web for exposure, but results": the idea was not only to show a product but to describe its characteristics and uses. In this perspective, the advertiser was paid not according to the number of visitors to the site (the equivalent of diffusion) but according to sales.
- "Customers must be rewarded when they disclose information about themselves": since the Internet allowed specific dialogue with consumers, businesses could take advantage of that to collect precise information about them. But they could gather such information only if they rewarded customers with discounts, complementary services or gifts.

Here we find Peppers and Rogers' idea of targeted and individualized marketing. Schwartz associated these ideas with the emergent characteristics of the Internet (Schwartz, 1997).

3.3.5   Virtual communities

By contrast, in *Net Gain* McKinsey consultants John Hagel and Arthur Armstrong considered webonomics from the point of view of a particular characteristic of Internet culture: virtual communities. As attentive observers of the Web, they knew that "most of these initiatives were motivated by passion not profit" (Hagel & Armstrong, 1997) and that "there was a strong anticommerce culture in the on-line world". Yet they considered that virtual communities were not necessarily averse to commerce. In their view, these communities were like individuals who shared the same interests and wanted to build real personal relationships or explore virtual worlds together. Balanced exchange resembling information bartering was one of the elements of the original Internet culture, codified in netiquette. Small ads had existed on the network from the outset. It was therefore natural for virtual communities to make space for commercial transactions. In fact, "commerce can actually reinforce community" (Kelly, 1997a).

Virtual communities thus became new economic tools enhancing consumers' power. This created a "reverse market" situation "where customers seek out vendors and deal with them on a much more level playing field in terms of information access" (Hagel & Armstrong, 1997). The virtual community was a device for aggregating buying power. Information on the product or service offering was collected by users and not by experts (specialized journalists, publishers of guides, etc.), who made their own quality assessments. But the community also provided information on the demand, which it could structure itself. It thus produced value (its members' commercial profile) that was normally produced by firms' marketing services. Hagel and Armstrong's intuition was that this economic activity of virtual communities could not be achieved in the context of information cooperation initially present on the Net. It was necessary to create commercial communities that were real business enterprises, with investors, managers and employees. These communities "will be the most competitive commercial on-line format" (Hagel & Armstrong, 1997), they said. "Virtual communities are not an opportunity that executives can choose to address or to ignore. They represent a profound change that will unalterably transform the business landscape and benefit only those who confront it head on" (Hagel & Armstrong, 1997).

This somewhat peremptory judgment on the future of commercial virtual communities was based essentially on an economic argument. It concerned an activity that, unlike most industries, had increasing returns and even combined several forms of increasing returns: low marginal costs (the initial investment is high but additional costs are limited), considerable learning effects (as the activity develops, organization improves and costs are reduced) and network effects (the greater the number of participants, the more attractive the community). To better understand the relevance of this reasoning, consider the way in which income was to be generated: subscriptions for use, advertising and commission on commercial transactions. It was primarily from the latter source of revenue that large-scale development of virtual communities could be expected.

This project was therefore based on an economic and sociological gamble. Although the dynamics of increasing returns could be highly profitable, they required continual investments, whereas income was low for a long time. Moreover, unlike other economic activities with the same characteristics, such as software and telecommunication networks, a first level of economic equilibrium could not be reached with high prices and a small customer base. In fact, like other economic projects on the Internet, the gamble was potentially very profitable but also very risky. To reduce this risk, Hagel and Armstrong suggested using the multiple non-commercial possibilities of the Net. Initially, to create traffic the initiator of a community could propose a repertory of available resources on related topics, with the relevant hypertext links. Next, "bulletin boards and chat areas are the elements of the community most effective in engaging members. A virtuous circle is often unleashed once members start contributing to these areas of the community. The act of contributing creates a feeling of involvement and ownership that draws members in more tightly to the community and motivates them to contribute even more actively over time" (Hagel & Armstrong, 1997). Since newsgroup moderators were usually volunteers, commercial communities fitted into the Internet culture and benefited from the outset from non-commercial services enabling them to reduce their initial losses. Creators of commercial communities thus had to maintain a delicate balance between seemingly antagonistic concerns: those of business and those of free exchange. Hagel and Armstrong concluded one of their chapters with the following advice: "The team should always remember the principle of 'community before commerce', to keep the organization's eye on what matters most – the members' interests and their relationships with one another" (Hagel & Armstrong, 1997).

This confusion between community life and commerce was also reported in a special issue of *Business Week* entitled "Internet communities: how they have shaped e-commerce". Robert Hof developed the idea that, faced with the confusion that was starting to reign on the Web, communities constituted landmarks and stabilized use of the medium. Several specialists of on-line communities, like Rheingold or Morningstar, explained that a community was a complex collective construct built up over time. An AOL executive who launched many newsgroup and chat services noted that "the community is the Velcro strip keeping people there" (Hof, 1997). But with these stabilized Internauts it was also possible to do business, provided one could play by the rules of collective life on-line.

Apart from on-line communities, the media started to forecast a great future for e-commerce – the "click here economy" as *Business Week* put it in a special issue entitled "Doing business in the Internet age". "Indeed, the Net is deconstructing the fundamental nature of business transactions. As every link in the supply chain is wired, the traditional roles of manufacturers, distributors and suppliers are blurring, and buyers will be the ultimate winners" (Hof, 1998). These profits reaped by both final consumers and businesses stemmed from increasing competition (buyers could compare prices more easily) and reduced transaction costs (negotiation between buyers and sellers was more direct).

To conclude this reflection on advertising and e-commerce, note that these two activities did not develop naturally as Canter and Siegel forecast, with the Internet being substituted for other media. Other forms of advertising and commerce were invented that were more in keeping with the history and culture of the network of networks, incorporated the new prospects of a more individualized form of marketing and corresponded to more general economic upheavals. In the final analysis, it seems that the Internet turned out to be less a new way of expanding traditional business than of actually doing business.

3.4   Towards a new economy

Although the free software perspective was initially radically opposed to that of the Internet commercial model, the two were to merge with the idea of a new economy. In 1994–95 the economy of the immaterial was an attempt to turn free sharing into a business strategy.

To explain this process, we need to revert to the early years of the network. Even though the pioneers of the Internet developed a world of free sharing and cooperation, they were less removed from the economic sphere than they seemed. This was particularly true of the hippie and community currents on the Net. As Stewart Brand notes: "Since we started dropping out of college, one of the things we missed was academia's disdain for business and money: 'do your own thing' translated into 'start your own business'. Carried by a vaster social movement, the hippies were readily accepted by the small business world" (Keegan, 1995).

We will proceed chronologically in our analysis of this nascent new economy ideology. Reflection on the economy of the immaterial, published in 1994–95, constitutes the base of the ideology that tried to merge free software with the commercial Internet model. In the years 1996 to 1998 the new economy as a topic appeared more and more explicitly and some authors tried to develop a theory. From 1999 the new economy theme was associated with the Internet boom, followed by the bursting of the bubble.

3.4.1   Conceiving an economy of the immaterial

One month before Canter and Siegel's ad operation, John Barlow published an article in *Wired* on the ideas economy in the digital era. This article, subsequently published in numerous collective volumes, was probably the first reflection by the digerati on intellectual property on the Internet and, more broadly, on the information economy. Barlow based his reflection on the fact that with digital techniques information is detached from a physical medium, so that the copy can no longer be distinguished from the original. "Notions of property, value, ownership, and the nature of wealth itself are changing more fundamentally than at any time since the Sumerians first poked cuneiform into wet clay and called it stored grain" (Barlow, 1994). Current intellectual property laws were totally unsuited to the situation and trying to apply them, regardless of that inappropriateness, would amount to limiting freedom of expression.

In order to lay the new foundations of intellectual property, Barlow defined his idea of information. For him, information differed fundamentally from a good that could be stored. It was action, movement. Similar to life itself, it was part of a dynamic, yet perishable. It was also fundamentally collective. The model of the author of a book could be considered an exception. In the modern digital culture, which in this respect Barlow saw as resembling yesterday's oral culture, he foresaw that "most information will be generated collaboratively by the cyber-tribal hunter-gatherers of cyberspace" (Barlow, 1994). Unlike material goods, there was no link between value and scarcity. The value of a software package, for example, increased with its diffusion. There were nevertheless cases where time created phenomena of scarcity, for instance the first to receive information could take advantage of it, compared with those who did not yet have it.

Based on these different characteristics of information, Barlow devised an economic model that articulated payment and gratuity, exclusivity and free dissemination, and emphasized additional services. Exclusivity was possible only if it corresponded to a particular service: priority in reception or a special quality. Cryptography was more appropriate for implementing it than legal weapons.[5] In respect of music, Barlow recalled the experience of his rock group, Grateful Dead, which charged for tickets to their concerts but let pirated recordings circulate. "Instead of reducing the demand for our product, we are now the largest concert draw in America, a fact that is at least in part attributable to the popularity generated by those tapes" (Barlow, 1994). For software, it was advisable to offer the latest version and various forms of assistance

---

[5] The previous year Richard Stallman had suggested authorizing copies of musical recordings and remunerating the musicians through a tax on machines used to make copies. See R. Stallman, "Copywrong", *Wired*, July 1993, pp. 48–49.

and training free of charge. "Once a program becomes central to your work, you want the latest version of it, the best support, the actual manuals, all privileges attached to ownership. Such practical considerations will, in the absence of working law, become more and more important in getting paid for what might easily be obtained for nothing" (Barlow, 1994).

That was exactly the strategy that Netscape (at the time called Mosaic) was developing at that stage. In an interview with *Wired* in October 1994, Jim Clark, one of the two founders, explained that he had provided the first version of his navigator freely and was preparing a more complete update that would then be sold (Goldberg, 1994). The effectiveness of that strategy was clear, since in the spring of 1995 6 million copies of the navigator had been downloaded. The new managing director later commented to *Wired*: "I don't know of a company that's created a brand quicker than we have. And by the way, over a period of a year and a half we have never run an ad" (Dyson, 1996).

Barlow's intuition, tested in a sense by Netscape, was presented in more complete form in an article by Esther Dyson. From the outset she asserted that content should be provided freely so that complementary services could be sold by building up a network of relations. This did not reflect the will to apply the ethical rules of the Net; rather, it was the result of a reasoned commercial strategy: "This 'generosity' isn't a moral decision: it's a business strategy" (Dyson, 1995). "The trick is to control not the copies of your work but instead a relationship with the customers – subscriptions or membership. And that's often what the customers want, because they see it as an assurance of a continuing supply of reliable, timely content" (Dyson, 1995).

What we have here is a "new economy" (the term appears in the text), in which "intellectual property" can be considered like ownership of land that produces no rents if it is not exploited in any way. It is the "intellectual value" that has to be sold. Dyson cited the case of a company that sold freeware of the Free Software Foundation. Its service consisted in installing software and training and advising users. "In the end, the only unfungible, unreplicable value in the new economy will be people's presence, time, and attention" (Dyson, 1995). To attract the attention of Internet users and make them spend their time, service providers would need mediators. One of "the most promising businesses in the Net world will be services and processes. They will include selecting, classifying, rating, interpreting, and customizing content for specific customer needs . . . Much chargeable value will be in certification of authenticity and reliability, not in the content. Brand name, identity, and other marks of value will be important; so will security of supply. Customers will pay for a stream of information and content from a trusted source" (Dyson, 1995).

In short, creators would be able to earn a living by proposing either choice content at a high price or additional services associated with free content. "Of course, this new world will distribute its benefits differently than how they are distributed today. But as long as the rules are the same for everyone – and predictable – the game is fair" (Dyson, 1995). Thus, in the information field, the new economy functioned on really different bases.[6]

The idea that in the Internet world free services had to be articulated to paid services also appeared at the first international conference on e-commerce (May 1994) which, incidentally, had a very explicit sub-title: "Making Money on the Internet".

In particular, Laura Fillmore developed the argument that with the advent of the Web, we had moved from an "economy of scarcity" to an "economy of abundance" in which very different intellectual services could be offered, from direct, "live" intellectual work, at very high prices, to standard knowledge that was already widely disseminated and proposed freely.

This idea of articulating free information to payable information was at the heart of the Web economic model. At the end of 1994, 42% of the 2.5 million host computers connected to the Internet in the US were business machines, while 39% were for educational purposes and 13% belonged to government organizations.[7] Five years later the proportion of commercial hosts had increased substantially, but 86% of Web pages were still non-commercial. These pages accounted for 51% of the audiences (i.e. pages read) (Gensollen, 2000). If we take into account the fact that the motive for visiting a large number of commercial sites (portals, search engines) was consultation of non-commercial sites created either by universities or on a voluntary basis, we see that the non-commercial sector was still central when it came to content on the Net. Moreover, the flourishing new Internet businesses were not, strictly speaking, media that transmitted information but rather intermediaries providing access to information collected and formatted in a non-market context. The peer-to-peer promoted by Barlow (see above) clearly fits this model.

But in *Wired* this position was also challenged. In May 2001 Charles Platt wrote an article headed "The Future Will Be Fast but Not Free".

---

[6] Dyson's thesis was to be adopted by various authors. It was, for example, the basis for the argument put forward by Andrew Odlyzko, "The Bumpy Road of Electronic Commerce" (http://curry.edschool.virginia.edu/aace/conf/webnet/html/ao/htm).

[7] Source: Network Wizard/SRI International.

He noted that Internauts "paid virtually nothing for almost anything". But this situation would be short-lived, not because of the failure of dot coms or media corporations' financial difficulties but because of technological trends. Broadband services allowed by the development of optical fiber networks made the hypothesis of free sharing unfeasible. The narrowband Internet had been subsidized by the copper wire telephone network; this was no longer the case with the optical fiber network. Platt asserted that this innovation would "destroy, once and for all, the egalitarian vision of the Internet" (Platt, 2001). He based his reasoning on the history of another medium by comparing the Internet to television. With the advent of cable and satellite, TV switched from scarcity to abundance and quality, from free programs to pay-to-view television. Platt's argument was rational. He never challenged the premises of Barlow's discourse that were, in a sense, part of the common culture at *Wired* but went further than Barlow. Whereas free sharing was the offspring of digital technology and the Internet, the new age of broadband introduced the return of payment.

3.4.2   Principles of the new economy

Until this point the main economic reflection on the Internet and computer technology concerned intellectual property rights. It was only from 1996–97 that the subject of the new economy started to appear, in another context. The term was first coined by *Business Week* (Mandel, 1996) in connection with skyrocketing high-tech stock prices and the sustained growth of the US economy under the impetus of information technologies. In 1997 Kevin Kelly, editor-in-chief of *Wired*, published an article headed "New Rules for the New Economy" (Kelly, 1997b). The central idea was that with the new digital world, new economic principles were emerging.

In the following year he expanded on the article in a book (Kelly, 1998). His "twelve dependable principles for thriving in a turbulent world" were less economic laws than precepts drawn from experience. Kelly's thinking was organized around two main themes: the first, technical and economic, consisted in analyzing all the impacts of the network's functioning; the second was a sort of radicalization of the Schumpeterian theme of creative destruction.

According to Kelly, the network's strength appeared primarily in its technical components, chips, which were connected to one another and proliferated not only in computers but also in many other machines. This law of increasing connection applied not only to chips but also, more generally, to humans. As the network expanded and "as the number of nodes increases arithmetically, the value of the network increases exponentially" (Kelly, 1997b). With the law of abundance, "more gives more". This exponential growth of the network, which had never really been proved, became one of the characteristics of the new economy. Thus, the law of increasing returns, which corresponded to self-reinforcing network effects, bore no relation to traditional economies of scale in the industrial era. The latter were linear, whereas the former corresponded to exponential growth. There was, moreover, a law of exponential value in terms of which the success of Net businesses was not linear. These different network effects resulted in a drop in prices of information and communication services as their quality increased. This law of inverse pricing led to the law of generosity in terms of which all information and communication services ended up being free.

Innovation was clearly fundamental in this type of model, for it allowed firms to make huge profits before the ineluctable drop in prices. Although Kelly had interviewed neo-Schumpeterian economists Paul Romer and Michael Cox in previous issues of *Wired* (Kelly, 1996a, 1996b), his view of innovation was inspired above all by biology. In a book published a few years earlier (Kelly, 1994) he had explained that the principles governing biological systems could also apply to technical systems and especially to networks, and he pursued that analysis in his new work. In terms of the law of devolution, goods and services inevitably deteriorated. At global level (law of displacement) "all transactions and all products tend to obey the network logic" (Kelly, 1997b). Firms therefore needed to be innovative all the time. This was the law of churn which was "like the Hindu god Shiva, a creative force of destruction and genesis" (Kelly, 1997b). Firms had to look for situations of "sustainable disequilibrium" and constantly create new spaces. The priority was no longer, as in the industrial era, to try to improve productivity and solve production problems (law of inefficiencies), but to find new opportunities afforded by networks.

Kelly was clearly not claiming to produce economic theories. His discourse was rather prospective. He cited very few economists (Paul Romer and Brian Arthur[8]) and based his reflection on such futurologists as Toffler, Gilder and Drucker who were often given space in the magazine, or on consultants like Hagel and Armstrong. Kelly's new economy was a technological utopia like virtual society or on-line democracy.

---

[8] Kedrosky, 1995.

Reflection in *Wired* was continued in 1998 in the March, April and May issues. These contained an "Encyclopedia of the New Economy" comprising a hundred or so articles classified in alphabetical order. The tone was more or less the same. In the introduction the two authors, John Browning and Spencer Reiss, stressed the key role of innovation and the fact that intelligence was becoming the main factor of production. This radically new world was presented as being fundamentally unsure: "We don't know how to measure this new economy . . . we don't know how to manage its companies . . . we don't know how to compete in it . . . A final thing we don't know is where – or how – the revolution will end" (Browning & Reiss, 1998). This was more than a treatise; it was advice for the pioneers of the new frontier.

Eleven of the terms used were general economic concepts: *capitalism, deflation, free market, monopoly*, etc., twelve others applied more specifically to the new economy (*technological lock-in, network externalities, winner takes all*) and eighteen defined the characteristics of the new networked world (*e-cash, e-commerce, electronic markets, information theory, narrowcasting*, etc.). Lastly, the encyclopedia also contained twelve technical terms (*PC, microprocessors, bandwidth, convergence*, etc.). Whereas this part of the encyclopedia was fairly close to Kelly's discourse, the remaining terms differed in so far as they applied the above-mentioned concepts to four particular domains: finance (nine terms), commerce (eight), corporate organization (seven) and knowledge management (five).

First, as regards finance, the authors pointed out the appearance of a world market (*big bang*) that was permanently open (*trading limits*) and functioned in real time (*Bloomberg box*). But they also covered development of *micro-finance* in third-world countries, in so far as these experiments were opposed to the banking establishment. Second, when it came to commerce, the encyclopedia put the accent on marketing: *brands, on-line communities, data mining, disintermediation*. Third, the principles of corporate organization proposed by Browning and Reiss corresponded essentially to contemporary managerial rules: *restructuring, outsourcing, decentralization* and "enabling people to continuously share information and coordinate themselves informally" (Browning & Reiss, 1998).

Lastly, in order to be able to run a business along these lines, knowledge management was necessary: "If knowledge is the only real asset, why not manage it like any other?" (Browning & Reiss, 1998). *Education* was therefore a requirement. "Training – acquiring the skills necessary to do a specific job – is the most important form of investment in an information economy" (Browning & Reiss, 1998). But this had to be done efficiently, through *just-in-time learning* which "delivers the right tools and parts when people need them. Instead of spending months in boring classrooms, people can use networks and clever databases to answer questions and solve problems as they crop up" (Browning & Reiss, 1998). Along with these four areas of application of the new economy, the encyclopedia noted several principles for state action, e.g. *deregulation* and *privatization*. The basic tenets of liberal economic policy were thus reaffirmed.

Of the hundred or so words in this encyclopedia, only six proper nouns – three firms and three economists – added a concrete dimension to the content. First, the breakup of AT&T marked the beginning of competition in the telecommunications sector and an international grasp of a nationally segmented market. Second, Microsoft was cited as an emblematic case of network externalities and technological lock-in, while Netscape is seen as "the new economy's corporate poster child" (Browning & Reiss, 1998). Adam Smith was described as "the grandfather of the new economy" (Browning & Reiss, 1998) since networks corresponded to a situation in which the invisible hand of the market was unquestionably at its optimum. Hayek was presented as the "free-market seer" (Browning & Reiss, 1998), and Schumpeter's "creative destruction" defined as "the battle cry of today's entrepreneurial Davids as they topple corporate Goliaths" (Browning & Reiss, 1998).

At first sight Browning and Reiss's new economy hardly seemed all that new. It was a collage of diverse considerations: neoliberalism, new marketing and management principles, and a vision of technological development. The link between these different elements was never demonstrated. But the strength of this discourse was precisely its assertion that the Internet could function efficiently only in a neoliberal economy and that network information technologies entailed a new mode of functioning of financial markets, a new organization of firms, direct relations between sellers and buyers, and new modes of access to knowledge. This discourse was intended not to enhance economic theory but to mobilize actors around these techniques and to give the new Davids the stones they needed to attack the incumbent Goliaths.

3.4.3   A new age of growth

In this respect *Wired*'s vision was not that different to the one found in *Business Week* during the same period. "By the New Economy," wrote Stephen Shepard, "we mean two broad trends that have been under way for several years. The first is globalization of business," which translates into "freer trade and widespread deregulation . . . The second trend is the revolution in information technology," which results in the appearance of new economic activities but "affects every other industry. It boosts productivity, reduces costs, cuts inventories, facilitates electronic commerce. It is, in short, a transcendent technology, like railroads in the 19th century and automobiles in the 20th" (Shepard, 1997).

It was the same long-term perspective that Chip Bayers proposed in a paper entitled "Capitalist Econstruction". He likened the changes under way to those observed by Braudel with the beginnings of the capitalist market. "As we re-create capitalism – this time, as one global market rather than the many regional exchanges Braudel chronicled – we are erasing the inefficiencies that have developed in the last 500 years" (Bayers, 2000). The idea was not to generalize the success stories of eBay or Amazon to the entire economy but to exploit the potentialities of the network economy in daily commercial activity. Consumers and traders could use bots to compare prices. Even the status of money could change. You could replace real money with virtual currency. And in the future, money itself might disappear. Some sectors of the economy would possibly become a new barter system.

Since the market and bartering mobilized far more information in the electronic world than in the brick and mortar world, would consumers be prepared to spend their time and energy on processing it, or would they prefer to trust the most well-known brands and companies? Today this e-construction of capitalism is still largely unfinished.

3.4.4   The Internet boom

The September 1999 issue of *Wired* devoted a large portion of its special report to the economic boom of the end of the century. A contributing writer, Peter Schwartz, presented his most recent book, *The Long Boom: A Vision for the Coming Age of Prosperity*, while an article headed "Prophets of the Boom" contained an interview with Harry Dent who had just published *The Roaring 2000s* (Kelly, 1999b). The leading article in the section, signed Kevin Kelly, was headed "The Roaring Zeros" (Kelly, 1999a). The oft-cited sub-title, "The good news is, you'll be a millionaire soon. The bad news is, so will everybody else", became the symbol of the aberrations of the new economy rhetoric. In subsequent issues, letters to the editor expressed some readers' indignation: "I'm flabbergasted that a seemingly educated, intelligent person could be so naive" (Frey, 1999).

Were the authors of this report really so naive? They did mention the possibility of a stock market crash and were aware of the cyclic nature of the stock market, but they saw slumps as periods of adjustment. It was therefore not on this point that they concentrated their reflection. Most important, for Kelly and his colleagues, was the fact that the Western economy was on the brink of a major change that would lead to a long period of growth. This growth would be based on four main conditions. The first was demographic. The US had well-educated and prosperous classes, capable of mastering productivity gains and attracted by new types of consumption. The second factor was new information and communication technologies. Not only was innovation developing very fast, the effects of the huge corporate investments in ICTs were expected to be strong. Third, the revolution in financial markets was far from over. Lastly, global openness was amplified very quickly. In the final analysis, this discourse was a continuation of that held in previous years on the new economy. The fact of being at the peak of the Internet bubble enhanced its euphoric character. Yet at the same time the September 1999 issue was, in a sense, the last shift in discourse on the new economy. It concerned no longer only the Internet or the digital economy but a new macro-economic perspective, and that was possible because digital technologies were generic technologies.

Not all the gurus of the Net shared Kelly's unshakeable optimism. In an article in *Red Herring*, Peter Schwartz studied several development scenarios of the new economy, from a rosy picture of "a world of mostly winners . . . where rewards are more often measured in equity than cash" to one "where the new economy is principally an illusion" or even a crash situation "where almost everyone is a loser" (Schwartz, 2000).

In 2001 *Wired* published an article headed "Death of the New Economy" in which the author seemed to believe that the crash scenario was happening. He noted that "the trouble with the term new economy is its McLuhanesque slipperiness. It means whatever you want it to mean. Too often, that has translated to wishful thinking: new rules, new paradigms, new riches" (Kelleher, 2001). But a few lines down he again stated that the economy had fundamentally changed in the previous few years and that the financial crisis of the early 2000s was simply a phase. Structurally, the US economy had experienced constant, substantial productivity gains from the mid-1990s, and in 2000–01 that was still the case. This trend, at the heart of the new economy, did not preclude sharply accentuated business cycles. "Job cuts are likely to be deeper and more frequent. An economy driven by equity investment is more vulnerable to excesses of speculation." Finally, for this author, as for the gurus of the new economy, the bursting of the Internet bubble was simply an episode that in no way undermined the development of the new economy.

A few months later *Wired* raised the question of whether "the new economy was a myth" (Surowiecki, 2002). The author noted that even if, in the public imagination, the new economy was associated with the stock market and in particular the Nasdaq, the real winners were in fact consumers and workers. Unemployment had decreased and in the private sector salaries had increased far quicker in the 1990s than in the previous decade. The gains of the late 1990s were sustainable; in the first quarter of 2002 productivity gains increased steeply. Thus, it seemed that the success of the new economy was not limited to a few cases directly related to the Internet, such as Amazon, Dell or Cisco, but affected all business. From this point of view the idea of a new economy made sense.

The author of an article published in August 2003, "Don't Worry About Deflation" (Delong, 2003), noted that US firms had bought more computer hardware and software than ever before. He was of the opinion that the stock market crisis was not the beginning of a Phase B in a Kondratieff cycle. "The boom of the 1990s continues."

In less than ten years, discourse on the new economy changed profoundly. Whereas at the outset the idea was to find a business model suited to the new technology that had developed outside the market economy, the discourse gradually got carried away. The new economy became the flag of all those who had developed a passion for the Internet, and finally it became a subject of more general reflection on the information society.

3.5   Ideologists and economists

Whereas most of the discourse on the new economy was produced by non-economists, from 1998 economists also joined the debate.[9] The scope of this chapter does not allow me to present all the debates on this topic in the economic community. I have taken only one example, the book by Carl Shapiro and Hal Varian, first because it was one of the earliest documents written by economists on these issues and second because it was intended for a broad public and was therefore reviewed and commented on in the media.

In 1998 Shapiro and Varian published a "strategic guide to the network economy" in which they considered that "you don't need a brand new economics" (Shapiro & Varian, 1998). Work on price discrimination, related sales, filters, licenses, lock-in and network economies, they said, provided a whole range of theoretical elements that were perfectly applicable to computer technology and to the Internet. The same was

---

[9] On this point see Eric Brousseau and Nicolas Curien (Chapter 1 in this book).

true a century ago when certain contemporary actors believed that electricity and the telephone completely undermined existing economic models. One point on which they agreed with the journalists of *Wired* was that major technological change was under way. But whereas Shapiro and Varian considered that economic laws applied perfectly to this new situation, Kelly, like Browning and Reiss, believed that they were dealing with entirely new economic principles. In fact, their disagreement related less to theory than to the presentation of the phenomena. The *Wired* team was familiar with some of the economic laws described by Shapiro and Varian, and had interviewed several prominent economists in the field,[10] but these laws seemed more meaningful when presented as the base of a new economy, as in *Wired*.

Shapiro and Varian's book, like the writings discussed above, was presented essentially as a guide offering advice to Internet entrepreneurs. The various economic principles described were illustrated by numerous practical examples. In certain respects this book on economics resembled Hagel and Armstrong's volume on marketing, but in addition a strong scientific ambition was affirmed. For example, in the introduction the authors expressed their wish to "seek models, not trends; concepts not vocabulary; and analysis not analogies" (Shapiro & Varian, 1998).

Shapiro and Varian, above all specialists in industrial economics, studied the ways in which firms could differentiate prices of goods or services in relation to their customers/clients, and in which standards were the instruments of cooperation or competition. They focused on the way in which a product or standard was imposed in a market through a feedback or snowball effect, and considered that self-realizing prophecies were one of the main components of this effect. "Companies participating in markets with strong network effects seek to convince customers that their products will ultimately become the standard, while rival, incompatible products will soon be orphaned" (Shapiro & Varian, 1998).

I believe that this theory of self-realizing prophecy can be extended beyond new products to the entire information technology and Internet sector. Discourse on the new economy also serves to promote these new IT activities and to discredit others, the "old economy". This manipulation of expectations serves to influence entrepreneurs and the general public alike, as potential consumers but also potential investors in the stock market.

[10] One year before Kelly's article, the magazine had published an interview with Brian Arthur in which he explained the principles of increasing returns and technological lock-in (Kedrosky, 1995).

3.6   Conclusion

In the early 1990s the Internet was used only in the academic world and in certain communities of the Californian counter-culture. Mass diffusion and integration into a market economy, that appeared from 1993–94, were not a natural development. On the contrary, they were a complete break that challenged the views of existing Internauts and brought new actors and practices to the fore. To mobilize those who were already immersed in the Net, they had to be shown that it was possible to develop the network of networks on the basis of other economic rules that took into account the specific characteristics of this new world (cooperation, free circulation, community, etc.). Doing business on the Net did not mean giving up former ideals and practices; it simply meant incorporating them into a new framework. It was also necessary to appeal to new actors, to show them that the Internet was far more than a new industrial sector, the base of a new way of functioning of the economy. Discourse on the new economy had precisely that function.

But that discourse also evolved. Gradually the initial Internet ideology waned. We could say that the early discourse on the new economy corresponded to a model where value is created by data processing and exchange tools. Discourse in the 2000s has been based primarily on another model in which value is related to the passive consumption of content. The Web is situated in the tradition of the press and television.

The second trend that appeared in discourse on the new economy in the early 2000s relates to the timing of the analysis. Whereas discourse in the late 1990s focused essentially on a short period of time – the Internet boom – that of the 2000s has taken into account a far longer period, the digitization of the US economy. This has enabled it to mask significant errors in the forecasting of certain Net ideologists. It has also brought the media's discourse closer to that of some economists who speak in terms of renewed growth or consider that the dominant economic model is not technology driven.

In the final analysis, discourse on the new economy continues to play its ideological role; it serves to mobilize the different actors around ICTs. At the same time, it has become more all-encompassing and a little more consensual. In this way it tries to cover up its excesses, its role in the Internet bubble. Yet with this evolution it has also lost its harshness, its ability to point out the economy's problems of adjusting to the world of digital technologies. *Wired*, for instance, no longer voices such strong opinions. It has become a more ordinary magazine that has to cater to the different sympathies of its readers as well as to the interests of its advertisers.

By launching the idea of a new economy, *Wired* and the general press that followed suit played a key part in the diffusion of the Internet. They enabled an academic communication tool to be turned into a universal system present throughout the corporate world and the public at large.

4   The Internet boom in a corporate finance retrospective

Ulrich Hege and Sébastien Michenaud

4.1   Introduction

Soon after the World Wide Web became popular in the second half of the 1990s, many expected the Internet to lead to a major technological revolution that would fundamentally transform consumer behavior and the mode of competition among firms. The ubiquitous term the "New Economy" epitomized the widely accepted idea that new Internet-based companies and business models had the potential to supplant existing firms and industries, and that they would give rise to a period of strong economic growth. These beliefs about the Internet, and more specifically the exuberant expectations about growth rates of the new sectors and the potential prize in a winner-takes-all competition, fed a wave of broad-based economic optimism that nourished, in the period 1998–2000, a major speculative bubble, the "Internet bubble". In New York, the Nasdaq, the major high-tech stock index, more than tripled in value between October 1998 and March 2000. The backlash was equally dramatic, with the Nasdaq index losing more than 75% in the following two years, and perhaps even excessive, considering that it subsequently increased by more than 80% from October 2002 to April 2004. With the Nasdaq index in April 2004 still accounting for only 40% of its peak value, it firmly looks today as if March 2000 marked indeed the peak of a speculative bubble. In the bubble period, there was a widespread belief among venture capital investors and financial markets that the economics of Internet-based networks would convey formidable market power to successful Internet start-ups. "Old economy" firms could hardly challenge that and this situation would enable hitherto unknown levels of growth. Venture capital funds aggressively injected capital into a wide array of Internet-related start-ups, and a flurry of Internet-related initial public offerings occurred with an unprecedented level of initial returns.

We are grateful to Hervé Tanguy, Nicolas Curien and an anonymous referee for many helpful comments.

In this chapter, we review some of the key developments of this remarkable period and offer an interpretation of the events from the viewpoint of corporate finance theory – with the benefit of hindsight, as we freely admit. Our goal is to elucidate the link between the new financial phenomena and the Internet, namely how the advent of the World Wide Web could give rise to such a transformative change in financial markets. More specifically, we focus on six aspects that we think are of peculiar importance: (i) the impact of the Internet on the role and the efficiency of the venture capital industry in Europe and the United States; (ii) financial markets' beliefs about Internet competition and Internet business models; (iii) valuation techniques applicable to these companies; (iv) agency conflicts between investors, in particular venture capital firms, and Internet entrepreneurs, as well as agency conflicts within venture funds, between fund providers and fund managers; (v) specific features in incentive compensation and financial policies of Internet firms; and finally (vi) the initial public offerings (IPOs) of these start-ups.

4.2   The Internet and venture capital

The arrival of the Internet and of Internet start-ups had dramatic effects on equity markets everywhere. In the United States, the largest and most developed market for venture capital, venture capital investments, saw strong and persistent growth throughout the 1990s and a virtual explosion during the two years between 1998 and 2000, with a fivefold increase of investments in these two years alone (see Figure 4.1). This abrupt development was largely driven by the Internet: in 2000, more than 80% of all venture capital investments were made in Internet-related companies, for a total of more than $56 billion (PricewaterhouseCoopers, 2001). By contrast, less than a quarter of all venture capital investments went to Internet-related firms prior to 1997. A rapid decline both in venture capital funding in general and in Internet investment in particular has taken place since, even though the share of Internet-related investments in venture capital disbursements is, with more than a third, perhaps surprisingly high. While other sources of funds, such as traditional bank loans, may be available to Internet start-ups, venture capital is widely believed to be more efficient relative to other financing modes when it comes to funding low-collateral, high-risk, high-return projects (see Ueda, 2004 for a convincing theory model on this topic). This interpretation is consistent with the strong growth since the 1980s, when bank lending to small firms was stagnant or even falling during this period (Ueda, 2002).

In Europe, a rather similar development took place, but it is worth reviewing the most important differences. First, Europe is a relative

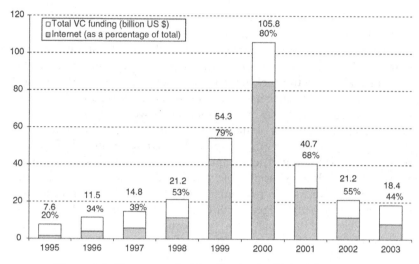

Figure 4.1. Venture capital funding in the United States and share of Internet start-ups.
Source: PricewaterhouseCoopers–Ventureconomics.

newcomer to venture capital funding, as the numbers published annually by the European Venture Capital Association (EVCA, 2003) show. In fact, the investment figures given by EVCA have traditionally been dominated by investments into more mature companies, like leveraged buy-outs or corporate restructurings, operations known as private equity. The arrival of the Internet led for the first time to a massive investment flow into start-up companies that jump-started venture capital funding in the American sense of the term. In 1999, venture capital investments in start-up companies in high-tech industries amounted to €8.9 billion. While this was only about a quarter of US investments during the same year, it indicates a dramatic catch-up compared with earlier years. In fact, venture capital funding for start-up companies increased by a staggering 166% in 1999 alone. The share of funds provided to high-tech start-ups, as a total of all venture capital and private equity investments, increased over the same period from 23% to 35%. This rapid evolution was largely driven by the advent of the Internet. In fact, as recent empirical work argues, the Internet revolution was the true starting point of a genuine venture capital industry in Europe dedicated to the financing of high-tech start-ups (Hege et al., 2006).

To understand the dramatic swings in venture capital commitments on both sides of the Atlantic, it is useful to put them into the historical context of the venture capital industry. The strong growth of venture funding in the US, and the appetite for similar investments elsewhere, have largely been fuelled by the astounding rates of returns of venture capital investments. While estimates on the long-run rates of returns vary, a typical estimate available prior to the take-off of the Internet bubble was that by Ibbotson Associates, which estimated the annual average return for American venture capital at 45% for the 1960–95 period. Moreover, a common argument was that venture capital returns appeared to be almost uncorrelated with the market return of the equity market, which – according to the Capital Asset Pricing Model (CAPM) – should mean that its expected return is close to the risk-free return, i.e., in the case of the American market, close to a 4% (nominal) return in the long run.[1]

Compared with the United States, rates of return have traditionally been lower in Europe. To give an example prior to the Internet bubble, NVP, the Dutch venture capital association, calculated a mean rate of return for its members of 15% for the 1989–98 period, and of only 6% for start-up financing activities (NVP, 2000). Just prior to the year 2000, a clear improvement in venture capital returns occurred, with the mean return of its member firms increasing from 11.9% in 1998 to 14.5% in 1999, and a particular sharp increase in *early stage* investments, according to EVCA. The reluctance of European investors to fund early stage activities, as well as their sudden interest in Internet start-ups during the bubble, must be seen against the backdrop of such numbers. A lot of money was piling into venture capital funds during a rather short period of time, and apparently rather indiscriminately; this is perhaps less surprising if one tries to adopt the vantage point of an investor in 1998.

Another element that helps in understanding the dramatic increase in available funds is that venture capital has always been a highly cyclical industry. The cyclicality appears not only in fund commitments but also in the industry sectors where investments occur.

Ultimately, the cyclicality in venture capital investments and returns is driven by what is known as the market conditions for venture "exits", the sale of venture capital investments, typically in the form of an initial public offering or a trade sale (i.e. selling it to another firm, usually an

---

[1] The stated numbers on returns on correlations are not uncontested, see e.g. Cochrane (2004) for different results. As far as the correlation with the market index is concerned, a major difficulty is that rates of returns are calculated from accounting figures and that venture capital firms tend to delay write-downs. Returns calculated from accounting figures probably tend to underestimate the return correlation.

industry incumbent). Venture capital depends very much on the exit market conditions since the bulk of venture capital returns is generated by a minority of projects. Typically, among the successful ventures, the best performers are sold in an IPO (see, for example, Cochrane, 2005). IPOs have known highly cyclical market conditions for many decades, with *hot issue markets* of intensive IPO activity and high first-day returns alternating with *cold issue markets* of low IPO activity and paltry or negative initial returns. The Internet bubble marked the last hot issue period from 1998 until summer 2000. The second important exit road for venture capital investments, acquisitions or *trade sales,* as they are known in the industry, are also intimately linked to the stock market. The current stock market conditions play a crucial role for the parameters that determine the valuation of any non-listed firm in an acquisition: for example, a peer group of comparable but listed firms is used to extract the multiples that determine the price range for the acquisition. In addition, the forecasts of future cash flows and their growth rates are certainly influenced by stock market conditions.

The arrival of the Internet and the concomitant explosion in investments had two clear consequences on the venture capital industry:

i. The strong increase in funds was followed by the market entry of new venture capital investors and the creation of new venture capital funds. Most of the new money inflow came from institutional investors, like pension funds and university endowments, that previously had a much smaller commitment in venture funding. The capital inflow meant that, for a few years, "money was chasing deals" and that the balance of power between fund providers and entrepreneurs shifted in favor of the latter.

ii. This large money inflow resulted in an increased scarcity of experienced venture capitalists. Being a successful venture capitalist requires substantial experience, and venture capital partners have typically garnered extensive knowledge as fund managers, investment bankers or former entrepreneurs before joining a venture fund. Venture capitalists learn their trade by costly trial and error rather than in business schools. This idea has been summarized bluntly in the saying that the training of a venture capitalist would be as expensive as crashing an airplane. In an interesting theory model, Michelacci and Suarez (2004) have highlighted the effect of a shortage of experienced venture capitalists by considering a venture capital sector that employs two complementary resources, capital and venture capitalists. While competitive financial markets guarantee an elastic supply of capital, experienced venture capitalists are in very inelastic supply

because of their lengthy training process. Thus, scarce venture capitalists are the factor ultimately limiting innovation and economic
growth.

At the same time, the practices of the venture capital business were
transformed by i) the advent of new players in the field, and ii) shortened
business cycles.

i. Concerning the type of players in the venture capital industry, there
   were both seemingly permanent and rather short-lived transformations. On the one hand, well-established large companies set up
   venture funds of their own, called *corporate venture capital funds*, with
   the double objective to better follow and control the new modes of
   innovation and to participate in the expected boon of returns. While
   many of the Internet-based corporate funds faltered as well, the trend
   of companies to spin off parts of their research funding into separate
   corporate venture funds clearly did not stop altogether with the
   bursting of the bubble. On the other hand, much of what was hailed
   as new practice was in fact the short-lived byproduct of the bubble,
   like venture capital incubators and venture catalysts. Instead of
   putting funds into clearly defined start-up firms, venture investors
   created research laboratories, called *incubators*, where individual
   researchers were assigned to projects and frequently reassembled to
   new teams in the hope of ultimately hatching successful start-up
   firms. *Venture catalysts* were essentially holding companies, like
   Softbank, CMGI and Internet Capital Group. They combined investments in newly started venture firms with holdings in stock
   market-listed Internet firms. Those firms were aiming for a public
   listing themselves, unlike venture funds that hitherto had chosen the
   form of closed-end funds. Incubators and venture catalysts quickly
   fell into oblivion after the Internet bubble burst.
ii. *An accelerated venture capital cycle and premature exits.* The prototyp-
   ical venture-funded start-up firm normally goes through a succession
   of *stages* that characterize different phases in its development, and
   each stage is normally associated with one or several financing
   rounds. In the first stage, called *seed financing*, typically the goal is
   to identify the potential of the initial innovative idea through the
   establishment of a business plan. The next stage is typically early-
   stage financing, followed by development and expansion stages
   (Gompers and Lerner, 2002) and, finally, the exit of the venture
   capitalists. Traditionally, the entire cycle used to last perhaps two to
   four years on average. Already from 1995, and even more so during
   the Internet bubble years, a clear acceleration in the venture capital

cycle could be observed; the data in Cochrane (2005), for example, document this trend very clearly in the US venture capital sector. This acceleration was closely linked to strategies of premature exits by venture capitalists, for which the tendency to take Internet companies public long before they were even close to reaching breakeven became a powerful symbol. Such a development was unconceivable even a few years earlier.

4.3   The Internet, network competition and superstar valuation

Looking back at the financial markets during the Internet bubble years, one may wonder what kind of rationale at the time was strong enough to persuade so many people, and to drive and sustain such a frenzy in start-up funding, initial public offerings and stock prices. While fully acknowledging that this is a difficult and inevitably subjective exercise, in this section we will attempt an interpretation, based on the economics of network competition. We hypothesize that market participants, or at least an influential segment of them, entertained a belief that *winner-takes-all* competition would become the norm across all Internet-based industries. This belief, so our argument goes, may have played a substantial role in the creation of the speculative bubble specific to Internet start-ups and, later, when contrarian evidence could no longer be ignored, in its precipitous downfall.

Network industries are characterized by the fact that a consumer's value of the goods and services depends on his use of the associated network, namely both on the state of the network and on the user's integration within the network. In addition, an agent's use of the network affects the state of the network for other users by creating *network externalities*. This will be the case for example because she increases the network's value through an increase in availability, quality and the diversity of the network's offerings, thereby creating *positive* externalities, or because she contributes to the network's congestion, which creates *negative* externalities. These effects are not specific to the Internet and have long been a prominent feature of traditional network industries such as electricity distribution, telecommunications and the railroad industry. The computer industry itself was hailed as the perfect example of a network industry long before the advent of the World Wide Web. In this market, the end users' requirements for compatibility between different systems gave rise to a strong demand for standardization in hardware as well as in software. This, in turn, gave a decisive advantage to the market leaders which could impose their technologies as de facto standards.

For Internet-related industries, network effects were expected to result in the emergence of players with strong market positions. These effects were created and sustained through a demand for compatibility, as well as a *club effect* related to both the size of the user base and its usage, along with the quantity and the quality of content that was generated. An early example that powerfully foreshadowed the demand for compatibility and network effects in Internet-based activities was the browser market. In 1994, when Netscape was launched, the browser market was considered as a natural monopoly market akin to the market for PC operating systems where Microsoft's Windows was then considered a near-monopoly product. In 1995, when Netscape went public on Nasdaq, financial markets seemed to be fully swayed by this logic, as the surge in the stock price following the IPO and the huge level of media attention attest. Microsoft's subsequent aggressive strategy to contest Netscape's initial market leadership, which consisted in providing for free Internet Explorer, its competing product, and bundling it with its Windows operating system, was viewed as further evidence to the power of network economics. Microsoft's strategy consisted essentially in increasing the installed base in order to marginalize Netscape, made possible by Microsoft's grip on the operating systems market and a policy of frequent upgrades. With its determined response, Microsoft made it clear that it viewed competition in the browser market as network competition, and its subsequent success in marginalizing Netscape seemed to demonstrate that an established market leader in the Internet era could not easily be challenged.

During the Internet bubble – which in this chapter we date to the period from summer 1998 to spring/summer 2000 – there was a widespread and indiscriminate belief in the network economics of any Internet-related business. In some cases, the belief in the network effects was fully justified; eBay's success is probably the best illustration of such a case. Valuations were largely overstated in most other cases. This was probably due to the lack of understanding of the future winning business models, a lack that in turn was owed to the large uncertainty with regard to customer behavior and innovation.

eBay is the perfect illustration of a successful Internet marketplace that has clearly benefited from a first-mover advantage and strong network effects. In 1995 eBay became the first player to launch an auction web site in the US and it quickly established a dominant position in its domestic market. In the following years it expanded internationally through acquisitions of, or partnership with, established local online auction companies and other similar companies. So far, it has managed to sustain its domestic leadership, and to a remarkable extent, to put it across other regions of the world. Likewise, Yahoo! was launched early in 1994. It clearly benefited from a similar first-mover advantage and emerged as an unchallenged portal leader in 1998–2000 – at least this was the belief that financial markets expressed with Yahoo!'s market valuation at the time. However, Google, started only in 1999, was able to capture a large share of the search engine business through its innovative technology and the build-up of a large market share in the Internet advertising market. It looks like a curiosity today that Google was initially not among the first players in the search engine market. Microsoft and Yahoo! were major competitors and claimed millions of users.

The success of Google shows that dominant market positions in the Internet era were often rather contestable. In the case of the market for web searches, one could argue that switching costs for a single end-user are low relative to other market segments such as Internet auctions. In the market for Internet auctions, a coordinated move among most or at least some of the agents linked to the network would be required to justify the decision by a single customer to switch to a competitor. Such a coordination problem is typical of a public good problem and naturally leads to the increased sustainability of a player's natural monopoly position. In addition, the value added by Google's technology had a huge impact on usage and justified uncoordinated switching from leading portals (Yahoo! and Microsoft's MSN) to the new entrant. As of early 2004, competition in this market seems to focus much more on new technological developments rather than on customer acquisition.

The economics of network effects were probably much less important for *e-commerce* start-ups. Nevertheless, during the Internet bubble, financial markets clearly assumed leadership in these markets to be a lasting advantage and valued it accordingly, notably for B2C and B2B Internet start-ups. In B2C, it now seems evident that market leadership was not a decisive factor for success, let alone survival, as the number of now-defunct e-commerce web sites suggests (famous examples include Pets.com and boo.com). There are, however, examples showing a role of network economics in Internet retailing. The case of Amazon.com is probably the most illustrative one. Closer examination of Amazon's success story suggests that a dominant market position was not sufficient; its success is probably as much rooted in the ability to build up massive capacities for logistics that guaranteed smooth and fast execution on an unrivalled range of books as in assembling a larger customer base than its rivals. The ability to build the initial business on a profitable market segment (books, and later music and media) also enabled Amazon.com to eventually turn a profit. As a result, it quickly established itself as the leading virtual bookstore and built on its initial leadership to extend activities in a large array of unrelated products such as clothing and consumer electronics.

The fate of B2B marketplaces was even more sobering than that of B2C companies: practically none of them proved capable of delivering a viable business model, contrary to the initial expectations. In 1999, the widespread belief was that marketplaces would match suppliers with purchasers, that they would exchange information on their products and prices and do business online. In this emerging industry, network effects were expected to be high, and large exchange platforms promised to deliver big savings for their customers on their procurement, the potential revenues of the platform being expected to draw from these savings. It turned out, however, that suppliers were reluctant to post their product catalogs online since this would have meant circulating sensitive information like prices and rebates in the public domain. At the same time, purchasers did not rush to join these marketplaces, considering that better prices were not all that mattered. Basically, it turned out that the B2B marketplace business model had a fundamental flaw in misjudging the incentives of both sides to participate. Interestingly enough, the financial markets erred as much as the media in their expectation of the B2B business model. By 2002 the large majority of players in this segment of the Internet economy had disappeared. Most of the companies that survived the B2B shakeout changed their focus, for example by providing web-based software for *private* marketplaces.

During the Internet bubble from 1998 to 2000, the prevalent belief in financial markets was that network effects would play a predominant strategic role for most Internet start-ups. Network effects would provide the leader with a very profitable position that would be difficult for any of its followers to challenge. As a result, any start-up that launched a new venture on the Internet had, first and foremost, to build a dominant market share in its target market. Because of the network effects described above, competition among start-ups was perceived as winner-takes-all (Noe and Parker, 2000), akin to a *patent race* where the lion's share of the profits is earned by the leader. This type of competition is very similar to that of entertainment and sports superstars who capture most of the rent available in their field, at the expense of second-tier competitors (Rosen, 1981). In the Internet economy, this meant *superstar valuations* of the market leaders by the financial markets. Players with a strong market share position and/or brand position in any Internet field earned a substantial market premium relative to their competitors.

With hindsight, equity markets were showing the right intuition when they identified network effects as the potential value drivers in the Internet economy: successful Internet business models were exclusively based on them. It even happened in a very small number of cases that the market initially underestimated the value premium that an Internet-based company could sustain, as the example of eBay's subsequent success suggests. In fact, in April 2004, eBay's stock price was more than 60% higher than at the height of the bubble in March 2000. But this is a rare exception, of course. The problem was that in the 1998–2000 period, market operators had a poor understanding of Internet economics, and were not (yet) capable of discerning the network-based economic models that would eventually be able to generate a profit. Instead, and certainly helped by fascination about all the possibilities that the Internet seemed to open, the value of network effects was generally overrated and indiscriminately applied to every business model alike, if only it showed some relation with the Internet. The near-total wipeout of companies that were once considered stars and uncontested market leaders in the most promising segments of the "new economy", such as Ariba (–98%) in the B2B market or AOL (now Time Warner) in the ISP market (–80%), is a stark reminder of this episode.

Whatever the financial markets' mistakes as they became obvious soon after, during the bubble years start-ups were all too willing to adapt their strategy to the stock market context. In order to command a high valuation and ensure survival, what mattered in those days was building market leadership and growing market share. Obviously, in a winner-takes-all competition, speed is a key success factor. However, unlike a patent race for a new prescription drug, say, the leading position in an Internet-based market is not determined by a single approval decision by a drug administration agency or patent office but by the independent decisions of a large number of customers. Their aggregate decision to adopt the service will convey a decisive advantage to an Internet company which will generally be highly valuable only if the customers' switching costs are so great that customers can effectively not be acquired or poached by competitors later on.

Differences in the character of network effects could also explain why companies fared so differently when adopting seemingly identical strategies with regard to the choice between the possibilities of growing organically or acquiring competing firms. eBay is a fine example of a rather successful acquisition strategy meant to rapidly capture and subsequently consolidate leadership positions in a slate of foreign markets. An intriguing lesson is that it proved impossible for eBay to arrive in a dominant position whenever the company shunned its usual acquisition strategy of taking over an already established local Internet auctioneer and instead tried to build its operations from scratch. This was the case in Japan: Yahoo! was able to hold on to its leading market position against a massive attempt by eBay to create a foothold, and eBay subsequently withdrew from the Japanese market. In countries where leadership was attained, however, the economics of Internet-based networks and the associated *club effects* played in full in eBay's favor. Width and depth of the offering attracted more buyers who, in turn, increased the quality and quantity of the goods offered by sellers. At the end of 2003, eBay boasted 95 million users worldwide and 45,000 categories of merchandise sold through its trading platform. More importantly, its business turned out to be very profitable, with operating margins in the range of 30% in 2002 and 2003.

In contrast to eBay's successful acquisition strategy, Amazon.com acquired a large number of companies in 1999 and 2000 that apparently were overvalued, and whose rationale for Amazon.com appeared to be rather doubtful after the Internet shakeout. Tellingly, most of these acquisitions were made when Amazon.com's stock price was at its peak and were paid for in stock or a combination of stock and cash. This suggests that opportunistic market timing may have played as much a role as sound business strategy. Taken together, the different tales of eBay and Amazon.com illustrate the nuanced character of network economics that led to almost opposite strategic effects in different market segments.

So while the eventual success of most of the Internet survivors was indeed ultimately grounded in network effects, only a fraction of the Internet business models that looked promising initially turned out to be sustainable. Financial markets went through a cycle of boom, bust and finally selective rehabilitation of Internet stocks between 1998 and 2004, during which the valuation of Internet stocks changed abruptly. We suggest viewing this cycle as a collective learning process of market operators grappling to understand and value the Internet phenomenon.[2] In this interpretation, we distinguish three different periods in stock markets:

- In the period 1998–2000, we observed extremely high valuations for a very large number of Internet start-ups. Two effects can explain these optimistic valuations: on the one hand, there was a strong belief in the natural monopoly value effect, as discussed above, and on the other hand, the financial markets expected high growth. In those times of overoptimism, the former effect was not challenged. Most of the investors believed that the winner-takes-all competition was a game where, on average, players would earn more profits than under traditional competition in spite of the risks associated.

---

[2] Our implicit theoretical reference is the semi-strong market efficiency hypothesis.

- In the period 2000–01, a drastic correction occurred that hit all dot. com and Internet-based stocks alike. This adjustment expressed the newfound skepticism that the hoped-for effects that had driven those superstar valuations would not materialize. Growth expectations were sharply revised downwards, and in addition the market accepted the idea that competition would be fiercer than initially anticipated, and that dominant market positions would be harder to sustain. The first effect hit all Internet firms more or less with the same magnitude, while the second effect naturally had a stronger impact on e-commerce, telecoms, network operators and ISPs, industries where the stock price drop was even more severe.
- Finally, starting in late 2002, a rehabilitation occurred for a selective group of surviving Internet stocks. In the 2002–04 period, Internet companies that were clear market leaders and managed to convincingly assert their leadership position and, above all, started to generate profits, outperformed the general market. This group includes Amazon.com and Yahoo! stocks. While both companies showed in spring 2004 market capitalizations still far below their peak valuations in 2000/2001, they commanded high valuation relative to their current financial results and fared much better than Nasdaq and the Dow Jones Internet Services index in the period 2003 to early 2004. Interestingly, eBay commanded a far higher valuation in 2004 than at its previous peak during the Internet bubble.

Our interpretation of the speculative Internet bubble is based on the idea that market participants overrated the benefits from network effects in Internet-based industries. A similar idea is at the heart of a theory model by Scheinkman and Xiong (2003) who show that heterogeneous beliefs among investors, in the form of overconfidence about a private signal, and the presence of short sales constraints alone suffice to generate a speculative bubble.

4.4   The valuation of Internet start-ups

During the Internet speculative bubble, issues related to the valuation of Internet start-ups and appropriate valuation techniques created an intensive debate among finance professionals, which inevitably spread to include academics as well.

In this debate, opinions were voiced purporting that traditional valuation techniques would no longer be applicable for Internet start-ups, typically based on the argument that (i) these methods would require forecasts of future expected cash flows, while a vast majority of the start-ups posted huge losses and did not even expect to break even in the medium term; (ii) Internet start-ups were deprived of operational and financial histories on which forecasts could credibly be built. With hindsight, however, this debate was clearly driven by an exaggerated belief in the rationality of stock markets: markets were considered to be infallible in their pricing of Internet stocks and market participants were desperately searching for the right valuation models that would justify what later turned out to be a bubble. A short review of this valuation debate is nonetheless interesting.

To put things straight, the valuation of a company rests on the general principle that a firm should be valued on the basis of its future expected cash flows to its investors, primarily equity- and debtholders. There is no valid reason to challenge this general principle. Only the methodology of how to forecast future expected cash flows or how to proxy for them can be the subject of legitimate discussion. The two traditional techniques against which objections were raised were, first, the discounted cash flow (DCF) technique that relies heavily on projections of future cash flows that the firm is expected to generate, and second, the technique of earnings multiples that relies on recent historical earnings of the firm or sometimes on consensus forecasts by analysts on these earnings.

The DCF technique, in essence, applies the net present value concept to the valuation of a firm, by discounting expected future cash flows at an appropriate rate of return that reflects the underlying non-diversifiable investor risk. The usefulness of the approach in practice depends on the ability to correctly estimate future cash flows. Generally, either these future cash flows are derived from historical financial data, when the firm is sufficiently mature, or growth rates are built into a model of future cash flows. Given the uncertainty surrounding most of the Internet start-ups and the lack of historical data to conduct the prerequisite financial analysis, the practical application of the DCF technique was difficult.

Another set of arguments against traditional valuation techniques was based on the idea that Internet start-ups are totally different from traditional firms and should therefore be valued with different tools. Their key assets were human capital and brand, not tangible assets. Their value no longer seemed to depend on their ability to generate cash flows from existing assets and existing, well-identified markets but rather on their ability to capture growth opportunities that had not yet materialized. This was precisely where *real options theory* appeared to provide significant insights.

The surge in interest in the real options method during the Internet boom was largely driven by the desire to justify astronomical stock prices (see Schwartz and Moon, 2000 for an example). However, adding real options techniques to the portfolio of valuation methods is certainly an interesting effort that should be dissociated from such misguided uses. Real options theory, which is based on the tools of financial option models, became popular in the 1990s (Dixit and Pyndick, 1994) but its use was largely confined to the valuation of technical natural resources projects (oil, mining). Real options theory has been useful in pointing out the shortcomings in the practical use of traditional valuation techniques, which are implicitly based on the notion of a single, perfect forecast of the firm's future. DCF valuation results will lead to a systematic downwards bias in the valuation of projects that feature both high-level uncertainty and managerial flexibility. However, it is difficult to make use of the option valuation technique since there are no methods to identify the most valuable real options in a systematic way. Even in a mining firm, which is a single-project firm, the analysis will be made difficult because numerous options are present. In the case of a technology start-up, which typically is a multi-project firm, the valuation of the implicit real options will be even more difficult. Not only is the number of available options multiplied in a multi-project firm, but real options are also more likely to create synergies so that their values interact and create compound options, i.e. options on options. A truly satisfying valuation of real options will be almost intractable analytically.

These practical difficulties help to explain why, since the Internet bubble has burst, the interest in using real options techniques for the valuation of start-ups has largely faded away. Copeland et al. (2000) probably expressed a general sentiment with their dictum that real option values can reasonably be approximated through a traditional decision-tree technique, keeping in mind that the implementation of even that simplified technique is not trivial. For the time being, real options valuation is likely to remain a marginal practice among professional bankers and investors, and the Internet boom will have produced little or no lasting change in the practice of valuation in the end.

4.5   Agency conflicts and the financing of Internet start-ups

The peculiar competitive environment of the Internet boom created challenges that fundamentally altered the relationship between start-ups and their financial backers. In this section, we investigate the nature of this change and the reaction of venture capitalists (VCs), entrepreneurs and investors.

Specifically, we explore the hypothesis that magnified agency problems constituted an essential part of these challenges. Agency costs should not be thought of as a constant tax on business operations, they are likely to get amplified in times of crisis, which is, in our view, what happened during the Internet bubble. We will discuss two distinct fault lines of agency conflicts. The first one concerns conflicts between the venture capital firm and the entrepreneur, the second one those between fund providers and fund managers, or between the general partners that run venture capital firms and their limited partners.

In any start-up, the entrepreneur or founding team uses funds provided by outsiders, the investors. This raises an agency problem, which is in principle no different from the agency conflicts in large companies and multinationals that are well known since Berle and Means (1932). But the magnitude of the agency conflicts between insiders (the founding team) and outside financiers depends on the ability of the latter to implement appropriate safeguarding mechanisms and to exert an appropriate level of monitoring.[3] In large and mature companies, addressing these issues is a matter of establishing a set of governance rules that creates an efficient balance of power between managers and their need for control, and shareholders who need to make sure funds are not diverted. In smaller businesses and start-ups, financiers will have to exercise monitoring in order to keep potential agency conflicts under control.

Innovative activities are in general associated with a high level of uncertainty and contractual incompleteness. For example it might be difficult or almost impossible to define unambiguously what determines success or failure of the project, or to define relevant benchmarks against which the managers' performance can be evaluated. The likelihood of conflicts between the founding team and the investors is larger than in more mature activities, where unforeseen contingencies can be more easily addressed, consistent with evidence that financial constraints have always been particularly elevated in high-tech industries (Himmelberg and Petersen, 1994). The venture capital industry has long resorted to a wide array of mechanisms to protect itself against such agency conflicts. Those mechanisms typically involve the presence of venture capitalists on the board of directors. They also provide the VC firm with the possibility of taking effective control of the start-up at any moment, should this be optimal (see Hellmann, 1998 and Sahlman, 1990 for more details).

---

[3] Too much monitoring may discourage the managers' investment in firm-specific effort while too little monitoring may induce managers to run the firm to maximize their own private benefits at the expense of shareholders (see Aghion and Tirole, 1997).

During the Internet boom, these well-known agency problems became further aggravated for the following reasons:

1. The winner-takes-all competition in Internet-related industries meant that a massive and prompt flow of funding was required. Most of the expenses were difficult to control through appropriate contracting, e.g. marketing expenses. As a result, it was hard to rein in any tendency to overspend. The founding team was naturally inclined to overinvest, a tendency that is in fact fuelled by overly optimistic views on the expected returns on investment and by a bias towards risk-taking. Both effects are classical agency costs. The former is a typical behavioral bias among entrepreneurs (see Landier and Thesmar, 2003 for a theoretical and empirical study), while the latter is rational as long as the entrepreneurs are equityholders protected by limited liability. Winner-takes-all competition can dramatically reinforce this effect: if all competitors behave in the same way, this will result in ever higher marketing expenditures all around, and each competitor will be convinced that a high stake in this race is indispensable to marginalize the competition and win the prize.

2. Tangible assets and tangible investments accounted for only a small share of total assets and total investments in most e-commerce start-ups. Typically, the costs related to hardware servers and to the web site's design and coding – the only expenditure that could be easily verified by an outsider or a court – are limited. Yet a large part of the initial investments and expenses are for items such as marketing expenses, customer base acquisition and retention costs (see Copeland et al., 2000 and Hand, 2000), which are not only intangible but also difficult to benchmark. To illustrate this point, eBay's marketing and product development expenses consistently accounted for around 70% of all operating expenses throughout the 1996–2003 period.[4] Like in the luxury goods industry, goods and services purchases on the Internet were believed to strongly depend on the "cash burn rate" to promote products and brands. This was best exemplified by boo.com (e-commerce) and World Online (ISP), which both disappeared through bankruptcy or acquisition.

3. The bargaining power relationship was turned upside down. Start-up entrepreneurs suddenly were in a strong position because of the massive funds inflow into the industry. Moreover, the start-ups could

---

[4] Source: eBay's SEC 10K filings. Total operating expenses were calculated excluding amortization of acquired intangibles and merger-related costs.

secure a disproportionate share of rights and cash flows because the bargaining power in the hands of employees was considerably increased at the expense of shareholders. In large part this was just a consequence of a tight labor market that put qualified and scarce staff in a strong bargaining position. In addition, in Internet start-ups, like in other firms whose business model and value are predominantly based on skill and creativity, the most valuable assets were easily human capital resources, i.e. employees (Zingales, 2000). As a result, a star employee who threatened to leave the company could extract a large rent from the firm and its investors.

Let us briefly discuss how the two probably most important agency conflicts in venture financing were magnified in Internet start-ups during the boom years.

1. *Bias towards independence.* Among the various available exit strategies, venture capitalists generally prefer the most profitable one, with a slight bias towards IPOs, as they are associated with a positive reputation effect. The situation is different for the founding team which systematically prefers the exit strategy that will uphold the start-up's independence. Indeed, there are private benefits associated with the managing of a company, and the founding team will always prefer to preserve its managing team status. This means that it will tend to avoid a trade sale and favor either an IPO or a management buy-out, and adopt product market strategies that commit the venture to remain independent (see Schwienbacher, 2005 for a theoretical model). During the Internet boom, this conflict became explosive, as the expectation of large fortunes in the wake of going public, coupled with the general tendency towards premature stock market listings, raised the stakes for entrepreneurs and made them even less neutral in respect of the choice of exit route.

2. *Bias towards continuation.* When the founding team is faced with the risk of failure, liquidation of the operations should be considered. However, it is inclined to, *ex ante*, favor continuation at any cost and avoid liquidation. This could be (i) because of the entrepreneurs' excessive optimism, (ii) because of the private benefits associated with the management of a company or (iii) because the founding team is an equityholder with a wealth constraint and is not asked to contribute to the next-stage financing. This effect arises because, as equityholders, the company founders are protected by limited liability against the downside while being able to take advantage of the upside. Cornelli and Yosha (2003) show that this bias towards continuation induces "window dressing" strategies by entrepreneurs,

i.e. short-term results manipulation, so as to favor investors' next-stage financing. Internet start-ups were particularly exposed to the possibility of such short-term manipulations. They had discretionary power over short-term expenses, as much of their expenditures accrued for items like marketing, and they could represent business activity through non-pecuniary measures of output such as unique web site visitors, etc. The manipulations in revenues by Lernout & Hauspie, a former market leader in voice recognition, or by Comroad, a supplier of navigation systems that invented 96% of its sales, were extreme cases illustrating the potential for abuse.

The amplification of agency conflicts between venture capitalists and entrepreneurs had dramatic consequences. On the entrepreneurial side, an Internet start-up without new financing from the venture capitalist can survive for an extended period of time by adjusting its *cash burn rate*, for example by cutting its marketing spending. Bias towards continuation is probably the main reason for start-ups exhausting all of their funds when possible. As a consequence, although bankruptcy filing began at the start of summer 2000, the Internet shakeout was a gradual and almost smooth process. On the financier side, one should have expected an increase in contractual provisions and other arrangements safeguarding against the moral hazard risk.

The second major fault line of agency conflicts during the Internet boom was the one between the ultimate providers of the invested funds, i.e. institutional investors, and the fund managers, i.e. general partners of venture capital funds.

First, general partners were all too willing to cooperate with entrepreneurs in nurturing unrealistic ambitions on scale and scope. For example, during the Internet bubble, most start-ups, including the smallest ones, expressed the strategic objective of operating on a European or even a global scale. Similarly, proven management rules, like those insisting on a clear corporate strategy that focuses on core activities and key markets, were ignored, or at least seemed not to be applicable to Internet start-ups. Like Amazon.com, a number of multi-market e-commerce sites appeared. Again, a strong belief in the network economics of the Internet provided a rationalization for both types of costly and over-reaching ambitions. But crucially, general partners in venture funds were probably willing to go along because their incentives were not aligned with those of fund providers. The structure of their compensation contracts, with typically a large (20%) retainer on profits and no penalty in case of losses, meant that they participated in the upside potential but barely had to suffer the consequences of investment failure. This may not be a big issue in normal times, but faced with the high level of risk that characterized the Internet boom, they were willing to take a gamble.

Second, why did fund managers accept all this money in spite of what turned out to be a paucity of "good" Internet projects? Certainly, as discussed in the previous section, fund managers and investors were overoptimistic and considerably overestimated the quality of their Internet projects. But importantly, given the compensation structure of a general partner in a venture fund, who typically received a percentage of managed funds plus a share in the ROI, it was obviously in their interest to accept as many funds as they could. With hindsight, obviously their incentives were no longer appropriate given the market conditions in this particular period. They clearly contributed to agency issues similar to the free cash flow problem described by Jensen (1986): general partners were mostly unwilling to return excess funds to their shareholders even when they could not identify enough sound projects. A compensation structure geared more heavily towards realized returns and including actual penalties for underperformance, with a cut in management fees, would have been more appropriate, together with provisions ensuring the swift return of "excess" funds.

The institutional investors' failure to implement adequate incentives, even though they must have been aware that the unprecedented level of capital inflows created additional risks, was perhaps itself sign of excessive optimism, in this case of the investors themselves as opposed to the entrepreneurs and general partners.[5]

The general partners' inadequate compensation structures probably continued to produce devastating consequences after the Internet shakeout unravelled. With most of their investments recorded in the books as ongoing projects, general managers largely had a free hand to window-dress the results of their funds. They could use this discretion to "gamble for resurrection" of distressed portfolio companies by keeping them alive. This probably meant often that good money was thrown after bad in order to mask problems with individual portfolio companies.

---

[5] Another argument would be that in the short term, it was rational to direct funds towards Internet start-ups to take advantage of the bubble. This explanation, however, cannot address the following question: why did the fund providers not insist on better compensation contracts for fund managers to make sure they would not lose too much with such a strategy later on?

4.6   Incentives and financial policies of Internet start-ups

As far as the capital structure and the financial policies of Internet start-ups are concerned, two salient differences compared with more traditional firms emerge: (i) the widespread use of stock options, and (ii) the surprising absence of debt financing.

4.6.1   Incentives

Internet companies quickly became champions in offering performance-related incentives not only to their executives but also to a wide array of employees. In fact, Internet firms, like other high-tech firms, had drastically "democratized" the use of performance-related pay and stock options. The use of equity-linked compensation was viewed as essential to attract and maintain talent at a time when not only executives with experience in high-tech start-ups but also programmers, web designers and other staff members had become a scarce human resource. Managers and key employees would often be granted compensation packages that overwhelmingly consisted of stock options and other performance-sensitive securities. Stock as a means of providing incentives was also offered to other groups of "stakeholders", like suppliers and customers. Incidentally, as far as suppliers were concerned, stock was also a convenient means of payment.

To understand the explanations given at the time for this startling development, let us start from the hypothesis that the nexus of contracts holding together a typical Internet start-up vastly differs from that of a more traditional firm. In a widely cited survey, Zingales (2000) coined the paradigm of the "new firm" to mark this difference, which he summarizes in three points: first, Internet start-ups are characterized by much more volatile boundaries than traditional firms; second, the contractual relationships that bind together company and employees are much looser and more temporary in nature, as is evident in the development of markets for temporary specialized workers; finally, whereas in a traditional firm the assets are first physical assets and only then intangible assets, for the new firm the overwhelming part of its valuable assets is the human capital of its employees, their knowledge and creativity. In the new firm the asset value of human capital assets is the "inalienable" property of the employees who can easily walk away. As a consequence, the bargaining power between companies and employees had shifted in favor of the latter, and companies appeared to have no choice but to offer generous incentives in order to create the employee loyalty and motivation that was seen as the essence of their valuable assets.

4.6.2 All-equity financing and absence of dividends

The large majority of Internet start-ups during the bubble years relied exclusively on equity financing, and tried to avoid the issuance of debt by all means.[6] During the Internet bubble, only a handful of Internet companies had issued debt, for example Amazon.com, but there are few other examples. The reliance on equity is in stark contrast with the classical financing pattern of start-up firms, where entrepreneurs, prior to the emergence of venture capital, used bank debt as the primary source of financing and switched to equity issuance only after reaching the limit of what they considered a sustainable debt level.

Three reasons might explain the exclusive reliance on equity financing during the boom years. First, as we have already seen, Internet start-ups placed a high value on financial flexibility. A company without debt obligation has an additional debt capacity to draw on if it wants to finance expansion. Moreover, financial flexibility included also the more defensive objective of avoiding fixed commitments in form of debt repayments that could be in harm's way in case of adverse contingencies. In fact, the brutal stock market reversal in 2000–01, as well as the ensuing difficulty for many companies to secure funding and their survival, can be viewed as an *ex post* justification of this instinctive prudence.

Second, according to the prominent capital structure theory of Jensen and Meckling (1976), the agency costs of debt, i.e. the incentives to take on risks even if they are value-destroying, is an increasing function of a company's leverage. Following up on our earlier argument that Internet start-ups were already operating in an environment of increased agency problems and de facto large risks (both upside and downside), the absence of debt financing ultimately was in the interest of shareholders as well.

Third, according to the more prosaic view expressed in Baker and Wurgler (2002), which has gained prominence in corporate finance since the bursting of the Internet bubble, the reliance on all-equity financing expressed merely an effect of shrewd "market timing". That is, managers tend to issue equity when they perceive equity as over-valued, and they rely on debt issuance when they view the stock price as low relative to its fundamental value. What other episode in recent financial history would be a stronger example than the Internet bubble for a clear case of managers perceiving their companies as overvalued,

---

[6] Moreover, their debt is rated as junk bonds or contains convertibility features and therefore is itself a security class with a strong equity-like risk component.

and opportunistically taking advantage of this situation by exclusively relying on equity issuance!

Finally, even though this discussion is not fully specific to Internet start-ups as such, we discuss the absence of dividend payouts during the Internet bubble as one of the more salient financial phenomena during this period. In fact, dividend payouts continuously decreased during the 1980s and 1990s, where many companies, in high-tech and also in traditional sectors, abandoned them in favor of accumulated earnings and share buybacks. Fama and French (2001) observe that the proportion of listed US companies with dividend payments diminished from 2/3 in the late 1970s to 1/5 in 1998.

What can financial theory tell us to make sense of such strong movements in the payout policy? Traditional theories on payout policy, based on "clientele" effects or tax advantages, seem hardly relevant. It is hard to see how tax clientele would have changed so much that they could explain a seismic shift in dividend payments, and if anything the tax legislation has become more favorable to dividends than it was 20 years ago.

By contrast, two other explanations seem relevant, and they are closely related to the prerogatives of Internet companies. First, the firms' payout policies were influenced by the extensive use of equity-based compensation awards and particularly of stock options. As a consequence, managers and employees had a direct interest in the stock price of their company, which determined the value of their stock option grants. This implied that they clearly preferred stock repurchases over dividend payouts to distribute income to shareholders, and their preference was amplified by the net dilution caused by stock options exercises. Indeed, when employees exercise their stock options, the company has to issue new stock, so that to avoid any net dilution many companies launched substantial buyback programs. In fact, in 2000–01, for the first time the value of share buybacks of US companies exceeded the value of total dividend payments. About half of the share buybacks were made with the latter goal in mind, i.e. in order to neutralize the dilution effect of newly issued shares in conjunction with employee stock options.

Second, profitable high-tech companies also avoided dividend payouts in order to build up cash reserves. This was viewed as strategically important in order to maintain maximum financial flexibility, in view of future investments such as mergers and acquisitions. The extraordinary investors' patience and tolerance regarding the non-payment of dividends is perhaps best understood as the expression of an optimistic belief that the build-up of internal funds reflected future "external" growth opportunities.

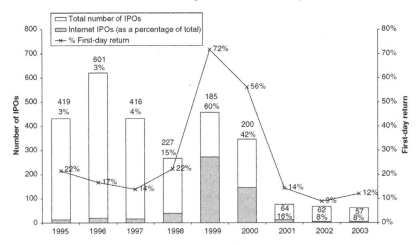

Figure 4.2. Total number of IPOs, share of Internet IPOs and first-day returns.
Source: Ritter (2004) and authors' calculations from data provided by Jay Ritter.

4.7   Initial public offerings

We can analyze in a bit more detail how the Internet bubble changed the character of IPOs, with the acceleration of the venture capital cycle and initial public offerings prior to breakeven.

The Internet bubble presented a classic *hot issue market* for IPOs, as Figure 4.2 shows. The brisk pace of initial public offerings in the years 1998–2000 shows all the typical signs that were previously seen in preceding hot issue markets (Ritter and Welch, 2003): strong volatility associated with unprecedented levels of underpricing, i.e. initial returns of the companies taken public surpassed everything seen in earlier hot issue markets (Loughran and Ritter, 2004; Demers and Lewellen, 2003), and finally a rather abrupt ending of the issue activity.

The massive wave of Internet-based stock market listings had also been a key to the initial success of new stock markets that had been created in Europe in the late 1990s to emulate the success of the Nasdaq market in the US. The Nouveau Marché in Paris, Techmark in London and similar markets in Amsterdam, Brussels and Milan were created to provide an outlet for such stocks. The German Neuer Markt became the most notorious poster-child of this short-lived success. It attracted almost 300 new listings in two years, only to be closed in 2003 after a drop in value of 97% of its leading NMAX index, many scandals and delistings.

To understand why public listings have become so popular with Internet start-ups, let us begin with the theoretical explanations for the decision to go public. The IPO marks in fact the exit of venture capital providers from the newly listed firm: even if they do not sell all of their stockholdings in the IPO immediately, venture capitalists will normally try to unwind their remaining holdings rather rapidly. Therefore, it also points out the transition from a mode of *relationship financing* to a form of *arm's length financing*. Chemmanur and Fulghieri (1999) and Pagano and Roell (1998), among others, argue that the advantage of relationship financing resides in valuable *monitoring* services provided by the venture capitalists. The benefit of a public listing is seen in the continuous production of information that the stock market offers through analysts' coverage and the efficient aggregation of information in the stock price. As soon as this informational role, together with the gains in transparency and stock liquidity conveyed by a market listing, outweighs the initial monitoring role, a firm will go public. So according to this view, for Internet companies the need for such a continuous stock market update arises early on in their life cycle.

Another explanation that seems particularly relevant to Internet start-ups emphasizes the advertising effect of an IPO. In this view, an important audience of an IPO is not the financial market but the product market where the newly listed firm sells its products. Stoughton et al. (2001) propose a model where start-up firms use the IPO as a device to credibly signal to their customers that their products are of high quality, whereas low-quality producers cannot adopt a similar strategy as it would be too costly. One can stipulate that the announcement effect linking IPO and free marketing with an audience of current or potential customers is even more pertinent for Internet start-ups: indeed, what better kind of publicity for a dot.com company than that of its stock market debut with its large media exposure. All the more so if the name of the newly listed firm happens to be identical to the URL of its company web site and if the IPO is accompanied by an investors' frenzy that leads to a first-day return of more than 100%. Some recent empirical studies supply evidence in support of this idea. Blass and Yafeh (2001) show that among Israeli firms undertaking an IPO, those with a large client base abroad show a clear preference for a listing on Nasdaq while those with a domestic customer base opt for a listing in Tel Aviv. Demers and Lewellen (2003) show that the web traffic of Internet companies significantly increases in the month following their IPO, and that the increase is all the more important as the IPO had substantial media exposure and generated a high first-day return.

In a more behavioral vein, the flurry of accelerated IPO activity can be seen as a rational response of company insiders to a market frenzy that generated a huge demand for Internet stocks at hugely inflated prices. According to Baker and Wurgler's (2002) idea, insiders opportunistically take advantage of market misperceptions, and they tend to issue shares when they are overpriced. Notice that the volume of primary shares issued in IPOs, which in the US alone reached a volume of around $65 billion in each of 1999 and 2000, about twice the average level of the 1990s, is only one side of the medal. In addition, newly listed companies issued large volumes of equity that were distributed to employees, former shareholders of acquired companies and other stakeholders.

Numerous Internet IPOs have chosen to accelerate the decision to go public. Until the late 1990s, it was conceived wisdom that companies could go public only if they had established a solid record of profitability. Compared with this traditional tenet, Internet firms have massively opted for early IPO dates. Only 21% of the companies listed in the US in 1999 were profitable at the moment of their IPO – compared with 68% in the 1983–98 period – and the IPOs of unprofitable companies generated a first-day return of 71.5% in those years compared with a return of 42.6% for profitable companies (Loughran and Ritter, 2004).

It is also interesting to relate this hot issue market and its characteristics with the formation and the burst of the speculative bubble as we interpreted it in section 2. Indeed, a prevalent IPO practice during this period was to lock up around 80% of the shares offered at IPO by insiders and other equityholders. As many of the Internet stocks were recent initial public offerings, the number of tradeable shares was thus limited, typically for a period of six months. After this lock-up period, insiders and other equityholders were no longer constrained by their inability to trade their shares, and this was known to all market participants in advance. Hong et al. (2006) discuss a theoretical model with such features. In their model, the market's limited risk absorption capacity, created by an artificially small free float of the newly issued equity, explains that prices could be pushed well above fundamental values even though the expiration of lock-up periods was anticipated by market participants. This model offers a rationale both for the very high underpricing observed during the boom period, when free floats were routinely limited to small fractions of the market capitalization, and for the dramatic correction in asset prices afterwards, when the asset float of Internet stocks often increased dramatically.

We will briefly mention another implication of the premature IPO wave that is directly linked to the likely agency conflicts in Internet start-ups that we mentioned earlier. Recall that we had postulated that in Internet start-ups, with their high cash burn rates and low average value of tangible assets, managers could easily manipulate accounting returns. In this context, the transition to a less flexible financing mode may become interesting as an incentive tool. Take the example of an ailing Internet start-up that has run out of cash and wants to raise a new round of financing. Its current financiers might be tempted to throw good money after bad, in order to rescue their past investments. At the same time, new investors are probably not inclined to provide funding, given the value of the securities already issued. Then, without an IPO, the company would normally be granted yet another round of cash injection. After an IPO, however, the presence of many dispersed shareholders can act as a powerful commitment device that prevents new financing from coming forward. In other words, relationship financing is *ex post* efficient, but arm's length financing can be in certain cases *ex ante* efficient. This will be the case if the incentives for the entrepreneurial team to finish the project successfully without burning more cash are sufficiently improved by the new, rigid financial contracts.

In this view, a positive aspect of the massive wave of premature IPOs for Internet start-ups was that it imposed a hard, non-renegotiable budget constraint, which prevented further cash injections once the company was publicly listed.[7] This hypothesis might appear far-flung, but it should be remembered that numerous Internet start-ups had little prospect of ever becoming profitable, especially towards the end of the 1998–2000 bubble. Those still held by venture capital funds stood a larger chance of securing additional, and likely wasteful, funding than those that had been taken public before.

4.8   Conclusion

This overview of the "Internet bubble" and its aftermath started out with its unique impact on venture funding. It argued that the European venture capital, in the sense of early-stage financing of innovative companies, was only truly started with the advent of the Internet, and the massive flows of funds that came with it. It remains yet to be seen whether early-stage financing in Europe will survive the demise of so many venture-backed Internet start-ups. We attributed the large flow of funds to Internet companies, the subsequent sharp correction and selective rehabilitation to a learning process about the true nature of Internet-based network economics in which winner-takes-all competition

---

[7] Dewatripont and Maskin (1995), among others, present a related formal model in a different context.

was overestimated. These beliefs drove the quest for alternative valuation techniques, based on Internet-specific performance metrics and real options techniques, which were largely a bubble-driven, temporary phenomenon. We argued that investors faced heightened agency conflicts, due to the need for flexibility and the perceived imperatives of a winner-takes-all competition in network industries. Institutional investors faced agency costs as well in their relationship with fund managers, in the form of excessive fund allocations and delayed value corrections. Finally, Internet start-ups were at the forefront of a premature IPO market, where for the first time companies were massively listed on the stock market while showing large operating losses. We suggested that premature IPOs might have acted as a commitment device against further cash burn of failing Internet companies.

Part II

On-line communities

5 Information goods and online communities

Michel Gensollen

Internet mass utilization developed during the years 1995–2000, especially via web and e-mail services. It was believed, perhaps a little too
quickly, that information and communication technologies (ICTs)
would improve markets' operation. It was wrongly imagined that business and social models of the real world would easily extend into the
virtual world. The collapse of the dotcoms showed that the transition
was not so easy and that a simple transposition of commerce into
e-commerce or of traditional media into a "multimedia" environment
was doomed to failure. The Internet deeply transforms market dynamics
and industrial organization. It is indeed a new economy which is slowly
taking root, but not the one that was dreamt up: not an old economy
using the Internet but an online economy.

In the beginning it was thought that groups of surfers in "virtual
communities" would follow the pattern of real communities and become
the online extension of the latter. It was imagined that, at best, online
communities would become almost as efficient as their real counterparts,[1] that they would induce relationships almost as intimate and
behavior almost as cooperative. According to the model of monopolistic
competition, it was concluded that more extensive and more mobile
communities would entail better segmentations of clients and more
accurate differentiation of products at both the production and the
distribution levels. As a sort of full-size clustering of consumers by
affinity, online communities would advantageously replace market

---

[1] Thus, in the pioneering Wellman–Gulia paper (1999), which forms part of a handbook
on "real" social networks (neighbor networks, social networks among urban poor in a
Latin American city, personal networks in France, network capital communist and
postcommunist countries, personal community networks in Japan, etc.), the authors
finally ask the question: how do Internet-based communities compare to real communities? Are they more specialized? Do they have weak ties and strong ties (in
Granovetter's sense [1973]), like real communities? Do intimate links exist in online communities? etc. Such an approach naturally leads the reader to conclude that virtual
communities are nothing more than a clumsy transposition of real communities, that
may improve over time and eventually become some substitutes for them.

173

analysis: customer segments would no longer appear as the uncertain result of statistical adjustments but as a reality that can be observed and possibly influenced. People dreamt of *community marketing*[2] and it was even thought that communities of consumers could issue grouped orders[3] that would benefit from discounted prices.

Yet sites which invested in community marketing have collapsed. The virtual communities which have finally emerged are new social structures that differ from those usually referred to by the term "community". ICTs do not transform real processes into similar virtual processes. This had already been noted for e-commerce or online media: retail purchasing, for example, does not simply morph into virtual shopping on commercial web sites. ICTs transform information networks which serve to regulate markets and hierarchies and by the same token they challenge production, distribution and consumption processes.

Original interaction structures are developing today on the Internet (referred to subsequently as "online communities"); they are already modifying the way consumer tastes evolve – perhaps in time they will close the loop between consumers and designers. In this chapter, we offer an analysis of this current development, based on actual examples of virtual communities that have recently been observed, i.e. communities hosted by vendor web sites (such as Amazon.com), communities which emerge from users' forums (e.g. free software distribution sites and user mailing lists) and finally communities that share digital files (e.g. peer-to-peer networks).

The chapter is organized as follows: after a short clarification of the concepts of information goods and informational infrastructure of markets (i.e. "meta-markets"), we characterize the economic role played by each type of virtual community, the type of information goods that it helps regulate and the market shortcomings and failures it could overcome. Finally, in each case, the operating mode of the communities, their governance problems and the motivations of their participants will be examined.

An overview will be given of:

(i) experience-sharing communities (i.e. sites where people can exchange reviews and advice) that make consumer choice easier for experience goods and in particular cultural goods; over time these communities could substitute for the top-down information model (mass media model);

---

[2] See the Hagel–Armstrong work (1997) on community marketing.
[3] Thus, group-buying web site Koobuy, which became KoobuyCity, or Clust, finally disappeared at the end of 2000.

(ii) epistemic communities (i.e. knowledge-sharing communities) which make it possible to disseminate the knowledge needed to use complex goods; in the future these communities may act as a communication channel between consumers who try to adapt complex goods to their particular needs and developers to design next-generation products;

(iii) file-sharing communities, dealing with cultural goods or software; these communities make it possible to achieve the productivity gains promised by ICTs, based on low-cost duplication, processing and storage of digital information; they challenge the editorial model of intellectual creation.

Lastly, we will point out what these three types of communities have in common: (i) an original sociality: *instrumental intimacy*, i.e. rationalization of the interpersonal link; (ii) a specific purpose that justifies their existence: the production and maintenance of a collective information corpus; (iii) a mode of participation that is less altruistic than proactive: participation in the community originates less from disinterested cooperation than from the wish to promote an opinion, a way of thinking or a model of society.

In this chapter we are not trying to analyze the various services, protocols and software that enable communities to develop and work technically. Apart from multi-player games (MUD) and chat rooms, these services offer *asynchronous* contacts on the basis of various protocols:[4] e.g. e-mail-based discussion lists, forums (bulletin board systems), discussion groups (e.g. Usenet newsgroups),[5] software made available by vendors on web sites (such as Amazon) or by distributors of free software (such as Debian), etc. The distinction between these various services is not always very clear and commercial sites can take advantage of services offered free on the Internet (as Amazon takes advantage of the IMDB – Internet Movie Data Base). Such services can also be used as a support for the online transposition of real communities: clubs or associations that develop a web site, support groups, etc. The analysis presented here is centered on the way online communities operate and on their economic role, whatever the precise type of online services used, as the same type of community can develop using

---

[4] For a precise description of newsgroup services on the Internet, see the article by Kollock and Smith, "Communities in Cyberspace", which is as an introduction to Kollock and Smith (1999).

[5] In particular see the description of these newsgroups in Smith (1999): "Invisible Crowds in Cyberspace: Measuring and Mapping the Social Structure of USENET".

various interaction applications (e.g. an experience community can use newsgroups, forums, discussion lists, personal pages or specific software offered by an online vendor, etc.).[6]

Finally, as we focus on the new regulations that the online communities can induce in the final market, we limit our scope to communities *on the Internet* without referring to working groups that companies can set up via their intranets. No mention is made here of the transformation of production processes resulting from a possible use of online communities inside companies (intranet), or between different companies (extranets, B to B platforms, etc.).

5.1   The role of ICTs in the current development of markets

5.1.1   *Markets and information processing*

Markets were first understood as exchange mechanisms which allow efficient allocation of resources without requesting a centralized understanding of each person's preferences. In this framework, production functions and consumers' utility functions are assumed to be exogenous. From a dynamic viewpoint, markets are considered as processes of reciprocal learning: demand progressively learns the constraints of the production function while the producers learn the features of the consumers' utility functions. The free market described by classical economists[7] is a means of inventing new forms: new products, new usages.

So, it may be surprising that market models do not explicitly take into account information exchange and the various institutions that allow the collective knowledge processing. As far as allocation of resources is concerned, the efficiency of a market obviously depends on the regulatory constraints that can weigh on physical exchanges, on the tax system, on the confidence in means of payment and in the security of transactions, etc; whereas the efficiency of a market that invents new forms tends to depend mainly on information networks: if the latter yield lower search and learning costs, qualitative matching between supply and demand will be improved.

Information and communication technologies act at two levels: on the one hand, at the level of physical exchange mechanisms, by simplifying

---

[6] Procedures and software are nonetheless crucial to shaping communities; some minimum changes in procedures can occasionally lead to significant consequences; in particular the role of the interface has been studied in the case of chat rooms: see the analysis of alternative chat interfaces (chronological presentation, conversation threads) in Smith, Cadiz and Burkhalter (2000).

[7] See, for example, Hayek (1978) or Kirzner (1985).

some transactions and by reducing the logistics costs for purchases (virtual shops), payment (electronic payment), delivery (management of delivery rounds); and on the other hand, at the level of information exchange mechanisms, which facilitate demand awareness and acculturation as well as innovation and product design.

5.1.2 Markets and meta-markets

From a static viewpoint, for ordinary products (i.e. standardized, easy to use and well known *ex ante* by consumers, when there is no fashion or imitation effects, etc.), the performances of markets do not heavily depend on information exchange between potential consumers and early adopters. All the goods are well known by all the consumers, even if these goods are not equally accessible due to transportation costs (these costs can be interpreted as information search costs: *search goods*).

From a dynamic viewpoint, when products are complex, when they change rapidly, when their utility is uncertain *ex ante*, consumers must be helped to search and collect data disseminated in the final market. The Internet and ICTs then allow for powerful information gathering and *collective* processing. User networks could be more or less spontaneous or controlled by producers and/or vendors. These user networks form new informational infrastructure that can improve the way retail markets operate. They will be subsequently called "meta-markets". They are not real markets as some economists presumed during the dotcom frenzy, when it was supposed that information on the primary market could form the staple product of a genuine secondary market and that *gatekeepers* could broker meta-information directly.[8] Thus, the knowledge of a price and the search for a better price would have its price in turn. Nevertheless, even if such information brokers managed to survive only according to a standard media model (e.g. banner advertising on sites offering price comparison or shopbots), it remains true that some networks or communities of consumers resemble markets: self-regulation mechanisms must develop to ensure fluidity of exchanges, permanence of the system (resistance to free-riders) and harmonious distribution of quasi-costs (e.g. the necessary balance between access time and writing time).

In the case of information communities, it would be simplistic to reason in terms of altruistic contributors and free-riders (*lurkers*) and undoubtedly naive to think that meta-information could simply be sold

---

[8] See the Baye–Morgan article (2001).

and bought as a product. Here, we focus on the mechanisms that allow these communities to function and on their role in regulating the associated final market.

5.1.3   The development of information goods

Meta-markets, i.e. the sophisticated information exchange systems needed for markets to operate, are all the more useful as the underlying primary markets relate to information goods. Here, "information goods" refers to the goods (or services) that incorporate information and/or that need information to be chosen and consumed. Of course, these two criteria are different: there are goods which contain information and that require little meta-information to be produced and consumed, just as there are goods, in particular those involving radical innovation, that require lengthy acculturation on the part of consumers, without however containing much information. Nevertheless, in practice, these two criteria often overlap: it is precisely information-rich goods (e.g. cultural goods or software) that also require exchanges of information either prior to purchase, to inform demand of the usefulness of their content, or after sale, to help utilization.

Information and communication technologies change the nature of information goods: on the one hand information becomes "free" information, i.e. it is no longer rigidly tied to the physical layer, while on the other hand, costs of handling meta-information fall, which facilitates the development of the latter and increases its efficiency. These two trends are not independent. Capturing the value of information goods cannot be efficiently based on the information they contain, because this free information becomes a collective product that is optimally priced at its marginal cost of reproduction (the no-charge economy). Yet the value of information goods might be extracted from the mechanisms they specifically need to meet the appropriate demand (attention and knowledge economy). In this sense, meta-information is the key to the value of information goods, even if it is not directly marketable.

Information goods will subsequently be broken down according to the type of market infrastructure (meta-market) which can serve to regulate them:

- In the case of experience goods, quality is not known *ex ante* by consumers. It could happen in a context of vertical or horizontal differentiation. In the case of vertical quality, all buyers agree on which of two different grades is the more desirable (e.g. the reliability of a transaction on a web site like eBay: everyone prefers a high degree of reliability). In the case of horizontal quality, products are not ordered in the same way by all the consumers (e.g. the quality of a cultural product, such as a DVD on a web site like Amazon.com, depends on each individual's tastes). In both cases, potential consumers must turn to early adopters for direction: in the case of vertical quality, they must trust them (e.g. the sellers' ranking system on eBay), while in the case of horizontal quality, they must be able to estimate the closeness between their tastes and those of the reviewers (e.g. customer reviews on Amazon.com).

• In the case of complex goods, the way of using the product and of adapting it to personal needs is not known *ex post*. After the purchase, consumption demands acculturation and learning; instructions for use supplied with the products and after-sales services are not sufficient; training sessions are both costly for producers or retailers to set up and, in many cases, off-putting for future consumers.

• In the case of dematerialized goods, information is freed from its physical layer: this information is either engraved on a CD or a DVD from which it can be extracted, or in files downloaded through the Internet. A bit stream is a collective product, with a very low or zero marginal cost of reproduction but with a very high initial fixed cost of production. Regulations must simultaneously allow widespread distribution, the financing of fixed costs and, above all, orientation of creation (which is no longer simply oriented through market reactions).

5.2   Experience goods and the limits of the mass media model

In the case of experience goods, ICTs, and in particular web services, have upgraded the markets' information setting by allowing consumers who have bought and appreciated a product to share their experience with potential customers who wonder about the quality and usefulness that they could derive from its consumption. In the past, customer information had to be disseminated[9] through a centralized review and

---

[9] Here the "top-down information model" refers to the overall mass media system (advertising, radio, television, newspapers, etc.) that makes it possible to inform the consumer today. Messages come not only from producers and distributors but also possibly from independent reviewers, critics and experts. Analysis of this system shows that to be really efficient the broadcast messages have to be relayed by intermediaries (opinion leaders): see, for example, the "two-step-flow" model by Katz and Lazarsfeld (1955). As a result, the top-down information model and the community model described here differ less in their final phase (influencing the final customer is ultimately through personal contact) than in their initial phase: a very small number of messages for the top-down information model (due to the mass media's narrow bandwidth) and a very large number of messages for the Internet (if the Internet is not used as a classic mass medium with a few portals playing the role of television channels).

advice system (mass media system). The transformation of this top-down informational infrastructure into a bottom-up one is likely to have multiple consequences upon the dynamics of the primary market.

5.2.1   Experience goods and the exchange of advice

When the quality of the experience good is objective (vertical differentiation of quality),[10] providing advice raises few difficulties, at least when compared with the case of horizontal differentiation. For example, setting up a reputation-reporting system demands the assurance that there is no cheating (e.g. dishonest vendors arranging to appear reliable through buyers who connive with them)[11] and a comparison of subjective scales: this involves, for example, correcting the excessively favorable advice generated by over-tolerant critics.

In contrast, in the case of cultural goods (e.g. a book or a film), when tastes and opinions are scattered (horizontal differentiation of quality), a review can be interpreted only when sufficient information is supplied about its author. It is then necessary to provide potential buyers with a large quantity of information, i.e. not only opinions on the goods themselves but also a description of the different reviewers.

In the case of rapidly renewed products, such a model of collective review will substitute completely for the top-down information model (i.e. the mass-media model) only if it can play a double role: both (i) draw attention to the goods recently issued on the market, and (ii) disseminate various estimations of their quality. Online communities seem more efficient today as regards the second dimension and distributors' sites have had to implement specific non-community procedures to focus consumers' attention: generally, statistical estimates of the product's proximity that can provide potential customers with short lists of new products (e.g. "Customers who bought this DVD also bought . . .). Nonetheless, there are attempts to enable communities to attract attention to products; thus, on the sites of some vendors the contributors can post lists of goods which, in their opinion, resemble each other and are quality products (e.g. in the form of a hit-list: the ten best science-fiction films, etc.).[12]

---

[10] More precisely we speak of vertical differentiation of quality when, in the absence of any price differentials, all potential buyers would adopt the same classification of goods.

[11] See the article by Paul Resnick and Richard Zeckhauser (2002): "Trust Among Strangers in Internet Transactions: Empirical Analysis of eBay's Reputation System" as well as the article by Chrysanthos Dellarocas (2001): "Building Trust On-Line: The Design of Reliable Reputation Reporting: Mechanisms for Online Trading Communities".

[12] On the Amazon.com web site and also on other sites, such as the BD Paradisio (http://www.bdparadisio.com/) web site, which advertises and sells comic books.

5.2.2   The limits of the top-down information model

Before the Internet, awareness and knowledge needed for consumption were mainly provided by the mass media top-down model. Such a procedure could be efficient if products are not changing too rapidly and if quality differentiation is vertical rather than horizontal (i.e. when consumers' tastes are close). When products and services differ and try to adapt very precisely to each customer segment, the costs of a centralized meta-information model become heavier. In the case of information goods, such as books or movies, a customization splitting the market into many cultural sub-markets can be undertaken only in the framework of a decentralized review system.

The top-down information model rests mainly on three elements: branding, advertising and professional reviewing. These elements are used differently depending on whether the experience goods are vertically or horizontally differentiated.

In the case of vertically differentiated quality (congruence of tastes), the producer is generally aware of and in control of the quality produced. Consumers' choices can be simply channeled by brand names and the advertising campaigns needed to make them known. For some goods, specialized publications give access to experts' opinions and the results of tests carried out by consumer associations. Some distributors, when they can make their objectivity credible, can also participate efficiently in informing potential clients (for example, this is often the case with electrical home appliances). For this type of product, online communities make little contribution and actually have a minor presence on the Internet.

In the case of horizontally differentiated quality (different tastes), the producers have difficulty in controlling the quality produced and the brand system becomes largely irrelevant. The top-down information model could then be based only on multiple reputation factors, with each one reducing the uncertainty concerning the quality, at least for certain segments of the customer base. Thus, one can try to assess the quality of a movie from the actors playing in it, the director, the producer or even the theaters where it is shown. When tastes are widely differentiated such a model is inefficient. That is why, in the case of cultural goods, producers try to focus consumers' attention on a very small number of easily identifiable goods. Thus, online communities could allow a wider variety of products and, over time, less homogenization of tastes.

5.2.3   The emergence of experience-sharing communities

The Internet was initially considered as an information infrastructure which could be used in the framework of the top-down information model, i.e. as a classic centralized mass media system characterized by advertising (e.g. advertising banners). During the anarchic growth of dotcoms, attempts were made to adapt the concepts of the top-down information model to the Internet and, for example, to argue in terms of web site audience or exposure of specific targets to advertising messages. However, the web does not provide clear advantages over newspapers, radio or television when it is used as a traditional medium. Here again, the Internet is more useful in inventing new services than in simply adapting existing ones.

"Experience-sharing communities" are specific *search communities* where early adopters provide valuable information on the quality of experience goods. These communities did not appear on media information sites (although this would have been logical) but in spontaneous discussion and opinion-exchange forums[13] or on cultural product vendor sites (in particular on the Amazon.com site, which has progressively refined its consumer interaction software).

The main difficulty these sites had to face came from the need to provide information that should be both precise enough to foreshadow the usages of the products and synthetic enough to limit the consumers' search time. A whole range of procedures and software has been designed, building on the interaction structures developed spontaneously on the Internet (Usenet newsgroups, bulletin board systems, discussion list by e-mail, personal web pages, etc.). The latter have been tested and gradually selected by the distributors' sites in order to permit ephemeral, intimate and efficient relationships between potential consumers and experts. In particular, those who issue reviews can often describe themselves in a specific space (e.g. a personal web page on the site). The reviews are in turn reviewed according to their usefulness and the reviewers are ranked according to the number and quality of their contributions, which can be considered as a form of symbolic remuneration.

Still, star products (i.e. products on which the mass media system has focused attention) have too many redundant reviews; this is inefficient and slows down searches, while the products that should benefit most from a decentralized review system usually get too few reviews. It is not certain that online communities have already created a greater differentiation of cultural products: the answer may depend on the type of goods considered (books, CD, DVD, etc.).

---

[13] For a description of such forums, see Smith (1999) and for a tentative modeling see Curien et al. (2000).

Moreover, in order for such a decentralized review system to be really useful, the potential customers must find sufficient advice about the products they are interested in: the community must therefore be very diverse. The distribution sites that offer such review services enjoy a scale-related competitive advantage: because of its size, Amazon.com has a dominant position on cultural products in the United States. But the vendors that edit reviews must also be able to link this service to actual buying or, at least, to offer prices and levels of service similar to the best market offers, in order to make the customers stick to their site.

5.2.4   *The construction of a review corpus to enlighten consumption*

Experience-sharing communities are characterized by the corpus they create and use. For a participant, the usefulness of the community depends on the quality of the corpus: relevant reviews, easy-to-access comments, meta-review system, efficient forum software, etc. Every product must have a sufficient number of reviews so that everyone can be efficiently guided, while star products must not have too many reviews which are time-consuming to skim through (or in this case, the reviews should be edited and presented according to their quality, which is itself estimated by feedback from readers). For reviewers, the incentives to contribute depend also on the nature of the corpus and on the quality of the audience, i.e. *in fine*, on the impact that publishing an opinion can have.

A "good" corpus of reviews minimizes the writing and reading times for a given level of quality; as there are for more readers than contributors, the greatest constraint comes from the reading process. So, reviews must be qualified by several comments and reviewers must be ranked according to the usefulness of their contributions.

Thus, for a virtual community, it is not possible to consider the contributors as being only altruistic and the readers as only taking advantage of the corpus as free-riders. On the contrary, the reviewers seek to promote their opinions and tastes and they are prepared to spend a considerable amount of time to do so.[14] Those who read the reviews undertake the complex and time-consuming task of selecting reviews which appear useful to them and seeking information about the issuers'

---

[14] For example, on Amazon.com, even if extreme cases are not considered (the first contributor wrote more than 4,500 reviews), the 50th expert wrote around 500 reviews and the 500th expert wrote more than 150 (classifying reviewers according to the number of reviews).

personal characteristics in order to fully understand their reviews. There is no altruism among reviewers: they try to increase the effective customer base for products that please them, so that these products multiply and gain quality. Readers do not exploit reviewers; on the contrary, the more numerous they are, the more the reviewers can promote their opinions.

The corpus of reviews created by an experience community therefore plays the same role as the "word of mouth" informal interaction system. But these virtual conversations are rationalized: long-term personal relationships turn to ephemeral, narrow and mediated social links.

Experience-sharing communities are fragile to the extent that the information corpus is under the control of an agent (the web master), who can edit the information (by withdrawing some texts or adding others) and who is supposed to do so because of his editorial responsibility. The web master's capacity to credibly commit himself to objectivity of the editing is then crucial for the survival of the community.

5.3   Complex goods and the limits of technology push innovation

In the case of complex goods, the Internet provides markets with information-processing social systems that contribute to the training of novice consumers: in epistemic communities, a newbie can benefit from the advice of experts or early adopters. As in the case of experience goods, this is a sort of mutual help among consumers; but epistemic communities are very different from experience-sharing communities because the tasks to be performed are much more complex: it is no longer a question of comparing tastes but of sharing new representations.

5.3.1   Complex goods and the dissemination of knowledge

Here a product will be called *complex* not only if its use is difficult to accomplish and, for example, entails reading a long set of instructions but also, more specifically, if:

- the potential consumers have not already formed the cognitive representations they would need to efficiently use the product; written instructions are not sufficient and prior training is essential;
- the product is not ready to use: it must be customized insofar as it is less expensive to produce a sort of "framework product" that will then be adapted by each consumer for his specific needs; this product fine-tuning is not always easy, precisely because all of the possible

adaptations could not have been tested during the production phase; this is generally the case with software.[15]

Complex goods could develop only because, at the production level, interface standardization improved (e.g. the case of video recorder, television, mobile telephone, etc.) and, at consumption level, users could benefit from training, generally at work; thus they can configure complex goods when these are identical for residential and professional usages (e.g. computers and basic interfaces such as Windows).

5.3.2   The limits of the technology-push innovation model

When innovation is driven only by technical progress, a new product is often designed without sufficiently taking into account the difficulties that the customers could encounter figuring out how to use it. Ergonomics and human factors recently came at the forefront of the discussions on the digital economy because of the growing awareness of both the scale of adaptation costs between supply and demand and the difficulties involved in financing them. It is now acknowledged that it is far more efficient to take into account the constraints imposed by final demand in terms of representations and user competence as soon as possible during the product design process. With the speed of technical progress and the development of complex goods, the technology-push innovation model comes to a crisis.

Communities offering mutual support for consumers of complex goods are original and very different from the experience-sharing communities insofar as they can play a double role: helping to train potential customers, but also allowing developers and designers to better understand customers' needs and representations in order to take them into account when designing products. Such a feedback would also be conceivable in the case of cultural goods; today it plays only a limited role[16] and sometimes comes up against the opinion that in cultural matters, taking account of demand at design level is not always judicious (independence of artistic creation, the mass audience's bad taste as illustrated by commercial television, etc.).

---

[15] This is the argument of James Bessen (2001) who wrote: "With complex software, standard products cannot address all consumer needs and proprietary custom solutions are not always offered. Open source allows consumers to create their own customizations. When such user-customizations are then shared, open source products grow in quality and features."

[16] Examples of such cooperation can be cited, for example on the previously described comic book distribution site, BD Paradisio (see note 12 above).

5.3.3   The emergence of epistemic communities

Proprietary software editors have been trying to replace instruction manuals by electronic documentation, which can be available as local support or as an online interactive service. For simple stable software, in a standardized context, such a procedure is consistent with mass consumption, when users have been trained in their workplace in the rudiments of information technologies (IT).

In the case of free software, the effort has tended to focus on providing user mailing lists and discussion forums, where users exchange clues and guiding information on installing and using the products and report bugs or documentation errors. Thus, in the case of Debian,[17] an operating system and application software based on the Linux core, more than 8,000 "packages" (i.e. 8,000 software components) are available. These packages can be in a stable form but they can also be released while being developed: "testing distribution" or even "unstable distribution". To enable users to install and test programs, detailed documentation is available online (made up of manuals, many HOW TO guides and frequently updated FAQs[18]) on the one hand and, on the other, discussion lists are opened where everyone can register to ask or answer questions and possibly to suggest corrections and improvements.

The common information corpus is thus composed of a rich documentation written by experts and of interactions between those seeking to solve practical problems, those who have already solved similar problems, and experts who can analyze these problems and recognize that some questions reveal bugs or limits in software applications (real bugs, documentation imprecision, poor interface design, etc.).

Thus, "epistemic communities" are specific *consumer communities* where early adopters can interact on the one hand with developers and designers to help them correct and improve complex products and on the other hand with beginners who cannot make do with the directions for use and the FAQs. For such "epistemic communities", where knowledge is unevenly distributed, the main problem comes from the heterogeneity of skills. The trade-off between contributors' and readers' times, already pointed out in the case of experience-sharing communities, becomes crucial here: novices must have read all the relevant documentation so that they do not ask obvious questions that clutter up the list and waste experts' time. Indeed, most of the contributors'

---

[17] http://www.debian.org/
[18] Manuals and documents are completed by online help: *Frequently Asked Questions* (FAQs).

time is not devoted to writing answers but to sorting out questions in order to identify those that are useful to deal with.[19] This issue is all the more important as the number of contributors is much lower than the number of questioners.

In user mailing lists, the difficulties involved in establishing an efficient allocation between the questioners' working time (time to prepare the question) and the experts' time to find the relevant questions in the list lead to numerous calls to order and even conflicting exchanges (*flaming*). These dysfunctions could even result in the splitting of the list into sub-lists according to the level of competence: for example, novices, beginners and some seasoned users on a low-level list and seasoned users, experts and software designers on a developer list. Such a segmentation may appear sensible; nonetheless, it breaks the loop between designers and customers, which is the main asset of epistemic communities.

5.3.4   Distributed knowledge and market-pull innovation

In mailing lists, if one sets aside simple precise questions which, by omission, have not been included in the FAQs, a large number of exchanges aim to dialectically clarify complex representations. Hence the importance of discussion threads: the first formulation of a question is generally not meaningful enough and this first draft must be inter-actively worked upon.

Beginners do not know what they do not know (to quote Hayek's formula on central planners): ignorance is not a lack of information but a lack of conceptualization. Someone who does not know how to run an application on his computer often does not know either how to explain what is happening and his questions can be enigmatic or even unintelligible for an expert.

A heterogeneous epistemic community on the Internet (e.g. user mailing lists) is characterized by an unequal distribution of knowledge among the various participants. In contrast to a community of experts with complementary skills,[20] the communities referred to here mix experts of very different natures: those who know the products and their

---

[19] Thus Eric von Hippel reports (see Lakhani and Hippel [2000]) that in the user list for Apache software (a list where most participants are software developers), 25% of the questions do not receive any answer, there are relatively few contributors and these spend a greater part of their time reading and filtering the relevant questions than answering them (to reply takes only between one and five minutes).

[20] The epistemic communities studied by Emmanuel Lazega (2001) in the case of a law firm or by Edwin Hutchins (1995) in the case of a ship's crew provide examples of communities of experts.

operating logic and those who know how they want to use these products. The fact that the "demand experts", in some ways "the experts in incomprehension", are considered as ignorant does not simplify the relationships between participants in discussion lists.

Thus, it is understandable why segmentation of user lists by levels of competence results in losing an essential advantage: orientation of innovation by the reporting of implementation difficulties. The most naive questions are occasionally the most useful for developers to ponder; the most badly formulated questions are precisely those that indicate a gap in representations between designers and users. But these questions are immersed under an ocean of naive questions, coming from beginners who save on reading documentation.

Ensuring smooth operation of heterogeneous epistemic communities is an essential condition for developing better free software. Open source applications that developers enjoy designing are rapidly written, whereas some applications that users need are never developed. Thus, closing the gap between experts and consumers is crucial for the very success of open source over proprietary software.

5.4   Dematerialized goods and the limits of intellectual property

In the case of dematerialized information goods, ICTs, and in particular peer-to-peer networks, have made efficient pricing possible: as the marginal cost of copying and transmitting a file is almost zero, a zero price ensures an optimum situation *once the good is produced*. Two problems must be solved: the financing of the fixed cost of production and the co-evolution of supply and demand.

The information available in digital form (bit streams) can be distributed by telecommunications networks at very low costs but the final customer must be equipped with several electronic terminals (computers, games consoles, MP3 players, etc.). There is thus a current conflict of interest between editors and ICT industries; there is also a conflict of interest between editors and consumers, the latter experiencing a drastic reduction of their digital fair use rights; finally there is a conflict of interest between telecommunications operators and editors, the latter wishing to keep a permanent link between information and its physical layer (CD, DVD).

Digitization is therefore happening very slowly not for technical but for economic reasons and online file-exchange communities (i.e. peer-to-peer networks) have developed in a particular context of fighting against obsolete legislation (copyright and patent).

5.4.1 Dematerialized goods and productivity growth

Information and communication technologies transform conditions of producing and consuming information goods. At the production level, better ICT equipment results in significant gains in quality (e.g. through digital processing) and major cost reductions: text and photo processing, digital cameras, camcorders, music recording equipment, etc. of professional quality are now readily affordable to individuals. At the consumption level, recording equipment, processing software and low-cost storage allow individuals to reuse digital products to create new ones by reassembling them.

"Open source" in the cultural domain is *technically* possible. Once a bit stream is made (text, music, movie, etc.), its duplication, compression, transmission and transformation by consumers over networks occur at almost zero costs: dematerialized information goods are collective goods.

The value of information products can be partially captured through various business models that can be characterized as follows:

- The "physical model" consists in rejecting digitization altogether (i.e. by ensuring that bit streams are permanently tied to their physical carrier). There is no information economy as such but an economy of physical objects or locked files.[21] Rejecting duplication means rejecting the gains in productivity and welfare permitted by digitization. It also naturally leads to confrontations between producers–publishers and consumers and, to a certain degree, authors. Finally, it places the consumption of cultural goods in an environment of suspicion, prosecutions and penalization which is at odds with the hedonism and creativity that are inherent to this type of consumption.
- The "servicization model" consists in shifting the value of cultural goods towards physical by-products or services. A movie can already draw a significant portion of its revenue today from (i) the sale of characters or images, just like brands (e.g. Mickey), and (ii) the transfer of its characters or script to other types of products, such as video games or texts (novelization). Such a strategy often requires the extension of copyright rules.

---

[21] It will be noted that the link between information and the physical carrier (CD, DVD) cannot only be obtained by encryption and anti-copying protection processes but also, straightforwardly, by increasing the quantity of information for the same service (supposedly of better quality); thus the very inefficient DVD video encoding, which does not offer better quality than DivX encoding designed by hackers (and used on peer-to-peer networks).

- The "customization model" consists in directly reducing the collective nature of information goods: when a product can be customized for a small number of consumers, its duplication becomes a lesser threat for publishers. An adapted information product does not need the same protections as a mass market product. However, in this case, the fixed costs have to be amortized over a small customer base: this limits this solution to luxury goods. This leads to separating production into two phases: the creation of a general pattern which can be amortized over large customer bases and an adaptation of these patterns to various customer segments, a phase in which the market value can be captured.
- The "matching and acculturation model" consists in placing the value less on information and more on meta-information, i.e. less on information content and more on software and services that can be used by customers for identifying goods that suit them. The shift of value from information to meta-information is a particular way of reducing the collective nature of information goods, as the relevant meta-information is specific to each individual. Thus, even if a work can be copied freely, it will finally take its value from the procedures that can attract the consumers who would like it. Today, a service like Musicmatch[22] provides this type of service: for each customer it designs successive bundles which are increasingly adapted to his/her specific tastes.

Thus, online communities play together an essential role in the development of information goods: peer-to-peer communities are forcing editors to change their business models, experience-sharing communities are developing meta-information and are shifting the value of goods towards matching procedures and, finally, epistemic communities make it possible to adapt innovation to consumer uses and representations.

5.4.2   The limits of the editorial model

Business models of editors and publishers are based on intellectual property rights, whether these rights specifically protect an expression (copyright) or a process (patents). When they were enacted, these regulations took great care not to harm innovation and the dissemination of knowledge: for patents, they set up protection length consistent with the then rather slow pace of technical progress and they stipulated very broad exceptions to copyright (fair use, private copy, right to quote, public libraries, etc.).

The speed of technical progress should have been reflected in a reduction in length and scope of patents. The low-cost transmission

---

[22] http://www.musicmatch.com/

and transformation of bit streams should have led to reduced authors' rights and copyright protection. In contrast, we are witnessing a counter-productive reinforcement of these constraints: copyright length has been considerably extended,[23] fair use is being more narrowly defined and home copying will soon be forbidden or made impossible.[24] Software, whether protected by copyright or patents, cannot be freely enhanced and customized; applications cannot evolve and adapt to new needs because the source is not open to scrutiny.

The editorial model, based on intellectual property rights, is linked to the top-down informational infrastructure (mass media); it is being challenged by the development of online communities. The model which will be induced by a bottom-up market infrastructure (virtual communities) is not perfectly clear yet. However, some of its features are foreshadowed by the current challenging of notions inherited from the industrial era (which in the domain of information goods starts with the invention of printing):

• The definition of a clearly identifiable work is no longer possible in a world where copying, reuse and hybridization can be done efficiently. Thus web pages do copy, use and freely adapt the components of others, like storytellers in oral tradition imitated each other to create a collective corpus.
• Similarly, the concept of original author is waning. It is no longer possible to consider an author as a demiurge, who is indefinitely the owner of his or her creation. Cultural works and scientific innovations are now created by teams rather than isolated individuals and these teams are well aware of what they owe to collective research and invention.
• Finally, in many cases, the traditional model of authorship is challenged: in this model the author is considered as a producer who has to be remunerated and the reader or viewer is seen as a customer who must pay the price to access the product. With many voluntary authors,[25] each working mainly for his pleasure and addressing narrow

---

[23] The US Congress recently extended the copyright period by 20 years via the Sonny Bono Copyright Term Extension Act; in its ruling *Eldred v. Ashcroft* of January 2003; the Supreme Court confirmed that Congress did indeed have the right to prolong the length of copyright under the Constitution.

[24] See, for example, the analyses by Lessig (2001) and Samuelson and Davis (2000) on the challenge to *fair use* in the United States.

[25] Authors are marginal in the information economy and at best gain only 5–15% of revenues (for texts and music; in the movie industry, it depends on the definition of "authors" and can reach 40%). When publishers hide behind authors to explain the price of information products, they are neglecting the fact that most costs are associated with publishing tasks and not creation itself. ICTs profoundly alter the publisher's work and have little effect on the process of creation.

audiences, it becomes less and less clear whether emitters or receptors should be remunerated, emitters for the works they conceive or receptors for the time and attention they agree to give.

5.4.3   The emergence of peer-to-peer file-sharing communities

Peer-to-peer networks (file-exchange communities) have recently got better media coverage than meta-information processing communities (i.e. experience-sharing communities or epistemic communities). Even though all of these communities challenge the top-down information model, peer-to-peer networks appear to harm publishers more directly by offering free substitutes (MP3 or DivX files) to expensive products (CD, DVD). The RIAA (Recording Industry Association of America)[26] played a driving role in the process that led to the prohibition of exchange sites[27] like Napster and their replacement by file-sharing software, less easy to attack. Publishers were unable to fully understand the advantage they could derive from the Internet and when they bought file-exchange platforms, they used them as supplementary radio stations.[28] In contrast, equipment manufacturers were more innovative in finding new markets for their products (CD copiers, MP3 players, etc.).[29]

File-sharing communities have become more efficient if less visible: they are based on community software that build a "commons" of files on the participants' hard disks; this is efficient only if there is a means of identifying the files currently available (with information on the bandwidth). It would be only natural over time for this technical meta-information to be extended to content-related meta-information, which could lead to a convergence of file-sharing communities and experience-sharing ones.

[26] See the site: http://www.riaa.org/

[27] The Net Act (16 December 1997) criminalizes the supply of files with copyright-protected content, even when supply is not done for profit (see the text at http://www.usdoj.gov/criminal/cybercrime/ip.html). On its site (http://www.riaa.org/Music-Rules-2.cfm), the RIAA states: "The No Electronic Theft law (the NET Act) sets forth that sound recording infringements (including by digital means) can be criminally prosecuted even when no monetary profit or commercial gain is derived from the infringing activity. Punishment in such instances includes up to 3 years in prison and/or $250,000 fines. The NET Act also extends the criminal statute of limitations for copyright infringement from 3 to 5 years." Recently, the RIAA tried to force Verizon to reveal the names of customers suspected of illegally downloading music from file-sharing networks.

[28] See, for example, the development of mp3.com after its purchase by a publisher (http://www.mp3.com).

[29] Today, Apple is becoming involved in distributing music (iTunes Music Store) and a software copying publisher, Roxio (which developed Easy CD Creator and owns the "Napster" name), has bought Pressplay, the platform that holds the rights of the Sony and Universal publishers.

With the development of broadband, file-exchange communities will soon extend to movies and threaten the movie industry's value chain. These communities will accelerate the value transfer from the primary market towards the meta-market, a transfer that will gradually occur for all goods but which is more advanced for information goods. If all movies or musical works are accessible free of charge via software like Gnutella or Kazaa, it becomes clear that the value is no longer based on the information itself but on the services and software that help the supply/demand matching procedures and the acculturation process.

5.4.4   *The construction of an efficient distribution system*

Like the above described epistemic or experience-sharing communities, peer-to-peer networks are characterized by a common information corpus: anybody may contribute to it and anybody can use it. In the case of file-sharing communities, all the files in the public directories at a given moment form the community corpus.

The cost of participation is very low: it involves placing a file in a person's public directory. In the case of a rare file that will interest a lot of people, this cost can include the upload cost that the Internet access provider (IAP) may charge (pricing or ceiling on upload volume). This constraint is all the more severe as the network has the structure of a physical broadcast network: cable networks are very quickly cluttered by upload flows whereas DSL networks are more resilient.

The motivation for participating actively (i.e. to offer files) is more altruistic than in the previous cases: the desire to promote works or to collect information does not really play a role. So, in the case of peer-to-peer networks, some procedures exist to detect free-riders, e.g. some participants check that those who are copying files have given access to interesting files in their own directory; if this is not so, the connection may be cut. This does not involve a negotiation between individuals but "altruistic punishment": some participants check that the behavior of other participants complies with a standard that ensures the survival of the overall system.

Up to now, the operation of exchange communities has been jeopardized less by free-riders than by the legal harassment of the publishing industry. As long as the editors, publishers and producers have not adapted their business model to new technical constraints, the communities will have to organize themselves to resist lawsuits and technical sabotage. This is currently an aspect that cements these types of communities and helps to enforce behavioral standards that ensure their survival.

Peer-to-peer networks, especially if they merge with experience-sharing communities, could result in a sort of reverse value chain and undoubtedly a more rational organization. In the case of music or movies, the communities could serve to initiate the audiences through free supply and collective meta-information; the "best" works, directly selected by the customers, would then be played in theaters (for movies) or would be promoted through major commercial campaigns (for CDs or DVDs).

5.5   Online communities: a new social interaction model?

The various online communities which have just been described, although apparently very different, share one common factor: they challenge the top-down information model by developing databases ("commons") that help to close the gap between innovation and customers' needs. They form original interaction patterns which differ from real communities. We will now try to highlight some aspects of this common feature.

5.5.1   Instrumental intimacy or the rationalized social link

The transition from real communities to online communities is very similar to the rationalization[30] process that can be exemplified by the transition from charismatic leadership to hierarchical and bureaucratic organization, or by the transition from informal bargaining to anonymous markets. In online communities, social links between individuals are similarly replaced by anonymous and asynchronous relationships.

Even if virtual communities are based on Internet services (e-mail, forums, newsgroups, web pages, etc.), there are no direct and lasting relations between individuals: contributors and users work on a common information corpus which they want to shape to their liking and to which they feel attachment and loyalty. An absence of inter-individual relationships is all the more surprising as, at least in the case of epistemic and experience-sharing communities, intimate knowledge is necessary at

---

[30] In the sense which Max Weber gives to this term: pre-eminence of the formal rule over the ethical value, of efficiency over justice, etc. which leads to disenchantment if not alienation.

some stage of the process. This sort of "instrumental intimacy"[31] is regulated by various procedures: asynchronicity,[32] the public nature of exchanges, anonymity protected by pseudonyms,[33] the rule of limiting exchanges to a precise subject, hosting of interactions by a third party, etc. In such a context, interaction protocols that would induce sustained relations between participants, far from adding to the integrity of the community, would rather tend to endanger its survival by making it less efficient and more time-consuming.

The rationalization of individual relationships in online communities does not occur without disenchantment. Just as managers speak of human relations and team spirit to counterbalance the inhumanity of rational relations induced by office work, and just as anonymous markets are described in terms of customer relationship management and customization, similarly online communities are very often described and studied as real communities, i.e. close groups of people in lasting intimate relationships.

Some real communities (clubs, associations, etc.) might also use Internet services (e-mail, web, instant mail services, etc.), but the resulting online communities do not have the specific structure or dynamics of real virtual communities, at least at the beginning. It would be interesting to analyze whether community software could transform real communities into virtual communities and whether in some specific cases online communities can give rise to real sub-communities. The clubs which appear among certain MMORPG (massively multiplayer online role playing game) players thus provide an example of real sub-communities emerging from repeated anonymous interactions (or which might exist prior to these interactions).[34]

5.5.2   The solitary construction of a collective virtual corpus

Unlike real communities characterized by clusters of interacting individuals, online communities are centered on a virtual meeting space, procedures, formal rules and a behavioral code tacitly accepted by everyone. This virtual space can be a web site (e.g. a site of a vendor of cultural

---

[31] Such an "instrumental intimacy" resembles the anonymous intimacy identified in *chats*, e.g. in Velkovska (2002).

[32] It should be noted that the majority of Internet services are asynchronous. Chat rooms and instant messaging, which are synchronous, primarily play a phatic role (clearly revealed by an analysis of their content): they build a sort of community illusion and thrive on it.

[33] On teleidentity, anonymity, multiple identities, pseudonyms, see the article by Judith Donath (1999).

[34] See Chapter 5 ("Multi-User Dungeons and Alternate Identities") in Rheingold (1993) for example.

products) but it can also be reduced to a simple software package, with all the data needed for interactions being distributed across participants' computers (e.g. as happens with peer-to-peer networks like Kazaa).

In virtual space, some participants build an information corpus and others come to use it. The efficiency of the community depends on the quality of this corpus: on its diversity, its relevance, its more or less frequent updating and, possibly, on its resilience to hijack or sabotage. Each contributor tries to modify the common corpus so that it serves a social goal; each user tries to optimize his consumption on the basis of information drawn from the information corpus. There is little altruism on anyone's part but some degree of coordination is nonetheless necessary, so that writing and reading tasks are efficiently distributed.

Indeed, the entire web meets this definition of online communities: not-for-profit personal web pages (i.e. most web pages) constitute an example of a common information corpus.[35] So it is understandable why attempts to identify communities of surfers based on the structure of hyperlinks between URLs have not been successful. It is the entire range of sites and the structure of the links between them that form the "commons" of the large community of Internet users. The web is a collectively built corpus with few commercial sites. Portals and search engines are essential to complement the links between sites and to help web surfers find their way towards what they seek.

The fact that the web is a community corpus but not a community of sites or URLs is illustrated by empirical studies on Internet connectivity and the structure of hyperlinks:[36] these do not form a "social graph" (i.e. a highly clustered graph with a very low average path length: *small world*[37])

---

[35] The Internet was used only by universities and research centers for a long time. Even today, over three-quarters of the pages are not profit oriented. The surfers form a scientific community rather than a customer base or an audience. See Flichy (1999): "Internet ou la communauté scientifique idéale".

[36] See the study by Michalis, Petros and Christos Faloutsos (1999) on the Internet topology.

[37] We have known since Milgram (1967) and Granovetter (1973) that social graphs are of the *small world* type (even if a formalization like this was not used in this first analysis), i.e. that they have an abnormally small diameter given their very high level of clusterization. In contrast, *scale-free* or fractal networks (the probability for a node to have k links is of the form k^{-P}) are graphs arising from a growth process, with each new node randomly connecting with highly connected nodes (*preferential attachment*). The diameter of a graph is the average number of edges that separate two nodes. A clusterized graph is characterized by the fact that two neighboring nodes of a same node have a greater chance on average of being connected. Milgram tried to determine the minimum number of steps linking two people taken at random (a step being defined as a relationship between two people who know each other). The experimental result was surprising: six steps were enough, i.e. two people taken at random are linked by a chain of six people

but in contrast a fractal graph (*scale-free network*), where it is possible to encounter very large hubs.

Similarly, attempts to help the construction of online communities based on hyperlinks or web pages organized as topic clusters have not given birth to very lively and thriving communities; "rings", that were supposed to constitute sub-graphs of sites that were closed in terms of content, or "virtual cities" introduced through free hosting by Geocity, did not succeed in designing virtual communities that imitated real communities. These companies were bought by Yahoo!, which terminated such experiments.

5.5.3 A participation pattern less cooperative than proactive

To explain why opportunist and selfish agents (*homo economicus*) may nevertheless engage in spontaneous cooperation and disinterested participation to the constitution of a collective good, economic literature offers three types of model:

- The observed cooperation is only apparent. Through peer recognition, the providers–contributors (e.g. developers of free software) are only trying to signal their talent and competence to possible employers in a domain where performances vary widely and are very difficult to estimate *ex ante*.[38] Such a mechanism, that may occasionally play a role in the case of software, can hardly be invoked for experience-sharing communities or peer-to-peer networks.
- Cooperation can be deemed rational in the framework of repeated games between the same individuals. When participants can recognize whether they are paired with a cooperator or a defector, it is clear that a stable community can emerge.[39] This type of mechanism is not suited to online communities, where lasting interpersonal relationships do not play a significant role.[40]

(knowing each other on a first-name basis). Granovetter had drawn attention to the essential role played by "weak ties", i.e. rare relationships (but sufficient to ensure a small diameter) between people who do not belong to the same cluster.

[38] See the model developed in the Lerner–Tirole paper (2002).

[39] See, for example, the formalization developed in the Sethi–Somanathan paper (2002).

[40] In his paper "Design Principles for Online Communities", Peter Kollock (1996) writes: "It is said that one of the attractive features of online interaction is the fluidity of identity – one can adopt a new persona with each and every interaction. But work on social dilemmas argues that identity persistence is a necessary feature of cooperative relations. Online worlds can eliminate the threat of theft and many forms of scarcity, but without risk online communities will be dull and will not provide the possibility for the development of high levels of trust."

- Apparent cooperation can also emerge when certain individuals are unconditional cooperators because they have internalized cooperative behavior standards. These norms can be transmitted, either through socialization institutions (oblique transmission) or by imitation within peer groups (horizontal transmission). Under certain conditions, the population of cooperators does not disappear and can stabilize.[41] In this type of model, altruist punishment (*strong reciprocity*) plays an important role. A formalization of this type seems to apply to online communities and could make it possible to characterize the conditions under which the latter can survive and develop.

As seen above, in the case of virtual communities, decisions to contribute are essentially explained by the willingness of contributors to set up an information corpus which, by its very existence, will lead to desirable consequences for them. For example, in experience-sharing communities, beyond the altruistic desire to provide relevant information on the quality of cultural goods, reviewers try to promote their consumption structure, which is a rational strategy because information goods are subject to direct externalities (creation of sub-cultures, groups of fans, specialist sites) and indirect externalities (due to fixed production costs). Thus, to paraphrase Adam Smith, "it is not from the benevolence of the contributors that the user expects his information, but from their regard to their own interest".[42]

Symmetrically, users are not free-riders and passive beneficiaries of the information corpus, the shape and content of which is affected by their demand. Their very presence on the community site is a means of pressure; they have often the possibility of reviewing the contributions (which makes them second-degree contributors).

Finally, it has been noted that contributors and users often wish to promote an alternative model of production (epistemic communities), distribution (peer-to-peer networks) or consumption (experience-sharing communities). This sort of activism has facilitated cooperative practices, at least in the initial phase of the community. Free software epistemic communities struggle for open source and against proprietary

---

[41] In this formalization, the cooperating individuals have payoff functions which could partially depend on how they behave but, of course, their survival depends only on the material component of the payoff. On this subject, apart from the pioneering work by Axelrod (1984), see the articles by Gintis (2003), Guttman (2000), Cox (2000) and the experiments by Fehr et al. (1997) and Henrich et al. (2001).

[42] This famous quotation is from *An Inquiry into the Nature and Causes of the Wealth of Nations* (1776): "It is not from the benevolence of the butcher, the brewer or the baker, that we expect our dinner, but from their regard to their own interest. We address ourselves not to their humanity, but to their self-love."

code, which handicaps scientific progress. Peer-to-peer networks and file-sharing communities try to create a direct link between artists and consumers. Experience-sharing communities are very proactive: they promote opinions and advice that oppose uniformity and conformism and very often challenge editorial reviews.

The "assertive" aspect of online communities makes them fragile: any editing by the site web master is suspected of censorship; it discourages participation. Moreover, challenging the dominant production/consumption model rapidly becomes political: the authorities are rediscovering, like at the time of the telegraph, that direct relations between individuals can be threatening if not riotous. Control of interaction platforms and software then becomes a political as well as an economic issue.

Finally, it is not obvious that the information corpus built by virtual communities resembles the commons of rural communities to which they are very often compared. The empirical rules identified by historians and sociologists who analyzed such real communities seem very different from those followed by virtual communities on the Internet:[43] the borders of virtual communities are not clearly defined, their participants cannot easily modify the interaction protocols, there is no graduated sanction system nor procedures for resolving conflicts, etc. It seems that the collective information corpus which online communities gradually constitute raises fewer appropriation and free-riding problems than the classically studied commons (common grazing, fishing reserves, irrigation systems, etc.).

5.6   Conclusion

In this chapter we have described interactive social structures which are currently developing on the Internet. No specific reference was made to communities on intranets and online working groups. It was not in the

---

[43] For example, Elinor Ostrom (1990) has studied real communities that manage "commons" (maintenance of common forest and grazing grounds in Swiss and Japanese villages, fisheries in Canada and Sri Lanka, irrigation systems in Spain and the Philippines, etc.) and has set forth several rules which appear to be necessary for such communities to sustain. For example, we find rules such as: "Group boundaries are clearly defined; most individuals affected by the rules of the community can participate in modifying these rules; the rights of community members to devise their own rules is respected by external authorities; a system for monitoring members' behavior exists; the community members themselves undertake this monitoring; a graduated system of sanctions is used; community members have access to low-cost conflict resolution mechanisms."

scope of this chapter to analyze whether ICTs could change coordination patterns at work and industrial relations between companies.

On the Internet, exchanges of information *between* consumers deeply change the way final markets operate; they also challenge the current business models for information goods and the technology-push innovation process.

The points emphasized more particularly in the chapter are as follows:

- To take full advantage of digitization (i.e. dematerialization of information goods) in terms of consumption dynamics, customer information cannot occur only via a top-down model, from producers to customers, via mass media channels.
- Meta-markets (i.e. exchanges of information between customers and producers) are migrating from mass media to virtual communities; this could lead to greater variety and better adaptability of products and services.
- Direct relationships between consumers are developing through the Internet. These links, complemented by relations between consumers and developers or product designers, could possibly implement a more demand-pull innovation.
- Virtual communities are original social structures; they are very different from real communities. There are no direct interpersonal links between participants who construct and use a common information corpus.
- The survival of virtual communities does not mainly depend on the altruism of the participants but on the shape of the corpus and its mode of continuous elaboration. It is essential to ensure (i) an efficient time allocation between contributors' and users' efforts, (ii) the possibility of intimate but very focused interactions between participants (*instrumental intimacy*), (iii) the objectivity of the corpus editor or moderator (participants must trust him).

6 Online consumer communities: escaping the tragedy of the digital commons

Nicolas Curien, Emmanuelle Fauchart, Gilbert Laffond and François Moreau

6.1 Introduction

In the early 1990s, the development of information sharing among individuals on the Internet seemed pervasive. Individuals started to share music files, to communicate word-of-mouth about products and the like. More than ever before a new technology enabled consumers to share information on a large scale and on a spontaneous basis. Most of the attention was then focused on the emergence of online consumers communities (OCCs) and their expected benefits (Wellman and Gulia 1999; Hagel and Armstrong 1997). According to Hagel and Armstrong (1997), OCCs were supposed to offer companies a chance to know their customers much better than ever before, through giving the latter the ability to easily interact with each other and with the company itself: firms organizing OCCs could use what they learned from communities to achieve "viral marketing" and merely create undreamed of customer loyalty.

However, rather little attention had been devoted to identifying potential obstacles to the sustainability of OCCs seen as economic entities providing an informational public good.[1] Yet, shared resources and public goods are shown to give rise to a "tragedy of the commons" (Hardin 1968) since agents' private interest dictates individual behaviors that are eventually harmful to general interest.[2] More precisely, individuals tend to under-invest in a public good because its non-excludability and

---

[1] Nicolas Curien et al. (2001) are among the rare exceptions.
[2] Hardin (1968) showed that the private interest of individual farmers shall drive them to over-exploit a common grazing resource due to the fact that they expect additional benefit from sending another cow to graze on the commons although uncoordinated such behaviors will inevitably spoil the resource. Formally, the tragedy of the commons refers to the over-exploitation of a shared resource. By extension, it also refers to the under-provision of a public good.

non-rivalry give private incentives to free-ride, free-riders expecting to benefit from the shared resource even if not contributing to its provision. This makes impossible, or at least unlikely, the decentralized provision of a public good, individuals failing to internalize general interest as they overlook the socially detrimental consequences of pursuing their own interest. Economic theory then states that the solution consists in coordinating individual decisions so as to "mimic" the taking account of social welfare.

Online consumers communities are indeed concerned with the issue of provisioning a common informational resource on a durable basis. As emphasized by Daniel McFadden (2001): "Digital information is the mirror image of the original grazing commons: information is costly to generate and organize but its value to individual consumers is too dispersed and small to establish an effective market." Thus, the failure of private incentives to provide adequate maintenance of public resources could prevail as well in the digital world. Our goal in this chapter is to examine to which extent OCCs are subject to the curse of under-participation, seemingly inherent to the management of shared resources. We argue that such communities might indeed succeed in escaping a "tragedy of the digital commons", due to the presence of a private interest in providing online information to other consumers. While in the standard literature on public goods, private interest only generates free-riding and precludes the uncoordinated management of the shared resource, conversely in the case of OCCs there exist some private incentives to contribute that trigger sufficient provision of the informational commons. Those who contribute getting higher benefits than those who do not, the amount of participation might prove consistent with a sustainable management of the shared resource.

In the next section, we present an overview of OCCs contrasting two types of such communities that differ in terms of interaction patterns among individuals, namely experience-sharing communities and user communities. We also propose a categorization of individuals likely to participate in OCCs with respect to the nature of their motivations. In section 3, we introduce the general arguments that the literature on shared resources puts forward as being relevant to the issue of sustainability. Section 4 then discusses those arguments in the particular case of digital information and examines how the respective interaction patterns and participants' characteristics within the two types of OCCs might affect the emergence of a sustainable management of the informational commons. Section 5 concludes with a re-visitation of the tragedy of the commons in the context of digital information and introduces a possible extension of the present research.

6.2 An overview of online consumers communities

Online communities are often split into three categories (Steinmueller 2000; Gensollen 2006): experience-sharing communities which make consumer choice easier for experience goods, epistemic communities (knowledge-sharing communities) which make it possible to disseminate the knowledge needed to use complex goods, and file-sharing communities which exchange cultural goods or software through peer-to-peer networks. In this chapter, we focus on the informative aspects of online communities, hence we are interested in communities as devices for sharing consumer-generated information on consumption goods. In this respect, we propose to distinguish *experience-sharing communities* from *user communities* (communities of practice). The latter may be considered as a subset of epistemic communities since user communities encompass only one of the two main features of epistemic communities.[3] We shall now describe these two types of communities and propose that they differ mainly along the way information is shared. What matters is the timing of information sharing (before or after consumption) as well as the process through which information is shared.

6.2.1 *"Experience-sharing" communities vs. "user" communities*

Experience-sharing communities aim at informing consumers about the quality and drawbacks of products, brands or sellers prior to making a purchase. Hence, experience-sharing communities usually consist in consumers posting reviews that rate the products they have experienced. Examples of such communities are those originated by Epinions, DealTime, ConsumerReview, Amazon, eBay, ReviewCenter, OpenTable, MSN, etc.

The rationale behind consumers searching for other consumers' opinions about products is twofold. First, information on the product provided by manufacturers may be incomplete – for instance consumers lack information about whether a product is easy to manipulate or

---

[3] As epistemic communities, user communities are devoted to knowledge sharing that allows a newbie to benefit from the competence and experience of experts or early adopters. However, focusing on information sharing *per se*, we do not consider the dimension of epistemic communities that consists in building up new information goods (open source software, for instance) or at least in producing consensus over the future design of products. Therefore, it is more appropriate to designate the communities we are interested in as user communities (communities of practice) rather than epistemic communities. Finally, we do not consider file-sharing communities in this chapter because the content that is shared is not consumer-generated content (though consumer owned).

Table 6.1. *A typology of online consumers communities*

	Experience-sharing communities	User communities
Timing of the information sharing	*Ex ante* to consumption	*Ex post* to consumption
Mechanism for information sharing	Information broadcasting	Direct communication

install – and second, this information is obviously biased towards selling the product. Though consumers can also find information from experts affiliated to specialized magazines or large retailers, this experts-generated information turns out to be complementary rather than a substitute to consumers-generated information. Experts may in fact lack the concrete and long enough experience with the products to be able to provide consumers with practical information about their advantages and drawbacks.

User communities aim at helping consumers to use at best products they have already purchased, by making them aware of all their potentialities and by helping them to solve problems. Most user communities focus on a specific brand or product, for instance Oracle Applications, Lego products, Paint Shop Pro software, Nikon cameras, Apple computers, etc. As emphasized in the literature on the economics of innovation (von Hippel 1988), users hold knowledge that even manufacturers do not have. An intensive and long-lasting use of products or technologies allow users to identify problems, bugs, drawbacks, inefficiencies, for which they may have found solutions. They also come up with efficient or convenient ways of using the goods. Hence, they hold information that is unique and typically unavailable in users' manuals. Besides this rather reactive role, online user communities may also try to play a more proactive role by submitting their requirements to manufacturers (the Lego community in Lugnet) or seeking to influence product design (the community of Oracle products in OAUG).

Of course, it should be underlined that online consumers communities are not systematically purely "experience sharing" or purely "user". For instance, user communities may provide information on experience goods for non (yet) users with the members posting reviews on products or retailers. However, this information is rather anecdotal. Conversely, experience-sharing communities may also provide user information. For instance, on PhotographyREVIEW.com, users of specific cameras may share user information in discussion forums, but here again it is rather anecdotal compared with the primary purpose of the information sharing.

6.2.2 Criteria of distinction

Two criteria distinguish experience-sharing communities from user communities along the way information is shared: the timing of the information sharing and the process through which information is shared.

Prior versus post purchase sharing
In experience-sharing communities, information sharing occurs *prior* to the consumption decision. These communities are indeed devoted to making the consumption choice easier when faced with an overwhelming number of goods the quality of which is not known *ex ante*. On the contrary, in user communities, the information sharing takes place *ex post* to the purchase decision, since the aim of such communities is precisely to help consumers make better use of the product they have purchased by sharing knowledge.

Information broadcasting versus direct communication
In experience-sharing communities, interactions among individuals are typically not direct but occur through the broadcasting of information. Consumers thus share a pool of information that is not generated as the result of a request but rather as the result of the willingness of some consumers to broadly communicate advices about products they have experienced. On the contrary, in user communities, interaction among individuals is direct and occurs through personal communication among members. Information is usually generated as a result of a request and is thus fitted to this particular need.

6.2.3 Different types of participants

We distinguish between different types of community participants:[4] pure contributors, reciprocal contributors, pure askers and lurkers. Pure contributors do not expect reciprocity from their contribution to the public good. Hence, their motivation does not stem from the collective benefit of their participation (which is to generate reciprocity and thus more contributions) but rather from its purely private benefit (reputation, learning, etc.). Conversely, reciprocal contributors do expect reciprocity from other participants. Their contribution is thus motivated by the quality or amount of the public good. Pure askers are individuals who

---

[4] Whereas the distinction between contributors, pure askers and lurkers is common in the literature, we add here the distinction between two categories of contributors.

request information directly from others without contributing themselves. Finally, lurkers are individuals who get information from the community without either contributing themselves or requiring direct effort from the others. The main difference between a pure asker and a lurker is that the former may be useful to the community, by raising issues that some contributors find interesting to answer, whereas the only usefulness of a lurker is to satisfy the compulsive desire of some contributors to broadcast their opinions on a very large scale.

6.3   Key issues for communitarian sustainability

We shall examine in this section issues that may be of importance to the sustainability of online consumers communities. These issues are derived from different streams of literature, namely the provision of public goods, the emergence of cooperation, information sharing and social dilemmas. All these topics are concerned with the issue of whether groups of individuals may be able to undertake collective action spontaneously without the intervention of a central authority. We argue in this section that two broad classes of problems have to be analyzed. The first refers to contribution issues (6.3.1.) and the second is related to the anonymity of online interactions (6.3.2).

6.3.1   Contribution issues

The contribution issue declines itself in different sub-problems: (i) incentives to contribute versus free-ride; (ii) the extent to which the collective good is prone to free-riding and the impact on the provision of the commons; (iii) the relation between individual efforts and the collective outcome.

Incentives to contribute

Incentives to contribute to a public good are twofold: reciprocation incentives and private incentives. The literature on reciprocation incentives, initiated by Robert Trivers (1971) and Robert Axelrod and William D. Hamilton (1981),[5] brings insight on the relation between the expectation of reciprocation by other individuals and the probability of cooperating with them. The main result is that cooperation among

---

[5] Trivers (1971) was the first to suggest reciprocation as an impetus for mutual assistance between individuals and introduced the prisoner's dilemma game to bring the problem into focus. Axelrod and Hamilton (1981) then proposed the repeated prisoner's dilemma game (see also Axelrod 1984).

individuals is all the more likely as (i) interactions are repeated rather than one-shot (Axelrod and Hamilton 1981), (ii) interactions are pairwise rather than among many individuals (Hauert and Schuster 1997), (iii) reciprocation is direct rather than generalized with interactions occurring within the neighborhood rather than randomly (Nowak and May 1992; Sigmund 1992; Durett and Levin 1994) and players having the possibility to refuse partners (Stanley et al. 1994). Another important result is that interaction patterns that are based on the expectation of indirect reciprocation may generate cooperation if information holders have sufficient information on the past cooperative behavior of requesters (Pollock and Dugatkin 1992).

Besides reciprocation incentives, the provision of a public good can also arise from purely private incentives. Such a motivation, known as "the warm glow effect" (Andreoni 1989) in the public good literature, has been documented by several studies on online participation. In particular, the latter has been shown to be motivated by the building of a reputation asset that then facilitates the obtaining of research grants or increases the value of the individual's human capital on the job market (Lerner and Tirole 2002); by learning benefits that accrue from being confronted with others' knowledge or from being challenged (Foray and Zimmermann 2001); by "recognition" (Chan et al. 2004; Wasko and Teigland 2002) which enhances self-esteem and sense of self-efficiency (Constant et al. 1994). In these cases, cooperation through contributing is quite independent of the utility of the public good for the contributor, and thus quite independent of the behaviors of the others as well.

The extent to which a good is prone to free-riding
An implicit assumption when dealing with free-riding is that free-riders can fully appropriate the benefits of using the public good. The properties of non-excludability and non-rivalry make all agents – those who contribute as well as those who free-ride – equal regarding the benefits they can individually accrue from the public good. Yet, Dietmar Harhoff, Joachim Henkel and Eric von Hippel (2003) emphasized that, particularly in the information case, free-riders have a big disadvantage over contributors: contributions are not tailored to their own needs but to those of the contributors. Hence, free-riders benefit less from the digital commons than contributors. Though information is a public good in the sense of being non-rival and non-excludable, entering into direct interactions generates specific benefits that may not accrue to those standing outside the interactions (lurkers). In a similar vein, Gensollen (2001) argues that individuals who post reviews on books or music on the

Internet may affect (or expect to do so) the structure of the supply of books and music in a way that benefits them. Thus, while anybody can read a review and benefit from others having bought the product and tried it, those who experiment and post their opinions affect future sales and thus modify the allocation of resources towards products that will fit their preferences.

Sandeshika Sharma (2003) precisely models the influence of the extent to which a good is prone to free-riding as the probability that cooperation emerges within a population of individuals who have to decide whether or not to contribute to the provision of the good. Her model shows that if a large part of the public good is prone to free-riding – hence if most of its value accrues to free-riders – then the region of successful collective action is limited. In other words, if free-riders and contributors equally benefit from the public good, it is likely that the group will not succeed in provisioning it. Conversely, if the information available has far less value for free-riders than for contributors, free-riding should be limited since individuals will have an incentive to contribute. Hence, in communities in which pure askers (who enter into direct interactions) get more value from information shared than lurkers (who just read information posted), lurkering should be discouraged.

The relation between individual efforts and the collective outcome
The literature on the provision of public goods identifies three types of relations linking individual efforts to collective outcomes (Hirshleifer 1983; Varian 1994, 2004): the "total effort" relation where the level of provision depends on the sum of the efforts exerted by the individuals; the "weakest link" relation where the level of provision depends on the minimum effort (on the smallest contribution); and the "best shot" relation where the level of provision depends on the maximum effort (the largest contribution). Relying on the example of a community seeking to improve the reliability of a computer system, Varian (2004) defines in the three configurations the amount of efforts and the characteristics of the contributor(s) at equilibrium. He shows that in the total effort case, the "quality" of the public good is determined by the agent with the highest benefit/cost ratio, all other agents free-riding on this agent. Conversely, in the weakest link case, all the agents contribute the same amount, this amount being determined by the agent with the lowest benefit/cost ratio. Eventually, the best shot case is equivalent to the total effort case, with only the agent with the highest ratio contributing and the others free-riding. Varian then shows that the probability of reaching the social optimum is lower in the weakest link case than in the two other cases. In the former case, all the agents indeed have to

increase their contribution whereas in the two other cases, only one agent has to do so. Finally, Varian underlines that as the number of agents increases, so does the provision of the public good in the total effort and best shot cases, whereas it decreases in the weakest link case.

The literature also emphasizes that sustainability of cooperation is influenced by an individual's beliefs on the behavior of other participants when facing her own participation. For instance, Bernardo Huberman and Natalie Glance (1994) distinguish "bandwagon" from "opportunistic" expectations. In the former case, the assumption is that individuals believe that their choice will tend to encourage similar choices (of cooperating or free-riding). With opportunistic expectations, it is assumed that individuals expect that their choice will encourage the opposite choice (free-riders expect that the others will contribute, whereas contributors fear that their choice will encourage free-riding). The authors analyze how the perception by the individuals of the relation between their personal effort and efforts of the others, and thus indirectly their beliefs as concerns the provision of the common good, may affect the probability of success in the provision of the good.[6] They derive two generic results: (i) for both types of expectations, there is an upper limit to the group size beyond which cooperation can no longer be sustained, and (ii) as long as delays in informing agents about the total provision of the good (and thus the utility of the good for them) are small, there is a range of group sizes for which the dynamics exhibit two fixed points, giving rise to abrupt transitions between cooperation and defection. The two fixed points for agents with bandwagon expectations are at either extremes of mutual defection or mutual cooperation, whereas for opportunistic agents, the second fixed point is mixed: a dominant cooperating group supports a defecting minority. In the case of opportunistic agents they also find that delays in information cause the cooperative fixed point to become unstable. The conclusion of Huberman and Glance is that to achieve spontaneous cooperation, a group should be structured into small units of individuals with well-designed diversity of beliefs: the small size of the units (communities) allows for the emergence of sustained cooperation, whereas diversity in beliefs hastens its appearance.

---

[6] Huberman and Glance (1993, 1994) model this issue as a repeated n-person prisoner's dilemma and cast the interaction as an asynchronous dynamic game in which each individual reconsiders its decision at a given average reevaluation rate using delayed information on the level of provision of the commons. The iterated game is of finite duration and individuals decide to cooperate or defect by determining which choice maximizes their expected share of the good for the remainder of the game. In addition, the relation between individual effort and group performance is subject to uncertainty in order to reflect uncertain information and individuals' bounded rationality.

6.3.2   Trust issues

The anonymity of online interactions raises different sub-problems as well: the confidence in advices received from strangers and the coherence (homogeneity in preferences) of interacting people.

Confidence

The success of mass interactions among strangers, and their ability to provision a common informational good, may be greatly affected by the ability to overcome anonymity and the subsequent uncertainty relative to the information provided. This issue is rarely examined in the literature on the provision of public goods since the participation of individuals is usually in the form of a monetary contribution. Here, the contribution is informational. Moreover, this information is usually provided (at least at the outset) by strangers, individuals about whom the others have no information. Information might well be released by firms trying to disseminate favorable information on their products. Similarly, a firm could try to destroy the reputation of its competitor through negative or irrelevant information, graffiti attacks, etc. A recent literature suggests that this issue is indeed stringent in the emergence of virtual communities in general. Trust has been identified as one of the most important factors that influences the level of participation in a virtual community (Andrews et al. 2001; Jarvenpaa et al. 1998; Kanawattanachai and Yoo 2002; Ridings et al. 2002; Tung et al. 2001) and one of the main risks threatening online interactions among strangers (Resnick et al. 2006).

The problem lies in the risk that "good" contributors – those aiming at providing the community with relevant and objective information – will be discouraged by "bad" ones – those who cheat on the community by providing irrelevant or biased information – giving rise to the "lemonization" of the digital commons. Good contributors could be discouraged both because they expect their information to be invisible, and thus useless to the other consumers, and because they expect nothing valuable in return to their contribution – if their probability of picking up good contributions is too small.

In this respect, reputation mechanisms have been suggested as a solution.[7] According to Resnick et al. (2000), reputation mechanisms can "unsqueeze the bitter lemon". Werner Güth and Hartmut Kliemt

---

[7] Though most of the literature concerns reputation mechanisms for sellers of goods of uncertain quality (such as on eBay), see for instance Resnick et al. (2003), Dellarocas (2003).

(2004) rely on the assumption that "in large anonymous interactions as today prevailing on the Internet, trustworthiness can survive if it can be detected with some reliability" to model the trust problem as a game. Their results show that if there is no reputation effect resulting from posting a good contribution, then the "trust predicament" will emerge. Every participant in a large transactions system will act in an opportunistic way behind the "veil of individual insignificance", hence behind the fact that none of the individual acts is significantly responsible for the general trust climate. For instance, if individuals or firms tempted to post biased messages – typically firms seeking to manipulate consumers (Maizlyn 2006; Dellarocas 2004[8]) – expect that those messages will not threaten the general trust climate, then they will pursue in posting such messages. If, despite their expectations, they do indeed affect the general trust climate, the community may vanish.

If trust can arise only from the ability to identify information providers, this suggests that repeated interactions favor the emergence of trust. However, interactions need not be pairwise: if A posted an information that has proved trustworthy to B in the past, C will be more willing to trust her next posting. Hence, the tracing of past information is essential to the building of trust in this respect. Resnick et al. (2000) give insights on the conditions required for information providers to be willing to provide trustworthy information (not biased, useful, etc.) to the community: (i) there must be expectation of future interactions, hence the information provider must expect to be involved again in the community; (ii) feedback about interactions must be captured and distributed; (iii) this feedback must have impact. In other words, trust in information provided will be higher if contributors post information more than once or expect to receive information later on, if there is a reputation mechanism, and if individuals take this reputation into account either for evaluating the "quality" of the information provided or for deciding whether to answer a request.

Coherence

The anonymity of interactions also raises the issue of matching among interacting people. Economists postulate that consumers choose goods that maximize their utility according to their given preferences. Then,

---

[8] Dellarocas argues that, as in a prisoner's dilemma, firms tend to have no choice as to how to manipulate information online when consumers are expected to use it to inform their purchases: good quality firms are forced to post online reviews in order to prevent competitors with lower quality products from persuading consumers that they sell good quality products, whereas bad quality firms must do the same in order to avoid being considered as even lower quality than they are.

when a consumer takes advice from another one, this advice will be useful only if this consumer has similar preferences. Yet preferences are not observable. Thus, if interactions are random, mismatching between consumers' preferences and advices received is likely and will lead to inappropriate choices. The point is whether consumers who have initially different preference patterns can spontaneously form coherent communities and thus minimize the cost of searching for relevant information. Curien et al. (2000, 2001), Curien and Emmanuelle Fauchart (2003) and Curien (2004) examine the conditions that must be fulfilled for heterogeneous consumers to self-organize in communities.

Curien et al. (2000, 2001) consider that an individual that has to choose among several varieties of a same good may take into account three types of information: (i) a possible private past experience of consumption of some of the varieties of this good; (ii) an advice retrieved from the online community he belongs to; or (iii) an information on bestsellers provided by an offline retailer. Self-organization is said to occur when each consumer is able to find and adopt a community that gives her relevant advices. More precisely, self-organization relies upon a twofold feedback: private consumption experiences aggregate into a collective expertise which, in turn, guides private consumption choices. Two conditions have to be fulfilled for self-organization to occur. On the one hand, there must be an optimal mix of the consumers' degrees of confidence in private information and in communities' advices. On the other hand, the initial number of online communities has to be low enough to generate sufficient initial differentiation across communities and avoid negative informational cross-externalities.

- *Private opinion/community advice.* The quality of self-organization, in terms of sorting out individuals into homogeneous segments, depends on two factors: (i) the weighting between past private consumption experiences and information signals sent by the community; (ii) individuals' level of requirement towards communities, that is the way consumers' loyalty to a given community is positively or negatively affected by "good" or "bad" advices. Two results have been stressed (Curien et al. 2001). *Result 1*: consumers can efficiently self-organize in online communities only if their trust towards communitarian advices is neither too low nor too high. In the former case, it is not worth belonging to a community the advices of which are weakly taken into account. In the latter case, when online advices are not weighted enough with private experiences, a community generates very noisy information leading to mis-consumption. *Result 2*: the more demanding individuals are towards advices provided by online communities, the higher the quality of self-organization. In other words, the quality of self-organization is all the higher as individuals remain in a community only if they collect relevant information.

- *Initial number of communities.* This number has to be lower than a threshold value for two reasons. Firstly, the initial differentiation among online communities has to be high enough. Curien (2004) shows that a minimal differentiation among forums is necessary for a self-organization dynamics of migration across forums to occur. The lower the initial number of forums, the less stringent this condition is. Secondly, a low enough initial number of forums prevents individuals from flitting around from one forum to another, which generates a negative externality. Indeed, at each period consumers visit other forums than the one they mainly trust, thus collecting some parasite information that confuses advices received from their favorite forum. The intuition is that the more numerous forums are, the more an individual will continue to flit around, even if she has already found her favorite. Indeed, when the number of forums grows, their density rises. Consequently, individuals are closer to alternative forums and can expect therefore to find a forum fitting better to their preferences.

6.4   Discussion

6.4.1   Contribution issues

Actually, each of the two types of community (experience-sharing communities and user communities) has similar "static" properties. Yet in experience-sharing communities the relation between individual efforts and the collective outcome is rather from the "total effort" type (all the reviews posted may be useful for consumers) whereas it is rather from the "best shot" for user communities (only the "good" answer to a given request is useful). However, whether the relation between individual efforts and the collective outcome is of the "total effort" or "best shot" type, the prediction about contribution is the same. There should be few contributors and many free-riders in both communities if agents simultaneously choose whether to contribute or not. However, the contribution issue fits better with a dynamic setting.

As shown by Huberman and Glance (1993, 1994), the introduction of "conditional reciprocity" in the framework changes significantly the prediction. Indeed, the models we referred to in the previous section show that if expectations are "bandwagon", then there are two possible outcomes: total defection or total cooperation. If expectations are "opportunistic", there are two possible outcomes as well: total defection or a mixed equilibrium with cooperators and free-riders. We assert that, in experience-sharing communities, expectations are likely to be of the bandwagon type. Each review posted may motivate others to give their opinion as well, in particular if they disagree. In this case, the bandwagon effect may trigger waves of cooperation and make the structure converge towards an equilibrium of large cooperation rather than large defection. On the contrary, in user communities, expectations are likely to be opportunistic. Once a request is answered, the utility of another answer decreases drastically. Since users do share knowledge, once one of them has brought her knowledge to a requester, there is no need for another user to bring the same knowledge as well.[9] Therefore, opportunistic expectations are likely to reinforce the static pattern and result in the prediction that the structure shall converge to large defection rather than towards a mixed equilibrium.

Yet those hypothetical predictions are deeply affected by the incentives to contribute in each type of community. Hence, the interaction pattern among the agents shall in fact affect greatly the ability of aggregation of consumers to achieve either one of those outcomes as well as to achieve it repeatedly across products or requests. We predict that, due to the properties of their interaction pattern, experience-sharing communities may in fact experience great difficulties triggering a bandwagon process of large contributions. Cooperation is threatened by non-pairwise interactions and thus the fact that reciprocity can at best be indirect and general. In an experience-sharing community, nobody contributes to reward an especially active and identified contributor, since contribution is spontaneous rather than an answer to a specific request. Moreover, those difficulties might be reinforced by the fact that the information shared in experience-sharing communities is a pure public good that any agent can fully appropriate. An active contributor and a lurker benefit exactly the same way from a review on a book or a CD posted on Amazon. com. Finally, in experience-sharing communities, private incentives to contribute are low. Only recognition may constitute an incentive to contribute since nobody can expect a gain in reputation from contribution[10]

---

[9] We could argue that knowledge is not so straightforward that another informant would be useless, but we think it is a good approximation to say that by and large there would be a large part of redundancy.

[10] It should be noted, however, that in the music industry, labels often rely on "street teams" (groups of fans) to generate positive feedback on a new CD in online communities. Those contributors are compensated with prizes such as free tickets (Maizlyn, 2006).

or the benefit from a learning effect. Hence, the sustainability of experience-sharing communities strongly depends on the presence of a few sub-sets of pure contributors who are willing to contribute to a large extent.

On the contrary, user communities have an interaction pattern that makes such communities prone to the emergence of cooperation despite the likely opportunistic nature of the expectations. First, users can choose at some degree whom they answer to. The ability to favor pair-wise interactions undoubtedly increases the incentive to contribute. Even general reciprocity may be favored by the ability to track past interactions, and thus the possibility to rate an anonymous requester as a cooperative or a non-cooperative one. Moreover, the only partial appropriation of the full value of the information shared reinforces that pattern, by making lurking quite insignificant and useless. More often than not, requests posted by other agents do not fit all the problems encountered by the lurker with the product at stake. Finally, private incentives to contribute in user communities are greater than in experience-sharing communities. A gain in reputation and learning from the issues raised by requesters can indeed be an incentive for some contributors, especially in software user communities.

6.4.2   Trust issues

We assert that experience-sharing communities are likely to encounter more difficulties than user communities in establishing trust among members. As suggested above, the interaction pattern characterizing user communities fits better with the three conditions necessary for cooperation as identified by Axelrod (1984): (i) repeated interaction; (ii) non-anonymity; (iii) information on past behaviors of other members. Given direct interactions that prevail in user communities and reciprocation incentives, even if anonymity still partially reigns (users seldom provide their full identity), interactions are likely to be repeated and non-anonymous and a reputation system that would provide information on past behavior of members is often seen as unnecessary. By contrast, in experience-sharing communities, the indirect feature of interactions reduces the trust on advices received from other members, although reputation systems do exist in communities like Amazon.com. Furthermore, since in experience-sharing communities consumers seek to get informed in order to make a purchase, the risk of manipulation by manufacturers is high. As pointed out by Dellarocas (2004), manipulation through anonymously supplying promotional chat or reviews in order to influence the consumers' evaluation of products is quite widespread.[11] In user communities, manufacturers may be tempted to be involved in order to ensure current users' loyalty but information itself is less likely to be manipulated since it does not have a direct impact on sales.

As far as the consistency issue is concerned, user communities also seem less threatened. User communities are indeed spontaneously organized around a topic of common concern. Thus, members can reasonably consider that advices and comments received in the community are likely to come from individuals with similar preferences. Conversely, models presented in section 3 predict that experience-sharing communities shall have difficulties getting self-organized. Experience-sharing communities do not fulfill the main condition for self-organization: the ability to learn on the usefulness of other members' advices through repeated interactions. Therefore, we predict that experience-sharing communities shall be able to get somewhat organized only if a central authority does establish some organizational principles.

6.5   Conclusion

6.5.1   Main results

The ability of online consumer communities to survive amounts to escaping the tragedy of the digital commons by securing the provision of online content. This issue was greatly overlooked in the early years of the Internet when it was believed that individuals would spontaneously share information on a durable basis. Information, however, has some character of a public good and therefore may be subject to issues of incentives and organization as suggested for a long time in economic theory. In this chapter, we showed that a relevant framework to discuss the sustainability of online communities consists in referring to interaction patterns and then relating those patterns to the main issues of contribution and trust.

---

[11] Maizlin (2003) reports that in August 1999, teenagers who frequented online bulletin boards of the singer Britney Spears began to receive messages that recommended a new singer, namely Christina Aguilera. The authors communicated in a style shared by the other members of the communities, which made it difficult for Britney's fans to distinguish whether the messages they received came from other fans or from marketers. Indeed, most of these messages came from Electric Artists, a firm specialized in buzz marketing. In February 2004, Amazon.com mistakenly disclosed the real identities of some of its book reviewers. This software error revealed that a sizable proportion of those reviewers were the books' own publishers, authors or even competitors (Dellarocas, 2004).

Table 6.2. *Contribution and trust issues in experience-sharing and user communities*

	Experience-sharing communities	User communities
Relation between individual effort and collective outcome	Total effort → few contributors and many free-riders	Best shot → few contributors and many free-riders
	Bandwagon expectations → shall possibly trigger large cooperation and inverse the previous pattern	Opportunistic expectations → shall reinforce the previous pattern of large defection
Incentives to contribute	Interactions not pairwise and indirect reciprocation + low private incentives → low incentives to contribute → unfavorable to trigger cooperation in a dynamic setting	Pairwise interactions and direct reciprocations + high private incentives → high incentives to contribute → favorable to trigger cooperation (from reciprocal contributors) in a dynamic setting
Extent to which the good is prone to free-riding	Full appropriation of information shared possible without contributing → high expected benefit to lurking	Full appropriation of information shared impossible without contributing → low expected benefit to lurking
Trust (confidence)	Indirect and pre-purchase interactions → unfavorable to confidence building and raises the risk of manipulation by manufacturers	Direct and post-purchase interactions → favorable to confidence building and lowers the risk of information manipulation
Self-organization (coherence)	Non-spontaneous (requires learning from interacting) → coherence hard to get	Spontaneous → coherence easy to get

We argue that experience-sharing communities are likely to experience some difficulties in making cooperation emerge because of their unfavorable interaction pattern (not pairwise interactions, indirect reciprocation, low private incentives to contribute) described in Table 6.2. Yet experience-sharing communities may escape the tragedy of digital commons thanks to the presence of a few "pure contributors" willing to intensively contribute due to the private benefits (self-esteem especially) that they derive from participating in online communities. It is indeed what we observe, with most communities being characterized by a small number of people contributing most of the reviews. Hence, on Amazon. com, the most prolific contributor writes more than 4,500 reviews a year, and the 500th more than 150! In this context, lurkers are not a problem and can even be necessary to the amount of private benefits that pure contributors get. However, experience-sharing communities are also affected by confidence and consistency issues. Hence, the observation shows that most of the experience-sharing communities created by shopping sites have been evaluated by their sponsors as of low value and substituted for communities professionally managed, such as the Epinions community. The latter was established quite late compared with other experience-sharing communities but with a clear purpose: to create a high-quality community by establishing voluntary and centralized mechanisms to palliate the drawbacks of spontaneity. In this respect, Epinions has developed a system to identify the good reviewers and to remunerate them.

User communities, on the contrary, benefit from an interaction pattern favorable to online cooperation (see Table 6.2) that allows them to quite easily escape the tragedy of digital commons, the usual pattern of user communities likely being a core (or cores) of users repeatedly interacting among themselves. Conversely to what holds for experience-sharing communities, pure contributors are not essential to community sustainability[12] and user communities are probably more threatened by over-contribution than by under-contribution. Hence, in user communities, members may be prone to answer some requests, without having the required expertise to do so, in order to benefit from a "learning by answering" effect. In such a setting, those members are likely to generate negative externalities for the community. Spotting the relevant answer to a given request will indeed become more difficult. This suggests that it is not worth paying contributors for their participation in the community and may even be counter-productive.[13] User communities, moreover, are much less prone to confidence and consistency issues than experience-sharing communities because the reciprocal contributors are able to build trust quite easily. As a matter of fact, empirical observation shows that user communities seldom incorporate reputation mechanisms to evaluate the contributors (as opposed to experience-sharing communities, at least successful ones).

6.5.2   OCCs and market concentration

Up to now, customer information had to be disseminated through a centralized review and advice system (mass media system). In that

---

[12] However, by answering requests issued by non-reciprocal members, they allow the survival of pure askers.
[13] On this topic see Godefroy Dang-Nguyen and Thierry Pénard (2006).

top-down information model, also called the prescription model by Pierre-Jean Benghozi and Thomas Paris (2006), the producers have difficulty in controlling the quality produced and therefore try to focus consumers' attention on a small number of easily identifiable goods through advertising and promotion (this is the Star-system model). However, when tastes are widely differentiated, such a model becomes inefficient. A common wisdom (Gensollen 2006) is that the rise of online consumers communities transforms this top-down meta-market into a bottom-up one: online communities could allow a wider variety of products and, over time, a lower homogenization of tastes. We claim that this would-say advantage of experience-sharing communities is highly questionable and that online communities may rather reinforce market concentration instead of reducing it. The online word-of-mouth within OCCs is indeed able to generate through network externalities a higher market concentration online than offline. Moreover, the "winner-takes-all" effect could be reinforced by a "path dependency" one, the selected variety being not known *ex ante*. The relevance of this scenario has been theoretically shown by Curien et al. (2001) who suggest that online communities could generate a market dynamic closer to the prescription model characterizing traditional mass media than to the bottom-up model that could allow greater diversity in consumption. The empirical validation of this theoretical scenario is on our agenda of further research in the field of OCCs.[14]

---

[14] To our knowledge, no papers explicitly deal with the impact of online consumers communities on market concentration. However, some works on the impact of reviews in the competition between Amazon.com and Barnes&Noble.com suggest interesting research perspectives. Chevalier and Maizlyn (2006) point out that the relative market share of a book across the two sites is related to differences across the sites in terms of number of reviews for the book and average star ranking of those reviews.

7   Network cooperation and incentives within online communities

Godefroy Dang Nguyen and Thierry Pénard

7.1   Introduction

Since its origins, the Internet has always been perceived as a world-wide collaborative network of information sharing, facilitating the emergence of various forms of online gifts and cooperation (Kollock, 1999; Dang-Nguyen and Pénard, 2001). Hence many academic or scholarly communities, many non-profit organisations and many individual users are accustomed to releasing and sharing free informational content or providing free advice and assistance. The increasing development of electronic commerce (B2C or B2B) could have endangered online cooperation and informational "gifts" via the Internet. Surprisingly, this did not occur and the well publicised phenomenon of the peer-to-peer exchange of files is the best illustration of the online cooperation vitality. Peer-to-peer (P2P) is a technology based on the direct exchange of resources from computer to computer at the edges of the network. In 2003, the world-wide P2P exchange of audio files was estimated at 150 billion and the exchange of movie files at 1 billion.[1] More than 7 million Internet users are simultaneously connected on P2P networks (Kazaa, eMule, etc.) every day.

However, many people consider cooperation on the Internet as a puzzle: how can one explain the extent of cooperative behaviours within and outside online communities, given that Internet users are generally anonymous, distant and too numerous to rely on mutual trust and reciprocity? What are the incentives behind cooperating and sharing information content on the Internet?

The aim of this chapter is to analyse the properties and the rationale of online cooperation through a game-theoretic framework. We focus on sharing communities such as file-sharing communities or discussion forums. The ease of entering and leaving such communities hinders the replication of the same cooperation patterns as in "physical" communities in which members are constrained in their movements (switching

---

[1] *Source*: IDATE.

costs due to location, social pressure, etc.). In these *offline* communities, long-term reputation and reciprocity are generally strong drivers for cooperative behaviour (Axelrod, 1984). By contrast, Internet-sharing communities appear to be loose-knit and cannot easily self-enforce cooperation by long-term reputation mechanisms.

To explain the vitality of online cooperative behaviour in virtual communities, we propose a model closely related to Krishnan et al. (2004). They constructed a model of content sharing in a P2P network where the users are heterogeneous in the content they own. They showed that both free-riding (consuming without contributing content) and sharing (consuming and contributing) can be observed at the equilibrium. They underlined that sharing can occur in the absence of altruism, motivated by self-interest because sharing content serves to offload traffic in the P2P network and increases the likelihood of accessing desired content. They also showed that under symmetric costs of sharing, high-value contents are shared before lower-value contents, this result being reinforced in a dynamic context where contents are replicated and propagated within the network.

Our model differs slightly from that of Krishnan et al. (2004). Here we consider an online community in which peers have the opportunity to send requests or queries to other peers (for example a request to download a given audio file, a request for assistance or advice, etc.). In such a community, contributing involves sending requests but also treating requests from other peers, whereas free-riding involves refusing to answer queries from the other members. The originality of our model comes from the heterogeneity in the costs of contribution (some peers are more competent or efficient in treating the requests) and from the presence of a delay cost when the requests are not immediately treated.

Like Krishnan et al. (2004), we highlight that online cooperation is characterised at the equilibrium by the coexistence of heavy contributors and free-riders when users are heterogeneous in their cost of contribution. Thus the presence of intense free-riding is not always a sign of cooperation breakdown and can durably persist in sharing communities. However, the level of free-riding is higher than the socially optimal level. We also consider the impact of external incentives on free-riding behaviours, examining monetary incentives and priority mechanisms. These external incentives can be a remedy to the excess of free-riding since online communities generally have no means to filter entry or exclude members from the services.

The remainder of the chapter is organised as follows. In the next section, we give more evidence about cooperative behaviour on the Internet and review the possible explanations. Section 7.3 develops a theoretical model of P2P community. Propositions and implications are discussed in section 7.4. Conclusions are given in section 7.5.

7.2   Theory and evidence

7.2.1   Evidence of free-riding in online communities

In a community, individuals always have a common interest and are collectively better when all members decide to cooperate or coordinate their efforts. Curien et al. (2004) distinguish different types of communities: *epistemic communities* where members produce knowledge, such as in a community of open source software developers; *communities of practice* where members exchange expertise or information, like in a technical support forum; and *content-sharing communities* where members directly share resources, as in a P2P network. Beyond this classification, all these communities share a commonality: their output is a public good, subject to potential free-riding or opportunistic behaviour. Each member of a community has a temptation to cheat, by consuming without contributing, letting the other members incur the cost of providing the public good. In these conditions, how do members of online communities overcome free-riding and sustain stable cooperation? What are the motivations to contribute?

There can be different answers to these questions, depending on the type of online community. Epistemic communities are characterised by high barriers to entry and exit and by a high cost to contribute (requiring rare specific competencies or skills). As their size is rather limited, they can efficiently rely on more classical mechanisms of cooperation, based on bilateral or multilateral reputation. In these communities, members realise that they are repeatedly interacting with the same partners and can suffer from retaliation in case of cheating. Indeed, it is difficult or costly to escape punishment, since leaving an epistemic community involves losing one's reputation and the benefits connected with it. Moreover, the small number of partners enables the community to quickly determine who has "cheated", and to personalise punishments (for example by using "tit for tat" (Axelrod, 1984) or a stick and carrot punishment (Abreu, 1988)). The possibility of "retaliation" is a strong incentive for maintaining cooperation, and largely explains the stability of epistemic communities. The relationships between Internet operators, also called Internet service providers (ISPs), illustrates this logic of cooperation. These operators form a club where each member decides with whom it accepts to interconnect at exchange nodes. Cooperation is materialised by peering agreements where each ISP agrees to convey all the traffic addressed to its network for free, and receives revenues only from the fees paid by its own subscribers.[2] These agreements are often not formalised (not written) and rely on mutual trust. Open source communities provide other examples of cooperation based on a direct multilateral reputation mechanism. In many open source projects, the number of members is limited (members are coopted) and each developer has a strong incentive to contribute honestly to encourage the others to contribute on the ongoing and future projects but also to signal their ability to future employers (Lerner and Tirole, 2002). (For a further analysis of open source cooperation, see Chapter 13 in this book.)[3]

In the remainder of the chapter, we will focus on the other two communities, i.e. practice and sharing communities, in which members exchange advice, expertise, information or other resources. These virtual communities are characterised by low barriers to entry and to exit, a huge number of members and an affordable cost to contribute. In these large communities, multilateral retaliation mechanisms cannot be applied easily or are less efficient. Some of these communities can include millions of people from everywhere who agree to share certain resources (information, content, advice, etc.) even if they do not physically know their partners. Since the ease of entering and leaving a community gives *prima facie* strong incentives to "cheat", the existence and stability of these large Internet communities represents a theoretical puzzle. However, these communities actually seem to manage the large presence of free-riding well. For example, Adar and Huberman (2000) observed in August 2000 that on the Gnutella P2P network, two-thirds of users did not contribute at all (namely by refusing to have their files downloaded by other peers) whereas the top 1% of users provided 50% of contents. Similarly, Asvanund et al. (2004) found in September 2002 that 42% of Gnutella peers were free-riders. Moreover, peers are less likely to contribute resources to the network as the network size increases. Asvanund et al. (2004) provided evidence of congestion effects that can counterbalance positive network externality resulting from a larger P2P community. Peers would have a higher propensity to free-ride as the size of the group rises, confirming the intuition of Olson (1965).

Similarly, Resnick and Zeckhauser (2002) found that on eBay, the Internet auction leader, 40% of buyers refuse to release an evaluation about their partners (positive or negative). This attitude can be assimilated

---

[2] It is a "sender keeps all" scheme. The network originating the traffic keeps all the money paid by its customers to access other networks (see Bailey, 1997).

[3] See Johnson (2002) on the impact of community size on the efficiency of open source projects.

to free-riding since the evaluation of the dealing partner is a public good that helps other buyers in the eBay community in their future transactions, e.g. these evaluations enable buyers to build a reputation for each eBay seller (Houser and Wooders, 2006; Friedman and Resnick, 2001). Likewise, Dellarocas et al. (2004) observed rare coin auctions on eBay and found that 23% of sellers and 33% of buyers did not leave feedback.

In all these examples, free-riding seems to be a common dominant norm, but apparently without threatening or ruining the existence and the stability of Internet communities. In these circumstances, why do some members agree to contribute intensively to the functioning of these communities and to the provision of public goods such as distributing information?

7.2.2   The motivations for contributing

One reason often put forward is linked to the origins of the Internet: cooperation is supposedly rooted in the "academic" origin of the Internet. The essence of academic life is publication (publish or perish), making one's own discoveries available to the whole community of scientists. This tradition of releasing and sharing freely one's own production of information has been progressively adopted by non-academic newcomers on the Internet: the latter seem to have been contaminated and converted to the academic spirit of free sharing. Hence the stability of cooperative behaviour within Internet communities could be analysed as an *evolutionary stable strategy* that has the property to resist the invasion of mutant strategies, in particular strategies of free-riding (Maynard-Smith, 1982).

Altruism can also be a driver for sharing and contributing in a virtual community. For example, Gu and Jarvenpaa (2003) empirically showed that members of technical support forums are largely motivated by a "warm glow" effect (a pure utility derived from contributing and helping the other members).[4] In the context of eBay, the feedback provided by buyers may similarly be motivated by a feeling of belonging to a community that promotes courtesy, fairness and truthfulness, exemplified by the large proportion of positive evaluation (only 1% of non-positive evaluation!).[5] Dellarocas et al. (2004) found that self-interest is an important motivating force behind the high level of evaluations. Indeed, many

---

[4] Warm glow effects have largely been evidenced in real communities, in particular through donation (see Andreoni, 1989).

[5] However, for Gross and Acquisti (2003), this hides a fear of retaliation and some unbalances among eBay "peers". See also Miller et al. (2005).

traders first send feedback to elicit a reciprocal response (selfish motivation).[6] But they also demonstrate some altruistic motivations, when eBay members agree to unconditionally evaluate their partner (a "warm glow" effect). Dellarocas et al. (2004) concluded that the motivation to contribute to eBay's review system is multifaceted (ranging from self-interest and reciprocity to altruism).

Online cooperation can also be explained by the nature of contributions that involves providing informational content. It is often more expensive to protect one's own information or to keep it secret than to share it freely. An Internet user needs to exert a costly effort if she does not want to participate in the public provision of information. This contrasts with a classical public good setting where the user supports a cost only if she contributes. The relative cost of contributing or not is indeed an important element in explaining the extent of cooperation within online communities: contributors are generally characterised by a higher personal cost when they refuse to contribute than when they agree to contribute. This happens in open source communities or technical forums where many members find it more profitable to make their information available, because this fosters technical improvements and innovation.

Cooperation can also be explained by the technical architecture or design of online communities. For example, in many P2P networks, each peer (client) is a server/contributor by default. When a peer downloads a file on a PC, this file becomes automatically available for uploading by other peers except if she explicitly forbids this. Hence being a free-rider (retrieving and hiding the downloaded files) requires certain technical competencies and can be time-consuming.

To summarise our discussion so far, cooperation tends to emerge and persist in large and loose-knit communities in which individuals are anonymous and do not have bilateral repeated relations, despite high levels of free-riding. In the following section, we propose a game-theoretic model to analyse more rigorously the dynamics of online cooperation.

7.3   A model of peer-to-peer cooperation

The model considers a community of Internet users or peers who are loosely linked by a common interest: for example, it can be a peer-to-peer community exchanging music files (Kazaa), or a community of software users exchanging programs and assistance, or a thematic community

---

[6] They find that the probability of contributing decreases if the partner has not yet released her evaluation.

exchanging ideas and opinions. Belonging to a community allows members to send requests or queries to the other members, expecting that some of them will respond. This can be a request for a music file, for assistance, or for advice. In this model, the online community is narrowly defined as an electronic network permitting the exchange of requests. An Internet user belongs to the community as long as she continues sending requests.

Technically, the transmission of a query or request can be either decentralised or centralised. In the latter case, all requests are sent to a server or a coordinator in charge of soliciting the different peers and finding those who will agree to treat the request. In a decentralised design, the sender solicits community members directly, either simultaneously or sequentially. The main advantage of a centralised network is efficiency in the processing of requests but the main drawback is vulnerability (in case of the shutdown of the central server, e.g. Napster). Thus a decentralised network (e.g. Kazaa, Morpheus, Gnutella) is more suited to large communities and can be a response to threats of prosecution, even if it demands much more of the community members (Gu and Jarvenpaa, 2003; Asvanund et al., 2003).[7]

Here we consider a decentralised community without making explicit the mechanism of request transmission. When members are solicited, they can either agree or refuse to process a request. Thus two types of members can emerge in a community: the contributors who send requests but also respond to some requests and non-contributors who content themselves with sending requests without treating the requests of other members.

Can the presence of many free-riders destabilise cooperation inside a virtual community? Our model makes it possible to understand how online cooperation can be sustainable when a large proportion of members never want to contribute to the provision of community services (by releasing and transmitting contents or files, or by answering requests). Let us now detail the assumptions of the model.

---

[7] For example, in recent P2P networks, the catalogue of contents is distributed among several peers who agree to be local servers. The users log in to one of these ultra-peers to submit their requests. Then the ultra-peers collect the list of contents of all connected peers who agree to share part of their resources. On the basis of this catalogue, the ultra-peer may answer or satisfy the request. If not, the latter transmits the requests to the other ultra-peers with whom she is connected. This is a hybrid solution between full centralisation and full decentralisation, relatively efficient and secure, which is assumed to reduce free-riding and improve performance. See Krishnan et al. (2003) for a more detailed presentation of P2P architectures with their advantages and weaknesses.

7.3.1   Assumptions

We assume that members incur a cost when they decide to contribute. This cost can correspond to the effort and time required to treat requests or to transmit the answer (files, information) to the other members of the community.[8] A key assumption is that peers face different costs. In other terms, they are heterogeneous in competencies or ability to treat requests. For example, if they experience a different quality of Internet access, it is likely that those who have a broadband connection will face lower costs in responding to requests.[9] We can also expect the more educated members to have better skills (and lower cost) to treat requests.

Let us assume that the individual costs are distributed between $[\underline{c}, \bar{c}]$, according to a density function f and a cumulative function F. A peer's decision to contribute or free-ride will straightforwardly depend on her cost. Indeed, the peer faces the following trade-off. Free-riding allows one to save the cost of participation, but it degrades the quality of community services by increasing the likelihood of congestion in the treatment of requests. So contributing can be a better strategy if the cost of participating is more than counterbalanced by the increasing quality of services provided by the community. By agreeing to treat requests, a peer knows that she is contributing to reducing congestion and aug-menting the probability of her own requests being treated rapidly.

If all members having a cost lower than $\hat{c} \in [\underline{c}, \bar{c}]$ agree to contribute, then the proportion of contributors will be $F(\hat{c}) = \int_{\underline{c}}^{\hat{c}} f(c)dc = \int_{\underline{c}}^{\hat{c}} dF(c)$.

We assume that peers send the same number of requests, this number being normalised to one by convenience. Moreover, N is the volume of requests sent simultaneously per period. We can interpret N as the intensity of community activity or the capacity of request transmission in the network. Obviously, N is positively linked with the size of the community (the number of peers).

Let $\alpha(\hat{c}, N)$ denote the probability that a request is instantaneously treated. We make the following assumptions on $\alpha(\hat{c}, N)$: i) $\alpha_{\hat{c}}(\hat{c}, N) > 0$, ii) $\alpha_{\hat{c}\hat{c}}(\hat{c}, N) < 0$, iii) $\alpha_N(\hat{c}, N) < 0$, iv) $\alpha_{NN}(\hat{c}, N) > 0$, v) $\alpha_{\hat{c}N}(\hat{c}, N) < 0$.

---

[8] The decision to contribute is binary. See Curien et al. (2004) for a model where peers can select the intensity of their contribution.

[9] Indeed, treating the requests implies a reduction of resources for other activities, and in particular a reduction of the contributor's bandwidth for other applications. Feldman et al. (2003) underlined the actual disincentive effects due to the symmetric treatment of uploading and downloading in P2P networks because the download latency is dominated by the sender's outgoing bandwidth: her computer link is often burdened by the provi-sion of service to peers at the expense of the fulfilment of her own requests.

The probability of request treatment is an increasing and concave function of $\hat{c}$. The higher the proportion of contributors inside the community, the more rapid the treatment of requests. But the positive effect of an additional contributor tends to diminish with the number of contributors and with the volume of requests (or the size of the community). Moreover, $\alpha(\hat{c}, N)$ is decreasing and convex in N: a larger community contributes to degrading the quality of request treatment, by reinforcing the risk of congestion. When the number of peers increases as well as the volume of requests, contributors are solicited much more and cannot satisfy all requests; consequently, the treatment is more likely to be delayed. Finally, let us assume that $\alpha(\underline{c}, N) = 0$ (in the absence of contribution, the online community is fully congested).

We also denote u as the utility for a member to send a request and to obtain immediately an answer or assistance. Facing a delay in the treatment of her request induces a disutility for the sender. Indeed, the utility of a request treated t periods after its transmission is $\delta^t u$, where δ is the discount factor (common to all members of the community).

When a request fails to be treated in the initial period, this request is resubmitted until it receives an answer. Thus sending a request yields an expected utility G defined by:

$$G = \alpha(\hat{c}, N)u + (1 - \alpha(\hat{c}, N))\delta G$$

After rearrangement, we obtain:

$$G = \frac{\alpha(\hat{c}, N)u}{1 - \delta + \delta\alpha(\hat{c}, N)}$$

G represents the expected benefit of belonging to a community (and of sending a volume of requests normalised to one) where a proportion $F(\hat{c})$ of peers actively contributes. G is increasing and concave in $\hat{c}$ (i.e. in the number of contributors).[10] This benefit also rises with the discount factor of the peer (her preference for the future). In the following proposition, we characterise the peers' equilibrium strategies in this virtual community.

---

[10] We have

$$G_{\hat{c}} = \frac{(1 - \delta)\alpha_{\hat{c}}u}{(1 - \delta + \delta\alpha)^2} > 0$$

and

$$G_{\hat{c}\hat{c}} = \frac{(1 - \delta)[\alpha_{\hat{c}\hat{c}}(1 - \delta + \delta\alpha)u - 2\delta(\alpha_{\hat{c}})^2]}{(1 - \delta + \delta\alpha)^3} < 0.$$

Proposition 1: Equilibrium conditions for online cooperation.
If

$$\underline{c} > \frac{(1-\delta)\alpha_{\hat{c}}\left(\underline{c}, N\right)u}{\left(1 - \delta + \delta\alpha(\underline{c}, N)\right)^{2}},$$

then all peers refuse to cooperate (no community)
If

$$\bar{c} < \frac{(1-\delta)\alpha_{\hat{c}}\left(\bar{c}, N\right)u}{\left(1 - \delta + \delta\alpha(\bar{c}, N)\right)^{2}},$$

then all peers contribute (no free-riding)
Otherwise there exists a $\hat{c} \in [\underline{c}, \bar{c}]$ defined by

$$\hat{c} = \frac{(1-\delta)\alpha_{\hat{c}}\left(\hat{c}, N\right)u}{\left(1 - \delta + \delta\alpha(\hat{c}, N)\right)^{2}}$$

such that a proportion $F(\hat{c})$ of contributors and a proportion $(1 - F(\hat{c}))$ of free-riders coexist in the same community.

Proof

A peer will agree to contribute if her cost of effort is inferior to her marginal gain. If $\underline{c} > \frac{(1-\delta)\alpha_{\hat{c}}(\underline{c},N)u}{(1-\delta+\delta\alpha)^{2}}$, then the most competent peer has no incentive to contribute and consequently this is the case for all the other less competent peers.

Now let us consider that $\underline{c} \leq \frac{(1-\delta)\alpha_{\hat{c}}(\underline{c},N)u}{(1-\delta+\delta\alpha)^{2}}$. Thus there exists at least one peer who agrees to contribute. Consider that there exists a peer with a cost $\hat{c}$ such that she is perfectly indifferent between accepting and refusing to treat requests, given that all the more competent peers are contributors. For this marginal peer, her additional gain from contributing $\frac{(1-\delta)\alpha_{\hat{c}}(\hat{c},N)u}{(1-\delta+\delta\alpha(\hat{c},N))^{2}}$ should be perfectly equal to her additional cost ($\hat{c}$). Then it can be recursively shown that any peer having a lower cost than $\hat{c}$ also has an incentive to contribute (because she knows that by refusing she will encourage all peers having a higher cost than herself to refuse). However, if $\bar{c} < \frac{(1-\delta)\alpha_{\hat{c}}(\bar{c},N)u}{(1-\delta+\delta\alpha(\bar{c},N))^{2}}$, even the less competent peer wants to contribute and there is no free-riding inside the community.

Proposition 1 underlines that inside the community the contributors are always the more competent or efficient peers. This result is similar to that of Krishnan et al. (2004), who showed that the contributors are the owners of the highest value contents. Hence, if members are widely heterogeneous ($\underline{c}$ sufficiently low and $\bar{c}$ sufficiently high), the community will be characterised by partial cooperation. The more competent members (those who have a cost below $\hat{c}$) will agree to contribute whereas the other members are mere consumers of community services.

So the presence of free-riders is not incompatible with a cooperative community. It may be in the interest of highly skilled members to continue contributing and maintaining the community activity because they are aware that they will be indirectly penalised if they stop treating the requests of their peers (meeting more congestion for their own requests). However, if the members of the community have a strong preference for the present $(\delta < 1 - \frac{\alpha_{\hat{c}}(\underline{c},N)}{\underline{c}} u)$, then no one will agree to contribute: in this case, no sustainable cooperation will emerge from this community. Online cooperation will be feasible only if members are sufficiently patient (high preference for the future).

7.3.2   The impact of community size

The world-wide expansion of the Internet has deeply impacted the functioning and activities of online communities. Most of them have welcomed many newcomers from all over the world and have dramatically grown (some Internet communities can bring together several million users). Does the boom in Internet communities represent a threat or an opportunity for them? We can expect that new members will be more free-riders due to their lack of competence or expertise. But it is also possible that the arrival of new members may incite some current free-riding members to contribute and counterbalance the negative effect of increasing request activity generated by newcomers. So it is debatable whether a larger community size may destabilise or reinforce cooperation.

By differentiating $\hat{c} = \frac{(1-\delta)\alpha_{\hat{c}}(\hat{c},N)u}{(1-\delta+\delta\alpha(\hat{c},N))^2}$, we obtain:

$$\frac{d\hat{c}}{dN} = \frac{-2(1 - \delta + \delta\alpha)\delta\hat{c}\alpha_N + (1 - \delta)\alpha_{\hat{c}N}u}{(1 - \delta + \delta\alpha)^2 + 2(1 - \delta + \delta\alpha)\delta\hat{c}\alpha_{\hat{c}} - (1 - \delta)\alpha_{\hat{c}\hat{c}}u}$$

The sign of the denominator is always positive, but the sign of the numerator is undetermined. A larger community can create new incentives to contribute and may increase the proportion of contributors if $2(1 - \delta + \delta\alpha)\delta\hat{c}\alpha_N < (1 - \delta)\alpha_{\hat{c}N}u$. This condition is likely to be satisfied if the risk of congestion is high (α_N high in absolute value) or if members have a strong preference for the future (δ high[11]).

---

[11] For $\delta=1$, the condition becomes $2\alpha\hat{c}\alpha_N < 0$ and is always true.

Proposition 2: An enlargement of the online community may reinforce cooperation if peers are sufficiently patient.

An increase in the size of the community (or in its activity) does not systematically threaten the stability of the community. As the risk of congestion becomes higher, some free-riders may realise that their efforts could be determinant to maintain cooperation and may decide to join the club of contributors.

7.3.3   The optimal level of cooperation

Does a decentralised online cooperation lead to an optimal level of contribution and request treatment? Are there too many or too few contributors? To address this question, we have to find the level of cooperation that maximises the collective surplus of the online community. This optimal level $\tilde{c}$ is given by:

$$Max_{\{\tilde{c}\}}\left(\frac{\alpha(\tilde{c},N)u}{1 - \delta + \alpha(\tilde{c},N)\delta} \int_{\underline{c}}^{\tilde{c}} f(c)dc - \int_{\underline{c}}^{\tilde{c}} cf(c)dc \right)$$

We notice that costs are supported by the contributors only $[\underline{c}, \tilde{c}]$ whereas gains $G(\tilde{c})$ are equally shared among all peers $[\underline{c}, \overline{c}]$. Thus $\tilde{c}$ is defined by:

$$\tilde{c}f(\tilde{c}) = \frac{(1 - \delta)\alpha_{\tilde{c}}(\tilde{c},N)u}{\left(1 - \delta + \delta\alpha_{\tilde{c}}(\tilde{c},N)\right)^2} \int_{\underline{c}}^{\tilde{c}} f(c)dc$$

The right-hand side stands for the marginal collective benefit if peers having a cost $\tilde{c}$ decide to actively contribute to the functioning of the activity, and the left-hand side shows the collective cost the type $\tilde{c}$ incurs.

Proposition 3: Decentralised online cooperation always induces an excess of free-riding when the community is heterogeneous.

    Proof

Since $\dfrac{f(\hat{c})}{\int_{\underline{c}}^{\overline{c}} f(c)dc} < 1$, then $\hat{c}\dfrac{f(\hat{c})}{\int_{\underline{c}}^{\overline{c}} f(c)dc} = \dfrac{(1 - \delta)\alpha_{\tilde{c}}(\tilde{c},N)u}{(1 - \delta + \delta\alpha_{\tilde{c}}(\tilde{c},N))^2} < \tilde{c}$ (i.e. $G_{c}(\tilde{c}) < \tilde{c}$).

Since $G_{c}(\hat{c}) = \hat{c}$ and $G_{cc} < 0$, then $\tilde{c} > \hat{c}$.

Note that optimal online cooperation does not imply a full participation (except if $\overline{c}\dfrac{f(\overline{c})}{\int_{\underline{c}}^{\overline{c}} f(c)dc} < \dfrac{(1 - \delta)\alpha_{\tilde{c}}(\overline{c},N)u}{(1 - \delta + \delta\alpha_{\tilde{c}}(\overline{c},N))^2})$ but the coexistence of contributors and free-riders. It may be sub-optimal to force all peers to contribute, especially the less competent (since the quality of their contribution is low).

The stake for an online community is to maintain and if possible strengthen cooperation in a context of membership growth, where screening of newcomers is difficult to implement. In the next section, we will consider different incentive designs that have already been experimented in online communities or have been debated.

7.4   How to stimulate online cooperation

There exists recent interdisciplinary literature that examines the means to reduce free-riding in P2P networks and online communities. What kind of incentives should members receive to be incited to provide resources, content or efforts? Some authors have proposed micropayment mechanisms (Golle et al., 2001), reputation systems (Tung et al., 2003), admission control systems (Kung and Wu, 2003) or priority systems (Krishnan et al., 2004). However, these systems generally rely on centralised administration and cannot be easily implemented in most online communities (based on a decentralised architecture). Nevertheless, it is worthwhile trying to understand how such systems could improve cooperation in our setting of a decentralised community.

We examine two cooperation-fostering mechanisms: first, the introduction of monetary incentives and second, the use of priorities for request treatment. Can these two mechanisms improve the performance of the community, enhance the matching and routing of requests and reduce the level of free-riding?

7.4.1   Monetary incentives

Let us consider that each non-contributor has to pay p to participate in the community and that the collected monetary sum is equally shared amongst contributors. Then each contributor receives $(\frac{1-F(\hat{c})}{F(\hat{c})})p$ where $F(\hat{c})$ is the proportion of a contributor.

Monetary incentives impact the trade-off between free-riding and cooperating. The level of cooperation is now determined by the following condition:

$$\hat{c}_p = \frac{(1-\delta)\alpha_{\hat{c}}(\hat{c}_p, N)u}{\left(1 - \delta + \delta\alpha(\hat{c}_p, N)\right)^2} + \left(\frac{1 - F(\hat{c}_p)}{F(\hat{c}_p)}\right)p$$

where $\hat{c}_p$ is the peer indifferent between contributing and free-riding.

A higher payment p leads to a larger proportion of contributors in the online community. However, monetary incentives have decreasing returns. Indeed, when p increases, then the proportion of contributors rises and tends to 100%, reducing the share claimed by each contributor.

Therefore there exists fees $\bar{p}$ such that $\hat{c}_{\bar{p}} = \bar{c}$. Hence fees rising above $\bar{p}$ create no more incentives inside the community.[12]

It is important to bear in mind that most online communities are decentralised and cannot technically or practically control access and exclude members. So membership fees are hard to enforce. Fees must be voluntary in an anonymous community. Obviously things would be different in a centralised community, sponsored and managed by either a non-profit or for-profit organisation (for example eBay, Amazon or Yahoo!).

Let us consider the incentives of non-contributors to voluntarily remunerate the contributors. The expected benefits of this voluntary transfer outweigh the cost when

$$\frac{\alpha(\hat{c}_p, N)u}{1 - \delta + \delta\alpha(\hat{c}_p, N)} - \frac{\alpha(\hat{c}_0, N)u}{1 - \delta + \delta\alpha(\hat{c}_0, N)} x > p$$

Proposition 4: If $\hat{c}_0 \geq 1/\frac{d\hat{c}_p}{dp}$, then a voluntary payment mechanism can be feasible even in a decentralised community.

Proof

The problem can be reformulated as follows. The benefit for a free-rider is defined by:

$$B(p) = \frac{\alpha(\hat{c}_p, N)u}{1 - \delta + \delta\alpha(\hat{c}_p, N)} - p$$

By differentiating with respect to p, we have:

$$\frac{\partial B(p)}{\partial p} = \left(\frac{(1 - \delta)\alpha_{\hat{c}}(\hat{c}_p, N)u}{\left(1 - \delta + \delta\alpha(\hat{c}_p, N)\right)^2} \right) \frac{d\hat{c}_p}{dp} - 1$$

As

$$\hat{c}_p = \frac{(1 - \delta)\alpha_{\hat{c}}(\hat{c}_p, N)u}{\left(1 - \delta + \delta\alpha(\hat{c}_p, N)\right)^2} + \left(\frac{1 - F(\hat{c}_p)}{F(\hat{c}_p)} \right) p$$

[12] In other terms, the differential in the marginal benefits of contributing with and without monetary incentives decreases and tends to zero as p becomes larger.

then

$$\frac{\partial B(p)}{\partial p} = \frac{d\hat{c}_p}{dp} \left(\hat{c}_p - \frac{1 - F(\hat{c}_p)}{F(\hat{c}_p)} p \right) - 1$$

At the neighbourhood of $p = 0$,

$$\left. \frac{\partial B(p)}{\partial p} \right|_{p=0} = \hat{c}_0 \frac{d\hat{c}_p}{dp} - 1$$

If

$$\hat{c}_0 < 1 \left/ \frac{d\hat{c}_p}{dp} \right., \text{ then } \left. \frac{\partial B(p)}{\partial p} \right|_{p=0} < 0$$

and non-contributors will refuse to voluntarily pay to send their requests.

A voluntary payment is more likely to exist if the proportion of free-riders is sufficiently low (if $1 - F(\hat{c}_0)$ is low or equivalently if $\hat{c}_0$ is high), but if there are too many free-riders, the benefit of monetary incentives does not counterbalance the cost.

Note that this proposition is useful to help understand why many communities are based on free interactions, without monetary compensation. For example, the community of Internet carriers is characterised by a predominance of peering agreements where each carrier keeps all the revenues from its customers and exchanges traffic with its peers without monetary compensation.

7.4.2   A priority system

Another mechanism to promote cooperation is to put priorities on the requests of contributors to encourage participation. Such a mechanism is examined by Krishnan et al. (2004). According to them, differentiating the quality of services provided to contributors and non-contributors could improve P2P network performance and can be easily implemented even in a decentralised environment. Indeed, Kazaa has developed a priority-like system where depending on the past behaviour of the peer, her requests will be treated as a priority or be delayed. Each peer has a kind of score related to the number of files she is currently offering to other peers and the number of files (requests) that have been downloaded on her own computer.

Let $q\alpha$ denote the probability of being served when the peer is a contributor ($q > 1$), and α the probability of obtaining a response when she is a free-rider. Here we implicitly assume that peers can distinguish between requests sent by a contributor and from a free-rider. Then the expected utility of a request sent by a contributor in an online community is defined by:

$$G = q\alpha(\hat{c}, N)u + (1 - q\alpha(\hat{c}, N))\delta G$$

meaning that for a contributor the expected utility is

$$G^c = \frac{q\alpha(\hat{c}, N)u}{1 - \delta + \delta q\alpha(\hat{c}, N)}$$

whereas for the non-contributor it is

$$G^{nc} = \frac{\alpha(\hat{c}, N)u}{1 - \delta + \delta\alpha(\hat{c}, N)}.$$

The marginal contributor is now determined by:

$$\hat{c}_q = \frac{(1 - \delta)q\alpha_{\hat{c}}u}{(1 - \delta + \delta q\alpha)^2} + \left(\frac{q\alpha u}{(1 - \delta + \delta q\alpha)} - \frac{\alpha u}{(1 - \delta + \delta\alpha)} \right)$$

The first term on the right-hand side corresponds to the marginal benefit of decreasing congestion and the second term the benefit with a right of priority.

The equilibrium level of contribution is higher with a priority system, as the incentives to contribute are reinforced: direct incentives through the priority label and indirect incentives through the reduction of congestion. We can observe that $\hat{c}_q$ is an increasing function in q (that measures the extent of priority).

However, in reality this system can have limited efficiency if free-riders can easily modify their profile and take on the appearance of a contributor. A network like Kazaa has faced this problem where some users have managed to replace their free-rider profile or score with a contributor's profile.

7.4.3   Taxation as a means to destabilise online communities

The taxation of upload flows on the Internet is strongly supported by music companies like Universal Music that are complaining about piracy and P2P networks that may be responsible for the drop in record sales. Several empirical studies have attempted to measure the impact of P2P on music sales. Most of them conclude the existence of a significant negative effect, but that only partially explains the CD sales decline these last few years (Peitz and Waelbroeck, 2004; Molteni and Ordanini, 2003; Boorstin, 2004; Hui and Png, 2003; Liebowitz, 2003; Oberholzer and Strumpf, 2004). Nevertheless music companies see taxation as a means to destabilise P2P communities by making active contribution more costly. Indeed, a tax would penalise those who agree to let their files be downloadable. Our framework enables us to understand the rationale of this taxation for record companies. Now the level of cooperation is defined by $\hat{c}_t$ where t stands for the tax applied to contributors:

$$\hat{c}_t + t = \frac{(1 - \delta)\alpha_\varepsilon(\hat{c}_t, N)u}{\left(1 - \delta + \delta\alpha(\hat{c}_t, N)\right)^2}$$

We can note that the threshold level of participation is decreasing in the tax t. If the goal of the record companies is to fully deter online cooperation on P2P networks, they should plead for a minimum tax $\underline{t}$ such that

$$\underline{c} + \underline{t} > \frac{(1 - \delta)\alpha_\varepsilon(\underline{c}, N)u}{(1 - \delta)^2}.$$

With a sufficiently large tax, all members of the community will refuse to contribute or to release content, files, information, etc.

7.5   Conclusion

This chapter has provided a survey of the recent economic literature on P2P systems, as well as a theoretical framework which has enabled us to give insights into issues which have been discussed in the literature. While many authors stress the point that the persistence of communities is a puzzle, given the large amount of free-riding which permeates them, we claim that a selfish attitude is perfectly consistent with cooperation because in such communities there exist heavy contributors. The large amount of free-riding is explained in our model by heterogeneity among community members. The main results provided are that monetary incentives may not be the proper way to reduce free-riding in these P2P networks, while prioritisation may be better suited in some cases. Thus, integrating the user's self-interest to cooperate in the design of computer networks is crucial. In Internet communities, free-riding problems can be more easily tackled by a technical response than in real communities (Schneidman and Parkes, 2003).

Part III

Network externalities and market microstructures

8 The Internet and network economics

Nicholas Economides

8.1 Introduction: the Internet and network economics

The Internet is the most important new network of the last part of the 20th century. As a global network of interconnected networks that connect computers, the Internet allows data transfers as well as the provision of a variety of interactive real-time and time-delayed telecommunications services. Originally developed through grants by the US Department of Defense (DOD) to connect disparate computers of its research division and its various contractors, the Internet served the academic community for over a decade before reaching the wide public in the mid-1990s. Internet communication is based on common and public protocols. Presently, hundreds of millions of computers are connected to the Internet.

The Internet exemplifies to the utmost "network effects", that is the fact that the value of a connection to a network increases with the size of the network. The Internet was not the first or last of electronic networks, but it is definitely the largest on earth in terms of hosts (computers) connected to it, content stored in them, and bits of traffic traversing it every day. Many electronic networks pre-dated the Internet, some with very sophisticated protocols compared with the Internet. But the strength of the Internet in terms of size and simplicity of its basic protocols forced pre-existing proprietary networks such as AOL, Prodigy, AT&TMail, and MCIMail to conform to the open standards of the Internet and become part of it. Competition in the provision of services is vigorous on the Internet.[1]

This chapter revives a paper originally published in the *IJIO*, "The Economics of Networks",[2] which was written in 1996 when the Internet was just reaching out to the mass market. A number of applications

---

[1] For a comprehensive discussion of competition issues on the Internet backbone, see Economides (2005a).

[2] Economides "The Economics of Networks", *International Journal of Industrial Organization*, vol. 14, no. 6, pp. 673–699 (October 1996).

benefiting from network effects mushroomed after that and were wildly successful "killer applications" on the Internet, including electronic mail, file transfers (Napster), interactive search, and interactive advertising. Telephone calls over the Internet, commonly called "Voice Over Internet Protocol" or VOIP, technically feasible for a number of years, are becoming a significant force in telecommunications and may, in the long run, become a "killer application".[3] VOIP converts voice calls to data and takes advantage of the very low cost of transmitting data over the Internet.[4]

Below we discuss in some detail the consequences of network effects for market structure in network industries, as well as the private incentives of each firm to deviate from common standards and make its product incompatible with those of competitors. In the extreme case, in telecommunications, incompatibility would mean refusal to interconnect. In the history of telecommunications, we have seen significant cases where a dominant firm refused to interconnect with others. From the expiration of its original patent before the turn of the 19th century until it was regulated in the 1930s and interconnection became mandatory, AT&T, leveraging its long-distance bottleneck position, refused to interconnect with independent telephone companies. This led to the absurd but then common situation of a customer having two different phones, each connected to a separate telephone network.

Even when each competitor potentially has its own bottleneck, as in the case of unique subscribers who need to be reached over the network by others, it can be shown that foreclosure of rivals can occur. In a local telecommunications network, if cost-based reciprocal compensation were not the rule, and networks were able to set prices for terminating calls at profit-maximizing levels, Economides, Lopomo, and Woroch (1996a,b) have shown that a large network will try to impose very high termination charges on an opponent's small network so that no

---

[3] In the United States, the growth of VOIP was significantly helped by the fact that, by the middle of 2004, the main alternative way (other than through the incumbent local exchange carrier) to traverse the "last mile" to reach residential customers (which was through leasing of parts of the incumbent's local network at cost-based prices) was practically eliminated as incumbents were allowed to charge commercial rates from such leases. See Economides (2005b), "Telecommunications Regulation: An Introduction", at http://www.stern.nyu.edu/networks/Economides_Telecommunications_Regulation.pdf. In many other parts of the world, VOIP has grown significantly as an alternative to extremely high long-distance, international, and interconnection rates.

[4] VOIP works best in a broadband connection. A significant limitation to wide adoption of VOIP in the United States is the fact that incumbent local exchange carriers typically do not allow access to a DSL loop unless they also provide voice service on the same line. Thus, most customers are unable to get their first line through VOIP.

calls terminate from the small network to the large one. Without the possibility of such across-networks calls, a small network will be able to provide only within-network calls and, being small, will be of little value to potential subscribers. As a consequence, large networks are able to offer subscribers more value and the small network is foreclosed. Starting from a regime of a large local incumbent and a small potential entrant, the large incumbent can set up termination access fees so that the entrant is kept out of the market.[5]

In the context of these historical examples of using bottlenecks to leverage market power and foreclose rivals, the Internet stands out as an example that breaks the rules. On the Internet, compatibility is the rule, pricing is independent of distance or direction of origination and does not even depend on the number, duration, and type of transactions – pricing depends only on the total bandwidth capacity bought. This feat is even more profound given the fact that the Internet is the least regulated part of the telecommunications world today. The success of competition on the Internet backbone is based on the public nature of Internet protocols, ease of entry, very fast network expansion, connections by the same Internet service provider (ISP) to multiple backbones (ISP multi-homing), and connections by the same large web site to multiple ISPs (customer multi-homing) that enhance price competition and make it very unlikely that any firm providing Internet backbone connectivity would find it profitable to degrade or sever interconnection with other backbones in an attempt to monopolize the Internet backbone.

On the "last mile" of the Internet, that is in reaching from the backbone to the customer's location, there is much less competition than on the backbone. There are two main avenues of residential broadband access, through "cable modems" that attach the cable TV wire and through digital subscriber lines (DSL) that use the higher frequencies of copper wire lines. Unfortunately, the United States lags behind countries like South Korea in broadband penetration. Wireless alternatives

---

[5] See Economides, Lopomo, and Woroch (1996a), "Regulatory Pricing Policies to Neutralize Network Dominance", *Industrial and Corporate Change*, vol. 5, no. 4, pp. 1013–1028, pre-publication copy at http://www.stern.nyu.edu/networks/96-14.pdf, and Economides, Lopomo, and Woroch (1996b), "Strategic Commitments and the Principle of Reciprocity in Interconnection Pricing", Discussion Paper EC-96-13, Stern School of Business, at http://www.stern.nyu.edu/networks/96-13.pdf. Note that this is not just a theoretical possibility. Telecom New Zealand (TNZ), operating in an environment of weak antitrust and regulatory intervention (so-called "light-handed regulation"), offered such high termination fees that the first entrant into local telecommunications, Clear, survives only by refusing to pay interconnection fees to TNZ, while the second entrant, BellSouth New Zealand, exited the local telecommunications market.

exist but presently are very expensive if done through traditional cellular carriers or very limited in geographic coverage if done through municipal WiFi networks. In such a context, our seminal work on the "Economics of Networks", presented below from section 2 to 7, examines the consequences of network effects for market structure and the various ways in which companies may attempt to take advantage of network effects by creating or leveraging bottlenecks.

8.2   Classification of networks[6]

Network industries play a crucial role in modern life. The modern economy would be very much diminished without the transportation, communications, information, and railroad networks. This chapter will analyze the major economic features of networks. In the course of the analysis it will become clear that many important non-network industries share many essential economic features with network industries. These non-network industries are characterized by strong complementary relations. Thus, the lessons of networks can be applied to industries where vertical relations play a crucial role; conversely, the economic and legal learning developed in the analysis of vertically related industries can be applied to network industries.

Formally, networks are composed of links that connect nodes. It is inherent in the structure of a network that many components of a network are required for the provision of a typical service. Thus, network components are complementary to each other. Figure 8.1 represents the emerging *information superhighway* network. Clearly, services demanded by consumers are composed of many complementary components. For example, interactive ordering while browsing in a "department store" as it appears in successive video frames requires a number of components: a database engine at the service provider, transmission of signals, decoding through an interface, display on a TV or computer monitor, etc. Clearly, there are close substitutes for each of these components; for example, transmission can be done through a cable TV line, a fixed telephone line, a wireless satellite, public cable network (PCN), etc.; the in-home interface may be a TV-top box or an add-on to a PC, etc. It is likely that the combinations of various components will not result in identical services. Thus, the information superhighway will provide substitutes made of complements – this is a typical feature of networks.

---

[6] The literature on networks is so extensive that it is futile to attempt to cover it. This contribution discusses only some issues that arise in networks and attempts to point out areas in which further research is necessary.

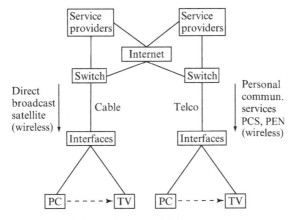

Figure 8.1. An information superhighway.

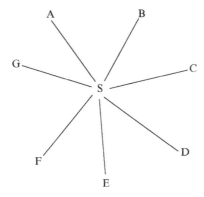

Figure 8.2. A simple star network.

Figure 8.2 shows this feature in a simple star telephone network. A phone call from A to B is composed of AS (access to the switch of customer A), BS (access to the switch of customer B), and switching services at S. Despite the fact that goods AS and BS look very similar and have the same industrial classification, they are *complements* and not substitutes.[7]

Networks where services AB and BA are distinct are named "two-way" networks in Economides and White (1994). Two-way networks

---

[7] AS and BS can also be components of *substitute* phone calls ASC and BSC.

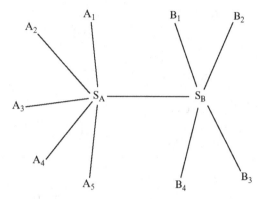

Figure 8.3. A simple local and long-distance network.

include railroad, road, and many telecommunications networks. When one of AB or BA is unfeasible or does not make economic sense, or when there is no sense of direction in the network so that AB and BA are identical, the network is called a one-way network. In a typical one-way network, there are two types of components, and composite goods are formed only by combining a component of each type and customers are often not identified with components but instead demand composite goods. For example, broadcasting and paging are one-way networks.[8]

The classification in network type (one-way or two-way) is not a function of the topological structure of the network. Rather, it depends on the interpretation of the structure to represent a specific service. For example, the network of Figure 8.3 can be interpreted as a two-way telephone network where S_A represents a local switch in city A, A_i represents a customer in city A, and similarly for S_B and B_j.[9] In this network, there are two types of local phone calls, $A_iS_AA_k$ and $B_jS_BB_l$, as well as long-distance phone call $A_iS_AS_BB_j$. We can also interpret the network of Figure 8.3 as an automatic teller machine (ATM) network. Then a transaction (say a withdrawal) from bank B_j from ATM A_i is $A_iS_AS_BB_j$. Connections $A_iS_AA_k$ and $B_jS_BB_l$ may be feasible but there is no demand for them.

We have pointed out that the crucial relationship in both one-way and two-way networks is the complementarity between the pieces of the

---

[8] The 1994 spectrum auction will allow for a large two-way paging network.
[9] In this network, we may identify end-nodes, such as A_i and B_j, end-links, such as A_iS_A and S_BB_j, the interface or gateway S_AS_B, and switches S_A and S_B.

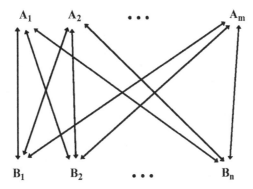

Figure 8.4. A pair of vertically related markets.

network. This crucial economic relationship is also often observed between different classes of goods in non-network industries. In fact, Economides and White (1994) point out that a pair of vertically related industries is formally equivalent to a one-way network. Figure 8.4 can represent two industries of complementary goods A and B, where consumers demand combinations A_iB_j. Notice that this formulation is formally identical to our long-distance network of Figure 8.3 in the ATM interpretation.

The discussion so far has been carried out under the assumption of *compatibility*, i.e. that various links and nodes on the network are costlessly combinable to produce demanded goods. We have pointed out that links on a network are potentially complementary, but it is *compatibility that makes complementarity actual.* Some network goods and some vertically related goods are immediately combinable because of their inherent properties. However, for many complex products, actual complementarity can be achieved only through the adherence to specific technical compatibility standards. Thus, many providers of network or vertically related goods have the option of making their products partially or fully incompatible with components produced by other firms. This can be done through the creation of proprietary designs or the outright exclusion or refusal to interconnect with some firms.

Traditionally, networks were analyzed under the assumption that each network was owned by a single firm. Thus, economic research focused on the efficient use of the network structure as well as on the appropriate allocation of costs.[10] In the 1970s, partly prompted by the antitrust suit

[10] See Sharkey (1995) for an excellent survey.

against AT&T, there was a considerable amount of research on economies of scope, i.e. on the efficiency gains from joint operation of complementary components of networks.[11]

Once one of the most important networks (the AT&T telecommunications network in the US) was broken to pieces, economic research focused in the 1980s and 1990s on issues of interconnection and compatibility. Similar research on issues of compatibility was prompted by the reduced role of IBM in the 1980s and 1990s in the setting of technical standards in computer hardware and software. Significant reductions in costs also contributed and will play a part in the transformation toward fragmented ownership in the telecommunications sector in both the United States and abroad. Costs of transmission have fallen dramatically with the introduction of fiber optic lines. Switching costs have followed the fast cost decreases of microchips and integrated circuits. These cost reductions have transformed the telecommunications industry from a natural monopoly to an oligopoly. The same cost reductions have made many new services, such as interactive video and interactive games, feasible at low cost. Technological change now allows for joint transmission of digital signals of various communications services. Thus, the monopoly of the last link closest to home is in the process of being eliminated,[12] since both telephone lines and cable lines (and in some cases personal communication services (PCS) and terrestrial satellites) will provide similar services.[13,14]

In a network where complementary as well as substitute links are owned by different firms, the questions of interconnection, compatibility, interoperability, and coordination of quality of services become of

---

[11] See Baumol, Panzar, and Willig (1982).

[12] It is already eliminated in some parts of the United Kingdom, where cable TV operators offer telephone service at significantly lower prices than British Telecom.

[13] These significant changes in costs and the convergence of communications services open a number of policy questions on pricing, unbundling, deregulation, and possibly mandated segmentation in this sector. It is possible that ownership break-up of local and long-distance lines is no longer necessary to improve competition. For example, European Union policy mandates open competition by 1998 in any part of the telecommunications network, but does not advocate vertical fragmentation of the existing integrated national monopolies; see the Bangemann Report. The reduction in costs and the elimination of natural monopoly in many services may make it possible for this policy to lead the industry to competition.

[14] Another important network, the airline network, faces significant change in Europe. Airlines have not benefitted from significant cost reductions and technological change; the reform is just the abolition by the European Union of the antiquated regime of national airline monopolies, and its replacement by a more competitive environment.

paramount importance. We will examine these issues in detail in the next few sections. We first focus on a fundamental property of networks, i.e. the fact that they exhibit *network externalities*.

8.3 Network externalities

Networks exhibit positive consumption and production externalities. A positive consumption externality (or network externality) signifies the fact that the value of a unit of the good increases with the number of units sold. To economists, this fact seems quite counterintuitive, since they all know that, except for potatoes in Irish famines, market demand slopes downwards. So the earlier statement "the value of a unit of the good increases with the number of units sold" should be interpreted as "the value of a unit of the good increases with the *expected* number of units to be sold". Thus, the demand slopes downward but shifts upward with increases in the number of units expected to be sold.

8.3.1 Sources of network externalities

The key reason for the appearance of network externalities is the complementarity between the components of a network. Depending on the network, the externality may be direct or indirect. When customers are identified with components, the externality is direct. Consider, for example, a typical two-way network, such as the local telephone network of Figure 8.2. In this n-component network, there are $n(n - 1)$ potential goods. An additional $(n + 1)$th customer provides direct externalities to all other customers in the network by adding 2n potential new goods through the provision of a complementary link say ES to the existing links.[15]

In typical one-way networks, the externality is only indirect. When there are m varieties of component A and n varieties of component B as in Figure 8.4 (and all A-type goods are compatible with all B-type), there are mn potential composite goods. An extra customer yields indirect externalities to other customers, by increasing the demand for components of types A and B and thereby (because of the presence of economies

---

[15] This property of two-way networks was pointed out in telecommunications networks by Rohlfs (1974) in a very early paper on network externalities. See also Oren and Smith (1981).

of scale) potentially increasing the number of varieties of each component available in the market.

Financial exchange networks also exhibit indirect network externalities. There are two ways in which these externalities arise: first, in the act of exchanging assets or goods, and second, in the array of vertically related services that compose a financial transaction. These include the services of a broker, of bringing the offer to the floor, matching the offer, etc. The second type is similar to other vertically related markets. The first way in which externalities arise in financial markets is more important.

The act of exchanging goods or assets brings together a trader who is willing to sell with a trader who is willing to buy. The exchange brings together the two complementary goods, "willingness to sell at price p" (the "offer") and "willingness to buy at price p" (the "counteroffer") and creates a composite good, the "exchange transaction". The two original goods were complementary and each had no value without the other. Clearly, the availability of the counteroffer is critical for the exchange to occur. Put in terms commonly used in finance, minimal liquidity is necessary for the transaction to occur.

Financial markets also exhibit positive size externalities in the sense that the increasing size (or thickness) of an exchange market increases the expected utility of all participants. Higher participation of traders on both sides of the market (drawn from the same distribution) decreases the variance of the expected market price and increases the expected utility of risk-averse traders. *Ceteris paribus*, higher liquidity increases traders' utility. Thus, financial exchange markets also exhibit network externalities.[16,17]

---

[16] For a more detailed discussion of networks in finance see Economides (1993a). Economides and Schwartz (1995a) discuss how to set up *electronic call markets* that bunch transactions and execute them all at once. Call markets have inherently higher liquidity because they take advantage of network externalities in exchange. Thus, transaction costs are lower in call markets. Economides (1994a) and Economides and Heisler (1994) discuss how to increase liquidity in call markets. The survey of institutional investors reported by Economides and Schwartz (1995b) finds that many traders who work in the present continuous market environment would be willing to wait a number of hours for execution of their orders if they could save in transaction costs, including bid-ask spreads. Thus, the time is right for the establishment of call markets in parallel operation with the continuous market.

[17] The increase of utility in expectation due to market thickness was pointed out by Economides and Siow (1988), and earlier and in less formal terms by Garbade and Silber (1976, 1979). The effects are similar to those of search models as in Diamond (1982, 1984).

8.3.2   The "macro" approach

There are two approaches and two strands of literature in the analysis of network externalities. The first approach assumes that network external-ities exist, and attempts to model their consequences. I call this the "macro" approach. Conceptually this approach is easier, and it has produced strong results. It was the predominant approach during the 1980s. The second approach attempts to find the root cause of the network externalities. I call this the "micro" approach. In industrial organization, it started with the analysis of mix-and-match models and has evolved to the analysis of various structures of vertically related markets. In finance, it started with the analysis of price dispersion models. The "micro" approach is harder, and in many ways more con-strained, as it has to rely on the underlying microstructure. However, the "micro" approach has a very significant benefit in defining the market structure. We discuss the "macro" approach first.

Perfect competition

As we have noted, network externalities arise out of the complementarity of different network pieces. Thus, they arise naturally in both one- and two-way networks, as well as in vertically related markets. The value of good X increases as more of the complementary good Y is sold, and vice versa. Thus, more of Y is sold as more X is sold. It follows that the value of X increases as more of it is sold. This positive feedback loop seems explosive, and indeed it would be, except for the inherent downward slope of the demand curve. To understand this better, consider a fulfilled expectations formulation of network externalities as in Katz and Shapiro (1985), Economides (1993b, 1996a), and Economides and Himmelberg (1995). Let the willingness to pay for the nth unit of the good when n^e units are expected to be sold be $p(n, n^e)$.[18] This is a decreasing function of its first argument because the demand slopes downward. $p(n, n^e)$ increases in n^e; this captures the network externalities effect. At a market equilibrium of the simple single-period world, expectations are fulfilled, $n = n^e$, thus defining the fulfilled expectations demand $p(n, n)$. Figure 8.5 shows the construction of a typical fulfilled expectations demand. Each curve D_i, $i = 1, \ldots, 4$, shows the willingness to pay for a varying quantity n, given an expectation of sales $n^e = n_i$. At $n = n_i$, expectations are fulfilled and the point belongs to $p(n, n)$ as $p(n_i, n_i)$. Thus $p(n, n)$ is constructed as a collection of points $p(n_i, n_i)$.

[18] In this formulation n and n^e are normalized so that they represent market shares rather than absolute quantities.

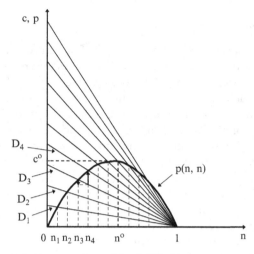

Figure 8.5. Construction of the fulfilled expectations demand.

To avoid explosions and infinite sales, it is reasonable to impose $\lim_{n \to \infty} p(n, n) = 0$; it then follows that $p(n, n)$ is decreasing for large n. Economides and Himmelberg (1995) show that the fulfilled expectations demand is increasing for small n if either one of three conditions hold: (i) the utility of every consumer in a network of zero size is zero, or (ii) there are immediate and large external benefits to network expansion for very small networks, or (iii) there is a significant density of high-willingness-to-pay consumers who are just indifferent on joining a network of approximately zero size. The first condition is straightforward and applies directly to all two-way networks. The other two conditions are a bit more subtle, but commonly observed in networks and vertically related industries.

When the fulfilled expectations demand increases for small n, we say that the network exhibits a positive critical mass under perfect competition. This means that, if we imagine a constant marginal cost c decreasing parametrically, the network will start at a positive and significant size n^o (corresponding to marginal cost c^o). For each smaller marginal cost, $c < c^o$, there are three network sizes consistent with marginal cost pricing: a zero size network; an unstable network size at the first intersection of the horizontal through c with $p(n, n)$; and the Pareto optimal stable network size at the largest intersection of the horizontal with $p(n, n)$. The multiplicity of equilibria is a direct result of the coordination problem that arises naturally in the typical network externalities model.

In such a setting, it is natural to assume that the Pareto optimal network size will result.[19]

In the presence of network externalities, it is evident that perfect competition is inefficient: the marginal social benefit of network expansion is larger than the benefit that accrues to a particular firm under perfect competition. Thus, perfect competition will provide a smaller network than is socially optimal, and for some relatively high marginal costs perfect competition will not provide the good while it is socially optimal to provide it.

One interesting question that remains virtually unanswered is how to decentralize the welfare-maximizing solution in the presence of network externalities. Clearly, the welfare-maximizing solution can be implemented through perfect price discrimination, but typically such discrimination is unfeasible. It remains to be seen to what extent mechanisms that allow for non-linear pricing and self-selection by consumers will come close to the first best.

Monopoly

Economides and Himmelberg (1995) show that a monopolist who is unable to price-discriminate will support a smaller network and charge higher prices than perfectly competitive firms. This is despite the fact that the monopolist has influence over the expectations of the consumers, and he recognizes this influence, while no perfectly competitive firm has such influence.[20] Influence over expectations drives the monopolist to higher production, but the monopolist's profit-maximizing tendency toward restricted production is stronger and leads it to lower production levels than perfect competition. Thus, consumers and total surplus will be lower in monopoly than in perfect competition. Therefore, the existence of network externalities does not reverse the standard welfare comparison between monopoly and competition; it follows that the existence of network externalities cannot be claimed as a reason in favor of a monopoly market structure.

Oligopoly and monopolistic competition under compatibility

Cournot oligopolists producing compatible components also have some influence over expectations. A natural way to model the influence of

---

[19] It is possible to have other shapes of the fulfilled expectations demand. In general, $p(n, n)$ is quasiconcave under weak conditions on the distribution of preferences and the network externality function. Then, if none of the three causes mentioned above is present, the fulfilled expectations demand is downward sloping.

[20] A monopolist unable to influence expectations will clearly produce less than a monopolist able to influence expectations.

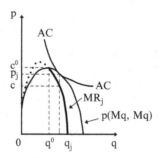

Figure 8.6. Monopolistic competition with network externalities and M compatible goods.

oligopolists on output expectations is to assume that every oligopolist takes the output of all others as given and sets the expectation of consumers of his own output. In this setting, M compatible Cournot oligopolists support a network of a size between monopoly (M = 1) and perfect competition (M = ∞). The analysis can easily be extended to monopolistic competition among compatible oligopolists if firms face downward-sloping average cost curves as shown in Figure 8.6. Firms produce on the downward-sloping part of the firm-scaled fulfilled expectations demand. At a symmetric equilibrium, firm j's output is determined at the intersection of marginal cost c and marginal revenue MR_j. Price is read off the fulfilled expectations firm-scaled inverse demand p(Mq, Mq). At a monopolistically competitive equilibrium, the AC curve is tangent to the fulfilled expectations demand at q_j.

Oligopoly under incompatibility

One of the most interesting issues in the economics of networks is the interaction of oligopolists producing incompatible goods. A full analysis of such a market, in conjunction with the analysis of compatible oligopolists, will allow us to determine the incentives of individual firms to choose technologies that are compatible or incompatible with others.

Given any set of firms S = {1, . . ., N}, we can identify a subset of S that adheres to the same technical "standard" as a coalition. Then the partition of S into subsets defines a coalition structure C_S = {C_1, . . ., C_k}. Compatibility by all firms means that there is a single coalition that includes all firms. Total incompatibility, where every firm adheres to its own unique standard, means that k = N.

A number of criteria can be used to define the equilibrium coalition structure. A purely non-cooperative concept without side payments requires that, after a firm joins a coalition, it is better off at the resulting market equilibrium, just from revenues from its own sales.[21] At a non-cooperative equilibrium with side payments, firms divide the profits of a coalition arbitrarily to induce firms to join a coalition. Yet firms do not cooperate in output decisions. Katz and Shapiro (1985) show that the level of industry output is greater under compatibility than at any equilibrium with some incompatible firm(s). This is not sufficient to characterize the incentives of firms to opt for compatibility.

Intuitively, a firm benefits from a move to compatibility if (i) the marginal externality is strong; (ii) it joins a large coalition; and (iii) it does not thereby increase competition to a significant degree by its action. Yet the coalition benefits from a firm joining its "standard" if (i) the marginal externality is strong; (ii) the firm that joins the coalition is large; (iii) competition does not increase significantly as a result of the firm joining the coalition. Clearly, in both cases, the second and the third criteria may create incentives that are in conflict; this will help define the equilibrium coalition structure.[22]

Katz and Shapiro (1985) show that if the costs of achieving compatibility are lower for all firms than the increase in profits because of compatibility, the industry move toward compatibility is socially beneficial. However, it may be true that the (fixed) cost of achieving compatibility is larger than the increase in profits for some firms, while these costs are lower than the increase in total surplus from compatibility. Then profit-maximizing firms will not achieve industry-wide compatibility while this regime is socially optimal. Further, if a change leads to less than industry-wide compatibility, the private incentives to standardize may be excessive or inadequate. This is because of the output changes that a change of regime has on all firms. Similarly, the incentive of a firm to produce a one-way adapter, that allows it to achieve compatibility without affecting the compatibility of other firms, may be deficient or excessive because the firm ignores the change it creates on other firms' profits and on consumers surplus.

Coordination to technical standards with asymmetric technologies
So far it has been assumed that the cost of standardization was fixed and the same for both firms. If standardization costs are different, firms play a standard coordination game. A 2×2 version of this game is presented in Figure 8.7. Entries represent profits.

[21] See Economides (1984), and Yi and Shin (1992a,b).
[22] Economides and Flyer (1995) examine the incentives for coalition formation around compatibility standards.

Player 2

	Standard 1	Standard 2
Standard 1	(a, b)	(c, d)
Standard 2	(e, f)	(g, h)

Player 1

Figure 8.7. Choice between compatibility and incompatibility.

In this game, we will assume that firm i has higher profits when "its" standard i gets adopted, $a > g$, $b < h$. Profits, in case of disagreement, will depend on the particulars of the industry. One standard assumption that captures many industries is that in case of disagreement profits will be lower than those of either standard, e, $c < g$; d, $f < b$. Under these circumstances, the setting of either standard will constitute a non-cooperative equilibrium.[23] There is no guarantee that the highest joint profit standard will be adopted. Since consumer surplus does not appear in the matrix, there is no guarantee of maximization of social welfare at equilibrium. For an analysis with continuous choice of standard specification, see Berg (1988).

8.3.3   The "micro" approach

The "micro" approach starts with an analysis of the specific micro-structure of a network. After identifying the physical aspects of a network, such as nodes and links, we identify the goods and services that are demanded on the network. We distinguish between the case where only end-to-end services are demanded and the case when there is also demand for some services that do not reach from end to end. The case when only end-to-end services exist is easier and has been dealt with in much more detail in the literature. However, many important networks, such as the railroad and telephone networks, provide both end-to-end and partial-coverage service. We examine this case later.

We start with a simple case where only end-to-end services are demanded. Suppose there are two complementary types of goods, A and B. Suppose that each type of good has a number of brands available, A_i, $i = 1, \ldots, m$, B_j, $j = 1, \ldots, n$, as in Figure 8.4. Let consumers demand 1:1 combinations $A_i B_j$. We call each of the

---

[23] Standard 1 is an equilibrium if $a > e$, $b > d$. Similarly, standard 2 is an equilibrium if $g > c$, $h > f$.

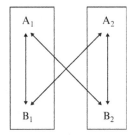

Figure 8.8. Mix-and-match compatibility.

complementary goods A_i or B_j *components*, while the combined good A_iB_j is called a *composite good* or *system*. Potentially all combinations A_iB_j, $i = 1, \ldots, m$; $j = 1, \ldots, n$, are possible. Thus complementarity exists in potential. Complementarity is actualized when the components A_i and B_j are combinable and function together without extra cost, i.e. when the components are *compatible*. Often it is an explicit decision of the producers of individual components to make their products compatible with those of other producers. Thus, compatibility is a *strategic* decision and should be analyzed as such.

Modern industrial organization provides a rich collection of environments for the analysis of strategic decisions; because of shortage of time and space, this chapter will discuss the decision on compatibility in only a few environments.

Mix and match: compatibility vs. incompatibility
The mix-and-match literature does not assume *a priori* network externalities; however, it is clear that demand in mix-and-match models exhibits network externalities. The mix-and-match approach was originated by Matutes and Regibeau (1988), and followed by Economides (1988, 1989a, 1991a, 1991b, 1993c), Economides and Salop (1992), Economides and Lehr (1995), Matutes and Regibeau (1989, 1992), and others. To fix ideas, consider the case of Figure 8.4 with m = 2, n = 2, technologies are known, coordination is costless, price discrimination is not allowed, and there are no cost asymmetries created by any particular compatibility standard. Figure 8.8 shows the case of compatibility. The incentive for compatibility of a vertically integrated firm (producing A_1 and B_1) depends on the relative sizes of each combination of complementary components. Reciprocal compatibility (i.e. simultaneous compatibility between A_1 and B_2, as well as between A_2 and B_1) increases demand (by allowing for the sale of A_1B_2 and A_2B_1) but also increases competition for the individual components. Therefore, when the hybrid demand is

large compared with the own-product demand (including the case where the two demands are equal at equal prices), a firm has an incentive to want compatibility.[24] When the demand for hybrids is small, a firm does not want compatibility. Thus, it is possible, with two vertically integrated firms, that one firm wants compatibility (because it has small own-product demand compared with the hybrids demand) while the other one prefers incompatibility (because its own-product demand is large compared with the hybrids demand). Thus, there can be conflict across firms in their incentives for compatibility, even when the technology is well known. The presumption is that opponents will not be able to counteract and correct all incompatibilities introduced by an opponent, and therefore in situations of conflict we expect that incompatibility wins.

These results hold both for zero-one decisions – i.e. compatibility vs. incompatibility – and for decisions of partial (or variable) incompatibility. The intuition of the pro-compatibility result for the zero-one decision in the equal hybrid- and own-demand is simple. Starting from the same level of prices and demand in both the compatibility and incompatibility regimes, consider a price increase in one component that produces the same decrease in demand in both regimes. Under incompatibility, the loss of profits is higher since *systems* sales are lost rather than sales of *one component*. Therefore, profits are more responsive to price under incompatibility; it follows that the residual demand facing firms is more elastic under incompatibility, and therefore firms will choose lower prices in that regime.[25] This is reminiscent of Cournot's (1838) celebrated result that a vertically integrated monopolist faces a more elastic demand and will choose a lower price than the sum of the prices of two vertically disintegrated monopolists.[26]

So far we have assumed that compatibility is reciprocal – i.e. that the same adapter is required to make both A_1B_2 and A_2B_1 functional. If compatibility is not reciprocal – i.e. if different adapters are required for A_1B_2 and A_2B_1 – the incentive of firms to achieve compatibility depends on the cross substitution between own-products and hybrids. Roughly, if the substitutability among A-type components is equal to the

---

[24] Matutes and Regibeau (1988) and Economides (1989a) find that compatibility is always the firm's choice because they assume a locational setting with uniform distribution of consumers in space that results in equal own-product and hybrid demands at equal prices. The exposition here follows the more general framework of Economides (1988, 1991a).

[25] These results also hold when firms can price-discriminate between buyers who buy the pure combination A_iB_i and buyers who buy only one component from firm i. Thus, firms practice mixed bundling. See Matutes and Regibeau (1992) and Economides (1993c).

[26] See Economides (1988) for a discussion of Cournot's result, and Economides and Salop (1992) for an extension of the result to (parallel) vertical integration among two pairs of vertically related firms.

substitutability among B-type components, the earlier results of the reciprocal setup still hold.[27] Nevertheless, if the degree of substitutability among the As is different than among the Bs, one firm may create an advantage for itself by introducing some incompatibilities. However, it is *never* to the advantage of *both* vertically integrated firms to create incompatibilities.

The issue of compatibility and coordination is much more complicated if there are more than two firms. A number of coalitions can each be formed around a specific technical standard, and standards may allow for partial compatibility, or may be mutually incompatible. Not enough research has been done on this issue. Research in this area is made particularly difficult by the lack of established models of coalition formation in non-cooperative settings. The analysis based on coalition structures is more complicated in the "micro" approach because of the specifics of the ownership structure.

The studies we have referred to this far take the ownership structure as given (i.e. as parallel vertical integration) and proceed to discuss the choice of the degree of compatibility. In many cases, vertical integration is a decision that is more flexible (and less irreversible) than a decision on compatibility. Thus, it makes sense to think of a game structure where the choice of technology (which implies the degree of compatibility) *precedes* the choice of the degree of vertical integration. Economides (1996b) analyzes the choice of asset ownership as a consequence of the choice of technology (and of the implied degree of compatibility). It posits a three-stage game of compatibility choice in the first stage, vertical integration in the second stage, and price choice in the third stage. Incentives for vertical mergers in industries with varying degrees of compatibility are compared. In analyzing the stage of compatibility choice, the influence of the anticipation of decisions on (vertical) industry structure on compatibility decisions is evaluated.

Changes in the number of varieties as a result of
compatibility decisions
Economides (1991b) considers the interplay of compatibility and the number of varieties of complementary goods. There are two types of goods, A and B, consumed in 1:1 ratio. There are two brands of good A, A_1 and A_2, each produced by an independent firm. The number of B-type brands, each also produced by an independent firm, is determined by a free-entry condition, so that industry B is in monopolistic competition.

---

[27] Economides (1991a), p. 52.

In a regime of compatibility, each B-type component is immediately compatible with either A_1 or A_2. In a regime of incompatibility, each brand B_i produces two versions, one compatible with A_1 and one compatible with A_2. The two cases are shown in Figures 8.10 and 8.11.

Under incompatibility, each B-type firm incurs higher fixed costs; it follows that *ceteris paribus* the number of B-type brands will be smaller under incompatibility. An A-type firm prefers incompatibility or compatibility according to the equilibrium profits it realizes in each regime. These profits, and the decision on compatibility, depend on the specifics of the utility function of consumers, and in particular on the impact of an increase in the number of varieties on utility. If industry demand is not sensitive to increases in the number of varieties of composite goods n (and does not increase much as n increases), then equilibrium profits of an A-type firm decrease in the number of firms; therefore profits of an A-type firm are higher at the smaller number of firms implied by incompatibility, and an A-type firm prefers incompatibility. Conversely, when consumers have a strong preference for variety and demand for composite goods increases significantly in n, equilibrium profits of an A-type firm increase in the number of firms; therefore its profits are higher at the larger number of firms implied by compatibility, and an A-type firm prefers compatibility.

Church and Gandal (1992b) and Chou and Shy (1990a,b,c) also examine the impact of the number of varieties of complementary

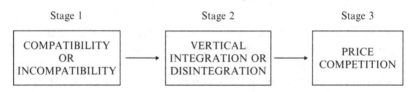

Figure 8.9. Compatibility decisions are less flexible than vertical integration decisions.

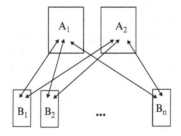

Figure 8.10. Compatibility.

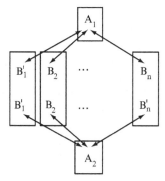

Figure 8.11. Incompatibility.

(B-type) goods on the decisions of consumers to buy one of the A-type goods under conditions of incompatibility.

Quality coordination in mix and match
The framework of mix-and-match models applies to both variety and quality features that are combinable additively in the utility function. That is, in the standard mix-and-match model, the utility accruing to a consumer from component A_i is added to the utility from component B_j. However, in some networks, including telecommunications,[28] the utility of the composite good A_iB_j is not the sum of the respective qualities. In particular, the quality of voice in a long-distance call is the minimum of the qualities of the component parts of the network, i.e. the local and the long-distance transmission. Thus, significant quality coordination problems arise in a network with fragmented ownership. Economides (1994b) and Economides and Lehr (1995) examine this coordination problem.

Let A and B be components that are combinable in a 1:1 ratio. Suppose that the quality levels of the components are q_A and q_B, while the quality level of the composite good is $q_{AB} = \min(q_A, q_B)$. Consumers vary in their willingness to pay for quality improvements as in Gabszewicz and Thisse (1979) and Shaked and Sutton (1982), and firms play a two-stage game of quality choice in the first stage, followed by price choice in the second stage. As mentioned earlier, Cournot (1838) has shown that an integrated monopolist producing both A and B will charge less than

---

[28] See also Encaoua et al. (1992) for a discussion of the coordination of the timing of different legs of airport transportation.

two vertically related monopolists, each producing one component only. This is because of the elimination of double marginalization by the integrated monopolist. Economides (1994b) and Economides and Lehr (1995) show that an integrated monopolist also provides a higher quality than the two independent monopolists. In bilateral monopoly, marginal increases in quality have a bigger impact on price. Being able to sell the same quality at a higher price than under integrated monopoly, the bilateral monopolists choose lower quality levels, which are less costly. Despite that, because of double marginalization, prices are higher than in integrated monopoly, a lower portion of the market is served, and firms realize lower profits.[29] Thus, *lack of vertical integration leads to a reduction in quality*. Note that this is not because of lack of coordination between the bilateral monopolists in the choice of quality, since they both choose the same quality level.[30]

In this setting, Economides and Lehr (1995) examine various ownership structures where for at least one of the types of components there is more than one quality level available. Clearly, a situation where all components have the same quality is not viable, since competition would then drive prices to marginal cost. Further, for a "high" quality composite good to be available, both an A- and a B-type good must be of "high" quality. They find that third (and fourth) "low" quality goods have a hard time surviving if they are produced by independent firms. In contrast, in parallel vertical integration (with firm i, i = 1, 2, producing A_i and B_i), firms prefer not to interconnect – i.e. to produce components that are incompatible with those of the opponent.

8.4   Network externalities and industry structure

8.4.1   *Invitations to enter*

In the presence of strong network externalities, a monopolist exclusive holder of a technology may have an incentive to invite competitors and even subsidize them. The realization of network externalities requires high output. A monopolist may be unable credibly to commit to a high output as long as he is operating by himself. However, if he licenses the technology to a number of firms and invites them to enter and compete with him, market output will be higher; and since the level of market

---

[29] Consumers also receive lower surplus in comparison to vertically integrated monopoly.
[30] The *reliability* of the network, measured by the percentage of time that the network is in operation, or by the probability of a successful connection, is measured by the product of the respective reliabilities of the components (another non-linear function).

output depends mainly upon other firms, the commitment to high output is credible.

The invitation to enter and the consequent increase in market output has two effects: a *competitive effect* and a *network effect*. The competitive effect is an expected increase in competition because of the increase in the number of firms. The network effect tends to increase the willingness to pay and the market price because of the high expected sales. Economides (1993b, 1996a) shows that if the network externality is strong enough, the network effect is larger than the competitive effect, and therefore an innovator-monopolist invites competitors and even subsidizes them on the margin to induce them to increase production.

8.4.2   Interconnection or foreclosure by a local monopolist?

Many telecommunications, airline and railroad networks have the structure of Figure 8.12. In a railroad network, there may be direct consumer demand for links AB, BC, as well as AC. This figure can also represent a telephone network with demand for local telephone services (AB) and for long-distance services (ABC); in that case, there is no direct demand for BC, but only the indirect demand arising from long-distance calls ABC. In many cases, one firm has a monopoly of a link that is necessary for a number of services (here AB), and this link is a natural monopoly. This bottleneck link is often called an essential facility. The monopolist can foreclose any firm by denying access to the bottleneck facility. What are his incentives do so?

Economides and Woroch (1992) examine intermodal competition in the context of a simple network pictured in Figure 8.13. S and R are local switches; AS and BR are local services (in different cities); SR and STR are alternative long-distance services. The diagram is simplified by eliminating R without any essential loss. Suppose that an integrated firm offers end-to-end service (ASB), while a second firm offers service of partial coverage only (STB). They find that although the integrated firm has the opportunity to foreclose the opponent, it prefers not to. In fact, the integrated firm is better off by implementing a vertical price squeeze on the opponent and charging a significantly higher price to the opponent for the use of the monopolized link than it "charges" itself.[31] Thus, foreclosure, although feasible, is not optimal for the monopolist.[32]

---

[31] This result is dependent on the linear structure of the demand system, and may not hold for any demand structure.

[32] Church and Gandal (1992a) find that sometimes firms prefer foreclosure, but their model does not allow for a vertical price squeeze.

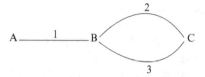

Figure 8.12. *AB* is a bottleneck facility.

Network in extensive and collapsed form

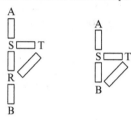

Figure 8.13. Intermodal competition.

Economides and Woroch (1992) also find that vertical disintegration is not desirable for the firm that offers end-to-end service. Once disintegrated, its constituent parts realize lower total profits. This is because, besides appropriating monopoly rents for its AS monopoly, the integrated firm (ASB) was creating a significant restriction of competition in the SB-STB market by its *de facto* price-discriminating strategy. After disintegration, the SB-STB market becomes much more competitive, even if AS price-discriminates between SB and STB. Thus, even if network ASB were to receive the full rent earned by the new owner of SB, its after-divestiture profits would be lower than before divestiture.[33]

Even in simple networks, there may be relations among firms that are neither purely vertical nor purely horizontal. Thus, the conventional wisdom about vertical and horizontal integration fails. Economides and Salop (1992) discuss pricing in various ownership structures in the model of Figure 8.8. They call the ownership structure of this figure, where each firm produces a component of each type, *parallel vertical integration*. They also consider the *independent ownership* structure, where each of the four components is owned by a different firm. In both of these structures, no firm is purely vertically or purely horizontally related

---

[33] This result is in contrast to Bonanno and Vickers (1988) because of the absence of two-part contracts in Economides and Woroch (1992).

to another firm. Thus, starting from independent ownership, or starting from parallel vertical integration, a merger to *joint ownership*, where all components are produced by the same firm, can either increase or decrease prices. Thus, simple prescriptions against mergers may easily fail.

In the model of Figure 8.13, Economides and Woroch (1992) consider the case where link ST is owned by a firm that owns a vertically related link (either AS or BT), or is owned by an independent firm. Clearly, the strategic structure of the game remains unaffected when link ST changes hands between two firms that also own a link that is vertically related to ST. Therefore, if ST has a fixed cost, it is a liability to such a firm; each firm would like the opponent to own it. However, if the link is owned by a third party, it has a positive value because of its monopoly position in the chain. Thus, each original owner has an incentive to sell ST to a third party. The direct implication is that the value of links depends on what other links a firm owns. Thus, general prescriptions on the desirability of unbundling of ownership are suspect.

Often parts of the network are regulated, while other parts are not. This is the typical arrangement in telephony in the US, where only local telephone companies are tightly regulated, since their market is traditionally considered a natural monopoly.[34] Baumol and Sidak (1994a,b) propose that to attract efficient entrants in the long-distance market and to discourage inefficient entrants, a local telephone company should charge them an *interconnection (or access) fee* equal to the marginal cost of provision of service plus any opportunity cost that the local telephone company incurs.[35] This is correct under a set of strict assumptions: first, that the end-to-end good is sold originally at the competitive price; second, that the entrant produces the same complementary good (long-distance service) as the incumbent;[36] third, that there are no economies of scale in either one of the complements. Economides and White (1995) discuss how the relaxation of these assumptions leads to different interconnection charges.[37] For example, if competition between an entrant and the incumbent reduces the market power of the incumbent, entry may increase social welfare even when the entrant produces at higher cost than the incumbent.

---

[34] This is changing for some customers through the existence of competitive access providers, which directly compete with the local telephone company for large customers, and the potential for competition from cable companies.
[35] Kahn and Taylor (1994) have very similar views.
[36] Armstrong and Doyle (1994) relax this assumption.
[37] See also Ergas and Ralph (1994).

8.5   Sequential games

In network markets, and more generally in markets with network externalities, when firms and consumers interact in more than period, *history matters*. Both consumers and firms make production and consumption decisions based on sizes of installed base and on expectations of its increases over time. The same underlying technology and consumer preferences and distribution can lead to different industrial structures depending on the way things start. Thus, strategic advantages, such as first-mover advantages, can have long-run effects.[38]

Network externalities and historical events are particularly important in the speed of adoption of an innovation that creates services on a network. Cabral (1990) discusses the adoption of innovations under perfect competition in the presence of network externalities. His main conclusion is that when network externalities are strong, the equilibrium adoption path may be discontinuous. This is another way of saying that there are two network sizes supported as equilibria at the same time. This may occur at the start of the network, and then it is called positive critical mass by Economides and Himmelberg (1995). It may also occur at other points in the network evolution. In practice, discontinuities in the size of the network over time do not occur since that would imply an infinite size of sales at some points in time. Continuity and smoothness of the network path is restored if instantaneous marginal production costs are increasing. Under this assumption, Economides and Himmelberg (1995) find that the adoption path is much steeper in the presence of externalities. Further, driven by the externality, in early stages the network can expand so quickly as to exhibit increasing retail prices even when marginal costs are falling over time. Their analysis is applied to the fax market in the US and Japan.

The analysis is more complex when we depart from the assumption of perfect competition. Accordingly, this analysis tends to be in the form of simple two-period models. We analyze it with reference to the standard simultaneous choice coordination game above, where we now interpret the first strategy as sticking to the old technology and the second as the adoption of a new one.

Network externalities for both technologies mean that a > c, e; b > d, f; g > c, e; h > d, f. If both firms are worse off when they are not coordinated, both the "new technology" (i.e. (N, N)) and the "old technology"

---

[38] See Arthur (1988, 1989) and David (1985). David argues that the QWERTY keyboard was adopted mainly because it appeared first while the DVORAK keyboard was superior. This is disputed by Liebowitz and Margolis (1990).

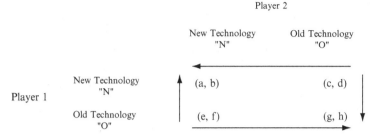

Figure 8.14. Choice between old and new technology.

(i.e. (O, O)) will arise as equilibria. Clearly, one of the equilibria can be inefficient. If the (O, O) equilibrium is inefficient and is adopted, Farrell and Saloner (1985) call the situation *excess inertia*. Similarly, if the (N, N) equilibrium is inefficient and it is adopted, the situation is called *excess momentum*.

Farrell and Saloner (1985) discuss a two-period model where consumers vary in their willingness to pay for the change of the technology, measured by θ. Users can switch in period 1 or 2, and switching is irreversible. Users fall into four categories according to the strategy they pick: (i) they never switch, whatever the behavior of others in the first period; (ii) they switch in period 2 if other users have switched in period 1 – jumping on the bandwagon; (iii) they switch in period 1; (iv) they switch in period 2 even if others have not switched in period 1. The last strategy is dominated by strategy (iii). Consumers of low θ use strategy (i), consumers of intermediate θ use strategy (ii), and consumers of high θ use strategy (iii). Consumers would like to coordinate themselves and switch in the first period (thereby getting the bandwagon rolling) but are unable to do so, thus creating excess inertia.[39] This inertia can be reduced through communication among the consumers, through contracts, through coordination in committees, or through new product sponsorship and special introductory pricing.[40]

In a sequential setting, preannouncement (i.e. announcement of a new product before its introduction) may induce some users to delay their purchase. Also penetration pricing can be important. Katz and Shapiro (1986a) examine the effects of sponsorship (allowing firms to

---

[39] See Katz and Shapiro (1992) for a different view arguing for excess momentum (which they call *insufficient friction*).
[40] See also Farrell and Saloner (1988) for mechanisms to achieve coordination, and Farrell and Saloner (1985) for a discussion of network product sponsorship.

price differently than at marginal cost). Katz and Shapiro (1986b) examine the effects of uncertainty in product adoption and introduction.

Nevertheless, there is much more work to be done on multi-period and on continuous-time dynamic games with network externalities. The issues of foreclosure and predation have not been sufficiently discussed in the context of network externalities. More generally, much more work is required on multi-period dynamic games in this context, especially for durable goods.

8.6   Markets for adapters and add-ons

Not enough research has been done on the economics of adapters and interfaces. One strand of the mix-and-match literature assumes that compatibilities introduced by one firm cannot be corrected by the other, so that adapters are unfeasible. Economides (1991a) assumes that adapters are provided by a competitive industry at cost, but firms' decisions determine the extent of incompatibility, and therefore the cost of the adapters. Farrell and Saloner (1992) assume that converters make the technologies only partially compatible, in the sense that hybrid goods that utilize incompatible components as well as an adapter give lower utility than a system composed of fully compatible components. In this framework, the availability of converters can *reduce* social welfare, since, in the presence of converters, some consumers would buy the converter and the "inferior" technology rather than the "best" technology, although the "best" technology gives more externalities.

8.7   Concluding remarks

In this chapter, we have noted some of the interesting issues that arise in networks and vertically related industries, especially in the presence of a fragmented ownership structure. Evidently, many open questions remain. One of the most important issues still largely unresolved is the joint determination of an equilibrium market structure (including the degree of vertical integration) together with the degree of compatibility across firms. The extent of standardization in markets with more than two participants and the structure of "standards" coalitions also remain open questions. Markets for adapters and add-ons have not been sufficiently analyzed. An analysis of market structure in multi-period dynamic games with network externalities is also unavailable. Further, issues of predation and foreclosure in networks have not been fully analyzed yet. On a more fundamental level, there is no good prediction yet of the "break points" that define the complementary components in a modular design structure. Even if these break points are known, little analysis has been done of competition in a multi-layered structure of vertically related components. Nevertheless, it is exactly this kind of modelling that is needed for an analysis and evaluation of the potential structures of the "information superhighway".

9 E-commerce, two-sided markets and info-mediation

Alex Gaudeul and Bruno Jullien

9.1 Introduction

As the Internet is spreading in our everyday life and business practices, it becomes clear that some of the major innovations that digital communication technologies have brought concern the process of intermediation. It is at that level of the production chain that the most radical changes affecting the organization of the exchange process will occur (see, for instance, *The Economist* (2000)). Traditional brick and mortar intermediation integrates several complementary functions. On one hand, it generates, processes and transmits various information flows that are necessary for transactions: this includes information about the existence, the characteristics and the location of the products or the terms of trade (the prices). On the other hand, it provides physical facilities that are used in the exchange process (transport, storage, exhibition, etc.). Digital technologies allow for an unprecedented separation between these two types of functions, due to the drastic reduction in the cost of information processing. One can then foresee a major impact on the distribution channels and on the vertical organization of industries. While it is hard to assess at what speed this will happen, it is clear that e-commerce and electronic intermediation will play a major role in the future. It then becomes imperative to understand how a sector specialized in information management (info-mediation) can organize itself when it incurs almost no variable costs, and how competition will operate in such a sector. For our purpose, the focus will be on two of the activities of intermediaries: identifying trading partners and determining the terms of trade.

The role of the intermediary can be divided into two parts: putting potential trading partners in contact, and providing each side of the trading relation with information about the other side. In the first function, clients of the intermediary, buyers and seller, value the diversity and breadth of offering of the intermediary. This can be because the higher the number of sellers present at the intermediary, the higher is the probability that one of them offers a low price, or because the higher the number of buyers coming to the intermediary, the higher is the probability that one will value the supplier's good highly. Network effects thus arise naturally if the intermediary is a matchmaker. The first part of this chapter is an introduction to the analysis of such network effects in two-sided markets, and to their translation into specific pricing strategies in monopolistic and competitive markets.[1] The second part examines further the role of the intermediary as a manager of the relationship between buyers and sellers. While in the first part the intermediary merely acts as a meeting point for potential traders, the second part examines how it can exploit its superior knowledge of each side of the market by selling information about one side of the market to the other side. The second part therefore deals with how the intermediary exploits asymmetric information in two-sided markets.

It is difficult to find a pure example of a market place, i.e. when the value of the intermediary comes only from being a simple meeting point and not from the information it gathers about participants in the market. It is similarly difficult to give a pure example of an expert whose role would be limited to gathering and publicizing information about the goods on a market. However, Amazon, on the one hand, and Google, on the other, do seem to stand at the opposite extremes.

As a bookseller, Amazon's role is to provide the widest variety of books to the largest audience. The role of Amazon as an expert for books is very limited, both because it is very easy for anybody to read a summary of the book and have an idea of its value, and because it is difficult for a writer or a publishing house to mislead the consumers about the value of the product. The role of Amazon as an adviser is also limited because most of the assessments of books on its web-site are written either by the publishing houses themselves or by readers. The value of the Amazon web-site is thus in its portfolio, not in its expertise.

Google, meanwhile, does not serve as a meeting place but as a thoroughfare: consumers use its search engine to find products. The only reason Google is valued by consumers is because it has a superior search algorithm that allows them to find information and products rapidly without fear that the search result may have been slanted toward one producer or another. Any search engine could have access to the same breadth of information as Google – the Internet is open – but Google is better at managing that information efficiently. Producers value advertising on Google because their ads will be finely targeted to

---

[1] See Rochet and Tirole (2004) for a more extensive survey on two-sided markets.

consumers who actually are searching for products in the category they are operating in. Merchants can indeed buy placement on the side of Google's pages of search results. Their product is displayed only when Google users search for specific keywords of their choice. This guarantees some relevance to the advertising to which the users are exposed. Google would therefore appear as an expert in matching consumers to producers and vice versa, while audience network effects play only a limited role.

These two examples, however, show how difficult it is to separate the role of the intermediary as an expert from its role as a market place. Indeed, the success of Amazon may be due in part to its expertise in categorizing its offering in ways that make finding books easy. Google draws part of its success from its ability to scour the whole of the Internet and provide search results that would not be available from other search engines. It could choose to ask for the exclusivity on some of its search results.

It was thus a choice for Amazon to limit itself to providing a market place; it did not believe it could build a competitive advantage by providing better buying advice than other sellers. Google realized in the same way it was not worth building a proprietary portfolio of merchants to which it would link in response to search queries by consumers. It preferred to emphasize its superiority as a neutral expert in web searching.

Most intermediaries thus choose to combine a role as an expert and a role as a market-maker. They build themselves both on their portfolio of clients and on their knowledge of the market they intermediate.

While the concepts and strategies that are studied in this chapter do not apply exclusively to the Internet markets, they hold specific relevance to the Internet, for two reasons. The first is that the Internet was thought to potentially lead to markets without intermediaries. Free access to the network and perfect information about each economic actor would make intermediaries irrelevant. Understanding why that "promise" was not fulfilled led to more reflection and a better understanding of the role of the intermediaries; an intellectual process which is reflected in the literature that is presented in this chapter. The second reason follows directly from the first: since intermediation is still necessary and Internet intermediaries do play an important role in the economics of the Internet,[2] studying their strategies and mode of functioning

---

[2] Henshaw (2001) reports that 80% of Internet users employ search engines to locate information. In January 2004, a Nielsen/Netrating survey ranked Google as the top Internet search destination before Yahoo!, MSN and AOL. Yahoo!, Amazon and eBay, all intermediaries, are among the few Internet success stories.

is necessary from a public policy point of view. One wants to understand what guides their pricing and what leads them to gather information on potential trading partners.

9.2   Network externalities, two-sided markets and intermediation

There are network externalities when the utility derived by a particular individual from a good or a service depends on the number of individuals using it. These network effects can play between similar users (direct network effects), in which case they are linked to the nature of the good or service offered. This is the case for a customer of Amazon, for instance, as the web-site offers recommendations on books to individuals based on the comparison between individual profiles and buying patterns. The more customers at Amazon, the larger the database and the more accurate the advice Amazon provides to its customers. This is one instance of a more general trend which sees the emergence of new ways to use the information generated within a consumption community to the benefit of this community. As another example, direct network effects are at stake in demand aggregators such as Mercata, which groups orders to negotiate favorable prices with suppliers: the ability to obtain a low price is related to the ability to attract a large number of buyers.

Network effects can also be at work between different groups of users (indirect network effects), in particular between users buying different services at different prices. This occurs for instance when one participates to an auction web-site such as eBay: on such a web-site sellers benefit from the participation of a large number of buyers as this ensures them a chance of selling and increases their chances of a higher expected selling price. At the same time buyers benefit from the presence of a large number of sellers as this increases their choice set.[3]

Such indirect network effects are one characteristic of intermediation activities. From a more general perspective, intermediation activities are characterized by asymmetric network effects. These network effects are to a large extent linked to the informational part of intermediation.[4] Buyers on an electronic platform care about the diversity of supply, while sellers care about the number of potential buyers they will have access to. There are two types of externalities involved: pecuniary externalities

---

[3] There are also negative externalities between buyers as the price depends on the level of supply on the market place (see Baye and Morgan (2001)).

[4] There may also be some consumption externality in transportation due to economies of scale, but they do not have the same asymmetric nature.

related to the way supply and demand affect the terms under which the exchange takes place, and non-pecuniary externalities coming from the extension of the range of products offered or demanded, and thus from the fact that at fixed exchange prices, there are more trade opportunities. Another important instance of asymmetric network effects concerns search engine and related services, where the externality is between the sites that are referenced and web-surfers. In what follows, only non-pecuniary externalities will be studied.

9.2.1   A model

The following model captures the nature of the interaction between the two parties. Consider one or several intermediation web-sites, referred to as *matchmaker/s*, performing an activity consisting in matching web-surfers with web-sites. On one side there is a unit mass of web-surfers forming a continuum. These web-surfers pay a price p to access the web-site. Denote by n the mass of web-surfers choosing to register. On the other side there is a unit mass of web-sites. The web-sites pay P to be listed by a matchmaker. Denote by N the mass of web-sites registering.

Matching is done as follows. For each client registering there is a cost c to collect and treat the client's information (for conciseness, it is assumed that the cost is the same for both sides). Assume that intermediaries are essential so that no match can be performed without the help of an intermediary. This is an extreme assumption but it makes sense in some cases where there are many agents supporting large search costs in the absence of some electronic intermediation.

Once an agent has registered with the intermediary, the latter introduces its characteristics within its database, and grants him access to a technology that performs a search in this database. The performance of the market under three scenarios will be compared:

- A competitive access to a global database: all intermediaries share their information. Any agent connected to the database has access to the whole information on all connected agents, and access is provided by all intermediaries under perfect competition. Intermediaries thus act as access providers.
- A monopoly intermediary: a monopoly builds a proprietary database of its customers. To be put in relation to a site or a web-surfer, it is necessary to register with the monopoly.
- Imperfect competition between several intermediaries: each intermediary builds a proprietary database of its customers. Only customers of the intermediary have access to its database.

Assume that when a web-site and a web-surfer are connected, they establish a non-merchant relationship, or the nature of the trade and the exchange price are not affected by the registration fees p and P. This supposes in particular that the intermediary performs only a matching function and does not intervene on the trading process between the web-site and the web-surfer.

To simplify, assume that payoffs are linear. A web-surfer receives an expected surplus fN from accessing a database with N web-sites, where f is the same for all web-surfers. The interpretation is that the probability of finding a partner is linear with the size of the population of web-sites and that the expected gain from trade is fixed, hence a linear relationship between the mass of web-site registering and the value of participating for a web-surfer. Web-surfers differ in their opportunity cost to participate in the market. This cost can be seen as the cost of time spent on the activity, or as the reflection of different values assigned to alternative activities. Each individual bears a personal cost of access that varies within the population. Individuals will access the market by increasing order of access cost. Define $a(n)$ to be the total access cost of the web-surfers when a mass n of them decides to access the market. The derivative $a'(n)$ is the access cost of the marginal participant: when the number of participants increases by dn, the new participants support an access cost $a'(n)$. In other words there is a mass n of web-surfers with an access cost smaller than $a'(n)$. Since the latter arrival incurs a higher cost than the former participants, the function $a(n)$ is convex and $a'(n)$ is increasing.

Consider here the case of a single large database, which obviously is efficient from a purely technical perspective.

Given a registration price p and a mass N of web-sites, a web-surfer will choose to register if its expected benefit is positive, where the benefit is the gross expected utility fN net of the price p and of the access costs. The number n of web-surfers participating is thus given by:

$$a'(n) = fN - p.$$

The net total surplus of web-surfers is then

$$s = fNn - a(n) - pn.$$

Similarly assume that each web-site derives a surplus Fn from its participation when this gives access to n web-surfers. Like for the web-surfers, the cost of registering and providing the relevant information to the intermediary is variable among web-sites. Let $A(N)$ be the total access cost of web-sites when a mass N of them registers. For the same reason as above, the total cost $A(N)$ is convex, and the mass of web-sites registering is related to the mass of web-surfers by the expression

$$A'(N) = Fn - P,$$

where P is the registration price for web-sites. The net surplus of web-sites is then

$$S = FnN - A(N) - PN.$$

In this set-up, the total profit is $(p - c)n + (P - c)N$, and the total surplus $W = s + S + (p - c)n + (P - c)N$ generated by the market is

$$W = (f + F)nN - a(n) - A(N) - c(n + N).$$

This shows that the market involves network externalities. The utility derived by a participant on one side of the market depends on the mass of participants on the other side of the market. This is referred to as a two-sided externality (see Armstrong (2002), Rochet and Tirole (2002)).

Ignoring any budget-balancing condition, the maximization of the total surplus requires that the participation levels verify

$$(f + F)N - a'(n) - c = 0;$$
$$(f + F)n - A'(N) - c = 0.$$

This is achieved by setting prices equal to

$$p = c - FN,$$
$$P = c - fn,$$

which accounts for network externalities. The participation of an additional web-site raises the utility of each web-surfer by an amount f. As a consequence, to achieve optimality, it is necessary to give to each web-site a subsidy equal to its total contribution fn. Total surplus maximization thus requires pricing access below cost and thus running a deficit.

When external subsidies are not available, the social optimum is obtained when maximizing the surplus W under the zero profit condition:

$$pn + PN = cn + cN.$$

A direct computation then shows that this leads to set prices such that the following conditions are verified:

$$p = c - FN + \frac{\lambda}{1 + \lambda} na''(n);$$

$$P = c - fn + \frac{\lambda}{1 + \lambda} NA''(N),$$

where λ is the shadow value of the zero profit condition. Optimal prices are not equal to marginal costs. Typically, since total profits vanish, the price faced by one side of the market should be below marginal cost, which is compensated by a positive margin on the other price. As emphasized in Armstrong (2002) or Caillaud and Jullien (2001): *The optimal pricing scheme involves cross-subsidies between the two sides of the market, a general characteristic of two-sided markets.* Which side of the market should be subsidized then depends on two considerations. The side of the market that generates the highest externality should claim for a subsidy. But this must be balanced by budgetary considerations of the Ramsey type, so that the price structure should also be shaped in favor of the side whose participation level is the most responsive to prices. A competitive access to a global database leads to access prices

$$p = c, \quad P = c.$$

The prices are equal to the marginal cost of including the customer in the network. Due to the presence of network effects, these prices are inefficient: *Competitive access pricing leads to an inefficient allocation of resources.*

The key point is that an access provider cannot recoup the entire surplus that its service generates since customers of other access providers benefit from the participation of its customers. Thus competitive access leads to complementarities between intermediaries that the market does not internalize. Achieving proper internalization would require creating a system of compensations, which would be equivalent to imposing access charges to the database of each intermediary.

Suppose now that the intermediation is ensured by a monopolist. Then the monopolist maximizes its profit:[5]

$$\Pi = (p - c)n + (P - c)N$$

or

$$\Pi = (F + f)nN - a'(n)n - A'(N)N - cn - cN.$$

The prices are then set at levels

$$p = c - FN + na''(n);$$
$$P = c - fn + NA''(N).$$

The monopolist internalizes the network effects but introduces a mark-up over the net social cost. It is easy to see that there are cases where

---

[5] Assume here that the monopolist can control quantities. Due to a coordination failure problem, there may exist several allocations compatible with a given price structure, so that price control may not suffice to achieve monopoly profits.

even a monopoly would choose to subsidize one side of the market by setting a price below cost (say $p < c$) and recovering the loss by having the other side pay a large fee for their participation. This will occur when the valuations that the two sides assign to the service are asymmetric.

One conclusion from the comparison between a monopoly and a competitive access system is that info-mediation markets are more complex than traditional "make and sale" markets, or even standard "buy and resale" intermediary markets. The complexity comes in part from the intermediary's ability to set different access prices for each side of the market. Suppose that the intermediary could not know the identity of customers nor the use they make of the database (for instance on stock exchanges, the same individual may be a buyer or a seller during the same session so that it is not possible to charge different registration fees). The monopolist charges the same price for all users and this price is above marginal cost. In this case, competition dominates a monopoly market structure unambiguously.

Thus the monopolist's advantage is the ability to set different prices and to cross-subsidize. That type of cross-subsidy calls for a more detailed discussion in the context of imperfect competition, for two reasons. First, the analysis suggests that the optimal market structure may obtain with a limited number of intermediaries under imperfect competition, as a way to balance coordination and the exercise of market power. Second, the use of cross-subsidies generates very aggressive pricing strategies to capture customers, which are specific to this type of market.

9.3   Competing intermediaries

Assume now that intermediation services are provided by two intermediaries, A and B. The intermediary k sets prices p_k and P_k for the web-surfers and the web-sites respectively. Unlike the competitive access case, a customer of an intermediary has access only to that intermediary's database and thus to its customers only. Assume in addition that a customer can register with only one intermediary (see the discussion below).

For this discussion, simplify matters further by assuming that access costs are constant and equal to zero. As this is the most interesting case, concentrate on the case where there is a strong asymmetry between the two sides so that $F > 2f$. Under those assumptions, a monopoly intermediary can charge maximum prices $p = f$ and $P = F$. The allocation is efficient but the entire surplus is captured by the monopolist. In this context a competitive access system would allow users to enjoy the full surplus but the allocation may be inefficient. In particular, if one side of the market has a low value for the connection to the other side (f smaller than c), there will be no exchange at all as no one participates. Consider the case of two competing intermediaries. Competition is taken under its extreme Bertrand type: each agent joins the intermediary offering the highest utility. Then, when the price differential between the two intermediaries is smaller for each side than the value of inter-mediation, f and F, the allocation of consumers is indeterminate due to network effects. There are two possible equilibria in the allocation of consumers: in both, all agents register with the same intermediary, but any of the two intermediaries can emerge as the winner. In such a setting, the outcome of competition will be affected by prices but also by the expectations of each individual on the behavior of the other side of the market: whether an individual registers with A or B depends on whether it expects the other side to do so. Our purpose here is simply to illustrate some of the mechanisms at work when info-mediaries compete.[6] To do so, an equilibrium which corresponds to the maximal profit equilibrium will be exhibited.

Notice that in our very simple set-up, an efficient equilibrium is one where all agents register with the same intermediary, say A. In equilibrium at least one of the prices of the intermediary A must be above cost. Given that web-sites attach a higher value to reaching the web-surfers than the latter attach to reaching a web-site, intuition suggests that web-sites should be the profitable side of the market. So let us take for granted that they face a price above c.

Given the prices of A, consider the options of the other intermediary in terms of tariffication. As follows from above, if the price differential with A is smaller than f and F respectively, B faces the risk of not attracting anybody. To be sure to attract some customers, B must thus undercut A by a large amount on at least one side. But then the possi-bility of cross-subsidy generates pricing strategies that are very con-trasted between the two sides of the markets. For instance, in order to attract the web-surfers with certainty, B must undercut the price of A for web-surfers by an amount f (implying a negative price and thus a subsidy or a gift). What is meant here by a negative price is not neces-sarily a payment to the web-surfers but rather translates into the fact that some services will be offered free of charge or that the intermediary will spend a lot in the acquisition of the audience. The subsidy here is chosen so that web-surfers join B even if web-sites register with A. Its purpose is for B to create a value for the web-sites and it is justified only if it allows

---

[6] See Caillaud and Jullien (2001) and Caillaud and Jullien (2003) for a more extensive analysis.

attracting the web-sites at a price that compensates the loss on web-surfers. Given that no web-surfers join A at this price if B decides to undercut by an amount f the price for web-surfers at A, A loses its value for the web-sites. Then the web-sites are willing to join B at a price up to F.

To summarize the discussion, by undercutting the price of web-surfers by f, the intermediary B can generate a profit $F - c$ on the web-sites. This implies that the profit generated by intermediary A on the web-surfers cannot exceed $f - (F - c)$. Given that $F - c$ is an upper bound on the profit obtained by the intermediary A on web-sites, the total profit that intermediary A can expect is less than or equal to f, the value of the service for the side of the market with the smallest willingness to pay for participation. Following the analysis in Caillaud and Jullien (2003), one can show that there is indeed an equilibrium in which the intermediary A monopolizes the market with this maximum profit. This can be achieved, for instance, with prices $f - (F - c) + c$ for web-surfers and a price F for web-sites.

This example illustrates that the nature of competition that takes place between intermediaries on electronic markets is quite different from the nature of the competition between producers of final goods, the difference coming from the network interactions inherent to the intermediation activity.

Competition reduces profits but may not eliminate them completely, even in the absence of any differentiation between service providers. In the relevant case where f is smaller than the monopoly profit, the profit cannot exceed the value of intermediation for any side of the market. In the simple case discussed before, this reduction in profit is not related to any efficiency consideration as the allocation is the same for a monopoly market structure or a duopoly (this obviously is not general). As suggested by the preceding section, an imperfectly competitive market structure with several intermediaries having proprietary databases may dominate a monopolistic market structure – which is not a surprise – but it can also dominate a competitive access system with a global database, which is more surprising. This occurs when the value of intermediation is small for the web-surfers, $f < c$. Indeed, in that case, competition between proprietary databases results in the participation of both sides in the market while a competitive global access system would not generate participation, and this is achieved with low profits for the intermediary, unlike in the monopoly case.

Thus, one conclusion from this analysis is that the optimal market structure for info-mediation markets is a situation of competition between a limited number of actors. This is true from a positive perspective, as due to network effects there are barriers to entry in these markets. This is also true from a normative perspective as this allows finding a compromise between the need to internalize network effects through some cross-subsidization and the distortions in the level of prices that market power induces. As usual when this occurs, one issue is obviously that if the competition is too intense with several intermediaries and there are significant entry costs, the market structure will not be optimal and may even turn out to be a monopoly, as no other firm may be willing to sink the entry cost to compete.

The analysis also provides a rationale for the common practice on the Internet of granting free access to one side of the market. Free access emerges when one side should be subsidized but the service provider cannot discriminate between potential users and money-grabbers.

More generally it shows that cross-subsidies are exacerbated by competition, a conclusion that contrasts with the analysis of traditional markets. Indeed, in markets with no network effects or any possibility of linking the price faced by a customer to the specific network externalities that its participation generates, competition tends to reduce the margins over marginal costs, and thus to reduce any form of cross-subsidy or more generally of price discrimination.

Exploring further the logic behind this type of model then shows that these conclusions are reinforced once other specificities of digital technologies are taken into account, such as sophisticated pricing, discrimination or multi-homing.

9.4   Asymmetric information and info-mediaries

Instead of looking at the role of the intermediary as a matchmaker, this section deals with the role of the intermediary as an expert. In a market where buyers are imperfectly informed about the value of the sellers' products, trade may not be possible. Suppose, for example, that the expected value of a product in a category in which there are many sellers is negative but some sellers have products with positive value. Suppose also that the seller cannot prove the value of its product to the consumer, as can happen if they trade exclusively over the Internet. Its product then cannot be sold as its expected value is negative; no claim that the product is valuable can be trusted, since all sellers are motivated to make that claim. On the Internet, those information asymmetries are exacerbated because the consumer cannot touch the product and assess its quality,[7]

---

[7] The consumer may have access to more information about the product via the Internet than it could through other channels, but the physical world will always potentially offer a wider range of learning experiences in a more credible way. "Those who have not seen and yet believe will be blessed", but more often than not they are deceived.

while guarantees are difficult to put in place: the seller's creditworthiness may be questionable. Even if the product is digital, a software for example, and could theoretically be tested before buying, it is not possible to monitor its use. A consumer would then be tempted to return the software and pretend it was not valuable, while continuing to use it on its computer, unchecked.

The intermediary may be relied on to prevent such a market failure: an intermediary, defined as a long-term market player with a superior knowledge of the supplier's good's quality and a large portfolio of clients, will be trusted to tell the truth about the supplier's good. Indeed, its interests are not linked to the welfare of any specific participant in the market, while it will want to provide objective advice to consumers: its reputation as a reliable information provider is its only stock in trade. Its profits being linked to the quality of the information it provides, it will also be motivated to invest in certification technologies that allow it to accurately assess the quality of the goods it intermediates.

There are therefore three main claims for the usefulness of intermediaries:

- *Neutral third parties:* intermediaries solve the adverse selection problem in markets with asymmetric information as they are not linked to any parties in the trade.
- *Reputation rent-seekers:* intermediaries will not lie about the seller's quality so as to preserve their reputation and the profits it engenders.
- *Experts:* intermediaries turn soft, unverifiable information about a supplier's product into hard, certifiable information.

The rest of this section examines those roles and how the intermediary plays them. A monopoly intermediary may want to profit from its information on a supplier's product not by revealing it but by hiding it in exchange for payment. This is the paradoxical "minimal information" result whereby all suppliers seek the certification of the intermediary but the intermediary's certification does not reveal any information to the customer beyond what it already knew about the supplier.

In a competitive setting, an intermediary will reveal the type of the supplier, but there will be concern about the motivation for suppliers to bribe the intermediary into lying about their type. This will be shown not to happen in equilibrium, unless consumers are naïve and do not anticipate bribe taking.

Before going on, note that the models presented here differ from the principal-agent models with an outside auditor who monitors the relationship (Khalil and Lawarree (1995) and Baron and Besanko (1984)): there is no hierarchical relationship between the trading parties, and no moral hazard from one or the other side. The type t of the good that is traded is not a variable in the model: effort in producing the good has already been expended.

The cases that are discussed here also differ from search and reputation models dealing with situations of asymmetric information in bilateral trade between buyers and sellers (Milgrom (1981), Grossman (1981), Crawford and Sobel (1982), Okuno-Fujiwara, Postlewaite, and Suzumura (1990) and Wolinsky (1993)). Instead of a situation where a player (seller, expert) wants to reveal its own type to another agent (buyer, decision maker), here an intermediary must try to find out the type of the supplier before revealing it to the buyer.

9.4.1   A model

The typical model of information intermediation that serves as the basic building block for the discussion is presented below. There are three types of agents: buyers, sellers and intermediaries. Buyers and sellers may use the services of the intermediary to assist them in their transactions. The seller owns a good of type t which it values at 0. The consumer values a good of type t at t. The seller knows t but cannot credibly reveal it to the consumer (soft information). The intermediary has a technology to test goods at cost c, which allows it to know t.

The timing of the game is as follows:

1. The intermediary sets an array of prices P and disclosure rules D to maximize its profits. P is the price vector for its service to consumers and sellers. Disclosure rules specify what information the consumer will be given about t.
2. The supplier decides whether to use the service of the intermediary, knowing P, D and its own type t.
3. If the supplier uses the service of the intermediary, then the intermediary may choose to pay cost c to discover t.
4. The consumer observes P, D, the decision of the supplier to use the service of the intermediary and the intermediary's revelation, $R(t, D)$.
5. The consumer decides whether to buy the seller's good.

9.4.2   The minimal information result

Suppose the intermediary is a monopoly. Note that the monopoly setting is not merely a way to introduce the more complicated competitive setting. Most papers study only a monopoly setting by arguing like Strausz (2003) that there are increasing returns to scale to certification: the bigger the potential loss from lying, the higher the motivation not to lie and the better the reputation of the intermediary, who can then out-price the competition. Intermediation would then be a natural monopoly. The certifier may also be a State-mandated monopoly, as happens if it is appointed the management of a government-mandated certification process.

Lizzeri (1999) will be used to study the base case scenario and is therefore presented in detail. There is an intermediary and many suppliers who want to sell goods valued at t by consumers, but consumers do not know t and know only its distribution among suppliers, F distributed over $[0, 1]$. The intermediary is able to certify the product of the supplier of type t and in that case, it can be sold at t. The intermediary sells its certification service at p, the same for each supplier. This is because it does not know 't' beforehand.

Suppose the intermediary tells t to consumers once the supplier has paid p. The supplier then makes profit of $t - p$. Since $p > 0$, not all suppliers will seek certification. Only suppliers with $t > t(p)$ will seek certification. The ones who do not must sell their goods to consumers who know that their type is below $t(p)$, and thus make a profit of $E[t/t < t(p)]$. The threshold type is thus $t(p)$ such that

$$t(p) - p = E[t/t < t(p)]$$

and the intermediary makes profits of

$$\Pi_I = p \times \left(1 - F(t(p))\right).$$

Note that an equilibrium where suppliers of type $t > t(p)$ go to the intermediary while others do not is sustained by consistent beliefs: if consumers believe suppliers conform to that equilibrium, then suppliers will do so, and conversely.

However, the intermediary may be able to manipulate beliefs in a more profitable way than by simply revealing t if p is paid. Looking at the profit function above, the intermediary wants many suppliers (potentially all) to use its service while charging them a positive price. This can be done by setting price $E(t)$ for its service and not revealing anything about the type of the supplier, except that it is not of type 0. In that equilibrium, consumers' beliefs are such that a supplier who does not get certified is assumed to be of type 0. That equilibrium is sustained by consistent beliefs.

The disclosure rule such that $D = \emptyset$ if $t > 0$, $D = 0$ if $t = 0$ thus supports an equilibrium that is optimal for the intermediary as it gets the whole surplus $E(t)$ from the market. However, the beliefs that sustain it may seem arbitrary, and indeed consumers may entertain other beliefs that get lower profits for the intermediary. (They may believe, for example, that no supplier goes to the intermediary except the lowest type, resulting in profit 0 for the intermediary.) Lizzeri (1999) shows that the intermediary can induce favorable beliefs under some conditions – see Appendix A.

Lizzeri (1999) thus shows that the intermediary may not reveal any information about t to the consumers. Even though there is no benefit for suppliers in using the service of the intermediary, all suppliers still are ready to abandon the whole surplus from trade to the intermediary. This is supported by the consumers' belief that a seller who does not go to the intermediary is of the lowest type. Not going to the intermediary is interpreted as a bad signal, and no buyer will buy from a seller that is not certified. Therefore, all sellers need to go to the intermediary to perform any sale. The intermediary sets its price as the difference between what the supplier will get by selling through the intermediary and what it would get if it was the worst type. The only information the consumer gets is that a supplier that is certified is not of the worst type. The intermediary thus acts like a parasite that both buyers and sellers would want to get rid of, but whose mere presence makes it indispensable. Is this what is observed on the Internet? No, as intermediaries do seem to provide information about products by ranking them, giving advice, etc. That information would not be accessible without them. Does this invalidate Lizzeri's point?

Not necessarily, as Guerra (2001) extends Lizzeri's minimal information result to explain why intermediaries give some (but not all) of their information. The consumer now has some information $t_e = t + \theta$ about the supplier's type t with θ i.i.d. The supplier can sell its product at $p(t_e)$ if t_e is the only information the consumer has, and at $p(t)$ if the intermediary certifies its product as t. The graph on the left in Figure 9.1 shows what happens when the consumer has no information about t: the intermediary's profit will be maximized by setting a threshold t_i under which it does not certify the product, and getting the supplier to pay for the difference between the expected value of its product without certification vs. its value with certification. The graph on the right shows what happens if t_e increases with t: setting a single threshold t_i results in suppliers with a high t not wanting to pay the price of certification because consumers will already know their type is higher than t_i. The intermediary is then better off setting several intervals of certification, $[t_1, t_2], [t_2, t_3], [t_3, t_4], \ldots$ with associated prices $p_1, p_2, p_3, \ldots$. The intermediary assigns suppliers into classes so as to offer the consumer

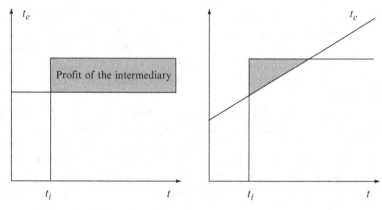

Figure 9.1. Lizzeri vs. Guerra.

just enough information to prevent the supplier from bypassing the intermediary.

The negative result in Lizzeri (1999) thus does not hold if the consumer has some information about the suppliers. It does not hold either if consumers are risk averse: Peyrache and Quesada (2004) show that in that case the intermediary will reveal information about t beyond simply saying whether trade is efficient or not. With risk aversion, t is revealed fully if it is above some threshold level, while nothing is said about those suppliers whose type is below that threshold. The disclosure rule is therefore such that t is revealed fully for $t \geq x$ for some $x > 0$, while nothing is revealed for $t < x$. The intermediary reveals more information than in Lizzeri (1999) because it plays an additional role which is to reduce uncertainty in the market. It thus can increase the expected surplus from trade by disclosing information about the supplier, a surplus from trade it then appropriates. As a monopoly, of course, it will set the threshold t such as to maximize its profit, and not the global surplus. This is why no information will be disclosed for t below a threshold. Peyrache and Quesada (2004) introduce another role for the intermediary: it relaxes price competition between the suppliers by allowing them to differentiate their product through certification. This leads it in the same fashion as above to disclose more information about the suppliers.

The monopoly intermediary thus reveals information about t when its role in the relationship buyer–seller is not only strategic (which side is going to get what share of the surplus of trade) but also productive (reducing uncertainty, alleviating competitive pressures, etc.).

9.4.3   Collusion

Lizzeri (1999) assumed that the intermediary could not lie about t: its disclosure rule was public. The monopoly intermediary would not disclose any information about t in equilibrium. However, consumers and suppliers are best served by an intermediary that reveals t and sets its fee to 0. Competition between intermediaries leads to the adoption of that strategy. There is thus revelation of information, and consumers pay t for a product that is certified as t while the intermediaries make zero profit. What happens then if the intermediary can lie about t? In a one-period setting, the intermediary will always want to take a bribe from a supplier to pretend that its type t is high. This adverse selection problem may then prevent trade from happening.

Peyrache and Quesada (2003) show, however, that if consumers correctly anticipate the risk of bribe taking and the game is repeated, there will be no bribe taking. Indeed, suppose consumers react to a lie about t by the intermediary by not using its service anymore in future periods. Suppose profit from accepting a bribe today is B while future discounted profits lost by lying is Π, and the intermediary accepts bribes with some probability λ. Either $B > \Pi$ in which case the intermediary will always accept bribes and its certificate does not convey any information, or $B = \Pi$ and $\lambda \in [0, 1]$. Knowing λ, consumers will update their belief about t based on the message of the intermediary. If, for example, it is profitable for a supplier of type t_1 to pay the bribe so as to obtain a certificate a, consumers will interpret a as t_1 and will not be ready to pay more than if the intermediary had told the truth. This can be generalized to say that the intermediary cannot sell a false report at any positive price, so $B = 0$ so that the intermediary will lie if and only if Π itself is 0. Therefore, in the general case, the intermediary never lies about t even if it is subject to bribes. That equilibrium is fragile however; the consumer must be able to estimate the profits of the intermediary and its incentive to accept bribes.

Those are strong assumptions since most consumers do not even know that many search results on search engines are sponsored. While sponsorships and bribes are two different things, this suggests that consumers are also unaware of the risk of getting biased reports. Most models of bribe taking thus assume that the consumer is naïve: it does not fully anticipate bribe taking. In that case, lying may be a profitable short-term strategy, and asking for bribes to do so is enticing. The consumer will deter such behavior by retaliating if it was lied to (when the supplier that was certified proved to be of another type than what the intermediary said). Instead of assuming that any consumer's report of a lie by an intermediary is immediately conveyed and believed by all, it is reasonable to assume that consumers can punish the intermediary only at their individual level. Indeed, if consumers believed any report of a misbehavior by an intermediary, a competitor would fabricate such a report.

Suppose therefore consumers take a report t at face value and do not have any other information about the type of the supplier than what the intermediary reveals. If no bribes are offered, and the intermediary sets the price of certification at p, then any supplier of type $t(p)$ such that

$$t(p) - p \geq E(t/t \leq t(p)) \tag{9.1}$$

will seek certification. Maximization of profit with respect to p leads to setting a certification threshold level at $t_I^{\star}$ and $p^{\star} = t_I^{\star} - E(t/t \leq t_I^{\star})$. Any supplier of type t more than t_I gets its product certified as t.

Suppose now, w.l.o.g., that the intermediary, before getting to know the type of the supplier, offers to certify the supplier as being of the highest type $\bar{t}$, and this at cost b (bribe). A supplier of type $t \geq t_I$ would then be able to sell its product at $\bar{t}$ and will bribe the intermediary if it can make higher profits that way than by paying p and being certified as being of type t:

$$\bar{t} - b \geq t - p. \tag{9.2}$$

Suppliers of type $t \leq t_I$ bribe only if:

$$\bar{t} - b \geq E(t/t \leq t_I). \tag{9.3}$$

Therefore, no supplier will bribe if $b \geq \bar{t} - E(t/t \leq t_I)$, all will if $b \leq p$, while for $b \in [p, \bar{t} - E(t/t \leq t_I)]$, some suppliers will choose to bribe the intermediary. The intermediary will then be trusted to reveal valuable information only if the maximum bribe $b = \bar{t} - E(t/t \leq t_I)$ it could get is low. That means p must be high as then, only suppliers with a high type t get certified, so that $E(t/t \leq t_I)$ is high and as a consequence b, the bribe that can be obtained, is low. Strausz (2003) shows that the intermediary will indeed react by setting a higher price for its certification than if it was not subject to bribes. The intermediary will thus exclude more suppliers from the market than if it was a monopoly unable to take bribes.

In competition the intermediary is forced to lower its price compared with the monopoly outcome. The previous analysis would seem to mean it is then more subject to bribe taking. There is then a potential degradation of the quality of certification due to competitive pressures. Gaudeul (2003) shows that competition may in fact improve the quality of certification. Suppose the intermediary has a portfolio of consumers (mass 1).

There are two types of suppliers – type high whose product can be sold to $\bar{t}$ consumers at price $\bar{p}$, and type low whose product can be sold to $\underline{t}$ consumers at price $\underline{p}$. Consumers buy a product if told to do so by the intermediary, and find out the type of the supplier afterwards. Suppose $1 > \bar{t} > \underline{t}$ and $\bar{p} < \underline{p}$. The honest intermediary can acquire hard information on the supplier's product at cost c and then get the appropriate number of consumers to buy it. The dishonest intermediary will announce a supplier of type $\underline{t}$ is of type $\bar{t}$. $\bar{t}$ consumers will then buy the product. $\bar{t} - \underline{t}$ will be disappointed and will not return to the intermediary the following period.

In the monopoly setting, intermediaries with a high discount factor will be honest because they want to keep customers. In competition, consumers who are not directed by an intermediary go to another. This will be shown to increase the incentive to be honest: when the intermediary announces a supplier of type $\underline{t}$ is of type $\bar{t}$, $1 - \bar{t}$ consumers go to another intermediary this period instead of $1 - \underline{t}$ if the intermediary had told the truth. While lying loses consumers for the next period, it also hurts competitors this period. Those competitors react to a deviation from truthfulness by offering suppliers or consumers more advantageous terms so as to discourage them from listing or buying at a deviating intermediary. This means that deviating starts a price war in addition to losing consumers. Any intermediary who would have been honest in a monopoly setting will therefore be honest in a competitive setting.[8] A competitive intermediation system is at least as stable as a monopolistic one as long as intermediaries are able to observe each other's pricing and recommendations strategies.

The models above apply to search engines, but there are other types of info-mediaries that are important to the functioning of the Internet – those companies such as Verisign that certify the compliance of a merchant's web-site with some pre-defined rules of operation (privacy policy, credit worthiness, etc.). Those intermediaries of trust either certify the web-site or do not. Hvide (2002) thus considers a situation where intermediaries offer only binary reports ("pass" or "fail") to the consumers. Instead of having a grid in which suppliers are ranked, the intermediaries

---

[8] For the same type of reason, an intermediary who would have incurred cost c to know the type of the supplier may not do so in competition. Indeed, knowing the type of the supplier allows the intermediary to better fine-tune its advice to consumers, and thus direct more consumers each period. As explained above, directing more customers each period exacerbates competitive pressure, which explains why this more efficient system is used less often in competition. The intermediary prefers giving less information to reduce competitive pressure with other intermediaries at the expense of directing fewer consumers each period.

disclose only whether the supplier passed or failed their test. Hvide (2002) shows a two-tiered system will arise in competition. Suppliers of a good type will get certified by the intermediaries who deliver certificates ("pass report") with lower probabilities, and information about the seller's type is thus conveyed by which intermediary it was certified by. The intermediaries who certify the highest type are the ones who make the highest profit, and those higher profits ensure they certify truthfully (they want to keep their reputation as a certifier of high-quality sellers). Suppliers self-select into each intermediary, as for example suppliers of a low type know they have low probability of passing the test of an intermediary of a high type. This explains how intermediaries of trust will compete based on the perception of the quality of the sites they certify.

Open questions

This chapter does not deal with the analysis of the incentive for suppliers to produce goods of a high quality when the intermediary confiscates some of their surplus. Albano and Lizzeri (2001) show that while the intermediary improves the information that buyers have about the quality of the supplier's good, quality is underprovided relative to full information.

The intermediary must limit its share of the surplus in order to provide an incentive for the supplier to produce goods of a high quality, which leads to a study of how the terms of trade are set between the supplier and the consumer after the intermediary put them in contact. There is indeed a problem of re-negotiation of the terms of trade between the buyer and the seller if those that were concluded at the intermediary cannot be monitored afterwards. Suppliers may use the intermediary to contact consumers, and then bypass it to conclude the transaction. There is indeed an information revelation problem as it may not be possible for the intermediary to prove that a trade took place and on what terms. This makes a commission-based contract difficult to implement.

This is why the intermediary will prefer getting the terms of trade determined at the same time as the two parties are put in contact; it will not leave this to negotiation between the two parties after matching. Alternatively, the intermediary can make sure all negotiations occur under its watch. The intermediary then determines the terms of trade through the choice of who is allowed to meet, whether they are allowed to break off negotiation, or by setting the level of compensation for the breakup of negotiations. eBay (Resnick and Zeckhauser [2002]) is a case study of the variety of choice an intermediary can propose to a consumer; buyers and sellers choose what selling/buying mechanism they are going to use (auction, fixed price, with insurance, without insurance, etc.) and then decide which buyer/seller to trade with, based at least in part on which mechanism was chosen. Nadel (2000) provides a discussion of how Internet intermediaries adopt different strategies that provide for different levels of objectivity in the advice given to consumers. Other interesting areas for research include the strategies of consumers, who may be able to take advice from several intermediaries (multi-homing) and gather multiple reports. They may also visit consumers' fora. Consumers' fora can be more credible than any intermediary, due to the number of reports gathered there and the lack of an incentive for any consumer to lie about their experience (Chen, Fay, and Wang [2003]). What then motivates consumers to report their experience? Can any one supplier influence the tone of the reports about its product or the product of competitors by posing as consumers?

Models also generally assume that a false report by an intermediary necessarily means it was lying. However, suppliers may be able to prevent the intermediary from gaining perfect knowledge of their type and it is then difficult to attribute a mistake to the intermediary or to the seller.

Finally, the government may adopt regulation and impose remedies to maintain and improve intermediation services. The government does play a role in the regulation of digital markets. It sets the allowed amount of advertising (anti-spam regulations), limits or encourages competition in markets for information, mandates the certification of products and ensures minimum levels of truthfulness in advertising. That role may also be partially left to private organizations that will set and monitor standards (see Lerner and Tirole (2004)). More broadly, Strömberg (2002) discusses the interplay between media and public policy.

9.5   Appendix A – Outline of Lizzeri's proof

If

$$E(t/t \geq x) - E(t) \geq E(t/t \leq x), \forall x \in [0, 1],$$

then the intermediary can use a certification method that ensures favorable beliefs by the consumer: it will certify the highest type 1 as type 1 with probability p close to 1, while certifying all other suppliers of type $t < 1$ as t with probability q close to 0. In that case, the type 1 supplier goes to the intermediary. It will not be alone to do so because if it was, then going to the intermediary would be a sure signal you are of type 1, and other suppliers would be motivated to go to the intermediary (indeed, q is low enough that their true type is not revealed often, while $p < 1$ makes it credible that a supplier who is not certified may still be of type 1). There is therefore a cutoff point x such that suppliers with $t > x$ go to I.

The condition on F ensures they make higher profits by getting certified and paying $E(t)$ than by not going to the intermediary. By progressive unraveling of suppliers' behaviors (any supplier of type $t = x - \varepsilon$, ε small, will want to get confused with suppliers of type $t \geq x$ and make higher profits), $x = 0$. Therefore, suppliers find themselves forced into a behavior that benefits the intermediary, and consumers cannot thus entertain alternative, less favorable, beliefs about the behavior of suppliers.

10   The economics and business models of prescription in the Internet

Pierre-Jean Benghozi and Thomas Paris

10.1   Introduction

A number of authors have helped to demonstrate the extent to which performance of e-commerce firms is based on their ability to design, control and manage an enormous amount of information on an ongoing basis so that consumers can easily grasp and understand goods and services provided. Thanks to the wide range of technologies made available by the Internet, along with methods for appropriating these technologies, highly diversified economic infrastructures and business models, autonomizing specific economic functions, can be mobilized for the purpose of marketing a single product or service.

Highlighting and revealing the informational aspect of transactions is useful but not helpful enough in explaining current market configurations or the strategies that economic agents deploy. Buzzel (1985) shows, for example, how distributors and intermediaries acquired power over producers and gained more influence as they moved from wholesalers engaged in buying and selling products to more complex forms of intermediation and prescription mobilizing information and communication technologies.[1] More specifically, allowing consumers to compare products directly without having to rely on supposedly knowledgeable experts, the Internet changed the traditional role of the intermediary;[2] it no longer functions as just a distributor or expert consultant but also regulates transactions, promoting and prescribing goods and services. As a consequence, many authors have attempted to describe and provide characterization of the various forms of intermediation (Spulber, 1996 and 1999; Chircu and Kauffman, 1999; Brousseau, 2002). For example,

---

[1] This analysis of the impact of distribution and other downstream activities in the manufacturing sector complements work in the field of information systems, notably by Steve Barley (1986).

[2] An idea that has received renewed attention owing to the growth of the Internet and other activities that reflect the expanding role of the knowledge economy (cf. Peter Kollock, 1999; Eric Brousseau, 2002).

Gensollen (1999) identifies several different actors who can play an intermediary role: attractors, aggregators, converters (i.e. those who convert an audience into customers) and prescribers.[3]

Our premise is that the mechanisms at work in distribution and intermediation at stake in the business models existing on the Internet should be assessed in terms of a *prescription economy*. By analyzing the markets in terms of prescription, i.e. the capacity of a firm to transform the potential request of a customer into a specific proposal of products, we can investigate the structure of a product or service supply, the decision-making process involved in purchasing, market configurations, and business strategies and models.

Analyzing intermediation and information markets in terms of prescription means considering three-pronged markets where prescribers are not simple intermediaries but third parties: they act alongside producers and consumers – not between them – in order to structure the product or service supply or to assume responsibility for some aspect of the consumer decision. If we proceed on this assumption, we can identify the market strategies and structures that characterize a prescription economy.

This chapter aims to propose a model for prescription on a three-pronged basis, and to explore the way it can be applied to explain the various strategies and business models used on the Internet. In the first part, we shall present our model for prescription and the strategic variables actionable by prescribers. In the second part, these results will help us to characterize the various existing forms of prescription and to propose a typology of prescribers. The forms of prescription provide a key to understand the economic structuring of the Internet. There, prescription assumes a wider range of forms (in terms of how users select content and in the nature of the relationship with consumers and sellers) insofar as the Internet is more complex: it offers a wider range of information products and greater variety with regard to value chains, economic players and business models.

10.2   The economic foundations of the prescription

In order to delineate the phenomenon at stake and to establish the economic foundations of prescription, we shall firstly describe more

---

[3] For Gensollen, prescribers do not truly exist but constitute the ultimate form of intermediation: the delivery of information from uniform groups of consumers to producers so that new products and services can be tailored to the tastes that these consumers have come to share over time.

precisely what can be considered as prescription. Discussing various examples will help us to discard the one-dimensional view of the market in which supply matches appropriately to demand, possibly via an intermediary or market platform.[4] Each component of prescription function (collection of information, selection of goods and services, support to the decision-making process of the consumer, assistance in the transactional process) influences the market configuration, the control of customer relations and emerging business models. It encourages us to replace it with a three-pronged model involving the supplier, the consumer and the prescriber. Using this model will help us to make out the various revenue sources for prescribers and the strategic levers at their disposal for gaining competitive advantage.

10.2.1 A widespread situation

The phenomenon of prescription is very diffused and can be found in several industries and professions, from doctors (who prescribe medications) to educators (who prescribe specific classroom textbooks), architects, contractors, financial advisers and asset managers. In each of these situations, responsibility for the purchasing decision is transferred; moreover, there is no longer a link between the market that brings together the product or service provider and the prescriber and the market that brings together the prescriber and the consumer – each of these two markets generates its own transactions and dynamics. For example, educators are in a position to recommend the textbooks that will be used on their courses: their role is not simply to inform or to influence but to actually issue an injunction. The same is true of physicians and the medications they prescribe to their patients. All these cases are putting on view different market structures where intermediaries are no more a mere link in the supply chain but contribute to more complex economic configurations.

Hatchuel (1995) has demonstrated how consumers disqualify themselves as decision-makers by relying on an outside prescriber, who defines how buyers perceive the goods to be searched, establishes the value assigned to these goods and points buyers toward one particular supplier over another. Hatchuel emphasizes how, in this case, knowledge is transferred to the end consumer, but he does not consider this a structural component of the market: when viewed as primarily a cognitive function, prescription is necessarily temporary in nature because

---

[4] See, in particular, developments made on two-sided markets by Jean-Charles Rochet and Jean Tirole, 2003.

consumers gradually acquire the knowledge that they previously lacked and, as a result, they have less and less need to rely on an expert. In this case, the relationship between seller and prescriber is limited to the domain of information and decision-making (i.e. the seller's attempt to influence the prescriber)[5] in a form of extra-market competition. In essence, this approach is very similar to the one advocated by authors who have studied electronic intermediation, which is characterized by the ability to take advantage of the correspondence between transactional flows and information resources. Our model aims precisely at modelling how such different flows and transactions articulate with one another.

10.2.2   A three-pronged model

We assume, in this chapter, that in the economics of prescription, there is no longer one sole market, operating between producers and consumers. Our main argument is that three markets work together wherein decisions are transferred, the decision-making process is compounded and the market is filtered by prescribers. These markets can be defined as follows, recapping the primary characteristics of our model (Figure 10.1):

1. A web of transactions among three groups:
   o suppliers (S), providing goods and services;
   o consumers (D), representing end demand;
   o prescribers, who offer or recommend goods and services.
2. A network of exchanges occurring in three separate markets:
   o the primary market of relevant goods and services, where consumers make a selection from a range of goods provided;
   o the prescriber market, which governs relations between consumers and the various prescribers;
   o the referral market, which regulates the acquisition of goods and the selection of information between prescribers and sellers.

The examples in Figure 10.2 show how this three-pronged structure provides a simple means of grasping the various configurations found in prescription-based markets.[6]

---

[5] Extensive marketing research has been conducted on this topic.
[6] For purposes of clarity, we have initially restricted ourselves to examples taken from outside the Internet.

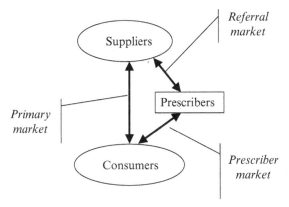

Figure 10.1. The prescription markets: a three-pronged structure.

10.2.3   The variables of prescription

Our model helps to establish prescribers as full-part economic actors in different markets. We propose, then, to identify the range of variables at their disposal to set their strategy and economic business models. They can be sorted into two main categories: first, the sources of revenue which support prescribers' activity, then their competitive leverages.

Sources of revenue for prescribers
Differentiating transactions, we can better understand how companies get revenue on each market and the opposing strategies they use. If the participants conduct a simple purchase or sale, their remuneration comes primarily from the profit yielded by the transaction. By contrast, if they facilitate the exchange or provide advice, their remuneration may be based on the commission that the seller or buyer is willing to pay in return (Hackett, 1992). As shown in Figure 10.2, prescribers participate in two different markets: the referral market and the prescription market. They can create value on both markets, performing information processing and certification on the first one, operating matching between consumer's request and product selection on the second one. The range of potential revenue sources and business models depends specifically on the prescriber's ability to become operative on these two markets.

In the prescription market, prescribers create value by explicitly selling the act of prescription to consumers.

Consumers can gain access to prescription via payment for a service (in the case of occasional access) or through a subscription that provides comprehensive access to the prescriber's services. The latter case relates

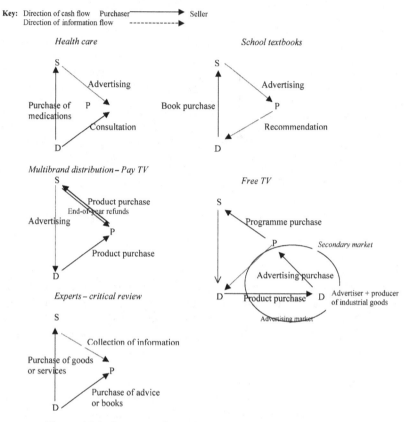

Figure 10.2. Some configuration of prescription markets.

quite directly to the business models used by publishers and content programmers. Its effectiveness is determined by the prescriber's ability to offer a quality product or service that is reliable, identifiable and discriminating (providing access to a complete and exclusive supply or to a specific type of goods). In addition, prescribers can create value from their expertise in related markets: for example, their ability to attract a large number of consumers will give them access to the advertising market.

In the referral market, prescribers create value by ensuring that sellers provide payment for referrals.

This form of marketing assumes that the prescriber is developing strategies for ensuring its selectivity rather than simply accumulating and enlarging the information base it provides. This is what major retail networks and shop bots have done on the Internet. Search engines are developing in the same way: after initially providing a basic service of locating and ordering existing pages on the Web, they are now becoming value-added directories that offer site selectivity, preferential listings and so on in return for payment from the sites that they list. This remuneration may be a one-time payment for a referral listing or it may be indexed to the number of contacts that the prescriber generated.

The effectiveness and justification for paying prescribers in return for selectivity will depend on the prescriber's ability to attract a large number of consumers or to reach a specific market segment or niche (through differentiation). To do this, prescribers must be able to guarantee consumers that their supply is of good quality and relatively complete or that it matches their specific interests (in the case of portals for virtual communities for instance).

Prescribers try to empower the primary market for goods whereas they are not initially directly involved.

The transaction that takes place on the primary market between the seller and the consumer does not necessarily entail the prescriber. For example, shop bots engines, classified advertising sites and auction sites bring together buyers and sellers who then negotiate directly. However, prescribers may receive compensations in the form of a commission on any transactions that take place, and get some profit on the referral market, in relation with the primary market. Any form of prescription may involve such remuneration, but the Internet particularly encourages this economic model since it can be used to track a consumer's browsing behavior and to identify any transactions that were generated with the help of a given prescriber.

Summary

As summarized in Table 10.1, the prescriber's competitive position and the range of eligible business models depend specifically on its ability to bring these various sources of revenue into play. Prescription can include

Table 10.1. *Sources of revenue for prescribers*

Market	Revenue source
Referral market	Sale of referral listings
	Profit sharing
	Marketing of customer data
	Sale of advertising space
Prescriber market	Sale of information and evaluations
	Distribution margin
Primary market	Commission on transactions

other functions as well (distribution, technical intermediation, etc.) to combine and enhance the various sources of revenue associated with these markets.

EXAMPLE: CLASSIFIED ADVERTISING SITES

Classified ad sites are not part of the primary market per se (i.e. the market for goods); instead, they offer a selection of available goods, providing referral opportunities and in some cases certification (eBay, for example, provides information on the reliability of vendors and buyers), assessing their quality (as does Amazon.com, which collects critiques submitted by web users) and providing related services (as with used car sites, which offer a warranty, after-sales service, insurance and support).

Competition among these classified ad sites stems largely from their ability to define their service and position themselves differently in each of the three submarkets in our model.

a. Some adhere to the principles that govern business models for classified advertising in newspapers. They ensure payment for the advertiser and offer a browser function for buyers free of charge. Under these circumstances, advertisers will give preference to the sites that attract the largest audience.

b. Therefore, in order to establish an advertising base, competitors can choose to reverse the usual roles in the referral market and compensate advertisers, perhaps in return for an exclusivity agreement to ensure that the same ads will not also appear on competing sites.[7]

c. Finally, some sites offer their prescription services at no charge and generate revenue solely by assessing a fee on the primary market (as with eBay and estate agent sites) or on related markets. Yet, prescribers can create classified ad sites in order to capture consumers at a sufficiently early stage so as to offer them a wide selection of products, ranging from financial services (loans, insurance, warranties and after-sales services) to related products that might be of interest (e.g. consumables for customers purchasing capital goods, similar products for those who buy cultural items and so on).

Competitive leverage

When the forms of economic organization are based on three-pronged structures involving sellers, prescribers and potential buyers, the decision-making process for consumers becomes more complex than economic

---

[7] When the US real estate market emerged on the Internet, RealSelect joined forces with one of the largest franchise networks in order to gain a solid point of access to the market. The site offered to provide equity capital for the network and to publish its advertising at no charge in exchange for access to information databases. Microsoft HomeAdvisor, meanwhile, entered the market by initially paying its advertisers $1.

theory suggests. Demand is no longer based solely on individual preference and pulled by supply structuring (price and product information, competition, etc.); it is also determined by prescription methods and strategies, the relationship with the prescribers and the price differentiation arising from the prescriber's cost structure. This complexity with regard to adjustment variables in supply and demand is reflected in both the decision-making process for consumers and the competitive mechanisms in the prescriber market.

The prescription supply is defined by a number of strategic variables that prescribers use to position themselves:

- The *range of services* that the prescriber develops and provides.
- The *cost of subscription services*, access to the service supply, consulting services, etc.
- The *production function* of prescription (the cost of acquiring information and producing the services provided to customers, the management costs of transactions and access, overhead costs and so on).

At the same time, consumer demand for prescription can be defined on the basis of:

- The quality, quantity and variety of the prescriber's supply.
- The cost of acquiring information on the products or services.
- The costs supported by the consumer (subscription, entrance fees, etc.).

To sum up, competition among prescribers is driven by two primary sets of factors and exists over two time dimensions. Prescribers compete on price (rates, payment terms) and on supply (the size and scope of the service, quality, customization level and exclusivity). Moreover, prescribers compete over time: to increase the instantaneous audience at each moment, to capture consumers through long-term subscriptions.

In some other cases, the prescriber is also a distributor and prescription takes place through the selection of products provided to consumers. As a consequence, competition may concern products offered on the primary market as well as the information provided about the products offered on the primary market. With banking and financial sites, for example, prescription involves selling selected financial products on the one hand and providing financial information or consulting services on the other.

Price competition
Whether they are just providing information or distributing selected goods, the same various strategies are available to prescribers for

differentiating their price structure and positioning below their competitors' prices:

- *Reduce the cost and quality of their supply:* while acting as intermediaries, it is less expensive for prescribers to acquire the products and services to be provided if they can limit the number offered (to reduce transaction costs) or develop an alternative supply of lower quality. This strategy is the only option available when overhead costs for customer management and acquisition and production costs are the same for all prescribers.
- *Establish an internal cost structure that is more favorable than that of competitors:* in order to improve productivity, prescribers will seek to implement economies of scale in distribution (promotional activities designed to increase the number of customers and reduce the administrative cost per customer, bundling and grouped sales, etc.) or create ancillary or by-product markets where they can apportion overhead costs and generate new resources on the referral market (providing services or customer data) or the prescriber market (through the sale of such by-products).
- *Offset costs between markets setting the direction of the referral market:* as described earlier, remuneration can be paid 1) by the supplier of goods to the prescriber (when sellers pay for preferential treatment for their products or, in the case of selective distribution, to ensure exclusivity) or 2) by the prescriber to the supplier (when prescribers are paying for exclusive information or access to the sellers' goods for the purpose of exclusive distribution). Prescribers that bring the direction of the market into play can offer a more attractive price structure by basing their economic model and remuneration on the referral market rather than on the prescriber market. In this way, they can wholly reverse and change the nature of their relationship with both customers and competitors.

The last outcome is one of the essential contributions of our three-pronged model; it does not merely reflect the existence of two different markets but demonstrates that the direction of the relationship between sellers and prescribers is a strategic variable.

Competition over supply of the services and products provided
Prescription can be the exclusive presentation of information aggregates, or it may be the result of a more complex selection process and expertise (as with guides to fine dining or search-engine portals, for example). In each case, the care with which the supply is structured is a critical competitive factor. There is a number of ways in which prescribers can enhance the appeal of their supply over that of their competitors:

– *Provide exclusive services:* this strategy has a direct impact on relations with goods and services providers[8] in terms of the acquisition of rights, exclusivity and production cost. The wider adoption of exclusive distribution rights has a noteworthy effect: it substantially increases the purchase price, since rare or appealing goods are the subject of intense bidding.[9] At the same time, the potential increase in the number of customers as a result of exclusive distribution rights can also lead to increased administrative costs.

– *Develop a specialized supply based on expertise:* specializing expertise (either in terms of its quality or its area of content) helps to target specific customer segments identified on the basis of marketing data and then to aggregate these segments. This strategy requires a policy of encouraging trade and consumption within virtual communities[10] as well as actions to encourage customer loyalty such as giveaways and discounts for major customers. However, it creates a significant risk that consumers may depart en masse for a more attractive prescriber.

– *Significantly expand the volume of the supply:* this strategy encourages customer loyalty, generates economies of scale and makes it difficult for new competitors to enter the market. It is attractive to buyers insofar as it reduces the price of comprehensive services and cuts transaction costs.

Competition based on acquiring customers

The third way that prescribers can improve their competitive position is by capturing consumers. This strategy makes use of the transfer of decision-making and the ability to make decisions at any time by prompting customers to make ex ante commitment to a prescriber before making a selection on the primary market.

In concrete terms, prescribers can increase their ability to capture consumers with the help of several economic and sales tools: by creating long-term subscriptions,[11] providing a technological platform (terminals, software), preventing defections (through rules and regulations or as a result of the learning curve that consumers must master) and establishing repeat-transaction incentives (such as customer loyalty and price discount programmes).

---

[8] This is the case for producers of original audiovisual works or those that hold the rights to such works (including sports federations and film producers, in particular).

[9] Meanwhile, goods with smaller market potential can be acquired, in some cases, for less than their manufacturing cost.

[10] See Gensollen in Chapter 5 of this book.

[11] For example, this is the strategy used by those mobile telephone operators and satellite television providers that offer a cell phone or satellite dish to customers who commit to a long-term subscription.

Consumers realize that this is in their best interests, since it leads to a reduction in both the fixed costs they must bear and the cost of acquiring information (as consumers master the learning curve and as prescribers increase their ability to customize supply) and provides rewards via direct incentives.

TELEVISION INDUSTRY: A PARADIGM FOR THE INTERNET?

The broadcast media industry offers a wealth of data for analysis of prescription. As a subset of a broader economic system that results from the convergence of telecommunications, information technology and audiovisual, it shares several characteristics with the Internet: the products exchanged via these media are information goods and incorporate significant value-added; the product supply is profuse, is conveyed to consumers via information and communications technology and can be consumed instantaneously online or at some future point by means of downloading. The importance of prescription through programming is central to the broadcast media industry and, thanks to wireless and high-speed Internet access, is becoming a more significant factor in the Internet-based economy and a focus of greater interest among access and service providers.

The dynamics of the television industry in the last decades can be read as an evolution of the role of the operators and the affirmation of the function of prescription.[12] In the earliest and most traditional television format – i.e. free television – prescription operates in the form of simple commercial intermediation, similar to what any distributor might provide. With the introduction of video-on-demand, consumers need no longer rely on the programming but can choose what they wish to see from a database of selected programmes. More complex scenarios emerged with the development of cable and satellite packages. Here, prescription is no longer just a matter of selecting and grouping the programmes: operators choose an appropriately diversified range of topical channels so as to create a complete, coherent programming line-up. As a result, more numerous distribution channels exist, greater competition takes place among operators, subscription options grow and network branding emerges. Networks are enlarging their role of prescribers by assuming control over a portion of their programme offerings and by actively structuring both the market and consumption models – consumers are then less concerned with locating a given programme than with each channel's identity, which confers a guarantee of the quality, the range and the type of programming as well as offering them access to exclusive programming matching their interests.

The Internet carries such a situation to extremes while consumers cannot, spontaneously, grasp all information and programmes available. The most important argument is that consumers' choice cannot be described as

---

[12] For a more detailed analysis, see Pierre-Jean Benghozi and Thomas Paris, 2003.

preference optimization from among existing content but as sorting out from a limited array of content. In this process, consumers entrust prescribers with some of their decision-making, since they do not choose content directly from among all those theoretically available: they choose a prescriber that itself selects the content.

10.3   Typical forms of prescription

In the first part of the chapter we defined a three-pronged market structure (primary-referral-prescription) between sellers, consumers and prescribers. We shall now see how this wide range of possibilities can be boiled down to a smaller number of typical configurations – each one based on a specific business model – depending on how the nature of the prescription is tailored to market characteristics.

In order to make out such configurations, we shall firstly make out three different market structures, depending on which of the markets of our three-pronged model are effective. Secondly, we shall characterize different natures of prescription, according to how the prescribers are restricting the supply and processing information on goods and services the consumers look at; it will lead us to identify specific limited types of prescribers. Thirdly, we shall use such a typology to outline the business models, strategies and dynamics associated with each form of prescription.

10.3.1 Market configurations

Each of the three markets we have identified may or may not be effective in our three-pronged model. The prescriber market is necessarily involved, but some configurations may not include one of the other two markets.

– There may or may not be a referral market between prescribers and sellers. Depending on the business sector, aggregator sites (e.g. search engines or sites that provide expert evaluations of other sites) may demand payment from companies that wish to be listed, while others may simply make their selections from existing information without the need for a transaction. A true referral market will emerge in the first case but not in the second.
– There may or may not be a primary market of goods and services. In some cases, the prescribers are also distributors and the transaction will involve them alone. For example, some real estate is accessible only through an agency, whereas other estate can be bought and sold among individuals and the prescriber's only function is to bring the parties together. In the first case, the primary market does not exist, since the consumers are never in contact with the suppliers.

Referral market		
	YES	NO
Primary market YES	*Prescriber-promoter*	*Prescriber-consultant*
Primary market NO	*Prescriber-distributor*	

Figure 10.3. Three forms of prescription.

Considering these various situations, three forms of prescription can be identified.[13] We can describe them using the terms distributor, promoter and consultant (see Figures 10.3 and 10.4).

10.3.2   The nature of prescription

We have just defined three configurations, each determining how specific relationships among economic agents are structured. However, they do not define just how the prescriptive information is conveyed or the way in which it plays a role in the consumer's decision-making process by restricting the consumer's scope to a greater or lesser degree. In fact, our second prescription variable involves the nature of the prescriber's recommendation – whether it is an injunction, a selection or an evaluation.

- The prescription may be an *injunction*: the prescriber singles out a product that responds to the consumer's requirements, as with television, a medical prescription or school textbooks. In this case, *the decision is transferred in full* from the consumer to the prescriber. An extreme example is the "I'm Feeling Lucky" function that Google offers on the Internet.
- The prescription is offered as a *selection*: the prescriber identifies a list of approved products that meet the consumer's requirements or grants certification consistent with its own criteria and accordingly provides a referral for a given product or company. The consumer still makes the final decision, but must choose from a product supply that has been winnowed down as part of an initial selection process conducted by

---

[13] We have not considered the scenario in which there is no prescriber market, since by nature it lies outside the scope of our analysis. We have also excluded the commonplace scenario in which there is neither a listings market nor a primary market.

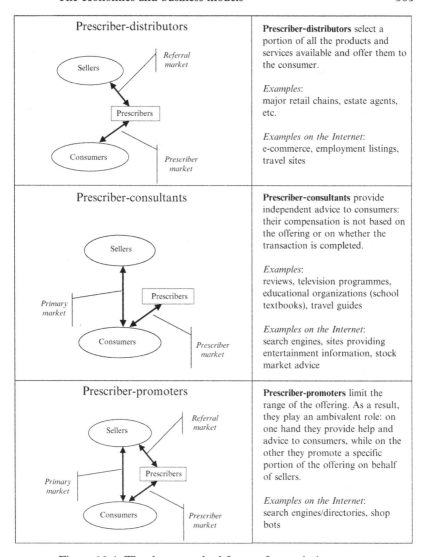

Prescriber-distributors	**Prescriber-distributors** select a portion of all the products and services available and offer them to the consumer.
	Examples: major retail chains, estate agents, etc.
	Examples on the Internet: e-commerce, employment listings, travel sites
Prescriber-consultants	**Prescriber-consultants** provide independent advice to consumers: their compensation is not based on the offering or on whether the transaction is completed.
	Examples: reviews, television programmes, educational organizations (school textbooks), travel guides
	Examples on the Internet: search engines, sites providing entertainment information, stock market advice
Prescriber-promoters	**Prescriber-promoters** limit the range of the offering. As a result, they play an ambivalent role: on one hand they provide help and advice to consumers, while on the other they promote a specific portion of the offering on behalf of sellers.
	Examples on the Internet: search engines/directories, shop bots

Figure 10.4. The three standard forms of prescription.

the prescriber. Wine retailers on the Internet are one example, offering a selected range of products.

– Finally, prescription may consist of an *evaluation* in the form of a ranking, a hierarchy or a list of proposed solutions accompanied by an assessment regarding essential and specific factors based on qualitative or quantitative criteria. In this case, consumers make their decision by relying on the selection factors provided by the prescriber. The Internet economy provides several examples: search engines that offer a list of items ranked on the basis of quality criteria (as specified in the query) and shop bots that rank available products according to price or other criteria.

Note that the form of the prescription is related to the nature of the intermediation and the organization of the market. In an injunction, therefore, the consumer is not aware of the range of the supplied products, whereas in the other two cases the supply remains partially visible.

10.3.3 Prescription business models

By combining the two variables we have just described (market configuration and nature of the prescription), we can identify various types of prescriber, each corresponding to a specific prescriptive method and revenue model. Table 10.2, wherein we have provided a term for each type of prescriber along with an example, summarizes this typology.

Table 10.2. *Types of prescriber*

Nature of the prescription configuration	Injunction	Selection	Evaluation
Prescription– distribution	PROGRAMMER (travel sites)	DISTRIBUTOR (selective e-commerce) *Wineonline*	DISTRIBUTOR- CONSULTANT *Amazon.com*
Prescription– promotion	—	WEB REFERRAL PROVIDER *Yahoo!*	SHOP BOT *Kelkoo*
Prescription– consulting	EXPERT	CERTIFICATION SERVICE *Google*	REVIEWER *Entertainment sites*

The preceding analysis has demonstrated that there is no single prescription model; instead, prescription is used in a variety of ways, which explains the wide array of examples that can be found on the Internet. When an economic actor takes place in the prescription market, it defines the variables that will govern its activity and the way it operates. Some of these variables are mutually exclusive. For example, web referral providers cannot also serve as consultants or experts, since consumers will not trust the independence of a third party that is compensated for promoting a product. In Table 10.3, we show how several factors are related: 1) prescriber's positioning within its business sector, 2) competition structure and competitive leverage and 3) sources of revenue (distribution and profit-sharing margins, charging of prescription services and referrals, audience value through the sale of marketing space and the marketing of customer data). We are now able to build on these different categories, developing their economic consequences and the strategic dynamics they encourage. Some of these categories sound different but will be presented altogether. This is the case for distributor and distributor-consultant, for referral and shop bots, for certification services and reviewer, as peculiarities concerning selection and evaluation activities have, at first sight, no noteworthy impact on their business model. Differences between these categories come into view when considering more precisely the production process and value-added of prescribers.[14]

Programmer

The programmer responds to consumer demand by providing a product. This is the type of prescription found on traditional broadcasting media. It can also be found on certain travel sites: consumers specify their travel requirements and the site then offers a proposed itinerary for purchase.

Programmers survive primarily on their profits from distribution and offer the prescription service free of charge. Their value-added lies in both the quantity of goods, information and services they can provide (i.e. their ability to respond to every request) and the quality of the products they sell. In addition, their ability to generate a large audience may enable them to sell advertising space.

Distributors/distributor-consultants

Distributors and distributor-consultants select several products and provide them to consumers, who make their own selection. Distributors earn their revenue primarily from the profits they make; distributor-consultants may be able to charge for their prescription services if they can link them to the retail process. Insofar as they make a selection, distributors and distributor-consultants can charge for referrals.

Referral providers/shop bots

Referral providers and shop bots participate in a transaction purely at an informational level. They do not distribute products, but instead help consumers to evaluate them on the basis of either cardinal and quantitative assessment (web referral) or hierarchical structure (price comparison). Their value-added stems from the quality of their evaluations,

---

[14] We shall not develop this point because of limited space.

which have the potential to build a significant audience that advertisers will find attractive; they also generate income by selling referral opportunities to sellers.

Experts
Experts have no economic ties to sellers. They are paid by consumers to make a selection on the consumer's behalf. Not-for-profit community-based websites are one of the few examples of this type of prescription on the Internet.

Certification services and reviewers
Certification services and reviewers have no financial relationship with sellers; they merely express an opinion. Their value-added is based on the quality and relevance of their views, their business model and their ability to generate and draw value from an audience.

Summary
Prescribers must address the strategic decision of where to position themselves among the options in Table 10.3 and what their source of revenue will be. Not every choice is open to them, however, since certain products or services may entail a specific positioning in the market. We showed, in Benghozi (2001), how information and communication

Table 10.3. *Prescription business models*

Prescriber type	Forms of competitive leverage	Business models/revenue source
PROGRAMMER	Supply structure	Distribution margins Sale of advertising space
DISTRIBUTOR	Price	Distribution margins Sale of referrals
DISTRIBUTOR-CONSULTANT	Supply structure Price	Distribution margins Sale of referrals (end-of-year refunds)
REFERRAL PROVIDER	Supply structure Capture of consumers	Sale of referrals Sale of advertising space
SHOP BOT	Supply structure	Sale of referrals Profit sharing
EXPERT	Supply structure Capture of consumers	Sale of information and evaluations Sale of advertising space
CERTIFICATION SERVICE	Capture of consumers	Sale of information and evaluations Sale of advertising space
REVIEWER	Supply structure Capture of consumers	Sale of information and evaluations Sale of advertising space

technologies can shape internal organizations and industrial sectors, creating new links between physical trades and information-based relations, and converting key assets (location, information, technology) into business economic models on the Internet.

Some market configurations lend to an injunction, while others do not. For example, a third party may define a travel itinerary and select an airplane company for a consumer in accordance with specific requirements (location, dates, price level).[15] By contrast, consumers make the final decision when purchasing a novel: in such a case, the prescription cannot serve as an injunction. For some goods, such as real estate or travel services, prescription and distribution are necessarily linked because of the existing market, but this is not always the case. Yet, the ability to combine prescription with another service, such as distribution, is essential for service providers who wish to charge customers for the prescription they are offering; otherwise, consumers can use the prescription and proceed to make their purchase from a retailer that does not impose a surcharge for the prescription.

10.4   Conclusion

The expansion of the Internet-based economy has prompted a realignment of value chains by severing the link between information functions and logistical functions. In this study, we have shown how the growing influence of distribution and intermediation functions reflects, in broader terms, the emergence of new business models that can be said to have their origins in a specific prescription economy. We have defined these models by identifying the structure of the prescription markets, the nature of the prescriptions and the competitive strategies adopted by these prescribers.

In addition to this prescription typology, we should emphasize a number of significant results. Despite available information on the Internet, customers have imperfect information, may face risks and have to be advised and backed up on their assessment of the quality of the supply. As information assumes a greater role in market organization, infomediaries are emerging and information markets are being created alongside existing markets for goods. More important, however, is the fact that the structure of transactions is being profoundly altered, as reflected in the transfer to prescribers of both expertise and – to a partial

---

[15] Low-cost companies are a noteworthy exception: they bypass prescribers such as travel agencies, selling their seats directly on the Internet and restricting the choice to their company.

extent – decision-making power. A consequence worth mentioning can be characterized as the "podium effect": prescribers contribute to concentrate demand on an ever more limited range of informations, goods or services. Such an effect is already well known in cultural industries and takes place progressively more on the Internet.[16]

The emergence of prescription services demonstrates how markets are becoming increasingly complex, coalescing around three-part structures that are opening up new strategic options. These structures are more than just intermediary market platforms.

An analysis of decision-making procedures and strategic challenges reveals that, in order to understand why prescription has emerged, we must consider the distinction that consumers draw between choosing a prescriber and choosing a product or service on the primary market. To do this, we must incorporate the timing of decision-making into our analysis. Time factor affects not only the individual decision-making process but also the nature of the competition that we find among prescribers.[17]

Prescription markets promote a form of competition that focuses simultaneously on information, price and consumer control. This explains why the Internet has prompted an increase in the number of business models, operating side by side to sell the same goods and services, rather than leading to simpler competitive structures based on price.

---

[16] As an example, in 2002, 54.1% of search engine users stopped their research on the first page of the results they got, compared with 28.6% in 1997 (Jansen, Bernard J. and Spink, Amanda (2003) "Analysis of web documents retrieved and viewed," *Proceedings of the International Conference on Internet Computing* (Humid R. Arabnia and Youngsong Mun (eds.)), Ic'03, Las Vegas, 23–26 June, vol. 1, pp. 65–9, CSREA Press).

[17] This phenomenon is generally overlooked in economics and business administration literature, except with regard to game theory.

Part IV
Producing, distributing and sharing
information goods

11 Bundling and competition on the Internet

Yannis Bakos and Erik Brynjolfsson

11.1 Introduction

11.1.1 Overview

The Internet has emerged as a new channel for the distribution of digital information such as software, news stories, stock quotes, music, photographs, video clips and research reports. However, providers of digital information goods are unsure how to price, package and market them and are struggling with a variety of revenue models. Some firms, such as America Online, have succeeded in selling very large aggregations of information goods – literally thousands of distinct news articles, stock reports, horoscopes, sports scores, health tips, chat rooms, etc. can all be delivered to the subscriber's home for a flat monthly fee. Such aggregations of content would be prohibitively expensive, not to mention unwieldy, using conventional media. Others, such as Slate, have made unsuccessful attempts to charge for a more focused "magazine" on the Internet even as similar magazines thrive when sold via conventional paper-based media.

Of particular interest are organizations such as Dow Jones, the Association for Computing Machinery (ACM) or Consumer Reports, which have successful offerings in both types of media, but which employ strikingly different aggregation and pricing strategies depending on the medium used to deliver their content. For instance, for a single fee Dow Jones makes available online the content of *The Wall Street Journal*, *Barron's Magazine*, thousands of briefing books, stock quotes and other information goods, while the same content is sold separately (if at all) when delivered using conventional media. The ACM and Consumer

Acknowledgments: We thank Nicholas Economides, Michael Harrison, Donna Hoffman, Richard Schmalensee, Michael Smith, John Tsitsiklis, Hal Varian, three anonymous reviewers and seminar participants at the 1998 Workshop on Marketing Science and the Internet and 1998 Telecommunications Policy Research Conference for many helpful suggestions. Any errors that remain are our responsibility only.

Reports Online follow similar strategies. These differences in marketing strategies for online vs. traditional media are indicative of the special economics of information goods when delivered over the Internet. As bandwidth becomes cheaper and more ubiquitous, we can expect that most publishers of text, data, music, videos, software applications and other digitizable information goods will confront similar issues in determining their marketing and competitive strategies on the Internet.

One of the most important effects of the Internet infrastructure has been the radical reduction in the marginal costs of reproducing and distributing information goods to consumers and businesses.[1] This low marginal cost typically results in significant production-side economies of scale for information goods distributed over the Internet. Furthermore, several information goods are characterized by network externalities, i.e., they become more valuable to consume as their market share increases, which leads to demand-side economies of scale. It is well known that such technological economies of scale have important implications for competition, favoring large producers, and can lead to winner-take-all markets (e.g., see Arthur 1996).

In this chapter we analyze "economies of aggregation", a distinct source of demand-side economies for information goods that can be created by certain marketing and pricing strategies that bundle access to large numbers of information goods. Specifically, we study the effects of large-scale bundling of information goods on pricing, profitability and competition. We show that bundling strategies can offer economies of aggregation favoring producers that aggregate large numbers of information goods, even in the *absence* of network externalities or economies of scale or scope. While earlier analyses (Bakos and Brynjolfsson 1999a, 1999b) focused on the implications of bundling and other forms of aggregation for a monopolist providing information goods, this chapter extends those models to consider the effects in competitive settings.

We demonstrate how marketing strategies that exploit these economies of aggregation can be used to gain an advantage when purchasing or developing new content. Firms can employ economies of aggregation to increase the value of new content, giving them an edge when bidding for such content. Economies of aggregation can also be used to discourage or foreclose entry, even when competitors' products are technically superior. The same strategies can also facilitate predation: a bundler

---

[1] In the remainder of this chapter, we will use the phrase "information goods" as shorthand for "goods with zero or very low marginal costs of production". In particular, our basic analysis is motivated by the way the Internet is changing the dynamics of publishing (broadly defined to include all forms of digital content).

can enter new markets and force a competitor with a higher quality product to exit. Finally, economies of aggregation can affect incentives for innovation, decreasing them for firms that may face competition from a bundler while increasing them for the bundler itself. The potential impact of large-scale aggregation will generally be limited for most physical goods. However, when marginal costs are very low, as they are for digital information goods, the effects can be decisive.

Our analysis is grounded in the underlying economic fundamentals of pricing strategy as applied to goods with low marginal cost. It can help explain the existence and success of very large-scale bundling, such as that practiced by America Online, as well as the common practice of hybrid publishers, such as *The Wall Street Journal*'s bundling of several distinct information goods as part of its online package even as it sells the same items separately through conventional channels. The same analysis can also provide insight into the proliferation of "features" found in many software programs. While our analysis is motivated by the pricing and marketing decisions that publishers face when they make their content available on the Internet, it may also apply in other markets where marginal costs are low or zero, such as cable television, software or even conventional publishing to some extent.

11.1.2 Bundling large numbers of information goods

Bundling may enable a seller to extract value from a given set of goods by allowing a form of price discrimination (McAfee, McMillan and Whinston 1989, Schmalensee 1984). There is an extensive literature in both the marketing and economics fields on how bundling can be used this way (e.g., Adams and Yellen 1976, Schmalensee 1984, McAfee, McMillan and Whinston 1989, Hanson and Martin 1990, Eppen, Hanson and Martin 1991, Salinger 1995, Varian 1997). Bakos and Brynjolfsson (1999a) provide a more detailed summary of the pertinent literature for large-scale bundling of information goods. Finally, the tying literature has considered the possibility of using bundling to leverage monopoly power to new markets (e.g., Burstein 1960, Bork 1978), with especially important contributions by Whinston (1990) on the ability of bundling to effect foreclosure and exclusion, and related recent work (e.g., Choi 1998, Nalebuff 1999).

This chapter builds on prior work by Bakos and Brynjolfsson (1999a) that considers the bundling of more than two goods and is focused on bundling information goods with zero or very low marginal cost. That article finds that in the case of large-scale bundling of information goods, the resulting economies of aggregation can significantly increase a monopolist's profits. The benefits of bundling large numbers of information goods depend critically on the low marginal cost of reproducing digital information and the nature of the correlation in valuations for the goods: aggregation becomes less attractive when marginal costs are high or when valuations are highly correlated. We extend this line of research by considering how bundling affects the pricing and marketing of goods in certain competitive settings. Furthermore, by allowing for competition we can consider how large-scale bundling can create a barrier to entry by competitors, enable entry into new product markets and change incentives for innovation.

The chapter is especially motivated by the new marketing opportunities enabled by the Internet. Most earlier work in this area – such as papers by Bakos (1997, 1998), Brynjolfsson and Smith (2000), Clemons, Hann and Hitt (1998), Degeratu, Rangaswamy and Wu (1998), Lynch and Ariely (2000) and Hauble and Trifts (2000) – has focused on the effects of low search costs in online environments. Others, including Hoffman and Novak (1996), Mandel and Johnson (1998) and Novak, Hoffman and Yung (1999), address how online environments change consumer behavior. In contrast, we focus on the capability of the Internet to actually deliver a wide class of goods, namely digitized information. The capability makes it possible not only to influence consumers' choices but also to consummate the transaction via the Internet, and typically at much lower marginal cost than through conventional channels. While bundling strategies might have been considered relatively esoteric in the past, they become substantially more powerful in this new environment, and specifically strategies based on very large-scale bundling become feasible.

While the focus of this chapter is on bundling strategies, the Internet clearly affects competition in many other ways. For instance, lower search costs, network externalities, high fixed costs, rapid market growth, changes in interactivity and other factors significantly affect marketing and competitive strategies. We abstract from these other characteristics of the Internet to better isolate the role of bundling on competition. Furthermore, we focus on equilibrium strategies, recognizing fully that many Internet markets are not in equilibrium as we write. As a result, it can be dangerous to extrapolate from current behavior, such as below-cost pricing, currently observed on the Internet. Executives at Buy.com, for instance, report that their current hyper-aggressive pricing strategy is driven by the need to establish a reputation for having low prices during the high-growth phase of the Internet, even if that means currently losing money on some items. After this reputation is established, they do not plan to be quite as aggressive (although they still expect to be positioned as a relatively low-price outlet for most goods) (Barbieri 1999). By analyzing and understanding the equilibria that result when firms compete in markets for information goods, we hope to gain insight into which outcomes are most likely when temporary phenomena and disequilibrium strategies have dissipated.

11.1.3 Approach in this chapter

In Section 2 we review the case of a monopolist bundling information goods with independent demands, and we provide the necessary background, setting and notation for the analysis of the competitive implications of bundling. In Section 3 we address upstream competition between bundlers to acquire additional information goods, as in the case of bundlers competing for new content. In Section 4 we analyze downstream competition for consumers in a setting with information goods competing in pairs that are imperfect substitutes, including the case of a bundle competing with one or many outside goods. In Section 5 we explore the implications of the analysis in Section 4, discussing how bundling strategies affect entry deterrence, predatory behavior and the incentives for innovation. Finally, Section 6 presents some concluding remarks.

11.2 A monopolist bundling information goods with independent valuations

We begin by employing the setting introduced by the Bakos-Brynjolfsson bundling model, with a single seller providing n information goods to a set of consumers Ω. Each consumer demands either 0 or 1 units of each information good, and resale of these goods is not permitted (or is prohibitively costly for consumers).[2] Valuations for each good are heterogeneous among consumers, and for each consumer $\omega \in \Omega$, we use $v_{ni}(\omega)$ to denote the valuation of good i when a total of n goods is purchased. We allow $v_{ni}(\omega)$ to depend on n so that the distributions of valuations for individual goods can change as the number of goods purchased changes.[3] For instance, the value of a weather report may

---

[2] We assume that the producers of information goods can use technical, legal and social means to prevent unauthorized duplication and thus remain monopolists. However, Bakos, Brynjolfsson and Lichtman (1999) have employed a similar framework to study a setting where users share the goods.
[3] To simplify the notation, we will omit the argument ω when possible.

be different when purchased alone from its value when purchased together with the morning news headlines, as they both compete for the consumer's limited time. Similarly, other factors such as goods that are complements or substitutes, diminishing returns and budget constraints may affect consumer valuations as additional goods are purchased. Even certain psychological factors which may make consumers more or less willing to pay for the same goods when they are part of a bundle (e.g., Petroshius and Monroe 1987) can be subsumed in this framework. However, for simplicity, we treat all goods as being symmetric; they are all assumed to be affected proportionately by the addition of a new good to the bundle.

Let $x_n = \frac{1}{n}\sum_{k=1}^{n} v_{nk}$ be the mean (per-good) valuation of the bundle of n information goods. Let $p_n^\star$, $q_n^\star$ and $\pi_n^\star$ denote the profit-maximizing price per good for a bundle of n goods, the corresponding sales as a fraction of the population and the seller's resulting profits per good respectively.[4] Assume the following conditions hold:

> A1: The marginal cost for copies of all information goods is zero to the seller.
>
> A2: For all n, consumer valuations v_{ni} are independent and uniformly bounded,[5] with continuous density functions, non-negative supports, means μ_{ni} and variances σ_{ni}^2.
>
> A3: Consumers have free disposal. In particular, for all $n > 1, \sum_{k=1}^{n} v_{nk} \geq \sum_{k=1}^{n-1} v_{(n-1)k}$.

Assumption A3 implies that adding a good to a bundle cannot reduce the total valuation of the bundle (although it may reduce the mean valuation).

Under these conditions, it can be shown that selling a bundle of all n information goods can be remarkably superior to selling the n goods separately.[6] For the distributions of valuations underlying most common demand functions, bundling substantially reduces the average deadweight loss and leads to higher average profits for the seller. As n increases, the seller captures an increasing fraction of the total area

---

[4] For bundles, we will use p and π to refer to *per-good* prices and gross profits, i.e., profits gross of any fixed costs. We will use P and Π to denote prices and profits for the entire bundle.

[5] I.e., $\sup_{n,i,\omega}(v_{ni}(\omega)) < \infty$, for all n,i ($i \leq n$), and $\omega \in \Omega$.

[6] In the remainder of the chapter, our focus will be on "pure" bundling – offering all of the goods as a single bundle. "Mixed" bundling, which involves offering both the bundle and subsets of the bundle at the same time for various prices, will generally do no worse than pure bundling (after all, pure bundling is just a special case of mixed bundling), so our results can be thought of as a lower bound for the profits of the bundler.

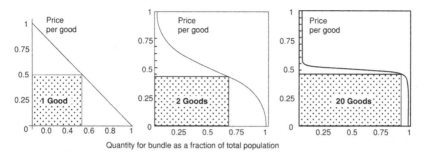

Figure 11.1. Demand for bundles of 1, 2 and 20 information goods with i.i.d. valuations uniformly distributed in [0,1] (linear demand case).

under the demand curve, correspondingly reducing both the deadweight loss and consumers' surplus relative to selling the goods separately. More formally:

Proposition 1
Given assumptions A1, A2 and A3, as n increases, the deadweight loss per good and the consumers' surplus per good for a bundle of n information goods converge to zero, and the seller's profit per good increases to its maximum value.

Proof
This is Proposition 1 of Bakos and Brynjolfsson (1999a).

The intuition behind Proposition 1 is that as the number of information goods in the bundle increases, the law of large numbers assures that the distribution for the valuation of the bundle has an increasing fraction of consumers with "moderate" valuations near the mean of the underlying distribution. Since the demand curve is derived from the cumulative distribution function for consumer valuations, it becomes more elastic near the mean and less elastic away from the mean. Figure 11.1 illustrates this for the case of linear demand for individual goods, showing, for instance, that combining two goods each with a linear demand produces a bundle with an s-shaped demand curve. As a result, the demand function (adjusted for the number of goods in the bundle) becomes more "square" as the number of goods increases. The seller is able to extract as profits (shown by the shaded areas in Figure 11.1) an increasing fraction of the total area under this demand curve, while selling to an increasing fraction of consumers.

Proposition 1 is fairly general. While it assumes independence of the valuations of the individual goods in a bundle of a given size, each valuation may be drawn from a different distribution. For instance, some goods may be systematically more valuable on average than others, or have greater variance or skewness in their valuations across different consumers. Furthermore, valuations may change as more goods are added to a bundle. As shown by Bakos and Brynjolfsson (1999a), Proposition 1 can be invoked to study several specific settings, such as diminishing returns from the consumption of additional goods, or the existence of a budget constraint. Thus, this analysis can also apply to the addition of new features to existing products; indeed, the line between "features" and "goods" is often a blurry one.

Even the assumed independence of valuations is not critical to the qualitative findings. As shown by Bakos and Brynjolfsson (1999a), many of the results can be extended to the case where consumer valuations are correlated. The key results are driven by the ability of bundling to reduce the dispersion of buyer valuations, and dispersion will be reduced even when goods are positively correlated as long as there is at least some idiosyncratic component to the valuations. In other words, valuations of the goods cannot all be perfectly, positively correlated. However, assuming zero correlation provides a useful baseline for isolating the effects of bundling and avoids the introduction of additional notation. Furthermore, we believe it is often a reasonable and realistic description for many online markets.

It is interesting to contrast the bundling approach with conventional price discrimination. If there are m consumers, each with a potentially different valuation for each of the n goods, then mn prices will be required to capture the complete surplus when the goods are sold separately. Furthermore, price discrimination requires that the seller can accurately identify consumer valuations and prevent consumers from buying goods at prices meant for others. Thus, the conventional approach to price discrimination operates by increasing the number of prices charged to accommodate the diversity of consumer valuations. In contrast, bundling reduces the diversity of consumer valuations so that, in the limit, sellers need to charge only one price, do not need to identify different types of consumers and do not need to enforce any restrictions on which prices consumers pay.

As the number of goods in the bundle increases, total profit and profit per good increase. The profit-maximizing price per good for the bundle steadily approaches the per-good expected value of the bundle to the consumers. The number of goods necessary to make bundling desirable, and the speed at which deadweight loss and profit converge to their limiting values, depend on the actual distribution of consumer valuations. In particular, it is worth noting that although the per-good consumers' surplus converges to zero as the bundle grows, the total consumers' surplus from the bundle may continue to grow, but only at a lower rate than the number of goods.

The efficiency and profit gains that bundling offers in the Bakos-Brynjolfsson bundling setting contrast with the more limited benefits identified in previous work, principally as a result of focusing on bundling large numbers of goods and on information goods with zero marginal costs. In particular, if the goods in the bundle have significant marginal costs then bundling may no longer be optimal. For example, if the marginal cost for all goods is greater than their mean valuation but less than their maximum valuation, then selling the goods separately at a price above marginal cost would be profitable. However, the demand for a large bundle priced at a price per good greater than the mean valuation will approach zero as the bundle size grows, reducing profits. Thus, because of differences in marginal costs, bundling hundreds or thousands of information goods for a single price online can be very profitable even if bundling the same content would not be profitable if it were all delivered through conventional channels.

11.3   Upstream competition for content

In the previous section, we focused on the case of a monopolist selling large numbers of information goods either individually or in a bundle. We now look at the impact of competition. In this section we analyze a setting with firms competing for inputs (e.g., content) and in the next section we analyze downstream competition for consumers in a setting with information goods competing in pairs of imperfect substitutes. In Section 5 we consider how downstream competition may further affect the incentives of a bundler in the upstream market.

Consider a setting similar to the one in Section 2 with n goods. There are two firms selling information goods, denoted as firm 1 and firm 2, which we refer to as the bundlers. These firms can be thought of as publishers selling information goods to the consumers, and we assume they start with respective endowments of n_1 and n_2 non-overlapping goods, where $n_1 + n_2 = n - 1$. We assume that consumers' valuations are independently and identically distributed (i.i.d.) for all goods. Thus different goods offered by the bundlers do *not* compete in the downstream market as they are not substitutes for each other.[7] For instance,

---

[7] In other words, the bundlers are monopolists in the downstream market, but not monopsonists in the upstream market. We disregard any effects by which one monopolist's sales might affect another monopolist via consumer budget constraints, complementarities, network externalities, etc.

a British literary online magazine might compete with an American online journal for the rights to a video interview even if they do not compete with each other for consumers, or an operating system vendor might compete with a seller of utility software to own the exclusive rights to a new data compression routine.

By postponing the analysis of downstream competition until Sections 4 and 5, we can highlight the impacts of bundling on upstream competition for content. Furthermore, the assumption that the goods are identically distributed makes it possible to index the "size" of a bundle by simply counting the number of goods it contains.

More formally we assume that:

Assumption A2': Consumer valuations v_{ni} are (identically distributed) i.i.d. for all n, with continuous density functions, non-negative support and finite means μ and variances σ^2.

In this setting we analyze the incentives of the two firms to acquire the n-th good in order to add it to their respective bundles. Specifically we consider a two-period game. In the first period the bundlers bid their valuations (y_1, z_1) and (y_2, z_2) for good n, where y denotes a valuation for an exclusive license and z denotes a valuation for a non-exclusive license.[8] In the second period the n-th good is acquired by one or both firms depending on whether y_1, y_2 or $z_1 + z_2$ represents the highest bid, provided that this bid is higher than the standalone profits that can be obtained by the owner of the n-th good. Subsequently, firms 1 and 2 simultaneously decide whether to offer each of their goods to the consumers individually or as part of a bundle (no mixed bundling is allowed), set prices for their offerings and realize the corresponding sales and profits[9].

In this setting, if the bundles are large enough, it is more profitable to add the outside good to the bigger bundle than to the smaller bundle. More formally, the following proposition holds:

---

[8] Because of the zero marginal cost of providing additional copies of the information good, we want to allow for the possibility that the information good is made available to both bundlers. We thank a referee for this suggestion.

[9] It would not be an equilibrium for the developer to sell the same good to two competing single-product downstream firms because monopoly profits are greater than the sum of duopoly profits in the single-good case. Thus the revenue that could be earned by selling an exclusive contract, thereby preserving the monopoly, is greater than the revenue that could be earned by selling the same product to two competitors. However, if the downstream firms are already selling bundles that include other competing goods, then the analysis becomes much more complicated and this result does not automatically hold. By requiring exclusive contract by assumption, we defer the issue of downstream competition among bundlers until later in the paper.

Proposition 2: Competition between bundlers for goods with i.i.d. valuations

Given assumptions A1, A2' and A3, and for n_1, n_2 large enough, then if $n_1 > n_2$, in the unique perfect equilibrium firm 1 outbids firm 2 for exclusive rights to the n-th good.

Proof

Proofs for this and remaining propositions are in the appendix to this chapter (page 340).

Proposition 2 builds on Proposition 1 by allowing for competition in the upstream market. It implies that the larger bundler (i.e., the one with the larger set of goods) will always be willing to spend the most to develop a new good to add to its bundle and will always be willing to pay the most to purchase any new good which becomes available from third parties. Proposition 2 can be easily extended to a setting with more than two bundlers although the incentives for exclusive contracting may diminish as the number of competing bundlers increases.

In settings where the bundlers compete for new or existing goods one at a time, Proposition 2 implies that the largest bundler will tend to grow larger relative to other firms that compete in the upstream market, unless there are some offsetting diseconomies.[10] Of course, if one or both bundlers understand this dynamic and there is a stream of new goods which can potentially be added to the bundles, then each bundler will want to bid strategically to race ahead of its rivals in bundle size and/ or to prevent its rivals from growing. In this way, strategies for bundling are very similar to traditional economies of scale or learning-by-doing, as analyzed by Spence (1981) and others. The far-sighted bundler with sufficiently deep pockets should take into account not only how adding a good would affect current profits but also its effect on the firm's ability to earn profits by adding future goods to the bundle.

In conclusion, large-scale bundling strategies may provide an advantage in the competition for upstream content. Large-scale bundlers are willing to pay more for upstream content and may come to dominate, because bundling makes their demand curve less elastic and allows them

[10] We conjecture that the implications of Proposition 2 would be strengthened if the goods bundled were complements instead of having independent valuations (e.g., because of technological complementarities or network externalities). In this case, the economies of aggregation identified in Propositions 1 and 2 would be amplified by the advantages of combining complements. Furthermore, while we assume no downstream competition in this section in order to isolate the dynamics of upstream competition, the upstream result would not be eliminated if we simultaneously allowed downstream competition. In fact, as shown in Sections 4 and 5, the ability to engage in large-scale bundling may be particularly valuable in the presence of competition.

to extract more surplus from new items as they add them to the bundle. Because the benefits of aggregation increase with the number of goods included in the bundle, large bundlers enjoy a competitive advantage in purchasing or developing new information goods, even in the absence of any other economies of scale or scope.

11.4   Downstream competition for consumers

It is common in the literature to assume that goods in a bundle have additive valuations (see e.g., Adams and Yellen 1976, Schmalensee 1984, McAfee, McMillan and Whinston 1989). This may not be realistic, especially when the goods are substitutes and thus compete with each other for the attention of consumers. In this section we consider a particular case of downstream competition, i.e., competition for consumers, by analyzing a setting where information goods are substitutes in pairs. In a setting similar to the one analyzed in Section 2, consider two sets of n information goods A and B, and denote by A_i and B_i the i-th good in A and B respectively ($1 \leq i \leq n$). For all i, goods A_i and B_i are imperfect substitutes (see below). For instance, A_1 might be one word processor and B_1 a competing word processor, while A_2 and B_2 are two spreadsheets, etc. For each consumer $\omega \in \Omega$, let $v_{Ai}(\omega)$ and $v_{Bi}(\omega)$ denote ω's valuation for A_i and B_i respectively. As before, we will drop the argument ω when possible. To simplify the analysis, we assume that the goods A_i and B_i have independent linear demands with the same range of consumer valuations, which we normalize to be in the range $[0,1]$. The independence assumption substantially simplifies the notation, but as noted above, as long as there is not a perfect positive correlation among the goods, bundling will still serve to reduce the dispersion of valuations and thus it will engender the competitive effects we model. Specifically,

Assumption A2'': For all i and all consumers $\omega \in \Omega$, all valuations $v_{Ai}(\omega)$ and $v_{Bi}(\omega)$ are independently and uniformly distributed in $[0,1]$.

Even though for each i the valuations for A_i and B_i are independent, the two goods are substitutes in the sense that a consumer purchasing both goods A_i and B_i enjoys utility equal only to the maximum utility that would have been received from purchasing only one of the two goods. In other words, the least valued good in each pair does not contribute to the consumer's utility if the other good is also owned. For example, a consumer who prefers Monday Night Football to the Monday Night Movie does not get any additional value if she has rights to view both programs than if she could watch only football. More formally,

Assumption A4: For all i and all $\omega \in \Omega$, consumer ω receives utility equal to $\max(v_{Ai}, v_{Bi})$ from purchasing both goods A_i and B_i.

Finally, we assume that development of the information goods involves a certain fixed cost:

Assumption A5: The production of good A_i,B_i involves a fixed cost of κ_{Ai},κ_{Bi} respectively.

We consider a two-period game with complete information. In the first period the firms invest κ_{Ai},κ_{Bj} for all goods A_i and B_j that will be produced.[11] In the second period, the firms decide whether to offer each of the goods individually or as part of a bundle (no mixed bundling is allowed), set prices for their offerings and realize the corresponding sales and profits.

As noted by Spence (1980), it is important to understand that goods may be substitutes yet still not have correlated valuations. In other words, one good may be less valuable if the other is simultaneously consumed but that does not necessarily mean that knowing the value for one good helps predict the value of the other, or vice versa. Substitutability and correlation of values are two logically distinct concepts. For instance, a boxing match and a movie on cable television may compete for a viewer's time on a Friday evening. Since consuming one reduces or eliminates the possibility of getting full value from the other, their values will not be additive, even if they are uncorrelated. Does making one program part of a large bundle give it a competitive advantage versus a standalone pay-per-view program? Similarly, websites compete for "eyeballs," music downloads compete for users' limited modem bandwidth and hard disk space and business software rented by application service providers (ASPs) competes for corporations' limited annual budgets. In each case, the purchase of one good reduces the buyer's value for a second good. How will bundling affect such competition?

11.4.1 Competitive and monopoly provision of two substitute goods

We begin by considering the base case in which there is no bundling and thus the goods compete in pairs. This provides a benchmark for the subsequent analysis and allows us to introduce the setting. First we analyze the case when for each pair of goods two separate, competing firms each offer one good in the pair. Because of the independence of consumer valuations for goods i and j if $i \neq j$, competition takes place only between the two goods in each pair. Thus our setting corresponds to n separate two-good markets. Dropping the subscripts indexing the pairs, suppose firm A provides good A and firm B provides good B. In this

---

[11] A good such as B_i that has no substitute can be modeled by setting the fixed cost of the corresponding good A_i to a value that would render its production uneconomical.

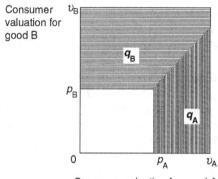

Figure 11.2. Competing imperfect substitutes.

case, if firm A prices at p_A and firm B prices at p_B, the line-shaded areas in Figure 11.2 show the corresponding sales q_A and q_B, assuming that $p_A \geq p_B$. The assumption of uniformly and independently distributed valuations implies that consumers are evenly spread throughout the unit square, making it easy to map from areas to quantities demanded.

As shown in the Appendix, the unique equilibrium has prices $p_A^\star = p_B^\star = \sqrt{2} - 1$, quantities $q_A^\star = q_B^\star = \sqrt{2} - 1$ and corresponding gross profit $\pi_A^\star = \pi_B^\star = (\sqrt{2} - 1)^2$, or approximately 0.17.

Given the above equilibrium in period 2, it is easy to see that any good with fixed cost less than $(\sqrt{2} - 1)^2$ will be produced when both firms offer competing goods. When a competing good is not produced, the remaining seller prices at the monopoly price of 0.5, selling to half the consumers and earning a maximum gross profit from a single good of 0.25. Thus, if a good has a fixed cost above 0.25, it will not be produced even by a monopolist. If one good has a fixed cost below $(\sqrt{2} - 1)^2$ and the other good has a fixed cost above $(\sqrt{2} - 1)^2$, only the low-cost good enters. Finally, if both goods have a fixed cost between $(\sqrt{2} - 1)^2$ and 0.25, there are two pure-strategy equilibria with either one or the other good entering, but not both.

If a single firm (monopolist) provides both goods A and B, for instance because firms A and B merge, it will set the prices p_A and p_B to maximize its total revenues $p_A q_A + p_B q_B$. As shown in the Appendix, this yields optimal prices $p_A^\star = p_B^\star = 1/\sqrt{3}$, and corresponding quantities $q_A^\star = q_B^\star = 1/3$. Revenues are $\sqrt{3}/9$ per good (approx. 0.19). It is worth noting that if the monopolist bundles A and B, he will price the bundle at $1/\sqrt{3}$, and sell quantity $q_A^\star + q_B^\star = 2/3$ for the same total revenues. This is a consequence of the fact that consumers do not derive additional value from their less preferred good. Thus the monopolist cannot increase his profits by bundling a single pair of such competing goods.

11.4.2 Competition between a single good and a bundle

To understand how bundling affects competition, we now analyze how prices and quantities are affected if firm B may include its good in a large bundle. Specifically, assume goods A_1 and B_1 compete as above. In addition firm B offers goods $B_2, B_3 \ldots B_n$ and has the option to include any subset of its goods in a bundle. No mixed bundling is allowed, in the sense that each good can be offered either separately or as part of the bundle, but not both ways simultaneously. This setting might be useful for modeling a situation such as a bundler of thousands of digital goods, for instance America Online competing with the seller of a single publication such as Slate, or an online music repository competing with an artist selling only his or her own songs.

Based on Propositions 1 and 2 of Bakos and Brynjolfsson (1999a), firm B increases its profits by including all goods $B_2, B_3 \ldots B_n$ in a bundle; let the optimal bundle price be $p_{B2\ldots n}^{\star}$ per good and the corresponding sales $q_{B2\ldots n}^{\star}$. The following proposition holds:

Proposition 3: Competition between a single good and a large bundle
Given assumptions A1, A2″, A3 and A4, for large enough n, firm B can increase its profits by adding good B_1 to its bundle, offering a bundle of n goods $B_1, B_2 \ldots B_n$.

In the Appendix we show that the optimal quantity for the resulting bundle of n goods will converge to one as the number of goods increases. In other words, Proposition 3 implies that as n increases, firm B's bundle, which includes good B_1, is ultimately purchased essentially by all consumers.[12] Thus firm A must set its price for good A_1 given the fact that almost all consumers already have access to good B_1. Figure 11.3 shows the fraction of consumers that will purchase A_1 at price p_{A1}, and thus firm A will choose p_{A1} to maximize $\frac{1}{2}(1 - p_{A1})^2 p_{A1}$, resulting in price $p_{A1}^{\star} = 1/3$, corresponding sales $q_{A1}^{\star} = 2/9$ and gross profit $\pi_{A1}^{\star} = 2/27$ or approximately 0.07. As shown in the Appendix, firm B will increase its gross profits by at least 0.28 by adding B_1 to its bundle.

Compared to competition in the absence of bundling, firm A has to charge a lower price (0.33 instead of 0.41), be limited to a lower market

---

[12] Under our assumptions, the quantity sold by the bundler grows monotonically (see Bakos and Brynjolfsson 1999a, Proposition 2). Thus the effect of bundling will be steadily diminished but not eliminated for smaller bundles.

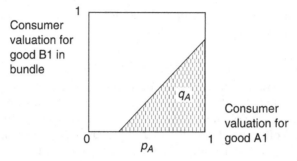

Figure 11.3. Good A_1, sold separately, competes with good B_1, part of a large bundle.

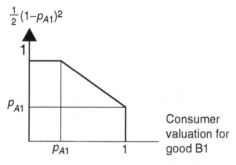

Figure 11.4. Distribution of valuations for good B_1 (including an impulse at the origin), when good A_1 is priced at p_{A1}.

share (0.22 instead of 0.41) and achieve substantially lower revenues (0.07 instead of 0.17). By contrast, by including good B_1 in a large bundle, firm B will increase the revenues from the bundle by at least 0.28 and achieve market share close to 100% for good B_1.

This phenonmenon can be observed in the software markets. For instance, Microsoft Office includes numerous printing fonts as part of its basic package. This is easy to do given the low marginal cost of reproducing digital goods. This strategy has drastically reduced the demand for font packages sold separately while allowing Microsoft to extract some additional value from its Office bundle.

Finally, although consumers' valuations are uniformly distributed for good B_1, the actual demand faced by firm B will be affected by the availability and pricing of good A_1. Figure 11.4 shows the derived distribution of valuations faced by firm B for good B_1 when firm A prices good A_1 at p_{A1}. The impulse at the origin represents the fact that a fraction $\frac{1}{2}(1 - p_{A1})^2$ of the consumers will purchase A_1 even if B_1

is offered at a price of zero. Given free disposal, we do not allow negative valuations. As expected, consumer valuations for good B_1 increase as p_{A1} increases.

11.4.3 Competition between multiple goods and a bundle

We now consider n pairs of competing goods, where one good in each pair may be part of a bundle. In particular, firm B offers goods $B_1, B_2 \ldots$ B_n as in the previous section, and has the option to combine them in a bundle. Goods $A_1, A_2 \ldots A_n$ are offered independently by firms $A_1, A_2 \ldots A_n$. Goods A_i and B_i compete just as A_1 and B_1 competed in the previous section ($0 \leq i \leq n$). As before, there is no private information and the setting has two periods, with firms $A_1, A_2 \ldots A_n$ and B deciding whether to invest κ_{Ai}, κ_{Bi} respectively in period one. In period two, firm B decides for each good $B_1, B_2 \ldots B_n$ whether to offer it as part of a bundle or separately, and all firms set prices and realize the corresponding sales and profits. No mixed bundling is allowed.

The analysis of the previous section is still applicable in this setting with many pairs of substitute goods, because valuations for goods in different pairs are independent. In particular, in each market i, if firm A_i prices good A_i at p_{Ai}, firm B faces a demand derived from the distribution of valuations shown in Figure 11.4. If good B_i is not offered as part of a bundle, then the equilibrium is as analyzed in Section 4.1. If B bundles B_1 with the other goods, $B_2, B_3 \ldots B_n$, then Proposition 1 applies and $\lim_{n \to \infty} \frac{1}{n} p_{B1\ldots n}^{\star} = \mu_B(p_A^{\star})$ and $\lim_{n \to \infty} q_{B1\ldots n}^{\star} = 1$, resulting at the limit in average gross profit of $\mu_B(p_A^{\star})$ per good, where $\mu_B(p_A^{\star})$ is the mean valuation of good B_i given that good A_i is priced at price $p_A^{\star}$. It can be seen from Figure 11.4 that $\mu_B(p_A^{\star}) = \int_{x=0}^{p_A^{\star}} x dx + \int_{p_A^{\star}}^{1} (1 - x + p_A^{\star}) x dx = \frac{1}{6} + \frac{1}{2} p_A^{\star} - \frac{1}{6} (p_A^{\star})^3$. As shown in Section 11.4.2, as n gets large, the seller of a free-standing good A_i that competes against good B_i that is offered in a bundle of n goods will maximize profits by charging approximately $p_A^{\star} = \frac{1}{3}$. The bundler thus faces a demand with mean valuation of about $\mu_B(p_A^{\star}) = \frac{53}{162} \approx 0.33$ and for large n realizes gross profits of approximately 0.33 per good. Since not bundling a good implies its contribution to gross profits will be at best 0.25 (when there is no competing good), Corollary 1 follows.

Corollary 1
If goods A_i and B_i compete in pairs and only firm B is allowed to bundle, bundling all B_is is a dominant strategy.

Goods A_i will be produced if $\kappa_{Ai} < 0.07$. Firm B will include good B_i in its bundle when $\kappa_{Bi} < 1/3$ in the presence of a competing good A_i, and when $\kappa_{Bi} < 1/2$ if there is no competing good. If fixed costs are between 0.07 and 0.33, then it is profitable for B to produce the good and sell it as part of the bundle even though it would be unprofitable for A to produce a similar good and sell it separately. Thus, a critical result of this analysis is that the bundler has an advantage competing in individual markets against individual outside goods. In Section 5.4 we offer a more complete discussion of implications for entry, exit and predation.

11.4.4 Competition between rival bundles

In the setting of Section 11.4.3, consider the case where goods $A_1, A_2 \ldots A_n$ are offered by a single firm A which, like firm B, has the choice of offering each of its goods individually as above or as a bundle of n goods priced at $p_{B1} \ldots n$ per good, with resulting sales of $q_{B1} \ldots n$. Proposition 1 now applies to both firms, and $\lim_{n \to \infty} q_{A1\ldots n}^{\star} = \lim_{n \to \infty} q_{B1\ldots n}^{\star} = 1$, i.e., almost all consumers purchase both bundles.[13] The valuation $v_{Ai}(\omega)$ for good A_i given that consumer ω already owns good B_i is 0 with probability 0.5, and has the probability distribution function $1 - v_{Ai}(\omega)$ for $0 < v_{Ai}(\omega) \leq 1$. The corresponding mean valuation is $\int_{v_{Ai}=0}^{1}(1 - v_{Ai})v_{Ai}dv_{Ai} = \frac{1}{6}$. As n gets large, the optimal price equals the mean valuation, i.e., $\lim_{n \to \infty} \frac{1}{n} p_{A1\ldots n}^{\star} = \frac{1}{6}$ and $\lim_{n \to \infty} \frac{1}{n} p_{B1\ldots n}^{\star} = \frac{1}{6}$. Thus, if the bundles are very large, in the unique equilibrium both A and B bundle at a price of $\frac{1}{6}$ per good and almost all consumers buy both bundles.

A consumer ω who owns both goods A_i and B_i enjoys utility equal to $\max(v_{Ai}(\omega), v_{Bi}(\omega))$, and thus her expected utility is $\int_{v_{Ai}=0}^{1}\left(v_{Ai}^{2} + (1 - v_{Ai})\int_{v_{Bi}=v_{Ai}}^{1} \frac{v_{Bi}dv_{Bi}}{1-v_{Ai}}\right)dv_{Ai} = \frac{2}{3}$ per pair of goods. Thus, in the case of rival bundles, as n gets large, the per-good deadweight loss converges to zero and consumers keep average surplus of 0.33 per pair of goods. If the bundlers merge, however, they can capture the consumers' surplus per Proposition 1 and in the process double their gross profit.

---

[13] Although consumers purchase both bundles, they do not necessarily use all the goods in each bundle. In our setting, a given consumer will use, on average, half the goods in each bundle – i.e., those that have higher valuations than the competing good in the other bundle.

11.4.5 Discussion

In this section, we have analyzed downstream competition in a setting with pairs of substitute goods with independently distributed valuations. This setting can be easily generalized to multiple competing goods. The independence assumption greatly simplifies the modeling, and it is a useful working assumption in the same way logit models of consumer choice assume independence of valuations to simplify the analysis (Guadagni and Little 1983), although this may not be strictly true. It should be pointed out, however, that the assumption of independent valuations is not essential for the results of this section. For instance, Proposition 3 states that a good facing competition is more profitable as part of a bundle. This strategic advantage to the bundler is derived by the ability to leverage the large market share of a large bundle; the bundler will extract higher profits from the outside good as long as the price of the bundle can be adequately increased when the outside good is added.

If consumers' valuations for the two goods are perfectly correlated, i.e., if the goods are perfect substitutes, Bertrand-Nash competition leads to zero prices when the goods are sold separately. In that case, the bundler will not be able to increase the price of the bundle when adding the outside good, and bundling will neither increase nor decrease the bundler's profit. If the valuations for the two goods are not perfectly correlated, as long as the bundler can charge for adding one of the goods to the bundle at least one half of the equilibrium price when the goods are sold separately, bundling will increase profits. Thus, while the results derived in this section may be weakened if the valuations for the goods are correlated, they will still be qualitatively valid for a range of correlations, depending on the precise functional form from which the valuations are derived.

An easy way to see this is to consider the distribution of valuations shown in Figure 11.5. This is a similar setting to the one analyzed in this section, except that we do not allow any consumer's valuations for the two goods to differ by more than $1 - r$ where $0 \leq r \leq 1$. When $r = 0$ we get the independent valuations of our earlier setting, while $r = 1$ corresponds to perfectly correlated valuations. Proposition 3 and the analysis in Sections 4.2 and 4.3 will still apply as long as $p_A > r$ and $p_B > r$. Thus as long as $r < 5/18$ the results in these sections will remain unchanged.

It is interesting to contrast our results with Whinston (1990). Using notation similar to our setting, Whinston considers a monopolist in good B_1 who is also offering good B_2, which faces actual or potential competition from an imperfect substitute A_2. Whinston shows that

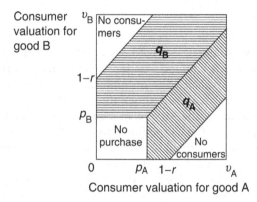

Figure 11.5. Correlated valuations: v_A and v_B cannot differ by more than $1 - r$, $0 \leq r \leq 1$.

low heterogeneity in valuations for B_1 and high differentiation in the valuations for A_2 and B_2 will help reduce the entrant's profits, and thus may allow the monopolist to deter entry for A_2. However, bundling may not be optimal after A_2 has entered, and thus may deter entry only if the monopolist can credibly commit to keep bundling if entry should occur. By contrast, in our setting, bundling a large number of information goods will be optimal whether or not entry occurs, and thus, as discussed in the following section, it will be more likely to effectively deter entry, increasing even further the incumbent's profits.

Nalebuff (1999) considers a model with an incumbent monopolist offering two goods, but where entry will occur in only one of the two markets. The entering product is a perfect substitute, i.e., its valuation by consumers is perfectly correlated to their valuation for the existing product in that market; furthermore, the incumbent cannot change prices post-entry. Nalebuff focuses on the ability of bundling to deter entry and his results are generally consistent with the ones derived in our setting, except that they apply to a case of perfectly correlated valuations. Nalebuff makes the argument that high correlation in valuations, while it may reduce the post-entry benefits from bundling, also reduces the entrant's profits and thus makes entry less likely. This reasoning also applies to our setting.

Finally, it should be noted that an incumbent bundler may find it possible to use predatory pricing to deter entry, while this practice may be hard to implement if the goods are sold separately, e.g., because of anti-trust considerations.

11.5 Implications for entry deterrence, predation and innovation

Summarizing the analysis of Section 4, Table 11.1 shows the market shares, prices and resulting revenues contributed by goods A_i and B_i when they compete under the different settings analyzed in Section 11.4. In this section we discuss the implications of the above analysis for how the strategy of marketing and selling information goods as a bundle can affect competition and profits.

11.5.1 Bundling and acquisitions

In the setting of Proposition 1 where all goods are independent of each other, as the number of goods in the bundle increases, revenues from the bundle increase monotonically. Because there are no fixed costs in this setting, the bundle becomes increasingly profitable. Interestingly, this result carries to the setting of Section 4, in which the added goods may compete with other goods in the bundle. In other words, in addition to bundling goods in B, the bundler will want to acquire goods in A. The following proposition holds:

Table 11.1. *Equilibrium quantities, prices and revenues in different settings*

Setting	A_i	B_i
Single goods A_i and B_i ($i = 1$) compete as standalone goods	$q_{A_i} = \sqrt{2} - 1 \approx 0.41$ $p_{A_i} = \sqrt{2} - 1 \approx 0.41$ $\pi_{A_i} = (\sqrt{2} - 1)^2 \approx 0.172$	$q_{B_i} = \sqrt{2} - 1 \approx 0.41$ $p_{B_i} = \sqrt{2} - 1 \approx 0.41$ $\pi_{B_i} = (\sqrt{2} - 1)^2 \approx 0.172$
Single goods A_i and B_i ($i = 1$) are both provided by a single monopolist who sells them as standalone goods	$q_{A_i} = 1/3 \approx 0.33$ $p_{A_i} = \sqrt{3}/3 \approx 0.58$ $\pi_{A_i} = \sqrt{3}/9 \approx 0.19$	$q_{B_i} = 1/3 \approx 0.33$ $p_{B_i} = \sqrt{3}/3 \approx 0.58$ $\pi_{B_i} = \sqrt{3}/9 \approx 0.19$
A_i as a standalone good ($i = 1$) competes with B_i that is provided as part of a large bundle of unrelated goods	$q_{A_i} = 2/9 \approx 0.22$ $p_{A_i} = 1/3 \approx 0.33$ $\pi_{A_i} = 2/27 \approx 0.07$	$q_{B_i} \approx 1$ $p_{B_i} \geq 5/18 \approx 0.28$ $\pi_{B_i} \geq 5/18 \approx 0.28$
Large number of standalone goods A_i ($i = 1, 2, \ldots$) each competing with corresponding B_i, where goods B_i are provided as a large bundle	$q_{A_i} = 2/9 \approx 0.22$ $p_{A_i} = 1/3 \approx 0.33$ $\pi_{A_i} = 2/27 \approx 0.07$	$q_{B_i} \approx 1$ $p_{B_i} \approx 52/162 \approx 0.33$ $\pi_{B_i} \approx 52/162 \approx 0.33$
Large bundle of goods A_i ($i = 1, 2, \ldots$) each competing with corresponding B_i, also provided as a large bundle	$q_{A_i} \approx 1$ $p_{A_i} \approx 1/6 \approx 0.167$ $\pi_{A_i} \approx 1/6 \approx 0.167$	$q_{B_i} \approx 1$ $p_{B_i} \approx 1/6 \approx 0.167$ $\pi_{B_i} \approx 1/6 \approx 0.167$

Proposition 4: Monotonic bundling profits

Given A1, A2″, A3 and A4, a bundler of a large number of goods from B will increase the profits extracted from any good A_i by adding it to its bundle, whether or not the bundle already contains the corresponding substitute good B_i.

Proposition 4 implies that large bundlers of information goods will be willing to acquire related (i.e., competing) as well as unrelated information goods to add them to the bundle. As a result, a bundle may include competing news channels, such as a cable TV bundle that includes both CNN and CNBC. When acquiring both items in a competing pair of goods, a firm will be able to extract more profit by selling the pair as a bundle (0.66 in total profits) than by selling each item in the pair separately (0.38 in total profits). This contrasts with the case of a bundler of only two competing goods, in which case no additional profits are gained by bundling. Furthermore, a firm's incentives to acquire a second good in such a pair are much higher if it intends to sell it as part of the bundle than if it plans to sell the good separately. The total revenues extracted from the pair of goods by all firms increase by over 0.26 when they are sold as a bundle.[14] The increase in profits is only 0.04 if the two goods continue to be sold separately.[15]

11.5.2 Bundling and entry deterrence

We now look at a bundler of a large number of goods facing a single potential entrant. For convenience we will focus on a potential entrant considering whether to offer good A_1, competing against good B_1 in the bundle. Because B_1 is part of a large bundle, the entrant in effect faces a more "aggressive" incumbent: as shown in Section 11.4.2, it is optimal for the incumbent bundler to price the bundle so that he maintains a market share of almost 100% even after entry. As far as the demand for the entrant's good is concerned, it is as if the incumbent is credibly willing to charge almost zero for good B_1. As a result, entry will be deterred for a broader range of entry costs.[16] For instance, if good B_1

---

[14] Before acquisition, the revenues are no more than 0.33 for the good in the bundle plus 0.07 for the outside good. After acquisition, they are 0.66 when they are sold as a bundle, for a gain of at least 0.26.

[15] The sum of the profits of the competing firms is 0.34 while the profits rise to 0.38 if both goods are sold separately by a single profit-maximizing firm.

[16] This is similar to the result in Whinston (1990) except that in our model, the power of the incumbent's bundle derives from the large number of goods in it, not an inherent characteristic of any particular good.

is part of a bundle, then it would be unprofitable for a potential competitor to enter and sell A_1 as long as his fixed costs exceed 0.07. In contrast, as shown in Sections 11.4.1 and 11.4.2, the entrant could profitably enter with fixed costs as high to 0.19 if B_1 were sold as a standalone good. Thus firms with fixed costs between 0.07 and 0.19 will be deterred from entry if B_1 is made part of the bundle. By continuity, this result can extend to the case where the bundling incumbent has slightly higher production costs than the single-product entrant, a product on the average valued less than the entrant's product (i.e., lower "quality") or both. In each of these cases, the entrant will not find it profitable to enter despite a superior cost structure or quality level.

This argument also applies in the case of a bundler of n goods facing n potential entrants. If the n goods $A_i \in A$ in the setting analyzed in Section 11.4.3 are seen as potential entrants competing with the goods B_i in set B, the following corollary follows for large values of n:

Corollary 2: Entry deterrence
Given A1, A2″, A3 and A4, if the goods A_i cannot be offered as a bundle, then there is a range of fixed costs κ_{Ai} for which none of these goods is produced, even though they would be produced if the products in B were offered separately.

It should be noted that the "aggressive" pricing of the bundler and the resulting entry deterrence are not based on any threats or dynamic strategies, e.g., artificially lowering prices in the short run to prevent entry. The bundler is simply choosing the price that maximizes profits in the current period. It happens that the optimal pricing policy for the bundler also has the effect of making entry very unattractive. Of course, this can make bundling even more profitable if it reduces competition.

11.5.3 Coordinated entry by offering a rival bundle

If the potential entrants can offer a rival bundle (e.g., if they merge or can coordinate their entry and pricing), they may be able to profitably enter the incumbent's markets. Specifically, if the entrants all enter simultaneously as a bundle, they can all gain sufficient market share to stay in business, even if they would have had to exit had they entered separately. The intuition for this result is that when the entrants offer their own bundle of products that compete with the original bundle, a large number of consumers will find it worthwhile to purchase *both* bundles, because there is no correlation among the valuations of the goods in each bundle, which means that for each pair of goods, each consumer is equally likely to find their preferred good in either bundle (see Section 11.4.4).

Corollary 3

In the setting of Sections 11.4.3 and 11.4.4, if the A_is can be offered as a bundle, for large n the total revenues for the entrants are maximized by bundling the A_i goods, and the unique equilibrium is characterized by two bundles, each selling at a price of 1/6 per good, and consumers buying both bundles.

Thus, if they can coordinate and offer a competing bundle of the A_i goods, the n A firms will find it profitable to enter even for fixed costs as high as 0.18. When fixed costs are between 0.07 and 0.18, it is unprofitable for the firms to produce the A_i goods and sell them separately, but it is profitable to produce and sell them as a bundle that competes with the B bundle. Consumer welfare is significantly increased by the availability of the competing bundle, increasing from little more than zero if only one bundle is sold with no competitors to about 0.33 if both bundles are sold.

11.5.4   Bundling, predation and exit

We now consider the case in which the incumbent firm sells a single information good and the entrant sells a large bundle of unrelated goods. This case is the reverse of the case in Section 5.2 if the incumbent sells good A_i and a bundler sells a large bundle of unrelated goods B – B_i, then the bundler can enter the new market by adding good B_i to its bundle, even if it would have been unprofitable to enter the market with a standalone good.

The reason is that, as shown in Section 11.4.2, the equilibrium for competition between a bundler and a seller of a single good with identical production costs and quality leaves the bundler with the majority of the market and higher profits while the profits of the single-product firm are reduced. If production were just barely profitable for a single-product firm selling good A_i competing with another single-product firm selling good B_i, then it would become unprofitable for a single-product firm selling good A_i competing with a bundler selling good B_i as part of a large bundle. For instance, in the setting of Section 11.4.2, the act of bundling could force a competing firm to exit if its fixed costs were greater than the 0.07 that would be earned when competing with a bundler. Without bundling, the same firm would not have exited as long as its fixed costs were greater than the 0.17 that could be earned when competing with another single-product firm.

Similarly, there is a range of fixed costs for which entry is profitable if and only if the entrant sells a bundle.

Corollary 4

An entrant who sells a large bundle can force a single-product incumbent firm to exit the market even if it could not do so by selling the same goods separately.

If there are fixed costs of production, the incumbent may find it unprofitable to remain in the market with a reduced market share. As a result, the bundler can successfully pursue a predatory strategy of entering new markets and driving out existing firms.

If the entrant did not have a superior product or cost structure, this strategy would not be credible or successful if the entrant sold its products separately. A threat to temporarily charge very low prices in an attempt to drive out the incumbent would not be credible if the entrant's goods were sold separately. If the incumbent did not exit, the entrant would not be willing to follow through on such a threat; it would not be a subgame perfect equilibrium strategy. However, the mere fact that the entrant has the option of including the new good as part of an existing bundle will immediately make it a more formidable predator. Now, it is credible for the entrant to charge low enough prices to maintain a very high market share. What's more, even with this "aggressive" pricing strategy, the entrant will be more profitable when it bundles its products than it would be if it did not bundle. Thus, even when the incumbent has lower fixed costs, lower marginal costs or higher quality than the entrant, it may be forced to exit when the entrant uses the bundling strategy.

11.5.5   Bundling and incentives for innovation

Assume that firm A is considering an investment in a market that does not currently face any competition. It can create an innovation at some irreversible cost and enter the market. Suppose a second firm could, for the same fixed costs and marginal costs and with a similar quality, follow the first firm into the market, leading to a competitive equilibrium between imperfect substitutes, as in Section 4.2. For a range of values, this equilibrium will result in sufficient profits for the first firm to undertake the innovation even in the face of potential entry by a similar firm. If fixed costs are somewhat higher, the equilibrium duopoly profits will be sufficiently lower than the monopoly profits that the first firm will enter the market, but the second firm will not. In either case, the innovation will be undertaken. While we assume that the costs and benefits of the innovation are deterministic, the analysis can be readily generalized to stochastic values.

However, now the second potential entry is a bundler of a set of similar goods in different markets. As in the analysis of predation above, an entrant who is a bundler can quickly capture most of the market share in the new market. Being aware of this possibility, what are firm A's incentives for innovating? Clearly, firm A will find it less profitable to innovate and create new markets since it cannot keep as large a share of the returns. Instead of earning the monopoly profits or half of the total duopoly profits, firm A will keep only a fraction of the market and much lower profits (0.07 in the setting above). Incentives for innovation by such firms will be reduced and fewer innovations will be funded and undertaken.

This result is consistent with claims by some entrepreneurs that venture capitalists will not fund their ventures if there is a significant risk that a competing product might be incorporated into a large bundle sold by a potential predator. The investors are rightly especially fearful of potential competition from a firm that already controls a large bundle of information goods. A potential competitor which merely sells a standalone good cannot as easily take away the market from the innovator.

It is important to note that the effect of bundling on innovation extends beyond the product markets in which the bundler currently competes. If a potential innovator believes that a bundler may choose to enter some *new* market that could be created by the innovator, the innovator's incentives will be reduced. Some innovations will be unprofitable in this situation even if they would have been profitable to undertake had there been no threat of entry by the bundler or if the only possible entry were by standalone goods.

However, this is not the end of the story. While the single-product firms will have reduced incentives to innovate, the bundler will have greater incentives. It can earn greater profits by entering new markets than the single-product firms could. Thus there will be a shift of innovative activity from standalone firms to bundlers. Whether the ultimate equilibrium will involve a higher or lower total level of innovation will depend on the ability of the different types of firms to succeed with innovations. Furthermore, the types of innovations that the bundler will undertake can be expected to differ systematically from the types of innovations pursued by standalone firms.

11.6   Concluding remarks

The economies of aggregation we identify are in many ways similar in effect to economies of scale or network externalities. A marketing strategy that employs large-scale bundling can extract greater profit and gain competitive advantage from a given set of goods. Economies of aggregation will be important when marginal costs are very low, as for the (re)production and delivery of information goods via the Internet. High marginal costs render large-scale aggregation unprofitable, which may explain why it is more common in Internet publishing than in publishing based on paper, film, polycarbonate discs or other relatively high-cost media.

Our analysis of bundling and competition showed that:

1. Large bundles may provide a significant advantage in the competition for upstream content.
2. The act of bundling information goods makes an incumbent seem "tougher" to competitors and potential entrants.
3. The bundler can profitably enter a new market and dislodge an incumbent by adding a competing information good to the existing bundle.
4. Bundling can reduce the incentives for competitors to innovate, while it can increase bundlers' incentives to innovate.

Although we analyze a fairly stylized setting in order to isolate the effects of large-scale bundling on competition, earlier work using the Bakos-Brynjolfsson bundling model (Bakos and Brynjolfsson 1999a, 1999b; Bakos, Brynjolfsson and Lichtman 1999) suggests that our framework can be generalized in a number of directions. In particular, Proposition 1 also applies, inter alia, to consumers with budget constraints, goods that are complements or substitutes, goods with diminishing or increasing returns, and goods that are drawn from different distributions (Bakos and Brynjolfsson 1999a). Furthermore, the existence of distribution or transaction costs, which are paid only once per purchase, will generally tend to strengthen the advantages bundlers have compared with sellers of separate goods (Bakos and Brynjolfsson 1999b). The effects we analyze are, by design, purely based on using bundling as a pricing and marketing strategy to change the demand for a collection of information goods without (necessarily) any change in any of their intrinsic characteristics or any change in their production technology. Naturally, bundling can be combined with changes in the goods to either reinforce or mitigate the effects we identify.

The development of the Internet as an infrastructure for the distribution of digital information goods has dramatically affected the competitive marketing and selling strategies based on large-scale bundling. As we show in this chapter, the resulting "economies of aggregation" for information goods can provide powerful leverage for obtaining new content, increasing profits, protecting markets, entering new markets and affecting innovation, even in the absence of network externalities or technological economies of scale or scope. Large-scale bundling was relatively rare in the pre-Internet era, but its implications for marketing and competition are an essential component of Internet marketing strategy for information goods.

11.7   Appendix: proofs of propositions

Proposition 1

See the proof for Proposition 1 in Bakos and Brynjolfsson (1999a).

Proposition 2

In the setting of Section 3, the following lemma states that if $n_1 > n_2$, then a bundle of n_1 goods will extract more value from exclusive rights to the single good than a bundle of n_2 goods.

Lemma 1

If n_1, n_2 are large enough integers, and if $n_1 > n_2$, then $y_1 > y_2$.

Proof

We first prove that if k is large enough so that the probability distribution for a consumer's valuation for a bundle of k goods can be approximated by a normal distribution, then a bundle with $k+1$ goods will extract more value from a single good than a bundle of k goods. The central limit theorem guarantees that in the setting of Section 3, the valuation for a bundle of k goods will converge to a normal distribution. The lemma then follows by induction and the application of an inequality from Schmalensee (1984).

Let x_k be the average (per-good) valuation for a bundle of k goods. Denote by $\pi_k(p)$ the per-good revenues of a bundler of k goods charging a price p per good and selling to a fraction q_k (p) of consumers. Let $p_k^\star$ be the profit-maximizing price, and denote $\pi_k(p_k^\star)$ by $\pi_k^\star$.

For the lemma to hold, it must be

$$(k + 2)\pi_{k+2}^\star - (k + 1)\pi_{k+1}^\star > (k + 1)\pi_{k+1}^\star - k\pi_k^\star, \text{ or } g(k + 1) - g(k) > 0 \quad (11.1)$$

where $g(k) = (k + 1)\pi_{k+1}^\star - k\pi_k^\star$.

For (1) to hold, it suffices that f is increasing in n, i.e.,

$$\frac{dg(k)}{dk} > 0 \tag{11.2}$$

Let $h(k) = k\pi_k^\star$. Then $g(k) = h(k + 1) - h(k)$, and $\frac{dg(k)}{dk} = \frac{d}{dk}[h(k + 1)] - \frac{d}{dk}[h(k)]$. Thus, for (2) to hold, it suffices that $\frac{d}{dk}[h(k)]$ is increasing in n, i.e., that

$$\frac{d^2}{dk^2}[h(k)] > 0 \tag{11.3}$$

From the definition of h, $\frac{d}{dk}[h(k)] = k\frac{d\pi_k^\star}{dk} + \pi_k^\star$ and $\frac{d^2}{dk^2}[h(k)] = k\frac{d^2\pi_k^\star}{dk^2} + 2\frac{d\pi_k^\star}{dk}$, and thus it suffices to show that

$$2\frac{d\pi_k^\star}{dk} + k\frac{d^2\pi_k^\star}{dk^2} > 0 \tag{11.4}$$

where $\pi_k^\star$ maximizes $\pi_k(p) = pq(q) = p(1 - F_k(p))$, and f_k is the pdf for the average valuation of a bundle of n goods, and F_k is the cumulative distribution of f_k.

Next, we show that (4) is satisfied in the case that $f_k = N(\mu, \sigma/\sqrt{k})$.

Let $x = \mu/\sigma$ and $\alpha_n = \frac{k\mu}{\sqrt{k}\sigma} = \sqrt{k}x$.

Then we can write

$$\frac{d\pi_k^\star}{dk} = \frac{d\pi_k^\star}{d\alpha_k}\frac{d\alpha_k}{dk} = \frac{1}{2}k^{-\frac{1}{2}}x\frac{d\pi_k^\star}{d\alpha_k} \tag{11.5}$$

and

$$\frac{d^2\pi_k^\star}{dk^2} = \frac{d}{dk}\left[\frac{1}{2}k^{-\frac{1}{2}}x\frac{d\pi_k^\star}{d\alpha_k}\right] = -\frac{1}{2}k^{-\frac{3}{2}}x\frac{d\pi_k^\star}{d\alpha_k} + \frac{1}{2}k^{-\frac{1}{2}}x\frac{d}{dk}\left[\frac{d\pi_k^\star}{d\alpha_k}\right]$$

$$= -\frac{1}{2}k^{-\frac{3}{2}}x\frac{d\pi_k^\star}{d\alpha_k} + \frac{1}{2}k^{-\frac{1}{2}}x\frac{d^2\pi_k^\star}{d\alpha_k^2}\frac{d\alpha_k}{dk}$$

$$\therefore \frac{d^2\pi_k^\star}{dk^2} = -\frac{1}{2}k^{-\frac{3}{2}}x\frac{d\pi_k^\star}{d\alpha_k} + \frac{x^2}{4k}\frac{d^2\pi_k^\star}{d\alpha_k^2}. \tag{11.6}$$

Substituting (11.5) and (11.6) into (11.4), we see that (11.4) is satisfied when $k^{-\frac{1}{2}}x\frac{d\pi_k^\star}{d\alpha_k} - \frac{1}{2}k^{-\frac{1}{2}}x\frac{d\pi_k^\star}{d\alpha_k} + \frac{x^2}{4}\frac{d^2\pi_k^\star}{d\alpha_k^2} > 0$, i.e., $\frac{1}{2}k^{-\frac{1}{2}}x\frac{d\pi_k^\star}{d\alpha_k} + \frac{x^2}{4}\frac{d^2\pi_k^\star}{d\alpha_k^2} > 0$.

It thus suffices to show that $\frac{d\pi_k^\star}{d\alpha_k} > 0$ and $\frac{d^2\pi_k^\star}{d\alpha_k^2} > 0$. The first condition follows from inequality (11a) in Schmalensee (1984) and the second condition follows from differentiating that inequality.

Proposition 1 implies that $\lim_{n_1 \to \infty} y_1 = \lim_{n_2 \to \infty} y_2 = \mu$. In the case of non-exclusive provision of the single good, if it is provided outside both bundles, Bertrand competition will result in a zero equilibrium price. As n_1 and n_2 get large enough, both bundles achieve a market share close to 100%. Thus if the good is provided as part of one bundle only, at equilibrium the outside good will realize revenues close to zero while the bundler will be able to incrementally extract lower revenues than when having exclusive rights to the good. If both bundles include the good, neither bundler will be able to extract revenues from it since (almost) all consumers will already have access to it via the other bundle. Thus it follows that as n_1 and n_2 get large enough, $y_1 > z_1$, and $y_2 > z_2$, and at least one of z_1 and z_2 converges to zero. Thus $\lim_{n_1, n_2 \to \infty} max(y_1, y_2, z_1 + z_2) = y_1$, which proves the proposition.

Section 11.4.1, equilibrium for competing substitute goods
At equilibrium, neither firm benefits from lowering its price, taking the price of the other competitor as given. The gray-shaded area in Figure 11.6 shows the additional sales for firm B if it lowers its price by δ, which equal $\delta p_A + \delta(1 - p_A)$, or δ. Thus if at price p_B firm B sells

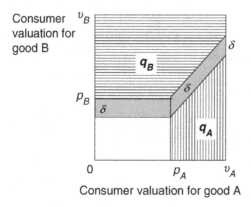

Consumer v_B
valuation for
good B

p_B

q_B

δ

δ

δ

q_A

0   p_A v_A

Consumer valuation for good A

Figure 11.6. Increase in sales by firm B from a small decrease in p_B.

quantity q_B, by lowering its price by δ, firm B realizes new revenues of δp_B and loses revenues δq_B from its existing sales. At equilibrium, $\delta p_B = \delta q_B$, or $p_B = q_B$. If firm A lowers its price by δ, it realizes new sales of $(1 + p_B - p_A)\delta$, corresponding revenues $(1 + p_B - p_A)\delta p_A$, and loses revenues δq_A from its existing sales. At equilibrium, this yields $p_A = q_A/(1 + p_B - p_A)$.

Then: $q_B = \frac{1}{2} + (p_A - p_B) - \frac{1}{2}p_A^2$ and $p_A = p_B$, and the unique equilibrium is characterized by prices $p_A^\star$ and $p_B^\star$ that are given by $p_A^\star = p_B^\star = \sqrt{2} - 1$, corresponding quantities $q_A^\star = q_B^\star = \sqrt{2} - 1$, and corresponding gross profit $\pi_A^\star = \pi_B^\star = (\sqrt{2} - 1)^2$, or approximately 0.17.

Section 11.4.1, monopoly provision of substitute goods
If both goods A and B are provided by a single firm, it will set the prices p_A and p_B to maximize its total revenues $p_A q_A + p_B q_B$. If the monopolist lowers p_B by an amount δ, the additional sales for good B are depicted in the gray-shaded area in Figure 11.6, and equal new sales of δp_A, and sales $\delta(1 - p_A)$ taken from good A. The corresponding increase in revenues is $\delta p_A p_B + \delta(1 - p_A)(p_B - p_A)$, and must be offset against a loss of revenues δq_B from existing sales of good B. Thus the monopolist will choose p_B so that $p_A p_B + (1 - p_A)(p_B - p_A) = q_B$. The corresponding condition for p_A is $p_A p_B + (1 - p_B)(p_A - p_B) = q_A$, and it can be seen that $q_A + q_B = 1 - p_A p_B$. In the unique equilibrium the monopolist maximizes $p_A(1 - p_A^2)$, yielding optimal prices $p_A^\star = p_B^\star = 1/\sqrt{3}$, and corresponding quantities $q_A^\star = q_B^\star = 1/3$. Revenues are $\sqrt{3}/9$ per good (approx. 0.19), for total revenues of $2\sqrt{3}/9$ (approx. 0.38).

Alternatively, the monopolist can sell only one good at a price of 0.5, with resulting sales of 0.5 and revenues of 0.25. Finally, as consumer valuations for the two goods are i.i.d., consumers do not derive additional value from their less preferred good and the goods have zero marginal costs; if the monopolist bundles A and B he will price the bundle at $1/\sqrt{3}$, and sell quantity $q_A^\star + q_B^\star = 2/3$, for the same total revenues of $2\sqrt{3}/9$. Thus the monopolist cannot increase his profits by bundling a single pair of competing goods.

Proposition 3

Proof

We know from Proposition 1 that $\lim_{n\to\infty} \dfrac{1}{n-1} p_{B2\ldots n}^\star = \dfrac{1}{2}$ and $\lim_{n\to\infty} q_{B2\ldots n}^\star = 1$.

Let $q_{B1}(p_{B1}, p_{A1})$ be the demand faced by firm B for good B_1 at price p_{B1}, when firm A sets price p_{A1} for good A_1. Define $\hat{p}_{B1}(p_{A1})$ so that $q_{B1}(\hat{p}_{B1}(p_{A1}), p_{A1}) = 1/2$. In other words, given a price p_{A1} for good A_1, $\hat{p}_{B1}(p_{A1})$ is the price at which good B1 achieves a 50% market share.

For large n if firm B adds good B_1 to the bundle of $B_2, B_3 \ldots B_n$ and raises the bundle price by $\hat{p}_{B1}(p_{A1})$, any change in the demand for the bundle will be second order, as marginal consumers are equally likely to drop or start purchasing the bundle when B_1 is added at a price of $\hat{p}_{B1}(p_{A1})$. The envelope theorem guarantees that gross profits will be approximately $\left(p_{B2\ldots n}^\star + \hat{p}_{B1}(p_{A1})\right) q_{B2\ldots n}^\star$, and thus for large n firm B can extract gross profit of at least $\hat{p}_{B1}(p_{A1})$ from good B_1 by including it in the bundle.

Since $\lim_{n\to\infty} q_{B2\ldots n}^\star = 1$, as n increases, good B_1 is eventually made available to essentially all consumers as part of the bundle. Thus firm A must set its price based to the fact that (almost all) consumers already have access to good B_1, and will thus choose p_{A1} to maximize $\frac{1}{2}(1 - p_{A1})^2 p_{A1}$ as shown in Figure 11.3, resulting in price $p_{A1}^\star = \frac{1}{3}$, corresponding sales $q_{A1}^\star = \frac{2}{9}$ and gross profit $\pi_{A1}^\star = \frac{2}{27}$ or approximately 0.07. The corresponding $\hat{p}_{B1}^\star(p_{A1}^\star)$ is $\frac{5}{18}$ or approximately 0.28.

Section 11.4.2, derivation of the demand for good B_1

If $p_{A1} \geq p_{B1}$, then $q_{B1} = \frac{1}{2}(1 + (p_{A1} - p_{B1}) + p_{A1})(1 - p_{B1}) - \frac{1}{2}(p_{A1} - p_{B1})^2 = \frac{1}{2} + p_{A1} - p_{B1} - \frac{1}{2}p_{A1}^2$.

If $p_{B1} > p_{A1}$, then $q_{B1} = 1 - q_{A1} - p_{A1}p_{B1} = \frac{1}{2} - p_{B1} + p_{A1} + \frac{1}{2}p_{B1}^2 - p_{A1}p_{B1}$. Thus, $\frac{\partial q_{B1}}{\partial p_{B1}} = -1$ for $p_{B1} \leq p_{A1}$ and $\frac{\partial q_{B1}}{\partial p_{B1}} = -1 + p_{B1} - p_{A1}$ for $p_{B1} > p_{A1}$. Furthermore, even if $p_{B1} = 0$, a fraction $\frac{1}{2}(1 - p_{A1})^2$ of consumers will purchase A_1 over B_1. The resulting distribution of valuations faced by firm B for good B_1 when firm A prices A_1 at p_{A1} is shown in Figure 11.4, and it has an impulse of measure $\frac{1}{2}(1 - p_{A1})^2$ at the origin. This distribution has mean $\mu_{B1}(p_{A1}) = \int_0^{p_{A1}} x\,dx + \int_{p_{A1}}^1 (p_{A1} + 1 - x)\,dx$, or $\mu_{B1}(p_{A1}) = \frac{1}{6} + \frac{1}{2}p_{A1} - \frac{1}{6}p_{A1}^3$.

Proposition 4

Proof

If B_i is not part of the bundle, this is easily shown based on Bakos and Brynjolfsson (1999a) Proposition 2, as adding A_i has the same effect as adding B_i. If both goods are produced, then introducing the second good in the bundle will allow the bundler not to worry about competition and extract nearly the full surplus created by the two goods. If a consumer values one of the two goods at x ($0 \leq x \leq 1$), then his value for both goods is x with probability x, and $\frac{1}{2}(1 + x)$ with probability $1 - x$, depending on which good is more valued. Thus the mean surplus created by the two goods as part of the bundle is $\int_0^1 (x^2 + (1 - x)\frac{1}{2}(1 + x))dx = \int_0^1 (\frac{1}{2} + \frac{1}{2}x^2)dx = \frac{2}{3}$. For a large enough n, the bundler can capture virtually the entire surplus by including both goods in the bundle, or gross profits of just under $\frac{2}{3}$. We showed in Section 4.2 that good A_i outside the bundle would generate gross profits of approx. 0.07. Since good B_i in the bundle will generate profits less than 0.5 (its mean valuation), the bundler will increase its gross profits by at least 0.16 by adding good A_i to the bundle. Therefore the bundler will be willing to acquire good A_i.

We also need to consider the case where the bundler acquires good A_i, but leaves it outside the bundle. In that case, if the bundler sets a price p_{A_i} for good A_i, the mean valuation for good B_i in the bundle will be $\mu_{B_i} = \frac{1}{6} + \frac{1}{2}p_{A_i} - \frac{1}{6}p_{A_i}^3$ and the quantity demanded for good A_i will be $\frac{1}{2}(1 - p_{A_i})^2$ as shown in Section 4.2. The bundler would thus maximize total revenues $\pi_{A_i} + \pi_{B_i} = \frac{1}{2}p_{A_i}(1 - p_{A_i})^2 + \frac{1}{6} + \frac{1}{2}p_{A_i} - \frac{1}{6}p_{A_i}^3 = \frac{1}{6} + p_{A_i} - p_{A_i}^2 + \frac{1}{3}p_{A_i}^3$ by setting $p_{A_i} = 1$, resulting in gross profit of 0.5. In other words the bundler would optimally price the outside good out of the market, maximizing B_i's contribution to the bundle. Thus the bundler maximizes his profits by including both goods in the bundle.

12 Pricing information goods: free vs. pay content

Marc Bourreau and Virginie Lethiais

12.1 Introduction

Various types of information goods are available on the Internet: business news, general news, entertainment content, games, music, software, etc. At the beginning of the World Wide Web, most content was free, but since 2002, content providers have begun to charge their customers. According to a study of the Online Publishers Association (OPA, 2004), US consumers spent $1.56 billion for online content in 2003,[1] an 18.8% increase over 2002.

The proportion of content offered for free varies a lot among content providers, as online press illustrates. At one extreme, some providers – like *The Wall Street Journal* online[2] – offer only pay content, while at the other extreme, some offer only free content – as the French journal *Libération* did for a while. In between, online press firms offer both free and pay content. For example, the online journal Salon.com offers roughly half of its content for free, and the other half to its subscribers only ($30 per year).[3] The French newspaper *Le Monde* provides some of its articles for free, but full access to content is available only to its subscribers. Combinations of free and pay content are also common for other types of content: degraded versions of software or video games can be downloaded for free, but the "full" version has to be purchased; excerpts of books or songs are also available at various online stores.

In this chapter, we suggest that providing a proportion of an information good for free, that is, a "free version", aims at signalling the quality

We would like to thank the editor, Nicolas Curien, for very useful comments and suggestions. We would like also to thank Pierre-Jean Benghozi, Thierry Pénard and Hervé Tanguy for their remarks.

[1] The OPA study excludes software.
[2] Headlines are free, but full articles can be accessed by subscribers only. The *WSJ* had 646,000 subscribers in June 2002. The price of the annual subscription to the online journal is $39 for subscribers to the print journal and $79 for non-subscribers.
[3] In 2002, Salon.com had only 39,500 subscribers for a total number of free users of 3.6 million. Free users have to watch an advertisement before reading the article.

of the good, and we provide a theoretical framework which accounts for this signalling strategy. Of course, there might be other motivations to provide free content. In particular, firms could provide free content to attract large audiences, and generate advertising revenues. In this respect, the presence of advertising revenues explains why, following the recent slowdown of advertising expenditure on the Internet, some content providers, such as online newspapers or portals, have stopped providing all content for free and started to charge. Nonetheless, these providers continue to provide both free and pay content.

Evaluation of quality before purchase is not a specific feature of the Internet. For instance, a sample of a beauty cream can be sent to potential consumers, or consumers can taste goods (like food) in supermarkets. However, evaluation of quality is much less costly both for the seller and for the consumer on the Internet than in traditional markets.

We analyze the incentives of a provider of information goods to offer a free version of his product. Consumers are uncertain about the quality of the product (it is an "experience good"). The free version discloses information about the quality of the product to potential consumers, though it does not give perfect information. Furthermore, the higher the proportion of the product which is offered for free – that is, the higher the size of the free version – the more accurate is the signal about the quality of the product. Hence, the free version acts as a partially informative advertisement, since it allows consumers to discover the quality of the product with some probability.

We assume that consumers derive utility only from the first consumption of content, which implies that the higher the size of the free version, the lower the willingness to pay for the whole product. This is consistent with what we observe in markets for experience goods. For instance, in the press industry, readers with low willingness to pay for information tend to visit only free sites to get informed. For a book, the possibility of reading the best excerpts can reduce the desire to read the whole book and hence the willingness to pay for it. This might be true for a film, too. In the software industry, every Internet user can download an "Acrobat reader" for free, and read pdf files using this software. However, Acrobat Reader does not allow users to create pdf files. One has to purchase the full "Acrobat" software for that. On the one hand, free access to one feature of the software ("read") may lead users to purchase the other feature ("write"), because they can evaluate the quality of the software. But on the other hand, it lowers the willingness to pay for the full set of features ("read" + "write").

This chapter is related to two strands of the economic literature. In media economics, free content ("programs") attracts audiences, which generates advertising revenues. A firm trades off between charging consumers and providing the good at a low price (maybe even for free) in order to increase its audience and hence its advertising revenues (see Baye and Morgan [2000], Gabszewicz, Laussel and Sonnac [2004], Ferrando, Gabszewicz, Laussel and Sonnac [2004]). Lethiais [2001] also proposes a model with two sources of revenues – subscriptions and advertising revenues – and studies competition between service providers on the Internet. Barros et al. [2002] construct a model of competition with advertiser-supported firms and ad-adverse consumers to analyze the incentives of Internet portals to form alliances with advertisers.

This chapter is also related to the economic literature about experience goods. Since disclosing information influences consumers' purchase decisions, Grossman [1981], Crémer [1984], Lewis and Sappington [1994], Che [1996] and, more recently, Gaudeul [2003] study whether firms should provide information to consumers about the goods prior to purchase. The decision of the firm to disclose information or not could also be a signal about the true quality of the firm. Milgrom [1981] and Okuno-Fujiwara et al. [1990] study the incentives for a firm to disclose information about its product in this context.

Advertising may not only reveal information about the good but also convince consumers that the good is of high quality. Nelson [1970, 1974], Milgrom and Roberts [1986] and Kihlstrom and Riordan [1984] study the incentives of a monopolist to invest in non informative advertising. They show, in a context of repeated purchases, that even if advertising reveals no information about the quality of the good, firms will advertise because advertising can modify buyers' perception about the quality of the good. Linnemer [2002] constructs a static model in which a monopolist can signal its quality through both its price and its investment in non informative advertising. He shows that, combined with price, advertising appears to be a useful signal of quality, and that a high quality firm makes greater profit than when only price is used to signal quality. Finally, advertising may also be informative: sellers can distribute free samples or propose demonstrations of their product. Moraga-González [2000] proposes a price signalling model with informative advertising, in which the seller chooses the proportion of the consumers to which he sends a signal, which is costly but completely informative. In his paper, the consumer receives two signals from the seller: the price of the good (which acts as a non informative signal) and the informative signal, which reveals the true quality of the good. He determines, in a static context, the conditions for advertising to arise in equilibrium.

In this chapter, due to the two opposite effects of the free version on consumers' preferences, a high quality supplier faces the following trade-off. On the one hand, if he provides a larger proportion of free content, he signals the quality of its content more accurately. On the other hand, he reduces the proportion of the product, which is available to pay consumers only. Consumers also obtain information by observing the strategy of the seller. Indeed, consumers receive two signals: the price and the proportion of free content offered by the seller. We determine the perfect Bayesian equilibria of this game.

We show that a high quality seller provides a free version of his product in any separating equilibrium. Price is not sufficient to signal quality. This result contrasts with the result of Moraga-González [2000], who shows that informative advertising never occurs in any separating equilibrium, hence that price suffices to signal quality. In our model, even when consumers do not discover the true quality of the product, they observe the size of the free version offered by the seller. Therefore, a free version is not only an informative signal for some consumers but also a signal of quality for all consumers. It differs from the model of Moraga-González, in which consumers who do not receive the signal do not know how many people have received it. This is why, in our model, a high quality seller has incentives to send this additional signal.

Moreover, we show that there is a unique separating equilibrium, which survives the intuitive criterion of Cho and Kreps [1987]. At this equilibrium, a low quality seller provides no free version and sets the perfect information optimal price, whereas a high quality seller offers a free version of his product to signal his quality and sets a price, which is lower than the perfect information optimal price. As a free version reduces the willingness to pay for the product, the high quality provider has to lower its price compared to the same setting with perfect information. An interesting implication of this result is that if the quality of the good is high, uncertainty about the quality of content implies higher consumer surplus. Finally, at the pooling equilibria of the game, both types of sellers propose a free version of their products.

The chapter is organized as follows. In Section 2, we begin by providing an empirical analysis of the strategies of online content suppliers. Our model is introduced in Section 3. We devote Section 4 to the determination of the demand for content. In Section 5, we determine the separating and pooling perfect Bayesian equilibria of the game. Finally, concluding remarks and possible extensions are presented in Section 6.

12.2 Online content strategies

Since the beginning of the Internet, some content has been offered for free. Various studies showed that consumers were reluctant to purchase online content, in particular because they felt that online payment was not secure, and that content was not attractive enough.[4] Exceptions – such as *The Wall Street Journal* online or software purchases – were rare.

However, since 2002, pay content has been developing on the Internet. A study of the Online Publishers Association (OPA, 2004) provides interesting information about the market for pay content, though it excludes software. According to this study, US consumers spent $1.56 billion for online content in 2003, an 18.8% increase over 2002. Table 12.1 shows the online content spending by category of content.[5] The top three categories in the OPA study are personals and dating, business content, and entertainment and lifestyle. They account for 64% of all consumer spending.

Table 12.1. *Content spending by category*

Content category	Examples	Spending in 2003 ($ millions)
Personals & dating	Dating sites	449.5
Business content	Business news, business research	334.1
Entertainment & lifestyle	Digital multimedia, erotica, humor	214.0
Research	Consumer research, people research	108.6
Personal growth	Motivational sites	90.7
General news	CNN.com, LeMonde.fr	87.5
Community directories	Virtual communities like IMDB.com	87.0
Games	Games played through web browsers	73.0
Greeting cards		40.6
Sports	Sports news, fantasy sports, etc.	38.2
Credit help	Access to consumer credit records	36.6
Total		**1559.8**

Source: OPA, 2004.

[4] According to the Pew Internet & American Life Project, in 2001, 17% only of US Internet users were willing to purchase online content. The two main factors to persuade consumers to buy content online are higher security and better content (source: PaymentOne, 2003).

[5] Apart from software purchases, the OPA study also excludes the following categories: pornographic sites, gambling sites, illegal drug-related sites, Internet service providers, business services and online games with non-web browser-based interface.

According to the OPA (2003), 10.5% of Internet users purchased online content in the first quarter of 2003. This is lower than the 17% of US Internet users who declared in 2001 that they were willing to purchase online content (according to the Pew Internet & American Life Project (http://www.pewinternet.org) in 2001). Subscriptions represent 89% of total pay content revenues, with an average monthly subscription amount of $11, whereas single payments represent only 11%, with an average single payment amount of $21.7.

Even though pay content is growing fast, most online content providers continue to offer free content. Below, we propose a few brief case studies, in which we analyze the motivations to propose free content.

12.2.1   Online press

In the online press, there is no "standard" business model. At one extreme, some providers offer all content for free. At the other extreme, some providers – like *The Wall Street Journal* online – offer no free content. The French newspaper *Libération* is a good illustration of this variety of content strategies. When it started to operate online, *Libération* offered all content for free. In October 2001, the journal decided to charge for content; only breaking news was proposed for free. But in 2002, *Libération* changed its strategy again and offered all content for free. Finally, since 2004, *Libération* has been providing a selection of articles for free, whereas the newspaper can be purchased online in digital (pdf) format.

When an online journal charges for content, the types of content which are sold to consumers vary a lot. Some newspapers, like *Libération*, sell only the newspaper in pdf format. The price of the pdf version is typically lower than the price of the paper version. For instance, another French journal, *Le Monde*, is sold for 1 euro in pdf format against 1.20 euros for the paper version.

Other online journals propose "premium" (i.e., higher quality) content to their online subscribers. For instance, for 5 euros per month, *Le Monde* offers a digital version of the newspaper (in pdf or html format), e-mail alerts, weather information, specific multimedia content (photos, videos), etc.[6] The online US journal Salon.com has adopted the opposite content strategy; the quality of free content is degraded by ads, pop-ups and a slower download speed, compared with the site available to subscribers. Besides, Salon.com offers additional benefits to its subscribers, which are not available on the free site (like access to *Wired* magazine or audio downloads).

---

[6] The subscription to the online version of the journal is cheaper than the subscription to the paper version, which is more than 15 euros per month.

In these examples, free content, when available, has two different roles. First, it attracts audiences and generates advertising revenues. Second, it allows consumers to evaluate the quality of content.

12.2.2 Portals

Portals offer a large range of services to Internet users, such as search tools, information services, webmail access, web pages, etc. Portals can be "independent" (like Yahoo! or MSN) or controlled by an Internet service provider. For instance, in France, Wanadoo.fr is the portal of the leading ISP, Wanadoo. Most of the revenues of portals come from advertising. However, some portals, like Yahoo.com, have begun to charge for content. For instance, in the fourth quarter of 2003, pay services represented 12.8% of Yahoo! total revenues (i.e., $85 million out of a total revenue of $663.9 million).

Some services are offered in both a free version and a vertically differentiated pay version. For instance, Yahoo.com offers a free mail account with web access and 4Mb storage, whereas its basic premium mail account service gives a 25Mb mailbox, POP access and other benefits for $19.79 per year. Vertical differentiation between the free and the pay version increases the willingness to pay and softens the cannibalization between the two versions. Vertical differentiation occurs either because the quality of the pay version is enhanced or because the quality of the free version is degraded. One example of quality degradation is Yahoo!'s home page service. In the free home page offer, Yahoo! incorporates ads to the user's web site. To get an ad-free site (and other benefits such as higher disk space for files, own domain name, etc.), one has to subscribe to the pay service (at the time of writing the basic offer is charged $8.95 a month plus a setup fee of $15).

In these two examples, the free service allows consumers to evaluate the quality of the service; consumers with high willingness to pay for the enhanced service can then switch to the premium service. Actually, most often, the services of Yahoo! are proposed in both a free and a pay version or a trial period is offered for free. Examples include fantasy sports (a free version is available with fewer features), bill pay service (basic plan with a limited number of billers), Yahoo! by phone (first month of service free).

Some ISP portals also offer pay services. For instance, in France, Wanadoo.fr proposes more than 100 pay services.[7] Examples include education services (English lessons, etc.), entertainment services,

---

[7] These services are available at http://servicesalacarte.wanadoo.fr

information services and professional services. Most of these pay services are not available in a free basic version.[8] In this case, the free services are used to attract audiences. Audiences generate advertising revenues, and some visitors might decide to purchase some of the pay services.

The portals of television channels in France have adopted the same strategy. They propose pay Internet services, which are related to popular television programs (like "Star Academy" and "Qui veut gagner des millions"). Free content serves to attract audiences for advertisers, and also to promote the programs and brand of the television channels.

12.2.3 Financial information

In 2001, in France, most online financial information services proposed only free services and derived revenues from advertising. As the advertising market shrank, most sites switched to a mixed business model; basic services are still offered for free but consumers are charged for premium services. Basic financial information services target consumers with low willingness to pay and allow consumers with a high willingness to pay to evaluate the quality of service. Premium services offer a higher quality of service (real time information, personalized advice, etc.).

In 2002, one French site, Serial-Traders, proposed only pay content for its financial information and advice to investors. The price of the service was relatively low, compared with other sites (15 euros per month, compared with 90 euros per month for the French site Boursorama). However, this site had the lowest number of subscribers in 2002 (10,000 subscribers, compared with 750,000 for Boursorama, for instance). It seems also that the quality of service was low; indeed some services proposed by Serial-Traders were offered for free by other sites. Eventually, Serial-Traders stopped its activity in April 2002.

12.2.4 Software

Some software producers offer free versions of their products on the Internet. The free version of a software might be a degraded version of the pay version, with fewer functionalities. For instance, Adobe's free Acrobat Reader does not have the "write" functionality of Adobe's pay Acrobat. Another strategy consists in offering a free trial version of the

---

[8] Some pay services (like weather information) are available both for free and as a paid service. But the free and the pay service do not appear on the same page, and Wanadoo does not indicate what is the differentiation between the two versions.

software for a limited time (typically one month). The same strategies are used by online games providers. Obviously, software firms provide free trial versions to allow potential consumers to try their products and evaluate their quality.

The case studies show that the proportion of the product offered for free is a strategic variable for the firms. Some content providers offer only free content/products, others propose only pay content/products, while between these two extreme cases some providers propose both free and pay content/products. In the following section, we construct a model which formalizes this strategic choice.

12.3   The model

12.3.1   Supply

A seller offers an information good, composed of different "elements", which can be consumed separately. For instance, the product could be an online newspaper composed of different articles, a book made of different chapters, a music CD with different music titles, or a software performing different functionalities or available at different time periods. For simplicity, we assume that the information good is composed of a continuum of "elements", and we normalize its total size to 1.

We assume that each "element" has the same true quality, denoted q. The seller can be either of low type, $t = L$, or high type, $t = H$. A seller of type L provides a low quality product ($q = q_L$), and a seller of type H provides a high quality product ($q = q_H$), where $q_H > q_L > 0$. The seller observes the true quality, but buyers don't. We assume further that $q_H \leq 2q_L$, i.e., that the high quality is not too high relative to the low quality.

The seller chooses the size $\alpha \in [0, 1]$ of the free version of his product, then chooses the price p of the product. We denote s_t a strategy of a seller of type $t = L, H$, that is, $s_t = (\alpha_t, p_t)$.

12.3.2   Consumers

Let μ denote the consumer belief about the quality of the product; consumers believe that quality is *low* with probability μ and that it is *high* with probability $1 - \mu$, where $\mu \in [0, 1]$. The expected quality of the product, conditional on the belief μ, is $E_\mu(q) = \mu q_L + (1 - \mu)q_H$. At the beginning of the game, consumers have the same prior belief, denoted by μ_0.

Each consumer has a taste θ for quality. The taste parameter θ is uniformly distributed on the interval $[0, 1]$. A consumer of type θ who pays price p for a proportion x of a product of expected quality $E_\mu(q)$ has an expected utility of

$$E_\mu(U) = \theta E_\mu(q)x - p.$$

If the true quality is q_t, he will receive utility of

$$U = \theta q_t x - p.$$

If available, consumers can use the free version of the product prior to deciding whether to purchase the product or not. When a consumer consumes the free version of the product, he obtains information about the quality. Formally, he receives a signal σ, which can take on the following values: $\sigma = H$ (quality is high), $\sigma = L$ (quality is low), $\sigma = \emptyset$ (no information). Quality evaluation outcomes are governed by the following signal structure:

$$\Pr\{L/q\} = \begin{cases} \gamma & \text{if} \quad q = q_L, \\ 0 & \text{if} \quad q = q_H \end{cases}$$

$$\Pr\{H/q\} = \begin{cases} 0 & \text{if} \quad q = q_L, \\ \gamma & \text{if} \quad q = q_H \end{cases}$$

$$\Pr\{\emptyset|q\} = 1 - \gamma.$$

We assume that γ is a function of α, i.e., of the size of the free version. We also assume that $\gamma(\alpha) \in [0, 1]$, $\gamma(0) = 0$, $\gamma(1) = 1$, $\gamma'(\alpha) > 0$ and $\gamma''(\alpha) \leq 0$. A higher α, hence a higher γ, corresponds to more precise information on the quality of the product. Consumers obtain no information when $\alpha = 0$ (no free version) and perfect information when $\alpha = 1$ (the product is free). The concavity of $\gamma(\alpha)$ means that consumers learn marginally less about the quality of the product as the size of the free version increases.

After receiving the signal σ, a consumer revises his belief according to the following rule: $\mu(\emptyset) = \mu_0$, $\mu(L) = 1$ and $\mu(H) = 0$.

12.3.3 Timing

The timing of the game is as follows:

1. Nature determines the type of the seller, L or H.
2. The seller chooses the size of the free version, $\alpha \in [0, 1]$, and the price of his product, $p \geq 0$.
3. Each consumer observes α and p, and revises his belief on quality. Then, he chooses whether or not to consume the free version. If he uses the free version, he receives a signal σ and revises his belief accordingly.
4. Finally, each consumer decides whether or not to purchase the product.

We look at the perfect Bayesian equilibria (PBE) of this game. Note that, in this setting, consumers obtain information about the quality of the product through two different channels. First, the strategy of the seller can convey information and signal his true quality. Second, consumers can obtain information by consuming the free version of the product.

12.4   Demand

In this section, we determine the demand, conditional on a belief μ. Assume that the seller provides both a free and a pay version of the product, that is, $\alpha \in (0, 1)$. A consumer has four possible strategies:

- He can use the free version first, then
  - if he anticipates a net gain from consuming the total product, he purchases the product (strategy FP),
  - otherwise, he stops (strategy F).
- The consumer can purchase the product, without using the free version first (strategy P).
- The consumer can neither use the free version nor purchase the product (strategy N).

By eliminating the dominated strategies, we show the following result.

Lemma 1
The consumer always uses the free version of the product.

Proof
We show that there are only two non dominated strategies: F and FP.

First, note that strategy F dominates strategy N. Indeed, any consumer is better off consuming the free version (strategy F) than consuming nothing (strategy N), since with strategy F the consumer gets $E(U^F) = \theta \alpha E_\mu[q]$, which is strictly positive, whereas he gets $E(U^N) = 0$ with strategy N.

Second, to prove that strategy FP dominates strategy P, remark that strategy FP is equivalent to strategy P if the consumer does not modify his purchase decision after consuming the free version. However, if he discovers that quality is low, the consumer has the possibility of not purchasing the product, which shows that $E(U^{FP}) \geq E(U^P)$.

Lemma 1 implies that when a free version is available, consumers always try to evaluate the quality of the product by using the free version. This has two implications. First, consumer choice is reduced to whether or not to purchase the product, after trying the free version. Second, given that there is a free version, a fraction of consumers will discover the true quality. Hence, we have to analyze the purchase decision, given the true quality, q.[9]

Demand for a low quality provider To begin with, assume that the supplier provides low quality content, i.e., $q = q_L$. With probability γ, a consumer of type θ discovers that quality is low; he then purchases the product if and only if

$$\theta(1 - \alpha)q_L - p \geq 0.$$

Indeed, the consumer derives utility from consuming the remaining $1 - \alpha$ parts of the product of quality q_L. Solving this condition for θ yields the equivalent condition $\theta \geq \theta_L^\star$, where

$$\theta_L^\star = \frac{p}{(1 - \alpha)q_L}.$$

With probability $1 - \gamma$ the consumer does not discover the true value of q; he decides to purchase the product if and only if $\theta(1 - \alpha)E_\mu(q) - p \geq 0$. Solving this inequality for θ yields $\theta \geq \theta^\star(\mu)$, where

$$\theta^\star(\mu) = \frac{p}{(1 - \alpha)E_\mu(q)}.$$

Note that $\theta^\star(\mu) \leq \theta_L^\star$, as $E_\mu(q) \geq q_L$. Besides, $\theta^\star(\mu)$ increases with μ, which means that, logically, the higher the belief that quality is low, the lower the demand.

To summarize, consumers of type θ such that $\theta \geq \theta_L^\star$ purchase the product whether they discover the quality or not. Consumers of type θ such that $\theta \in [\theta^\star(\mu), \theta_L^\star]$ purchase the product only if they do not discover that $q = q_L$ (which occurs with probability $1 - \gamma$). Finally, consumers of type θ such that $\theta < \theta^\star(\mu)$ do not purchase the product in any case. Therefore, when $q = q_L$, the demand for the product, conditional on the belief μ, is given by

$$D(q_L, \mu, \alpha, p) = \begin{cases} 1 - \theta^\star(\mu) - \gamma(\alpha)(\theta_L^\star - \theta^\star(\mu)) & \text{if} \quad \theta_L^\star \leq 1 \\ (1 - \gamma(\alpha))(1 - \theta^\star(\mu)) & \text{if} \quad \theta^\star(\mu) \leq 1 < \theta_L^\star. \quad (12.1) \\ 0 & \text{if} \quad \theta^\star(\mu) > 1 \end{cases}$$

The demand function shows that a low quality seller is harmed by the revelation of the true quality. The higher the size of the free version, α, hence the higher $\gamma(\alpha)$, the lower the demand for the seller. Besides, demand decreases when μ increases.

---

[9] If there were an opportunity cost of using the free version, consumers with low taste for quality might not consume, and consumers with high taste for quality might purchase the product, without using the free version.

Demand for a high quality provider Now suppose that $q = q_H$. With probability γ, a consumer of type θ discovers that $q = q_H$; he purchases the product if and only if $\theta(1 - \alpha)q_H - p \geq 0$, or $\theta \geq \theta_H^\star$, where

$$\theta_H^\star = \frac{p}{(1 - \alpha)qH}.$$

With probability $1 - \gamma$, the consumer does not discover the true value of q; he decides to purchase the product if and only if $\theta(1 - \alpha)E_\mu(q) - p \geq 0$, i.e., if and only if $\theta \geq \theta^\star(\mu)$.

Note that $\theta_H^\star \leq \theta^\star(\mu)$, as $E_\mu(q) \leq q_H$. To summarize, consumers of type θ such that $\theta \geq \theta^\star(\mu)$ purchase the product whether they discover the true quality or not. Consumers of type θ such that $\theta \in [\theta_H^\star, \theta^\star(\mu))$ purchase the product only if they discover that $q = q_H$ (which occurs with probability γ). Finally, consumers of type θ such that $\theta < \theta_H^\star$ do not purchase the product. Therefore, when $q = q_H$, the demand, conditional on the belief μ, is given by

$$D(q_H, \mu, \alpha, p) = \begin{cases} 1 - \theta^\star(\mu) + \gamma(\alpha)(\theta^\star(\mu) - \theta_H^\star) & \text{if} \quad \theta^\star(\mu) \leq 1 \\ \gamma(\alpha)(1 - \theta_H^\star) & \text{if} \quad \theta^\star(\mu) > 1 \geq \theta_H^\star . \\ 0 & \text{if} \quad \theta_H^\star > 1 \end{cases} \quad (12.2)$$

In contrast with a low quality seller, a high quality seller always benefits from the revelation of his true quality. Indeed, the higher α, hence the higher $\gamma(\alpha)$, the higher the demand for the seller. However, when the belief, μ, that quality is low increases, the demand for the product decreases.

12.5   The equilibria

In this section, we characterize the perfect Bayesian equilibria of the game. We start by computing the optimal price for a given belief, μ, and a given size of the free version, α. Then, we analyze the equilibrium with perfect information. Finally, we determine the separating and pooling perfect Bayesian equilibria of the game.

12.5.1   Price determination

To characterize the equilibria of the game, it is useful to determine the optimal price of the product, when the size α of the free version is given and the belief μ is fixed. Let $\Pi(q, \mu, \alpha, p)$ denote the profit of a seller of true quality q. For $\alpha \in (0, 1)$, the supplier has the following maximization problem,

$$\max_p \Pi(q, \mu, \alpha, p) = pD(q, \mu, \alpha, p). \quad (12.3)$$

We distinguish two cases: $q = q_L$ and $q = q_H$.

Optimal price for a low quality provider ($q = q_L$) We insert (12.1) into the maximization program (12.3) of the supplier. Solving this program yields the following result.

Lemma 2

If $q = q_L$ and $\alpha \in (0, 1)$, the profit maximizing price is

$$p_\mu^\star(q_L, \alpha) = \frac{(1 - \alpha)q_L E_\mu(q)}{2[q_L + \gamma(E_\mu(q) - q_L)]}.$$

Proof See Appendix.

Replacing for $p_\mu^\star(q_L, \alpha)$ in $\Pi(q_L, \mu, \alpha, p)$ gives the profit of the supplier,

$$\Pi(q_L, \mu, \alpha, p_\mu^\star(q_L, \alpha)) = \frac{(1 - \alpha)E_\mu(q)q_L}{4[q_L + \gamma(E_\mu(q) - q_L)]}. \tag{12.4}$$

Equation 12.4 shows that the larger the size of the free version, i.e., the higher α, the lower the profit of the seller. Indeed, for a low quality seller, providing a free version has two negative effects on the willingness to pay. First, as we have already mentioned, providing free content reveals to some consumers that quality is low, hence the average expected quality decreases. Second, it reduces the proportion of the product which is available to pay customers only.

Optimal price for a high quality provider ($q = q_H$) When the true quality is high, demand is given by equation 12.2. We solve the maximization program of the supplier and we obtain the optimal price as a function of α.

Lemma 3

If $q = q_H$ and $\alpha \in (0, 1)$, the profit maximizing price is

$$p_\mu^\star(q_H, \alpha) = \frac{(1 - \alpha)E_\mu(q)q_H}{2[q_H - \gamma(q_H - E_\mu(q))]}.$$

Proof See Appendix.

Replacing for $p_\mu^\star(q_H, \alpha)$ in $\Pi(q_H, \mu, p, \alpha)$, we obtain the profit of the supplier,

$$\Pi(q_H, \mu, \alpha, p_\mu^\star(q_H, \alpha)) = (1 - \alpha)\frac{E_\mu(q)q_H}{4[q_H - \gamma(q_H - E_\mu(q))]}. \tag{12.5}$$

A larger α has two opposite effects on the willingness to pay. On the one hand, as above, a larger free version, that is, a higher α, reduces the amount of the product available to pay customers only, which decreases the willingness to pay. This corresponds to the first term of the right-hand side in equation 12.5. On the other hand, trying the free version gives the information that quality is high with probability $\gamma(\alpha)$, which makes a fraction of consumers revise their beliefs and increases the average willingness to pay.

12.5.2 Perfect information

For further comparison, we derive the equilibrium in perfect information. If quality is low, we have $\mu = 1$. The size of the free version and the price which maximize profit are $\hat{\alpha}_L = 0$ and $\hat{p}_L = q_L/2$, respectively; the low quality seller obtains $\hat{\pi}_L = q_L/4$. If quality is high, we have $\mu = 0$, and profit is maximized for $\hat{\alpha}_H = 0$ and $\hat{p}_H = q_H/2$; the high quality seller obtains $\hat{\pi}_H = q_H/4$.

Since consumers observe the quality of the product perfectly, a free version has no positive effect on the willingness to pay (through the revelation of the quality of the product); only its negative effect operates (it diminishes the proportion of product available to pay customers only). Hence, the seller offers no free version and charges the profit maximizing price, which depends on the quality of content.

12.5.3 Separating equilibria

Assume that there is a separating equilibrium, such that a low quality seller plays strategy s_L, a high quality seller plays strategy s_H, and $s_L \neq s_H$. Since he observes the strategy played by the seller, a consumer can infer whether it is a low or a high quality provider. Let $\mu(s)$ denote the revised belief after the observation of the strategy s of the seller. We have therefore $\mu(s_L) = 1$ and $\mu(s_H) = 0$. We also denote $\Pi_t^\star$ the equilibrium profit of a seller of type $t = L, H$.

Replacing for $\mu(s_L) = 1$ into lemma 2 and equation 12.4 shows that a low quality seller sets necessarily $\alpha_L = 0$ and $p_L = q_L/2$, and obtains $\pi_L = \hat{\pi}_L = q_L/4$. The high quality seller sets $s_H = (\alpha_H, p_H)$ and obtains a profit of $\pi_H = p_H D(q_H, 0, \alpha_H, p_H)$.

Lemma 4 There is a multiplicity of separating equilibria. At any separating equilibrium, a seller of type L plays his perfect information strategy, $(\hat{\alpha}_L = 0$ and $\hat{p}_L = q_L/2)$, and a seller of type H plays a strategy (α_H, p_H), such that a seller of type L has no incentives to play (α_H, p_H) and a seller of type H has no incentives to play $(\hat{\alpha}_L, \hat{p}_L)$.

Proof See Appendix for a formal proof.

In a separating equilibrium, quality is perfectly inferred by consumers. A low quality seller acts as in perfect information. A high quality seller distorts his choice of price and size of free version, compared to perfect information. Indeed, suppose that the high quality seller plays the perfect information strategy $(\hat{\alpha}_H, \hat{p}_H)$. A low quality seller would gain from imitating a high quality seller, because if consumers believe that it is a high quality seller it obtains a profit of $q_H/4$, which is higher than $\pi_L = q_L/4$. Therefore, the equilibrium in perfect information is not a separating equilibrium of the game of imperfect information.

A more general question is whether a high quality seller can use his price *only* to separate from a low quality seller. In the following, we show that it is not the case.

Corollary 1
At a separating equilibrium, a high quality seller always proposes a free version of his product.

Proof
Suppose that there is a separating equilibrium, such that $\alpha_H = 0$. The profit of the high quality seller, if he plays (α_H, p_H), is

$$\pi(p_H) = p_H D(q_H, 0, 0, p_H) = p_H \left[1 - \frac{p_H}{q_H}\right].$$

Assume that $\pi(p_H) > \pi_L$, which means that the high quality seller has no incentive to mimic the low quality seller. If the low quality seller imitates the high quality seller, he obtains at best $\pi(p_H)$, since there is no free version, and hence everything is as if it were a high quality seller. As $\pi(p_H) > \pi_L$, the low quality seller has incentives to imitate the other type, which is not possible at a separating equilibrium. This proves that there is no separating equilibrium such that $\alpha_H = 0$.

This corollary shows that, at any separating equilibrium, a high quality seller proposes a free version of his product to signal that his quality is high. This contrasts with the setting of Moraga-González [2000], in which informative advertising never occurs at any separating equilibrium. This is because price signals quality, and advertising is redundant, as consumers receive informative advertisements but do not observe the advertising effort. In our chapter, the free version is an informative signal in itself for some consumers, because it reveals the true quality of content with some probability. As it is observed by all consumers, it can also serve as a signal of high quality.

Though lemma 4 characterizes an infinity of separating equilibria, all of them are not equally convincing. Indeed, in a separating equilibrium, a high quality seller signals his quality by offering a free version, such that a low quality seller has no incentive to imitate his strategy. But since the profit of the high quality seller decreases with the size of the free version, a high quality seller obtains maximum profit when it offers the smallest free version, such that there is still separation at the equilibrium.

The "intuitive criterion" of Cho and Kreps (1987) helps us to formalize this intuition. The intuitive criterion requires the following. Assume that there is a deviation to an out-the-equilibrium strategy that is not in the interest of a low quality seller, but that there are beliefs that it could pay for a high quality seller. Then, consumers should believe that they face a high quality seller. Formally, for any out-the-equilibrium strategy, s, we have $\mu^\star(s) = 0$ if $\Pi(q_H, 0, s) > \Pi_H^\star$ and $\Pi(q_L, 0, s) < \Pi_L^\star$.

The only separating equilibrium that survives this criterion is such that the high quality seller sets α_H and p_H so as to maximize his profit, given that a low quality seller has no incentive to imitate this strategy.

Proposition 1

The unique separating equilibrium, consistent with the intuitive criterion of Cho and Kreps (1987) is characterized by the following strategies:

$$s_H = \left(\alpha_H^\star, \frac{(1 - \alpha_H^\star)q_H}{2} \right),$$

$$s_L = \left(0, \frac{q_L}{2} \right),$$

where $\alpha_H^\star$ is the smallest α_H that satisfies

$$\alpha_H \geq 1 - \frac{q_L}{q_H \left(1 - \gamma(\alpha_H)\left(\frac{q_H}{q_L} - 1 \right) \right)}.$$

Proof
Consider that the high quality seller chooses a size $\alpha_H > 0$ for his free version and sets the optimum price given that separation occurs at the equilibrium, i.e., we have $p_H = (1 - \alpha_H)q_H/2$. The profit of the high quality seller, $\Pi_H(\alpha_H) = (1 - \alpha_H)q_H/4$, obviously decreases with α_H. Therefore, the high quality seller sets the maximum α_H such that

$$\Pi(q_L, 0, \alpha_H, (1 - \alpha_H)q_H/2) \leq \pi_L \tag{12.6}$$

still holds. Since we have

$$\Pi(q_L, 0, \alpha_H, p_H) = p_H \times D(q_L, 0, \alpha_H, p_H)$$

$$= (1 - \alpha_H)\frac{q_H}{2} \times \frac{1}{2}\left[1 - \gamma\left(\frac{q_H}{q_L} - 1\right)\right],$$

equation 12.6 is equivalent to

$$(1 - \alpha_H)\frac{q_H}{2} \times \frac{1}{2}\left[1 - \gamma\left(\frac{q_H}{q_L} - 1\right)\right] \leq q_L/4.$$

As $\Pi_H(\alpha_H)$ decreases with α_H, the solution α_H of the optimization problem is the smallest α_H that satisfies the following condition,

$$\alpha_H \geq 1 - \frac{q_L}{q_H\left(1 - \gamma(\alpha_H)\left(\frac{q_H}{q_L} - 1\right)\right)}. \tag{12.7}$$

Finally, we check that this equilibrium exists. By construction, α_H is such that the low quality seller has no incentive to imitate the high quality seller. The high quality seller has no incentive to adopt the same strategy than the low quality seller if and only if

$$\frac{(1 - \alpha_H)q_H}{4} > \frac{q_L}{4} \tag{12.8}$$

or

$$\alpha_H > 1 - \frac{q_L}{q_H},$$

which is true as (12.7) holds. Therefore, the unique separating equilibrium is the one characterized by the proposition. ∎

In the unique separating equilibrium, beliefs are given by $\mu^*(s_L) = 1$ and $\mu^*(s_H) = 0$, and for any other strategy $s \neq s_L, s_H$, $\mu^*(s)$ is sufficiently high such that neither type of seller gains from deviating to s.

In this equilibrium, the high quality seller offers a free version of his product to signal his quality. The price of a high quality seller is lower than under perfect information. This implies that consumer surplus is higher in the separating equilibrium of proposition 1 than under perfect information.

Illustration
Assume that $\gamma(\alpha) = \alpha$, and let $\lambda = q_H/q_L$. The solution of (12.7) is

$$\alpha_H^* = \frac{\lambda^2 - \sqrt{\lambda^4 - 4\lambda^3 + 8\lambda^2 - 4\lambda}}{2(\lambda^2 - \lambda)}.$$

We observe that α_H^* increases with λ, and that α_H^* goes to 0 when λ goes to 1, and α_H^* goes to 0.29 when λ goes to 2. Otherwise stated, the higher q_H relative to q_L, the higher the size of the free version provided by the high quality seller. This is because the incentives of a low quality seller to mimic a high quality seller become stronger, hence a high quality seller has to provide a larger free version to separate.

12.5.4 Pooling equilibria

Now, we characterize the pooling equilibria of the game. In a pooling equilibrium, a low and a high quality supplier choose the same strategy $s^\star = (\alpha^\star, p^\star)$, hence consumers are not able to revise their beliefs. A low quality supplier obtains $\Pi(q_L, \mu_0, \alpha^\star, p^\star)$, whereas a high quality supplier obtains $\Pi(q_H, \mu_0, \alpha^\star, p^\star)$. We assume that, for any strategy s such that $s \neq s^\star$, beliefs are given by $\mu(s) = 1$.

This equilibrium is valid only if the low quality supplier has no incentive to deviate to his perfect information strategy, $(\hat{\alpha}_L, \hat{p}_L)$, i.e., only if

$$\Pi(q_L, \mu_0, \alpha^\star, p^\star) > \hat{\pi}_L = q_L/4,$$

and if a high quality seller has no incentive to deviate either, that is, if

$$\Pi(q_H, \mu_0, \alpha^\star, p^\star) > \max_{\alpha, p} \Pi(q_L, 1, \alpha, p).$$

The intuitive criterion eliminates some pooling equilibria, but not necessarily all. A given $s^\star \in S_L$ is not a pooling equilibrium any more if there exists $s \neq s^\star$, such that $\Pi(q_H, 0, s) > \Pi_H^\star$ and $\Pi(q_L, 0, s) < \Pi_L^\star$.

Proposition 2
In any pooling equilibrium, sellers propose a free version of their products.

Proof
Suppose that this is not the case, that is, there is a pooling equilibrium such that $\alpha^\star = 0$. A seller of high quality obtains

$$p^\star(1 - \theta^\star(\mu_0)) \qquad (12.9)$$

at the pooling equilibrium, with

$$\theta^\star(\mu_0) = \frac{p^\star}{E_{\mu_0}(q)}.$$

and

$$p^\star(1 - \theta^\star(0)) \qquad (12.10)$$

if he deviates by offering a free version of size α, with

$$\theta^\star(0) = \frac{p^\star}{(1 - \alpha)q_H}.$$

If α is sufficiently small, then $\theta^{\star}(0) < \theta^{\star}(\mu_0)$, which implies that (12.10) is greater than (12.9), hence that the high quality seller has an incentive to deviate from the equilibrium. This proves that in any pooling equilibrium, sellers offer a free version of their products, i.e., $\alpha^{\star} > 0$.

To summarize, if we apply the intuitive criterion, the separating equilibrium of proposition 1 is the unique separating equilibrium of the game. A low quality seller proposes no free version and sets the perfect information optimum price, whereas a high quality seller proposes a free version to signal his (high) quality. The greater high quality relative to low quality, the higher the size of the free version. Besides, there are pooling equilibria, such that both types of sellers propose a free version of their product.

12.6   Conclusion

In this chapter we have studied the incentives a seller of information goods has to offer a proportion of his product for free when consumers are uncertain about the quality of the product. We have shown that a unique separating equilibrium survives the intuitive criterion of Cho and Kreps [1987]. In this equilibrium, a low quality provider offers no free version of his product and sets the perfect information optimal price, whereas a high quality content provider offers a free version to signal that he offers a high quality product, and sets a lower price than the optimal price in perfect information. We have also shown that price does not suffice to signal quality; offering a free version is necessary for a high quality seller to separate from a low quality seller. As the free version acts as a partially informative signal, the low quality seller has no incentive to imitate the high quality seller, as some consumers would discover that he provides a low quality product. There are multiple pooling equilibria of this game too, in which both types of sellers propose a free version of their products.

Our results seem to be consistent with what we observed in the online financial information market. On the one hand, Serial-Traders proposed a low quality service at a fair price. On the other hand, Boursorama offered a high quality service and a proportion of it for free, which allowed consumers to evaluate the quality of the service and to be more informed when deciding whether to switch to the expensive "premium" service or not.

We analyzed only one aspect of the markets of information goods, namely, the "experience good" nature of information goods. Other features of markets of information goods, such as the importance of advertising revenues or the presence of network externalities, also play an important role and might explain why some suppliers offer free versions of their products. For instance, an online journal could provide free content to obtain advertising revenues. Integrating one of these features into our model would probably lead to a wider range of strategies for each type of seller, and account for some sellers' behaviors that we outlined in the empirical study of Section 2, but that do not appear as solutions of our model.

12.7 Appendix

12.7.1 Proof of lemma 2

The demand, given by equation 12.1, is composed of two parts. We begin by optimizing the supplier profit on each demand segment. Then, we will show that only one local optimum is attained, hence it is the global optimum.

First, assume that $\theta_L^{\star} < 1$. The first-order condition for profit maximization gives the following local optimum,

$$p_{L1}^{\star} = \frac{(1-\alpha)q_L E_\mu(q)}{2[q_L + \gamma(E_\mu(q) - q_L)]}.$$

The second-order condition is always satisfied. This local maximum exists if and only if $\theta_L^{\star} < 1$. We show that this condition holds always. Inserting $p_{L1}^{\star}$ into $\theta_L^{\star}$ shows that $\theta_L^{\star} < 1$ if and only if

$$(1 - 2\gamma)E_\mu(q) < 2(1 - \gamma)q_L. \tag{12.11}$$

If $\gamma \geq 1/2$, this condition is always satisfied as the left-hand side is negative. When $\gamma < 1/2$, condition (12.11) can be rewritten as

$$E_\mu(q) < \frac{2(1 - \gamma)}{1 - 2\gamma} q_L,$$

which holds always, as $2(1 - \gamma) / (1 - 2\gamma) \geq 2$ when $\gamma \in [0, 1/2)$, $E_\mu(q) \leq q_H$ and $q_H \leq 2q_L$.

Second, assume that $\theta_L^{\star} > 1 > \theta^{\star}$. The first-order condition for profit maximization gives the following local optimum,

$$p_{L2}^{\star} = \frac{(1 - \alpha)E_\mu(q)}{2}.$$

The second-order condition is always satisfied. This local maximum exists if and only if $\theta^{\star} < 1$ and $\theta_L^{\star} > 1$. We show that this local optimum is not attained. By inserting $p_{L2}^{\star}$ into $\theta^{\star}$, we find that $\theta^{\star} = 1/2$, hence $\theta^{\star} < 1$ holds always. But we have $\theta_L^{\star} > 1$ if and only if

$$E_\mu(q) > 2q_L,$$

which is never satisfied as $E_\mu(q) \leq q_H$ and $q_H \leq 2q_L$. Therefore, $p_{L1}^\star$ is the global maximum of the profit function.

12.7.2   Proof of lemma 3

The demand, given by equation 12.2, is composed of two parts. We begin by optimizing the supplier profit on each demand segment. First, assume that $\theta^\star \leq 1$. The first-order condition for profit maximization gives

$$p_{H1}^\star = \frac{(1-\alpha)E_\mu(q)q_H}{2[q_H - \gamma(q_H - E_\mu(q))]}.$$

The second-order condition is always satisfied. This local maximum exists if and only if $\theta^\star \leq 1$. Inserting $p_{H1}^\star$ into $\theta^\star$ shows that $\theta^\star \leq 1$ if and only if

$$E_\mu(q) > \left(1 - \frac{1}{2\gamma}\right)q_H, \qquad (12.12)$$

which is always satisfied as $E_\mu(q) \geq q_L \geq q_H/2$ and $1 - 1/2\gamma < 1/2$.

Second, assume that $\theta^\star > 1 > \theta_H^\star$. The first-order condition for profit maximization gives

$$p_{H2}^\star = \frac{(1-\alpha)q_H}{2}.$$

The second-order condition is always satisfied. This local maximum exists if and only if $\theta_H^\star < 1$ and $\theta^\star > 1$. But we have $\theta^\star > 1$ if and only if

$$E_\mu(q) < \frac{q_H}{2},$$

which never holds as $E_\mu(q) \geq q_L \geq q_H/2$. Therefore, $p_{H1}^\star$ is the global optimum of the profit function.

12.7.3   Proof of lemma 4

Separation occurs at the equilibrium only if the low (resp., high) quality seller does not find it profitable to imitate the high (resp., low) quality seller.

First, consider that a low quality seller imitates the strategy of a high quality seller. In the best case for the low quality seller, consumers infer that the quality of the product is high and the seller obtains a profit of $\Pi(q_L, 0, \alpha_H, p_H)$. The low quality seller has incentives to imitate the strategy of a high quality seller if he obtains a higher profit under the most favorable beliefs (that is, consumers believe that he is a high quality seller) than under the worst beliefs (that is, consumers believe that he is a low quality seller), which occurs when $\Pi(q_L, 0, \alpha_H, p_H) \geq \pi_L$. Otherwise stated, if a high quality seller plays strategy $s = (\alpha, p)$ such that $\Pi(q_L, 0, \alpha, p) < \pi_L$, a low quality seller has no incentive to imitate this strategy. We can now define S_L as the set composed of the strategies of a high quality seller that a low quality has no incentive to imitate. We have

$$S_L = \{s = (\alpha, p) | \Pi(q_L, 0, \alpha, p) < \pi_L\}.$$

Now, consider the incentives for a high quality seller to imitate a low quality seller. If the high quality seller plays a strategy $(\alpha, p) \neq (\alpha_H, p_H)$, consumers infer, at worst, that he is a low quality seller and he obtains a profit of $\Pi(q_H, 1, \alpha, p)$. Let S_H denote the set of strategies that give a high quality seller a higher profit under the most favorable beliefs than the maximum profit he can earn under the worst beliefs. We have

$$S_H = \{s = (\alpha, p) | \Pi(q_H, 0, \alpha, p) \geq \max_{\alpha', p'} \Pi(q_H, 1, \alpha', p')\}.$$

The intersection of S_L and S_H, $S_L \cap S_H$, is the set of strategies of a high quality seller, such that he has no incentive to deviate and that a low quality seller has no incentive to imitate.

We can now characterize the separating equilibria: a pair of strategies $\{(\alpha_L, p_L), (\alpha_H, p_H)\}$ is a separating equilibrium if $(\alpha_L, p_L) = (\hat{\alpha}_L, \hat{p}_L)$, (α_H, p_H) belongs to $S_L \cap S_H$ and the beliefs are $\mu^\star(\hat{\alpha}_L, \hat{p}_L) = 1$, $\mu^\star(\alpha_H, p_H) = 0$, and for any other (α, p), $\mu^\star(\alpha, p)$ is sufficiently high such that neither type finds it profitable to play (α, p).

13 Open software: knowledge openness and cooperation in cyberspace

Dominique Foray, Sylvie Thoron and
Jean-Benoît Zimmermann

13.1 Introduction

An "open source" software is a software whose source-code, that is the sequence of instructions that forms the program, is openly available to anyone and cannot be privately appropriated and sold or rented. The development of open source software, also called "free software", is based on the contributions of voluntary and benevolent developers. This within a cooperative mode of organization that largely draws its efficiency from the organization and communication commodities which have arisen from the Internet structure.

The star product of free software today is the operating system Linux that was designed from the initial kernel conceived by a young programmer called Linus Thorvald, then developed and progressively improved through a cooperative and open process of coordination. Linux, inspired by the basic concepts of Unix, has been mainly dedicated to implementation on micro-computers but in fact has a wider scope for potential uses on larger systems. Many other products are now available from specialized suppliers or freely downloadable on the Internet: web servers, office applications, scientific programs, image processing . . . Some of them have achieved very important market shares, like Apache which holds first place in the field of web servers; the main tools for the Internet also belong, in their majority, to the open source world.

The cooperative mode of development of free software, often called the "bazaar" model (Raymond, 1998), gives to any programmer the possibility of making any improvement or change that might be useful for him. But from a collective point of view, such modifications have an interest only if he publicizes them, opening the opportunity to integrate them in a global common construction.

In this chapter we focus our attention on what motivates individual programmers to contribute, according to these basic rules, to the production process of such collective creation. As we shall see, the "open source" world appears very similar to that of "open science". For economists, knowledge accessibility is viewed as a mechanism generating efficiency. The welfare implications are clear: no monopoly distortion, spillovers do not reduce but rather increase the innovator's incentives. These welfare implications are magnified in the case of open source because software benefits from unlimited increasing returns in production as well as in diffusion.

The basic problem when considering incentives is to understand why voluntary spillovers occur at all. For any system promoting knowledge accessibility, incentives have to motivate people to reveal their knowledge freely to others, but also to make it more profitable to be an innovator than a free-rider. Such incentives are generally found in the field of learning and signalling. On the one hand, programmers are actually confronted with a rich and wide community of developers whose knowledge they can use to improve their own skills very efficiently. On the other hand, the "copyleft" principles that govern the world of open source software do not deny intellectual property of contributions; it thus permits programmers to publicize their contributions and hence their competence.

But today, open source software can generate business and private returns. This market orientation is the consequence of the success of open source software on a larger market. Today users are not confined to developers and hence possible contributors. The question is then to analyze this new unprecedented situation and to understand to what extent it can change the conditions and nature of incentives and possibly require a new level of incentives that can be of private (firms) or public (technological policy) origin.

13.2   The economics of knowledge accessibility

13.2.1   Welfare implications

Knowledge accessibility and sharing behavior do not only express some kind of ethical or moral attitude (although ethical conviction certainly plays a role). Knowledge accessibility is viewed, above all, as a mechanism to generate economic efficiency. There is a host of positive effects on the dynamics of innovation which are generated by knowledge accessibility. The latter facilitates coordination between agents, reduces the risk of duplication between research projects, and functions as a sort of "quality assurance". Above all, by disseminating knowledge within a heterogeneous population of researchers and entrepreneurs, it increases the probability of subsequent discoveries and innovations and decreases the risk of this knowledge falling into the hands of agents incapable of exploiting its potential.

The free revelation of new solutions and ideas is a necessary condition for the functioning of communities of users. In these communities multiple potential sources of innovation are identified and each member of the community can benefit from them. Developers interact in a community which functions within a certain sector of the economy, designing and building innovative products for their own use and freely revealing the design of these others. Others then replicate and improve the innovation that has been revealed, and freely reveal their improvements in turn (von Hippel, 2001). If the conditions of free revelation were not met, each user would be obliged to make all the modifications he needs by himself, which would substantially increase the overall cost of the process. It would consequently have no chance of competing with "average" solutions (more or less suited to everyone) at a lower cost, derived from commercial systems. The sharing and circulation of innovation is therefore essential to ensure a minimum of efficiency.

These positive effects on efficiency are magnified in the case of open source because:

- software is a very complex system that generates almost unbounded learning processes, so that a system of thousands of developers working for a long time on the same software still continues to show increasing returns;
- it is a technology which is informational, meaning that there is no difference between transferring the technology and transferring information on the technology. This makes it possible to increase the efficiency of the collective learning process by exploiting the potential of the new electronic infrastructure;
- software belongs to a certain class of technologies that has the particular property of bringing consumers and knowledge production close together. In the case of software or scientific instruments, users are, very often, also developers.

The welfare implications of knowledge accessibility are obvious. First of all, there is no dead-weight loss from above-marginal cost pricing. A second positive welfare effect is that knowledge accessibility may induce sellers of competing commercial products to reduce their prices, thus indirectly leading to another reduction in dead-weight loss. Finally, knowledge accessibility removes the restrictions imposed on second generation innovators.

13.2.2 A dual incentive structure

Making one's knowledge freely available is not a "rational" action in standard economics. As observed by Allen (1983), "it is extremely puzzling why firms released information and knowledge to potential rivals. If the industry is competitively organized, it would appear that this action could only rebound to the disadvantage of the firm." Actually, the model of knowledge accessibility involves a major deviation from the private investment model of innovation, which assumes that returns to innovation result from excluding other manufacturers from adopting it (von Hippel and von Krogh, 2003): here innovators freely reveal the proprietary knowledge that they have developed at their private expense.

There are, however, particular circumstances that make it more likely to occur. One clear factor in favour of accessibility and free distribution is that in many cases the benefits from free revelation exceed the benefits that can realistically be derived from strategies of control and access restriction. In such circumstances, the private benefits of free revelation knowledge are greater than the costs of losing exclusivity.

We have thus to explain why in many cases the benefits from intellectual property rights that can actually be obtained are very low, while the private benefits from free revelation may be higher.

Incentives to freely reveal information and knowledge
Others often know something close to "your secret"
Here, we follow von Hippel's argument developed in his most recent work (2004). An obvious condition for a successful intellectual property strategy is that others do not know very similar things. If multiple individuals or firms have similar information, and if at least one information holder expects no loss or even a gain from a decision to freely reveal, then the secret will probably be revealed. In such a case the private value of maintaining secrecy is very low.

Little ability to profit from patenting
Even if one agent is the only information holder and wants to legally protect it via a patent grant and copyright, it is difficult in general for a large class of innovators (typically independent innovators, small companies, users) to effectively profit from an intellectual property strategy. Such a strategy is costly, in terms of both time and resources, and the protection afforded by a patent is neither automatic nor free. If the patent owner believes that his rights have been usurped, the onus is on him to identify the counterfeiter and take the matter to court, where it will be assessed and interpreted. The effectiveness of property rights is therefore inseparable from the creator's capacity to watch over them. Such capacities are typically not easy to develop and maintain.

Given these two arguments, we may conclude that in practice, little profit is being sacrificed by most innovators that choose to forego the possibility of legally protecting their innovations in favour of free revelation.

Positive returns from free revelation

While strategies of secrecy and access control can be simply ineffective in many situations (above), a range of private benefits can be derived from the free revelation of information and knowledge (Foray, 2004a):

- When *reward systems* specifically address the issue of knowledge diffusion and reproduction. This requires a mechanism designed to give credit to inventors without creating exclusivity rights. This is the case of the reward system based on the accumulation of collegial reputation: here, the need to be identified and recognized as "the one who discovered" something forces people to release new knowledge quickly and completely (Dasgupta and David, 1994). Such reputation capital can then be exploited in academic science (for members of the academic profession) or on specific labour markets (for software developers).
- When agents or companies create *general reciprocity obligations* in order to capture external knowledge: that is, the right to continue obtaining information from others (e.g. a scientific network, engineers or users working on similar problems) is conditional on sharing one's own information.
- When a private agent can *benefit from increased "free" diffusion*. A direct result of free revelation is to increase the diffusion of that innovation over and above the level that would obtain if it were licensed or kept secret. Increased diffusion may be beneficial to private agents when (i) they are interested *in setting a standard advantageous to them*, and which would induce other agents (including rivals) to adopt it as well; or (ii) they are interested in *inducing manufacturers to make improvements*. This last strategic use of free dissemination is particularly important for users: by free revelation of an innovative product, a user makes it possible for manufacturers to adopt that innovation.

Low diffusion costs

There is a final condition for free revelation, which involves the cost of transmitting and communicating information and knowledge. Users/practitioners are not especially altruistic and they receive competing demands on their time during working hours. This means that time spent diffusing solutions, ideas or innovations within the community or to a particular partner should be not too costly.

The Internet can dramatically reduce diffusion costs, but only for innovations that can be expressed in digital form – literally a bit string, a long sequence of 0s and 1s. But in many cases low cost diffusion is more likely to be available because users can meet in real places for conferences, contests, tournaments or social events. Where electronic diffusion is possible, diffusion cost is at a constant low level; where diffusion is through people meeting, it is episodically low.

*Positive incentives for continuing to contribute (instead of free-riding)
in an open system*

We have just made the case that in some circumstances expected private benefits from a strategy of free revelation are higher than the expected benefits which can be obtained in reality from secrecy or intellectual property. These simple arguments create a rationale for cooperative behavior leading to information and knowledge sharing. Now, might such cooperation encourage "free-riding" behavior (a large number of members of the system giving up any creative effort because they can free-ride), undermining the whole innovative capacity of the system? The answer is striking and counter-intuitive: no, because the private rewards to those who contribute to collective developments are much higher than those available to free-riders.

Several such "selective incentives" which encourage project participation have been identified in the case of open source projects (von Hippel and von Krogh, 2003): although a freely revealed code (in an open source development project) becomes a public good, its production also creates some spin-off private benefits, such as learning and enjoyment, and a "sense" of ownership and control over the final product. In many cases, innovations are created by individuals for their own private purposes and are tailored to their individual needs. They are, then, openly revealed and contributed to the community as public goods for other individuals to use as they see fit. If the use to which a contributor wishes to put the public good is different from that of free-riders, the contributor is in a more favorable position than those free-riders to gain private benefit from the code he contributes.

Any system promoting knowledge accessibility involves a dual incentive structure: positive incentives to freely reveal knowledge and positive incentives to keep "contributing" (rather than free-riding) in a system in which free revelation is the dominant norm. Thanks to such a complex incentive structure, the model of innovation involving an open and distributed system offers the best of the two main models of innovation – that based on private investment and that based on collective action: "New knowledge is created by private funding and then offered freely to all" (von Hippel and von Krogh, 2003).

13.3   Legal framework to protect the commons

The question of intellectual property protection (IPP) for computer software was raised as soon as software products could, in the mid 1970s, be considered as commercial goods in their own right and not only as application technologies tied to the market for computer systems.

Following the United States in this regard, Europe and Japan adopted various frameworks of copyright laws which differed according to national legal context as well as differing cultural attitudes towards intellectual property.

13.3.1 Knowledge accessibility, copyright and patents

In the early years of software development, software got very limited protection through intellectual property rights. Two factors explain such a situation (Foray, 2004b):

1. Firstly, initial software developers were members of the open science/ academic research community that had evolved a different approach to rewarding inventors and managing spillovers than that suggested by the use of intellectual property right (IPR) to exclude potential users – one based on rapid publication and dissemination in order to achieve a prior claim as the inventor.
2. Secondly, most software was custom-designed for internal use. It would not work elsewhere without significant modifications and thus exhibited some kind of "natural excludability" that made IP protection superfluous.

The computer industry began to move away from custom-designed software towards standardization and then mass production (packaged software). Firms began to purchase more software and more firms began to develop software with the intention of selling it. This trend created a rationale for extending copyright protection to software. However, copyright as an intellectual property mechanism has two drawbacks when it comes to protecting "inventions":

1. Copyright affords relatively narrow protection to software – allowing rivals to offer very similar products without infringing the copyright. The nature of copyright as an intellectual property right does not make it particularly well adapted to the protection of inventive activity: copyright protects only the expression of an idea. It is an effective means of guarding against the pure reproduction of software but it does not protect the substance of inventive activity, which deals with the invention of new functions.
2. There is no legal provision in the copyright regime for public disclosure because it is taken for granted that authors and artists are eager to disclose and circulate their works and certainly do not want to keep them as their "secrets". It is, thus, a right with no necessary benefit for society (on the contrary, patent protection involves a constraint on

the patent holder to disclose their work). Such a right without compensation makes sense when copyright application is limited to literary and artistic contributions. However, the use of copyright to protect software creates a distortion, since companies can enjoy protection while keeping secret the object of this protection. "For the first time since Sybaris, 500 B.C., who imposed public disclosure in exchange for the legal protection of recipes, private property and secret are reconciled!" (Vivant, 1993). The problem here is to extend copyright protection to an object which is fundamentally different from artistic and literary works. The purpose of software is not to communicate the expression of ideas and inspiration but to command and control a machine.

The fragile balance between the private interest of innovators and the public interest of society is thus hampered by such an extension of copyright.

The next step is, therefore, quite naturally the extension of patent protection to software. The private rationale is that a patent as a legal asset will offer better and stronger protection. The public rationale is that patents will create information spillovers, since the granting of a patent creates a legal obligation to publicly disclose the invention.

13.3.2 The question of source-code accessibility

Most publishers do commercialize their software products only in the form of object-codes, that is compiled programs, in internal machine language, ready to be directly installed on a computer. They do not, in general, reveal the "source-code" of the programs, that is the explicit expression of the program architecture, procedures and algorithms. But even if the debate as to the relative merits of copyright and patents as modes of software protection raises very important issues, both of them rely on the willingness to impose barriers to the diffusion of knowledge embedded in software products and to base the commercial activity of software firms on the private appropriation and confidentiality of the code. This opposition between private property of the codes, that gave rise to the software industry, and the free circulation of the sources considered as pure knowledge, that corresponds to the tradition of "open science", had already proved to be divisive in the software developers' community, like in the MIT in the mid 1970s (Smets-Solanes and Faucon, 1999). It is at the origin of the birth of a "free software" movement at the beginning of the 1980s that aimed to preserve the diffusion of ideas and the combinatorial and cumulative nature of technical progress, both in terms of concepts and tools and in terms of algorithms for problem resolution and methods of coding.

From that situation stems the definition of an "open source" software product as a program whose source-code has to be freely accessible and cannot be privately appropriated. In that sense open source software fits the definition of public good insofar as it is a non-rival and non-exclusive product. With the birth of the "Free Software Foundation" and the launching of the GNU[1] project by Richard Stallman in 1984, the first collective development project had as its aim an open Unix equivalent platform. It appeared necessary to build up the legal framework that could guarantee these principles of "copyleft"-based intellectual property of software. Next, the GPL or "GNU-General Public License" was designed in order to protect the foundations of cooperative work development and to prevent any private appropriation of part or all of the concerned code lists, as can be done with software which can occur in the public domain. Hence, through the GPL, intellectual property is not rejected, authors do not renounce their rights but just the monopoly rent, which such rights would produce in a copyright regime. The main legal aspect is that when a program is declared under GPL license, any code derived from it or integrating GPL code lines must also be available under GPL license. Hence GPL status is "contagious" in the sense that this status attached to any number of lines is automatically transmitted to the whole program into which they are incorporated. The authors authorize anyone who wants to make use of their work (modifications, improvements, additional features, etc.) to do so under the sole condition that the new product must also circulate freely.

This does not exclude a possible commercialization of these programs and does not limit "open source software" to the non-marketable sphere. As a result, firms have recently joined the world of cooperative development and of free access to sources-codes. This enlargement involves two types of strategy. On the one hand, as with Californian RedHat Software or the French Mandrake, firms have built their activity on the improvement and distribution of open source programs in order to make them accessible for an enlarged base of users who are not software specialists. Their contribution has taken the form of man–machine interfaces, new functions, tutorials, documentation, but does not impede the acquisition of their products by simply copying or downloading them rather than paying for them. In fact, these firms make a large part of their cash flow from the services they offer jointly with their

---

[1] GNU's Not Unix.

products: training, adaptation to specific cases or contexts, hotlines, maintenance, updating. On the other hand, a second type of firms decided to "open" some of their software products which they previously had the option of protecting, like Netscape with its "Communicator" in 1998, or Sun with its communication protocol named "Jini", etc. These strategies seek to draw benefits from the development potential of the free software community or to promote the large-scale diffusion of a key product, thereby imposing it as a de facto standard and subsequently profiting from the commercialization of proprietary complementary products.

But these strategies did not fit very well with terms of the GPL as they were and this increase in the number of actors involved has led to an extension of the legal arrangements beyond the strict framework of the GPL. Many "hybrid" licenses have been designed in order to reconcile cooperative development and private interests in a variety of specific contexts. They involve different ways of combining the copyright and copyleft rules in different proportions (Smets-Solanes and Faucon, 1999).

Hence, when opening the access to its Communicator, Netscape developed two complementary licenses: NPL (Netscape Public License), which authorizes the integration of new features into its servers without requiring that they be placed in the field of copyleft, and the MPL (Mozilla Public License)[2] which concerns the development of new modules. Then any modification of Communicator source-code has to be published, but Netscape keeps the choice as to whether to integrate proprietary modules into its Communicator or whether to use Communicator modules in its own proprietary products range. Similarly, Sun has designed the SCSL (Sun Community Source License) granting free access to its Jini communication protocol and then keeps the exclusivity of compatibility certification for any products derived from Jini and which it wishes to commercialize. Other firms like Novell and IBM have designed their own solutions, combining in a variety of ways the use and integration of open source software with proprietary products, and whether or not they are commercialized. The general objective is to achieve a certain compatibility between a model of free access to technology, aimed at increasing knowledge, and/or the standard model of adoption, with exclusion applied to some modules or products, thereby ensuring a source of profits.

---

[2] Mozilla is the name of the cooperative development project issued from the Communicator opening.

Such approaches, based on a partition between non-commercial development activities and business-oriented products, appear as short term solutions allowing computer software firms to benefit from the open source dynamics while preserving their source of income. It is difficult to forecast the future of such hybrid forms of intellectual property protection. But the recent development of private firms contributing to open source software development seems to confirm the limits of such mixed legal tools which try to combine divergent principles of intellectual property. On the contrary, business activity does not appear to be in contradiction with free software development insofar as commercial activity and software development seek complementary aims, products and services.

13.4   Three alternative contribution games to model open software

Production of open source software should then be analyzed as a public good. It is based on individual contributions and generates the production of a value to the user which depends neither on the contribution nor on its level. Furthermore this externality exists solely as a result of individual contributions and its value is increasing with the total amount of these contributions. But the marginal cost of an individual contribution to a public good generally remains higher than the marginal change in the level of the externality and this gives an incentive to defect and to adopt free-riding strategies. In reality, in the case we are considering, things do not work like that. This is firstly because the marginal cost of a contribution is often very low, for example when developers already have on their own shelves the answer to the question posed (von Hippel, 2001). Secondly, by contributing to open source, developers earn a reward in terms of both learning and reputation. Working within the open context, learning through contributing to a free software project can be considered as more efficient than it would be in the context of a closed firm. This can be explained by the multiple interactions with a wide variety of programmers using a wide scope of methods and programming styles, from which a developer benefits. Today, with the use of the Internet, such an interaction effect has increased the individual returns any developer can expect from their contribution.

In the early years of open source software, these products were developed for the use of professionals alone. Their free availability within the programmers' community did not generally depend on whether individuals had contributed to the project or not. As in the case of a pure public good, all of them were able to benefit from the externality when deciding whether to contribute or to free-ride. History has proved that, in spite of individual profit motives, this cooperative system has generated a significant production and proved its sustainability.

By contributing, a given programmer helps to improve the product, but when she free-rides, she benefits from the product in any event, as it is without her contribution. Hence, the individual trade-off can be expressed in terms of opportunity costs. It confronts, on the one hand, the expected benefits of the contribution (externality improvement plus individual returns) with, on the other hand, the expected benefits of devoting equivalent effort to another activity (consulting, individual production, etc.).

It seems likely that, since developers are heterogeneous, the individual level of contribution will vary with the individual characteristics of the programmers. Apart from personal motivations and ethics, we shall restrict this heterogeneity to the individual level of competence. This will allow us to establish a direct link between individual contributions and the global quality of the software developed. It should also be the case that better individual incentives, like learning, will entail higher levels of individual contributions.

Today, with the diffusion via the Internet, the success of open source software has reached far beyond the population of developers alone. Free software products are being progressively adopted by simple users that would not be able to contribute and do not necessarily have the technical skills needed to master their installation and use. Hence these new users need assistance, either from their social or professional environment or from specialized providers that will supply them with appropriate services or products (training, advice, graphic interfaces, tutorials, etc.). This demand creates a market and can be the source of private profits. Hence the problem of building a stable community for producing open source software has to be seen quite differently. The agents that are able to contribute to the production are precisely those that are in the best position to satisfy this new demand, and by doing so they can make profits at the expense of other benevolent contributors. In this case, the trade-off is no longer between internal and external value of contribution effort but on the individual allocation of resources between benevolent contribution to open source software and commercial activity based on open software products diffusion. Here our model elucidates the consequences of this new deal, which produces a shift towards more commercial open source software diffusion, for the distribution of the levels of individual contributions and for the building of stable communities.

Therefore, the aim of this section is to study the nature and properties of the equilibrium depending whether or not any commercial activity is involved. We shall stress the effect of learning on the developers' contributions given their level of competence and the way in which market-oriented activities tend to alter the equilibrium, and finally the sustainability of the software production pattern.

13.5   A simple game of contribution to a public good

As a first step, we model open software as a simple game of contribution to a public good. We consider a finite set of software developers $I = \{1, \ldots, I\}$ with heterogeneous competences. Each developer's competence is measured by her production capability, for instance the number of standard code units she can write per unit of time. We assume developers are indexed in order of increasing competences. Therefore, if developer i and j's competences are respectively ω_i, $\omega_j \in [\underline{\omega}, \bar{\omega}]$, then, $\omega_i < \omega_j$ if and only if $i < j$. Each i-developer has to choose the level of effort $n_i \leq \omega_i$ she is willing to put into her contribution to open software. Open software, denoted by $G(n)$ with $n = \sum_{i \in I} n_i$, is considered as a public good generated by the sum of individual contribution efforts. We assume that each developer increases the value of her remaining competence $\omega_i - n_i$ using an outside option which is identical for all of them. The developer's benefit derived from this outside option is then given by the function $O(\omega_i - n_i)$. One interpretation is that there is a price per code unit which is set before any contribution. Competent developers are paid more because they can produce more code units per unit of time. In a simple contribution game (see for example Bergstrom, Blume and Varian (1986), Gradstein (1994)), preferences are additively separable in the public good and the private good. We consider that there is a delay between the time an i-developer contributes and the time he can enjoy the externality generated by open software. In other words, the game we propose is a two-stage one. At each stage, each developer i has a competence ω_i. In the first stage, she chooses the level of effort $n_i \leq \omega_i$ devoted to open software production. She uses the competence left to benefit from the outside option, $O(\omega_i - n_i)$. In the second stage, the open software is available and developer i benefits from $G(n)$. She also benefits from her current competence $O(\omega_i)$ through the outside option. Then, her total payoff can be written:

$$\Pi_i(n_1, \ldots, n_I) = O(\omega_i - n_i) + \delta[O(\omega_i) + G(n)] \qquad (13.1)$$

where δ is a discount factor. We assume that $O(.)$ and $G(.)$ are twice differentiable functions, which are increasing and concave. Therefore, if we do not take into account the two-sided constraint $0 \leq n_i \leq \omega_i$, there is a unique equilibrium characterized by the following first order conditions:

$$G'(n) = \frac{1}{\delta} O'(\omega_i - n_i), \forall i \in I \qquad (13.2)$$

An immediate consequence is that, at the equilibrium, $O'(\omega_i - n_i) = O'(\omega_j - n_j)$ for all i and $j \in I$. Therefore, the different developers have the same marginal utility of the outside option and as a consequence, the most competent developers are willing to contribute more. This is conveyed by the following proposition.

Proposition 1
If O is linear, there is a multiplicity of equilibria since any division of the equilibrium total contribution n^* solution of (13.2) is solution. If $O(.)$ is not linear, for two developers i and $j \in I$, $n_i = n_j + \omega_i - \omega_j$ and contributions are an increasing function of competences.

When we take into account the two-sided constraint $0 \leq n_i \leq \omega_i$, there is still a unique equilibrium but two cases can occur. If $\omega_i - n_i \leq 0$ each developer devotes all his ability to open software. If $\omega_i - n_i > 0$, contributions are not necessarily a strictly increasing function of competences since it may be the case that the less competent developers do not contribute at all (see Figures 13.1 and 13.2).

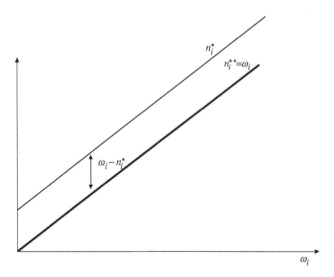

Figure 13.1. Pure contribution game with $\omega_i - n_i \leq 0$: each developer devotes all his ability to open software.

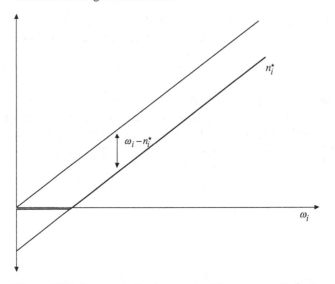

Figure 13.2. Pure contribution game with $\omega_i - n_i > 0$: the less competent developers do not contribute at all.

13.5.1 Learning

Now, we can add a learning function as a new ingredient of this public good contribution game. The idea is that a contribution effort to open software increases the developer's future competence. Consider the following learning function derived from Alchian (1963)[3] where ω_i^+ is the increased competence through contribution n_i:

$$\omega_i^+ = (\omega_i^{\frac{1}{\alpha}} + n_i)^\alpha \text{ with } 0 < \alpha < 1 \tag{13.3}$$

When a software developer i contributes at level n_i, she benefits from the externality of open software but she can also benefit from a private effect, since she can exploit the value of her increased competence. Her total payoff is then:

$$\Pi_i(n_1, ..., n_I) = O(\omega_i - n_i) + \delta[O(\omega_i^+) + G(n)] \tag{13.4}$$

When a developer i increases her contribution n_i, it decreases her current payoff $O(\omega_i - n_i)$ but increases her future payoff $\delta[O(\omega_i^+) + G(n)]$ now

---

[3] Following Alchian's (1963) formulation, $\tau = \lambda x^\rho$ with $\rho \in [-1, 0]$ is the time taken by the production of an additional unit after a cumulated production x.

in two different ways. If, as a first step, we do not take into account the two-sided constraint $0 \leq n_i \leq \omega_i$, the first order conditions are:

$$G'(n) = \frac{1}{\delta}O'(\omega_i - n_i) - O'(\omega_i^+)\alpha(\omega_i^{\frac{1}{2}} + n_i)^{\alpha-1}, \; \forall i \in I \qquad (13.5)$$

Remember that $0 < \alpha < 1$ and that $G(.)$ and $O(.)$ are increasing and concave functions. We can easily verify that the second order conditions are satisfied:

$$G''(n) + \frac{1}{\delta}O''(\omega_i - n_i) + O''(\omega_i^+)\left(\alpha(\omega_i^{\frac{1}{2}} + n_i)^{\alpha-1}\right)^2$$

$$+ O'(\omega_i^+)\alpha(\alpha - 1)(\omega_i^{\frac{1}{2}} + n_i)^{\alpha-2} < 0, \forall i \in I$$

Therefore, it is clear that at the unique equilibrium characterized by Equation (13.5) and in comparison with the equilibrium of the simple contribution game described in the previous subsection, the learning effect increases the incitation to contribute. This is shown by the following proposition.

Proposition 2
At the equilibrium without constraints, the sum of contributions $n^\star$ is higher in the game with learning than in the simple contribution game.

Proof
Remember that $O(.)$ is an increasing function and compare Equations (13.2) and (13.5) which give the first order conditions in the simple game and the learning game respectively. Then the proof is immediate since we deduce from the first order condition that the slope of the concave function $G(n)$ is smaller here than in the previous case of a simple contribution game.

This first result is rather intuitive and not surprising. However, we would like to know more about the relative contributions of the different developers. Consider the case in which the payoff function is quasi linear, that is when $O(\omega_i - n_i) = \omega_i - n_i$. We obtain the following lemma.

Lemma 1
The production effort a developer is willing to contribute is a decreasing function of his initial competence.

Proof
From the first order conditions given in Equation (13.5) we deduce:

$$n_i^\star = h(n^\star) - \omega_i^{\frac{1}{2}}, \forall i \in I \text{ with } h(n^\star) = \left(\frac{1 - \delta G'(n^\star)}{\alpha\delta}\right)^{\frac{1}{\alpha-1}} \qquad (13.6)$$

Then, $n_i^\star$ is a decreasing function of ω_i.

The result is that, at the equilibrium without constraints, the different developers target the same increased competence: $\omega_i^+ = (h(n))^\alpha$, $\forall i \in I$. Therefore, developers who are initially less competent are willing to contribute more because they have more to learn. However, this is no longer true when we take into account the two-sided constraint $0 \leq n_i \leq \omega_i$. On one hand, less competent developers, limited by their capacity, cannot contribute as much as they would like. On the other hand, negative contributions are not feasible and developers who do not want to contribute a positive amount do not participate in the game. This two-sided constraint changes the total amount of contributions $n^\star$. In this case, there is still a unique equilibrium (cf. Appendix 1) but contributions are no longer a monotonic function of competences.

Proposition 3

At the unique equilibrium constrained, there exists a pair of critical values of competences $(\tilde{\omega}, \tilde{\tilde{\omega}})$ such that contributions are an increasing function of competences for $\omega \leq \tilde{\omega}$ and a decreasing function for $\tilde{\omega} \leq \omega \leq \tilde{\tilde{\omega}}$. The most competent developers do not contribute at all (cf. Figure 13.3).

Proof
cf. Appendix 1.

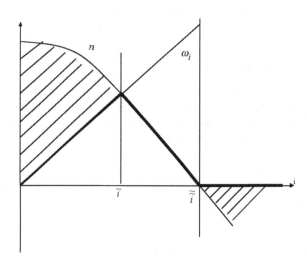

Figure 13.3. Contribution game with learning: contributions are a non-monotonic function of competencies – the most competent developers do not contribute at all.

The intuition for the proof is illustrated in Figure 13.3. The less competent developers who have a high willingness to contribute devote all their effort to open software. As a result, contributions are first increasing as long as competences are below a critical value $\tilde{\omega}$. Above this critical value, contributions are a decreasing function of competences. As a consequence, the new competences are not the same for all the developers. New competences are identical for developers whose initial competence is above this critical value but increasing for those for whom the initial level was below that value.

13.5.2 Market for open software

Now, we introduce the third ingredient, which is a market for open software. There is a finite set U of potential users who have no competence as software developers and need some assistance to access open software. We consider a model of vertical differentiation in the spirit of Shaked and Sutton (1982). Each potential user $k \in U$ is characterized by a positive real number θ_k which is a taste parameter. He has the following utility function:

$$u_k = \begin{cases} \theta_k s - p & \text{if she pays a price } p \text{ for an access to software} \\ & \text{with quality } s \\ 0 & \text{if she refuses to pay for the access} \end{cases}$$

The positive real number s describes the quality of the software to which the user gets access. We assume that this quality depends on the level of the available open software $G(n)$, and on ω_i, the competence of the developer who sells her the access services. In this sense, the more competent a programmer is, the better the interfaces she is able to develop for simple users. The quality of the access delivered by an i-developer is $s_i = (\omega_i - n_i)G(n)$. For simplicity of presentation, we assume that there are only two software developers, 1 and 2, and that 2 is initially the most competent, $\omega_1 < \omega_2$.

All users prefer high quality for a given price but a user with a high θ is willing to pay more to obtain high quality. We assume that θ is uniformly distributed on the interval $[\underline{\theta}, \bar{\theta}]$. We now derive the demand for developer i. Note first that a θ-user is willing to pay for access if and only if $Max_{i=1,2}(\theta_k s_i - p_i) \geq 0$. Now, given s_1, s_2, p_1 and p_2, we consider the user characterized by a taste parameter $\theta^\star$, who is indifferent between buying the access services proposed by developers 1 and 2. He is defined by the following equality:

$$\theta^\star s_1 - p_1 = \theta^\star s_2 - p_2 \Rightarrow \theta^\star = \frac{\Delta p}{\Delta s}$$

with $\Delta p = p_2 - p_1$ and $\Delta s = s_2 - s_1$

The demand for developer 1 is given by:

$$D_1(s_1, s_2, p_1, p_2) = U \int_{\underline{\theta}}^{\theta^\star} \partial\theta = U\left(\frac{\Delta p}{\Delta s} - \underline{\theta}\right)$$

and the demand for developer 2 is given by:

$$D_2(s_1, s_2, p_1, p_2) = U \int_{\theta^\star}^{\bar{\theta}} \partial\theta = U\left(\bar{\theta} - \frac{\Delta p}{\Delta s}\right)$$

Here, we do not consider two periods. We consider that there is no delay between the time developers contribute and the time they can enjoy the externality generated by open software. However, we model the strategic interaction of developers as a two-stage game, since there are two strategic variables, the contribution n_i and the price p_i. In the first stage, each developer i chooses a contribution to open software n_i, as in the simple contribution game or in the contribution game with learning. The second stage is a price competition to sell access services to users. Each developer chooses a price p_i. Developer-i's payoff is then:

$$\Pi_i(n_1, n_2, p_1, p_2) = G(n) + D_i(s_1, s_2, p_1, p_2)p_i,$$
with $s_1 = G(n)(\omega_1 - n_1)$, and $s_2 = G(n)(\omega_2 - n_2)$

Note that this case cannot be considered as a simple contribution game since $G(n)$ appears in the function $D_i(s_1, s_2, p_1, p_2)p_i$. In other words, preferences are not additively separable in the "public good" $G(n)$, and the "private good" $\omega_i - n_i$. This game must be solved by backward induction. At the equilibrium of the second stage, prices and profits are as follows:

$$p_1^\star = \frac{\bar{\theta} - 2\underline{\theta}}{3}\Delta s \text{ and } p_2^\star = \frac{2\bar{\theta} - \underline{\theta}}{3}\Delta s \tag{13.7}$$

$$\Pi_1(n_1, n_2, p_1^\star, p_2^\star) = G(n) + U\left(\frac{\bar{\theta} - 2\underline{\theta}}{3}\right)^2 \Delta s, \tag{13.8}$$

$$\text{and } \Pi_2(n_1, n_2, p_1^\star, p_2^\star) = G(n) + U\left(\frac{2\bar{\theta} - \underline{\theta}}{3}\right)^2 \Delta s \tag{13.9}$$

Note that prices and payoffs are increasing functions of the differential in qualities $\Delta s = G(n)((\omega_2 - n_2) - (\omega_1 - n_1))$. Indeed, the vertical differentiation reduces competition and increases payoffs. We obtain the following proposition.

Proposition 4

In the model with a market for open software, the most competent developer contributes more, fixes a higher price and has a bigger payoff.

Proof
cf. Appendix 2.

Indeed, we can easily check that, for any differential in qualities Δs, the higher quality access seller's price and profit are higher than the price and profit of the lower quality seller. Furthermore, we note that developer 1's payoff is an increasing function of his contribution n_1. The more he contributes to open software, the more he increases the externality *and* the differential in qualities. However, there is a limit to this improvement. If he devoted all his effort to open software, the quality of the access he could propose would be zero and the demand for his access services would disappear. However, when the most competent developer increases his contribution, the utility of open software $G(n)$ increases but the differential in qualities decreases, since he can spend less effort on selling access services. As a consequence, we show in Appendix 2 that, at the equilibrium of the first stage and in contrast with the learning model where contributions are a decreasing function of competences, here the most competent developer contributes more.

13.6   Conclusion

In this chapter we have stressed the similarity of open source software production to the "open science" paradigm. We have seen that, in the case of free software, there are particularly favorable conditions for knowledge accessibility. These "good properties" are due to the informational nature of software, the unlimited scope for improvements and the close connection between developers and users. The existence of the Internet structure, with the powerful connections that it allows, within the community of developers and with users, also increases the efficiency of these good properties.

Considering the open system as a public good production process leads immediately to the question of incentives for developers to contribute rather than to adopt a free-riding attitude, which would allow them to benefit from the externality without contributing. We have seen that learning provides a good incentive for contribution, especially for less skilled developers who can in this way efficiently improve their technical competence and hence their human capital.

But the foundations of open source software are not in contradiction with a possible commercialization of open products or complementary products and services, and hence with private benefits gained from making open software products available. The question is now as to how the introduction of business transforms the nature of the contribution game equilibrium. Assuming that contribution to open software development makes developers more competent in complementary business activities, we have shown that the introduction of business incites the most competent agents to contribute more than their less experienced counterparts.

Hence, learning and business have complementary incentive effects that need to be better understood so that they can be incorporated in a technological policy whose object is to favor larger open source software production and diffusion.

13.7   Appendix 1

Proof of Proposition 3: We saw that the willingness to contribute represented by the vector $N^1 = (n_i^1)_{i \in I} \in \Re^I$ is an equilibrium when we do not take into account the two-sided constraint $0 \leq n_i \leq \omega_i$. It is the solution of Equation (13.6), which are the first order conditions: $n_i^1 = h(n^1) - \omega_i^{\frac{1}{2}}, \forall i \in I$, with $n^1 = \sum_{j \in I} n_j^1$ and $h(n^1) = \left(\frac{1 - \delta G'(n^1)}{\alpha \delta}\right)^{\frac{1}{\alpha - 1}}$. As can be seen in Figure 13.3, this equilibrium cannot be implemented in reality since the less competent developers are willing to contribute at a level above their real competences. However, the more competent developers have a negative willingness to contribute. Let $\bar{i}^1$ be the least competent developer whose competence is strictly larger than his willingness to contribute, $\bar{i}^1 = Inf\{i \in I | n_i^1 < \omega_i\}$ and $\approx^1_i$ be the more competent developer whose willingness to contribute is strictly positive, $\approx^1_i = Sup\{i \in I | n_i^1 > 0\}$ (cf. Figure 13.3).

We denote by ϑ the transformation from $\Re^I$ to $\Re^I$ which maps to each $N^p = (n_i^p)_{i \in I} \in \Re^I$ a given $N^{p+1} = (n_i^{p+1})_{i \in I} \in \Re^I$ with:

$$n_i^{p+1} = h\left(\sum_{j < \bar{i}_p} \omega_j + \sum_{\bar{i}_p \leq j \leq \approx_{\bar{i}_p}} n_j^p\right) - \omega_i^{\frac{1}{2}}, \forall i \in I$$

in which $\bar{i}^p = Inf\{i \in I | n_i^p < \omega_i\}$ and $\approx^p_i = Sup\{i \in I | n_i^p > 0\}$, $N^1 = (n_i^1)_{i \in I} \in \Re^I$ are solutions of $n_i^1 = h(n^1) - \omega_i^{\frac{1}{2}}, \forall i \in I$, with $n^1 = \sum_{j \in I} n_j^1$.

Denote by $g(N^p) = \sum_{j < \bar{i}_p} \omega_j + \sum_{\bar{i}_p \leq j \leq \approx_{\bar{i}_p}} n_j^p$, the h-function's argument, then, the previous equality can be written: $n_i^{p+1} = h \circ g(N^p) - \omega_i^{\frac{1}{2}}, \forall i \in I$. We note that both functions g and h are continuous and $\Re^I$ is compact. As a consequence, we can apply the Brouwer's fixed point theorem, and the transformation ϑ admits a fixed point.

13.8   Appendix 2

Proof of Proposition 4: Solving the contribution game with a market for open software by backward induction, we first consider the first order condition for each developer in the price competition game.

$$\frac{\partial \Pi_1}{\partial p_1} = 0 \Rightarrow \frac{p_2 - \theta \Delta s}{2} = p_1 \text{ and } \frac{\partial \Pi_2}{\partial p_2} = 0 \Rightarrow \frac{p_1 + \bar{\theta}\Delta s}{2} = p_2$$

Therefore, the equilibrium of the second stage is characterized by the following prices and payoffs:

$$p_1^\star = \frac{\bar{\theta} - 2\theta}{3}\Delta s \text{ and } p_2^\star = \frac{2\bar{\theta} - \theta}{3}\Delta s \tag{13.10}$$

$$\Pi_1(n_1, n_2, p_1^\star, p_2^\star) = G(n) + U\left(\frac{\bar{\theta} - 2\theta}{3}\right)^2 \Delta s, \tag{13.11}$$

$$\text{and } \Pi_2(n_1, n_2, p_1^\star, p_2^\star) = G(n) + U\left(\frac{2\bar{\theta} - \theta}{3}\right)^2 \Delta s \tag{13.12}$$

Note that prices and payoffs depend only on the differential in qualities $\Delta s = G(n)((\omega_2 - n_2) - (\omega_1 - n_1))$. They are increasing functions of the differential in qualities Δs. Indeed, vertical differentiation reduces competition. We can easily check that the higher quality access seller's price and profit are higher than the price and profit of the lower quality seller. In the following we show that, in contrast with the learning model, where contributions are a decreasing function of competences, here the most competent developer contributes more. Note first that developer 1's payoff is an increasing function of his contribution n_1. The more he contributes to open software, the more he increases the externality *and* the differential in qualities. However, there is a limit to this improvement. If he devoted all his competence to open software, the quality of the access he could propose would be zero and the demand for his access services would disappear. The demand for access 1 is strictly positive if $\theta s_1^\star > p_1$. This imposes the following condition on the quality of access 1:

$$\omega_1 - n_1 \geq \frac{\bar{\theta} - 2\theta}{2\bar{\theta} - \theta}(\omega_2 - n_2)$$

We denote by $n_1^\star(n_2) = \omega_1 - \frac{\bar{\theta} - 2\theta}{2\bar{\theta} - \theta}(\omega_2 - n_2)$, the reaction function of developer 1. developer 2's first order condition leads to:

$$G'(n) + U\left(\frac{2\bar{\theta} - \theta}{3}\right)^2 [G'(n)((\omega_2 - n_2) - (\omega_1 - n_1)) - G((n))] = 0$$

$$\tag{13.13}$$

A consequence of developer 1's reaction function is that:

$$(\omega_2 - n_2) - (\omega_1 - n_1) = \frac{\bar{\theta} + \underline{\theta}}{2\bar{\theta} - \underline{\theta}}(\omega_2 - n_2) \tag{13.14}$$

Introducing this equality in developer 2's first order condition leads to:

$$n_2 = \omega_2 - \frac{2\bar{\theta} - \underline{\theta}}{\bar{\theta} + \underline{\theta}}\frac{G(n)}{G'(n)} + \frac{9}{U(2\bar{\theta} - \underline{\theta})(\bar{\theta} + \underline{\theta})}$$

and:

$$n_2 + \frac{2\bar{\theta} - \underline{\theta}}{\bar{\theta} + \underline{\theta}}\frac{G(n)}{G'(n)} = \omega_2 + \frac{9}{U(2\bar{\theta} - \underline{\theta})(\bar{\theta} + \underline{\theta})}$$

We note that the left side of this equality is an increasing function of n_2.

14 Simulating code growth in Libre (open source) mode

Jean-Michel Dalle and Paul A. David

14.1 Introduction

The initial contributions to the social science literature addressing the phenomenon of Libre (open-source, free) software have been directed primarily to identifying the motivations underlying the sustained and often intensive engagement of many highly skilled individuals in this non-contractual and unremunerated mode of production.[1] That focus reflects a view that widespread voluntary participation in the creation and free distribution of economically valuable goods is something of an anomaly, at least from the viewpoint of mainstream microeconomic analysis.

A second problem that has occupied observers, and especially economists, is to uncover the explanation for the evident success of products of the Libre software mode in market competition against proprietary software – significantly on the basis not only of their lower cost but their reputedly superior quality.[2] This quest resembles the first, in reflecting a

The research reported in this chapter was made possible by grant awards to the Stanford University (SIEPR) Project on the Economics of Free and Open Source Software and its European academic partners by the National Science Foundation program on Digital Technology and Society: IIS-0112962 (2001–04) and IIS-0329259 (2003–05). [http://siepr.stanford.edu/programs/OpenSoftware_David/OS_Project_Funded_Announcmt.htm.]
Our research has also been supported by *CALIBRE*, an EU FP6 Coordination Action. We have benefited from discussions with participants at the EPIP3 and OWLS seminars, which convened at Scuola Superiore Sant'Anna in Pisa, Italy on 2–3 April 2004, and at the Oxford Internet Institute in Oxford, UK on 25–26 June 2004, respectively. Fabio Arcangeli, Robin Cowan, Brian Fitzgerald, Alfonso Gambardella, Rishab A. Ghosh, Jesus Gonzalez-Barahona, Bronwyn H. Hall, Jim Herbsleb, Eric von Hippel, Brian Kahin, Mathieu Lacage, Karim Lakhani, Juan Mateos-Garcia, Stephen M. Maurer, Jean-Charles Pomerol, Gregorio Robles, Walt Scacchi and Ed Steinmuller all had a helpful hand in shaping this work. But the views expressed and the defects that remain are ours.

[1] See, among the salient early contributions to the "economics of open source software," Ghosh (2003), Harhoff, Henkel and von Hippel (2003), Lakhani and von Hippel (2000), Lerner and Tirole (2000), Weber (2000), Kogut and Metiu (2001).
[2] In this particular vein, see, for example, Dalle and Jullien (2000, 2003), Bessen (2001), Kuan (2001), Benkler (2002).

state of surprise and puzzlement about the apparently greater efficiency that these voluntary, distributed production organizations have been able to attain *vis-à-vis* centrally managed, profit-driven firms that are experienced in creating "closed" software products.

Anomalies are intrinsically captivating for intellectuals of a scientific or just a puzzle-solving bent. Yet, the research attention that has been stimulated by the rapid rise of a Libre software segment of the world's software-producing activities during the 1990s owes something also to the belief that this phenomenon and its relationship to the free and open software movements could turn out to be of considerably broader social and economic significance. There is, indeed, much about these developments that remains far from transparent, and we are sympathetic to the view that a deeper understanding of them may carry implications of a more general nature concerning the organization of economic activities in networked digital technology environments. Of course, the same might well be said about other aspects of the workings of modern economies that are no less likely to turn out to be important for human well-being.

Were the intense research interest that Libre software production currently attracts to be justified on other grounds, especially as a response to the novelty and mysteriousness of the phenomena, one would need to point out that this too is a less than compelling rationale; the emergence of Libre software activities at their present scale is hardly so puzzling or aberrant a development as to warrant such attention. Cooperative production of information and knowledge among members of distributed epistemic communities who do not expect direct remuneration for their efforts simply cannot qualify as a new departure. There are numerous historical precursors and precedents for Libre software, perhaps most notably in the "invisible colleges" that appeared among the practitioners of the new experimental and mathematical approaches to scientific inquiry in western Europe in the course of the 17th century.[3] The professionalization of scientific research, as is well known, was a comparatively late development, and as rapidly as it has proceeded, it has not entirely eliminated the contributions of non-professionals in some fields, optical astronomy being especially notable in this regard; communities of "amateur" comet-watchers persist, and their members continue to score – and to verify – the occasional observational coup.

"Open science," the mode of inquiry that emerged and became formally institutionalized during the era of the Scientific Revolution under systems of public and private patronage, thus offers an obvious

---

[3] See, for example, David (1998a, 1998b, 2002a, 2002b, 2004) and references to the history of science literature supplied therein.

cultural and organizational point of reference for observers of contemporary communities of programmers engaged in developing free software and open-source software.[4] The "communal" ethos and norms of "the Republic of Science" emphasize the cooperative character of the larger purpose in which individual researchers are engaged, stressing that the accumulation of reliable knowledge is an essentially social process. The force of its universalistic norm is to render entry into scientific work and discourse open to all persons of "competence," while a second key aspect of "openness" is promoted by norms concerning the sharing of knowledge in regard to new findings and the methods whereby they were obtained.

Moreover, a substantial body of analysis by philosophers of science and epistemologists, as well as theoretical and empirical studies in the economics of knowledge, points to the superior efficiency of cooperative knowledge-sharing among peers as a mode of generating additions to the stock of scientifically reliable propositions.[5] In brief, the norm of openness is incentive compatible with a collegiate reputational reward system based upon accepted claims to priority; it also is conducive to individual strategy choices whose collective outcome reduces excess duplication of research efforts and enlarges the domain of informational complementarities. This brings socially beneficial spill-overs among research programs and abets rapid replication and swift validation of novel discoveries. The advantages of treating new findings as *public goods* in order to promote the faster growth of the stock of knowledge are thus contrasted with the requirement of restricting informational access in order to enlarge the flow of privately appropriable rents from knowledge stocks.

---

[4] This has not gone unrecognized by observers of the free and open-source software movements. In *The Magic Cauldron*, Raymond (1999) explicitly notices the connection between the information-sharing behavior of academic researchers and the practices of participants in Libre projects. Further, Raymond's (1998b) illuminating discussion of the norms and reward systems (which motivate and guide developers' selections of projects on which to work) quite clearly parallels the classic approach of Robert K. Merton (1973) and his followers in the sociology of science. This is underscored by Raymond's (1999) rejoinder to Bezroukov's (1999) allegations on the point. See also DiBona et al. (1999) for another early discussion; Kelty (2001) and David, Arora and Steinmueller (2001) expand the comparison with the norms and institutions of open/academic science. Nevertheless, one should observe that the parallel is by no means exact: formal professional accreditation and institutional affiliation are salient de facto requirements for active participation in modern academic and public sector research communities, yet the computer programming and other software development tasks – whether in the commercial or the free and open-source spheres – remain activities that have resisted becoming "professionalized."

[5] See Dasgupta and David (1994), David (1998b, 2002a, b) on the cognitive performance of open science networks in comparison with that of proprietary research organizations; and David (2003) on the interaction between modern "open science" and proprietary R&D.

The foregoing functional juxtaposition suggests a logical basis for the existence and perpetuation of institutional and cultural separations between two normatively differentiated communities of research practice. The open "Republic of Science" and the proprietary "Realm of Technology" on this view constitute distinctive organizational regimes, each of which serves a different (and potentially complementary) societal purpose. One might venture farther to point out that the effective fulfilling of their distinctive and mutually supporting purposes was for some time abetted by the ideological reinforcement of a normative separation between the two communities; by the emergence of a distinctive ethos of "independence" and personal disinterestedness ("purity") that sought to keep scientific inquiry free to the fullest extent possible from the constraints and distorting influences to which commercially oriented research was held to be subject.

It follows that if we are seeing something really new and different in the Libre software phenomenon, that hardly can inhere in attributes shared with long-existing open science communities.[6] Rather, it must be found elsewhere, perhaps among the more distinctive items in the following list: (a) the sheer scale on which these activities are being conducted, (b) the global dispersion and heterogeneous backgrounds of the participants (and the related absence of mandatory professional certification requirements), (c) the rapidity of their transactions, and (d) the pace at which their collective efforts reach fruition. This shift in conceptualization has the effect of turning attention to a constellation of technical conditions whose coalescence has especially affected this field of endeavor. Consider just these three: the distinctive immateriality of "code," the great scope for modularity in the construction of software systems, and the enabling effects of advances in digital (computer-mediated) telecommunications during the past several decades. Although it might be thought that the intention here is merely to portray the historically unprecedented features of the Libre software movement as primarily an "Internet phenomenon," we have in mind something less glib than that.

---

[6] The phenomenon of free and open-source software is perceived by Benkler (2002: pp. 1–2) as exemplifying "a much broader social-economic phenomenon . . . the broad and deep emergence of a new, third mode of production in the digitally networked environment." This mode he labels "commons-based peer production" to distinguish it from the property- and contract-based modes of firms and markets. Its central characteristic is that groups of individuals successfully collaborate on large-scale projects following a diverse cluster of motivational drives and social signals rather than either market prices or managerial commands. Anyone at all familiar with the history of open science since the 17th century will be disconcerted – to say the least –by this particular imputation of novelty and significance to Libre projects.

It is true that resulting technical characteristics of both the work product and work process alone cannot be held to radically distinguish the creation of software from other fields of intellectual and cultural production in the modern world. Nevertheless, they do suggest several respects in which it is misleading to interpret the Libre software phenomenon simply as "another sub-species of 'open science.'" The knowledge incorporated in software differs in at least two significant respects from the codified knowledge typically produced by scientific and technical work groups. Computer software is a form of information that is at the same time a "technological artifact," which is to say that it has immediate functional effectiveness without requiring further expenditures of effort upon development.[7] This immediacy has significant implications not only at the micro-level of individual motivation but for the dynamics of collective knowledge-production. Indeed, because software code is "a machine implemented as text," its functionality is peculiarly self-exemplifying. Thus, "running code" serves to short-circuit many issues of "authority" and "legitimation" that traditionally have absorbed much of the time and attention of scientific communities, and to radically compress the processes of validating and interpreting new contributions to the knowledge stock.[8]

In our view Libre software production activities warrant systematic investigation not as a sub-species of the unusual class of technological objects called "computer software" but because its relationship with a conjunction of a particular set of trends in the modern economy may give this development significant implications for the future of the advance of knowledge, and consequently for knowledge-driven economic growth. The first of those trends is that information goods that share many of the special properties of software have been moving more and more to center stage among the drivers of sustainable economic development. Secondly, the enabling of peer-to-peer organizations for information distribution and utilization is an increasingly obtrusive consequence of the direction in which digital technologies are advancing. Thirdly, the "open" (and cooperative) mode of organizing the generation of new knowledge has long been recognized to have efficiency properties that are much superior to institutional solutions to the public goods problem that entail the restriction of access to information

---

[7] This property of software, incidentally, accounts for its anomalous treatment under intellectual property law. Software, being "a machine" implemented as "text," is unique in being both patentable and copyrightable.

[8] Therefore, at the risk of re-circulating a tired bromide, it might well be said that in regard to the sociology and politics of the open-source software communities, "the medium is the message."

through secrecy or property rights enforcement, but poses a problem inasmuch as it seemingly requires a rising volume of public funding for basic research. Fourthly, and of practical significance for those who seek to study it systematically, the Libre software mode of production itself is generating a wealth of quantitative information about this instantiation of "open epistemic communities." This latter development makes Libre software activities a valuable window through which to study the more generic and fundamental processes that are responsible for its power, as well as the factors that are likely to limit its domain of viability in competition with other modes of organizing economic activities.

Proceeding from this re-framing of the phenomenon, one is led toward a conceptual approach that highlights a broader, ultimately more policy-oriented set of issues than those which hitherto have dominated the economics literature concerning Libre software. A corresponding re-orientation of research agendas would appear to be called for.[9] Its analytical elements are in no way novel, however, but merely newly adapted to suit the subject at hand. It is directed to answering a fundamental and interrelated pair of questions: First, by what mechanisms do Libre software projects mobilize the human resources, allocate the participants' diverse expertise, coordinate the contributions and retain the commitment of their members? Second, how fully do the products of these essentially self-directed efforts meet the long-term needs of software users in the larger society and not simply provide satisfactions of various kinds for the developers? These will be recognized immediately by economists to be utterly familiar and straightforward – save for not yet having been explicitly posed or systematically pursued in this context.

Pursuing these concrete, classic economic questions compels a detailed examination of the workings of the system of social organization that actually allocates software development resources among the various software systems and applications projects that are being undertaken by "communities" of distributed and sometimes anonymous volunteers – which is the situation typical of the larger projects in the world of Libre

---

[9] This is the approach being pursued by the members of the project on the Economic Organization and Viability of Open Source Software at Stanford University and its research partners at academic institutions in France, the Netherlands and Britain. Many of the researchers associated with this project come to this particular subject matter from the perspective formed by their previous and on-going work in "the new economics of science," which has focused attention upon the organization of collaborative inquiry in the "open science" mode, the behavioral norms and reinforcing reward systems that structured the allocation of resources, the relationships of these self-organizing and relatively autonomous epistemic communities with their patrons and sponsors in the public and private sectors. See Dalle, David, Ghosh and Steinmueller (2005) for the scope of this integrated research agenda.

software. How does the ensemble of developers collectively "select" among the observed array of projects that are launched? What processes govern the mobilization of sufficient resource inputs to enable some among those to attain the stage of functionality and reliability that permits their being diffused into wider use – that is to say, use beyond the circle of programmers immediately engaged in the continuing development and "debugging" of the code itself?

Indeed, it seems only natural to expect that economists would provide an answer to the question of how, in the absence of directly discernible market links between the producing entities and "customers," the output mix of the open-source sector of the software industry is determined. Yet, surprisingly, this question does not appear to have attracted any significant amount of attention. This curious lacuna, moreover, is not a deficiency peculiar to the economics literature, for it is notable also in the writings of some of the Libre software movement's pioneering participants and popular exponents.[10] Although enthusiasts have made numerous claims regarding the qualitative superiority of products of the open-source mode when these are compared with software systems tools and applications packages developed by managed commercial projects, scarcely any attention is directed to the issue of whether the array of completed Libre software projects also is "better" or "just as good" in responding to the varied demands of software users.

It is emblematic of this gap that the metaphor of "the bazaar" was chosen by Eric S. Raymond (1998a) to convey the distinctively unmanaged, decentralized mode of organization that characterizes open-source software development projects. Here is a representative reading of this aspect of Raymond's widely influential essay by an otherwise perceptive commentator, Ko Kuwabara (2000):

... The Cathedral and the Bazaar, is a metaphorical reference to two fundamentally different styles of software engineering. On the one hand, common in commercial development, is the Cathedral model, characterized by centralized planning enforced from the top and implemented by specialized project teams around structured schedules. Efficiency is the motto of the Cathedral. It is a sober picture of rational organization under linear management, of a tireless watchmaker fitting gears and pins one by one as he has for years and years. On the other hand is the Bazaar model of the Linux project, with its decentralized development driven by the whims of volunteer hackers and little else. In contrast to the serene isolation of the Cathedral from the outside, the Bazaar is the clamour itself. Anyone is welcome – the more people, the louder they clamour,

---

[10] See, for example, Raymond (1998b, 1999), Stallman (1999), Dibona, Ockman and Stone (1999) and the statements of contributors collected therein.

the better it is. It is a community by the people and for the people, a community for all to share and nurture. It also appears chaotic and unstructured, a community where no one alone is effectively in charge of the community. Not all are heard or noticed, and not all are bound to enjoy the excitement. For others, however, the Bazaar continues to bubble with life and opportunity.

But "the bazaar" remains a peculiar metaphor for a system of production: the stalls of actual bazaars typically are retail outlets, passive channels of distribution rather than agencies with direct responsibility for the assortment of commodities that others have made available for them to sell. Given the extensive discussion of the virtues and deficiencies of "the bazaar" metaphor that was stimulated by Raymond's essay, it is all the more remarkable that what has managed to pass with scarcely any comment is rhetorical finesse of the problem of aligning the activities of producers with the wants of the needs and wants of the final, non-specialist users of these information goods.[11]

In contrast, the tasks set in our project on free and open-source ("Libre") software represent an explicit response to the challenge of providing *non-metaphorical* answers to the classic economic questions of whether and how this instance of a decentralized decision resource allocation process could achieve coherent and socially efficient outcomes. What makes this an especially interesting problem, of course, is the possibility of assessing the extent to which institutions of the kind that have emerged in the free software and open-source movements are enabling them to accomplish that outcome – without help either from the "invisible hand" of the market mechanism driven by price signals, or the "visible hands" of centralized managerial hierarchies.[12] Meeting this challenge requires that the analysis be directed ultimately toward providing a means of assessing the social optimality properties of the organization and management of "open science," "open-source" and kindred cooperative knowledge-creating communities. In all such circumstances where specialized expertise of those participating is critical for the effective conduct of the work, and prior evaluations are made difficult by the asymmetric distribution of the pertinent bodies of expert knowledge and knowledge about expertise, one would expect to find a greater reliance upon *ex post* verification and validation of the work product rather than on formal management tools for selecting the producers and monitoring

---

[11] See, for example, Kuwabara (2000), and references in the notes accompanying Raymond (1999: pp. 19–63): "Cathedrals and Bazaars."

[12] Benkler (2002) has formulated this problem as one that appears in the organizational space between the hierarchically managed firm and the decentralized competitive market, focusing attention primarily on the efficiency of software project organizations rather than considering the regime as a whole.

the quality or intensity of their contributions. When considering the issues surrounding the nature and efficacy of the coordination, governance and quality-regulating mechanisms that have emerged in the context of large and complex Libre software projects, it is therefore relevant to recognize the potential tensions between the product control devices that can be readily implemented by expert developers and those which may be of importance to the end-users in society at large.

14.2   Modeling Libre communities at work

The parallels that exist between the phenomena of "open source" and "open science," to which reference has been made already, suggest a modeling approach that builds on the generic features of non-market social interaction mechanisms. These involve feedbacks from the cumulative results of individual actions, and thereby are capable of achieving substantial coordination and coherence in the collective performance of the ensemble of distributed agents. This approach points in particular to the potential significance of the actors' consciousness of being "embedded" in peer reference groups; and therefore to the role of collegiate recognition and reputational status considerations as a source of systematic influence directing individual efforts of discovery and invention.

Our agent-based modeling framework has been structured with a view to its suitability for subsequent refinement and use in integrating and assessing the significance of empirical findings about patterns of resource allocation within large and more complex F/LOSS projects, well-known exemplars of which are the Linux operating system, the Mozilla web browser and the Apache web server. Systematic empirical evidence about the participants in such projects, their behaviors, patterns of communication and the internal modes of project organization has only lately begun to be collected.[13] Nonetheless, to guide initial

---

[13] Pioneering studies of large projects include the work of Koch and Schneider (2000), Tuomi (2000, 2001), Dempsey et al. (1999, 2002), S. Krishnamurthy (2002). More recent studies have sought to exploit new methods of automated data-mining from source code repositories, and to build links between that information and data on communications flows among project participants. On patterns of authorship and the structure of code within large projects, obtained using the CODD data-extraction algorithm (developed by R. A. Ghosh and V. V. Prakash and described first to measure the code size of projects in the Orbiten Free Survey (2000) – see http:www.orbiten.org/codd), see Ghosh (2003); for findings from the application of CODD to studies of sequential releases of the the Linux kernel, see Ghosh and David (2003). See also Gonzalez-Barahona and Robles (2003, 2004), Robles, Koch and Gonzalez-Barahona (2004), Gonzalez-Barahona, Lopez and Robles (2004).

specifications it is possible to draw upon insights provided by experienced project leaders and descriptive generalizations about micro-level incentives from survey- and interview-based studies regarding the nature of the community norms that might not only affect the mobilization of participants but guide the allocation of software developers' efforts within particular projects. Nothing in that approach invites hypothesizing the operation in the representative, "ideal-type" open-source community of a system of social norms which mimics the particular features of collegiate reputational reward systems such as are found in the Republic of Science. Yet, postulating that an equivalent functional structure does exist provides an entirely plausible basis upon which we may proceed. Further, it is equally clear that provision eventually will need to be made to incorporate functional equivalents of the conventions and institutions governing recognized claims to scientific "priority" (being first), as well as the symbolic and other practices that signify peer approbation of exemplary individual performance.

A systems analysis perspective such as is familiar in general equilibrium economics suggests that within such a framework we should be capable also of asking how the norms and signals available to micro-level decision-takers in the population of potential participants will shape the distribution of resources among different concurrent projects, and direct the attention of individual and groups to successive new projects. That, in turn, will affect the growth and distribution of programmers' experiences with the code of particular projects, as well as the capabilities of those who have gained familiarity with the norms and institutions (e.g., software licensing practices), and the coordination and communication styles specific to individual projects, as well as the more widely shared practices of the Libre software regime. Obviously, the formation of generic knowledge and capabilities provides potential "spill-overs" to other areas of endeavor – including the production of software goods and services by commercial suppliers. From this it follows that to fully understand the dynamics of the Libre software mode and its interactions with the rest of the information-technology sector, one cannot treat the expertise of the software development community as a given and exogenously determined resource.

From the foregoing it should be evident that the task upon which we are embarked is no trivial undertaking, and that to bring it to completion we must hope that others can be drawn into contributing to this effort. We report here on initial progress toward that goal: the formulation of a highly stylized dynamic model of decentralized, micro-level decisions that shape the allocation of Libre software programming resources among project tasks, and across distinct projects, thereby generating an evolving array of Libre software system products, each with its associated qualitative attributes. In such work, it is hardly possible to eschew taking account of what has been discovered about the variety of prospective rewards – both material and psychic – that may be motivating individuals to write free and open-source software, because it is only reasonable to suppose that these may influence how they allocate their personal efforts in this sphere. At this stage, it is not necessary to go into great detail on this matter, but among the many motives enumerated it is relevant to separate out those involving what might be described as "independent user-implemented innovation."[14] Indeed, this term may well apply to the great mass of identifiably discrete projects, because a major consideration driving many individuals who engage in the production of open source would appear to be the direct utility or satisfaction they expect to derive by using their creative outputs.[15] The power of this motivating force obviously derives from the property of immediate efficacy, which has been noticed as a distinctive feature of computer programs. But, no less obviously, this force will be most potent where the utilitarian objective does not require developing a large and complex body of code, and so can be achieved quite readily by the exertion of the individual programmer's independent efforts. "Independent" is the operative word here, for it is unlikely that someone writing an obscure driver for a newly marketed printer that he wishes to use will be at all concerned about the value that would be attached to this achievement by "the Libre software community." The individuals engaging in this sort of software development may use open-source tools and regard themselves as belonging in every way to the free software and open-source movements. Nevertheless, it is significant that the question of whether or not their products are to be contributed to the corpus of non-proprietary software, rather than being copyright protected for purposes of commercial exploitation, really is one that they need not address *ex ante*. Being essentially isolated from active collaboration in production, the issue of

---

[14] The term evidently derives from von Hippel's (2001, 2002) emphasis on the respects in which open-source software exemplifies the larger phenomenon of "user innovations."
[15] Just how great a mass these independent projects represent in the total remains unclear, as the most readily available indications are those obtained by studying the characteristics of the just *publicly announced* open-source projects. On the basis of gathered data from Sourceforge.net on the 100 most active projects observed in the "mature stage" (i.e. the final stage of a project's development, when it is almost fully functional and distributed), Krishnamurthy (2002) reports finding that the modal project has only one identified developer; among the most active projects – a mere fraction of the 40,000 or so listed on that site – the median number of developers was four.

the disposition of authorship rights can be deferred until the code is written.[16] That is an option which typically is not available for projects that contemplate enlisting the contributions of numerous developers, and for which there are compelling reasons to announce a licensing policy at the outset.

For all intents and purposes, software production activity in such circumstances stands apart from the efforts that entail participation in collective developmental process, involving successive releases of code and the cumulative formation of a more complex, multi-function system. We will refer to the latter as Libre software production in "community-mode" or, for convenience, *C-mode*, contrasting it with software production in *I-mode* (Dalle and David, 2003). Since *I-mode* products and producers, almost by definition, tend to remain restricted in their individual scope and do not provide as direct an experience of social participation, the empirical basis for generalizations about them is still very thin; too thin, at this point, to support interesting model building. Consequently, our attention here focuses exclusively upon creating a suitable model to simulate the actions and outcomes of populations of Libre software agents that are working in *C-mode*.

It would be a mistake, however, to completely conflate the issue of the sources of motivation for human behavior with the separable question of how individuals' awareness of community sentiment, and their receptivity to signals transmitted in social interactions, serves to guide and even constrain their private and public actions; indeed, even to modify their manifest goals. Our stylized representation of the production decisions made by Libre software developers therefore does not presuppose that career considerations of "ability signaling," "reputation building" and the expectations of various material rewards attached thereto are dominant or even a sufficient *motivation* for individuals who participate in *C-mode* projects. Instead, it embraces the weaker hypothesis that awareness of peer-group norms significantly influences (without completely determining) micro-level choices about the individuals' allocation of

---

[16] In this respect it can be argued that the decision of the individual developer working in *I-mode* to participate in Libre software production actually is not a decision about the mode of production but instead a matter of making an *ex post* choice of whether or not to disclose the source code, and whether or not it is worth trying to exploit the resulting program as protected intellectual property. The economics of such post-production decisions certainly are of interest, and the normative force of the open-source and free software movements may come into play at this stage. This represents a promising line for future research, but it is a line of inquiry quite different from the one we are pursuing here.

their code-writing inputs, whatever assortment of considerations may be motivating their willingness to contribute to those efforts.[17] Our model-building activity aims to provide more specific insights not only into the workings of Libre software communities but also into their interaction with organizations engaged in proprietary and "closed mode" software production. It seeks to articulate the interdependences among distinct sub-components of the resource allocation system, and to absorb and integrate empirical findings about micro-level mobilization and allocation of individual developer efforts both among projects and within projects. Stochastic simulation of such social interaction systems is a powerful tool for identifying critical structural relationships and parameters that affect the emergent properties of the macro system. Among the latter properties, the global performance of the Libre software mode in matching the functional distribution and characteristics of the produced software systems to the evolving needs of users in the economy at large, obviously, is an issue of importance for our analysis to tackle.

It is our expectation that in this way it will be feasible to analyze some among the problematic tensions that may arise between the performance of a mode of production guided primarily by the internal value systems of the participating producers, and that of a system in which the reward structure is tightly coupled (by managerial direction) to external signals deriving from the satisfaction of end-users' wants. Where the producers are the end-users, of course, the scope for conflicts of that kind will be greatly circumscribed, as enthusiasts of "user-directed innovation" have pointed out.[18] However, the latter solution is likely to serve the goal of customization only by sacrificing some of the efficiencies that derive from producer specialization and division of labor. The analysis developed in this chapter is intended to permit investigations of this classic "trade-off" in the sphere of software production.

---

[17] It will be seen that the probabilistic allocational "rules" derive from a set of distinct community "norms," and it will be quite straightforward within the structure of the model to allow for heterogeneity in the responsiveness to peer influence in this respect, by providing for inter-individual differences in weighting within the rule set. This may be done either probabilistically, or by creating a variety of distinct "types" of agents and specifying their relative frequencies in the population from which "contributions" are drawn. For the purposes of the basic model presented here, we have made a bold simplification by specifying that all potential contributors respond uniformly to a common set of allocational rules.

[18] See von Hippel (2001), Franke and von Hippel (2002), on the development of "user toolkits for innovation," which are specific to a given production system and product or service type, but within those constraints enable producers to transfer user need-related aspects of product or service design to the users themselves.

14.3   The model[19]

14.3.1   Structure and rationale

The core of the stochastic simulation model of open-source software production presented here is a behavioral kernel: heterogeneous developers face an existing set of software modules[20] – about the state of which we assume they are fully informed[21] – and they choose the module they will contribute to stochastically, according to their effort endowments and to the reward that each module can grant them. Heterogeneity, represented here by the existence of a stochastic (discrete) choice function, classically accounts for all the unobserved characteristics of each developer. Each developer will prefer to undertake the most rewarding tasks, according to a reward system still to be determined: however, this is not a deterministic choice as there are necessarily unobserved heterogeneous characteristics which drive this choice, and for which no model can account if it wants to avoid the absolute contingency trap in which it would fall if it assumed it could take all relevant variables into account. A simple and now relatively traditional way to handle this (Anderson, de Palma and Thisse, 1992) is to consider that the more rewarding modules will be chosen with a higher probability – or, in the statistical physicist's language now common in most disciplines including economics, to consider rewards as weights and to compute the probability that each module is chosen according to a ratio between its weight and the sum of all weights, possibly distorted by various parameters and coefficients. Namely:

---

[19] The current version of this model, and its exposition, have benefited enormously from comments and criticisms we have received from various people after we previously opted for an "early" release (Dalle and David, 2003/2005), precisely to elicit comments both from the academic community and from participant observers in open-source projects. Any modeling exercise like this one implies some conscious level of abstraction and simplification: however, the modelers might not be immediately accurate in their modeling attempts, over-estimating some parameters while underestimating others, and therefore critically need insights and inputs from many other experts. Needless to say, this basic assumption still completely holds here.

[20] Which would probably correspond more to packages than to individual files according to the terminology current in most open-source projects.

[21] Which implies that each new contribution is immediately made accessible to all developers. We do not account here for the fact that some contributions do not automatically become "commits" (entering the code), due to the decisions of maintainers at the module level.

$$\mathbf{P}\left[chosen\ module = (virtual)\ module\ m\right] = \frac{\rho_m(\alpha)}{\sum_{i=1}^{all\ modules}\rho_i(\alpha) + \sum_{i=1}^{all\ virtual\ modules}\rho_{i'}(\alpha)}$$

(14.1)

where $\rho_\bullet(\alpha)$ stands for the prospective reward for code-amount α contributed to that module. An important caveat to be mentioned here concerns the fact that the precise nature of the technical problems faced by each developer in his or her own idiosyncratic situation is part of the unobserved characteristics that influence behaviors. This feature of the choice situation is reported to be a significant determinant of a developer's action in "selecting" among the multiplicity of open-source projects on which they could work. Eric S. Raymond (1998a) encapsulated that view aphoristically and normatively: "Every good work of software starts by scratching a developer's personal itch." But, subsequently, its importance has received confirmation from a variety of more systematic empirical studies of software "user innovation" and surveys of open-source developers' experiences.[22] This is a consideration which is dealt with only by stochastic representation of project selection in the model's present formulation: we "account for" it among all the other unobserved characteristics. Subsequent versions of this model should involve the development of an improved behavioral kernel, which would account for the matching process between developer and module characteristics, including the possibility that developers might acquire greater facility in specific technical classes of software such as network drivers, or knowledge of the subtle features of the architecture of a particularly complex software system, such as the Linux kernel, that would influence the dynamics of their contributions.[23]

---

[22] For studies motivated by Eric von Hippel's "user innovation hypothesis" see Harhoff, Henkel and von Hippel (2000), Franke and von Hippel (2002), von Hippel (2002). For survey-based quantitative evaluations of this motivation that qualify the universalistic claims, but nevertheless document the importance of individual use motivation even among participants in large projects, see, for example, Ghosh, Glott, Kreiger & Robles (2002), David, Waterman and Arora (2003), Lakhani, Wolf, Bates and DiBona (2003).

[23] We do not underestimate the added complexity of the resulting simulation structure and the necessity of increasing the number of simulation experiments required to assure that the results reported were reasonably robust. One problem is that by increasing the heterogeneity of actors who make choices at random moments in time, and by allowing for endogenously formed heterogeneity of individual skills, the evolution of the model is likely to become more "historically contingent" or "path dependent" (David, 2001b). Without the introduction of some very strong "viability" condition that greatly restricts the number of stable attractors, a modeling step for which there is no immediately evident a priori or empirical warrant, studies of the resulting non-ergodic system would require much more extensive and exhaustive computational explorations.

Of course, inasmuch as not all the functions required for a full operational software system can be instantaneously provided for, the existence of a virtual architecture for the project would imply that for much of the early history of the project new modules, such as those for network drivers, printer drivers, file systems, would remain to be added. Consequently, the option of adding a new module, rather than expanding or replacing the code of an existing model, may attract development contributions. Indeed, that is exactly what open-source software development generally implies, since open-source developers build upon the structure of existing code to extend its functionality both vertically (adding new levels of applications) and horizontally (for example, by building variant applications that may be better suited to different machine architectures).

The incentives to add modules that are defined by community recognition of the generic need to that functionality – as distinct from the idiosyncratic technical interests of the developer in question, like the prospective "rewards" of contributing existing modules – constitute the mechanism that we have implemented to simulate the dynamics of the growth of code growth within a given project. For this purpose we have relied upon the following modeling finesse: we suppose that to each existing module is associated a "virtual" module, which stands for the eventuality that a new module could be created from the existing one, either by developing an existing functionality out of it, in the form of an external module, or simply by adding a new one which would supplement this module. Clearly then, the new module and the existing one would be technically linked,[24] the new external module would typically be included in the existing during the compilation process, or sometimes simply called. Figure 14.1 represents the growth of a software system according to this rule: at each step, red lines and circles represent the last created module, while dotted blue lines and circles represent virtual modules attached to each existing one, and black lines and circles represent older modules created during earlier steps.

In this framework, the emerging architecture of the modules is indeed mathematically a tree, since, by construction, there are no loops and each module is linked to only one (parent) module. This tree does not completely correspond to the actual directory tree, nor to the full set of technical and functional dependencies, which are usually known as the architecture of a software system per se (Bass, Clements and Kazman,

---

[24] Also in the sense of the wording of the GPL license, for instance, which implies that if the "parent" module was GPLd, then the new one would be also.

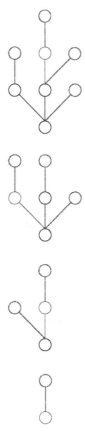

Figure 14.1. Graphical representation of a software system's growth as an upwards-evolving tree.

1998), since some technical dependencies are not accounted for here, namely the fact that some modules can be called by several others. We have rather characterized it here as an emerging architecture, i.e. the one which stems from the fact that developers generally decide to create a new module to solve a technical problem they face while working on a particular existing one, or as a development or part of an existing module. Therefore, this emerging architecture here has much to do with the kind of phenomenon that Herbert A. Simon (1962) famously characterized years ago in a seminal article on the "architecture of complexity" to which we clearly are intellectually indebted, all the more so as the emerging architecture that Simon considered was also a tree-like "hierarchical system."[25] Indeed, Simon explicitly indicated that the emerging architectures of complex systems tended often to be spontaneously tree-like, *because complex systems were born out of simple ones, and because simple systems then tend to be somehow included in more complex ones.* As for our modeling of open-source software development, the rationale for the emergence of a hierarchy of modules is strongly similar: a complex system is dynamically born out of a simple one; new modules are created out of existing ones to supplement them by developing existing functionalities or adding new ones; and these new modules can be included in higher ones during the compilation process or at least are called as sub-systems. We are also very close here to the recent research on design modularity (Baldwin and Clark, 2000), and extending the model further in this direction, notably by studying more extensively, and modeling more accurately, the actual technical interactions between modules would also be a fruitful research avenue.

This model then allows us to test one of the main hypotheses that have been suggested about software development in open-source mode, namely, what we suggest calling the "peer-regard" hypothesis. According to this theory, developers are significantly influenced by reputation effects. Eric S. Raymond (1998a, b) was among the first to emphasize this idea in the famous essays he wrote as a participant observer in open-source communities, and it has been since suggested repeatedly by several other important studies of open-source software development, also as a more general attempt to analyze the striking similarities between open-source and open science communities.[26] In a companion paper to this chapter (Dalle, David, Ghosh and Wolak, 2004), we build upon Raymond's (1999) insights to suggest that open-source software development processes are a manifestation of a broader class of socio-economic organizations that have been described as "economies of (peer) regard."

Our allusion to the concept of "the economy of regard" in this connection should not be understood simply as a reference to the motivation that individuals may derive for participation in open-source software development from instrumental evaluation of material rewards to professional, career reputation-building actions – the sort of considerations that are readily assimilated into the corpus of conventional microeconomic theorizing (see Lerner and Tirole, 2002).

---

[25] But not in the traditional sense of hierarchy, just as a description of an architecture with several levels; indeed, so as to avoid misunderstanding, the French version of this text employs, in place of "hierarchy", the word arborescent, meaning "tree-like".

[26] See Benkler (2001), Kelty (2001), Dalle, David and Steinmueller (2002); on the economics of open science, specifically, Dasgupta and David (1987, 1994), David (1998a, b, 2000).

As introduced by Offer (1997), "the economy of regard" is conceptualized as a system of reciprocated exchanges that is situated "between the gift and the market," providing a distinctive and less individualistic framework for understanding recurring voluntary transactions that are not highly personalized and in which pecuniary compensation plays little if any significant part. It therefore serves to point the discussion of collective production organizations away from the essentially atomistic mode of analysis familiar in cartel theory and public finance economics, where agents are depicted as passively deciding whether to free-ride or join a pre-existing organization whose existence they view to be independent of their personal actions. Instead, it invites analysis of the intrinsic satisfactions that people may derive from interactive, community-creating aspects of participation – particularly in middling and large Labour software projects. It thus subsumes the influence exerted on individuals' behaviors of the construction of elements of personal identity through participation in, and public subscription to, the ethos and expressed *mores* of the organizations to whose "causes" they voluntarily devote their efforts. Through the internalization of the community-generated value norms, the actions undertaken by developers *at the margin* of choice will – in this view – be shaped significantly by their *ex ante* consideration of the relative measure of peer-group approbation (or disapprobation).[27]

14.3.2   Peer regard and the relative normative valuation of development tasks: a specification

A formalization of such a normative system fits easily enough into the framework of a system of probabilistic weights attached to the elements of the set of marginal decisions with which individual members of an open-source project are presented. To make this very concrete we posit that the typical developer tends (statistically) to prefer lower-level modules to higher-level ones in the hierarchical structure presented above, since the former, more general ones, are regarded as more generally relevant by their peers than more specialized ones, and also because their visibility being higher, it will automatically grant their contributors more regard from their peers. Contributing to the "kernel"-module within the Linux operating system therefore would be deemed a potentially more rewarding activity than contributing to the file system, and the latter still dominates writing a driver for a new sound sound system.

---

[27] Especially when they are in C-mode, as opposed to I-mode.

Stated differently, we postulate here that there is a strong dependency between the emerging hierarchical architecture of the software system and the associated hierarchy of peer regard. Or, in still other words, we postulate that there is lexicographic ordering of rewards based upon a discrete, mainly technically based "tree-like" structure formed by the successive addition of modules. Some empirical support for this important assumption is provided by the finding that the pattern of signed and unsigned contributions in the Linux kernel project is not random, but is systematically affected by the structure of technical dependencies among the Linux modules (see Dalle, David, Ghosh & Wolak, 2004).

Still, in keeping with the "peer regard" hypothesis, and to also account for other observations by Raymond and others, we add the two further properties influencing developer choice:

1. Launching a new project is more rewarding than contributing to an existing one, all the more so when several contributions have already been made: namely, the first contributions to a given module are more rewarding than later ones – while this resembles the "first to publish" rule in open science communities, but in this context the payoff is not strictly "all-or-nothing".
2. Contributing to an active project is more rewarding than contributing to a stagnant or dormant one, as contributions will simply be more noticed by a larger number of peers.

This last property could be considered as a second-order effect, since it supposes that developers and contributions will be attracted by modules that already have drawn more numerous contributions, inasmuch as developers take signals from one another's behavior as to which modules are "interesting." But it also is a relevant consideration for individuals seeking peer regard that one's contributions, however technically astute, should have a contemporaneous audience.[28]

---

[28] The empirical study by Dalle, David, Ghosh and Wolak (2004) of the proportions of unsigned (uncredited) code in modules of the Linux kernel finds that the number of developers contributing to the package exerts no appreciable *independent* effect on the probability that code is signed (credited). This result – and other related findings – are interpreted in the paper as reflecting the greater importance for developers of signing contributed code when they are making comparatively smaller contributions to a multiple project which they join in the later, mature state, rather than for major core developers who become identified with a project during its early stages by virtue of their extensive contributions to its technically critical modules. Were it to be thought that an enlarged audience of "spectators" would induce a larger proportion of code to be signed in the expectation of gaining greater "peer regard," that would presuppose that there had been an *exogenous* increase in the size of the relevant audience – i.e. in the total number of developers engaged in contributing to the module in question. Yet, the findings on the joint determination of average code-signing propensities and developer participation in

14.3.3 Mathematical description

In mathematical terms, we therefore have the specifications:

$$\forall m \ \text{ a } \ \text{module} : \rho_m(\alpha) = r_m(x_m + \alpha) - r_m(x_m), \qquad (14.2)$$

where $\rho_m(\alpha)$ still stands for the expected[29] reward of contributing α to module m, $r_m(\cdot)$ is the cumulative reward function, i.e. the total reward associated with the sum of all contributions to module m, x_m is the current improvement of module m, i.e. precisely the sum of all past contributions, and α is a potential contribution for a developer's given effort endowment. Clearly then, by construction, for m' the virtual module associated with m:

$$\forall m' : x_{m'} = 0 = r_{m'}(x_{m'}). \qquad (14.3)$$

Thus:

$$\forall m' \ \text{the virtual module associated with module } m : \rho_{m'}(\alpha) = r_{m'}(\alpha) \qquad (14.4)$$

where $r(\cdot)$ is a (positive) increasing convex function in coherence with rule [1] above, which imposes that the first contributions are more rewarded than the later ones.
We will further consider here that:

$$r_m(x_m) = r_{d(m)}(x_m) = v_{d(m)}(x_m)d(m)^{-\lambda}\Big((1 + c(m))^{\gamma}\Big) \qquad (14.5)$$

where $d(m)$ is the distance of module m from the first "root" module; $v_{d(m)}(x_m)$ is the function which gives the version number of module m at distance $d(m)$ from the root from its current improvement x_m; $c(m)$ is the number of contributions received by module m, and $\lambda \geq 0$ and $\gamma \geq 0$ are parameters.

This simplification of $r_m(\cdot)$ into $r_{d(m)}(\cdot)$ is a direct consequence of the hierarchical and lexicographic assumption presented above – the reward associated with module m depends on its location in the software architecture only, as it depends on the height of the module in the hierarchical module tree, $d(m)$. This dependency is then given according to

---

the modules of the Linux kernel do not support such a supposition of exogeneity. Rather, it appears that larger modules (measured in terms of code size) exert a selective drawing power that results in larger average contributions of code per developer. If considerations of peer regard underlay the bias in the selectivity effect on contributors, that would suggest that the number of developers contributing to a given module was an endogenous variable, and that the selectivity effect (itself an indirect reflection of considerations of peer regard on the part of early contributors of larger blocks of code) worked to vitiate the emergence of a positive statistical association between the proportion of code that was signed and the total number of developers in the module.
[29] Part of the reward at least, especially for new modules, depends upon other contributions to be added later: therefore its expected nature.

characteristic exponent λ: when $\lambda = 0$ all modules are similarly rewarded, whatever their height $d(m)$, while as λ goes to infinity the effect on rewards of the module's height is increased:

$$r_0(x_m) = v_0(x_m)\left((1 + c(m))^\gamma\right) \text{ and } \forall m \neq root : r_m(x_m) \rightarrow 0 \text{ as } \lambda \rightarrow +\infty. \quad (14.6)$$

Since, by construction, the height of a virtual module is the height of its parent plus one, (14.4) and (14.5) above imply that:

$$\forall m : \rho_{m'}(\alpha) = r_{m'}(\alpha) = r_{d(m)+1}(\alpha) = v_{d(m)+1}(\alpha)\left(d(m) + 1\right)^{-\lambda} \quad (14.7)$$

where we note also that:

$$\forall m : \left(\left(1 + c(m')\right)^\gamma\right) = 1 \text{ since } \forall m : c(m') = 0. \quad (14.8)$$

By construction, the term in $c(m)$ in (14.5) above allows us to account for rule [b], namely, to render the more active projects – the "hot spots" – more rewarding for further contributions – even more and more so as γ increases, while this effect disappears completely when $\gamma = 0$. It is therefore not relevant for potential virtual modules, and the mathematical expression has been chosen in consequence.

We then define also:

$$v_{d(m)}(x_m) = \log(1 + x_m d^\mu), \quad (14.9)$$

where $\mu \geq 0$ is another characteristic exponent, which simply implies that it is easier to increase version numbers for high modules than for lower ones, and we easily verify that $v_{d(m)}(x_m)$, and therefore $r_\bullet(x_m)$ are positive increasing convex functions of x_m.

To complete the description of the model, what we are finally missing is a distribution of effort endowments α within the population of independent developers,[30] normalized by individual productivities to directly translate into potential "commits" (in equivalent lines of code) to some project module. We characterize this distribution of the sizes of contributions[31] on the basis of the relative sizes of the high- and low-activity

---

[30] Whatever their unit of measurement, typically in SLOC or in KLOC: if such a measure was to be selected, it should be noted that we do not differentiate here between lines added, replaced and deleted. As a consequence, a more appropriate measure of improvement would then be the sum of all lines added, replaced and deleted.

[31] Since, as we mentioned above, this model is for now a model of contributions and not a model of contributors: the heterogeneity of contributions is a consequence of the heterogeneity of contributors, and we do not track for now for individual developers or for instance for the history of their contributions, which would necessarily imply attaching idiosyncratic characteristics to each individual developer. As a consequence, the model presented here is not strictly agent-based, but is more stochastic in its nature,

segments of the developer population reported by the major web-surveys of developers, but simplify the specification so that the "code endowments" follow an exponential distribution function.[32] Using the classical inverse transformation method on the cumulative distribution (e.g. Ross, 2003), we then compute the following exponential random number generator, which generates contributions α from a uniformly distributed probability:

$$\alpha = -\frac{1}{\delta} \ln (1 - p), \qquad (14.10)$$

where $p \in [0,1]$ is uniformly distributed and δ is a parameter which controls for the mean of the distribution. Straightforward calculation will show that $\langle \alpha \rangle = \frac{1}{\delta}$, where $\langle \cdot \rangle$ denotes the expectation operator.

Simulation experiments can then be run easily according to this model: in discrete time, at each time step a new contribution is simply added to the existing system,[33] i.e. either an existing module is improved or a new one is created. The procedure is the following:

i. A random contribution is given by (14.10).
ii. The rewards of all existing modules, considering their current improvements, and of all virtual modules are computed according to (14.5), (14.7) and (14.9).
iii. A module is chosen according to (14.1), and the system is then modified in consequence.

Figure 14.2 represents a typical evolution of the project's code, and therefore corresponds to the abstract depiction in Figure 14.1, above (numbers for each module are version numbers).

To complete the mathematical account of the model, we should recall that the goals of this exercise include evaluating some properties of the emerging software. In particular, we are interested in measuring how sensitive their morphology (software-tree forms) is to parameter variation. Stretching the tree metaphor further, the obvious trade-offs of

---

accounting better for the intrinsic heterogeneity of economic actors through the observable heterogeneity of their actions.

[32] For the FLOSS-EU and FLOSS-US surveys, see Ghosh et al. (2002), and David et al. (2003), respectively. No distinction is made here for now, we do not make any distinction between different types of contributions, be they patches to correct bugs or the addition of new features – which Raymond (1998a) indeed characterizes as the correction of "bugs of omission." Nor do we account for the involvement of a small population of commercially sponsored developers, whose distribution of "contribution endowments", and module selection behaviors are most likely different from the rest of the project community.

[33] As in all the experiments presented here, the simulation starts with only the root module with initial improvement 1.

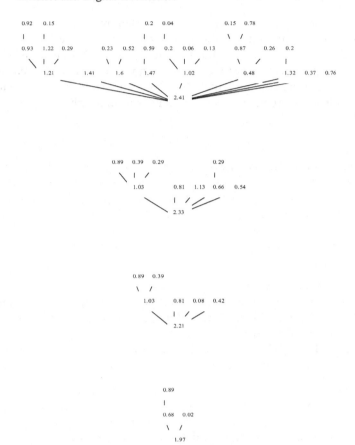

Figure 14.2. A simulation of the growth of a software project.

interest are those between the intensive development of a few main branches with big "leaves," i.e. modules, which may be supposed to be highly reliable and fully elaborated software systems whose functions in each case are nonetheless quite specific, or, alternatively, the formation of a "dense canopy" containing a number and diversity of "leaves" that, typically, will be less fully developed.

A simple way to characterize this morphology, which we will use below, is to compute the Gini coefficient of the distributions of the sizes of all the "leaves" – modules – of the code-tree. One motivation for taking this approach is the empirical observation of very high concentration of the code-size distribution of modules in large open-source projects, as indicated by high values of the Gini coefficient. This striking feature means that there are relatively few modules that attract numerous contributions, and a very large number that receive a limited number of contributions; indeed, quite possibly only one.[34]

A second consideration for examining features of the code-tree's morphology is that its variations would not be perfectly neutral in their implications for the social utility of the software product. Although this raises complex and potentially contentious issues, they are obviously important: the global performance of development in open-source mode in matching the functional and other characteristics of the variety of software systems that are produced with the needs of users in various sectors of the economy and polity, will affect the long-term viability and growth of this mode of organizing production and distribution. In taking a first step onto this hazardous terrain, we can use the simulation model to investigate the ways in which the specific norms of the reward system and organizational rules can shape emergent properties of software systems, such as its range of functions and reliability, that have a bearing on their social utility.

For this purpose we posit the following three "project evaluation criteria":

1. Lower modules are more socially valuable than higher ones because more users use them, and also because of the range of other modules and applications that eventually can be built upon them.
2. A greater diversity of functionalities is more valuable because it provides software solutions to fit a wider array of user needs.
3. Users value greater reliability, which is likely to increase as more work is done on the code, leading to a higher number of releases. Releases that carry higher version numbers are likely to be regarded as "better" in this respect.

We capture these principles mathematically and use them to assess the project code – according to the following social utility function:[35]

$$u = \sum_{m}^{(modules)} [(1 + v_d(m))^{\nu} - 1]d^{-\xi} \qquad (14.11)$$

---

[34] See Ghosh and David (2003) for code-size distribution of the Linux kernel's modules. Similarly, high concentration measures are found for the distribution of "commits" among modules of other large projects (e.g. KDE, Gnome, Apache) at http//libresoft/ dat/escet/urjc/cvsanal. One-contribution (and therefore one-contributor) modules could be created in *I-mode* and subsequently contributed to a project – following the global process-rules for *C-mode* behavior.

[35] Future versions of the model might introduce a clearer differentiation between functionality and reliability, with the idea also that different users might typically value both aspects differently.

where $v \in [0,1]$ and $\xi \geq 0$ are parameters, again in the form of characteristic exponents, obviously v controls rule (3) above, while ξ controls rule (1) and while the summation in itself accounts for rule (2).

14.4   Simulating the allocation of efforts in open-source software development

For the sake of the exposition, Figure 14.3 presents a typical assortment of trees generated in the context of the simulation experiments presented in this section. Like all the simulations reported in this chapter, they have been generated with a fixed set of "background" parameter values, excepting the values of λ and γ which control the main "reward system" – relating to peer-regard – we wish to study here. The fixed parameter set, namely

$$\begin{cases} \delta = 3 \\ \mu = 0.5 \\ v = 0.5 \\ \xi = 2 \end{cases}$$

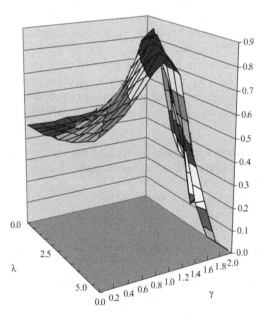

Figure 14.3. Gini coefficient for module size distribution.

can be considered as reasonable for this purpose, especially because results similar to those presented below are obtained with other values in their respective neighbourhoods. The one exception is that larger values of ξ tend to eliminate the existence of a non-corner maximum for social utility because their effect is to drive the maxima of the surface in Figure 14.4 toward a region with very high λ-values.

14.4.1 Simulation results on project architecture and the distribution of module sizes

Table 14.1 and Figure 14.3 present Gini coefficients of the module-size distribution for various values of λ and γ, i.e. showing that measure's dependence on the strengths of the two main "regard" effects in the model: λ controlling the influence of the inner hierarchy of modules within the project, and γ controlling the attractivity of "hot spots" – active modules. Clearly, there is a region of the parameter space within which both coefficients exert a positive influence on the Gini coefficient: one can see the boundary of that region describes a steeply rising "ridge line" in Table 14.1 along which the entries for γ attain a maximum in the neighborhood 0.86–0.88. The row maxima and column maxima for the Gini coefficient, which coincide along that ridge line, are marked in bold face in the table. In other words, there is a linear combination of λ and γ that constitutes a limit, above which the software system fails to

Table 14.1. *Gini coefficient for module size distribution*

		γ									
		0.0	0.2	0.4	0.6	0.8	1.0	1.2	1.4	1.6	1.8	2.0
λ	0.0	0.47	0.47	0.47	0.48	0.47	0.48	0.50	0.55	0.61	0.70	0.68
	0.5	0.48	0.47	0.47	0.47	0.49	0.50	0.54	0.60	0.70	0.83	**0.73**
	1.0	0.48	0.48	0.48	0.49	0.51	0.53	0.58	0.67	0.82	**0.87**	0.67
	1.5	0.48	0.49	0.50	0.52	0.53	0.57	0.65	0.75	0.85	0.72	0.41
	2.0	0.50	0.50	0.51	0.54	0.58	0.61	0.74	0.86	**0.87**	0.71	0.32
	2.5	0.50	0.52	0.53	0.57	0.61	0.69	0.79	**0.88**	0.81	0.43	0.30
	3.0	0.52	0.53	0.56	0.60	0.65	0.74	0.85	0.87	0.61	0.38	0.17
	3.5	0.53	0.56	0.59	0.63	0.70	0.79	**0.88**	0.72	0.58	0.15	0.17
	4.0	0.55	0.57	0.61	0.66	0.75	0.84	0.86	0.61	0.56	0.22	0.05
	4.5	0.57	0.60	0.65	0.70	0.79	**0.87**	0.83	0.52	0.22	0.05	0.00
	5.0	0.59	0.62	0.67	0.74	0.82	**0.87**	0.79	0.46	0.25	0.05	0.00

develop, so that virtually all the code growth is confined to a single (root) module.[36]

We certainly do not generate Gini coefficients as high as those found in actual open-source project code (sometimes over 0.99), because this would have been impossible due to the limitations of our stylized simulation. Furthermore, we do not account for the technical peculiarities of some specific modules in a software project like Linux – where the modules providing a great variety of "drivers" result in a multiplicity of comparatively small code packages, which contribute to the project's high Gini coefficient. Other simulation experiments were performed by altering the structure of the model and repeating the exploration of the same parameter ranges (as those in Table 14.1). These yielded results in which Gini coefficients typically remained low (i.e. rarely exceeding 0.5). This was, for instance, the case when we grew software systems:

i. Without rule [2] above, i.e. without the "hot spot" effect;
ii. Without rule [2], but with another rule, positing a negative effect that as the number of modules stemming from m increases, the incremental reward from adding further modules decreases.

These findings – and others to be presented below that exhibit high Gini coefficients – suggest that there is a positive association between the existence of certain "regard-based" reward structures and the observed characteristics of package size distributions within large open-source software projects.

14.4.2 Simulation results on developers' choices, project "release" rules and social utility

To turn now to results about social utility, Table 14.2 and Figure 14.4 show that social utility varies systematically with λ and γ. But the effect of higher values of γ, raising the attractiveness of "hot spots" of developer activity among the modules, monotonically reduces the social utility of the overall project code. In Table 14.2 only the column maxima are marked in bold face, to highlight the fact that these occur at successively lower values of λ as the attractiveness of "hot spots" is increased, and that the value of the column maxima themselves decreases. It will be seen, therefore, that the locus of column maxima, and therefore the maxima of social utility, *nowhere correspond* to the ridge-line region of Gini coefficients that appears in Table 14.1 and Figure 14.3. (Note that

---

[36] A close approximation to this boundary line is found as: $max\text{-}Gini = (0.1)\lambda + (0.43)\gamma$. As one may see, this relationship begins to break down for values of $\lambda < 1$.

Table 14.2. *Social utility*

	γ										
	0	0.2	0.4	0.6	0.8	1	1.2	1.4	1.6	1.8	2
λ 0	5.1	5.2	5.0	5.1	4.7	5.1	5.2	5.0	4.6	**4.3**	2.4
0.5	7.1	6.3	7.0	6.8	6.7	6.4	7.0	5.6	**5.4**	3.5	2.3
1.0	8.4	8.4	7.8	8.6	8.2	8.2	7.2	**6.5**	4.3	3.0	2.0
1.5	10.0	9.5	10.1	9.5	9.4	8.8	**8.0**	6.2	3.4	2.1	1.7
2.0	11.2	11.4	11.0	10.5	10.1	**9.2**	6.9	4.3	2.6	1.9	1.7
2.5	12.3	12.1	11.4	11.4	10.2	8.6	6.4	3.2	2.2	1.7	1.7
3.0	13.3	13.2	12.3	11.4	**10.5**	8.0	4.8	2.8	1.9	1.7	1.6
3.5	13.8	13.4	12.4	**11.9**	9.6	7.0	3.7	2.0	1.8	1.6	1.6
4.0	14.4	13.8	**12.6**	11.5	8.8	5.7	2.7	1.8	1.7	1.7	1.6
4.5	14.6	**14.1**	12.4	10.6	7.8	4.6	2.4	1.8	1.6	1.6	1.6
5.0	**15.0**	13.8	12.2	9.7	6.9	3.4	2.2	1.7	1.6	1.6	1.6

the γ axis has been inverted between Figures 14.3 and 14.4, in order to obtain greater clarity in the perspective imposed by the 3-D view.)

Although these results remain tentative, it is difficult to escape the conclusion that the "regard" motivations which we have hypothesized to operate within the open-source software communities of large projects are not conducive to generating socially optimal or even second-best optimality in the emerging functional design of software systems. To put it differently, and still more hypothetically, if the motivations of independent developers drive them to take decentralized decisions that are responsive to "peer regard" and imitative of "social fashion" within the project community (which would correspond to specifying parameters λ and γ in the "high Gini" zone), then the results could be considered as a less socially beneficial global outcome – at least compared with other situations where fashion and "regard" effects would typically have less potency in guiding developers' decisions.

Needless to say, this rather striking conclusion rests entirely on the specification of the social welfare criterion and the model's behavioral specifications. That it reverses some results on social utility effects, reported by Dalle and David (2003/2005) on the basis of a previous version of the model, is not in itself problematic. The present model, as has been seen, incorporates a previously overlooked "externality effect" – in the form of mimetic behaviors affecting individual selection of the location of code contributions that reinforce "herding" or "hot-spot" activity. While this enables the model to reproduce the skewed distribution of module sizes, it tends to restrict the development of a more diverse range of functionalities based on contributions closer to the

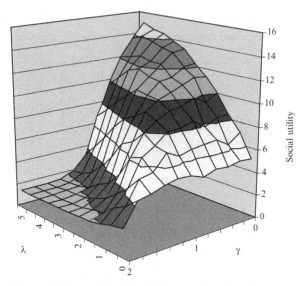

Figure 14.4. Social utility (without maintainers).

root of the system. But it is clearly premature to assign any finality to these results and unwarranted to accord them any significance for policies affecting the conduct of open-source software projects. Further developments in this still rather primitive model are needed, so that its structure and parameterization can first be fitted to other empirical regularities – such as the distributions of individual developer contributions to each of the modules.

Nevertheless, in view of the importance and intrinsic theoretical interest of understanding the factors that will affect the assessment of open-source project performance from the viewpoint of external evaluators, and final users in particular – which our social welfare function seeks to represent – we believe it is appropriate to call attention to the foregoing results. At the very least, it exposes the "instability" of the results yielded by the model during this still early phase of the sequential modification of its specifications. Indeed, one can do no less than report such reversals in results if we are to adhere to the general scientific norm of "full disclosure" – placing one's trust in the latter's efficacy in promoting rapid, cumulative advances in knowledge.

14.5   Conclusion

In this chapter we have reported an effort to construct a simulation model of software development in Libre (open-source) mode.

Obviously, the next steps can be taken in either of two directions. Following the empirical path and an iterative mode of development, we can seek to calibrate the model more precisely by using the empirical regularities (e.g. on the types and sizes of modules, and the overall architectural morphology) observed in a number of large open-source projects of various kinds. But there clearly are numerous research agenda items in view on the analytical path, many having been set out by our first report on this undertaking (Dalle and David 2003/2005), with several new ones being added in the course of the foregoing discussion. Perhaps the most important discrete elaboration will be the steps from modeling the tree to modeling a forest – adding typically a second "project tree" that may compete with the first for developers' contributions but also may benefit from experience that they gain in working on the "rival" project. Next we envisage exploring whether the dynamics of the system become markedly more complex when the forest expands to beyond two trees, allowing some projects to have relationships marked by complementarity whereas other pairs are substitutes as far as the production relationships are concerned.

Looking ahead on both paths, it seemed obvious that it will be beyond our power to adequately pursue on our own even the principal items in the vast research agenda that we have opened – at least not at a rate that can keep up with the proliferating sources of empirical data that a fully specified model could illuminate, and the multiplying policy questions that a carefully parameterized model could be used to analyze. Consequently, in a somewhat self-referential fashion, we are moving toward facilitating the conduct of the simulation project in the distributed open-source manner. The next version (release) of the model will provide not only the mathematical structure of a modularized simulation structure but also the source code we are running, and which others may use to replicate our results and modify the model – perhaps on general "share-and-share-alike" terms.

Whether this should formally become an experiment in the organizing of this kind of research on open source as an open-source-like project (with all that this implies about claims to licensing terms and governance norms) is an intriguing question. But, for the present, the "open science" mode seems to be a powerful and attractively familiar way in which to move forward, inviting others to join in the collective advancement of knowledge.

Part V

How e-markets perform

15 Economic insights from Internet auctions

Patrick Bajari and Ali Hortaçsu

15.1 Introduction

Electronic commerce continues to grow at an impressive pace despite widely publicized failures by prominent online retailers. According to the Department of Commerce, total retail e-commerce in the United States in 2002 exceeded $45 billion, a 27 percent increase over the previous year. Online auctions are one of the most successful forms of electronic commerce. In 2002, more than 632 million items were listed for sale on the web behemoth eBay alone, a 51 percent increase over the previous year. This generated gross merchandise sales of more than $15 billion.

The rapid development of these markets is usually attributed to three factors.[1] The first is that online auctions provide a less costly way for buyers and sellers on locally thin markets, such as specialized collectibles, to meet. Cohen (2002, p. 45) states, "It would be an exaggeration to say that eBay was built on Beanie Babies, but not by much."[2] In May 1997, nearly $500,000 worth of Beanie Babies was sold on eBay, totaling 6.6 percent of overall sales. While it may be difficult to find a particular Beanie Baby locally, such as Splash the Whale or Chocolate the Moose, you have a good chance of finding it online. Collectibles such as Beanie Babies, first edition books, Golden Age comics, and Elvis paraphernalia are among the thousands of categories actively traded in online auctions.

A second factor is that online auction sites substitute for more traditional market intermediaries such as specialty dealers in antiques, sports

We thank the editor, two anonymous referees, Ginger Jin, Axel Ockenfels, David Reiley, Paul Resnick, and Alvin Roth for their very detailed and insightful comments on various drafts of this document. Bajari and Hortaçsu would like to thank the National Science Foundation for partial research support, grants SES-0012106 (Bajari) and SES-0242031 (Hortaçsu).

[1] There are several interesting accounts of the early development of Internet auctions. Cohen (2002) chronicles the development of eBay through in-depth interviews of eBay founders, executives, and users. Lucking-Reiley (2000b) provides an insightful description of Internet auction sites and auction mechanisms across different market segments.

[2] Beanie Babies are stuffed dolls that are popular among collectors.

cards, and other collectibles. For instance, an antique dealer from Seattle explained why he closed his store on an eBay message board:

A couple of years or so ago my best buyers started spending their money at eBay. Then my pickers started selling on eBay instead of selling to me. Then when I went to the flea market and asked how much an item was, I got quoted what one sold for on eBay, not what the seller wanted for the item. I have a toy show that sold out for years, but nowadays all my vendors sell on eBay, and all the buyers are spending their money on eBay. I used to buy and sell a lot in the toy magazine before they got reduced to mere pamphlet-sized rags . . . Get my drift?   (Cohen, 2002, p.110)

Online auctions have extensive listings and powerful search technologies that create liquid markets for specialized product categories. The resulting reduction in transaction costs forced some intermediaries, like the antique dealer above, to exit the market.

Finally, online auctions can be fun! Many bidders clearly enjoy contemplating the subtleties of strategic bidding and sharing their insights with others. Most online auction sites have active message boards where one can learn the fine points of collecting. The boards also provide a sense of community for diehard collectors.

In this chapter, we shall survey recent research concerning online auctions. First, we describe the mechanics of the auction rules used on the most popular sites and some empirical regularities. An especially interesting regularity is that bidders frequently snipe, that is, they strategically submit their bids at the last seconds of an auction that lasts several days. Several authors have empirically examined sniping and proposed explanations.

We then survey a growing literature in which researchers have attempted to document and quantify distortions from asymmetric information in online auction markets. As pointed out by Kazumori and McMillan (2003), the "information asymmetry" problem constitutes perhaps the biggest limitation posed to the impressive growth of online auctions. In online auctions transactions take place between complete strangers who may not live in the same state or the same country, making it very difficult for buyers to directly inspect the good, or to make sure that the good will be delivered at all. This creates opportunities for misrepresentation of objects and fraudulent behavior by sellers, which may limit trade in these markets.[3]

---

[3] A number of high-profile incidents of fraud have occurred in online auctions. For instance, the FBI launched an investigation called "Operation Bullpen" that led to an indictment of twenty-five people for selling tens of millions of dollars of forged collectibles such as forged signatures from Babe Ruth and Lou Gehrig (Cohen, 2002, p. 308).

The informational asymmetry may manifest itself as a "winner's curse" problem, in which bidders recognize that winning an auction is conditional on them being the most optimistic among their competitors regarding the honesty of the seller. Auction theory then predicts that bidders will respond strategically to the "winner's curse" by lowering their bids, thus leading to lower prices and volumes in these markets. In section 15.4, we will survey empirical work that uses detailed data from online auction sites to test whether bidders indeed act strategically in the face of a possible "winner's curse," and whether this strategic response is large enough to prevent fraudulent sellers from extracting (short-term) rents.

Given the above discussion, a very important component of the online auction business is to decrease the informational asymmetries between market participants. A particularly popular method, pioneered by eBay, is the use of feedback mechanisms that allow buyers and sellers to leave publicly available comments about each other. In section 15.5, we will survey a rapidly growing empirical literature that utilizes data from the feedback mechanisms of online auction sites to quantify the market value of online reputations as defined by various summary statistics of user feedback.[4]

Auction theory, with its sharp predictions about the optimal way to design and conduct auctions, has become one of the most successful and applicable branches of microeconomic theory. Internet auction sites, with their abundance of detailed data on bidding and selling behavior, provide fertile ground to test some of these theories. On many Internet auction sites, sellers are allowed to fine-tune their auctions by experimenting with minimum bids or secret reserve prices. Several sites also allow the sellers to make choices regarding which auction format to use. Thus, empirical researchers can utilize such natural sources of variation, along with a newfound ability to set up randomized "field experiments" to test predictions of auction theory. In section 15.6, we discuss several strands of research addressing this purpose. We first discuss the use of Internet auction sites as a medium for randomized field experiments, and survey empirical work that has utilized this methodology to compare bidder behavior across alternative auction formats. Second, we discuss the use of both field experimentation and structural econometric modeling techniques to investigate the question of how sellers should set reserve prices for their auctions. In particular, we focus on the question of why reserve prices are kept secret in many Internet auctions. Third, we discuss the prevalence of ascending auctions on the Internet.

---

[4] Another article that provides a more in-depth survey of theoretical models of reputation is Dellarocas (2003). See also the survey by Baron (2002).

We consider alternative theoretical explanations, along with a discussion of new experimental evidence motivated by this empirical observation. Finally, we discuss the importance of taking into account endogenous participation decisions when conducting theoretical and empirical comparisons of different auction rules, since online auction sites typically feature multiple auctions that are taking place at the same time (and the sites themselves can be thought of as competing with each other through their site designs). We conclude with a brief discussion of open research questions that remain to be explored.

15.2   Buying and selling in online auctions

On any given day, sellers list millions of items on online auctions. These sites include business-to-business (B2B) sites and sites where the typical buyer is a consumer.[5] We will concentrate on the latter category since this has been the focus of most empirical research. On the largest sites, such as eBay, Amazon and Yahoo!, bidders can choose from a mind-boggling array of listings.[6]

These sites facilitate search in two ways. First, the sites have a carefully designed set of categories and subcategories to organize the listings. For instance, eBay's main page lists general categories that include automobiles, real estate, art, antiques, collectibles, books, and music. Within a subcategory, there are multiple layers of additional categories. For instance, the subcategory of paintings includes Antique American and Modern European. These categories are carefully designed by the auction site to facilitate buyers' searches. Second, users can search the millions of listings by keywords, category, price range, and completed items. This allows users to gather considerable information about similar products which is useful for forming a bid.

The search process eventually leads one to a listing page providing a detailed description of the item of interest. The descriptions are based on a

---

[5] See Lucking-Reiley and Spulber (2001). Examples are MuniAuction.com, which conducts auctions of municipal bonds, ChemConnect.com, for trade in chemicals, and Wexch.com, for electricity contracts.

[6] Lucking-Reiley (2000b) surveyed 142 online auction sites that were in operation in fall 1998. Exact estimates of the number of auction listings are few and far between. Lucking-Reiley (2000b) reported that in summer 1999, 340,000 auctions closed on eBay every day, as opposed to 88,000 on Yahoo! and 10,000 on Amazon (most auctions last seven days). Park (2002) reports, based on Nielsen/NetRatings surveys, that eBay had 5.6 million listings and Yahoo!, 4.0 million listings as of fall 2000. When we counted the number of active listings on January 25, 2004, we found 14.5 million listings on eBay and only 193,800 listings on Yahoo!. Our counts of Amazon listings were much more inexact, since the website does not divulge this information as visibly as eBay or Yahoo!; however, our estimate is between 500,000 and 1.5 million listings.

template supplied by eBay, but can be customized by sellers, and are often enriched by photos of the item. The user can see the current highest bid, the time left in the auction, the identity of the seller, and the highest bidder. The listing also displays the seller's feedback immediately next to the seller's identity. Users on eBay can leave each other feedback in the form of positive, neutral, or negative comments. The total feedback is the sum of positive comments minus the number of negative comments. eBay also computes the fraction of positive feedback received by the seller.[7]

The listing page also displays the minimum bid and whether the seller is using a secret reserve. The minimum bid is analogous to a reserve price in auction theory – that is, the seller will not release the item for less than the minimum bid. A secret reserve price functions similarly except that it is not publicly displayed to the bidders. Bidders can see only whether or not the secret reserve is met. Sellers on eBay pay an insertion fee and a final value fee. The insertion fee is based on the minimum bid set by the seller. For instance, if the minimum bid is between $25 and $50, at the time of writing the insertion fee was $1.10. The final sale fee is a non-linear function of the final sale price. For items with a final sale price of less than $25, the fee is 5.25 percent of the final sales price. Higher sales prices are discounted at the margin. Also, eBay has additional fees if a secret reserve is used or if more than one picture is used.[8]

At the bottom of the listing page, buyers can submit their bids. All three major online auction sites use some variant of proxy bidding.[9] Here's how it works. Suppose that a seller lists an Indian head penny for sale with a minimum bid of $15. At this price level, eBay requires a bid increment of 50 cents to outbid a competitor.[10] If bidder A places a proxy bid of $20, the eBay computer will submit a bid of $15, just enough to make bidder A the highest bidder. Suppose that bidder B comes along and submits a bid of $18. Then the eBay computer will update A's bid to $18.50 (the second highest bid plus one bid increment). The proxy bidding system updates A's bid automatically, until A is outbid by another bidder. If this occurs, the bidder will be notified by email and given a chance to update her bid.

---

[7] Similar mechanisms are used on Yahoo! and Amazon. Yahoo!'s feedback pages look almost exactly like eBay's. Amazon uses a slightly different five-star system to summarize the comments.

[8] The fees that eBay charges have been updated several times, with vocal dissent from eBay sellers in certain instances, such as when the site decided to charge a $1 fee to use the secret reserve option (Wolverton (1999)). Also, see Park (2002) for some evidence on the impact of network effects on the competition (in listing fees) between eBay and Yahoo!.

[9] Yahoo! also allows "straight bidding," i.e. bidding precisely the price you want to pay.

[10] eBay has a sliding scale of bid increments, based on the current price level in an auction.

Although all three sites use the proxy-bidding mechanism, they differ in how they end the auction. eBay auctions have a fixed ending time set by the seller, who chooses a duration between one, three, five, seven, and ten days and the auction closes exactly after this duration has passed.[11] On Amazon, if a bid is submitted within the last ten minutes of the previously fixed ending time, the auction is automatically extended for ten minutes. Furthermore, for every subsequent bid, the ten-minute extension still applies. Hence, the auction ends only if there is no bidding activity within the last ten minutes. Interestingly, Yahoo! takes the middle ground and allows sellers to choose which one to apply to their auction. As we will see in the next section, this seemingly innocuous difference in ending rules is associated with strongly divergent bidding behaviors across auction sites.

15.3   Last-minute bidding

Bids commonly arrive during the final seconds of an Internet auction that lasts as long as several days. For instance, Roth and Ockenfels (2002) and Ockenfels and Roth (2003) found in a sample of 240 antique auctions on eBay, 89 had bids in the last minute and 29 in the last 10 seconds. Other researchers, including Wilcox (2000), Bajari and Hortaçsu (2003), and Schindler (2003), have documented similar patterns. In this section, we summarize some of the proposed explanations for last-minute bidding and the related empirical work.

Last-minute bidding is difficult to explain using standard auction theory. Proxy bidding bears a strong similarity to the second-price sealed-bid auctions since, in both cases, the payment by the winning bidder is equal to the second highest bid. Vickrey (1961) observed that in a second-price sealed-bid auction with private values, it is a weakly dominant strategy for a bidder to bid her reservation value. The intuition is simple. If the bid is less than her private value, there is a probability that she will lose the auction. However, the payment the winning bidder makes depends only on the second highest bid. As a result, bidding one's valuation weakly increases ones payoff. Thus at first glance, it appears that bidders can leave their proxy agents to do their bidding and not need to wait until the last seconds of the auction.

However, this is clearly not what happens in practice and therefore several explanations for late bidding have been proposed in the literature. A first explanation, which departs only slightly from the independent

---

[11] There is a 10 cent charge for running a ten-day auction on eBay.

private values environment, is proposed by Ockenfels and Roth (2003) to argue that late bidding may be a form of "tacit collusion" by the bidders against the seller. In their model, bidders can choose to bid early or late. However, a late bid might not be successfully transmitted due to network traffic. There are (at least) two possible equilibria in their model. In the first, agents bid early in the auction and in the second agents bid only at the last second. Bidding late is a risk because the bids may not be successfully transmitted. However, late bidding softens competition compared with the first equilibrium.

Ockenfels and Roth (2003) demonstrate that this "tacit collusion" explanation of last-minute bidding equilibrium hinges on the assumption that there is a hard deadline for submitting bids. However, as mentioned in the last section, while eBay auctions have a hard deadline, Amazon auctions are automatically extended if a late bid arrives. Ockenfels and Roth (2003) then demonstrate that late bidding is no longer an equilibrium in Amazon-style auctions. They conclude that there are more powerful incentives for late bidding in eBay auctions than in Amazon auctions.

As a test of this theory, Roth and Ockenfels (2002) and Ockenfels and Roth (2003) compare the timing of bids for computers and antiques on Amazon and eBay. They find that late bidding appears to be more prevalent on the eBay auctions. On eBay, bids are submitted within the last five minutes in 9 percent of the computer auctions and 16 percent of the antique auctions. On Amazon, about 1 percent of the auctions in these categories receive bids in the last five minutes. Bidder surveys reveal late bidding on eBay is a deliberate strategy meant to avoid a bidding war. Similar evidence comes from Schindler (2003), who studies bidding in Yahoo! auctions for computers, art, and cars. In these auctions, the sellers can choose to have a hard close or an automatic extension, similar to Amazon auctions, if late bids arrive. She finds that, consistent with the Ockenfels and Roth theory, the winning bidder tends to arrive later in the auctions with a hard ending for all three product categories.

We should note that the empirical finding by Roth and Ockenfels (2002), Ockenfels and Roth (2003), and Schindler (2003) that there is less sniping in flexible ending rule auctions is not confirmed in all studies. Ku, Malhotra, and Murnighan (2003) study bidding in online auctions in several US cities for art that has been publicly displayed. The proceeds of the auctions were donated in part to charitable causes. The authors observe online auctions with both hard endings and flexible endings. They observe substantially less late bidding than the previously mentioned studies. Only 1.6 percent of the bids arrive in the last five minutes of the auctions with hard deadlines and 0.5 percent in the auctions with flexible endings. Also, Ku, Malhotra, and Murnighan find that for auctions with flexible endings, a greater percentage of the bids arrive in the last hour and the last day than for auctions with hard endings. This is not qualitatively consistent with Ockenfels and Roth's prediction. However, it is important to note that the authors have limited controls for heterogeneity across auctions that are held in different cities.

Several other empirical researchers have further examined the tacit collusion hypothesis of Ockenfels and Roth. Hasker, Gonzalez, and Sickles (2003) test the Ockenfels and Roth theory by examining bids for computer monitors on eBay. If late bids soften competition and lower the probability of price wars, then the distribution of the winning bids conditional upon a snipe should not equal the distribution of the winning bids if no snipe occurs. Hasker et al. find that in most of the specifications they examine, they are unable to reject the equality of these two distributions. They argue that this is inconsistent with the "tacit collusion" theory. Similarly, in a data set of bidding for eBay coin auctions, Bajari and Hortaçsu (2003) find that reduced-form regressions suggest that early bidding activity is not correlated with increased final sales prices. Schindler's (2003) study also casts some doubt on the tacit collusion hypothesis on the revenue front. Under private values, the Ockenfels and Roth model predicts that a hard close will decrease revenues for the seller.[12] Schindler finds that sellers more frequently use auctions with automatic extensions for art (82% vs. 18%), cars (73% vs. 27%), but not for computers (91% vs. 9%). Therefore, under the Ockenfels and Roth theory, the first two categories are consistent with seller revenue maximization while the last category is not.

A second theoretical explanation, also offered by Ockenfels and Roth (2003), is the presence of naive bidders on eBay who do not understand the proxy-bidding mechanism and hence bid incrementally in response to competitors' bids.[13] Ockenfels and Roth (2003) demonstrate that last-minute bidding is a best response by rational bidders against such naive bidders. They present empirical evidence that more experienced bidders are less likely to place multiple, incremental bids on eBay. This

---

[12] However, this revenue ranking may be reversed in an affiliated interdependent values environment.

[13] Based on survey data, Ku, Malhotra, and Murnighan (2003) also find that some bidders may be driven by emotional factors, which they label as "competitive arousal." For instance, one survey respondent from Cincinnati who purchased a ceramic pig explained her actions as follows: "[I] really wanted the pig, and probably also got caught up in the competitive nature of the auction." Another respondent explained her behavior by stating, "Auction fever took over."

evidence is complemented by survey evidence reported in Roth and Ockenfels (2002). Furthermore, Ariely, Ockenfels, and Roth (2003) conduct a controlled laboratory experiment in which one of the experimental treatments is an eBay-type fixed-deadline auction, where the probability of "losing" a bid due to transmission error is zero. Notice that this feature rules out the tacit collusion explanation; however, it is still a best response against naive incremental bidders to bid at the last second. Accordingly, Ariely, Ockenfels, and Roth (2003) find a significant amount of late-bidding activity in this experimental treatment.

A third explanation is based on a common value. In a common value auction, such as Wilson's (1977) mineral rights model, the item up for sale has a true value V that is not directly observed by the bidders. For example, the common value V could be the resale value of a collectible. Each bidder receives an imperfect signal x of V which is private information. By bidding early, a bidder may signal information about x to other bidders and cause them to update their beliefs about V. Conditional on winning, this may increase the price that a bidder has to pay for the item. Bajari and Hortaçsu (2003) formalize this intuition and demonstrate that last-minute bidding occurs in models of online auctions with a common value – in fact they show that in a symmetric common value environment, the eBay auction can be modeled as a sealed-bid, second-price auction. A similar result is also provided in Ockenfels and Roth (2003) in a simpler setting. This explanation also finds some support in the data. Roth and Ockenfels (2002) and Ockenfels and Roth (2003) report that there is more last-minute bidding on eBay antiques auctions than in eBay computer auctions. They argue that antiques auctions are more likely to possess a common value element than computer auctions, and hence the observed pattern is consistent with the theoretical prediction.

A fourth explanation for late bidding is proposed by Wang (2003), who studies a model in which identical items are simultaneously listed, as opposed to the usual assumption that only a single unit of the item is up for sale. Last-minute bidding is part of the unique equilibrium to his model. Peters and Severinov (2001) argue that their model of bidding for simultaneous listings of identical objects is also qualitatively consistent with late bidding. Taken together, these two papers suggest that the multiplicity of listings is another explanation for late bidding. However, it is not clear whether the Wang (2003) and Peters and Severinov (2001) models predict that last-minute bidding should be less prevalent on Amazon as opposed to eBay.

A fifth explanation is given by Rasmusen (2001), who considers a model in which bidders have uncertainty about their private valuation for an item. As in the model of Levin and Smith (1994), he assumes that some bidders must pay a fixed fee to learn their private information. This is not an unreasonable assumption in online auctions. In order to learn their private valuations, bidders will inspect the item and may search for sales prices of previously listed items. The fixed fee can be thought of as the opportunity cost of time required to do this research. Rasmusen demonstrates that late bidding can occur because bidders wish to economize on the costs of acquiring information.

The multiplicity of explanations provided in the literature regarding the causes of a seemingly innocuous phenomenon like last-minute bidding is a great example of how the analysis of online auctions enables us to appreciate the richness and complexity of strategic interaction in markets. The preceding discussion also illustrates how a seemingly simple empirical regularity can have multiple explanations, and that it is not easy to tell between these explanations without creative exploitation of sources of variation in the data. In this regard, the experimental study of Ariely, Ockenfels, and Roth (2003) is a good demonstration of how laboratory experiments can complement data obtained from real markets to help explain complex strategic interactions.

15.4   The winner's curse

In online markets, buyers are not able to perfectly observe the characteristics of the goods for sale. In the market for collectibles and other used goods, buyers value objects that appear new. Scratches, blemishes, or other damage will lower collectors' valuations. Since a buyer cannot directly touch or see the object over the Internet, it may be hard to assess its condition. This introduces a common value component into the auction and therefore bidders should account for the winner's curse.

The winner's curse can be illustrated by the following experiment discussed in Coy (2002):

Paul Klemperer . . . illustrates the winner's curse to his students by auctioning off a jar with an undisclosed number of pennies. The students bid a little below their estimate of the jar's contents to leave a profit. Every time, though, the hapless winner of the jar is the student who overestimates the number of pennies by the greatest amount, and therefore overpays by the most.

The winner's curse occurs when bidders do not condition on the fact that they will win the auction only when they have the highest estimate. If there is a large number of bidders, the highest estimate may be much larger than the average estimate. Therefore, if the winner bids naively, he may overpay for the item. In addition to the classroom experiment above, a number of experimental studies find that inexperienced bidders frequently are subject to the winner's curse (see Kagel and Roth (1995) for a survey of the experimental literature). Several authors empirically examine whether bidders are subject to the winner's curse and, more generally, measure distortions from asymmetric information in online markets. Two main methodologies have been utilized to answer this question so far. The first method, utilized by Jin and Kato (2002), is to sample goods in an actual market and determine whether the prices reflect the ex post quality of the goods they buy. Online auctions present perhaps a unique opportunity in the utilization of this methodology, since items sold in these markets are inexpensive enough to allow researchers to "shop" out of their own pockets or research grants.

In particular, Jin and Kato (2002) study fraudulent seller behavior in an Internet market for baseball cards. Fraud on the Internet is a problem. The Internet Fraud Center in the US states that 48 percent of the 16,775 complaints lodged in 2001 were from online auctions. In this market, Jin and Kato find that sellers frequently misrepresent how baseball cards will be graded.

Professional grading services are commonly used for baseball cards. Grading services produce a ranking from 1 to 10 based on the condition of the card. Cards that are scratched or have bent corners are assigned lower grades than cards that are in mint condition. Jin and Kato bid on eBay auctions for ungraded cards and then submitted the cards to a professional graded service.[14] Their sample contained 100 ungraded baseball cards. Of these, 19 claimed that they had a ranking of 10 (gem mint), 47 claimed mint (9 or 9.5), 16 near mint-mint (8 or 8.5), 7 near mint (7 or 7,5), 11 had no claim.

Many sellers of ungraded cards misrepresented the card quality. Among sellers who claimed that their cards were grade 9 to 10, the average grade was 6.34. In comparison, the average grade of cards claiming 8.5 or below was 6.87. The price difference between a grade 10 and a grade 6.5 for some cards could be hundreds or thousands of dollars. Jin and Kato find evidence that some buyers were misled by these claims. Buyers were willing to pay 27 percent more for cards that were self reported as 9 to 9.5 and 47 percent more for cards that were reported as 10. They conclude that some buyers have underestimated the probability of fraud and therefore have fallen prey to the winner's curse.

---

[14] They attempted to bid just enough to win the auction and to have a minimal effect on the actions of other players.

To establish whether the winner's curse problem is more of an issue on online as opposed to offline markets, the authors employed male agents between 25 and 35 years of age to purchase the same types of cards from retail collectibles stores in 11 metropolitan districts, and found that the fraud rate there (3.2%) was much lower than online (11%). Moreover, in their retail purchases, the authors found that retail sellers were more reluctant to quote the likely grade of the cards when one was not available.

Does this mean that online auctions for baseball cards are fraught with fraudulent sellers and naive buyers – a market that could use further regulation and intervention by third parties to operate more efficiently? Before we jump to this conclusion, we believe that a cautious interpretation of Jin and Kato's findings is in order. In our opinion, the main finding of this paper is that "while online bidders account for the possibility of misrepresentation, they might make mistakes when assessing the probability of fraudulent claims." It should be pointed out that the "mistakes" that buyers make are not likely to lead to very large monetary losses, since most items in this market are mundanely priced (between $60 and $150). Even for more valuable items, the estimated losses from buyer naivete are not very large. For instance, Jin and Kato report that the average eBay price for a graded 10 Ken Griffey Jr.'s 1989 Upper Deck Card (the most actively traded card on eBay) is $1,450. An ungraded Griffey with a self claim of 10 sold for only an average of $94.26. Jin and Kato's estimates imply that this self claim generated an extra $30 in revenue for a fraudulent seller. If bidders naively took the claims at face value, this would have generated a mistake of over $1,300 – hence the Ken Griffey example shows that bidders by and large do correct for the winner's curse. The issue is whether the bidders correct for this enough. Furthermore, the authors did manage to purchase a card of mint quality (grade 9) from their ungraded group. Apparently, taking a chance with ungraded cards sometimes does pay off.

Regardless of how one may interpret Jin and Kato's (2002) findings, their methodology to assess the prevalence of fraud and the magnitude of the corresponding winner's curse suffered by buyers is a direct and effective way to get precise measurements. Unfortunately it would be difficult, if due only to budget constraints, to replicate this methodology to examine markets for more expensive items like computers or automobiles (which are actively traded on eBay). Hence, the second set of papers we will survey utilize more "indirect" methods that rely on testing the implications of strategic bidding in common value auction models (in which bidders account for the presence of a winner's curse).

The first study we will summarize in this regard is Bajari and Hortaçsu (2003), who examine the effect of a common value on bidding for collectible coins on eBay auctions. The authors first argue that bidding in an eBay auction in the presence of a common value element can be modeled as bidding in a second-price sealed-bid auction with common values (and an uncertain number of opponents). The reasoning is based on the observation of sniping in these auctions: the presence of a common value element in an eBay auction suggests that bidders should wait until the last minute in order to avoid revealing their private information. If all bids arrive at the last minute, a bidder will not be able to update his beliefs about the common value V using the bids of others – hence his bidding decision will be equivalent to that of a bidder in a sealed-bid second-price auction.

Given this argument, the authors then test for the presence of a common value element using an idea first proposed by Paarsch (1992).[15] If the auction environment is one with purely private values, it is a dominant strategy for bidders to bid their private values, independent of the number of competitors that they face. If there is a common value element, however, the bids will depend on the number of bidders present. This is because when there are more bidders, the possibility of suffering a winner's curse conditional on winning the auction is greater, further cautioning the bidders to temper their bids to avoid the curse.

Bajari and Hortaçsu (2003) implement this using cross-sectional regressions of bids on the number of bidders, and apply various instruments to account for the endogeneity of the number of bidders in the auction. Consistent with the presence of a common value element, they find that bids decline with the number of competing bidders. They test whether bidders with little eBay experience tend to bid systematically higher, by regressing individual bids on total eBay feedback. While they find a statistically significant effect on bids, it is very small in magnitude. This is not consistent with experimental evidence that suggests inexperienced participants overbid and hence are more likely to suffer from a winner's curse.

Next, the authors attempt to directly measure the distortions from asymmetric information by estimating a structural model. In their structural model, the data-generating process is a Bayes-Nash equilibrium

---

[15] We should note, however, that Paarsch (1992) implemented his idea in the context of first-price auction, where the comparative static with respect to the number of bidders in the auction is ambiguous. See Athey and Haile (2002) and Haile, Hong, and Shum (2003) for more rigorous derivations of this comparative static result in the context of second-price and ascending (button) auctions.

where: 1) there is a common value, 2) bidders have to pay a fixed cost to learn their signal x, and 3) entry is endogenously determined by a zero-profit condition. Given this structural model, they estimate the parameters for the distribution of the common value V, the distribution of bidder's private information x, and the parameters that govern entry decisions.

The authors find that bidder's prior information about V is quite diffuse. In their model, ex ante beliefs about V are normally distributed. The standard deviation is 0.56 times the book value of the coin if there is no blemish and 0.59 time the book value if there is a blemish. For instance, the standard deviation of V for a coin with a book value of $100 with no blemish is $56. However, the distribution of x has much lower variance than V. For instance, the distribution for x for the coin described above would be normally distributed with a mean equal to V and a standard deviation of $28. After a buyer has spent the time and effort to research a coin, his estimate x is considerably more precise than his prior information about V.

Given their parameter estimates, the authors simulate their structural model to quantify the distortions from asymmetric information. First, they compute the equilibrium bidding strategies for an auction where all of the covariates are set equal to their sample averages (most importantly, the book value is equal to $47). The bid functions are roughly linear. In this auction, bidders shade their bids to be $5.50 less than their signals x. Given their uncertainty about V, the buyers bid 10 percent less than their signals to compensate for the winner's curse. Second, they simulate the impact of adding an extra bidder on expectation (since bidders arrive at random). When the expected number of bidders increases, the winner's curse is more severe. Bajari and Hortaçsu find that for an auction with all characteristics set equal to their sample averages, adding an additional bidder reduces equilibrium bids by 3.2 percent as a function of the bidder's signal x. Finally, they study the effect of lowering the variance of V from 0.52 times the book value to 0.1. They find that the bid function shifts upwards by $2.50.

There are two main limitations to their analysis. First, the results depend on correctly specifying both the game and the parametric assumptions used in the structural model. The common value model that they use is fairly strict. All players are perfectly rational, symmetric, and have normally distributed private information. However, they note that it is not computationally tractable, with current methods, to generalize the model since computing the equilibrium involves high-dimensional numerical integration. Second, unlike Yin (2003) or Jin and Kato (2002), the authors do not have rich ex post information about the realization of the common value or for bidder uncertainty.

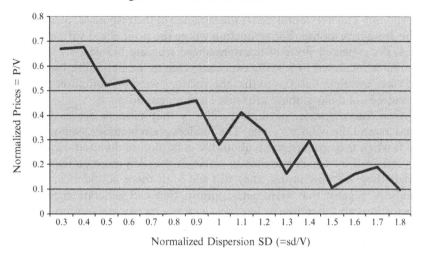

Figure 15.1. Bidder uncertainty and winning bids.

In a related study, Yin (2003) utilizes comparative static predictions of the common value second-price auction model to test for the presence of common values in eBay auctions for used computers. Based on numerical simulations, Yin establishes that bidding strategies in the common value second-price auction model respond strongly to changes in the variance of x, a bidder's private signal about V. Holding V fixed, if the variance of x increases, the bidder is more likely to be subject to the winner's curse. Conditional on winning, the value of x should be larger holding V fixed. Therefore, bidders should behave more conservatively.

Yin supplements her data set with survey information in order to understand how changing the variance of the signal x influenced bidding. To do this, she downloaded the web pages for 223 completed auctions and asked survey respondents from the Internet to reveal their estimates, x, purging information about the bids and the reputation of the seller from the web page so that the survey responses would primarily reflect bidders' ex ante beliefs about the item for sale and not the seller characteristics. By computing the variance of an average 46 such responses per auction, she constructed a proxy for the variance of x. The highest variance occurred in the auctions where the seller poorly designed the web page or where the object for sale had inherently ambiguous characteristics.

Yin finds that the winning bid is negatively correlated with the normalized variance of the survey responses. This is illustrated in Figure 15.1. The vertical axis is the winning bid divided by the average survey response. The horizontal axis is the variance of the responses, divided by the average response. For an auction where the normalized variance was 0.4, the expected value of the normalized winning bid was 0.7. As the variance increased to 1.3, the expected value of the normalized winning bid was less than 0.2. Given that the auctions were for computers worth hundreds of dollars, these are fairly large magnitudes.

One interpretation of these results is that bidders act as if they understand the winner's curse. The bidders are reluctant to submit high bids when they are uncertain about the condition of the used computer, as reflected by a high variance in x. Yet, if they are more certain about what they are purchasing, they will bid with more confidence. These findings suggest that asymmetric information can generate significant distortions and therefore sellers have a strong incentive to communicate what they are selling by designing a clear web page to reduce bidder uncertainty.

A potential limitation to Yin's analysis is that the variance of x for survey respondents may be an imperfect measure of the variance of x for the real bidders. The survey respondents' reservation values are roughly twice the final sales price on average. Perhaps they are not well informed about used computer prices. However, if the winner's curse is a strong possibility, it may be an equilibrium for a bidder to shade his bid to be one half of his estimate x.

Conditional on their caveats, all three papers surveyed in this section suggest that the winner's curse is an important concern in the eBay markets analyzed (baseball cards, collectible coins, used computers). Two of the three papers – Bajari and Hortaçsu (2003) and Yin (2003) – find evidence that bidders strategically respond to the presence of a winner's curse. Jin and Kato (2002) also present similar evidence of strategic "bid shading," but, through their ex post appraisal of cards sold on eBay, they argue that the amount of bid shading by bidders in the baseball cards market is not large enough.

As pointed out in the introduction, an important implication of these results, noted by Kazumori and McMillan (2003), is that depressed prices due to the winner's curse may limit sellers' use of online auctions to items for which informational asymmetries do not play a very large role. Kazumori and McMillan (2003) report that after several years of experimentation with running art auctions on the Internet in partnership with eBay, Sotheby's decided to discontinue selling art on the Internet as of May 2003. As the authors note, there may have been several factors that led to the failure of Sothebys.com. Fortunately, this still leaves the investigation of the question "which goods can be sold using online auctions?" open for further empirical and theoretical analysis.

15.5 Reputation mechanisms

Perhaps the most important source of information asymmetry in online auctions, aside from the inability to physically inspect goods, is the anonymity of the sellers. For instance, eBay does not require its users to divulge their actual names or addresses; all that is revealed is an eBay ID.[16] There are also very few repeat transactions between buyers and sellers. For instance, Resnick and Zeckhauser (2002), using a large data set from eBay, report that fewer than 20 percent of transactions are between repeated buyer-seller pairs within a five-month period.[17] This obviously limits a buyer's information about the seller's reliability and honesty.

To ensure honest behavior, online auction sites rely on voluntary feedback mechanisms, in which buyers and sellers alike can post reviews of each other's performance. On eBay, a buyer can rate a seller (and vice versa) by giving her a positive (+1), neutral (0), or negative (−1) score, along with a text comment.[18] eBay records and displays all of these comments, including the ID of the person making the comment. eBay also displays some summary statistics of users' feedback. The most prominently displayed summary statistic, which accompanies every mention of a user ID on eBay's web pages, is the number of positives that a particular user has received from other unique users, minus the number of negatives.[19] eBay also computes and reports the number of positives/neutrals/negatives that a seller has received in her lifetime, along with those from the last week, month, and six months.

A prospective buyer on eBay therefore has access to a considerable amount of information about the reputation of a seller. For instance, almost all of the feedback on eBay is positive. Resnick and Zeckhauser (2002) report that only 0.6 percent of comments left on eBay by buyers about sellers was negative or neutral. One interpretation of this result is that most users are completely satisfied with their transaction. However, another interpretation is that users are hesitant to leave negative feedback for fear of retaliation. For instance, Cabral and Hortaçsu (2003)

---

[16] Sellers are also required to list a valid credit card number.

[17] Resnick and Zeckhauser (2002) had data on transactions conducted on eBay in a five-month period, hence they cannot track transactions preceding this period. Within this time period, however, repeat transactions, if they occurred at all, happened in a very short time period.

[18] Other auction sites such as Amazon allow for more nuanced feedback. Amazon, for example, utilizes a scale of 1 to 5.

[19] In March 2003, eBay also began displaying the percentage of positive feedbacks along with the total score.

report that a buyer who leaves a negative comment about a seller has a 40 percent chance of getting a negative back from the seller (whereas a neutral comment has a 10 percent chance of being retaliated against).[20] Another factor limiting the potential usefulness of feedback, reported by Resnick and Zeckhauser, is that feedback provision is an arguably costly activity that is completely voluntary, and that not all buyers (52.1 percent) actually provide reviews about their sellers.

15.5.1   Empirical assessment of feedback mechanisms

Do online reputation mechanisms work? The fact that we observe a large volume of trade on sites like eBay, Yahoo!, and Amazon may suggest that the answer to this question is affirmative. However, there have also been a number of attempts to answer this question in a more direct manner, by estimating the market price of reputation in online auctions through hedonic regressions to estimate the response of market prices or stated willingness to pay to variation in measures of reputation.

Figure 15.1, which is adapted from Resnick, Zeckhauser, Swanson, and Lockwood (2003), summarizes these empirical studies. The first ten studies on this list have used data on completed auctions on eBay to run cross-sectional hedonic regressions of the sale price or sale probabilities of similar objects on sellers' observable feedback characteristics. The (log) number of positive and negative comments is used as a right-hand-side variable in almost all of these studies. Some of these studies also attempted to account for non-linearities in the functional relationship by putting in dummy variables for the existence of negatives, or dummy variables for different ranges of feedback. Some studies also explicitly recognize the truncation problem caused by auctions that did not end in a sale, and estimated a "probability of sale" equation either separately or jointly with the (log) price regression.

As Figure 15.1 shows, although the signs and statistical significance of the regression coefficients are mostly of the expected kind, the empirical results from these studies are not easily comparable, since some of them are reported in absolute terms and some are reported in percentage

---

[20] Resnick and Zeckhauser (2002) also report in a smaller sample that in 18 out of 87 cases (20 percent) where a buyer left negative feedback about a seller, the seller responded with a negative for the buyer. There is also the possibility that some buyers are more critical than others – although eBay allows users to observe the feedback that a user has left about others, it does not provide summary statistics of left feedback, hence making it quite costly for a prospective buyer to gauge the attitude of a particular commentor (other sites that provide user reviews, such as Amazon, allow readers of a comment to rate that comment on the basis of its usefulness).

terms. We should also note that the absolute number of feedback comments received by sellers follows a highly skewed distribution, reflecting a Gibrat's Law type effect. Given this, however, the starkest differences appear to be between sellers who have no feedback records and those with a very large number of positive comments. For example, Melnik and Alm (2002) report that the difference between 452 and 1 positive comment is $1.59 for $33 items, implying a price premium of 5 percent. Livingston's (2002) estimates imply a price premium of more than 10 percent for sellers with more than 675 positive comments, as opposed to those with no feedback. Similarly, Kalyanam and McIntyre (2001) report that a seller with 3,000 total feedback and 0 negatives is estimated to get a 12 percent higher price than a seller with 10 total comments and 4 negatives. The presence of a price premium of up to 10–12 percent between an "established" eBay seller (with hundreds or thousands of feedback comments) and a seller with no track record appears to be the most robust result among these studies, especially in light of the 8.1 percent price premium uncovered by a recent "field experiment" conducted by Resnick et al. (2003) to account for some of the more obvious factors inherent in the hedonic regressions, which we shall discuss now.

The first confounding factor is that the estimate of reputation may be subject to an omitted variable bias. Since there is very little negative feedback, the number of positives is essentially equal to the number of transactions that a seller has completed on eBay. More experienced eBayers are on average more adept at constructing a well-designed web page and responding to buyer questions. The work of Yin (2003) suggests that a well-designed web page has a sizeable effect on final sales prices by reducing buyer uncertainty about the object for sale. As a result, more experienced sellers (as measured by positive feedback) will have higher sales prices for reasons that have nothing to do with reputation.[21] Obviously, these factors could lead to biased estimates that overstate the market value of reputation scores obtained by sellers on eBay.

Ba and Pavlou (2002), Cabral and Hortaçsu (2003), and Resnick et al. (2003) attempt to reduce this confounding factor by manipulating feedback indicators independently of other characteristics of auction listings. For example, Resnick et al. (2003) conduct a "field experiment" with the help of an established eBay seller (2,000 positives, 1 negative), by selling matched pairs of postcards both under the seller's real name

[21] Standard models of dynamic industry equilibrium, such as Hopenhayn (1992) and Ericson and Pakes (1995), suggest that survival is positively correlated with measures of seller productivity.

and under newly created identities. They report that the established seller received, after correcting for non-sales, 8.1 percent higher prices than his newly formed identity. Ba and Pavlou (2002), meanwhile, asked a sample of eBay bidders to state their willingness to pay for eBay auction listings obtained from the website, with the twist that seller feedback characteristics were manipulated by the experimenters.[22] Cabral and Hortaçsu (2003) exploited a change in eBay feedback reporting policy: as mentioned before, eBay began displaying the percentage of positives starting in March 2003. Cabral and Hortaçsu run a hedonic regression where they interact different feedback summary statistics with a dummy variable for the policy change and show that the negative correlation between prices and the percentage of negatives is larger after the policy change, whereas the correlation between prices and total feedback score and the seller's age in days is smaller.

A second limitation of hedonic studies is that there is very little variation in certain independent variables, particularly negative feedback. For instance, in Houser and Wooders (2003), the maximum number of negative feedbacks in their data set is 12. Similarly in Melnik and Alm (2002) the maximum number of negatives is 13. In the data set analyzed in Bajari and Hortaçsu (2003), we found that only very large sellers with hundreds if not thousands of positive feedbacks had more than a handful of negative feedbacks. Obviously, it is hard to learn about the value of negative feedback when there is not much variation in this variable.

A third limitation is that the objects analyzed in the hedonic studies mentioned above are fairly inexpensive and standardized. Researchers prefer using standardized objects because it is fairly easy to collect book values, which are an important independent variable in hedonic regressions, for such items. Fairly inexpensive items are typically used because they are representative of the objects bought and sold in online markets.

However, it is arguable that the role of reputation is most important when a buyer is considering the purchase of a very expensive item of potentially dubious quality. When a buyer is purchasing a new, branded, and standardized object (e.g. a new Palm Pilot), there is probably little uncertainty about the item up for sale. When the item is expensive, used, and of uncertain quality, such as a hard-to-appraise antique, reputation might play a more important role. A buyer in such an auction might be

---

[22] There may have been some other confounding factors that Resnick et al. might not have been able to remove with their experimental design. In particular, some buyers may have been repeat customers of the established seller ID, and some buyers may even have searched (or had automatic watches) for sales by that seller and not even looked at the matched listings from the new buyer. We thank Paul Resnick for pointing this out.

reluctant to bid thousands of dollars when the seller has only limited feedback. However, such items have typically not been included in previous studies since it is difficult to construct appropriate controls for the value of such an item. In particular, book values for such items are probably not very meaningful.

A final limitation, which applies equally to both the hedonic regressions and the field experiment studies, is that it is difficult to interpret the "implicit prices" as buyer valuations or some other primitive economic object. In the applied econometric literature on hedonics, such as Rosen (1974) and Epple (1982), there is a fairly simple mapping from "implicit prices" to buyer preferences. The implicit price can typically be interpreted as the market price for a characteristic. Hence the implicit price is equal to the marginal rate of substitution between this characteristic and a composite commodity. This straightforward mapping breaks down when there is asymmetric information.

The winning bid in an auction is a complicated function of the underlying private information of all of the bidders. Only fairly stylized models of auctions would let the economist directly interpret the coefficient on feedback as a marginal rate of substitution between reputation and a composite commodity. In the framework of Rezende (2003), if the economist makes the following assumptions, then the standard hedonic interpretation of implicit prices is valid:

1. There are private values and there is no asymmetric information among the bidders about the marginal value of the observed product characteristics.
2. There are no minimum bids or reserve prices.
3. All bidders are ex ante symmetric.
4. The bidders cannot observe characteristics. The economists can.
5. Entry is exogenous and a dummy variable for the number of bidders is included in the regression.

Clearly, these may be strong assumptions in many applications. In particular, a large fraction of online auctions use minimum bids or secret reserve prices. Also, it could be argued that uncertainty about quality naturally induces a common value component into the auction.

Many of the papers in the literature do not articulate a primitive set of assumptions under which the regression coefficients can be interpreted as a measure of buyers' willingness to pay for characteristics (such as reputation) or some other primitive economic parameter. While this limits the generality of the conclusions, it is nonetheless interesting to know the conditional mean of the sale price as a function of characteristics.

15.5.2   Other tests of the theory

In addition to measuring the market price of a reputation, several other empirical observations have been made about feedback mechanisms. For example, Ba and Pavlou (2002) report that the impact of variation in feedback statistics is larger when the value of the object being sold is higher. This is consistent with economic intuition – the value of a reputation is more important for "big ticket" items. Jin and Kato (2002) and Ederington and Dewally (2003) find that for collectible objects for which professional grading is an option, sale prices of ungraded objects respond more to eBay's feedback statistics than graded objects. This is consistent with our conjecture above – reputation is more important the less certain the buyer is about the quality of the item that is for sale.

Cabral and Hortaçsu (2003) investigate whether sellers respond to the feedback mechanism. They use the feedback profiles of a cross section of active sellers to construct a backward-looking panel data set that tracks the comments received by the sellers. They find that, on average, the number of positive comments received by a seller until her first negative is much larger than the number of positive comments received between her first and second negatives. They investigate a number of alternative hypotheses for this phenomenon, in particular the possibility that buyers may be reluctant (possibly due to altruistic reasons) to be the first one to "tarnish" a seller's reputation. They find that buyers who place the first negative are not, on average, more likely to give negative comments than the buyers who gave the subsequent negatives. Moreover, they do not find an observable difference between the textual content of first vs. subsequent comments.

15.5.3   Do reputation mechanisms work?

Given the various results in the literature, it is natural to attempt to reach a judgment as to whether reputation mechanisms achieve their purpose of reducing trading frictions on the Internet. The robust growth in the number of users and transactions on eBay could be regarded as a testament to the fact that fraud is not perceived as a huge deterrent on these markets. However, a number of authors express skepticism about the effectiveness of the feedback systems used on online auctions. For example, the study by Jin and Kato (2002), which we discussed in section 15.4, takes the stance that the observed patterns of trade cannot be explained by rational buyers. The conclusion they reach in their study is that the prices ungraded cards were fetching on eBay were higher than could be rationalized by the frequency of fraudulent claims in their graded sample. They also found that although reputable sellers were less likely to make fraudulent claims and were also less likely to default or deliver counterfeits, the premium that buyers pay for reputation (after correcting for sales probability) is much lower than the premium that buyers pay for self claims. Hence they conclude that "in the current online market, at least some buyers drastically underestimate the risk of trading online" and that "some buyers have difficulty interpreting the signals from seller reputation." The study by Resnick et al. (2003) also concludes with the statement: "Nevertheless, it is hardly obvious that this reputation system would work sufficiently well to induce reliable seller behavior."

We believe the jury is still out on the effectiveness of the reputation systems implemented by eBay and other online auction sites. There is still plenty of work to be done to understand how market participants utilize the information contained in the feedback forum system, and whether some of the seemingly obvious deficiencies of these systems, such as the free-riding problem inherent in the harvesting of user reviews and the presence of seller retaliation, are large enough to hamper their effectiveness. As in the analysis of the "late-bidding" phenomenon, perhaps controlled laboratory experiments can help shed more light on how different components of this complex problem work in isolation of each other.[23]

15.6 Design insights from Internet auctions

Perhaps the most central question that auction theorists try to answer is: "What kind of an auction should I use to sell my goods?" Since William Vickrey's seminal paper (Vickrey (1961)), a large body of theoretical literature has investigated how various informational and strategic factors in the auction environment affect the decision of how one should design auctions.[24] Economic theorists studying auctions have also been influential in the design of important, high-profile auctions such as wireless spectrum auctions, and the design of deregulated energy markets across the world.

---

[23] A pioneering attempt in this direction is a laboratory experiment by Bolton, Katok, and Ockenfels (2004), which shows that while reputation mechanisms induce a substantial improvement in transactional efficiency, they also exhibit a kind of public goods problem in that the reporting of honest or dishonest behavior has external benefits to the community that cannot be internalized by the individual making the report.

[24] See the survey articles by McAfee and McMillan (1987), Klemperer (1999), and the recent textbook by Krishna (2002).

The dramatic development of our theoretical understanding of auction theory and the increasing scope for real-world applications also drive a natural need for empirical assessment of how these theories perform in the real world. To this date, most empirical research on auctions has been conducted in laboratory experiments. Such experiments are well suited for this purpose, since the empirical researcher has control over the design of auction rules and the flow of information to participants.[25] However, most laboratory experiments employ as their subjects college students, who are typically not experienced bidders and are given relatively modest incentives (by the yardstick of corporate wages). Hence, empirical researchers hailing from non-experimental branches of economics have frequently questioned the extent to which laboratory experiments can replicate "real-world" incentives.

There are, however, important difficulties with the use of data from non-experimental, "real-world" auctions for empirical testing of theories. First, in most field settings of interest, it is very costly to conduct controlled, randomized trials; hence statistical inferences based on non-experimental data are typically subject to much stronger assumptions than inferences from experimental data. Second, detailed transactions data from real markets are typically not easy to get, since such data are sensitive and confidential information in many industries.

Internet auctions provide an interesting and promising middle ground between controlled laboratory experiments conducted with student subject pools and large-scale field applications such as wireless spectrum auctions or energy auctions. First, data on bids are readily available from online auction sites, lowering this important "barrier to entry" for many empirical researchers. Second, as discussed in section 15.3, there are differences among the auction rules utilized across different auction sites or even within an auction site, and these differences can be exploited to empirically assess whether one mechanism works better than another. Third, empirical researchers can actually conduct their own auctions on these sites, which allows them to run randomized "field experiments" with experienced, real-world subject pools.

We now survey several examples of how the study of Internet auctions has provided novel and potentially useful insights regarding economic theories of auction design.

---

[25] For a comprehensive survey of experimental work on auctions, see Kagel and Roth (1995), Chapter 7.

15.6.1 Field experiments on the Internet

In a set of "field experiments," David Lucking-Reiley (1999a) tests two basic hypotheses derived from auction theory: 1) the strategic equivalence[26] between the open descending price (Dutch) and sealed-bid first-price auction, and 2) the strategic equivalence between second-price and English auctions.[27] As discussed in Milgrom and Weber (1982), the strategic equivalence between Dutch and sealed-bid first-price auctions follows quite generally, since the only piece of information available to bidders in a Dutch auction that is not available to bidders in a sealed-bid first-price auction is whether a bidder has claimed the object. But this information cannot be incorporated into bidding strategies, since its revelation causes the auction to end.

The strategic equivalence between second-price and English auctions applies only in a private values environment, where bidders would not modify their personal willingness to pay for the object even if they knew how much other bidders were willing to pay. It can be shown that with private values, bidding one's value or staying in the auction until the price reaches one's valuation is a (weakly) dominant strategy in both the second-price auction and the English auction. In an interdependent values or common value environment, however, seeing another bidder's willingness to pay may affect the inference one makes regarding the value of the object and hence changes her willingness to pay. Hence, as shown by Milgrom and Weber (1982), bidding strategies may be very different in an English auction in which drop-out points of rival bidders are revealed as opposed to sealed-bid second-price auctions, where bidders do not observe each other's actions and hence cannot update how much they are willing to pay for the object during the course of the auction.

Lucking-Reiley's experiment used the above auction formats to sell trading cards for the role-playing game *Magic: The Gathering* on an

---

[26] According to Krishna (2002), page 4, footnote 2: "Two games are strategically equivalent if they have the same normal form except for duplicate strategies. Roughly this means that for each strategy in one game, a player has a strategy in the other game, which results in the same outcomes." In this context, strategic equivalence means that fixing the valuation constant, bids should be the same across the two auctions.

[27] Briefly, the auction formats are the following: in the sealed-bid first-price auction, the highest bidder wins the auction and pays the price bid. In the sealed-bid second-price auction, the highest bidder wins but pays the second-highest bid. In the Dutch auction, price decreases continuously from a high starting value, and the first bidder to claim the object wins the auction and pays the price at the instant she called in. In the English auction considered here, price rises continuously and all bidders indicate (by pressing a button, for example) whether or not they are still in the auction. The auction ends when the second-to-last bidder drops out and the winner pays the price at which this final drop-out occurs. Bidders cannot rejoin the auction once they have dropped out.

Internet newsgroup that was organized as an online marketplace for enthusiasts in "pre-eBay" days. Lucking-Reiley invited participants to his auctions using e-mail invitations and postings on the newsgroup. To minimize differences across participants' distribution of values for the auctioned cards, Lucking-Reiley used a "matched-pair" design. For example, in the comparison of first-price and Dutch auctions, he first auctioned a set of cards using the first-price auction; a few days after his first set of auctions ended, he sold an identical set of cards using a Dutch auction. To account for temporal differences in bidders' demand for these cards, Lucking-Reiley repeated the paired experiment about four months later but this time selling the first set using Dutch auctions and the second set using first-price auctions.

Lucking-Reiley found that Dutch auctions yielded 30 percent higher average revenue than the first-price auctions, and rejected the strategic equivalence of the two auction formats. In the second-price vs. English auction experiment, he found that the auction formats yielded statistically similar revenues. However, he found less convincing evidence for the hypothesis that the two auctions were strategically equivalent. In particular, he found that in 81 out of 231 cases where the same bidder placed a bid for the same card on both an English auction and a second-price auction, the bidder's highest English auction bid exceeded her bid on the second-price auction.[28]

We should note that previous studies using laboratory experiments, by Coppinger, Smith, and Titus (1980) and Cox, Roberson, and Smith (1982), also rejected the strategic equivalence of first-price auctions with descending auctions. However, these experiments reported higher prices in first-price auctions than Dutch auctions, with Dutch auctions yielding 5 percent lower revenues on average. Similarly, Kagel, Harstad, and Levin (1987) report the failure of strategic equivalence of the second-price and English auctions in the laboratory setting. In particular, they report a tendency for subjects to bid above their valuations in the second-price auction, whereas they rapidly converge to bidding their values in the English auction, yielding 11 percent higher revenue for the second-price auction.

What explains the differences across Lucking-Reiley's results and results from laboratory experiments? First of all, as Lucking-Reiley notes, his field experiment cannot control for the entry decisions of the bidders: he reports that Dutch auctions attracted almost double the number of bidders as his first-price auctions, and it is not hard to see

---

[28] This finding does have an alternative explanation in that bidders have decreasing marginal valuations for the cards.

that an increase in the number of bidders would increase revenues. The cause of the higher participation in the Dutch auction remains a mystery: Lucking-Reiley argues that this is not due solely to the novelty of the Dutch auction mechanism, since market participants had been exposed to Dutch auctions before. One wonders, however, whether a "taste for novelty" effect may persevere over longer periods of time.[29]

Second, Lucking-Reiley's experiment cannot control for the informational structure of the auction. In the laboratory, the researcher can choose whether to run a common/interdependent value or a private value auction; however, Lucking-Reiley cannot predetermine whether bidders will regard his trading cards as private value or common value objects. This may affect the interpretation of his second-price vs. ascending auction results: in a common value environment, the second-price auction is predicted to yield lower average revenues. This factor, compounded with the experimentally reported bias of the bidders to overbid, may result in the observed revenue equivalence result.

One may think that the online marketplace utilized by Lucking-Reiley is populated by veterans of previous auctions, who are experienced enough not to overbid in a second-price auction – hence the theoretical prediction of revenue equivalence is more likely to be borne out in the field than in the laboratory. Lucking-Reiley briefly mentions this possibility, though more direct evidence comes from elsewhere. Garratt, Walker, and Wooders (2002) invited experienced bidders on eBay to take part in second-price auction experiments conducted in a laboratory setup. In contrast to previous experimental findings, Garratt, Walker, and Wooders found that bidders experienced on eBay do not overbid in second-price private value auctions, and very often give the correct reasoning to their action. Hence, field experiments conducted on online auction sites may indeed provide a more qualified subject pool for auction experiments.

Another argument for the field experiment methodology, as pointed out by Lucking-Reiley (1999b), is that in practical settings where a seller is trying to assess the proper auction mechanism to use, controls for endogenous entry decisions and on the informational environment will typically not be present. For example, the fact that a Dutch auction may lead to higher bidder participation may be an outcome variable of

---

[29] Lucking-Reiley also discusses whether the speed at which prices decline in Dutch auctions may have led to a difference between his results and laboratory results – in his field experiment, prices declined much slower than in the laboratory. Interestingly, Katok and Kwasnica (2000) find, in a laboratory setting, that slower price declines in Dutch auctions led to increased revenues as compared with sealed-bid auctions, suggesting that bidder impatience may have played a role in the field experiment setting.

interest to a seller considering switching to this auction format, especially since it leads to higher revenues. Hence, Lucking-Reiley argues that for practical or policy applications, results of field experiments may provide more insights regarding the outcome of a possible policy change.

The field experiment methodology also has advantages over non-experimental analyses of outcomes across different auction formats. As Lucking-Reiley notes, a non-experimental analysis of whether a first-price or a second-price auction yields higher revenues may have to worry about why some auctions were conducted using a first-price auction and others using a second-price auction.[30] We should note that the field experimentation methodology, as used by Lucking-Reiley, can shed light only onto partial-equilibrium responses to changes in mechanism design. For example, his finding that Dutch auctions yield 30 percent higher revenues than first-price auctions may not apply if every seller on an auction site decides to use a Dutch auction as opposed to a first-price auction.[31]

Whatever its pros and cons, Lucking-Reiley's paper is a good example of how online auction sites can be used as a laboratory for creative field experiments. Last but not least, we should point out that a very important advantage of this "field laboratory" is that it was relatively inexpensive to use: Lucking-Reiley's experiment had an initial cost of $2,000 to buy about 400 trading cards, which he claims to have recouped with a profit (in addition to a published thesis chapter) after selling them. Moreover, at the cost of some lack of customizability, online auction sites make it easy for the researcher to set up and track experiments instead of requiring her to spend a significant amount of programming time writing software for her own experiments.

15.6.2   Should reserve prices be kept secret?

Auction design is not only about choosing between formats such as first-price, second-price, English, or Dutch. As first shown by Myerson (1981), a seller may significantly increase her revenues by optimally setting a publicly observable reserve price or, equivalently, a minimum bid.

A look at sellers' practices of setting reserve prices on eBay reveals an interesting regularity: as noted by Bajari and Hortaçsu (2003), many

---

[30] Lucking-Reiley quotes Hansen's (1986) finding of systematic differences in timber lots sold using sealed-bid vs. ascending auction by the US Forest Service.

[31] Lucking-Reiley notes that the marketplace was active enough that his 80 auctions would not have a "market-wide" impact.

sellers on eBay, especially those selling higher-value items, choose to keep their reserve price secret, as opposed to publicly announcing it. This immediately brings up the question: "When, if ever, should one use a secret reserve price, as opposed to a publicly observable minimum bid?"

Auction theory has been relatively silent regarding this question, with two notable exceptions. Li and Tan (2000) show that with risk aversion, secret reserve prices may increase the auctioneer's revenue in an independent private value first-price auction, but in second-price and English auctions, regardless of the bidders' risk preferences, the auctioneer should be indifferent between setting a secret vs. observable reserve price. Vincent (1995) provides an example in which setting a secret reserve price in an interdependent value second-price auction can increase the auctioneer's revenues. Vincent's basic intuition is that the minimum bid censors some bidders, and the inference drawn by participants in the auction from this censored distribution may lead to lower bids than inference from the uncensored distribution.

Given the above theoretical results, especially that of Vincent (1995), Bajari and Hortaçsu (2003) estimate bidders' common value and private signal distributions in a symmetric common value second-price auction model of eBay coin auctions, and use these parameter values to numerically compute optimal minimum bid and secret reserve price levels to compare the revenues expected from these two pricing policies. They find that, at its optimal level, a secret reserve price can yield the seller 1 percent higher expected revenue.

Katkar and Lucking-Reiley (2000) question the validity of the behavioral assumptions used in Bajari and Hortaçsu's (2003) structural econometric model and attempt to answer the same question using a field experiment. In their experiment, the authors bought and sold 50 matched pairs of Pokemon trading cards on eBay, auctioning one card in the pair using a publicly announced minimum bid and the other using a secret reserve price that was set equal to the minimum bid. They found that the secret reserve price auctions yielded 60 cents less revenue on average (average card value was approximately $7). They also reported that secret reserve price auctions were less likely to end in a sale.

Although Katkar and Lucking-Reiley (2000) have a valid point in questioning the structural econometric approach of Bajari and Hortaçsu (2003), especially with regards to its imposition of fully rational behavior by the bidders, the field experiment approach they utilize is also subject to important caveats. For example, an important feature of Katkar and Lucking-Reiley's experiment is that the minimum bids and the secret reserves were assigned arbitrarily and were kept constant across treatments. However, under the assumption of seller rationality, a more appropriate comparison should be between the ex ante revenue maximizing values of the minimum bid and the secret reserve price, which might not necessarily be the same. Unfortunately, deriving ex ante revenue-maximizing values of the choice variables above is actually not a very straightforward exercise, since, as first derived by Myerson (1981), a calculation of the revenue-maximizing minimum bid depends on the distribution of bidders' valuations – which must be estimated from bidding data.

The previous discussion emphasizes some of the subtleties underlying the analysis and interpretation of experimental or non-experimental data from online auction sites for the purpose of evaluating mechanism design alternatives. The treatment effects estimated using a randomized field experiment, such as Katkar and Lucking-Reiley (2000), may not always have a clear interpretation within the context of a theoretical model. Structural econometric models, as utilized in Bajari and Hortaçsu (2003), have the advantage that their estimates can be readily interpreted within the context of a theoretical model, but their results may not always be robust to specification error or problems associated with the non-experimental nature of the data. The user of either approach should be very clear about the shortcomings of the respective methods and, if possible, use the two methodologies in a complementary manner.

Coming back to the question of whether empirical studies have taught us anything about the use of reserve prices, we should note that both of the papers surveyed here are unable to provide a very satisfactory answer to the question "if one reserve price mechanism revenue dominates the other, why do sellers persist in using the dominated mechanism?" Katkar and Lucking-Reiley quote an additional "benefit" of the secret reserve price strategy that their experiment does not account for – by setting a very high secret reserve, a seller may first screen out the bidders with the highest valuations for the object and later contact them away from eBay to run a private transaction for which he does not have to pay commission to eBay. On the flip side, Bajari and Hortaçsu (2003) mention an additional "cost" of using a secret reserve price auction: some buyers, especially new participants who do not quite understand the rules of eBay, may get angry upon not winning an auction due to a secret reserve and place a negative comment on the seller's record.[32] However, neither

---

[32] We should note that this is no longer possible on eBay, since feedback is restricted to being transaction specific.

paper provides a satisfactory reconciliation of these various costs and benefits to explain the patterns of usage of different reserve price strategies on eBay. We believe this may be an interesting avenue for future research.

15.6.3 The prevalence of ascending auctions

A casual observer of online auction sites will immediately observe the following pattern: all three major online auction sites (eBay, Yahoo!, Amazon) use the proxy-bidding format (albeit with differing ending rules, as discussed in section 15.3). In a much more comprehensive survey, Lucking-Reiley (2000b) found that 121 of the 142 Internet auction sites he surveyed in 1998 used an ascending auction format. Seven sites used a first-price sealed-bid auction and eight used a second-price sealed-bid auction.[33]

What is so special about the proxy-bidding mechanism, or open-ascending auction formats in general? A similar question was posed in an earlier survey article by McAfee and McMillan (1987) regarding the prevalence of ascending auction formats in the "brick-and-mortar" era preceding the Internet. McAfee and McMillan (1987) suggest an explanation based on the theoretical results of Milgrom and Weber (1982). As discussed in section 15.4, in many of the auctions conducted on these sites, a common value or interdependent values element may be present. As shown by Milgrom and Weber (1982), the open-ascending English auction yields higher expected revenues than its sealed-bid counterparts – intuitively due to the fact that a lot of information about other bidders' valuations is revealed during the course of an English auction and hence bidders are not as compelled to shade their bids to combat the winner's curse. This does not automatically mean, however, that ex ante, bidders expect to gain less surplus from participating in an English auction as opposed to a sealed-bid auction. The English auction can yield more revenue to the seller because more information is revealed during this auction, as opposed to in a sealed-bid auction. Left to their devices, bidders in a sealed-bid auction might have chosen to buy some of this information. Hence, from the perspective of sellers, buyers, and the site operator alike, the use of an open-ascending auction format such as the English auction yields benefits to all: the sellers gain higher revenues, the

---

[33] We should note that although first-price sealed-bid auctions are quite common in offline contexts such as procurement, second-price auctions are quite rare. For an historical account of the use of second-price or Vickrey auctions, see Lucking-Reiley (2000a).

buyers avoid the winner's curse, and the site operator gains higher commissions.[34]

Several alternative explanations for the prevalence of ascending auctions have been suggested in the literature. The Milgrom and Weber (1982) explanation applies to isolated, single-unit auctions. However, as Lucking-Reiley (2000b) points out, on sites like eBay there are many sellers trying to sell the same type of good simultaneously. Hence, one intuition suggested by Lucking-Reiley is that with open-ascending auctions, bidders may have an easier time deciding which auction to bid on. Peters and Severinov (2001) make this intuition more rigorous. In an independent private values setting where there are many simultaneous English auctions of the same good, they show that the following is a perfect Bayesian equilibrium strategy for a bidder: place a bid in the auction with the lowest current price and raise your bid as slowly as possible, until you reach your valuation.[35] The resulting equilibrium will then lead to all bidders paying a uniform market-clearing price, which is equal to the valuation of the highest losing bidder. Thus, there is no need for an active market-maker to solicit bids and offers from buyers and sellers and match them using a rule such as Walrasian market-clearing – the decentralized equilibrium leads to an ex post efficient allocation (one in which no buyer regrets the price at which she bought). Observe that although Peters and Severinov's prescribed equilibrium strategy requires bidders to be very attentive (or utilize the help of automated bidding software, versions of which are available on the Internet), the decision problem of a bidder facing multiple simultaneous sealed-bid auctions is considerably more complicated, leading in many cases to randomized entry decisions.[36]

However, there are also several reasons why sealed bid auctions may be preferred to open-ascending auctions. As shown by Holt (1980) and Matthews (1995), if bidders have DARA (decreasing absolute risk aversion) preferences, equilibrium bids, and hence the seller's expected revenue in the sealed-bid first-price auction, are higher than in the English auction. Moreover, as shown by Robinson (1985) and McAfee

---

[34] We should note, however, that the use of a hard-deadline ending rule can nullify this benefit of using an ascending auction, since rampant sniping leads to much less information revelation during the auction.

[35] We should note that in Peters and Severinov's model, all auctions end at the same time.

[36] This is not to say that there are not mixed strategy equilibria in the game constructed by Peters and Severinov; however, in many plausible versions of the simultaneous sealed-bid auction game, there are no symmetric pure strategy equilibria.

and McMillan (1992), collusion may be more difficult to sustain in sealed-bid first-price auctions as opposed to English auctions.[37]

Motivated by this empirical pattern, Ivanova-Stenzel and Salmon (2003) ran an experiment in which they allowed bidders to choose, for an entry fee, between a sealed-bid first-price auction and an English auction.[38] The authors report that when entry prices for the two auction formats were the same, the subjects overwhelmingly preferred the English auction. By varying the entry prices across the formats, the authors attempted to measure bidders' willingness to pay for the English auction. The observed willingness to pay for the English auction, however, was much higher than the profit differential implied by the risk-aversion explanation, which led the authors to conclude that there is a yet unexplained "demand" component that drives bidders' revealed preference for the English auction.

We believe that Ivanova-Stenzel and Salmon's (2003) study is an important first step toward understanding the economic forces shaping the demand for different types of trading mechanisms. Auction theory is almost exclusively couched in a "partial equilibrium" framework, where competition between different trading mechanisms is seldom studied.[39] Studying demand and supply patterns on the Internet may prove quite fruitful in future research in this area, since data on prices and quantities are relatively easy to obtain, and wide variation across markets/types of goods can be observed.

15.6.4 Endogenous entry decisions of bidders

Another theoretical question that has been put under empirical scrutiny by both field experimentation and structural econometric modeling is the endogenous entry decisions of bidders. As noted by Levin and Smith (1994), most theoretical revenue comparisons between auction formats take the number of participants in the auction as given. However, even on eBay, bidders may incur costs to bid in an auction, albeit due to the time they spend searching for the right auction or the time they spend watching the bidding come to a close (though some may also derive enjoyment from the process). Hence, a more realistic model of bidding

---

[37] This may explain why sealed-bid auctions are prevalent in procurement contexts, where there is repeated interaction within a small group of bidding firms. On Internet auction sites, free entry, geographic dispersion, and anonymity of bidders may make collusion much harder to sustain.

[38] The experiments were independent private value auctions, with the distribution of valuations kept constant across auction formats. The subjects did not observe their valuations prior to choosing the auction format to participate in.

[39] Two notable exceptions are by McAfee (1993) and Peters and Severinov (1997).

in an auction should endogenize the number of participants, where the bidders weigh the expected benefit from winning the auction against the cost of participating. This, in turn, means that auction mechanisms that offer different expected surpluses to the bidders will attract different number of bidders and hence the revenues generated by the alternative auction designs cannot be compared under the assumption that the same number of bidders participates in both. In fact, Levin and Smith (1994) argue that this may lead to a more general revenue equivalence principle, since expected payments to bidders should be equalized across two auction mechanisms when the choice is present, so the expected revenues of the sellers should also equalize.

The analysis of online auctions suggests that entry costs, and hence the endogenous entry decisions of bidders, are indeed quite important and should be taken into account when modeling the performance of alternative trading rules in such environments. Lucking-Reiley (1999b) once again uses the field experiment method to assess the entry costs of bidders in online auctions. He notes that when he auctioned several trading cards simultaneously, with zero minimum bids on each, very few bidders placed bids on every item, and argues that this is consistent with the presence of bidding costs. He also finds, not surprisingly, that higher minimum bids on otherwise comparable auctions resulted in fewer participants (a finding also corroborated by correlations reported by McAfee, Quan, and Vincent (2002), Bajari and Hortaçsu (2003), Lucking-Reiley et al. (2000)).[40]

15.7   Conclusion

Internet auctions are the subject of a rapidly growing body of research. Interest in these markets stems from two factors. First, Internet auctions are an inexpensive source for high-quality data. In empirical economics, our data are often an incomplete representation of the markets that we study. Often, the researcher cannot measure important product characteristics that determine consumers' choices. Also, we cannot always observe all of the relevant actions of buyers and sellers. In online

---

[40] A quantification of the magnitude of these entry costs, however, requires the imposition of a model of entry to calculate the trade-off between the expected benefit from participation and the cost of bidding. Bajari and Hortaçsu (2003) use their structural model to estimate the implied cost of bidding on eBay coin auctions to be around $3 – a significant cost, given that the average object in their sample was worth $47. It is interesting to note that several Internet services like eSnipe and AuctionWatch, along with eBay itself, have invested in developing technologies to make it easier for bidders to search listed auctions, to monitor progress in simultaneous auctions by creating watch-lists, and to place "snipe" bids in the auctions in which they are participating.

auctions, the economist is able to observe almost all of the product information that is available to the bidders. Also, the actions of buyers and sellers are recorded in minute detail. The exact time and amount of the proxy bids and the sellers' reserve price policies can easily be downloaded. Second, online auctions are a natural testing ground for auction theory. A substantial body of economic theory studies how to optimally design an auction. In online auctions, we can see how the mechanisms examined in theory perform in the field.

Given the easy access to high-quality data and constant evolution of these trading mechanisms, we predict that the study of Internet auction markets will continue to generate interest among many researchers. In particular, we believe that the study of these markets provides an exciting interface for experimental, theoretical, and econometric researchers to bring their methodological toolkits together. Some important research areas remain to be explored. For example, we believe that current research on the design of reputation mechanisms and rating systems to help resolve information asymmetries on online trading environments is still in its infancy. Such a research program will undoubtedly open new questions regarding how people process and transmit information, and how incentives affect these; we believe there are many interesting insights to be gained by observing the experimentation of Internet auction sites with different "reputation" mechanisms. The design of reliable feedback and quality-enforcement systems is of central importance to Internet auction businesses, and insights from this research program can have a lasting influence on the way their websites are designed.[41] We also observe many businesses sell their goods through eBay and other auction sites, often using fixed-price mechanisms (such as the "Buy It Now" feature on eBay) rather than auctions. In our opinion, the economic trade-offs between fixed prices vs. auctions are still largely unexplored, and the analysis of this question will benefit very much from careful observation of what happens on the Internet. We also think that important theoretical and econometric challenges exist in the analysis of markets with multiple simultaneous auctions – which is a more accurate characterization of market clearing on large Internet auction sites like eBay. Pioneering attempts like the work of Peters and Severinov (2001) exist, but we believe much more needs to be done in this area.

---

[41] In fact, as discussed in section 15.5.1 and in Cabral and Hortaçsu (2003), eBay has already changed the way it calculates and reports feedback statistics. The most recent site change, in response to user comments and internal development efforts, was implemented in late 2003. See http://pages.eBay.com/services/forum/newfb.html for the details of this change.

16 Consumer search and pricing behavior in Internet markets

Maarten C. W. Janssen, José Luis Moraga-González and Matthijs R. Wildenbeest

16.1 Introduction

Throughout economic history, changes in technology have had a substantial impact on consumers' search and transportation costs and, consequently, on the size of the relevant market. One example is the progressive decline in transportation costs that historically has taken place through the use of faster means of transportation (sailing ships, machine ships, trains, cars, airplanes, etc.). This reduction in transportation costs has made it possible for consumers to search for products in markets that were previously beyond their horizon. In our present times, the increased use of the Internet can be viewed in a similar way. Due to a reduction in search costs, the Internet allows consumers to become active in markets where they were not active before.

The general consensus among academics and leading businessmen seems to be that increased use of the Internet will lower consumers' search costs and consequently intensify price competition. The Internet is thus regarded as reducing commodity prices and promoting economic efficiency. Bakos (1997) argues:

> Electronic marketplaces are likely to move commodity markets closer to the classical ideal of a Walrasian auctioneer where buyers are costlessly and fully informed about seller prices . . . We expect that electronic marketplaces typically will sway equilibria in commodity markets to favor the buyers, will promote price competition among sellers, and will reduce sellers' market power.[1]

This chapter is a thoroughly revised and extended version of an earlier working paper that the first two authors circulated with the title "Pricing, consumer search and the size of Internet markets". We thank the editors, E. Brousseau and N. Curien, and an anonymous referee for their useful comments. We also thank J. Cáceres, C. Mazón, P. Pereira and S. Roy for their helpful remarks on previous versions of this chapter. The chapter benefited from presentations at Brussels (ECARE), Crete, Erasmus, Tilburg (CentER) and at the XVI Jornadas de Economía Industrial (Madrid).

[1] See also Bailey and Bakos (1997) and Vulkan (1999: F69–70).

Moreover, Jeff Bezos, founder of Amazon.com has argued:

We on the Internet should be terrified of customers because they are loyal to us right up to the point that someone else offers a better service. The power shifts to the consumer online.[2]

This chapter is an attempt to put these quotations into perspective. We first give an overview of the relevant empirical literature. This literature provides a mixed view of the effectiveness of online markets in bringing down prices to competitive levels. We then present a simple endogenous search model that identifies basic market conditions that may help explain and organize the mixed empirical evidence. By doing so, we develop a more cautious view on the economic implications of electronic market-places than the consensus view expressed in the above quotes.

The model's economy has firms producing a homogeneous product at a unit cost r and competing to sell their good to a number of consumers. There are two types of consumers: *informed* buyers who incur no search cost and *less informed* consumers who have positive search cost c. We shall use the percentage of informed consumers in the economy as a proxy for the rate of adoption of search engines. For simplicity, all consumers have identical willingness-to-pay $v > c + r$. We will refer to $(v - r)/c$ as the *relative size of the purchase*. Firms simultaneously choose prices and announce them on the web. Less informed consumers decide how many searches to make before buying. These buyers can also abstain from searching when they expect the search not to be worthwhile. In equilibrium, consumer expectations are fulfilled. Hence, the interaction between firms and buyers is modeled as a simultaneous move game, where (in equilibrium) consumers' search activity impinges on the prices quoted by firms, and the price-setting behavior of firms influences buyers' search activity.

There are three types of price-dispersed equilibria in our economy: (i) an equilibrium with *low* search intensity, i.e., where less informed consumers randomize between one search and no search; (ii) an equilibrium with *moderate* search intensity, i.e., where less informed buyers search for one price; and (iii) a *high* search intensity equilibrium, i.e., where consumers randomize between one search and two searches. Relative size of the purchase and the rate of adoption of search engines in the Internet market determine buyers' search incentives. A first lesson our analysis yields is the existence of a correlation between buyers' search propensity and the product's value. That is, a high search intensity equilibrium arises when the relative size of the purchase is large, ceteris paribus. In contrast,

---

[2] Quoted in Victoria Griffith (1999).

a low or a moderate search intensity equilibrium results when the search cost is relatively important compared with the size of the purchase.

Our second main observation pertains to comparative statics results. We find that the impact of improved search technology on market transparency critically depends on market characteristics. We pinpoint the nature of this dependence in more detail below. Consider first that improved search technology results in a decline in search cost c, ceteris paribus. When both the size of the purchase and the search engines adoption rate are low, expected price-to-cost margins rise as c falls because more consumers who do not compare prices enter the market. Price dispersion, in contrast, increases when search cost is high initially, and falls otherwise. However, when the relative size of the purchase is high, expected price-to-cost margins and price dispersion unambiguously decline with c because more buyers exercise price comparisons in this case. In between, when the relative size of the purchase is not very low and not very high, price-to-cost margins and price dispersion are unaffected by a change in c.

Second, consider that improved search technology results in an increase in the search engine rate of adoption. When the size of the purchase is low and the adoption rate of search engines is also low initially, an increase in the number of informed buyers leaves expected price-to-cost margins and price dispersion unchanged. When the rate of adoption of search engines in the market is quite high initially, in contrast, an increase in the number of informed buyers reduces average price-to-cost margins and price dispersion. Finally, when the size of the purchase is large, expected price-to-cost margins and price dispersion are (again) insensitive to changes in the number of informed buyers.

The remainder of the chapter is organized as follows. Section 16.2 provides a more detailed overview of the relevant literature. Here, we first discuss the different empirical studies that have been carried out so far concerning prices and price dispersion on the Internet. We then briefly discuss the consumer search literature and other more theoretical approaches to studying online markets. Section 16.3 describes the simple search model we use and its equilibria. Section 16.4 gives the comparative statics analysis of the model and relates the results to the findings of other studies. We conclude in that section that the mixed empirical evidence found in other studies can be explained by our finding from the comparative statics that firms' pricing behavior depends on market characteristics. However, other studies do not take into account the specific market characteristics that we find to be important. In Section 16.5 we conclude and we discuss some of our ideas for an empirical analysis that is able to control for the theoretical forces that are relevant.

16.2   Overview of the relevant literature

A study of the implications of the easiness with which consumers may search and compare firms' offerings on the Internet on the competitiveness of online markets has two main branches of literature to discuss. First, there is a large and relatively recent empirical literature on prices and price dispersion in online markets. Second, there is a large theoretical literature on consumer search. In this section, we first discuss these two branches of literature before we briefly dwell upon other issues related to online markets that have attracted the attention of economists.

The turn of the millennium has seen many empirical studies investigating whether Internet markets bring market prices closer to their competitive levels. The commonly held theoretical point of view, as indicated by the two quotes from the Introduction, seemed to be that as it is easier for consumers to compare firms' offerings, consumers will exercise more countervailing market power, which should lead to lower market prices and less price dispersion. Below, we will see that empirical studies do not unambiguously support this view. Concerning *price levels* in electronic markets, some studies, notably Lee (1998) and Lee et al. (1999) on cars, and Bailey (1998) on books and CDs, find that they are higher than corresponding prices in conventional markets. Lee (1998) was one of the first to study the impact of the Internet on price levels. He compares prices in online auctions for second-hand cars to similar prices in conventional auctions. The fact that he found higher online prices should be considered with some care as (i) second-hand cars are not a homogeneous good (and quality may be higher in online auctions compared with conventional auctions), and (ii) auctions may very well function in a different way from retail markets due to the fact that in auctions the good is sold to the bidder with the highest valuation. These potential problems with the interpretation of the results do not arise in Bailey (1998), since books and CDs are entirely homogeneous goods. His observations could be due to a low rate of adoption of search engines in Internet markets at that point in time. Other analyses – Friberg et al. (2000) and Clay et al. (2002) on books – report that prices in online and physical stores are quite similar. The study of Friberg et al. (2000) is interesting in this context as they take into account the shipping and handling fees that are charged on online purchases. Not taking these additional fees into account results in the conclusion that online prices are lower, the difference being very well accounted for by the size of the shipping and handling fees that are charged. Finally, Brynjolfsson and Smith (2000) in a study on books and CDs find prices to be lower in electronic markets, even when taking into account the additional online fees that are charged.[3]

On *price dispersion*, the effect of moving markets online also seems to be empirically ambiguous. Price dispersion is typically explained in the literature with reference to search costs and arises as some consumers do not search more than once while others search more often. A reduction in search costs associated with online sales should bring search costs down and therefore should reduce (at first sight) the amount of price dispersion. Bailey (1998) and Brynjolfsson and Smith (2000), however, find that price dispersion for books and CDs is not lower online than in traditional outlets. According to Brynjolfsson and Smith (2000), online price differences average up to 33% for books and 25% for CDs. Bailey (1998) notes that the opposite holds for software and that in these markets online price dispersion seems to be lower. Other studies also emphasize that online prices exhibit substantial dispersion (Baye and Morgan, 2001; Brown and Goolsbee, 2002; Clay et al., 2002).[4] The study by Clemons et al. (2002) is also interesting in this respect. They find that online airline tickets may differ as much as 20% across different agents, even when controlling for observable product heterogeneity.

Another interesting observation in the context of search and online markets can be found in the empirical study by Eric Johnson et al. (2004). These authors study data on how many times people search (i.e., how many sites they visit) before making a purchase. Johnson et al. (2004) report that travel shoppers search substantially more than CD shoppers and book purchasers. Incipient research accounting for consumers' search behavior on the Internet finds that 70% of CD shoppers, 70% of book purchasers and 36% of travel buyers were observed to visit just one site. The main issue to note is that it is easy to visit an Internet site, but it still takes some time to find a particular book or CD and to order it. For a few dollars purchase, it does not seem to be worthwhile to search over and over again. Since higher search activity is naturally associated with lower price levels, one would expect lower price-cost margins for products whose value is higher. This may explain an empirical result found by Clay et al. (2001), namely that bestseller books in online markets are generally more discounted than books at random.

---

[3] Reports by consultant companies Ernst & Young, Forrester Research and Goldman Sachs have also reached opposite conclusions (OECD, 1999: 73).

[4] See Smith et al. (2000) for an overview of some of these empirical findings and a discussion of the different methodologies employed.

From the viewpoint of our analysis, search is more intense in the market for bestseller books as buyers value them more.[5] The other literature that is relevant to our study is the one on consumer search. There is a vast literature on this subject and we refer to Stiglitz (1989) and Stahl (1996) for surveys of the early literature. We will restrict ourselves to an overview of two classic papers in the search literature: Burdett and Judd (1983) and Stahl (1989).[6] Burdett and Judd present a competitive market with firms pricing non-strategically and consumers search non-sequentially, i.e., they have to decide how many firms to sample before they see the results of their search activities. The model has only less informed consumers who get a first price quotation for free. They show that equilibrium price dispersion may occur in competitive markets when consumers randomize between searching for two prices and searching for one price, in a non-sequential fashion. Our analysis presented in the next two sections also studies non-sequential search and the price-dispersed equilibria we obtain are similar in nature. Our model is, however, more suited for studying the implications of the growth of Internet use for the following two reasons. First, we allow for the presence of fully informed consumers (consumers without search costs). This implies that, in contrast to Burdett and Judd, our model does not have a monopoly price equilibrium and that all the equilibria of our model exhibit price dispersion. More importantly, the increase in the search engine rate of adoption makes it important to study the impact of a growing number of fully informed consumers. Second, Burdett and Judd assume that each consumer makes at least one search. As argued above, consumers are steadily entering electronic markets and thus we think that in the context of the Internet discussion, it is important to allow for the possibility that consumers (previously) were not searching, or were searching with low intensity.

Stahl (1989) studies a search model where firms price strategically and less informed buyers search sequentially, i.e., they first observe one price and then decide whether or not to observe a second price, and so on. The first price quotation is observed for free, which implies that every buyer makes at least one search. Moreover, under the optimal sequential

---

[5] Sorensen (2000) presents similar evidence in a study of price dispersion in *physical* markets for prescription drugs. He finds that mean prices and price dispersion are sensitive to the characteristics of the drug therapy. In particular, long (multi-month) prescriptions mean prices and price dispersion are lower compared with regular drug therapies. Seen from our model viewpoint, the market for long treatment drugs would be in an equilibrium with relatively lots of search compared with the market for regular prescriptions.

[6] An early paper with a model similar to ours is Varian (1980); however, he did not consider endogenous non-sequential consumers' search. Fershtman and Fishman (1992) study a dynamic version of Burdett and Judd (1983).

search rule a consumer continues searching if, and only if, the observed prices are above a certain reservation price. This implies that in equilibrium no firm charges prices above the reservation price so that, in fact, in every equilibrium buyers search only once. The unique equilibrium of Stahl's model displays properties that are qualitatively similar to properties of our moderate or high search intensity equilibrium. The sequential search model cannot, however, explain why there is more search in some markets than in others, a feature that is captured in our model by the presence of low and high search intensity equilibria. Using the qualitative properties of these two equilibria allows us to explain some of the empirical findings concerning electronic marketplaces.[7]

Of course, apart from changes in search parameters in a homogeneous market there are many other issues that are relevant when comparing online to more conventional markets. Recently, a few papers have appeared that reflect in a more formal way on the changes in the nature of price competition due to the introduction of the Internet. Some of these papers, Bakos (1997) and Lal and Sarvary (1999) among others, study heterogeneous goods markets, as they argue that in homogeneous markets it is evident that a reduction in search cost will intensify price competition. As already indicated, our chapter argues that this is not necessarily the case.

16.3   Results from a simple search model

We present a simple search model which is used to explain some of the different observations concerning Internet markets. Consider a market for a homogeneous good. On the supply side of the market there are two firms.[8] Firms produce the good at constant returns to scale with identical unit cost equal to r. There is a unit mass of buyers who wish to purchase at most a single unit of the good. A fraction λ of the consumers search for prices costlessly, $0 < \lambda < 1$. We will refer to these buyers as *informed* and we will use this variable as a proxy for the rate of adoption of search engines. The other buyers must pay search cost $c > 0$ to observe a price quotation. These buyers, referred to as *less informed*, may decide to obtain several price quotations, say $n \geq 0$, in which case they incur search cost equal to nc. Informed consumers buy the good

---

[7] Morgan and Manning (1985) have derived optimal search strategies which combine features of the fixed-sample-size search strategy and the sequential search strategy. Our search method seems more adequate when price observations come after some delay. One of the authors has been recently looking for an apartment in Rotterdam. In this market one must first register electronically at a number of real estate agents to be able to receive offers.

[8] A full analysis of the N firm case including all the derivations of some of the claims we make here can be found in Janssen and Moraga-González (2004).

from the lowest priced store, while less informed ones acquire it from the store with the sampled lowest price. The maximum price any buyer is willing to pay for the good is v, with $v > c + r$. We shall refer to $(v - r)/c$ as the *relative size of the purchase*.

Firms and buyers play a simultaneous moves game. An individual firm chooses its price taking price choices of the rivals as well as consumers' search behavior as given. Buyers form conjectures about the distribution of prices in the market and decide how many prices to observe before purchasing from the store with the lowest observed price. Let $F(p)$ denote the distribution of prices charged by a firm. Let μ_n denote the probability with which a less informed buyer searches for n price quotations. Let $\pi(\cdot)$ be the profits attained by a firm. We consider only symmetric equilibria. An equilibrium is a pair $\{F(p), \{\mu_n\}_{n=0}^N\}$ such that (a) $\pi(p) = \bar{\pi}$ for all p in the support of $F(p)$, (b) $\pi(p) \leq \bar{\pi}$ for all p, and (c) $\{\mu_n\}_{n=0}^N$ describes the optimal search behavior of less informed buyers given that their conjectures about the price distribution are correct.

Janssen and Moraga-González (2004) show that the following alternatives exhaust the equilibrium possibilities of less-informed buyers' search behavior: (a) they search with *low intensity*, i.e., $0 < \mu_1 < 1$, $\mu_0 + \mu_1 = 1$, (b) they search with *high intensity*, i.e., $0 < \mu_1 \leq 1$, $\mu_1 + \mu_2 = 1$, finally (c) they search with *moderate intensity*, i.e., $\mu_1 = 1$. This holds for an arbitrary number of firms N. We will study each of these three equilibrium configurations in turn.

Case a: Low search intensity
Consider that less informed buyers randomize between searching for one price and not searching at all, i.e., $\mu_0 > 0$, $\mu_0 + \mu_1 = 1$. Let $F(p_i)$ be the probability that a firm charges a price that is smaller than p_i. The expected payoff to firm i of charging price p_i when the rival chooses a random pricing strategy according to the cumulative distribution $F(\cdot)$ is in this case

$$\pi_i(p_i, F(\cdot)) = (p_i - r) \left[\frac{(1 - \lambda)\mu_1}{2} + \lambda(1 - F(p_i)) \right]. \tag{16.1}$$

This profit expression is easily interpreted. Firm i obtains a per consumer profit of $p_i - r$. The expected demand faced by a firm stems from the two different groups of consumers. Firm i attracts the fully informed consumers when it charges a lower price than the rival, which happens with probability $1 - F(p_i)$. The firm also serves the less informed consumers whenever they actively search for one price, which happens with probability μ_1, and, particularly, when they visit its store, which occurs with probability one half.

In equilibrium, a firm must be indifferent between charging any price in the support of F. The maximum price a firm will ever charge is v since no buyer who observed a price above his/her reservation price would acquire the good. Further, the upper bound of the price distribution cannot be lower than v because a firm charging the upper bound would gain by slightly raising its price. Thus, it must be the case that $F(v) = 1$, and $F(p) < 1$, for all $p < v$. Any price in the support of F must then satisfy $\pi_i(p_i, F(\cdot)) = \pi_i(v)$, which yields

$$F(p) = \frac{2\lambda + (1 - \lambda)\mu_1}{2\lambda} - \frac{(1 - \lambda)\mu_1}{2\lambda} \frac{v - r}{p - r}. \tag{16.2}$$

Since F is a distribution function there must be some $\underline{p}$ for which $F(\underline{p}) = 0$. Solving for $\underline{p}$ one obtains the lower bound of the price distribution $\underline{p} = ((1 - \lambda)\mu_1(v - r))/(2\lambda + (1 - \lambda)\mu_1) + r$.

A mixed strategy over the support $\underline{p} \leq p \leq v$ according to the cumulative distribution function F specified above is an equilibrium if and only if consumers are indeed indifferent between searching for one price and not searching at all. Therefore, it must be the case that $v - E[p] - c = 0$, where E denotes the expectation operator.[9] In other words, the following condition must be satisfied:[10]

$$1 - \frac{(1 - \lambda)\mu_1}{2\lambda} \ln\left(\frac{2\lambda + (1 - \lambda)\mu_1}{(1 - \lambda)\mu_1}\right) = \frac{c}{v - r}. \tag{16.3}$$

The LHS of this equation represents the additional gains to a consumer from searching once (given that he does not search at all). The RHS gives the relative cost of an additional search. In a low search intensity equilibrium, these two must be equal. Figure 16.1 gives a graphical representation of the two sides of the equation, where the LHS of equation (16.3) is denoted as $\Phi(\mu_1, \lambda)$. It is easy to see that whenever $c/(v - r)$ is not too small, a low search intensity equilibrium exists.

Case b: High search intensity

We now turn to the case where less informed consumers randomize between searching for one price and searching for two prices.[11] The expected payoff to firm i from charging price p_i when the rival chooses

---

[9] It must further be checked that it is not profitable for consumers to search more than once, i.e., that $v - E[\min\{p_1, p_2\}] - 2c < 0$.

[10] For current and future reference, let $H(p) = a - b(v - r)/(p - r)$ be a distribution function in the support $b(v - r)/a + r \leq p \leq v$, with $a - b = 1$. Then $E[p] = b(v - r)\ln[a/b] + r$, $E[\min\{p_1, p_2\}] = 2b(v - r)(1 - b\ln[a/b]) + r$ and $E[\max\{p_1, p_2\}] = 2b(v - r)[(1 + b)\ln[a/b] - 1] + r$.

[11] For ease of exposition, we maintain the notation used so far in the sense that μ_1 denotes the probability with which less informed buyers search for one price. However, unlike in Case a above, $1 - \mu_1$ denotes now the probability with which these consumers search for two prices, i.e., μ_2.

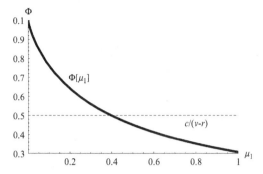

Figure 16.1. Buyers randomize between one search and no search ($\lambda = \frac{1}{3}$).

a random pricing strategy according to the cumulative distribution function $F(\cdot)$ and less informed consumers search as specified above is

$$\pi_i(p_i, F(p)) = (p_i - r)\left[\frac{(1 - \lambda)\mu_1}{2} + (\lambda + (1 - \lambda)(1 - \mu_1))(1 - F(p_i))\right]. \quad (16.4)$$

This function is easily interpreted along the lines explained above.

In equilibrium, a firm must be indifferent between charging any price in the support of F. The same arguments employed above allow us to argue that $F(v) = 1$, and $F(p) < 1$, for all $p < v$. Any price in the support of F must satisfy $\pi_i(p_i, F(\cdot)) = \pi_i(v)$, which yields

$$F(p) = \frac{2 - (1 - \lambda)\mu_1}{2(1 - (1 - \lambda)\mu_1)} - \frac{(1 - \lambda)\mu_1}{2(1 - (1 - \lambda)\mu_1)}\frac{v - r}{p - r}. \quad (16.5)$$

Solving $F(\underline{p}) = 0$ for $\underline{p}$ yields the lower bound of the equilibrium price distribution.

In this case, a mixed strategy over the support $\underline{p} \leq p \leq v$ according to (16.5) is an equilibrium if and only if less informed buyers are indeed indifferent between searching for only one price and searching for two prices.[12] Therefore it must be the case that $v - E[p] - c = v - E[\min\{p_1, p_2\}] - 2c$, which yields (see footnote 10):

$$\frac{(1 - \lambda)\mu_1}{2(1 - (1 - \lambda)\mu_1)}\left[\frac{1}{1 - (1 - \lambda)\mu_1}\ln\left(\frac{2 - (1 - \lambda)\mu_1}{(1 - \lambda)\mu_1}\right) - 2\right] = \frac{c}{v - r}. \quad (16.6)$$

This equilibrium condition has a similar interpretation as the one for the low search intensity equilibrium. The LHS of this equation represents the additional gains to a consumer from making one search more (given that he has already searched once), while the RHS gives the relative cost

---

[12] We must additionally be sure that no consumer gains by making no search, i.e., it must be the case that $v - E[p] - c > 0$. This is trivially satisfied.

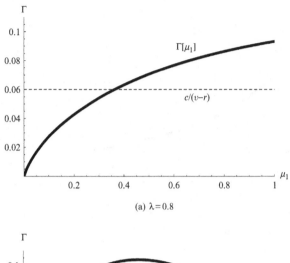

(a) $\lambda = 0.8$

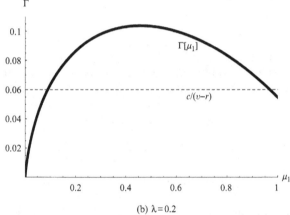

(b) $\lambda = 0.2$

Figure 16.2. Buyers randomize between one search and two searches.

of an additional search. To represent condition (16.6), let us denote its LHS by $\Gamma(\mu_1, \lambda)$. When the percentage of informed consumers is large enough, Γ is an increasing and concave function of μ_1, as represented in Figure 16.2(a) ($\lambda = 0.8$). A high search intensity equilibrium is given by the intersection of curve Γ with the line $c/(v - r)$. When, in contrast, the percentage of informed consumers is small, the curve $\Gamma(\mu_1)$ is first increasing and then decreasing. The shape of Γ when λ is relatively small is illustrated in Figure 16.2(b) ($\lambda = 0.2$).

Case c: Moderate search intensity
We finally turn to the case where less informed consumers search for one price with probability one. Derivations for this case are similar to the

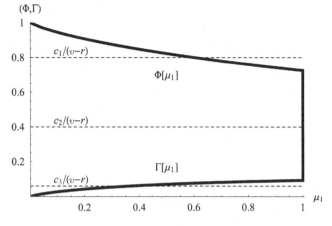

(a) High search engine rate of adoption ($\lambda = 0.8$)

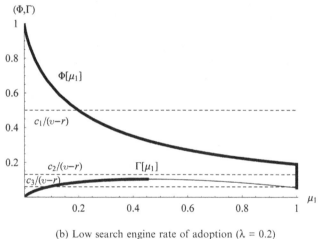

(b) Low search engine rate of adoption ($\lambda = 0.2$)

Figure 16.3. Equilibrium conditions.

computations above and therefore omitted. The equilibrium distribution function for this case can be obtained by plugging $\mu_1 = 1$ in either
of the Cases a and b discussed above. A mixed strategy distribution
function $F(p) = (1 + \lambda)/2\lambda - (1 - \lambda)(v - r)/(2\lambda(p - r))$ is part of an
equilibrium if less informed consumers indeed find it optimal to search
only once. Therefore, the following two conditions must hold: (i) $v -
E[p] - c \geq 0$ and (ii) $v - E[p] - c \geq v - E[\min\{p_1, p_2\}] - 2c$.

The three possible equilibria are illustrated in Figures 16.3(a) and
16.3(b). Figure 16.3(a) exhibits a market where $\lambda = 0.8$. In this case, for

large search cost parameters, for instance $c_1/(v - r)$, there is a unique equilibrium where less informed buyers search with low intensity. As search cost falls, these consumers find it beneficial to search more intensively. Indeed, for intermediate search cost levels, for example $c_2/(v - r)$, the only equilibrium is such that less informed buyers search for one price with probability one. Finally, when search cost is sufficiently low, for instance $c_3/(v - r)$, buyers search with high intensity in equilibrium. The bold lines depict the loci of equilibrium points.[13]

Figure 16.3(b) illustrates a case where the rate of adoption of search engines is low ($\lambda = 0.2$). In this case, for high and intermediate search cost, for example $c_1/(v - r)$, there is a single equilibrium where consumers search with low intensity. However, for a relatively low search cost $c_2/(v - r)$, there is a single moderate intensity equilibrium. For $c_3/(v - r)$, there are two equilibria: one in which buyers search with moderate intensity and another in which they search with high intensity. Finally, for extremely low search costs, there is just one equilibrium with high search intensity. As before, the bold lines depict the loci of equilibrium points.[14]

The analysis above yields the insight that whether the economy is in a low, moderate or high search intensity equilibrium depends on two critical model parameters: (i) the size of the purchase compared to the search cost $c/(v - r)$, and (ii) the search engine rate of adoption λ. In real markets, there is a marked difference between buyers' search intensity for different products (cf. the reference to Johnson et al. (2004) in Section 16.2). Our basic model is able to explain this difference in terms of the exogenous parameters.

16.4   Comparative statics

In this section we study the impact of changes in the parameters of the model. As argued above, a change in the search technology can be captured in our model either by a decline in c or by an increase in the rate of adoption of search engines λ. We shall see that the influence of these parameters depends on the intensity with which less informed buyers search in equilibrium.

[13] To help to interpret these graphs recall that $1 - \mu_1 = \mu_2$ in a high search intensity equilibrium, while $1 - \mu_1 = \mu_0$ in a low search intensity equilibrium.

[14] We note that for very low rate of adoption of search engines and for very low search costs, there may be an equilibrium with low search intensity and an equilibrium with high search intensity.

Table 16.1. *Summary of comparative statics results*

	Low				Moderate				High			
	p^e	p^d	π	W	p^e	p^d	π	W	p^e	p^d	π	W
$\downarrow c$	↑	↑↓	↑	↑	−	−	−	↑	↓	↓	↓	↑↓
$\uparrow \lambda$	−	−	↑	↑	↓	↑↓	↓	↑	−	−	−	↑

The comparative statics results of a change in search technology are summarized in Table 16.1. In the table expected prices, price dispersion, profits and welfare are represented by p^e, p^d, π and W respectively. An upwards (downwards) arrow means that the variable under consideration increases (falls); two arrows together means that the variable may increase or decrease and this depends on the initial value of the parameter; the symbol − means that the variable remains constant. In the discussion below explaining the results summarized in the table, we focus on explaining the empirical studies. Therefore, we concentrate on the implications of a change in search technology on expected prices and price dispersion. As a measure of price dispersion we take the difference between the expected maximum price and the expected minimum price.[15] The implications for firms' profits and social welfare are discussed in the footnotes.

The following facts prove useful in the discussion that follows. Both price distributions given in (16.2) and (16.5) are of the form $H(p) = a - b(v - r)/(p - r)$ with support $b(v - r)/a + r \leq p \leq v$, and with $a - b = 1$. Then:

Fact 1: $\frac{dE[p]}{db} > 0$

Fact 2: $\frac{dE[\min\{p_1, p_2\}]}{db} > 0$

Fact 3: $\frac{d(E[\max\{p_1, p_2\}] - E[\min\{p_1, p_2\}])}{db} > 0$ if and only if $b < \overline{b} \simeq 0.28763$.

From equations (16.2) and (16.5) it follows that b is a measure of the equilibrium fraction of consumers who search only once relative to the number of consumers who search twice. In other words, it measures the fraction of active buyers over which firms have monopoly power.

---

[15] There is a mathematical property that makes this measure attractive in our setting, namely, $E[\max\{p_1, p_2\}] - E[\min\{p_1, p_2\}] = 2(E[p] - E[\min\{p_1, p_2\}])$. Many of the aforementioned empirical papers have used this measure of dispersion; considering price variance instead complicates the analysis without bringing about additional insights.

16.4.1   The effects of a reduction in search cost c

Expected prices

Consider first that less informed consumers search with low intensity in equilibrium. Since $v - E[p] - c = 0$ in a low search intensity equilibrium, the price that less informed buyers expect increases as c falls. To understand the intuition behind this surprising result let us point out that, as Figure 16.1 shows, the intensity with which less informed consumers search in this type of equilibrium rises as c falls. Note further that these consumers are precisely those who do not exercise price comparisons, and thus they are prepared to accept higher prices. Consequently, a fall in c gives sellers incentives to charge higher prices more frequently, which in turn raises expected prices. Our next observation has to do with the expected price faced by the informed consumers, i.e., $E[\min\{p_1, p_2\}]$. It turns out that increased activity of the less informed buyers exerts a negative externality on the informed ones. Indeed, a decline in c also increases the expected minimum price. This is readily seen by employing Fact 2 and noting that $b = (1 - \lambda)\mu_1/2\lambda$ in this equilibrium.[16]

Suppose now that less informed consumers search with moderate intensity in equilibrium. Observe that a small change in c leaves less informed buyers' behavior unchanged. Consequently, expected prices remain constant.[17]

Finally, consider that less informed consumers search with high intensity in equilibrium. Figures 16.2(a) and 16.2(b) show that a decline in c raises the probability with which less informed buyers search for two prices, i.e., $d\mu_1/dc > 0$. Since price comparisons are more frequent as c falls, price competition between firms is fostered. Thus, one would expect prices to fall with c. Indeed, $b = (1 - \lambda)\mu_1/[2(1 - (1 - \lambda)\mu_1)]$ in this type of equilibrium and it is readily seen that $db/d\mu_1 = (1 - \lambda)/[2(1 - (1 - \lambda)\mu_1)^2] > 0$. This together with the Facts above prove that mean prices for both types of consumers decrease with c.[18]

---

[16] It is straightforward to see now how firms' profits and social welfare are affected by a decline in c in a low search intensity equilibrium. Note that profits are proportional to the intensity with which less informed buyers search: $\pi = (v - r)(1 - \lambda)\mu_1/2$ (see equation (16.1)). Then it is obvious that firms' profits rise with c. Social welfare, $W = \lambda(v - r) + (v - r - c)(1 - \lambda)\mu_1$ in this case, also increases. Note, however, that the additional surplus generated by a fall in c is fully captured by the firms!

[17] It is also obvious that firms' profits remain constant with c in a moderate search intensity equilibrium. Social welfare, $W = \lambda(v - r) + (v - r - c)(1 - \lambda)$ in this case, however, rises because less informed consumers incur lower costs to discover prices.

[18] Note that equilibrium profits in a high search intensity equilibrium are $\pi = (v - r)(1 - \lambda)\mu_1/2$ (see equation (16.4)). As expected, profits decline with c because μ_1 does so.

Price dispersion

Consider first that consumers search with low intensity in equilibrium. As previously noted, a decline in c increases the shopping activity of the less informed buyers μ_1. Since $b = (1 - \lambda)\mu_1/2\lambda$, this implies that b increases as c decreases. Using Fact 3, it is easy to see that price dispersion rises as c decreases if and only if b is small. The fraction of consumers b who search only once can be small for two reasons: first, when λ is large, and second, when many less informed consumers do not find it worthwhile to search (which occurs when c is relatively large). A search cost reduction brings more price-insensitive buyers to the market, which gives incentives to raise prices. Recall that price dispersion arises due to the existence of two groups of consumers who are asymmetrically informed, and that firms make substantial profits basically by expropriating the less informed consumers. When there are many informed consumers, an individual firm will try to keep them and thus will randomize prices to balance these two conflicting interests. As a consequence, price dispersion increases. In contrast, when there are few informed consumers firms do not need to care so much about them and thus price dispersion does not necessarily increase with a fall in c.

Suppose now that less informed buyers search with moderate intensity in equilibrium. As observed previously, a small change in c leaves less informed consumers' behavior unchanged and thus price dispersion remains constant.

Finally, consider that less informed consumers search with high intensity in equilibrium. Since $E[p] - E[\min\{p_1, p_2\}] = c$ in this equilibrium, from footnote 15 it follows that $E[\max\{p_1, p_2\}] - E[\min\{p_1, p_2\}] = 2c$. Consequently, price dispersion decreases as the search cost falls.

Interestingly, a fall in c does not increase social welfare necessarily. The reason is that the increased search activity of the less informed consumers may be excessive from a social welfare viewpoint. This can be seen by noting that welfare is $W = \lambda(v - r) + (1 - \lambda)$ $(v - r - 2c + \mu_1 c)$ in this case. Thus $dW/dc = (1 - \lambda)(-2 + \mu_1 + cd\mu_1/dc)$. The sign of this derivative depends on the parameters of the model. To provide an instance in which welfare declines after a decrease in c, consider a market setting where $\lambda = 14/15$, $v = 1$ and $r = 0$. Consider that search costs are initially $c = 0.055$. In the equilibrium with high search intensity, less informed buyers would search for two prices with probability 0.0756452, and social welfare would be 0.996056, approximately. A reduction in search cost from 0.055 to 0.054 would increase the incentives to search of the less informed consumers, who would thus search for two prices with higher probability, 0.105676 approximately. From a social perspective, however, the increased search intensity brought about by the search cost reduction is excessive and welfare attains a lower level, 0.99602 approximately.

Overview of partial results

Previous observations regarding the impact of a search cost reduction on expected prices and price dispersion are gathered in Figure 16.4(a) and 16.4(b). In Figure 16.4(a) we have simulated an economy where the number of informed consumers is large ($\lambda = 0.8$). This graph depicts expected price (thicker curve) and expected minimum price (thinner curve) as a function of relative search cost. As noted above, for any given value of $c/(v - r)$, the vertical distance between the two lines constitutes a measure of actual price dispersion. When search cost lies in the interval ($\Phi(1)$, 1), less informed consumers search with low intensity in equilibrium. In this region, expected prices and price dispersion increase as the search cost falls, as indicated above. For search cost values in between $\Gamma(1)$ and $\Phi(1)$ it pays less informed consumers to search for one price with probability one. In this region a decline in search cost has no impact on expected prices and price dispersion. Finally, when search cost lies in the interval $(0, \Gamma(1))$, it pays less informed consumers to search for two prices with positive probability. As the search cost falls in this region the frequency with which price comparisons occur in the market increases, which fosters competition between the firms. Consequently, expected prices and price dispersion decline. Eventually, as search cost approaches zero, mean prices converge to marginal cost.

It might be argued that moving markets online does not marginally decrease search costs but does so dramatically. Upon observing Figure 16.4(a) one sees that even a dramatic change in search cost does not necessarily decrease price dispersion and mean prices. To see this, consider for instance a search cost reduction from A to B. Even though this is an enormous decline of about 80%, mean prices and price dispersion increase. In contrast consider a smaller cost fall from B to C of about 60%. This cost reduction decreases mean prices and price dispersion. These observations illustrate that one cannot conclude that a large search cost reduction will enhance market efficiency without taking into account the market status quo.

Figure 16.4(b) complements our previous exposition by presenting equilibrium expected prices for a case with a lower rate of adoption of search engines ($\lambda = 0.2$). Figure 16.4(b) has the distinctive feature that for some parametrical values there are multiple equilibria. In particular, when search cost lies in the interval $(\Gamma(1), \Gamma^{max})$ one may have a moderate search equilibrium with high expected prices, or a high search intensity equilibrium with lower mean prices. (This is the reason why Figure 16.4(b) exhibits a discontinuity in expected prices; see also Figure 16.2(b).) Thus, less informed consumers face a coordination problem. It pays to search intensively if the others do so, otherwise it is

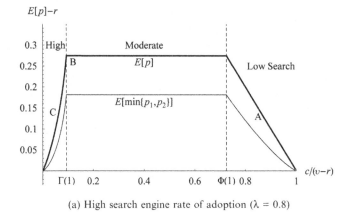

(a) High search engine rate of adoption ($\lambda = 0.8$)

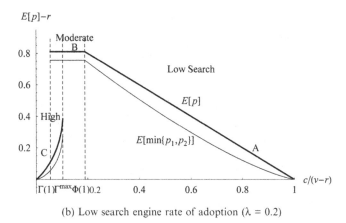

(b) Low search engine rate of adoption ($\lambda = 0.2$)

Figure 16.4. The impact of lower search cost c.

worth searching only once. As argued above, observing price dispersion and expected prices at the search cost levels A, B and C one can state that a dramatic decline in search cost need not increase market transparency.

As explained in Section 16.2, we see these results as a possible explanation why Bailey (1998) found higher online prices for books and CDs compared with off-line, while almost equal online and off-line prices for software. For books and CDs the relative size of the purchase is small compared with the search cost, and in 1996 and 1997 the rate of adoption of search engines was probably low. Thus, one would expect a low or a moderate intensity equilibrium to be in place. In such a case, the comparison between the online channel and the off-line one would be captured by a decline in c and thus would produce higher or equal expected prices. In contrast, for software one may reasonably expect a moderate or a high search intensity equilibrium, since product value and rate of adoption of search engines seem to be greater for this product. This may explain why software online prices were not found to be much higher compared with their off-line counterparts and, further, why price dispersion was found to be lower. Brynjolfsson and Smith (2000) found book and CD prices to be lower online than off-line. Since they took a sample of prices much later than Bailey did, it may be the case that they were looking at a market with a larger search engine rate of adoption. This market may be in a high search intensity equilibrium and thus a decline in search cost would lower expected prices and price dispersion.

16.4.2   An increase in the rate of adoption of search engines λ

Another manner to capture changes in search technology is to consider that the fraction of consumers using search engines increases.

Expected prices

Consider first that less informed consumers search with low intensity in equilibrium. Since $v - E[p] - c = 0$ in equilibrium, and since neither v nor c varies, expected price must remain constant. It is worth disentangling the incidence of changes in λ on less informed consumers' search incentives and firms' pricing decisions. Notice first that an increase in the search engine rate of adoption has in principle a pro-competitive effect. Ceteris paribus, firms would tend to charge lower prices with higher probability. One can apply the implicit function theorem to equation (16.3) to obtain

$$\frac{d\mu_1}{d\lambda} = \frac{\mu_1}{\lambda(1 - \lambda)} > 0, \qquad (16.7)$$

which means that an increase in λ results in an increase in the search intensity of the less informed consumers μ_1. This is obviously due to the fact that more informed consumers in the market makes searching more attractive for the less informed consumers, as the former buyers put pressure on firms to reduce prices. This in turn implies that the number of price-insensitive buyers rises, which gives firms incentives to raise prices. Interestingly, these two opposite forces cancel out so that expected prices remain constant. We also observe that the price informed consumers expect, i.e., $E[\min\{p_1, p_2\}]$, does not change with λ either. To see this, note that in this case $b = (1 - \lambda)\mu_1/2\lambda$. Using equation (16.7), just a little algebra shows that $db/d\lambda = 0$, which implies that the expected minimum price remains constant too.[19]

Suppose now that less informed buyers search with moderate intensity. Notice that an increase in λ does not alter the behavior of less informed buyers. Consequently, since more consumers exercise price comparisons, the economy becomes more competitive. The price expected by the less informed consumers obviously falls. This is readily seen using the Facts above and noting that $b = (1 - \lambda)/2\lambda$ in this case, and therefore $db/d\lambda = -1/2\lambda^2 < 0$. Analogously, using Fact 2, one proves that the price expected by the informed buyers also declines.[20]

Finally, consider that less informed buyers search with high intensity in equilibrium. As noticed above, when λ goes up firms tend to charge lower prices with higher probability. Applying the implicit function theorem to equation (16.6), one obtains

$$\frac{d\mu_1}{d\lambda} = \frac{\mu_1}{1 - \lambda} > 0, \tag{16.8}$$

which means that less informed buyers search less intensively as λ rises. The decreased search activity of these consumers implies that the frequency with which price comparisons occur diminishes. Surprisingly, it turns out that the behavior of less informed buyers compensates away the pressure that the presence of relatively more informed consumers puts on the firms to cut prices. To see this, note that $b = (1 - \lambda)\mu_1/[2(1 - (1 - \lambda)\mu_1)]$ in this case. Using equation (16.8), it is easily seen that $db/d\lambda = 0$. This implies that neither the price expected by less informed consumers who search only once, nor the price expected by buyers who search twice, changes.[21]

---

[19] Since expected prices remain constant and more less informed consumers are active when λ rises, one would expect firms' profits to increase. Remember that $\pi = (v - r)$ $(1 - \lambda)\mu_1/2$ in this case. The impact of an increase in λ is given by $d\pi/d\lambda = (v - r)[(1 - \lambda)$ $d\mu_1/d\lambda - \mu_1]/2$. Using (16.7) we obtain $d\pi/d\lambda = (v - r)\mu_1(1 - \lambda)/2\lambda > 0$, i.e., an increase in λ increases firms' profits!

We finally observe that social welfare increases with λ due to the increased activity of the less informed consumers (note that $(1 - \lambda)\mu_1$ rises). To see this, remember that $W = \lambda$ $(v - r) + (v - r - c)(1 - \lambda)\mu_1$ in this case. Using (16.7) we can compute $dW/d\lambda = v - r$ $+ (v - r - c)\mu_1(1 - \lambda)/\lambda > 0$. Note, however, that a great deal of the increase in social welfare is captured by the firms.

[20] From the previous remarks it is readily understood that firm profits, $\pi = (v - r)(1 - \lambda)/2$ in this case, decline with λ. In contrast, social welfare, $W = v - r - c(1 - \lambda)$ here, rises with λ since fewer consumers incur search costs.

[21] An increase in λ also turns out not to have influence on firms' profits. Remember that $\pi = (v - r)(1 - \lambda)\mu_1/2$ in a high search intensity equilibrium and it is readily checked that $d\pi/d\lambda = 0$. With regard to social welfare, remember that $W = \lambda(v - r) + (1 - \lambda)(v - r - 2c + \mu_1 c)$

Price dispersion

Consider first the economy is in a low search intensity equilibrium. As shown above, the pro-competitive effects of an increase in λ are offset by the increased activity of less informed consumers. This in turn implies that changes in λ have no incidence on price dispersion.

Suppose now that less informed buyers search with moderate intensity in equilibrium. As shown above, $db/d\lambda < 0$, which implies that the influence of λ on price dispersion is ambiguous (Fact 3). When the number of informed consumers is large initially then an increase in λ decreases price dispersion. In contrast, when λ is small initially then an increase in λ raises price dispersion. The intuitive argument has been explained above.

Finally, consider the economy is in a high search intensity equilibrium. In this case the pro-competitive effects of an increase in λ are entirely offset by a decrease in the search activity of the less informed buyers. Consequently, changes in λ have no impact on price dispersion.

Overview of partial results

Previous discussions regarding the influence of changes in the number of informed buyers on expected prices and price dispersion are gathered in Figures 16.5(a) and 16.5(b). Figure 16.5(a) simulates an economy where a product's valuation is relatively low compared with search cost $(c/(v - r) = 0.5)$. The figure depicts expected price (thicker curve) and expected minimum price (thinner curve) as a function of λ. Recall that for any given λ, the vertical distance between the two curves provides a measure of price dispersion. Observe that when λ lies in the interval $(0, \Phi(1))$ market equilibrium exhibits low search intensity. In this case, the pro-competitive effects of an increase in λ are entirely offset by the search behavior of less informed buyers and so expected prices and price dispersion remain constant. When the rate of adoption of search engines is large enough, $\Phi(1) < \lambda < 1$, less informed consumers search with moderate intensity in equilibrium and prices decline smoothly to marginal cost as λ rises.

In Figure 16.5(b) we have simulated an economy where search cost is low $(c/(v - r) = 0.05)$. We first observe that there may be multiple equilibria in this case. For instance, for a λ level depicted by point A

---

in this case. A little algebra shows that $dW/d\lambda = 2c > 0$, which implies that welfare rises with λ. Two factors explain this. First, observe that fewer consumers pay search costs when λ rises. Second, less informed consumers search less intensively and the economy further saves in search costs. Remarkably, the additional surplus is captured by the consumers.

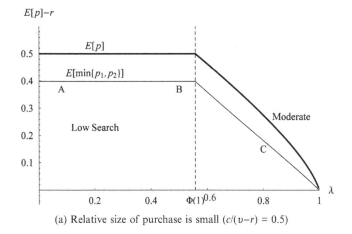

(a) Relative size of purchase is small $(c/(v-r) = 0.5)$

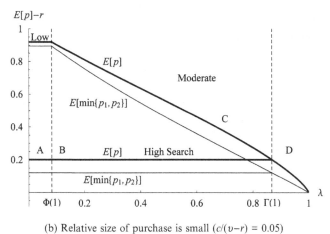

(b) Relative size of purchase is small $(c/(v-r) = 0.05)$

Figure 16.5. The impact of the search engine rate of adoption λ.

there are two equilibria: one with low search intensity and one with high search intensity. For λ levels given by the points B and C there are also two equilibria: one with moderate search intensity and one with high search intensity. Finally, for a λ level given by point D there is a single moderate search equilibrium. Observe that when there is multiplicity of equilibria a high search intensity equilibrium leads to lower expected prices. Thus, less informed consumers face a coordination problem. If a high search intensity equilibrium prevails in the economy, expected prices and price dispersion are insensitive to changes in λ, as noted above. It may also happen that the nature of buyers' coordination is such that they do not search so much. Then, if λ lies in the interval $(0, \Phi(1))$, the economy would be in a low search intensity equilibrium and changes in λ have no influence on expected prices and price dispersion. If, instead, λ lies in between $\Phi(1)$ and $\Gamma(1)$, consumers would search with moderate intensity and an increase in λ would reduce mean prices. However, it would decrease price dispersion only if λ is sufficiently great to begin with. In summary, Figure 16.5(b) illustrates that while price levels do not increase with respect to λ, it may very well be the case that price dispersion rises.

A final remark regarding Figure 16.5(b) is that a high search intensity equilibrium may exhibit greater price dispersion than a low or moderate search intensity equilibrium. Therefore, mean prices and price dispersion need not be perfectly correlated.

We believe that search engine rate of adoption may explain why Bailey (1998) found higher online prices for books and CDs sold in 1996 and 1997 while Brynjolfsson and Smith (1999) found the opposite for a sample of books sold in 1998 and 1999. The same applies to the study of Brown and Goolsbee (2002), who argue that there is no evidence that Internet usage reduced prices of life insurance policies before comparison websites emerged and proliferated. When the rate of adoption of search engines is low, we note that the pro-competitive effects of marginal increases of informed buyers are entirely offset by economizing behavior of less informed buyers. As the adoption rate of search engines increases, search propensity rises and further increases in λ result in greater transparency.

16.5   Conclusions and discussion

In a model that concentrates on the search aspect of (online) markets, we have investigated whether improved search technology fosters competition and consequently lowers commodity prices and raises social welfare, as commonly argued. We have found that the impact of Internet usage on the efficiency of commodity markets may be more subtle than previously thought.

Our first primary finding relates to the intensity with which buyers search in equilibrium. We have found that a product's value relative to search cost as well as the search engine rate of adoption are the determinants of consumers' search incentives. More precisely, for a given search cost, buyers' search incentives are (weakly) monotonic in a product's value and non-monotonic in the search engine rate of adoption. The direct implication of this observation is that price-cost margins and price dispersion need not be low in all online commodity markets.

Whether they are low or high depends on how much buyers search, which in turn depends on market characteristics. Our second major finding is that the comparative statics effects of improved search technology on commodity markets depend on the manner in which it is modeled, i.e., on whether improved search technology is regarded as lowering unit search costs or as increasing search engine rate of adoption. Moreover, these effects are influenced by the intensity with which consumers search in the status quo equilibrium, and hence by initial market characteristics. A unit search cost reduction may result in higher, equal or lower mean prices and price dispersion depending on whether consumers initially search with low, moderate or high intensity, respectively. In contrast, expected prices and price dispersion (weakly) decrease as the search engine rate of adoption rises, irrespective of the buyers' search activity. The latter two remarks suggest that the long-run impact of Internet usage on commodity markets will be sensitive to the extent to which search engines are adopted and become central places of information exchange.

As argued in the main body of this chapter, our results may help understand the controversial empirical findings reported so far. Perhaps more interesting is the fact that, as suggested by our research, future empirical studies assessing the impact of Internet usage on market efficiency should take into consideration more explicitly market characteristics such as a product's value and the search engine rate of adoption. A first attempt to such an analysis is provided by Janssen, Moraga-González and Wildenbeest (2004). Contrary to most empirical studies carried out so far, this paper adopts a fully structural approach. The theoretical restrictions derived from firm and consumer behavior in a consumer search model similar to the one discussed in Section 16.3 of this chapter are directly tested using price data collected from the Internet. The parameters of the model are first estimated by maximum likelihood and in turn used to test whether the model does well in explaining real-world data. Moreover, using the equilibrium conditions on search behavior, it is possible to estimate the search cost of uninformed consumers. Then, provided that the model does well in explaining the data, the estimates shed light on how market characteristics affect consumer and firm behavior. Janssen, Moraga-González and Wildenbeest (2004) find that the high search intensity equilibrium is particularly capable of explaining observed prices of online computer hardware in a manner that is consistent with the underlying theoretical model for almost all products included in the analysis.

17 Are neighbors welcome? E-buyer search, price competition and coalition strategy in Internet retailing

Jacques Laye and Hervé Tanguy

17.1 Introduction

When electronic commerce started to grow, understanding the novelty the Internet brought to business economics became a major issue, considering relations with suppliers and clients as well as among competitors. "Bricks and mortar" firms operating in distribution had to decide whether or not to enter the Internet retailing channel, at what pace and whether to be with or without partners. This chapter focuses on the nature of competition within the online distribution channel once this channel becomes a significant way for firms to access customers. Although many questions under study also make sense for business-to-business (B-to-B) relationships, we will keep in mind the world of business-to-consumer (B-to-C) retailing, which although it still played a minor role in 2003, enjoyed a high growth rate and already accounted for a large share of sales in some sectors.[1] We will put aside problems related to vertical relationships and competing distribution channels – our general objective is to contribute to the understanding of the differences induced on the structuring of markets between selling through physical stores and selling through web-sites. More precisely, we will modelize the forces driving aggregation of shops on the Internet.

When the business press or the economics and management literature deal with the new features of web retailing, "one to one" marketing opportunities on the sellers' side and exchange of information among potential buyers and their network effects (communities) seem to be the most significant factors that could change the rules of the competition game. The prominent role of these two phenomena is yet far from being confirmed when we consider the development of the e-sales and the

We wish to thank Maximilien Laye and Charis Lina for their invaluable comments. This work has been supported by the I-Cities project, IST, 11337, Information Cities.

[1] For example in France, already in 2001 travel and hotels accounted for €300 million of the €680 million generated by B-to-C, followed by computers and multi-media (€90 million), food and drink (€80 million). Source: Benchmark Group, July 2001.

most important B-to-C sites. We do not have plenty of Amazon-like sites in fields other than the entertainment and edition sector, but we find a huge growth in e-tourism sales, for example. In addition to this, the reasons for Amazon's success remain to be elucidated: the hyper-mediatization of the site, the quasi-exhaustiveness and easy access to its database of books could be as important as the availability of customers' comments or the profile-related suggestions and other targeted dynamic marketing devices. Communities suppose discipline and frequent visits to the web-sites, while occasional transactions by customers looking for some type of goods at a given moment represent a great share of the B-to-C sales (think, for instance, about the Christmas peak), in which case inter-actions among users are obviously less likely to appear.[2] What is left, then, of the Internet attractiveness that could foster this new distribution channel? According to us, simply a more efficient search without trans-portation costs involved. Direct sales through catalogs and mail (or phone) already avoided transport before the Internet era but we gained through the web both a huge broadening of the scope of search and higher quality information on the goods offered. Of course, it is always possible to get higher quality in a physical store through face-to-face contact with the goods and the sellers, but enlarging the search scope leads the transportation costs and the opportunity cost of time to rapidly explode. Thus, our objective is to give a diametrically opposed and complementary view of the forces that drive the evolution of the Internet landscape, compared with the world of Internet users who enjoy spending their time surfing the web, chatting and being willing to belong to some communities, and then eventually giving in to unexpected temptations through advertising or advice. Our proposed view originates in the sole e-retailing area and considers web users looking for some good to buy and having a high opportunity cost for the time spent searching that good.

For Internet consumers the search process is a key issue. With some rare exceptions (like Amazon and its few competitors in the edition sector), such an e-customer does not *a priori* know where the right door is to ring the bell. Then, searching on the web is not *per se* an easy task and can quickly become tedious and time consuming. Though the

---

[2] In this book, Curien et al. notice that "online consumers' communities do not represent the dominant business model of online communities" and Gensollen, on the emergence of experience-sharing communities, states: "The distribution sites that offer such review services enjoy a scale-related competitive advantage: because of its size, amazon.com has a dominant position on cultural products in the United States. But the vendors that edit reviews must also be able to link this service to actual buying or at least to offer prices and level of service similar to the best market offers, in order to make the customers stick to their site."

Internet often remains more attractive than other distribution channels regarding this point, e-customers' search costs may well be one of the main competitive key drivers of the demand each Internet shop will meet at the end of the day. The most puzzling empirical fact from the e-customer's point of view is that they generally do not find *ex post* a convenient web-site where they could easily compare all the available offers close to their preferences and then fine-tune their choice, using a specialized search engine. Why? While the Internet may remain more attractive than other distribution channels for lowering search costs, why, with the availability of all the necessary technology, is it still so painful for customers who ignore the true availability of the potential goods and services among providers and their price and precise characteristics to find and buy what they are looking for?

Coalitions of Internet sites can be a solution to lower the cost of search for e-customers. It is the case for portals with a specialized search engine or electronically linked independent sites that are examples of what we will call a coalition. These coalitions are far more easily built than in the physical world (the street of the fish shops). Whereas in the physical world the size of the required specific investments, the limitation of geographical locations available and the widespread location of customers put the brake on the coalition of independent firms (localization in the same area) and may instead favor true mergers and specialized chain store developments, the coalition of independent mono-product firms on the web is by far the easiest aggregation move. So putting aside mergers that, of course, also happen on the web for many reasons (most of them being not web specific), we intend to treat these two main questions:

1. What is the motivation for a web retailer to enter a coalition and why would it be accepted or not by insiders?
2. What is the coalition structure that is likely to appear: firms offering close substitutes grouped together or firms offering differentiated products?

17.2   Related literature

The closest literature to these subjects deals with the aggregation of "true" shops in some locations (Schulz and Stahl 1996, Henkel and Stahl 2000) in the presence of search costs. Two main forces are considered in these papers: on one hand, the lowering of search costs for consumers who may ignore the prices and characteristics of goods but know *a priori* the number of shops/products that are offered in a given location (or "marketplace"), and on the other hand, the increased competition due to the proximity of shops. The first force drives aggregation of shops by directly adding up to the demand of a fair number of consumers who want to cut down search costs. The second one limits this aggregation when the decrease in prices (resulting from the increased number of firms) – which may happen more or less quickly according to the differentiation of products – is no more counterbalanced by the increased demand accruing to each shop. Once a limited number of existing shops is reached, it can become more profitable for a shop to choose a distant location.[3] Finally, entry sunk costs in a given location determine the number of viable firms.

Though the seminal papers on search costs (Stigler 1961) emphasized the subsequent choice of spatial monopolies by firms (maximum dispersion), the empirical evidence of concentration phenomena (Nelson 1970, Stuart 1979) led to the introduction of differentiation among the products offered by competing firms (Stahl 1982), or the focus on coordination on volume or prices (organization of the marketplace, mergers, collusion). The main interesting result is that, due to the search costs of consumers, prices may increase with the number of firms in a given location (entrants are more than welcome). Not surprisingly, when the entry or coalition formation process is part of the model, the more the products are substitutes in the eyes of the customers, the less the "big coalition" on a unique marketplace is likely to appear.

In all those models, every product has the same level of differentiation with the other products (the value of this level being a parameter) and the questions under study are only the number of products offered in a marketplace, or the number of marketplaces.[4] As a consequence, if we understand well the forces driving aggregation/disaggregation of firms in the physical world – and we will discuss later the differences on the web – we do not have insights or discussions yet on our second question: what is the coalition structure of the firms located in the same place? Do groups of close substitutes prefer to aggregate on the same locations or the opposite? Competition among firms that are more or less close in the sense of search but also more or less close in the sense of product offering is hardly intuitively predictable.

This idea of coalition structure, related to the relative differentiation of products taking part in the coalition, exists in another stream of the

---

[3] Except when price coordination is made possible in the marketplace, for instance through mergers or more or less tacit collusion.

[4] The tractability of such models in a context of imperfect competition is an issue, of course, and explains this assumption of symmetry.

literature, where regrettably search costs are absent from the scope of the models. For instance, Giraud-Héraud, Hammoudi and Mokrane. (2003) look for the optimal product range in a coalition game where mono-product firms can merge in the sense that they will coordinate their pricing decisions. As these authors do not consider a bi-dimensional space (spatial location and product characteristics), the only sense aggregation can take is a merger among firms.[5] They find that the coalition at the equilibrium includes close-substitute products, in order to capture captive customers with relatively high prices in the core offering and then be more aggressive on the border of the product range.

Let us now focus more precisely on the assumptions of our model. We consider the mechanisms of competition among integrated (production-distribution) mono-product firms selling through the Internet to imperfectly informed consumers. We will restrict our analysis to the competition among firms within a given sector of goods or services (products are more or less substitutes). As long as delivery to customers does not alter the relative costs of competing firms, these goods do not need to be digital ones. We need to include both search costs of imperfectly informed consumers and a measure of differentiation among goods offered by firms. Moreover, we must clearly distinguish search costs *per se* and adaptation/transportation costs that consumers incur when the goods they find do not perfectly match their preferences.[6] We choose a circular differentiation model similar to that of Bakos (1997) rather than the classical linear one first proposed by Hotelling (1929), since, in our model, it is more convenient that all the locations in the differentiated market are *a priori* equivalent. In this way, the choice of a partner with which to make a coalition depends only on whether the partner site is highly differentiated from the location of the initiator or not, and not on whether the partner's location is a privileged one, which is the case for the firms that are located in the extremities of the linear city.

Let us establish what a coalition is. As in the works of geographical economy with the presence of search costs, to search within a coalition will induce a lower search cost to discover all the products offered by the

---

[5] Most of the analysis concerning the formation of coalitions considers the primary objective of companies to be agreeing on the prices and quantities sold on the market. All the works built on the models of Salant, Switzer and Reynolds (1983), Perry and Porter (1985), Deneckere and Davidson (1985), Farrell and Shapiro (1990) are based on this assumption.

[6] In the mono-product models with spatial differentiation and consumers imperfectly informed about prices (see, for instance, Gabszewicz and Garella 1986), search cost is a transportation cost (or an adaptation cost) and the preferred location of a firm for customers is their own location.

members of the coalition. This is the case when a consumer searches through a portal with a specialized search engine. We suppose that firms belonging to a coalition remain free to choose their prices. In other terms we exclude price coordination that arises when firms merge or when a single firm chooses more than one location on the circle (multi-product firm). This allows us to isolate the effect of lowering search costs for the consumer in the optimal choice for the initiator of a coalition between two different coalition structures: one involving partners selling close substitutes and, conversely, one formed with partners selling goods with highly differentiated characteristics.

The rest of this chapter is organized as follows. After an example of the kind of problem treated in this chapter, we present the modelization of the differentiated market and the search procedure of the consumer, and we describe the different coalition structures. We first examine the preferred coalition structure when prices are fixed at the level given by the game without coalitions and, second, when sites compete in price. Finally, we analyze the results of the model and finish with some concluding remarks.

17.3   An example of search within coalitions

The example of "online booking" serves to justify our motivation for building a specific model for Internet retailing where search costs and adaptation costs are clearly separated and where firms coalesce without price coordination. Let us describe the search procedure of a (rich) traveller willing to book online a luxury hotel in Paris. Luxury hotels are mainly located in a few neighborhoods of Paris (Champs-Elysées, Opéra, Bastille, etc.) that will be a criterion of differentiation for consumers. Firstly, because the system of stars guarantees a type of service, so that a consumer searching on the Internet (rather than directly making reservations in a hotel chosen for its reputation, for example) can be considered to be indifferent towards two hotels in terms of quality. Secondly, the fact that travellers might have different reasons to visit Paris gives them preferences in terms of location (proximity to a person, a meeting, a conference center). Thus, both the hotel characteristics and the consumers' preferences are defined in terms of location. A choice of hotel category (number of stars) also corresponds to an anticipated price that the consumer is ready to pay, say €300 per night, but discovering a lower price could be a motivation to accept a hotel located farther than the maximum acceptable distance for a price of €300 if the difference in price counterbalances the adaptation cost.

The search procedure begins by typing a request in a search engine (such as google.com, altavista.com, excite.com). To a request equivalent to "luxury hotels in Paris", the search engine will return a great number of sites, so the consumer invests an amount of time and energy picking out a suitable site among the list and visiting this site in order to get the information about price and location. Therefore a search cost is incurred in order to get complete information about one site (one hotel). If the hotel is "close enough" to the consumer's preference, the transaction can take place, otherwise it is preferable to perform a new search in the hope of finding a better alternative. The decision depends on the characteristics of the current hotel, on the priors on the characteristics of future hotels to discover and on the cost of searching further.

The results from the search engine are of different kinds. The consumer gets sites of a single hotel (Bristol, Le Crillon, Meurice, Ritz, Scribe, Westminster, Hilton, Intercontinental, etc.), but also sites that refer to several hotels. In their more simple version these collective sites, to which we will refer as "coalitions", have only an electronic link to the sites of single hotels: Le Crillon and Bristol, for example, feature at lodging-france.com with two other luxury hotels. Another kind of collective site also offers the opportunity to reduce the consumer's search cost through the development of specialized search engines. By sorting the results of the site by category, it is possible to find "in one click" a number of luxury hotels that may vary from one site to another (none at hotel-paris.com or hotelus.com, two at parishotelreservation.com, four at paris.book-online. org, five at hotel-paris-tobook.com and hotelclub.org, six at 0800paris-hotels.com). By visiting such a site, the consumer gains access to more results corresponding to their search by incurring a lower cost than the one required to extract the information from the entire web.

The reduction of search costs is considered to be the result of the coordinated efforts of the coalesced sites to develop more efficient search tools helping Internet consumers to find goods closer to their preferences. But from the hotels' point of view, the interest of forming a coalition is to increase the probability of being visited, thereby increasing the expected demand. Developing a site for a group of hotels (or agreeing to appear in a portal site made by a specialized firm) also has the advantage of being a very low-cost device if we compare it to the cost of merging in the physical world. In this kind of coalition, hotels remain independent (in particular in their price policy) and benefit only from the increase in visits of those consumers that book online. Since we are interested in the outcome in terms of emerging coalition structure, we observe that in most of the cases, inside a coalition hotels belong to different neighborhoods – for instance, in the 0800paris-hotels.com coalition, the six luxury hotels proposed by the site are located in six different districts of Paris.

The results we obtain with the model presented in the next section are consistent with these findings: firms prefer to coalesce with differentiated partners. But we obtain more when we look at the Nash equilibrium prices of highly differentiated firms belonging to a coalition compared with the prices of close-substitute ones grouped in a coalition: in the configuration we modelized, prices are lower within a coalition of highly differentiated firms than in the other case. This goes against the intuitive explanation for the preference for highly differentiated partners, which would highlight the fear of increased competition because of perfect information for consumers once they have reached a coalition of firms offering close substitutes without coordinating their prices. We also show that this preferred coalition structure can be beneficial to consumers.

17.4   The model

As in Bakos's (1997) model, we consider a market with a continuum of Internet consumers and m B-to-C sites. m is supposed to be common knowledge. Each site j sells a unique good at price p_j and the characteristics x_j of the goods are differentiated along the unit circle as in Eaton's (1976) pioneering work and subsequent models (D'Aspremont, Gabszewicz and Thisse (1979), Salop (1979), Novshek (1980), Eaton (1982), Stahl (1982), Economides (1989b)). Consumers' tastes x_i are heterogeneous and uniformly distributed along the same circle. When buying a unit of good that does not perfectly match their preferences, consumers incur an adaptation cost t per unit of distance ($t > 0$) between their location (or preference) and the location of the site chosen for transaction (characteristic of the good). Therefore, the utility function if consumer i buys a unit offered by site j is $U(i,j) = r - p_j - t|x_i - x_j|$, where r is the reservation utility of each consumer.

Consumers' search procedure
Consumer i acquires information on the location and the price of one of the m sites of the electronic market by incurring a constant search cost $c > 0$. We consider this search cost to be both the cost associated with the discovery of the site on the web, for example through a search engine, and the cost of visiting the site to find out about its characteristics: sell price S and distance D. The utility of the consumer in case of a transaction is $U(S, D) = r - S - tD$. If the consumer decides to search further and finds another site located at distance x and with price p, the utility in this case is $U(p, x) = r - p - tx$. Thus, $(U(x, p) - U(S, D))^+ = (S + tD - xt - p)^+$ represents the increase of utility for the consumer if $U(x, p) - U(S, D) > 0$ (otherwise it is 0).

We suppose that the consumers are risk neutral. The calculation of the expected gain in utility based on the priors on the distributions of sites' locations and prices allows the consumer to decide on the opportunity to continue the search procedure.

Consumers' priors

Concerning the priors on prices, the consumers believe that at equilibrium all sites choose the same price $p^\star$. More precisely, the distribution of prices is such that $f(p) = 1$ if $p = p^\star$, and $f(p) = 0$ if $p \neq p^\star$. Concerning the priors on locations, the consumers believe that sites locate according to a uniform distribution over the unit circle. We also suppose that consumers find sites according to a random trial with replacement. These assumptions are related to the fact that consumers are considered to leave unchanged their priors on the distributions of locations or prices after finding each site.

Stopping rule

The expected gain in utility obtained in this case is $g(S, D) = \int_{x=0}^{1} (\int_{\Re} (S + tD - xt - p)^+ f(p) dp) dx$. According to the priors of the consumers on the locations, we find like in Bakos (1997) that $g(S, D) = (S + tD - p^\star)^2/t$. Next, the consumer has only to compare its expected gain in utility with the search cost c. If $g(S, D) > c$, the consumer will prefer to continue its search. If $g(S, D) < c$, the consumer will choose to buy a unit of the good located at a distance D and at price S. At equilibrium with rationale expectations for the consumers, $S = p^\star$. For each consumer i located in x_i, we have $g(p^\star, D) < c$ on the interval $[x_i - L, x_i + L]$, where $L = \sqrt{c/t}$. Consequently, if the consumer discovers a site at a distance smaller than L, the transaction will take place. Symmetrically, from the point of view of a site, the most distant potential client is located at distance L. We obtain an interval of length $2L$ around any site, which will be referred to as "natural territory".[7]

Definition 1

The natural territory of a site corresponds to the interval around the location of the site in which consumers will stop their search and buy from this site if they find it.

Let us now describe the simplest framework needed to capture the effects we want to describe once it is possible for sites to coalesce. We consider that $m = 4$, that the sites are located according to the principle

---

[7] It is clear that the length of the natural territory depends on consumers' anticipations. For other scenarios on consumers' anticipations in an agent-based environment, see Laye, Lina and Tanguy (2004).

of maximum differentiation and that they sell at price $p^\star$, which is also the price anticipated by the consumers. We restrict the study in terms of length of natural territories by supposing that $\underline{L} < L \leq \overline{L}$ such that no consumer is priced out of the market[8] and the natural territory of a site intersects only with those of its neighbors. In the case of four sites, we have $\underline{L} = 1/8$ and $\overline{L} = 1/4$. On one hand, this intersection of natural territories will be crucial once there is a coalition on the market (as we will see in the next section), since the consumers belonging to this intersection are the ones that are targeted by the coalition through the reduction of the search cost. On the other hand, when $\underline{L} < L \leq \overline{L}$, the price equilibrium we find is identical to the one found in the basic Salop model (without search cost) for four firms on the circle.

Proposition 2
There is a unique symmetric price equilibrium with rational expectations: $p_j = p^\star = t/4$.

Proof
Let us first compute the expected demand of each of the four sites. For a consumer that belongs to the natural territory of only one site, the search procedure will continue until this site is found. A consumer that belongs to the intersection of two natural territories will buy at the first of the two sites to appear during the search procedure. As a result, each site has an interval around its location in which it does not share the consumers (of length $1/4 - L$), followed by the intersection of the natural territories of length $2L - 1/4$ where the site shares consumers with one competitor. Since no consumers are priced out, the expected demand is $D = 2(1/4 - L) + 2(2L - 1/4)/2 = 1/4$. Next, we search a non-cooperative symmetric price equilibrium $p^\star$. Since the expected demand is $1/4$, the expected profit of a site is $\Pi^\star = p^\star/4$. Let Π^δ be the profit resulting from a price deviation δp of one of the sites, *i.e.* $p = p^\star - \delta p$, resulting in a variation of natural territory by $\delta p/t$: $\Pi^\delta = p/4 + 2p\delta p/2t = p/4 + 2p(p^\star - p)/2t$, leading to: $d\Pi^\delta/dp = 1/4 + 2p^\star/2t - 4p/2t$. The condition $d\Pi^\delta/dp|_{p=p^\star} = 0$ provides the equilibrium price: $p^\star = t/4$.

We see that the equilibrium price increases with the adaptation cost and does not depend on the search cost[9] as long as $\underline{L} < L \leq \overline{L}$, where $L = \sqrt{c/t}$. L and $p^\star$ are in fact two aspects of the same reality at equilibrium based on the assumption of rational expectations. We can show that there exists a

---

[8] The range $L < \underline{L}$ does not make sense here since these priced-out consumers would indefinitely take advantage of the low search cost without ever finding any satisfying site, which, knowing that there are only four sites, severely challenges the assumption of no revision of the priors on the location of the sites.

[9] More precisely, $p^\star$ is independent from c in each interval of study, but increases with c through $L = \sqrt{c/t}$ as follows: if $L < 1/8$, then $p^\star = \sqrt{ct} < t/8$; if $1/8 \leq L < 1/4$, then $p^\star = t/4$; if $1/4 \leq L < 3/8$, then $p^\star = 3t/8$ and if $3/8 \leq L < 1/2$, then $p^\star = 3t/4$.

bijection between the set of possible prices and the set of possible natural territories: since $g(S, D) = (S + tD - p^\star)^2/t$, if $S = p^\star$, then $g(p^\star, D) = tD^2$ and the transaction takes place if $D < \sqrt{c/t}$. If a site situated at a distance D offers a different price $p' = p^\star - \delta p$, then $g(p', D) = (-\delta p + tD)^2/t = (t(D - \delta p/t))^2/t$. This expected gain has to be compared with the search cost: $g(p', D) < c \Leftrightarrow D - \delta p/t < \sqrt{c/t} \Leftrightarrow D < \sqrt{c/t} + \delta p/t$. If we define $l = L + (p^\star - p)/t$, where l is half the length of the natural territory that results from a price p, the corresponding space of strategy for l is the interval $[0, 1/2]$.

17.4.1 Coalition structures

The setting with four sites we described is also the minimal setting required to differentiate coalition structures: a site willing to coalesce can choose two kind of partners defining the two different categories of coalitions.

Definition 3

A coalition will be called "connex" if the natural territories of its members intersect, otherwise the coalition will be called "non-connex".

For $\underline{L} < L \leq \overline{L}$, a coalition is connex if its members are located consecutively on the circle (little differentiation) and non-connex otherwise (high differentiation) – see Figure 17.1.

From the point of view of the consumers, visiting a coalesced site allows the consumer, who has incurred only the search cost c for a search on the entire web, to visit other sites by incurring a lower cost $c' < c$ within the coalition. We normalize c' to zero. We suppose that consumers benefit only *ex post* from the reduction of the search cost: they do not

connex coalition   non-connex coalition

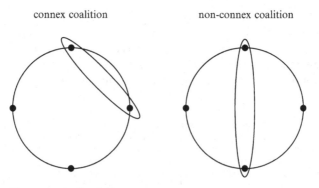

Figure 17.1. Coalition structures.

anticipate the presence of a coalition on the market and if one coalition is discovered the search procedure continues without modifying their priors accordingly. Modifying the priors would be equivalent to considering that after discovering a coalition (without finding a site to make the transaction), the search cost is lower for the rest of the search procedure. In other words, the expected gain is increased since there is more chance of finding a site that matches the preferences of the consumer from now on, in a market with coalitions. Therefore, after the first discovery of a coalition and for the rest of the search procedure we would be in an equivalent situation without this simplifying assumption. Therefore the results are not affected qualitatively by this assumption.

From the point of view of sites, a coalition is a possibility to increase their expected demand. To analyze the incentives to choose a connex or a non-connex partner, we do first the static comparative of the two coalition structures, putting aside price competition.

Proposition 4
With fixed prices, a site willing to coalesce has more incentives to choose a non-connex partner.

Proof
Without loss of generality, the price is fixed at the equilibrium price without coalition $p^\star$. As we have already shown, without coalitions, the expected demand of each of the four sites is 1/4. Depending on the coalition structure, the expected demand will be modified. In the connex case, if I denotes the length of the intersection of the natural territories, the expected demand is $1/4 - I/2 + 2I/3 = 1/4 + I/6$ for each coalesced site and $1/4 - I/6$ for the non-coalesced ones. In the non-connex case, the expected demand is $1/4 - I + 4I/3 = 1/4 + I/3$ for coalesced sites and $1/4 - I/3$ for independent sites. And $1/4 + I/6 < 1/4 + I/3$.

Concerning the robustness of this result, on one hand, for $m > 4$, the equilibrium price is different and the values of the $\underline{L}$ and $\overline{L}$, so that no consumer is priced out of the market and the natural territories of the sites intersect only with those of their neighbors, also change. The length of the intersection of natural territories will be modified but the qualitative result holds. On the other hand, for any m, if we do not suppose that $\underline{L} < L \leq \overline{L}$, then either the natural territories have no intersection or the territory of sites first intersects with those of their neighbors but also with the one of at least two other sites. In the first case $(L < \underline{L})$, some consumers are priced out and will never accept making the transaction, while the others belong to the natural territory of only one site. The search procedure of a consumer will continue until this site is found and the demand is deterministic. The coalition has no effect on the expected demand and consequently this situation is not interesting to study. In the second case $(L > \overline{L})$, not only are the immediate neighbors potential connex partners but it is still a non-connex partner (if it exists since if L is big enough or if m is small enough, all the sites can be connex) that the initiator of a coalition will prefer. It is still the fact that the natural territories intersect or not that will drive the choice of a partner to coalesce. As a consequence, the qualitative result in terms of preferred coalition structures does not depend on the assumptions $m > 4$ and $\underline{L} < L \leq \overline{L}$.

17.4.2 Coalition strategy with price competition

In the previous section, all sites sell at a fixed price $p^\star$ (equilibrium price without coalitions). Given the strength of this assumption, it is necessary to study in what way strategic pricing for the sites influences the choice of coalition structure. For each coalition structure, we find that, at equilibrium, sites deviate from $p^\star$. Here we provide only the expressions of the prices in the intervals in which there is no multiplicity of equilibria. See the appendix for details about the multiple equilibria. Coalesced sites choose their price (denoted by π_{nc} in a non-connex coalition and π_c in a connex coalition) and the members of the fringe choose p_{nc} and p_c.

Proposition 5

In the non-connex coalition case, there exists $\tilde{\varepsilon}$ so that if $L \in [\underline{L}+\tilde{\varepsilon}, \overline{L}]$, we obtain a unique and symmetric price equilibrium:

$$\left| \begin{array}{l} \pi_i = \pi_{-i} = \pi_{nc} = p^\star - \Delta/6 \\ p_i = p_{-i} = p_{nc} = p^\star + \Delta/3 \end{array} \right.$$

If $L \in [\underline{L}, \underline{L}+\tilde{\varepsilon}]$, there is a multiplicity of symmetric equilibria.[10]

In the connex coalition case, there exists $\hat{\varepsilon}$ so that if $L \in [\underline{L}+\hat{\varepsilon}, \overline{L}]$, we obtain a unique price equilibrium:

$$\left| \begin{array}{l} \pi_i = \pi_{-i} = \pi_c = p^\star - 10\Delta/69 \\ p_i = p_{-i} = p_c = p^\star + 14\Delta/69 \end{array} \right.$$

If $L \in [\underline{L}, \underline{L}+\hat{\varepsilon}]$, there is a multiplicity of eventually non-symmetric equilibria but there always exist symmetric equilibria,[11]

$$\text{where } \Delta = p^\star - tL > 0 \text{ for } L \in [\underline{L}, \overline{L}].$$

---

[10] In this case, for a price chosen by a type of site (coalesced or non-coalesced), the other type will choose a price so that their natural territories are adjacent.

[11] These strategies correspond to prices leading to adjacent natural territories for the non-coalesced sites.

Proof

See the appendix.

The proposition[12] shows that for both coalition structures (connex and non-connex), coalesced sites have an incentive to lower their prices from the one obtained without coalitions ($p^\star = t/4$) in order to increase their natural territories (and therefore the length of the intersection of natural territories). The opposite tendency is observed for the non-coalesced sites: they increase their price in order to decrease the length of this intersection. Furthermore, we see that the non-connex coalition is more aggressive than the connex one. The fact that non-connex partners decrease their prices more than if they were in a connex coalition shows that it is not the increase in the competition between the coalesced sites that drives the price decrease. Decreasing the price reflects only the opportunity to gain market share from the non-coalesced sites. When the coalition is connex, a coalesced site gains market shares from the territory shared with a non-coalesced site (on one side of its location) and shares equally the rest of the consumers with its partner (on the other side of its location), which brings no additional demand. The gain of market shares is far better exploited when the coalition is non-connex since it occurs on both sides of coalesced sites' locations, without interacting with their partner.[13]

17.4.3 Welfare analysis

Let us introduce the notations for the different profits and consumers' surplus. Π denotes the profit of a site and W the total consumers' surplus when there is no coalition. In the non-connex coalition case, Π_{nc} and Π_{nc}^f correspond to the profit of a coalesced site and the profit of a member of the fringe respectively, and W_{nc} denotes the total consumers' surplus. In the connex coalition case, the corresponding notations are Π_c, Π_c^f and W_c. The aggregated profit of the retail sector is $\Pi^{total} = 4\Pi$ if there is no coalition, $\Pi_{nc}^{total} = \Pi_{nc} + \Pi_{nc}^f$ in the non-connex case and $\Pi_c^{total} = \Pi_c + \Pi_c^f$ in the connex case. Finally, the total welfare in the three cases is

---

[12] For both coalition structures, the analysis that follows is made over the analytical expressions of the symmetric equilibria (unique or multiple).

[13] We can remark in the non-connex case that the price adjustment of the non-coalesced site $\Delta/6$ is half the one of the coalesced site $\Delta/3$. However, the probability of attracting consumers belonging to the intersection of natural territories for a non-coalesced site is also half the probability of attracting them for a coalesced site. We can also remark in the connex case that the ratio of price adjustment due to the presence of a coalition is equal to the ratio of the probability of obtaining, for each type of site, a consumer belonging to the intersections of natural territories (this ratio is 7/5).

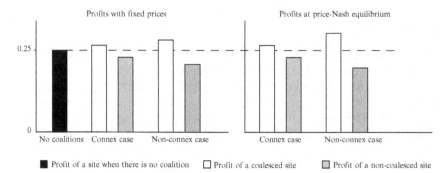

Figure 17.2. Profits comparison.

$W^{total} = \Pi^{total} + W$ (no coalition), $W_{nc}^{total} = \Pi_{nc}^{total} + W_{nc}$ (non-connex), $W_c^{total} = \Pi_c^{total} + W_c$ (connex).

By comparing the profit of the coalesced sites depending on the coalition structure, it is possible to decide which coalition structure is preferred by a site willing to initiate a coalition thanks to the following proposition.

Proposition 6

For $\sqrt{c/t} = L \in [\underline{L}, \overline{L}]$, the profit of a coalesced site in a non-connex coalition is greater than the profit of a coalesced site in a connex coalition, i.e. $\Pi_c \leq \Pi_{nc}$.

Proof

See the static comparative of the coalition structures in the appendix.

Consequently, with price competition, the result we obtain with fixed prices still holds: the initiator of a new coalition always prefers the non-connex structure. In addition to the relative level of prices presented in the previous section (no coalition, firms within or outside the connex and the non-connex coalition), the main results are summarized in Figure 17.2,[14] which makes it easy to compare the profits in the various situations (fixed prices, price competition), for each coalition structure (connex or non-connex), and for the two types of sites (coalesced sites, which are represented first, and non-coalesced sites).

The results of the comparisons of the profit functions depending on the coalition structures are summarized in the next proposition, in which

[14] For the parameters $t = 4$ and $c = 9/16$, leading to $L = \sqrt{c/t} = (\underline{L} + \overline{L})/2 \in [\underline{L}, \overline{L}]$ and to $p^\star = 1$, we obtain a profit for each of the sites of 1/4 when there is no coalition.

we restrict the welfare analysis to the unique symmetric price equilibria described in proposition 5.

Proposition 7

It is always to the benefit of a site to coalesce and the non-connex structure is preferred ($\Pi \leq \Pi_c \leq \Pi_{nc}$ *for the coalesced sites*). *The opposite goes for the members of the fringe* ($\Pi_{nc}^f \leq \Pi_c^f \leq \Pi$). *However, from an aggregated profit point of view, the gain of the coalesced sites is bigger than the loss of the remaining sites when there is a coalition in the market* ($\Pi^{total} \leq \Pi_c^{total} \leq \Pi_{nc}^{total}$).

The consumers' surplus is always increased when there is a coalition on the market ($W \leq W_{nc}$ *and* $W \leq W_c$), *but depending on the length of the natural territory without coalition L, the coalition structures (connex and non-connex) can have different effects. For small values of L, the non-connex coalition is preferable for consumers, but for large values of L, it is the connex coalition that favors them. More precisely,* $\exists \hat{L} \in [\underline{L}, \bar{L}]$ *so that* $W_{nc} \leq W_c$ *if* $L \leq \hat{L}$ *and* $W_c \leq W_{nc}$ *if* $L \geq \hat{L}$.

Finally, concerning the total welfare, the presence of a coalition is always beneficial ($W^{total} \leq W_{nc}^{total}$ *and* $W^{total} \leq W_c^{total}$), *but we also observe a switching value* $\hat{L}$ *when we compare the coalition structures, that is to say,* $\exists \hat{L} \in [\underline{L}, \bar{L}]$ *so that* $W_{nc}^{total} \leq W_c^{total}$ *if* $L \leq \hat{L}$ *and* $W_c^{total} \leq W_{nc}^{total}$ *if* $L \geq \hat{L}$.

Proof

See the appendix.

Comments

Any coalition is preferable for the coalesced sites compared with the profit they obtain without coalition, while it is the opposite for the members of the fringe. However, the aggregated profit of the four sites is increased when there is a coalition on the market. The non-connex coalition that we have shown in proposition 6 to be the best from the coalesced sites' point of view is also the best for the aggregated profit. Consumers are also always better off when there is a coalition on the market. This is due to the fact that the presence of a coalition lowers their expected time for finding a site in which they can buy. Added to this, there is a higher probability of discovering a coalesced site (with a lower price) which also increases consumers' surplus compared with a market without coalitions and with a unique price. Concerning the comparison of the two coalition structures from the consumers' point of view, we see that there is a switching value of the length of initial natural territory L. For smaller values of L, which can be the case when c is relatively small or t is relatively high, the non-connex coalition is better for consumers. But if L is high, it is the connex coalition that is better for consumers. This same effect is transferred to the total welfare. For $L \geq \hat{L}$, it is interesting to notice that firms' interests coincide with those of consumers, not only in coalescing *per se* but also in the optimal choice of coalition structure (non-connex).

Although the analytical model is built with only four firms, some qualitative results can be drawn for more general situations within the same corpus of assumptions (no community effect on the demand side, no price coordination on the supply side):

- If a site initiates a coalition for gaining visibility, it will prefer a differentiated partner (whose natural territory does not intersect with its own one) rather than its neighbors.
- If an individual site wonders whether or not to belong to a portal with already coalesced members, the answer will be yes: to be in a coalition is better than staying alone.
- But if an insider firm offers a product with a close characteristic, otherwise said, if its natural territory intersects with that of the potential entrant in the coalition, it will be worse off and thus it will reject the candidate (if it is entitled to do so).
- We expect firms within coalitions to price lower than single web-sites, and firms within non-connex coalitions to be even more aggressive than firms within connex coalitions.
- Consumers always benefit from the reduction of search costs brought by coalitions, but it is difficult to know whether the non-connex coalition structure is the best for them. In any case the increase in consumers' surplus is always greater than the loss of the members of the fringe, leading to the fact that coalitions improve the total welfare.

17.5   Concluding remarks

Even though starting from a static comparative allows us to make conjectures on the consequences of introducing dynamics and a huge number of sites (see the above section),[15] we have not yet taken into

---

[15] Within the same framework, a simulation model with n sites and m customers has been built with some natural rules for the game of the coalition formation (multiple initiators, random choice of partners, individual profit criterion and veto right). The results obtained by simulation confirm the qualitative trend suggested by the analytical model in terms of coalition structures: few connex components in the coalitions present at a stabilized regime, although some may appear as a response to competition with many coalitions. The rejection criterion of a new member based on the fact that, after having joined the coalition at least one of the previous members is worse off, is sufficient for stopping the coalition formation process after a finite number of simulation steps. The final outcome is typically one or a few "big" non-connex coalitions, many small ones and the remaining individual sites. For more details, see Laye, Lina and Tanguy (2004).

account the various processes of coalition formation, the opportunity to belong to many coalitions or the effects of competition among several coalitions. Nevertheless, we have already captured some mechanisms that could be fundamental in the differences between the structuring of e-retailing markets and the structuring of traditional ones.

A first main difference, when we associate web coalitions to geographical locations, is that entering a coalition, in the sense we have used here, is a decision that can be completely separate from the decision of entering the market. In the usual retail markets, building a shop and choosing a location are the same decision. It is therefore not surprising that we observe a lot of individual, say mono-product, web-sites (the supply can be very fragmented on the differentiation axis) and also a lot of coalitions whose structure can evolve rapidly.[16]

Another main difference is the nature of search costs. In the "real" world, we have clearly two dimensions for horizontal differentiation, which must be taken into account to explain the structuring of the supply side: distance between customers and shops (transportation costs) and characteristics of products (adaptation costs). When consumers' search cost is an issue, transportation cost is at least a big part of it and, moreover, consumers know *ex ante* the location of the marketplaces as well as the importance of the product offering (number of products is the proxy used in the models).[17] In the web-retailing world, the distance component of the differentiation space disappears and the search cost becomes independent from any "location" issue for the aggregation phenomenon. Moreover, we assumed that consumers ignore the existence of coalitions: when the web user unwittingly enters in

---

[16] Portals specialized in a given sector, or sub-parts of multi-sector portals, best exemplify the coalitions we are speaking about. But the results and discussion can be extended to several other forms of coalitions, such as sites that play the role of an intermediary (such as Anyway.com for travel services), and while taking a percentage of the sales, do not distort the prices proposed by their suppliers or "partners". Finally, we can also consider the situation of on-line multi-product distributors whenever their price policy is constrained by suppliers: having been referred to at this distribution site, suppliers indeed appear not far from other competitors (as in a coalition) and keep some control over the pricing of their products as is the case in the "selective" distribution channels where minimum or "advised" prices can be legally enforced by the suppliers.

[17] In spatial competition models without search costs, firms are generally spread over the differentiation line at the equilibrium. Coalition is therefore often associated with price coordination between firms belonging to different locations. To our knowledge, if double horizontal differentiation has already been used, for instance for studying pricing issues between two distant firms offering one or two differentiated products (with price coordination), the structure of the supply has not been treated *per se* so far, certainly not in a world of imperfectly informed consumers (search costs). Where independent mono-product firms locate and what product they choose to produce remains an open question in the real world.

some "city", the search cost for the characteristics of the products offered there is suddenly dramatically reduced.

However, if we consider that search costs to find the product whose characteristics on the Internet are equivalent to transportation costs in the physical world (that is to say, if we consider the geographical location as a characteristic of the good), a parallel can be made between what we call connex coalition and an aggregation of shops in the world of bricks and mortar, such as shopping malls. In both cases the aggregation is aimed at reducing consumers' search cost: by reducing the transportation cost that is a component of the search cost in the real world or by reducing the search cost of searching on the web. In both cases the firms have close locations (corresponding to a geographical proximity in the real world). In this case, the new phenomenon brought by the world of Internet retailing is the possibility for sites to coalesce with a distant partner (non-connex coalition), for which there is no equivalent in the real world. Moreover, we have shown that this structure of coalition is preferred. In the shopping mall, in the usual sense, the (complementary) goods offered by each shop belong to different markets (different circles in our model) and the coalition formation issue is drawn back to the optimal number of shops, in the real world as well as on the web. If we consider now, more interestingly, that a shopping mall often includes groups of branded goods (perfume, jewelry) in competition with the remaining shops in the city, like in our model for B-to-C sites, then the goods offered in a shopping mall will have two dimensions (their geographical location and their characteristic, say their brand name), while in our model we consider only one space of differentiation (characteristics of the products), which, once again, makes the comparison quite difficult, beyond the fact that coalition in both geographical and web space is better than single-brand shops.

All the specific features of the Internet retailing we incorporated in the model are necessary to obtain the main intriguing result: lower prices in the non-connex coalition than in the connex one. When eliminating search costs within the coalitions, the possible gain of market shares against non-coalesced sites is therefore the main force that drives the lowering of prices. This force is dominating the increased competition among firms which is due to the frictionless price comparison. Actually, this result can be obtained because we made a distinction between the situation in which both neighbors, close in terms of product differentiation, are "far away" because of search costs (non-connex case), and the situation in which one of the two neighbors is also close from the search cost point of view (connex case). Obtaining the same type of topology with transportation costs as the main component of search cost remains to be done and we hardly see the empirical facts that could be matched with such situations: in the connex case, the firm must compete both with close substitutable firms in the same city and other ones spread alone in the countryside, in the non-connex case, the shops within the city would be highly differentiated, each one competing with isolated shops, out of the city, offering more similar products.

Finally, and maybe more interestingly still, the model and its results presented should be seen as an inquiry device on the evolving landscape of the web retailing sector, while questioning the relevancy of the assumptions that have been voluntarily left out of the model. As long as tough competition for market shares in a fast-growing market will occur, and new entries of individual sites are possible, we expect that price coordination will not hold within coalitions and we also expect that sites grouped in coalitions will go on competing with single sites. Consequently, we remain in the competition framework of the model. So we do not expect the emerging of a global coalition, nor of several big connex coalitions in those séctors that drive the development of e-retailing. The consequence is that an under-optimization of the search process for e-buyers should continue unless other mechanisms take place, such as:

- strong community effect that alters the utility function of web users. These ones would then reject all the non-connex coalitions where potential buyers are too different and therefore provide poor additional gains in terms of information exchanges, driving in turn connex sites to get together to obtain higher demand;[18]
- search costs of web users that are dramatically altered by massive advertising or word of mouth about sites that are a "must" in each sector and directly capture the e-buyer. The assumption of imperfectly informed consumers could also be progressively irrelevant with the maturation of the sector (few new entrants or landscape changes), a clever use of bookmarks and other learning effects.[19]

Of course, with the maturation of e-retailing and decreasing forces to challenge market shares, the opportunity of price coordination and best taking advantage of that within connex coalitions could reverse the trend. If we add into the picture the costs of developing efficient search engines equipped with the right level of sophistication according to the size of the coalition, free riding on this common good is less likely to

---

[18] See Curien et al. (Chapter 6 in this book) for a discussion on the conditions that may drive the rise of user communities.

[19] For a model that links the maturation of the sector with search behavior of consumers in the case of non-differentiated goods, see Chapter 16 this book.

happen in a well-organized coalition where discussions on prices would also take place. At this stage, it is still unclear to what extent our e-customer would be worse off with a highly efficient search and higher prices.

17.6   Appendix

17.6.1   Proposition 5: price equilibria

Notations

In order to compute the price equilibrium it is more suitable to use an equivalent strategic variable (half natural territories): λ_i corresponding to price π_i is set by a coalesced site; λ_{-i} is set by the other coalesced site (partner in the coalition); l_i corresponding to price p_i is set by a non-coalesced site; l_{-i} is set by the other non-coalesced site. We also define an auxiliary variable $K = L/2 + 1/8$ in order to simplify the expressions at equilibrium.

The first step of the demonstration consists in showing that in both the connex and non-connex case, price strategies corresponding to natural territories that exceed $1/2$ (i.e. with $l > 1/4$) are dominated. In order to compute the Nash equilibrium strategy of a coalesced site, we suppose that the strategies of the other sites are fixed and we search the best reply strategy of this site. We can remark that its profit for $l \in [0, 1/4]$ depends on the configuration of the overlapping with the natural territories of its neighbors that determines the probability of capturing consumers, thus the expected demand. We can point out three different intervals depending on whether there is an intersection with none, one or both neighbors' natural territories. In each of these intervals the expected demand is a continuous linear function of l, therefore the profit on each interval is the restriction of a continuous and concave function. As a result we can reduce the study of the best reply to finding the maximum of three points, each of them corresponding to the unique optimum of the profit function on each interval. For each coalition structure (connex or non-connex) there are many cases to be treated depending on how the strategies of the remaining sites are fixed. The method consists in treating them exhaustively.

In the non-connex case, the profit function is concave-like. In this case we know that the maximum of the profit function in $[0, 1/4]$ is unique. Since the two coalesced sites face the same situation, they choose this unique optimal strategy. The same happens for the non-coalesced sites. Thus $\lambda_i = \lambda_{-i} = \lambda$ and $l_i = l_{-i} = l$. The best reply functions verify $\lambda^{BR}(l) = \max(1/4 - l, K - 1/16 + l/4)$ and $l^{BR}(\lambda) = \max(1/4 - \lambda, K - 1/4 + \lambda)$.

Solving this system shows that if $K \geq 5/26$, there is a *unique symmetric equilibrium* in which the coalesced sites have a larger natural territory than the non-coalesced sites: $l_i = l_{-i} = 8K/3 - 5/12$ and $\lambda_i = \lambda_{-i} = 5K/3 - 1/6$. And if $K < 5/26$, there is a *multiplicity of symmetric equilibria* that correspond to adjacent territories (sites avoid to intersect and to price out consumers) given by: $l_i = l_{-i} \in [K/2, 1/4 - 4K/5]$ and $\lambda_i = \lambda_{-i} = 1/4 - l_i$. By applying the bijection $l = L + (p^* - p)/t$, we find the price equilibrium and the definition of K gives $\tilde{\varepsilon} = 1/104$.

In the connex case, let us identify a player with its strategic variable. When we consider a coalesced site λ_i, we denote by λ_{-i} its neighbor and partner in the coalition, and by l_i its non-coalesced neighbor. In the same way, when we consider a non-coalesced site, we denote it as l_i and its neighbors as λ_i and l_{-i}. We compute the three candidates for optimality and we eliminate strongly dominated strategies in the different configurations of natural territories ($\lambda_{-i} \geq l_i$, $\lambda_{-i} \leq l_i$, $l_{-i} \geq \lambda_i$, $l_{-i} \leq \lambda_i$). We find that the Nash equilibrium must verify simultaneously the two systems:

$$(E) \begin{cases} \lambda_i = K - 5/56 + 3\lambda_{-i}/14 + l_i/7 \\ \lambda_{-i} = \max(K - 5/56 + 3\lambda_i/14 + l_{-i}/7, 1/4 - l_{-i}) \\ l_i = \max(K - 7/40 + 3l_{-i}/10 + 2\lambda_i/5, 1/4 - l_{-i}) \\ l_{-i} = \max(K - 7/40 + 3l_i/10 + 2\lambda_{-i}/5, 1/4 - l_i) \end{cases} (I) \begin{cases} \lambda_i > 1/8 \\ \lambda_{-i} > 1/8 \\ l_i \geq 1/8 \end{cases}$$

We check all the possible cases by replacing each expression containing a "max" by an equality with one of the two terms and the corresponding inequality. More precisely, in case k, (E) will be replaced by a linear system (E_k) of equalities containing no "max" and a system of inequalities (I_k), and the Nash equilibria verify simultaneously (E_k), (I_k) and (I).

Case 1

We suppose that $\lambda_{-i} = K - 5/56 + 3\lambda_i/14 + l_{-i}/7$, and $l_i = K - 7/40 + 3l_{-i}/10 + 2\lambda_i/5$ and $l_{-i} = K - 7/40 + 3l_i/10 + 2\lambda_{-i}/5$. These assumptions impose the inequalities $K - 5/56 + 3\lambda_i/14 + l_{-i}/7 > 1/4 - l_{-i}, K - 7/40 + 3l_{-i}/10 + 2\lambda_i/5 > 1/4 - l_{-i}$ and $K - 7/40 + 3l_i/10 + 2\lambda_{-i}/5 > 1/4 - l_i$. The set of solutions is non-empty and if $K \in [3/16 + 7/664, 1/4]$, there is a *unique equilibrium* in which the coalesced sites have a larger natural territory than the non-coalesced sites, defined by: $l_i = l_{-i} = 166K/69 - 97/276$ and $\lambda_i = \lambda_{-i} = 118K/69 - 49/276$.

Case 2

We suppose $\lambda_{-i} = K - 5/56 + 3\lambda_i/14 + l_{-i}/7$, and $l_i = 1/4 - l_{-i}$. The corresponding system has an infinity of solutions. More precisely, *if* $K \in [3/16, 3/16 + 7/664]$, there is a *multiplicity of eventually non-symmetric equilibria* (even though there exists a unique symmetric equilibrium), parameterized by $\delta \in [0, 4471/18744 - 2822K/2343]$: with $\lambda_i = 14K/11 - 1/11 + 2\delta/17$, $\lambda_{-i} = 14K/11 - 1/11 - 2\delta/17$, $l_i = 1/8 + \delta$ and $l_{-i} = 1/8 - \delta$.

Remaining cases

The set of solutions is empty in all the other cases. By applying the bijection $l = L + (p^\star - p)/t$, we find the price equilibrium and the definition of K gives $\hat{\varepsilon} = 7/332$.

17.6.2 Proposition 6: static comparative of the coalition structures

By comparing the profit of the coalesced sites depending on the coalition structure, it is now possible to decide which coalition structure is preferred by a site willing to initiate a coalition. We have shown that there always exists a symmetric equilibrium in both the connex and the non-connex cases. This equilibrium is unique in the connex case. We provide the profit function at this equilibrium in each case in order to show that a non-connex coalition is preferred by the initiator of a coalition. It is easy to show that for the non-symmetric equilibria of the connex case, the non-connex coalition is preferable as well. In fact, the non-symmetric equilibria are close enough to the symmetric equilibrium and the profit function is almost the same.

In the non-connex case, for $K < 5/26$, we consider the values $l = 5/52$ and $\lambda = 1/4 - l = 2/13$. The natural territories do not intersect. Thus, the profit function is given by: $\Pi_{nc} = (2K - \lambda) 2\lambda = 8K/13 - 8/169 \simeq 0.615K - 0.047$. For $K \geq 5/26$, the unique equilibrium is given by $l = 8K/3 - 5/12$ and $\lambda = 5K/3 - 1/6$. The natural territories intersect and the profit function is given by: $\Pi_{nc} = (2K - \lambda)(2 (1/4 - l) + 4/3(\lambda - 1/4 + l)) = 4/27 (K^2 + K + 1/4) \simeq 0.148K^2 + 0.148K + 0.037$.

In the connex case, for $K < 3/16 + 7/664$, we consider the unique symmetric equilibrium: $l_i = l_{-i} = 1/8$, $\lambda_i = \lambda_{-i} = 14K/11 - 1/11$. The profit function is given by: $\Pi_c = (2K - \lambda)(1/4 + 2/3 (\lambda - 1/8)) = 56/363 (4K^2 + K + 1/16) \simeq 0.617K^2 + 0.154K + 0.001$. For $K \geq 3/16 + 7/664$, the unique equilibrium is given by $l_i = l_{-i} = 166K/69 - 97/276$, $\lambda_i = \lambda_{-i} = 118K/69 - 49/276$. The profit function is given by: $\Pi_c = (2K - \lambda)(1/8 + 1/4 - l + 2/3(\lambda - 1/4 + l)) = (1400K^2 + 1715K + 16807/32)/14283 \simeq 0.098K^2 + 0.120K + 0.036$. We see that for all $K = L/2 + 1/8$, $\Pi_c \leq \Pi_{nc}$.

17.6.3 Proposition 7: sites' profits and consumers' surplus

We restrict the welfare analysis to unique symmetric price equilibria described in proposition 5. To compute the average cost $c(x)$ for finding a site to buy a product depending on the consumer's location x and the coalition structure, we must first know the average number of "clicks" needed to discover this site.

Lemma 8

Let τ be the average number of clicks needed to find the correct site and P the probability to find such a site in one click of cost c. Then $\tau = 1/P$ and, therefore, $c(x) = c/P$.

Proof

$$\tau = \sum_{k=1}^{\infty} k(1-P)^{k-1}P = -P\sum_{k=1}^{\infty}[(1-P)^k]' = -P\left[\frac{1-P}{1-(1-P)}\right]' = 1/P$$

The consumer surplus is given by $S = r - p(x) - c(x) - t\delta(x)$, where $p(x)$ and $t\delta(x)$ are the price and the adaptation cost for a consumer located on x. The consumer has at most two possible sites, in which case $p(x)$ and $\delta(x)$ are computed as an average price and distance weighted by the probability of finding each site.

No coalition case

We suppose that one of the four sites is located in $x = 0$. The symmetry of the problem allows us to reduce the study to $x \in [0, 1/8]$. The length of the intersection of natural territories is $I = 2L - 1/4$. Consumers located in $[0, L - I]$ belong to the territory of only one site and the probability of finding it is $1/4$. In $[L - I, 1/8]$, consumers can buy at either of the two sites around their locations and the probability of finding a site is now $1/2$. We have:

$$W = 8\left[\int_0^{L-I}(r - p^\star - 4c - tx)dx + \int_{L-I}^{1/8}\left(r - p^\star - 2c - t\left(\frac{x + (1/4 - x)}{2}\right)\right)dx\right]$$

$$= r + 2c(8L - 5) + t\left(L - \frac{3}{8}\right)\Pi = p^\star/4 = t/16$$

Non-connex coalition case

We suppose that one of the two coalesced sites is located in $x = 0$. The symmetry of the problem allows us to reduce the study to $x \in [0, 1/4]$. The length of the intersection of natural territories between a coalesced and a non-coalesced site is $I_{nc} = \lambda_{nc} + l_{nc} - 1/4$. In $[0, \lambda_{nc} - I_{nc}]$, the consumers belong only to the territory of the coalesced site, but the fact that it is coalesced increases the probability of finding it to $1/2$. In $[\lambda_{nc} - I_{nc}, \lambda_{nc}]$, the consumers belong to the territory of a coalesced site and a member of the fringe. The probability of finding a site where they can buy is now $3/4$. Finally in $[\lambda_{nc}, 1/4]$, the consumer can buy only at the non-coalesced site found with probability $1/4$. We have:

$$W_{nc} = 4\left[\int_0^{\lambda_{nc}-I_{nc}}(r - \pi_{nc} - 2c - tx)dx \right.$$

$$\left. + \int_{\lambda_{nc}-I_{nc}}^{\lambda_{nc}}\left(r - \left(\frac{2\pi_{nc}}{3} + \frac{p_{nc}}{3}\right) - \frac{4c}{3} - t\left(\frac{2x}{3} + \frac{1/4 - x}{3}\right)\right)dx\right.$$

$$+ \int\limits_{\lambda_{nc}}^{1/4} \left(r - p_{nc} - 4c - t\left(\frac{1}{4} - x\right)\right) dx \Bigg]$$

$$= r + \frac{16}{9}c(7L - 5) + \frac{1}{72}t(88L - 29)$$

$$\Pi_{nc} = 2\pi_{nc}\left[(\lambda_{nc} - I_{nc}) + \frac{2}{3}I_{nc}\right] = \frac{1}{432}\left(16c + 5t(5 + 8L)\right)$$

$$\Pi^f_{nc} = 2p_{nc}\left[(l_{nc} - I_{nc}) + \frac{1}{3}I_{nc}\right] = \frac{2}{27}(c + t - 2Lt)$$

Connex coalition case

We suppose that one of the two coalesced sites is located in $x = 0$. The symmetry of the problem allows us to reduce the study to $x \in [0, 1/2]$, or for simplicity reasons to $[-1/8, 3/8]$. The length of the intersection of natural territories between a coalesced and a non-coalesced site is $I_c = \lambda_c + l_c - 1/4$. The length of the intersection of natural territories between the two coalesced sites is $\mathcal{J}_c = 2\lambda_c - 1/4$. The length of the intersection of natural territories between the two non-coalesced sites is $K_c = 2l_c - 1/4$. In $[-1/8, \lambda_c - I_c]$, consumers belong only to the natural territory of a coalesced site discovered with probability 1/2. In $[\lambda_c - I_c, \lambda_c]$, consumers belong to the intersection of the natural territories of a coalesced site and a non-coalesced site and, therefore, discover a site where they can buy with probability 3/4. In $[\lambda_c, 1/4 + l_c - K_c]$, consumers belong only to the natural territory of a non-coalesced site discovered with probability 1/4. Finally, in $[1/4 + l_c - K_c, 3/8]$, consumers belong to the intersection of the natural territories of the two members of the fringe, each one found with probability 1/2.

$$W_c = 2\Bigg[\int\limits_{-1/8}^{\lambda_c - I_c} (r - \pi^c - 2c - t|x|)dx$$

$$+ \int\limits_{\lambda_c - I_c}^{\lambda_c} \left(r - \left(\frac{2\pi_c}{3} + \frac{p_c}{3}\right) - \frac{4c}{3} - t\left(\frac{2x}{3} + \frac{1/4 - x}{3}\right)\right) dx$$

$$+ \int\limits_{\lambda_c}^{1/4 + l_c - K_c} \left(r - p_c - 4c - t\left(\frac{1}{4} - x\right)\right) dx$$

$$+ \int\limits_{1/4 + l_c - K_c}^{3/8} \left(r - p_c - 2c - \frac{t}{2}\left(\left(x - \frac{1}{4}\right) + \left(\frac{1}{2} - x\right)\right)\right) dx \Bigg]$$

$$= r + \frac{32}{4761}c(1633L - 747) - \frac{t}{304704}(146608L + 61231)$$

$$\Pi_c = \pi_c \left[(\lambda_c - \mathcal{J}_c) + \frac{1}{2}\mathcal{J}_c + (\lambda_c - I_c) + \frac{2}{3}I_c \right] = \frac{7t}{457056}(40L + 59)^2$$

$$\Pi_c^f = p_c \left[(l_c - K_c) + \frac{1}{2}K_c + (l_c - I_c) + \frac{1}{3}I_c \right] = \frac{5t}{457056}(83 - 56L)^2$$

Comparison of coalition structures

All the profit and surplus functions are continuous and strictly monotonous. Most of the comparisons of the propositions are trivial. Let $d(L) = W_c - W_{nc}$. Since $d(L)$ is a continuous strictly decreasing function for $L \in [\underline{L}, \overline{L}]$ and $d(\underline{L}) \geq 0$ and $d(\overline{L}) \leq 0$, we know that there exist $\tilde{L}$ such that $d(\tilde{L}) = 0$. The same goes for $d^{total}(L) = W_c^{total} - W_{nc}^{total}$ which leads to the switching value $\hat{L}$.

18 Bidding and buying on the same site

Marc Bourreau and Christian Licoppe

18.1 Introduction

E-commerce is growing steadily today despite the setbacks of the "new economy". As consumers become accustomed to this type of market mediation, new ways of configuring trade appear. In the received view of e-commerce, on-line consumption seems to be a process compacted in time and space, condensed into the interval of an Internet session and focused on the space of a computer screen. A consumer seeking a particular good such as a tour can compare the offers of several agencies by consulting them either individually or simultaneously on the same screen, via several navigation windows opened at the same time. In the same way he or she can explore different ways of purchasing products, for example by buying an air ticket either directly from an airline or from a last-minute travel discounter or, alternatively, on specialized auction sites. In the "bricks and mortar" world of shops, agencies and counters, this type of exploration requires the customer to visit different places and often involves significant amounts of time and preparation. The "search costs" limit the scope of the exploration, making visits to distant points of sale an exception. The telephone and call centers facilitate this type of exploration without allowing the same kind of focusing as with e-commerce where everything can happen simultaneously on the same screen.

In this chapter we consider the effects of e-commerce on consumption practices when such an activity (consuming), and related courses of action (exploring the offer), and operations (web surfing routines) can all be performed on a single screen within the same connected session. We adopt an original approach, which combines a sociological analysis and an economic analysis to study the effects and rationale of two different modes of commercialization.

We have chosen a case study in which proximity effects on consumption are particularly salient: an on-line travel agency offering the same good in two different ways, from the home page of its site. Once a week this firm auctions a number of trips and tours on its website. Its development of on-line auctions was designed more for advertising purposes than to build a distribution channel in its own right (that is, with a turnover comparable to selling on catalog). Initially the idea was essentially to use electronic auctions to build an innovative, high-tech image. The same flights and holidays are sold simultaneously on the site by auctions, and at the standard catalog price. Consumers thus have the possibility of buying the same good, on the same site, commercialized in two different ways and at two different prices. From an economic point of view, auctioning and selling on catalog are two distinct commercial approaches.

When the same good can be bought at either a set price or by auction (e.g. in the wine market), different actors commercialize it in one way or the other. The example that we are about to study is extreme in the sense that e-commerce produces a twofold proximity: a) proximity on the screen for the consumer (who, with a few clicks, can buy an auctioned tour at a listed catalog price) and b) organizational proximity for the sellers (because as the firm is commercializing the same goods in two ways, its agents are in contact with customers who have been exposed simultaneously to both alternatives on the site and have bought flights and/or tours in either way).

This research question is a continuation, in the e-commerce context, of empirical studies over the past two decades on the anthropology of consumption and economic sociology, on the relationship between trade and the concrete environments in which it takes place. A first current was characterized by the historical and ethnographic study of the encounter between consumers and goods in very different places and situations, from the souk (Geertz, 1979) to the provincial market (De la Pradelle, 1996), the supermarket (Miller, 1998) or the flea market (Sciardet, 2003). The economics of conventions introduced into the economic and social sciences the analysis of conventional arrangements on which the qualification of goods is based (Eymard-Duvernay, 1986; Boltanski and Thévenot, 1991). Part of economic sociology has applied these different research currents to illuminate the concrete modalities of commercialization (Barrey, Cochoy and Dubuisson-Quellier, 2000; Cochoy, 2002) and to analyze the devices that market professionals use to adjust and co-produce consumers' preferences and the qualities of goods (Hennion, Maisonneuve and Gomart, 2000; Mallard, 2002; Teil, 2004).

In this chapter we treat websites and e-commerce as a particular, highly instrumented form of commercialization. We highlight and analyze the economic, pragmatic and moral consequences of the kinds of screen-based propinquities created by e-commerce sites.[1] This question of proximity effects within commercial arrangements has, as yet, been studied only from the very different angle of the problems raised by the proximity of quasi-identical products on the same shelves and the consumer's dilemma when faced with the choice between identical goods: this dilemma is the basis for the "economics of qualities" (Cochoy, 2002). In our case, the consumer's dilemma lies in his access to two distinct pricing mechanisms for the same good. Situations in which, in the same place and at precisely the same time, the consumer is able to buy the same product in one of two different ways, and at two different prices, are exceptional. E-commerce gives an opportunity to study empirically the effects of "proximity" and availability of different pricing mechanisms. As such, it constitutes a laboratory to search for the possibility of some "economics of pricing".

We shall analyze the consequences of the proximity of catalog selling and on-line auctions in three respects. We examine:

- how the rules of auctions and the final prices of products are reframed to make them compatible with distribution on catalog. The key issues concern the qualification of the frame in which a particular transaction is likely to take place. The proximity of auctions and catalog sales generates ambiguity between two different ways of juxtaposing those two modes of commercialization: on the one hand, we have a model of radical, regulated separation and on the other hand, a model of negotiated hybridization;
- how consumers' behaviors and rationality depend on whether they are based on one or the other of the two available commercial mediations, or on both (in which case strategies are developed that explicitly rely on the co-availability of auctions and catalog selling);
- how the proximity of these two forms of selling creates latitude in the sales agents' treatment of customers and how this is put to the test, especially in certain hybrid configurations of the demand. This is the case mainly when certain consumers would like to travel in a group exceeding the number of tickets bought by auction and try to negotiate

---

[1] Internet sites are characterized by the density of pragmatic resources they present for action, interaction and exchange. They act as "interactional artefacts" (de Fornel, 1994) or "communicational affordances" (Hutchby, 2000). Though they look like digital documents, essentially organized as texts, they interweave semiotic and pragmatic dimensions. Their "active" or "interactive" surface is intended to condense and make accessible an apparently inexhaustible quantity of information and possible links on the limited space of the screen page (Jeanneret, 2000). The Internet portals and home pages of e-commerce sites are typical of this tendency towards saturation of communication environments and media with resources for action.

a compromise on the total cost, while the salespeople try to optimize the deal from a professional point of view, in the name of their sales ethos.

The sociological analysis provides detailed evidence that the costs associated with the organization of labor increase when the travel firm provides its customers with the opportunity to trade off between two competing online pricing mechanisms for the same goods. Are there also benefits to the simultaneous provision of two different pricing mechanisms? We shall use an economic model to show that this is indeed the case, from an economic standpoint. To understand why, remark that the sale of tours through a catalog and by auctions has two different timings. Whereas a tour can be purchased from the catalog in advance, only last-minute tours are available in the auction. We assume that consumers value last-minute tours less than tours which are sold in advance; this is because consumers value the flexibility in organizing their tours. Otherwise stated, if we define "quality" as the amount of time left before the travel occurs, last-minute tours are "low" quality tours and tours purchased well in advance from the catalog are "high" quality tours. If, besides, consumers have different tastes for quality, the seller has the possibility to "price discriminate", that is, to sell two qualities at different prices instead of a single quality. We build a simple model of price discrimination for the sale of tours, with two categories of consumers (with low and high taste for quality, respectively). We begin by showing that price discrimination is a profitable strategy when there is a sufficiently low proportion of consumers with low taste for quality. When there is price discrimination, consumers with high taste for quality purchase well in advance tours at a relatively high price, whereas consumers with low taste for quality purchase last-minute tours at a relatively low price.

Another important benefit of selling tours at different dates is the posibility for the tour operator to sell unsold high-quality tours at the last minute and at a lower price. We extend our model of price discrimination to account for this strategy by introducing uncertainty about demand. More precisely, the seller does not know whether demand is "low" or "high" when it offers its high-quality tours. We show that it is rational for the seller to sell a high quantity of high-quality tours. Indeed, if a low demand is realized, the seller has the possibility to sell his unsold high-quality tours at the last minute. Hence, we can conclude that uncertainty increases the incentives to price discriminate.

The rest of the chapter is organized as follows. To begin with, we present the case study on which we will base our analysis. Then, we show

how the rules of the auctions are affected by the proximity of the traditional distribution channel and how consumers trade off between these two different channels. An analysis of the organizational costs and economic benefits of providing two different channels on the same screen follows. Finally, we provide some concluding remarks.

18.2   Screen proximity and two forms of commercialization

The field work on which this study draws was part of a larger research project on the evolution of call centers. In this chapter we focus on a mass distributor in the tourism sector which we will call Travels & Tours. This firm has a national network of agencies and sells both its own tourism products and flights and tours that it buys in batches from suppliers. The aim is to sell everything, as quickly as possible.

Travels & Tours, which has a call center for telephone sales, has been developing its website for e-commerce for the past few years. The site is devoted primarily to the sale of flights and tours at listed catalog prices but the firm also offers consumers two other ways of buying its products. First, a service which we will call "buy and go" enables it to clear unsold products at the last minute, with prices that shrink as the departure date approaches. This service corresponds directly to a current trend in the tourism market where the proportion of tickets and tours bought a few days before the departure date has been rising steadily over the past few years. This form of buying is used primarily by regular Internauts (Licoppe, Pharabod and Assadi, 2002).

The other mode of consumption offered by the site is an on-line auction service. Once a week the site auctions flights and tours, usually close to the departure date. The managers of the company are proud of having developed this service and see the firm as a pioneer in on-line travel sales in France. The auctions are above all a matter of image and publicity. They have enabled the firm to enjoy considerable media visibility and recognition, especially on television, and contribute to the innovative image it tries to build. The amount of money generated by the sales of tickets put up for auction is still low, however, compared with that coming from direct catalog sales. Hence auctions are not really considered as a distribution channel in their own right. This partly explains the relative leeway left to tele-advisers in dealing with problems concerning the auctions. It seems likely that if the firm was to put up more tickets for auction in the future, more rigid rules and procedures would be established in this respect.

The questions raised by the behavior of consumer-bidders stem from the fact that at exactly the same moment the same tickets or tours can be reserved and bought "normally" on the site at the listed price. Thus, at any point in time two prices coexist and these are sometimes so different that the two modes of transaction can no longer be considered comparable. The call center tele-advisers consider auctioned tickets can be sold so cheaply compared with the catalog price that they are more like a gift given to the fortunate or skilled bidder than an actual sale.

The site's home page is occupied mainly by the functions giving access to the catalog offer, with the search engine figuring prominently. In the top right-hand corner two hyperlinks labeled "auctions" and "buy and go" highlight these two specific services for selling at non-standard prices. Since they are written in hypertextual mode, the customer simply has to click on them for access to the corresponding screen. The word "auctions" on the screen can be interpreted as one of the affordances described by the ecological theory of perception, since engagement in the auction process seems to follow on directly from reading the word, with nothing but a click separating the two. But a consumer engaged on his screen with this purpose is simultaneously confronted with other consumption affordances, such as the search engine, or other links and "clickable" images enabling him or her to buy a product at the standard catalog price. We can say that these two modes of commercialization – selling on catalog and selling by auction – are in a situation of "screen proximity" on the home page. They are very close to each other in the consumer's environment of perception and action. How does such a proximity influence consuming practices? To account for empirically observable on-line behavior should on-line auctions and on-line catalog sales be treated as independent mediations – which would amount to considering that this consumer's behaviors are not affected by the proximity of the home page hypertextual links that give access to them? Or should they, by contrast, be considered as a single commercial device equipping the situation of electronic consumption and whose hybrid properties differ from the sole juxtaposition of the commercial mediations comprising it? This is what we set out to do by exploring its consequences, way beyond the luminous surface on which this proximity is so glaringly set.

Our work is based on a series of interviews, observations and recordings made in a call center responsible for telephone relations with on-line customers. This center constitutes an ideal point of entry to reconstruct the interactional and organizational work required to adjust consumption behaviors to situations of co-availability of auction and catalog buying. Such work constitutes the hidden side of this screen proximity and that cannot be dissociated from it.

18.3   How the rules of an auction system are affected by the proximity of the traditional distribution channel

Since auctions are accessible only from the website, they are managed by the service that supervises the site and its content (T&T Online). This service has outsourced the software part of the auction system. After closure of each auction the subcontractor records the process and provides an ordered list of winners.

The on-line auctioning of tickets and tours also available in the Travels & Tours general catalog leads to constraints on price determinations that would not be observed in a pure auction system. At the bottom of the scale a reserve price of one quarter the catalog price is set on tickets – a cut price since profits on tourism products typically range between 5% and 25%. This reserve is not apparent on the site, where starting prices are usually much lower. The auction process (as seen from the consumer side) therefore mimicks a free auction dynamic at play in which the seller takes the risk of letting the product go at a virtually token price, unrelated to its real value. In reality, the site managers have to agree to a set reserve price (i.e. a minimum price under which the good cannot be sold) negotiated on an ad hoc basis with the sales managers. At the top of the scale, in some cases the consumers bid higher than the catalog price, the price at which they could also buy the same product directly on the site at the very same moment. However, since it is illegal to sell a flight or tour for more than the catalog price, the winners are informed accordingly and the price eventually paid has an upper limit, set to the catalog price. These constraints on price determination are the results of pressure on the auction system created by the nagging proximity of the regular selling procedure.

This proximity is felt not only as constraints on final prices. Often batches of tickets or tours have to be totally cleared in a single auction where each bidder can bid on a maximum of only one or two tickets. This configuration differs from auctions for the general public where each good is singular and can be bought only once (e.g. an art auction), or from cases where the seller auctions identical batches of a given product, but where batches are auctioned one after the other, as in the "au cadran" auctions sales of strawberries on the wholesale markets of central France (Garcia, 1986). In the latter case the same bidder can make a clean sweep of all the batches by bidding on each.

Here, Travels & Tours' aim is to sell batches of tickets and tours, but an entire batch is sold in a single session and no consumer may buy more than one or two trips in this way. The managers of T&T Online fear that if all the tickets in a batch of 100 identical tickets were sold by separate auctions, there would not be enough interested bidders to ensure the necessary dynamic in each session. A large number of the 100 tickets would then be likely to be bought at little more than the reserve price. With a single auction, however, one usually does not allow for multiple bidding, even if 100 similar tickets are to be sold. If the bidders were allowed to bid several times they would be able to calculate and would honor only the lowest bids. In the system opted for here, each bidder can buy only two places at the most. At closure of the auction T&T goes down the list of bids, starting with the highest one, and sells tickets to the successive bidders at a price corresponding to their highest bid, until the stock has been cleared. Hence, there is the apparent winner but also the eligible successful bidders, that is, all those who will be contacted by decreasing order of bids, until there are no places left. The higher the number of identical tours thus auctioned, the more the auction service functions like a system for clearing stock. It is then a commercial tool that, like the last-minute on-line sales service where the price drops as the departure date approaches, is part of yield management practices currently used in the tourism industry. The proximity between auctioning and ordinary distribution has a quite significant consequence here, in that the visible winner of the auction game is not the winner in the market sense. The one who, in the end, pays the least is the last of the eligible successful bidders, whose bid was just high enough to enable him or her to buy the last available place.

These effects of proximity embedded in home page design are amplified by the way in which the organization manages relations with consumers. It is the same call center that processes telephone calls corresponding to all the transactions performed on the site (purchases, auctions, etc.). The work is organized in multi-skilled teams (a supervisor and usually six to eight tele-operators). One team deals with a certain type of call for a week and changes its mission by rotation. From week to week, a tele-operator will be confronted with all types of consumer and consumption accessible on the site. The week in which they process calls relating to the auctions follows or precedes the week in which they process mainly ordinary sales, so that the different types of activity and interaction are present in their minds, irrespective of the type of request they are busy dealing with at a given time. Processing calls related to on-line selling and calls related to auctions are thus entangled procedures. The proximity of commercial mediations on the Internet site is reinforced by the propinquity of their handling in the tele-operators' work as well.

In the management of telephone interactions related to auctions, "winners" (i.e. those with the highest bid) are treated differently to eligible successful candidates. The operators make direct contact with the former, whose places have automatically been reserved. However, these winners are not legally committed until the firm has received signed confirmation by letter or fax. The operators' difficulty lies in ensuring that the winners send in this signed form, while talking to them as though they were already committed to honoring their bid. They know, however, that if their customer is unsatisfied or very well informed of his or her rights as a consumer and insists on not honoring his or her bid, they have to backtrack to avoid exposing themselves to accusations of forced sales. The eligible bidders, meanwhile, are not called directly; they are informed of their eligibility by email. The operators wait for them to call to validate their bid, depending on their rank and the number of places still available.

As the operators move down the list of eligibility the status of the transactions becomes more ambiguous. The expression of this ambiguity wavers between the ludic rationality of the auction and commercial rationality, especially when the auction price is distant from the catalog price. For the bidder who is eligible in fourth or fifth place and for the operator who confirms the transaction, is this a game in which the customer has been very lucky to win at so low a price and in which the firm accepts the risks and agrees to reward him or her? Is it a transaction corresponding to a purely commercial rationality, another way of clearing unsold tours at the last minute? In every case the meaning of the interaction as well as the actors' roles and commitments have to be renegotiated. This repetitive and cumulative process of qualification and negotiation weaves the fabric of a social order that determines a special kind of geometry of proximities for the market coordinations at play. It is these interactions behind the screens that we analyze in the following section.

18.4   Mediated constructions of the consumer

Our initial question concerned the proximity between commercial mediations on the screen. The home page of the website that we are studying here offers multiple affordances for engaging in on-line transactions. A high density of links with a large degree of redundancy between them is a characteristic of the home pages of e-commerce sites and Internet portals in general (Beaudouin et al., 2002). The on-line consumer is therefore faced with a complex environment that allows very different navigation and courses of action for comparable efforts. It is to be expected that the pragmatic complexity of sites will lead to a greater variety of their uses. The screen proximity alone of on-line sales and auctions introduces enough complexity into the organization of the home page to result in significant dispersion of user behaviors – as attested by our observations at the call center.

The call center operators encounter a wide range of consumer engagements in the incoming calls they process. At one extreme some consumers play the auction game to the full. A very specific behavior that characterizes auctions is the tendency to collaborate in hectic bidding sequences just before closure (Muniesa, 2003). Here, customers do bid at the last minute and they also protest when they discover that the bid they thought was late enough to be the last one was actually superseded a minute after the official closing time. At the other extreme are those customers who treat the auction as if it were an ordinary form of sale and seem to disregard its ludic aspect. In their calls they demand the right to be served simply because they made a bid that was higher than the starting price and because there are still places available. These Internauts shape their behavior on the expectations and obligations characterizing ordinary distribution. In a shop, when the product is there for all to see, customers consider that they have the right to be served immediately with such a displayed good if they offer an acceptable sum. The possibility of alternating between those who are unable to see that auctions may also be a form of game and those who get too carried away by them clearly reflects the ambiguity of such a bidding process in the context of its uncertain proximity with ordinary sales.

Some consumer tactics are explicitly based on the co-availability of the two types of selling. The day before the auction they reserve the ticket they want and the next day they bid for the same ticket at a lower price. If their bid is not eligible they keep the ticket reserved at the listed price; if it is, they try to cancel the reservation. This manipulation is apparent only if the sales staff who cancel the ticket at the catalog price are skilled enough to notice in the records that the customer has another file open for the same destination, corresponding to the successful bid.

Some calls highlight users' skills in exploiting the resources offered by the complex electronic environments in which on-line sales and auctions are embedded. To bid, one has to register and give a name and email address. Since the entire procedure revolves around their electronic address, some Internauts open several mail boxes and make several different bids, under different email addresses. If they are eligible for several bids they understandably refuse to honor any, save the lowest one. It therefore seems possible to correlate the growing complexity of e-commerce environments with an increasing dispersion and variety of consumer uses, and with the development in some users of real skills in trying to exploit this complexity to the best advantage. The coexistence of different forms of transaction in consumption environments is favorable to the development and mobilization of suitable forms of calculation, among consumers and operators alike. This is an example of how the equipments organizing trade situations influence market rationalities (Callon, 1998).

Because of such calculations by users, a significant cognitive load weighs on tele-operators. They constantly have to interpret bidders' behaviors, both retrospectively (by using the customer information available on computer records) and during telephone conversations. It is necessary for them to evaluate customers' competencies and intentions and to make appropriate decisions in situations of interaction. They therefore valorize "the smartest", those who have chosen to bid for products available in large quantities, at a low enough price to have a good chance of getting the flight well below the catalog price. By contrast, they stigmatize the incompetence of those who, through ignorance, self-absorption or an excess of enthusiasm, bid higher than the catalog price. On the whole, a representation emerges among them of consumer-bidders as mostly experienced, competent and prone to "roguish" behavior. In this context telephone conversations reveal the figure of a typical consumer who is skilled at operating in a complex environment and at exploiting any leeway. It is therefore necessary to be able to evaluate customers' behavior and to determine whether their game is acceptable in relation to the moral economy of the commercial transaction.

18.5   Commercial proximity and tele-operators' autonomy

This work of interpretation and evaluation of consumers by tele-operators is particularly evident in the most uncertain cases, especially the lowest eligible bids. These cases test the various qualifications and justifications used to legitimate the relevant transactions, and they allow for some margin in choosing the interpretive frame in which a given transaction should be concluded. They often require the salesperson to take decisions and to accept or refuse certain transactions without these choices being determined beforehand by a rigid system of rules. In a sense the proximity on the screen of regular sales and auctions allows tele-operators leeway and opportunities for initiative, which are particularly visible in these cases where eligible bids get very low with respect to the catalog price, there is still a significant quantity of goods to be attributed and the customer wants to buy more than what her successful bid allows.

18.5.1   The perfect test of proximity between regular sales and auctions: a winner buys additional tickets

Such a situation, that we frequently observed, puts the sales staff's engagement and autonomy to the test. It often happens that eligible bidders are prepared to honor their bid but wish to make the trip with friends or family, i.e. in a group of three or more, whereas the auction system allows them to buy only two tickets. What should the consumer do in this situation? Agree to buy the additional tickets at the catalog price? This would amount to acknowledging that the auction is simply a limited commercial gesture, embedded in an essentially commercial world, and accepting a framework in which the regular sales service and the auction service are totally disjoint and the former must eventually prevail. Or, alternatively, try – like almost all consumers – to minimize the overall expense by attempting to convince the tele-operator to let them have the additional tickets at the same price as their successful bid? To justify the latter approach, consumers often refer to the necessity to treat each traveler in their family or group equally as regards price. They often refuse to honor their initial bid if this is not granted. This is also a reminder that in almost all cases on-line transactions concern not isolated consumers but a small close-knit group characterized by solidarity and a community spirit.

This simple alternative raised by the question of the purchase of additional tickets corresponds to a rift of larger proportions: the industrial modernity/reflexive modernity divide (Beck, 2001). With industrial modernity, mass distribution allows consumers to buy as many goods as they wish at the same price (here tourism services). The very principle of mass distribution is compatible with social structures such as the family. Reflexive modernity is marked, by contrast, by the emancipation of behaviors relative to traditional social relations and by the rise of individualism. Paradoxically, in this context the individual actor is increasingly dependent on the technico-economic environment proposed to him or her, and compelled more and more to manage his or her daily life like a project that also relies on this complex environment. The proximity and hybridization of commercial mediations tilts the corresponding transactional frame towards reflexive modernity. This can be attributed to the growing complexity of the consumer environment, the limited places available by auction and the corresponding necessity for the consumer, in this plural context, to negotiate the best way of obtaining all the places required for a tour that will either be collective or will not be.

On the tele-operators' side, various interests conflict. Sales staff are not individually interested in auction sales to the difference of catalog sales. The auctions are considered to be an operation for prestige and publicity, as much as a distribution channel in its own right. The company has chosen to associate the corresponding turnover with the unit that manages the site, T&T Online, and it is therefore not treated as cash generated by the call center salespeople. Therefore, unlike on-line sales, for which they are paid an individual commission, the tele-operators receive no commission on auction sales – unless they manage to sell additional services to bidders, at ordinary rates. Thus their individual interest would be to sell additional tickets at catalog price. But if they try to impose that on consumers, they often renege on their bids, and the operator has to move towards the next bidders (and lower bids). But if all operators do so, most tickets will be sold very low and the amount of cash globally generated by the auction will be too low and unsatisfactory to the management, which will comment back on that kind of poor performance. This is internalized as a collective sales ethos to which the operators refer and in which they display their personal commitment in the collective effort to generate cash turnover (and therefore not start a downward spiral where too many tickets will remain unsold or will be sold too low) in the name of the firm's global commercial interests. These cases where bidders ask for additional tickets are never clear-cut.

Hence, the consumer-bidder's negotiation for additional tickets is a trial (*épreuve*) in the pragmatic sociological sense, that is, "a point at which entities are qualified or requalified in relation to a salient issue" (Dodier, 2003). Most particularly at play in this trial, and in the confrontation between the salesperson and the tele-operator in which it is resolved, is the negotiation of a relevant frame for the interaction. Buyers and sellers collaborate to decide, in a situated context, which of the two ways of juxtaposing on-line sales and auctions is to be applied: the model of radical separation on the one hand and of negotiated hybridization on the other. It is because regular sales and auctions are found on the home page of the commerical site, and because of the way in which consumers are treated in each case by the same call center operators, that the problem exists and constitutes a trial for possible commercial frames. Choosing one frame of interaction over the other one is economically consequential. Depending on the frame eventually negotiated for the transaction, the sale goes through or not since the consumer can choose to withdraw by not buying additional tickets or even honoring his or her bids. If the transaction does go through, the consumer's expenditure and the firm's profits will differ, depending on whether the additional tickets are sold at a catalog price or an auction price.

The corresponding conversational work is accomplished during telephone calls made by the tele-operators. Such dialogs constitute rich sources that reveal the economic, pragmatic and ethical consequences of the electronic proximity of on-line sales and auctions, in situated contexts.

18.5.2   From the test of the additional ticket to the moral economy created by the proximity of different forms of commercialization

In practice it is largely up to the salesperson to decide whether to grant the additional tickets requested. Moreover, the information asymmetry is enough to ensure that the consumer rarely has the opportunity to challenge this decision. This type of tricky situation generally allows two alternatives. Either the salesperson tries to enforce and legitimate the application of the auction rules, so that he refuses to sell additional tickets at a price different to that of the catalog. In this case he runs the risk of the bidder declining. The salesperson will then have to sell the same tickets to the next eligible customers on the list, at a lower price. Alternatively, the salesperson can grant the customer's wish and agree to sell the additional places at the same price as the successful bid. In this case the difference between the catalog price and the relevant auction price will be lost. In the former case regular sales and auctions are kept separate, whereas in the latter they are allowed to "hybridize" and to "contaminate" one another to some extent.

From both a financial and an ethical point of view, the difference between the two alternatives is very slim when the auction price is close to the catalog price. In this case the bidder almost becomes a customer (buying at the catalog price). Granting her the requested additional ticket at the auction price is then of little consequence from an accounting point of view. This small commercial gesture does not in any way undermine the salesperson's engagement in the collective maximization of the company's turnover. Salespeople commented in interviews that they were indeed prepared to make such an effort for bidders when their successful bid was slightly less than the listed price. The bidders themselves internalize this moral economy of commercial situations. On several occasions they asked whether it was because they were not the winners (i.e. did not have the privileged status of the necessarily unique winner, and were not the ones who paid the most) that they were refused additional tickets at the same price. When, however, the gap is too wide and the auction price bears no relation to the usual price, the salespeople adopt the accounting logic and seem to consider that simply the fact of honoring the bid is already a fair enough gift from the firm. Asking for an additional ticket is then considered excessive and they tend to refuse.

Between these two extremes less clear-cut situations exist where the tele-operator has to mobilize multiple evaluation repertoires. They are the cases where a limited number of tickets is available and where the relevant bids are significantly lower than the normal price but not so low that the goods seem to be sold for next to nothing, at a provocative price that would cause the salesperson to appear incompetent. Then nothing is determined in advance. It is during the telephone conversation that bidders and tele-operators raise this question of additional tickets at prices that are neither too low nor too high, and negotiate their roles, expectations and obligations with varying degrees of courtesy and mutual empathy. The constitution of the test and its resolution is a conversational accomplishment.

One of the cases that we observed involved an eligible customer who wanted an additional ticket for her daughter at the auction price. The supervisor himself had taken the call and had refused. The customer then decided not to honor her bid. After the conversation the supervisor, normally an outgoing person, was visibly uncomfortable. Without any questions being asked he started to justify himself to the observer. He recalculated the two alternatives and showed that there was a difference of a few hundred francs. Since this calculation done after the phone call clearly failed to satisfy him (the difference was substantial compared with the price of a ticket but not that much compared with the five tickets lost), he discussed the problem publicly, addressing everyone in general in the call center. He then called one of his interlocutors in the T&T Online management team. From these different conversations it emerged that he could have been more flexible. He then moved on directly to the next call. This example confirms that the operator has a fair amount of leeway in dealing with this type of case. The resolution of such problems mobilizes varied and complex evaluation repertoires, the use of which is rooted in the dynamic of the telephone conversation and requires conversational competencies. It also shows the extent to which the initiatives taken within the latitude available to operators correspond to a distributed and ever-present professional collective. Telephone conversations are treated in an open-space configuration, where neighboring operators can hear what is going on, while there are frequent telephone interactions between the supervisor and the T&T Online site manager.

The sales and auction context involves an effort at interpretation and evaluation by the tele-operators who mobilize individual competencies and collective solidarity. For transactions that the proximity of on-line bidding and catalog selling renders ambiguous, they have sufficient leeway to negotiate their answer to consumers' requests during the conversation and in so doing to set the meaning of the transaction concerned. The Internet home page vicinity of such different commercial modes of coordination leads to individual and collective empowerment of tele-operators that runs counter to the trend towards rationalization and even Taylorization of interactional practices that have often been described as characteristic of call centers (Boutet, 2001; Buscatto, 2002; Cousin, 2002). This autonomy and empowerment may be only temporary and likely to be crushed by organizational rationalization, especially if the auctions, victims of their own success, soon become a distribution channel in their own right. We can also believe that the continuous innovative redesign of Internet sites might lead to new forms of screen proximity for different consumption mediations, and more generally that the proliferation of ICTs will lead to a greater complexity of consumers' pragmatic environment with respect to commercial transactions. Such an effervescence might also stimulate the constant appearing of new forms of autonomy and competencies for salespeople in call centers.

18.6   Benefits of selling tours through two different mechanisms

Whereas a tour can be purchased from the catalog in advance, only last-minute tours are available in the auction. We assume that consumers value last-minute tours less than tours which are sold in advance; this is because consumers value the flexibility in organizing their tours. Otherwise stated, if we define "quality" as the amount of time left before the travel occurs, last-minute tours are "low" quality tours, and tours purchased well in advance from the catalog are "high" quality tours. If, besides, consumers have different "tastes" for quality, the seller has the possibility to "price discriminate", that is, to sell two qualities at different prices instead of a single quality.

In the following, we provide a model of price discrimination for the sale of tours. We start by introducing a standard model of price discrimination (as in Belleflamme, 2004). Then, we introduce uncertainty about demand and show that demand uncertainty increases the incentives to price discriminate.

18.6.1   A basic model of discrimination

Travels & Tours sells mainly "tours" (hotel plus flight) at the last minute. For this type of product, we assume that consumers' willingness to pay increases when the tour is sold at an earlier date. Our idea is that, for tours, consumers value the time they have to organize their trip. Therefore, the quality of a tour is characterized by the amount of time left before the travel occurs. More specifically, if a tour is commercialized at date t and occurs at date $T \geq t$, we assume that its quality is $s = T - t$; hence, the higher t, the lower the quality of the tour. There are two types of consumers: consumers of type "1" have a low "taste" for quality, θ_1, with $\theta_1 > 0$, and are in proportion ρ_1; consumers of type "2" have a high "taste" for quality, θ_2, with $\theta_2 > \theta_1$, and are in proportion ρ_2, with $\rho_1 + \rho_2 = 1$. We denote by M the number of potential consumers. Since $\rho_1 + \rho_2 = 1$, there are $N_i = \rho_i M$ consumers of type $i = 1$, 2. When consuming a tour of quality s, a consumer of type i obtains gross utility of $V(s, i) = k + \theta_i s$, where $k > 0$ is a fixed utility obtained from consuming tours.[2]

We consider a monopolist who sells tours. The marginal cost of production is constant and denoted by c. We assume that $c \leq k$, which implies that it is viable to sell tours. The monopolist knows the distribution of the taste parameter but is unable to identify a particular consumer's type. He has two options: he can either sell a unique quality at a single price, or price discriminate by offering two qualities at different prices. In the following, we examine the two options in turn. Profits are denoted by π^s when the monopolist offers a *single* quality and π^t when he offers *two* qualities.

Single quality

Assume that the monopolist offers a single quality, s, at price p. The monopolist's program is to maximize his profit with respect to p. He has two options: he can either sell tours to consumers of type 2 only at price $p = k + \theta_2 s$ and obtain a profit of

$$\pi_2^s = N_2(k + \theta_2 s - c)$$

or sell to both types of consumers at price $p = k + \theta_1 s$ and obtain a profit of

$$\pi_{1+2}^s = (N_1 + N_2)(k + \theta_1 s - c).$$

The monopolist serves all consumers if and only if $\pi_{1+2}^s \geq \pi_2^s$ or

$$\frac{N_2}{N_1 + N_2} \leq \frac{k + \theta_1 s - c}{k + \theta_2 s - c}.$$

This condition means that the monopolist covers the market if there is a high proportion of consumers with high taste for quality (that is, N_2 is high compared to N_1) and/or the willingness to pay of consumers of type 2 is high compared to that of consumers of type 1 (that is, θ_2 is high compared to θ_1).

---

[2] Though consumers purchase a tour of quality $s(t)$ at date t, we do not discount utility. The preference for travel that is commercialized earlier is accounted through the s term in the utility function.

Quality choice

Since π_2^s and π_{1+2}^s are both increasing in s, whether he chooses to cover the market or not, the monopolist chooses the maximum quality, that is, he sets $s^\star = T$ (or $t^\star = 0$).

Two qualities

Now, assume that the monopolist offers two different qualities, denoted by s_1 and s_2, with $s_2 > s_1$. We determine the prices (p_1, p_2) which maximize the profit of the monopolist and such that a consumer of type i chooses quality s_i at the equilibrium.

The monopolist faces two types of constraints: "individual rationality" constraints and "self-selection" or "incentive" constraints. The individual rationality constraint means that the monopolist must set a sufficiently low price for a tour of quality s_i so that consumers of type i prefer to purchase that tour rather than not to purchase. Formally, a consumer of type i purchases quality s_i at price p_i only if he gets higher utility from purchasing than from not purchasing, i.e.

$$k + \theta_i s_i - p_i \geq 0.$$

The incentive constraint means that, for $i \neq j$, the price differential between quality s_i and quality s_j is sufficiently large so that a consumer of type i prefers to purchase quality s_i than quality s_j. Formally, a consumer of type i decides to purchase quality s_i at price p_i only if he gets higher utility than from purchasing quality s_j at price p_j, i.e.

$$\theta_i s_i - p_i \geq \theta_i s_j - p_j.$$

To summarize, the monopolist chooses prices (p_1, p_2) to maximize his profit, with respect to four constraints:

$$p_1 \leq k + \theta_1 s_1, \tag{18.1}$$

$$p_1 \leq p_2 - \theta_1(s_2 - s_1), \tag{18.2}$$

$$p_2 \leq k + \theta_2 s_2, \tag{18.3}$$

$$p_2 \leq p_1 + \theta_2(s_2 - s_1). \tag{18.4}$$

Conditions (18.1) and (18.2) are the individual rationality and incentive constraints for consumers of type 1, and conditions (18.3) and (18.4) are the individual rationality and incentive constraints for consumers of type 2. We solve the maximization problem of the monopolist, which yields the optimal prices under price discrimination.

Lemma 1
Under price discrimination, the optimal prices are $p_1^\star = k + \theta_1 s_1$ and $p_2^\star = k + \theta_1 s_1 + \theta_2(s_2 - s_1)$.

Proof
Since monopoly profit is increasing in p_1 and p_2, the monopolist raises prices p_1 and p_2 as long as the four constraints hold. Therefore, at the optimum, either (18.1) or (18.2) is binding and, similarly, either (18.3) or (18.4) is binding.

To begin with, suppose that condition (18.3) is binding, that is, we have $p_2 = k + \theta_2 s_2$. Then, condition (18.4) implies that $p_2 \leq p_1 + p_2 - k - \theta_2 s_1$, i.e., $k + \theta_2 s_1 \leq p_1$. Since $\theta_2 > \theta_1$, this implies that $p_1 \geq \theta_2 s_1 + k > k + \theta_1 s_1$, which contradicts (18.1). As condition (18.3) is not binding, condition (18.4) is, that is, we have

$$p_2 = p_1 + \theta_2(s_2 - s_1).   \qquad (18.5)$$

Now, consider conditions (18.1) and (18.2). If condition (18.2) were binding, we would have $p_1 = p_2 - \theta_1(s_2 - s_1)$. Substituting for p_2 in (18.5), we obtain

$$p_1 = p_1 + \theta_2(s_2 - s_1) - \theta_1(s_2 - s_1),$$

or

$$\theta_2(s_2 - s_1) = \theta_1(s_2 - s_1).$$

Since $s_1 \neq s_2$, this equality is equivalent to $\theta_2 = \theta_1$, which contradicts our assumption that $\theta_2 > \theta_1$. Therefore, condition (18.2) is not binding, hence condition (18.1) is. Therefore, we have $p_1^\star = k + \theta_1 s_1$. Replacing for $p_1^\star$ in (18.5) yields $p_2^\star$. ∎

Optimal prices can be interpreted as follows: the monopolist extracts all surplus from consumers of type 1 and sets a price not too high for consumers of type 2, such that they prefer purchasing quality s_2 than quality s_1. It can be checked that conditions (18.1)–(18.4) hold when the monopolist sets prices $p_1^\star$ and $p_2^\star$.[3]

Quality choice
Replacing for optimal prices $p_1^\star$ and $p_2^\star$, profit can be rewritten as a function of s_1 and s_2,

$$\pi^t(s_1, s_2) = (k + \theta_1 s_1 - c)N_1 + [k + \theta_1 s_1 + \theta_2(s_2 - s_1) - c]N_2.$$

Since, for any s_1, profit is increasing in s_2, the monopolist sets high quality at its maximum, that is, he sets $s_2^\star = T$. Furthermore, profit decreases with s_1 if and only if $\theta_1(N_1 + N_2) < \theta_2 N_2$ or $N_2/(N_1 + N_2) > \theta_1/\theta_2$.

---

[3] Conditions (18.1) and (18.3) hold by construction. Condition (18.2) holds if $p_1^\star \leq p_2^\star - \theta_1(s_2 - s_1)$, that is, $\theta_1(s_2 - s_1) \leq \theta_2(s_2 - s_1)$, which is always true. Condition (18.4) holds if $p_2^\star \leq p_1^\star + \theta_2(s_2 - s_1)$, that is, $\theta_2(s_2 - s_1) \leq \theta_2(s_2 - s_1)$, which is also true.

Therefore, $s_1^* = 0$ if $N_2/(N_1 + N_2) > \theta_1/\theta_2$ and $s_1^* = T$ otherwise. Since there is price discrimination only if the monopolist sells two different qualities, we obtain the following result.

Proposition 1
There is price discrimination if and only if $N_2/(N_1 + N_2) > \theta_1/\theta_2$.

The intuition is the following. Increasing quality s_1 has two opposite effects on profit. First, it increases the surplus of consumers of type 1, which can be extracted through price p_1, hence it increases profit. Second, since quality is bounded, a higher s_1 reduces the differentiation between the high quality and the low quality. This implies that the monopolist has to reduce his price for consumers of type 2, to ensure that they choose quality s_2. The second negative effect dominates the first positive effect, hence there is price discrimination, when N_2 is high relative to N_1 and/or θ_2 is high relative to θ_1.

Optimal product strategy
To summarize, when he sells a single quality, the monopolist gets a profit of

$$\pi^s = \begin{cases} (k + \theta_2 T - c)N_2 & \text{if} \quad \rho_2 \geq (k + \theta_1 T - c)/(k + \theta_2 T - c), \\ (k + \theta_1 T - c)M & \text{otherwise} \end{cases}$$

whereas, if he sells two qualities, he gets

$$\pi^t = \begin{cases} (k - c)M + \theta_2 T N_2 & \text{if} \quad \rho_2 \geq \theta_1/\theta_2 \\ \pi^s & \text{otherwise} \end{cases}.$$

Note that $(k + \theta_1 T - c)/(k + \theta_2 T - c)$ increases with $k - c$, hence, for $k \geq c$ (as assumed), we have

$$\frac{k + \theta_1 T - c}{k + \theta_2 T - c} \geq \frac{\theta_1 T}{\theta_2 T} = \frac{\theta_1}{\theta_2}.$$

Therefore, we have two cases.

Case 1
If $\rho_2 \geq \theta_1/\theta_2$, there is price discrimination; the monopolist sells tours in advance (that is, high-quality tours) at a relatively high price, and the same tours at the last minute (that is, low-quality tours) at a relatively low price.

Case 2
If $\rho_2 < \theta_1/\theta_2$, there is no price discrimination; the monopolist only sells tours in advance (that is, high-quality tours) at a relatively low price.

Note that, in the first case, if price discrimination were not possible, the monopolist might sell tours to consumers of type 2 only (if $\rho_2 \geq (k + \theta_1 T - c)/(k + \theta_2 T - c)$).

18.6.2 Uncertainty on demand

In this section, we introduce uncertainty about demand. More precisely, we assume that the number of potential consumers, M, is high ($M = H$) with probability μ and low ($M = L$) with probability $1 - \mu$, where $\mu \in (0, 1)$ and $0 < L < H$. When the monopolist makes his decisions, at date 0, demand is uncertain. Uncertainty is resolved at a later date, denoted by $\hat{T}$, where $\hat{T}$ is very small but not equal to zero. Consumers start to purchase tours after date $\hat{T}$.

Along with price and quality, at date 0, the monopolist commits on the quantity of tours, Q, he provides for each quality of tour. We assume that a tour of quality s, which is not sold at its commercialization date, can be sold later as a lower quality tour. We also assume that consumers pay only if they get a tour, which implies that uncertainty does not affect willingness to pay.

Single quality

As above, a monopolist who offers a single quality, s, has two options: he can either sell at price $p = k + \theta_2 s$ to consumers of type 2 only or sell to both types of consumers at price $p = k + \theta_1 s$. First, if the monopolist sells to consumers of type 2 only, his expected profit is

$$E[\pi_2^s] = (k + \theta_2 s)\min(Q, \rho_2 E[M]) - Qc$$

As $E[\pi_2^s] = (k + \theta_2 s - c)Q$ when $Q \leq E[M]$ and $E[\pi_2^s] = (k + \theta_2 s - c)\rho_2 E[M]$ when $Q > E[M]$, $E[\pi_2^s]$ increases with Q for $Q \in [0, E[M]]$, and decreases with Q when $Q > E[M]$, hence the optimal Q is $Q^\star = E[M]$, and

$$E[\pi_2^s] = (k + \theta_2 s - c)\rho_2 E[M].$$

Second, if the monopolist sells to consumers of both types, his expected profit is

$$E[\pi_{1+2}^s] = (k + \theta_1 s)\min(Q, E[M]) - Qc.$$

A similar analysis as above shows that $Q^\star = E[M]$, hence

$$E[\pi_{1+2}^s] = (k + \theta_1 s - c)E[M].$$

Price and quality choice

We have $E[\pi_{1+2}^s] > E[\pi_2^s]$ if and only if $(k + \theta_1 s - c)E[M] > (k + \theta_2 s - c)\rho_2 E[M]$ or

$$\rho_2 < \frac{k + \theta_1 s - c}{k + \theta_2 s - c}.$$

As in the section without demand uncertainty, since $E[\pi^s_{1+2}]$ and $E[\pi^s_2]$ are both increasing in s, whether he chooses to cover the market or not, the monopolist chooses the maximum quality, that is, $s^\star = T$ (or $t^\star = 0$).

After demand is realized, supply can be either too high or too low. In the former case, the monopolist does not sell all his tours. In the latter case, consumers get a tour or no tour randomly.

Two qualities

Now, assume that the monopolist offers two qualities, s_1 and s_2, and commits at $t = 0$ to Q_1 and Q_2 quantities of tours for qualities s_1 and s_2, respectively.

Rationing

When demand is low (that is, $M = L$), every consumer gets preferred quality, as the monopolist has incentives to offer at least $\rho_i L$ tours of quality s_i. However, when demand is high (that is, $M = H$), some consumers do not get their preferred tour if $Q_1 + Q_2 < H$. Let r_i denote the probability of getting a tour of quality s_i.

The fact that a consumer might not get his preferred tour might affect his purchase strategy. In particular, a consumer of type 2 who does not get a tour of quality s_2 could try to get a tour of quality s_1, as tours of quality s_1 are available at a later date than tours of quality s_2. In what follows, we will consider this possibility, but we will assume that a situation in which a consumer of type 1 applies for a tour of quality s_2 because he is not sure to get a tour of quality s_1 does not occur (we will check that it is indeed not possible at the equilibrium).

To summarize, we have the following situation. Consumers of type 2 apply for tours of quality s_2. With probability μ, a proportion $1 - Q_2/(\rho_2 H)$ of these consumers does not get a tour. Consumers of type 1 and consumers of type 2 who did not get a tour apply for a tour of quality s_1. With probability μ, there are Q_1 places for $\rho_1 H$ consumers of type 1 and $(1 - Q_2/(\rho_2 H))\rho_2 H$ consumers of type 2 who did not get a tour of quality s_2. Hence, a proportion

$$1 - Q_1/(\rho_1 H + (1 - Q_2/(\rho_2 H))\rho_2 H) = 1 - Q_1/(H - Q_2)$$

does not get a tour. Therefore, we have

$$r_1 = \min\{Q_1/(H - Q_2), 1\},$$

and

$$r_2 = \min\{Q_2/(\rho_2 H), 1\}.$$

Pricing

The willingness to pay is not affected by rationing, as consumers pay only if they get a tour. Therefore, the monopolist faces the same individual and incentive constraints as in the previous section, which implies that

$$p_1^\star = k + \theta_1 s_1$$

and

$$p_2^\star = k + \theta_1 s_1 + \theta_2(s_2 - s_1).$$

Replacing for $p_2^\star$ shows that the utility of a consumer of type 1 who consumes a tour of quality s_2 is strictly negative. Therefore, no consumer of type 1 applies for a tour of quality s_2 because he is not sure to get a tour of quality s_1. Besides, since consumers of type 2 get higher utility with quality s_2 than with quality s_1, they all apply for a tour of quality s_2 first.

Profit maximization

Last-minute tours provide the monopolist with some flexibility: he can either commit to last-minute tours at date 0, or commit to a larger number of high-quality tours, which he can later transform into last-minute tours if realized demand is low. Since the margin is higher with a consumer of type 2 than with a consumer of type 1, that is,

$$k + \theta_1 s_1 + \theta_2(s_2 - s_1) > k + \theta_1 s_1,$$

the monopolist has incentives to substitute high-quality tours for low-quality tours. Indeed, if a high level of demand is realized (that is, $M = H$), the monopolist makes more profit by selling tours at a high price to consumers of type 2 than by selling at a low price to consumers of type 1. If a low level of demand is realized (that is, $M = L$), then some high-quality tours are not sold, but can be transformed later into low-quality tours.

We have two cases, depending on whether or not all low-quality tours are transformed into high-quality tours.

(i) First, suppose that $\rho_1 E[M] \leq \rho_2(H - E[M])$. In this case, the monopolist transforms all low-quality tours into high-quality tours, that is, he chooses $Q_1 = 0$ and $Q_2 = \rho_2 E[M] + \rho_1 E[M] = E[M]$. With probability μ, demand is high; no low-quality tour is sold, while all the high-quality tours are sold. With probability $1 - \mu$, demand is low; $\rho_1 L$ low-quality and $\rho_2 L$ high-quality tours are sold. Therefore, the monopolist's expected profit is

$$
\begin{aligned}
E[\pi^t(s_1, s_2)] = {} & (k + \theta_1 s_1)(1 - \mu)\rho_1 L \\
& + [k + \theta_1 s_1 + \theta_2(s_2 - s_1)][\mu E[M] + (1 - \mu)\rho_2 L] \\
& - cE[M].
\end{aligned}
\tag{18.6}
$$

(ii) Second, suppose that $\rho_1 E[M] > \rho_2(H - E[M])$. In this case, the monopolist chooses $Q_1 = \rho_1 E[M] - \rho_2(H - E[M])$ and $Q_2 = \rho_2 H$. With probability μ, demand is high; all low- and high-quality tours are sold. With probability $1 - \mu$, demand is low; $\rho_1 L$ low-quality and $\rho_2 L$ high-quality tours are sold. Therefore, the monopolist's expected profit is

$$E[\pi^t(s_1, s_2)] = (k + \theta_1 s_1)[\mu(\rho_1 E[M] - \rho_2(H - E[M]))$$
$$+ (1 - \mu)\rho_1 L] + [k + \theta_1 s_1$$
$$+ \theta_2(s_2 - s_1)]\rho_2 E[M] - cE[M]. \tag{18.7}$$

We can now state our main result.

Proposition 2
Incentives to price discriminate are higher with demand uncertainty.

Proof
The profits given by (18.6) and (18.7) are both increasing in s_2, hence the monopolist has incentives to set the high quality at its maximum, that is, $s_2^* = T$. Now, remember that, in the same setting without uncertainty, we had price discrimination, that is, $s_1^* = 0$, if and only if

$$\frac{\theta_1}{\theta_2 - \theta_1} < \frac{\rho_2}{\rho_1}.$$

We are going to show that, with demand uncertainty, we get a similar condition but that it is more easily met. The profit function in (18.6) is decreasing in s_1 if

$$(1 - \mu)\rho_1 L \theta_1 - (\theta_2 - \theta_1)[\mu E[M] + (1 - \mu)\rho_2 L] < 0,$$

or

$$\frac{\theta_1}{\theta_2 - \theta_1} < \frac{\mu E[M] + (1 - \mu)\rho_2 L}{(1 - \mu)\rho_1 L}.$$

Since the right-hand side is greater than ρ_2/ρ_1, we have price discrimination for a larger set of parameters than without demand uncertainty. Similarly, the profit function given by (18.7) is decreasing in s_1 if

$$[\mu(\rho_1 E[M] - \rho_2(H - E[M])) + (1 - \mu)\rho_1 L]\theta_1 - (\theta_2 - \theta_1)\rho_2 E[M] < 0$$

or

$$\frac{\theta_1}{\theta_2 - \theta_1} < \frac{\rho_2 E[M]}{[\mu(\rho_1 E[M] - \rho_2(H - E[M])) + (1 - \mu)\rho_1 L]}.$$

Note that the denominator can be written as $\rho_1 E[M] - \mu\rho_2(H - E[M]) - (1 - \mu)$ $\rho_1(E[M] - L) < \rho_1 E[M]$, hence the right-hand side is greater than ρ_2/ρ_1. ∎

With this model, we have shown that a tour company benefits from price discrimination when demand is heterogeneous with respect to the willingness to pay for in-advance tours. We also introduced demand uncertainty in this setting. We showed that demand uncertainty increases the incentives to price discriminate. This is because a tour company has the possibility to transform standard (in-advance) tours into last-minute tours.

18.7   Conclusion

The screen proximity between ordinary sales and on-line auctions cannot be reduced to the few centimeters separating the corresponding hypertext links on the home page of the e-commerce site. Continuity on the screen cannot be separated from proximity in the consumers' activity space and in the salespeople's professional work of articulation and organization. It is accompanied by a shift in the rules of the transactional game. The functioning of auctions is in a sense "contaminated" by proximity with ordinary sales. Consumers consequently range from those who take the auction game too seriously to those who deny it and treat it simply as a special kind of direct sale. Some consumers show real skills in trying to take advantage of the multiplicity of affordances offered by the socio-technical system in which the transaction is embedded. The salesperson's interpretive workload is therefore increased since they constantly have to assess consumers' intentions with respect to requests that explore the whole range of possible configurations entwining auction-based transactions and direct sales, on the basis of electronic records and telephone conversations.

The salesperson's interpretive work and leeway are particularly important since one of the characteristics of screen proximity is the production of highly uncertain or ambiguous situations that test the separation between regular sales and auctions. This is the case, for instance, when a couple that is eligible to buy two tickets by auction at a relatively low price wants to buy two additional tickets for their children. Depending on whether the salesperson takes the initiative of selling the tickets at the catalog price (at the risk of the couple refusing to honor the bid) or at the auction price, the transaction and its meaning change. This situation is a trial in so far as it requires an effort at qualifying all the entities composing the situation. This qualification is of an economic order (calculation of the amounts involved), a pragmatic and imperative order (evaluating the position and intentions of both the consumer and the tele-operator on the basis of the auction sequences and the course of their conversation) and, finally, a moral order (what are the expectations, obligations and leeway of each party, and how can the qualification of the transaction and the positions of the consumer and salesperson be co-produced in a way that saves face for all concerned?). It is also to a large degree a mutual conversational accomplishment.

There is not on the one hand a digital document on which hyperlinks towards two distinct forms of sale are situated, and on the other a proliferation of commercial conversations in which services and prices are negotiated and the consumer's and salesperson's positions constructed. The two are inextricably co-constructed. In other words, including an "auction" link on the home page of an e-commerce site means not only creating screen proximity but also allowing an affordance for a wide range of consumption practices based on that proximity. These constitute trials of the commercial transaction that require the actors concerned to qualify all the entities involved in the situation of consumption and to reach an agreement on the regimes of economic, pragmatic and moral justification through which the transaction is likely to have meaning. If there is stability here it is dynamic. The screen proximity can endure only if this work of qualification of situations of transaction and interaction stabilizes it. The two last or change together. Consumption as an activity is embedded in the equipped environments that support it, and it co-evolves with them.

Finally, it seems that in the case studied here, this screen proximity between sales and auctions makes the forms of transaction more complex. It renders a wide range of commercial situations relevant and possible. The management and evaluation of these situations produce a skilled and enthusiastic consumer on the one hand, and a subtle seller with more leeway and decision-making power on the other. Although this does not really amount to a re-enchanting of the consumption process by e-commerce, the use of the e-commerce sites calls for creative exploration by consumers of all the possible behaviors that can be supported by them, behaviors whose complexity and sophistication increase with the complexity of Internet design. This observation can probably be generalized to other contexts where the saturation of environments with interactional mediations is increasingly evident.

Part VI

Evolving institutional infrastructures

19   An economic analysis of conflicts resolution in cyberspace

Bruno Deffains, Yannick Gabuthy and Philippe Fenoglio

19.1   Introduction

The development of the Internet is accompanied by legal risks which induce law and economics scholars to study the question of the appropriate judicial order for efficiently treating the conflicts originating in cyberspace. It is generally accepted that public regulation, which deals with the majority of offline conflicts, is unsuitable or inefficient in the virtual world. A private regulatory system would offer a number of advantages. It is frequently justified by arguments such as the territorial incompetence of classical courts of jurisdiction, and their technical incompetence when faced with anonymous subjects such as those found in cyberspace. Public justice is also characterized by slow management and settlement of conflicts and by high administrative costs, notably in cases where conflicts concern small amounts of money.

The argument about the inefficiency of public regulation of cyberspace has led its authors to think about the ways in which a decentralized and "dejudiciarized" regulation could emerge, and what its organizational structure could be. The main question is how to attain better governance in cyberspace outside governmental control. A commonly studied idea is based on an analogy between the development of private rules, which are common to all cybernauts, and the adoption of the Lex Mercatoria which formed the mode of regulation of commercial activity in the Middle Ages (Deffains and Fenoglio, 2001). Some authors add that the Internet will indeed be regulated. Left to itself, Lessig (2000), for example, says that cyberspace will become a "perfect tool of control" not for the government but for software programmers.

This chapter discusses the more general relationship between technology and law. Dealing especially with the emergence of online dispute resolution (ODR), it explores the idea that technology might be the "fourth party" in conflict resolution. More precisely, we examine the feasibility and efficiency of online negotiation. In practice, we observe an increasing offer, by specialized companies, of private solutions which use

539

technologies of the Internet to settle the conflicts online. The growing world of ODR draws its main themes and concepts from alternative dispute resolution (ADR) processes in the real world such as negotiation, mediation and arbitration. So, ODR exists on a continuum from online arbitration to pure *automated negotiation*. The opportunities provided by the Internet are used not only to employ these processes in the online environment but also to enhance them when they are used to resolve conflicts in an offline environment. Moreover, both private and public agents are involved in ODR. They constitute an open and developing field that changes as new online tools and resources are developed. The general idea is to provide dispute resolution in a more flexible and efficient manner than is usually found in courts and litigation: "These two factors, dispute resolution and information technology, have combined into an important new tool, a new system, a new way of doing business that is more efficient, more cost effective, and much more flexible than traditional approaches" (Rule, 2002, p. 3). The success of this type of product, especially in North America, is explained mainly by profit opportunities which attract new operators into the business of "electronic justice".

Most of the literature evaluating the potential of ODR can be best characterized as a collection of facts and anecdotes transmitted by electronic medium. Scholars have not sufficiently looked into the rich economic literature on the effects of computer-negotiated communications. We hope to begin to rectify this neglected interdisciplinary area by applying lessons of bargaining theory to online negotiation. For this reason, we will focus on automated negotiation, which constitutes the most specific form of ODR supported by the Internet.

Our aim is to evaluate the economic performance of this form of ODR. The first part of the chapter is devoted to the emergence of ODR. The second part analyzes the efficiency of a process elaborated by one of the prominent companies in the ODR world: Cybersettle.[1] Of course, this procedure is specific to Cybersettle but we consider that it is highly representative of the methods put on the market by private operators. We conclude with a general discussion about private regulation of the Internet *via* ODR.

19.2   The emergence of ODR

A basic attraction of the Internet is the ability to do at distance what previously required physical presence. The word cyberspace suggests, however, that as the exchanges accelerate and multiply, so what occurs is

---

[1] http://www.cybersettle.com/

more than the accumulation or rapid transformation of data. Access to new spaces allows users anywhere to accomplish many tasks that might have previously occurred in physical spaces. One of these is a virtual dispute resolution space which includes ODR.

19.2.1 Problems with courts

The rapid growth of B2C electronic commerce over the past few years has raised a number of concerns for businesses and consumers alike, chief among which is the problem of the relevant forum and the applicable law (and enforcement thereof) in an increasing number of transactions. Cross-border online shopping is rife with problems, including non-delivery of goods and difficulty obtaining refunds. The lack of effective consumer redress when the parties are in different countries is a major barrier to consumer confidence in dealing with all but the most well-known and trusted brands. All parties (businesses, consumers and governments) recognize that, in order to facilitate the continued growth of electronic commerce, consumer confidence and trust in it must be improved. In order to improve consumer confidence, the problem of consumer redress in the event of cross-border disputes must be resolved.

The emergence of the Internet as a commercial phenomenon has resulted in an explosion of interest in ODR. Soon after goods and services started to be sold over the Internet, it became obvious that online transactions need the same support as face-to-face transactions. It was acknowledged that the growing cyberspace required institutions much like the offline world. Here, the consumer can return to the store to get a defective product replaced. If the store refuses to replace it, the consumer can take the matter to court. Online there are no such institutions to resolve the dispute.

It is interesting here to note that ODR was in fact developed by two sides, both the commercial side and the governmental side, generating a kind of complementarity between public and private regulation. In practice, private companies were founded to provide ODR services (including Cybersettle, InterSettle,[2] SquareTrade[3]). But at the same time, public and para-public organizations also issued standards calling for e-commerce companies to integrate ODR into business practices (ECODIR, ICC, ICCAN, NAFTA).

Auctions websites were the first e-commerce environments to make use of ODR. These sites are particularly vulnerable to conflict because

---

[2] http://www.intersettle.co.uk/   [3] http://www.squaretrade.com/

the transaction environment usually connects the buyers and sellers and then leaves them alone to work out the details. It is difficult to identify the sellers and to know whether or not they are telling the truth about the item they want to sell. There are rarely repeat relationships between buyers and sellers, so most of the exchanges take place between strangers. Because of this lack of personal contact it is difficult to interact in a relationship of trust. As a consequence, auction sites have developed a variety of tools to reassure buyers and sellers. Escrow accounts, where money is held by a neutral third party until the goods are delivered, help to solve the problem of fraudulent sellers. Ratings show transaction partners who do not know each other a record of the other side's positive or negative feedback from prior transactions. Because these methods are not always sufficient to prevent conflicts, auctions websites have also developed ODR (for example, SquareTrade for eBay).

19.2.2 Forms and nature of ODR

The Internet is often said to reduce the importance of space and distance. This is true in the sense that communication can occur easily among persons in different places, and information can be accessed quickly from anywhere. Space and distance interfere less with the process of communication than they used to. If information is online, we can find it quickly and conveniently. In another sense, however, the Internet makes space more important and the use of space more complicated. It allows the creation of a new kind of space, not physical but online and in virtual form. In this space, agents can de facto create new kinds of jurisdictions which benefit from an important autonomy because they imply specific rules and enforcement instruments. Conflict resolution in virtual space is already the focal point of great activity. However, the problem is to build and design efficient mechanisms.

The tools and techniques of dispute resolution can be viewed along a spectrum, ranging from options where the parties are totally in control of the process and the outcome, to options where a third party decision-maker is totally in control of both the process and the outcome. Mediation and arbitration are the more frequent ADR. They involve a range of processes that allow a third party to work with the parties in dispute. A large part of the expertise of any third party consists of information management. In arbitration, there is a fairly clear process of receiving information, evaluating information and reaching a judgment. In mediation, the process is more flexible.

Katsh and Rifkin (2001) have introduced the idea that technology acts as a "fourth party". Arbitrators and mediators are often referred to as "third parties" in a dispute because they are the third participants in the process, in addition to the two litigants. When ODR is introduced, technology can also play a major role in managing the process and setting the agenda, so it becomes the fourth party. This idea is interesting because it indicates the significant role technology can play in guiding litigants toward agreement. Technology is not just about replicating face-to-face interactions. In addition to facilitating the process, online practitioners need to think through the various communication options available and design a communication environment that can address the issues under discussion and the dynamic between the parties.

ODR system designers came to realize that, in addition to playing a crucial role in shaping the environment around the parties' interaction, ODR technology could itself also play a facilitative role. New methods for helping the parties reach agreement began to appear online, methods that did not require human involvement to operate. This development is significant because many of the rules that were developed regarding effective ADR practice presumed that the process was being run by a human (arbitrator or mediator). If the process is instead being run by a machine, the challenges are entirely different.

While face-to-face negotiations are usually fairly uniform, online negotiations can vary widely. The ODR environment changes the frame of the negotiation significantly. Online negotiation can parallel face-to-face negotiation by putting the parties into an unstructured communication environment which simply uses technology as the communication medium for a traditional process such as arbitration or mediation. But online negotiations can also place parties into automated negotiation procedures which use algorithms to drive the negotiation process. For example, in automated arbitration, both parties assent to using an automated algorithm to handle their dispute. In recent years, ODR companies have emerged to offer such a process of dispute resolution: a *blind-bidding* process in which an automated algorithm evaluates bids from each party. If the two bids are within a prescribed range (for example 20%), then the case is settled at the median value. If the cases are not within the prescribed range, then the bids are annulled and neither side knows the other's offer. Before it begins, both parties are fully informed of the way the process works and they agree to abide by the outcome.

19.2.3 Online and offline disputes

ODR is not only a valuable resource for online activities, business and dispute resolution for professionals, it also offers added-value offline undertakings. Whereas ODR's origins lie in disputes that arose online and for which traditional means of dispute resolution were largely unavailable, it has also come to be used in offline-based arbitrations and mediations.

In practice, operators rapidly realized that what works for online disputes can also be applied to offline disputes. One of the most publicized examples of technology-facilitated dispute resolutions, the blind-bidding system, can be used for insurance claims. These blind-bidding processes illustrate that if we can identify interactions that are difficult or inconvenient offline, we have to evaluate the relevance of developing online processes to improve them. Once an accident occurs, the insurance companies deal first with the parties involved and then with each other. Negotiation between insurance companies to resolve differences over payment obligations, called subrogation, is a complex and costly process. The majority of these negotiations between insurers are successful in reaching a resolution (in the United States only one-third of claims become lawsuits and only 2% of these lawsuits are decided by a court verdict). Awards in insurance cases are also very important. Unlike e-commerce disputes, where claim values in the B2C context are usually less than €500 and in B2B less than €10,000, insurance disputes are often much higher in value (€100,000 and above, especially in medical or environmental cases). The industry is under enormous pressure due to costs. Consequently, integrating ODR into the insurance claims resolution process could save important administrative costs.

This is probably the reason why the insurance industry has become the largest user of automated dispute resolution mechanisms. Moreover, because so many cases involve monetary values, it is relatively simple to build a technology-administered process that allows participants to resolve their conflict despite the depersonalized process. The largest ODR companies that have emerged so far, such as Cybersettle and ClickNsettle, have focused primarily on this market. Cybersettle is, at the time of writing, the most prominent company in bringing ODR to the attention of the insurance industry. During 2002 and 2003, this company facilitated settlements of more than $30 billon. We will now study the efficiency of the Cybersettle patented technology.[4]

---

[4] For more details, see Cybersettle's website.

19.3   The model

19.3.1   Strategic environment

Following the pioneering approach of Chatterjee and Samuelson (1983), we frame the Cybersettle settlement tool as a finite-horizon bargaining model with two-sided incomplete information and focus on the resulting set of equilibrium outcomes.

Framework

We consider two players, a defendant and a plaintiff, who bargain over the price at which the plaintiff will set his claim at the lawsuit, $N = \{D, P\}$. Let v_D denote the defendant's reservation price (i.e. the greatest sum he is willing to pay for the damage). Similarly, let v_P denote the plaintiff's reservation price (i.e. the smallest monetary sum he will accept in exchange for the damage). The valuations of the damage of the defendant and plaintiff are their private information. The incomplete information of the bargainers is modeled by the following assumption: each individual knows his own reservation price, but is uncertain about his adversary's, assessing a subjective probability distribution over the range of possible values that his opponent might hold. Specifically, each party regards the opponent's reservation value as a random variable drawn from an independent uniform distribution defined as $[0, 100]$, and these distribution functions are *common knowledge*.[5] Therefore, the type spaces are respectively $V_D = \{0 \leq v_D \leq 100\}$ and $V_P = \{0 \leq v_P \leq 100\}$. Following Harsanyi (1967–1968), one imagines that *Nature* first chooses v_D and v_P according to these distributions, and then reveals v_D to the defendant and v_P to the plaintiff, but not vice versa. We focus on the case of incomplete information essentially because the requirement of the complete information approach that each bargainer is assumed to know the other's preferences and payoffs is often regarded as an idealization, incapable of concrete realization.[6] In this framework, bargaining behavior depends on a player's reservation price, his assessment of the opponent's reservation price, the knowledge of the opponent's assessment and the bargaining rule considered by the Cybersettle process.

---

[5] That is, each side knows these distributions, knows that they are known by the other side, knows that the latter knowledge is known, and so forth (Aumann, 1976).

[6] For example, the plaintiff may have more accurate information on the value of the damages and the defendant may know whether or not he was negligent.

Bargaining rule

Acting independently and without prior communication, the defendant submits an offer b_D while the plaintiff enters a demand b_P, defining the action spaces $B_D = \{b_D \geq 0\}$ and $B_P = \{b_P \geq 0\}$. The Cybersettle software then analyzes these proposals and adds $\delta = 20\%$ to b_P in order to create a *settlement range* between the plaintiff's demand and the calculated *maximum settlement amount*.[7] If the defendant's offer is strictly greater than the maximum settlement amount (i.e. $b_D > b_P(1 + \delta)$), then the case is settled for this amount (i.e. $b = b_P(1 + \delta)$). If the defendant's offer is within the settlement range (i.e. $b_P \leq b_D \leq b_P(1 + \delta)$), then the case is settled for the average of the two proposals (i.e. $b = (b_P + b_D)/2$). In this latter case, the bargaining rule determines the settlement price by splitting the difference between the parties' proposals. If the proposals diverge (i.e. $b_D < b_P$), then there is no agreement for this period. In this case, the process repeats with the parties making new proposals in the next period: Cybersettle provides three rounds to the parties for reaching an agreement. Therefore, if the parties disagree at the third period, there is no settlement and no money changes hands (each player's payoff from disagreement is zero). In order to illustrate this bargaining rule, let us take an example by considering the three cases mentioned above:[8]

Case	Offer (b_D)	Demand (b_P)	Maximum settlement	Result
1	$28,000	$22,000	$26,400	Settlement for $26,400 $b_D > b_P(1 + \delta) \rightarrow b = b_P(1 + \delta)$
2	$24,000	$22,000	$26,400	Settlement for $23,000 $b_P \leq b_D \leq b_P(1 + \delta) \rightarrow b = (b_P + b_D)/2$
3	$18,000	$22,000	$26,400	No settlement $b_D < b_P \rightarrow$ No agreement for this period

Our principal aim is to investigate the efficiency properties of equilibrium strategies and to study how the parties fare, individually and collectively, under the Cybersettle bargaining rule. In order to conduct our analysis in a simplified manner, we deliberately omit from our model various other elements of the Cybersettle procedure that would also have

[7] The parameter δ will be called the *settlement factor*. Although Cybersettle considers that $\delta = 20\%$, we keep a general value for this parameter (i.e. $\delta \in [0, 1]$) in order to present comparative statics results indicating the effect that δ may have on bargaining behavior.
[8] For more details, see the general demonstration available on the Cybersettle website (http://www.cybersettle.com/demo/generaldemo.asp).

some role and impact on the issue under study. In particular, some restrictive assumptions are made in order to develop understanding and intuition about the role of the forces under study in a more precise manner.[9]

First, we assume, without loss of generality, that there is no direct cost for the parties from using the settlement service – this is a simplifying modeling assumption. Currently, the Cybersettle system uses a wide range of fee structures – that is, a submission fee (incurred only by the defendant or claims professional) and a settlement fee (incurred by both parties if and only if a successful settlement is reached) – the amounts of which depend essentially on the type of claim and on the settlement value.

Second, we implicitly assume throughout this chapter that the agreement struck *via* the Cybersettle process is binding for both parties. Indeed, the actual users of such a service have to agree in writing to be legally bound by all settlements arising from the negotiations. Therefore, settlements are binding for both parties and preclude them from seeking redress in court for the same claim. In addition, parties are barred from bringing any other suit arising from the same facts as those from which the claim arose.

19.3.2 Properties of Cybersettle

This section presents a number of results characterizing the equilibrium strategies of the parties and the welfare properties of the settlement mechanism provided by Cybersettle. We start by temporarily considering the one-shot (unrepeated) version of Cybersettle. This analysis is useful as a benchmark to highlight the "pure" effect of the settlement factor on the parties' bargaining behavior (which stays relevant in the repeated version of the game) and to derive further results indicating how the likelihood of a settlement is affected by the dynamic nature of Cybersettle.

Equilibrium strategies

A *pure strategy* for player i is a function $b_i(v_i)$, where for each type v_i in V_i, $b_i(v_i)$ specifies the action from the feasible set B_i that type i would choose if drawn by Nature $(i = D, P)$. In other words, a pure strategy for the

---

[9] However, we will see that the simple model of this analysis is rich enough to capture several important elements of the Cybersettle bargaining process: the role of the settlement factor, the effects of uncertainty and the way information is transferred over the dynamic interaction.

defendant is a function $b_D(\cdot)$ specifying a proposal b_D for each of his possible valuations v_D. Similarly, $b_P(\cdot)$ is a pure strategy for the plaintiff specifying a proposal b_P for each of his reservation prices v_P.

In the event of an agreement, each player earns a profit measured by the difference between the agreed price and his reservation value ($v_D - b$ for the defendant and $b - v_P$ for the plaintiff). In the event of no agreement, each earns a zero profit. The payoffs to both the defendant and the plaintiff are then:

$$\phi_D = \begin{cases} v_D - b_P(1 + \delta) & \text{if } b_D > b_P(1 + \delta) \\ v_D - (b_P + b_D)/2 & \text{if } b_P \leq b_D \leq b_P(1 + \delta) \\ 0 & \text{if } b_D < b_P \end{cases}$$

$$\phi_P = \begin{cases} b_P(1 + \delta) - v_P & \text{if } b_D > b_P(1 + \delta) \\ (b_P + b_D)/2 - v_P & \text{if } b_P \leq b_D \leq b_P(1 + \delta) \\ 0 & \text{if } b_D < b_P \end{cases}$$

Suppose that the parties are risk-neutral, so that, for a given pair of strategies $b_D(\cdot)$ and $b_P(\cdot)$, the respective *expected utilities (profits)* are:

$$\Pi_D = E\phi_D \tag{19.1}$$

$$\Pi_P = E\phi_P \tag{19.2}$$

where the expectation is based on the probability distributions of v_D and v_P.

The set of equations above determines a Bayesian two-person game. As usual, a pair of strategies (b_D, b_P) is a *(Bayesian) Nash equilibrium* if $b_D(\cdot)$ is a best response to $b_P(\cdot)$ and $b_P(\cdot)$ is a best response to $b_D(\cdot)$. $b_P(\cdot)$ is a best response to $b_D(\cdot)$ if, conditional on the plaintiff's beliefs, the defendant's strategy $b_D(\cdot)$, and the realization of v_P, $b_P(v_P)$ maximizes the plaintiff's expected utility for each value of v_P. Similarly, $b_D(\cdot)$ is a best response to $b_P(\cdot)$ if, conditional on the defendant's beliefs, the plaintiff's strategy $b_P(\cdot)$, and the realization of v_D, $b_D(v_D)$ maximizes the defendant's expected utility for each value of v_D. In other words, a Nash equilibrium is a pair of strategies such that neither player can increase his expected gain by unilaterally altering his chosen strategy (Nash, 1951). The pair of strategies which together form an equilibrium of the Cybersettle game is stated in the following Lemma.[10]

---

[10] In order to get a unique equilibrium, we restrict attention to linear (strictly monotonic and differentiable) strategies. Multiplicity of equilibria is, of course, a frequent phenomenon in game theory. For example, it is possible to construct other pure-strategy equilibria involving discontinuous strategies that can have arbitrarily many jumps (Leininger et al., 1989). These equilibria imply that players with different valuations may post the same propositions. However, Radner and Schotter (1989) show in an

Lemma 1

In the one-shot version of Cybersettle, the equilibrium strategies of the defendant and plaintiff are respectively

$$b_D(v_D, \delta) = \alpha(\delta)v_D \text{ and } b_P(v_P, \delta) = \beta(\delta)v_P + \gamma(\delta)$$

where $\alpha(\delta) = 2(1 + \delta)^2/(3\delta^2 + 6\delta + 2)$, $\beta(\delta) = 2/(3\delta^2 + 4\delta + 4)$ and
$\gamma(\delta) = 400(1 + \delta)^3/(3\delta^2 + 4\delta + 4)(3\delta^2 + 6\delta + 2)$.

Proof

See 19.5.1.

The defendant's offer is biased downward with his reservation price while the plaintiff's asking compensation is biased upward with respect to his valuation: the Cybersettle bargaining rule does not promote honest behavior, implying that each party makes a truthful proposition (i.e. $b_i = v_i$ for all v_i, $i = D, P$). Furthermore, given that an agreement is reached if and only if $b_D \geq b_P$, manipulating the equilibrium strategies in Lemma 1 shows that an agreement occurs in the equilibrium if and only if:

$$v_D \geq \frac{3\delta^2 + 6\delta + 2}{(3\delta^2 + 4\delta + 4)(1 + \delta)^2}v_P + \frac{200(1 + \delta)}{3\delta^2 + 4\delta + 4}$$

In other words, even when the defendant values the damage more highly than the plaintiff (that is, $v_D \geq v_P$), a successful settlement may be impossible. One can understand intuitively why a number of mutually beneficial agreements will be lost in the first period of the Cybersettle process.

In fact, the *design* of Cybersettle creates two possible sources of inefficiencies: the existence of incomplete information and the impact of the settlement factor on the defendant's bargaining behavior.[11]

Proposition 1

The settlement factor puts a downward pressure on the defendant's offer which moves away from his true valuation and becomes more aggressive.

experiment that the linear assumption is consistent with the observed strategies of the players.

[11] The inefficiency due to incomplete information is a well-known result in bargaining theory which has been demonstrated by Myerson and Satterthwaite (1983). The authors consider bargaining problems of bilateral monopoly under uncertainty and show that it is generally impossible to have an *allocation mechanism* that is incentive-compatible, individually rational, and *ex post* efficient (in the sense that it transfers the object to the buyer if and only if his valuation for the object is higher). In other words, with incomplete information, Coase's Theorem fails to apply and even the *optimal* mechanism will lead to inefficient outcomes with strictly positive probability (Coase, 1960).

Proof

A comparative statics analysis confirms that, as δ increases, the slope of the defendant's strategy decreases causing his bargaining position to become more aggressive:

$$\frac{\partial b_D(v_D, \delta)}{\partial \delta} = -\frac{4(1+\delta)}{(3\delta^2 + 6\delta + 2)^2} v_D \leq 0, \text{ since } \delta > 0 \text{ and } v_D \in [0, 100].$$

The defendant's equilibrium strategy is naturally sensitive to changes in the settlement factor. In the case where $\delta = 0$, it is straightforward to show that the defendant's strategy coincides with his reservation value (i.e. $b_D = v_D$ for all v_D). The intuition behind this result is the following. When an agreement is reached, the case is settled at price $b = b_P$, therefore the rule is equivalent to granting the plaintiff the right to make a first and final offer that the defendant can accept or reject. In this case, the transaction price is determined solely by the plaintiff's demand, while the defendant's offer serves only to determine whether there is an agreement or not. The defendant's dominant strategy is then to make a truthful offer in order to maximize the probability of settlement. On the contrary, in Cybersettle (where $\delta = 20\%$), the defendant faces a trade-off since his proposal determines both his profit and the probability of conflict resolution. Therefore, he adopts an under-efficient behavior which consists of offering a compensation lower than his valuation. The impact on the defendant's bargaining behavior of the settlement factor is characterized in Figure 19.1 which represents the defendant's equilibrium strategy with $\delta = \{0, 20\%\}$.

Concerning the plaintiff's demand strategy, one could think intuitively that the defendant's aggressiveness would force the plaintiff to adopt a more concessionary behavior in order to increase the probability of reaching an agreement. This is, however, not the case because a more

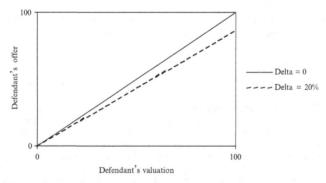

Figure 19.1. The impact of δ on the defendant's equilibrium strategy.

compromising bargainer, while enhancing his chances of reaching an agreement, does so at the expense of lowering his expected payoff. The key point is that Cybersettle creates a bargaining situation similar to the prisoner's dilemma. Both parties know that while their optimal independent behavior is to play strategically, they could both be better off by bidding truthfully. However, they also know that each proposal they make involves a trade-off between increasing the odds of a successful agreement (accomplished by placing a bid closer to their reservation value) and increasing their share of the joint gain should a settlement be reached (the gain is enhanced by placing a more aggressive bid). In this context, honesty does not pay: it is rational for both defendant and plaintiff to sacrifice some feasible settlements if they desire to maximize their equilibrium expected profits. The results indicate that the parties have correctly perceived the strategic implications of the settlement factor and have incentives to adopt aggressive bargaining positions.

In the next section we derive further results, indicating to which extent the efficiency of Cybersettle may be shaped by a multi-stage representation. The central issue is that the sequential nature of Cybersettle has a crucial impact on its ability to generate efficiency and induce the parties to reach a settlement.

Welfare analysis
Let the efficiency of Cybersettle be defined as the ratio of the expected gains from the agreement in the equilibrium (i.e. the expected total profits of the two parties) to the potential maximum expected gains from agreement (the latter would be realized if each party bidded his true valuation in the *first-best* situation). As stated in the following proposition, dividing the equilibrium combined expected profits by the potential combined expected profits shows that the Cybersettle procedure extracts 78.1% of the potential group profit in the first period and 98.9% in the last one.[12]

Proposition 2
The portion of the potential combined expected profits the parties are able to capture via Cybersettle is drastically increasing over time.

Proof
See 19.5.2.

The proof of this proposition is somewhat tedious but the idea behind the conclusion is simple and intuitive: the efficiency effect of repetition is

---

[12] The Cybersettle system is 95.4% *ex post* Pareto-efficient in period 2.

related to the learning process that the dynamic nature of Cybersettle creates. While no proposal is ever revealed to the opposing party in the Cybersettle mechanism, the occurrence of a disagreement is regarded as a signal which must be used to update the other bargainer's private information and thus to adjust subsequent actions. In other words, when no agreement is reached in period j, each party might infer from it some information concerning his adversary's type (i.e. reservation value) and adjust his strategy (i.e. proposal) in period $j + 1$ ($j = 1, 2$). The plaintiff (resp. defendant) might use a failure in period j as an indication that the defendant's (resp. plaintiff's) valuation is below (resp. above) a certain value and therefore should adopt a more reasonable behavior in period $j + 1$ in order to increase the chances of reaching an agreement. The key point is that the occurrence of a disagreement leads the *prior* beliefs to be updated pessimistically and the likelihood of concessionary behavior to be enhanced. The efficiency effect of the length of the bargaining process in Cybersettle is plotted in Figures 19.2a and 19.2b where the settlement zone is represented by the shaded area (which increases over time).

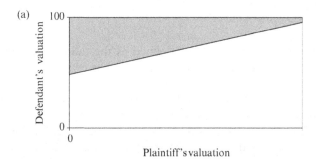

Figure 19.2a. The first-period settlement zone in Cybersettle.

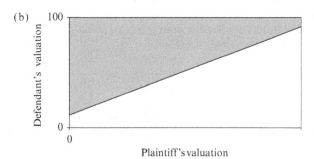

Figure 19.2b. The last-period settlement zone in Cybersettle.

As a conclusion, the possible signaling role of the disagreement (induced by the sequential feature of Cybersettle) is a central issue that seems to improve the efficiency of the settlement mechanism by partly offsetting the perverse effect of the settlement factor on the bargaining strategies. However, this conclusion concerning the positive welfare properties of Cybersettle has to be put into perspective since, as shown in Figure 19.2a, a number of mutually beneficial agreements are lost in the first period which induces 21.9% loss in expected profit and implies that the settlement is likely to be delayed (delay is required for the learning process to occur). Delay is usually costly due to the opportunity costs of the parties' delayed receipt of their gains from the settlement and to expenses incurred during the bargaining process. Following these arguments, the key question is whether a part of the inefficiency can be eliminated by choosing a different mechanism of conflict resolution. The answer is *yes* since Myerson and Satterthwaite (1983) show that the Chatterjee-Samuelson procedure is *second-best* (in the sense that it extracts the maximum group expected profit for all possible bargaining mechanisms).[13] In other words, parties would be better off using the bargaining mechanism developed by Chatterjee and Samuelson (1983) than by entering Cybersettle.

Proposition 3
Individuals would be able to capture a larger portion of the potential gains from agreement by using the Chatterjee-Samuelson mechanism rather than Cybersettle.

Proof
See 19.5.3.

This result suggests that the Cybersettle resolution process is not a relevant settlement tool, while the Chatterjee-Samuelson mechanism (which surprisingly is not used in practice) has a strong welfare property.[14] The central idea is that the Cybersettle bargaining rule in

---

[13] Furthermore, the Chatterjee-Samuelson mechanism is very simple since it considers the following settlement rule: if $b_D \geq b_P$, then the case is settled at price $b = (b_P + b_D)/2$ (i.e. the average of the two proposals). If $b_D < b_P$, then the agreement is not reached.

[14] Furthermore, the dynamic aspect of Cybersettle may also induce a perverse effect from an *equity* standpoint by providing the defendant with a significant bargaining advantage: following the results stated in 19.5.2, it is easy to show that the defendant is able to capture 41.7% of the equilibrium combined expected profits in the first period and 86.5% in the last one (leaving only 13.5% to the plaintiff). On the contrary, the *split-the-difference* rule which is considered in the Chatterjee-Samuelson procedure provides incentives for the parties to reach a symmetric agreement: the results stated in 19.5.3 show that each party obtains an equal share of the equilibrium total expected profits whenever an agreement is reached. The *distributive* consequences of the Cybersettle

combination with the behavioral processes of decision-making under uncertainty determines the environment within which the parties negotiate and hinders human interaction by creating some crucial inefficiencies. These results have important implications and suggest that maintaining such a design is not a good way for increasing the likelihood of a settlement and promoting economic welfare.

19.4   Discussion: private regulation and ODR

The analysis of the Cybersettle procedures gives some elements of reflection to determine whether such an online negotiation can easily be generalized for different forms of conflicts which could appear, for example in B2C relations.

First of all, decentralized solutions offered by private companies are, by definition, contractual. In other words, it is only through the establishment of a contract between parties to a conflict that the latter agree to enter into this type of procedure and to respect the settlement. Nevertheless, the problem is to know to which extent a private electronic constraint can ensure acceptance of disputing parties to engage in this type of procedure and to accept the settlement, particulary if we consider its distributive consequences. Currently, nothing can force an agent to settle a conflict by a private electronic system. This is reinforced by the precise fact that agents have alternative solutions represented by courts in the real world. When an agreement is achieved by electronic means, there is not absolute guarantee the litigants will accept the decision, even when they are engaged by contract to respect the agreement. Indeed, it is useless to think that a private electronic constraint will be able to substitute the public one, court intervention which could remain necessary to obtain the execution of a decision when a party refuses to conform to it (Cachard, 2002). In fact, the lack of coercion, inherent to private companies, could be problematic in the case of ODR proposed by private operators.[15]

To mitigate this problem, authors defending the cyberspace private regulation thesis assume that a reputation mechanism can be a powerful

---

bargaining rule should provide a strong incentive for the plaintiff to *renegotiate* the settlement in order to share the gains from agreement in a different manner and raise the crucial question of how to *enforce* this type of agreement. As discussed in 19.4, this element may have important implications concerning the potential role of the public intervention and the *reputation* mechanisms in cyberspace.

[15] Of course, the problem is different acording to the type of ODR. For online arbitration, one can imagine that, as in the real world, the sentence of the arbiter could be executed without any changes by courts.

way to enforce contracts. In fact, when reputation plays a role in the activity of an agent, its profit is supposed to be an increasing function of its reputation. For example, the reputation of a cyber-merchant who delivers bad-quality products, does not respect the delivery deadline, or generates a great number of conflicts with consumers, will decrease. Consumers will avoid contracting with him. Thus, if one of the parties to the contract does not respect the decision of the decentralized regulation mechanism, a *naming and shaming* strategy, for example, would be powerful enough to enforce it. Nevertheless, effectiveness of reputational enforcement implies that the agent is engaged in repeated relations and that contractors can evaluate the quality of the relation in which they are engaged. Moreover, the generated information must be reliable and public. If, however, even though agents on the Internet are generally engaged in repeated relations and they can evaluate the quality of their relations with the other agents in cyberspace, the reliability of public information concerning the reputation of an agent remains problematic. For example, nothing prevents a cyber-merchant disseminating false information on a competitor on the Web, in order to degrade the latter's reputation and thus to destroy his business. The Internet private regulation mechanism advocates the use of technologies used on the Web (search engine, news group, label, etc.), enabling the collection of information on cyber-agents' reputations in a much more efficient way than in the real world. In parallel, other technologies (in particular technologies concerned with cryptography) ensure the reliability of information thus disseminated on the Internet. Consequently, cyberspace can offer solutions to the criticism addressed to the reputational enforcement.

If we suppose that these technologies effectively enable us to overcome the problem of information reliability, we have to know whether reputation creates strong incentives to respect commitments. In the case of Cybersettle, parties are users specialized in judicial questions or institutional agents who have the capacity and means to implement this type of procedure. Repeated relations between these agents, the "closed" world in which they do business and the fact that the Canadian Bar Association and the Association of Trial Lawyers of America are associated to Cybersettle imply that reputation plays an extremely powerful role enforcing agents to respect their commitments. It is, in fact, rather interesting to note that examples drawn from the real world which describe reputation as a coercive means are very often based on extremely "closed" communities where reputation plays a major role. What, however, happens in the case of a cyber-merchant who enters into a relationship with millions of consumers who each buy DVDs or books on the Internet? Is the coercive mechanism as powerful as in the case of "closed" communities where agents know each other and are closely connected with each other? In fact, if one can accept that in B2B markets reputation can be regarded as a powerful tool to enforce agents to respect their commitments, it appears that a reputational mechanism is a much less powerful constraint in B2C and C2C markets. Indeed, if the Internet technologies make it possible to obtain information about cyber-agents' reputations, the collection and use of this information is not free of cost to the consumer. Transaction costs on the Internet imply that the research process ends when the marginal cost of research equals its marginal benefit. This mechanism generates a selection of the sites according to the characteristics of the consumers.

One can also link the concept of reputation to that of brand image or quality. Models of differentiation based on quality show that the price of the products is an increasing function of quality. Thus, various qualities coexist on the market due to the fact that consumers do not have the same level of income. By applying a similar reasoning, it appears that obtaining a high reputation implies a certain cost: the price of the products sold on better reputation sites will be higher than those of the worse reputation ones. Consequently, the lower income consumers will choose to enter into relations with the latter, and it is thus useless to think that reputation allows the elimination of all the bad sites in order to keep only the good ones.

These various arguments show why reputation cannot always constitute a powerful way to enforce contracts and that the lack of coercion, inherent to private companies, is problematic in the case of ODR offered by decentralized operators. Thus, it appears that a mechanism like Cybersettle cannot easily be generalized to various kinds of conflicts such as, for example, a conflict which would emerge in a relation of B2C type.

Concerning the efficiency of these mechanisms, we can observe that the reputation mechanism does not necessarily represent the optimal solution to solve the enforcement problem inherent to online negotiation developed by private companies. First of all, reputation can be regarded as a form of *barrier to entry*. This argument rests on the fact that reputation requires time to build. It thus appears that the first mover has an indisputable advantage in comparison with a potential player who wishes to enter into the market. This argument, concerning reputation as a barrier to entry, is reinforced when the entry implies engaging in important investments to acquire the same level of reputation as that of the insider. Indeed, the amount of investment necessary to enter into the market, related to the weakness of its market share, gives the potential entrant a cost disadvantage in comparison with the insider. The latter can thus invest as much as the new entrant in order to keep constant (or even to increase) his level of reputation, but amortize his investments on much more important volumes. Finally, the risk is to create undesirable market powers from an economic point of view.

A final argument concerning the relevance of decentralized regulation of the Internet is based on the technology properties of Cybersettle. In fact, the development of the Internet and of the associated judicial risks inevitably leads to an increasing number of conflicts in cyberspace. In parallel, assuming a private and decentralized regulation of the Internet implies that a market for "electronic justice" exists. One can suppose that profit opportunities generated in this new market lead to the entry of new companies, offering alternative technologies to those already supplied by installed firms. However, each proposed technology is set up in order to maximize the profit of the technology's owner and not the social surplus. In this case, if a strong network effect in participating in one ODR system exists, the optimal strategy for a firm to develop its ODR system is to get the bigger market share and protect its technology, in order to avoid new incumbents and pricing competition. This multiplication of the number of private operators and adopted strategies between firms in order to capture the market can lead to an inefficient allocation of resources. Moreover, duplication and coexistence of private and public regulation to treat the same risks in cyberspace could lead to a waste of resources. In other words, this multiplicity of offers leads to the mobilization of incessantly increasing resources for the same activity and for an altogether dubious effectiveness. Obviously, some authors will argue that competition allows for the elimination of bad technologies (the least effective) from the market to retain, *in fine*, only the good technologies (the most effective). This competition should not only eliminate private offers which are economically least desirable but will also favor private regulation to the detriment of public regulation (or conversely) according to their respective effectiveness. In fact, we know that competition between technologies does not inevitably lead to the emergence of better "quality" products (Arthur, 1988, 1989). Various examples show that the most efficient technology is not inevitably chosen by the market, technologies of varying effectiveness being able to obtain a positive market share. On this point, the Cybersettle example is, here again, a good illustration. Indeed, the fact that the patented solution supplied by this private operator appears ineffective does not prevent it from being the world leader on the automated negotiation market. Even if we suppose that a more effective competitor appears to be one that uses, for example, the Chatterjee-Samuelson procedure, it is difficult to conclude that Cybersettle will lose its leadership, or that the offer of the competitor will succeed in surviving in the market. This chapter shows that Cybersettle technology is suboptimal or at least dominated by an obvious mechanism (Chatterjee-Samuelson). But the Cybersettle mechanism is not obvious for the "men of the art" and, consequently, is patentable whereas the Chatterjee mechanism is not. Even though the Cybersettle mechanism is suboptimal, it is defendable and creates a significant barrier to entry.

Globally, arguments in favor of private regulation seem to be based on aspects concerned with communication and information technologies. If ODR has undeniable advantages compared with traditional conflict resolution (low cost, speed, etc.), it is not based on its private character but on the technologies used.

19.5   Appendix

19.5.1   Proof of Lemma 1

Considering linear strategies (Gibbons, 1992), we assume that the player i's strategy is $b_i(v_i) = a_i + c_i v_i$ ($i = D, P$). Then, following (19.1) and (19.2), the maximization problems for the defendant and plaintiff are respectively

$$\max b_D \left(v_D - \frac{b_D(4+3\delta)}{4(1+\delta)} \right) \left(\frac{\delta b_D}{c_P(1+\delta)(\bar{v}_P - \underline{v}_P)} \right)$$

$$+ \left(v_D - \frac{b_D + (1+\delta)(a_P + c_P \underline{v}_P)}{2} \right) \left(\frac{b_D - (1+\delta)(a_P + c_P \underline{v}_P)}{c_P(1+\delta)(\bar{v}_P - \underline{v}_P)} \right)$$

$$\max b_P \left(\frac{b_P(4+\delta)}{4} - v_P \right) \left(\frac{\delta b_P}{c_D(\bar{v}_D - \underline{v}_D)} \right)$$

$$+ \left(b_P(1+\delta) - v_P \right) \left(\frac{a_D + c_D \bar{v}_D - b_P(1+\delta)}{c_D(\bar{v}_D - \underline{v}_D)} \right)$$

The first-order conditions for which yield

$$b_D = \frac{2(1+\delta)^2}{3\delta^2 + 6\delta + 2} v_D \tag{19.3}$$

$$b_P = \frac{2}{3\delta^2 + 4\delta + 4} v_P + \frac{2(1+\delta)}{3\delta^2 + 4\delta + 4}(a_D + \bar{v}_D c_D) \tag{19.4}$$

By manipulating (19.3) and (19.4), we obtain the following linear equilibrium strategies:

$$b_D(v_D, \delta) = \frac{2(1+\delta)^2}{3\delta^2 + 6\delta + 2} v_D \tag{19.5}$$

$$b_P(v_P, \delta) = \frac{2}{3\delta^2 + 4\delta + 4} v_P + \frac{4(1+\delta)^3}{(3\delta^2 + 4\delta + 4)(3\delta^2 + 6\delta + 2)} \bar{v}_D \tag{19.6}$$

By assuming that $\bar{v}_D = 100$, it is straightforward to determine the equilibrium strategies stated in Lemma 1.

19.5.2   Proof of Proposition 2

We proceed in two steps. We begin by determining the (updated) beliefs of the parties and infer from this their equilibrium strategies in each period (step 1). Next, we compute the total expected gains from agreement in each period and compare these gains with that in the first-best situation (step 2).

Step 1: The learning process
-First period-
The information structure has not evolved and each party has the same prior beliefs:

$$v_P \in [\underline{v}_P^\star, \bar{v}_P^\star]; \underline{v}_P^\star = 0; \bar{v}_P^\star = 100$$

$$v_D \in [\underline{v}_D^\star, \bar{v}_D^\star]; \underline{v}_P^\star = 0; \bar{v}_P^\star = 100$$

Using (19.5) and (19.6), the first-period equilibrium strategies of the defendant and plaintiff are

$$b_D^\star(v_D, \delta) = \frac{2(1+\delta)^2}{3\delta^2 + 6\delta + 2} v_D \tag{19.7}$$

$$b_P^\star(v_P, \delta) = \frac{2}{3\delta^2 + 4\delta + 4} v_P + \frac{400(1+\delta)^3}{(3\delta^2 + 4\delta + 4)(3\delta^2 + 6\delta + 2)} \tag{19.8}$$

-Second period-
The negotiations achieve the second period if and only if the parties fail to reach an agreement in the first one. No agreement in the first period implies that $b_D^\star(v_D, \delta) < b_P^\star(v_P, \delta)$ and, given (19.7) and (19.8), the parties' beliefs are revised as follows:

$$v_P \in [\underline{v}_P^{\star\star}, \bar{v}_P^{\star\star}]; \underline{v}_P^{\star\star} = \frac{(3\delta^2 + 4\delta + 4)(1 + \delta)^2}{3\delta^2 + 6\delta + 2} v_D - \frac{200(1 + \delta)^3}{3\delta^2 + 6\delta + 2}; \bar{v}_P^{\star\star} = 100$$

$$v_D \in [\underline{v}_D^{\star\star}, \bar{v}_D^{\star\star}]; \underline{v}_D^{\star\star} = 0; \bar{v}_D^{\star\star} = \frac{(3\delta^2 + 6\delta + 2)}{(3\delta^2 + 4\delta + 4)(1 + \delta)^2} v_P - \frac{200(1 + \delta)}{3\delta^2 + 4\delta + 4}$$

Using (19.5) and (19.6), the second-period equilibrium strategies of the defendant and plaintiff are

$$b_D^{\star\star}(v_D, \delta) = \frac{2(1 + \delta)^2}{3\delta^2 + 6\delta + 2} v_D \tag{19.9}$$

$$b_P^{\star\star}(v_P, \delta) = \frac{6(\delta^2 + 2\delta + 2)}{(3\delta^2 + 4\delta + 4)^2} v_P + \frac{800(1 + \delta)^4}{(3\delta^2 + 4\delta + 4)^2(3\delta^2 + 6\delta + 2)} \tag{19.10}$$

-Third period-

The negotiations achieve the third (last) period if and only if the parties fail to reach an agreement in the second period. No agreement in the second period implies that $b_D^{\star\star}(v_D, \delta) < b_P^{\star\star}(v_P, \delta)$ and, given (19.9) and (19.10), the parties' beliefs are revised as follows:

$$v_P \in [\underline{v}_P^{\star\star\star}, \bar{v}_P^{\star\star\star}]; \underline{v}_P^{\star\star\star} = \frac{(1 + \delta)^2(3\delta^2 + 4\delta + 4)^2}{3(\delta^2 + 2\delta + 2)(3\delta^2 + 6\delta + 2)} v_D$$

$$- \frac{400(1 + \delta)^4(3\delta^2 + 4\delta + 4)}{3(\delta^2 + 2\delta + 2)(3\delta^2 + 6\delta + 2)}; \bar{v}_P^{\star\star\star} = 100$$

$$v_D \in [\underline{v}_D^{\star\star\star}, \bar{v}_D^{\star\star\star}]; \underline{v}_D^{\star\star\star} = 0; \bar{v}_D^{\star\star\star} = \frac{3(3\delta^2 + 6\delta + 2)(\delta^2 + 2\delta + 2)}{(3\delta^2 + 4\delta + 4)^2(1 + \delta)^2} v_P$$

$$+ \frac{400(1 + \delta)^2}{(3\delta^2 + 4\delta + 4)^2}$$

Using (19.5) and (19.6), the third-period equilibrium strategies of the defendant and plaintiff are

$$b_D^{\star\star\star}(v_D, \delta) = \frac{2(1 + \delta)^2}{3\delta^2 + 6\delta + 2} v_D$$

$$b_P^{\star\star\star}(v_P, \delta) = \frac{2(9\delta^4 + 30\delta^3 + 58\delta^2 + 56\delta + 28)}{(3\delta^2 + 4\delta + 4)^3} v_P$$

$$+ \frac{1600(1 + \delta)^5}{(3\delta^2 + 4\delta + 4)^3(3\delta^2 + 6\delta + 2)}$$

Step 2: The welfare analysis
We first determine the total expected gains from an agreement in the first-best situation. In the first-best situation, the parties reach an agreement if and only if $v_D \geq v_P$ and the transaction price is given by the average of the two propositions $b = (v_P + v_D)/2$ (Myerson and Satterthwaite, 1983).

Therefore, the defendant's *ex ante* expected gain is given by

$$\Pi_D^e = \frac{1}{100} \int_0^{100} (\Pi_D^e/v_P)dv_P \simeq 8.333$$

where Π_D^e/v_P is the defendant's expected gain, for some value of v_P, and is given by

$$\Pi_D^e/v_P = \frac{1}{100} \int_{v_P}^{100} (v_D - b)dv_D = \frac{1}{400}v_P^2 - \frac{1}{2}v_P + 25$$

Similarly, the plaintiff's *ex ante* expected gain is given by

$$\Pi_P^e = \frac{1}{100} \int_0^{100} (\Pi_P^e/v_P)dv_P \simeq 8.333$$

where Π_P^e/v_P is the plaintiff's expected gain, for some value of v_P, and is given by

$$\Pi_P^e/v_P = \frac{1}{100} \int_{v_P}^{100} (b - v_P)dv_D = \frac{1}{400}v_P^2 - \frac{1}{2}v_P + 25$$

The total expected profit in the first-best situation is defined as:

$$\Pi_D^e + \Pi_P^e \simeq 16.67 \tag{19.11}$$

We now determine the *per-period* equilibrium expected gains from agreement in Cybersettle.

-First period-
The defendant's expected gain, for some value of v_P, is given by

$$\Pi_D^*/v_P = \frac{1}{100} \int_{b_P^*}^{b_P^{*(1+20\%)}} (v_{D}-b_1)dv_D + \frac{1}{100} \int_{b_P^{*(1+20\%)}}^{100} (v_D - b_2)dv_D$$

$$= \frac{195299}{156857472}v_P^2 - \frac{10375}{45387}v_P + \frac{1773750}{139523}$$

where $b_P^\star$ and $b_D^\star$ are the first-period equilibrium strategies, while b_1 and b_2 are the corresponding transaction prices:

$$b_1 = \frac{b_P^\star + b_D^\star}{2} = \frac{25}{123}v_P + \frac{36}{83}v_D + \frac{7200}{3403}$$

$$b_2 = b_P^\star(1 + 20\%) = \frac{20}{41}v_P + \frac{172800}{3403}$$

Therefore, the defendant's *ex ante* expected gain is given by

$$\Pi_D^\star = \frac{1}{100}\int_0^{100}(\Pi_D^\star/v_P)dv_P \simeq 5.4337$$

Similarly, the plaintiff's expected gain, for some value of v_P, is given by

$$\Pi_P^\star/v_P = \frac{1}{100}\int_{b_P^\star}^{b_P^{\star(1+20\%)}}(b_{1-v_P})dv_D + \frac{1}{100}\int_{b_P^{\star(1+20\%)}}^{100}(b_2 - v_P)dv_D$$

$$= \frac{83}{35424}v_P^2 - \frac{21}{41}v_P + \frac{86400}{3403}$$

Therefore, the plaintiff's *ex ante* expected gain is given by

$$\Pi_P^\star = \frac{1}{100}\int_0^{100}(\Pi_P^\star/v_P)dv_P \simeq 7.5898$$

Using (19.11), we state that the Cybersettle system is 78.1% *ex post* Pareto-efficient in period 1:

$$\frac{\Pi_D^\star + \Pi_P^\star}{\Pi_D^e + \Pi_P^e} \simeq 78.1\%$$

-Second period-
The defendant's expected gain, for some value of v_P, is given by

$$\Pi_D^{\star\star}/v_P = \frac{1}{100}\int_{b_P^{\star\star}}^{b_P^{\star\star(1+20\%)}}(v_D - b_1)dv_D + \frac{1}{100}\int_{b_P^{\star\star(1+20\%)}}^{100}(v_D - b_2)dv_D$$

$$= \frac{726707579}{263677410432}v_P^2 - \frac{41018840}{76295547}v_P + \frac{6670332150}{234538163}$$

where $b_P^{\star\star}$ and $b_D^{\star\star}$ are the second-period equilibrium strategies, while b_1 and b_2 are the corresponding transaction prices:

$$b_1 = \frac{b_P^{\star\star} + b_D^{\star\star}}{2} = \frac{1525}{5043}v_P + \frac{36}{83}v_D + \frac{1440000}{139523}$$

$$b_2 = b_P^{\star\star}(1 + 20\%) = \frac{1220}{1681}v_P + \frac{3456000}{139523}$$

Therefore, the defendant's *ex ante* expected gain is given by

$$\Pi_D^{\star\star} = \frac{1}{100} \int_0^{100} (\Pi_D^{\star\star}/v_P)dv_P \simeq 10.746$$

Similarly, the plaintiff's expected gain, for some value of v_P, is given by

$$\Pi_P^{\star\star}/v_P = \frac{1}{100} \int_{b_P^{\star\star}}^{b_P^{\star\star(1+20\%)}} (b_1 - v_P)dv_D + \frac{1}{100} \int_{b_P^{\star\star(1+20\%)}}^{100} (b_2 - v_P)dv_D$$

$$= \frac{35441}{19849248}v_P^2 - \frac{26901}{68921}v_P + \frac{107136000}{5720443}$$

Therefore, the plaintiff's *ex ante* expected gain is given by

$$\Pi_P^{\star\star} = \frac{1}{100} \int_0^{100} (\Pi_P^{\star\star}/v_P)dv_P \simeq 5.1645$$

Using (19.11), we state that the Cybersettle system is 95.4% *ex post* Pareto-efficient in period 2:

$$\frac{\Pi_D^{\star\star} + \Pi_P^{\star\star}}{\Pi_D^{e} + \Pi_P^{e}} \simeq 95.4\%$$

-Third period-

The defendant's expected gain, for some value of v_P, is given by

$$\Pi_D^{\star\star\star}/v_P = \frac{1}{100} \int_{b_P^{\star\star\star}}^{b_P^{\star\star\star(1+20\%)}} (v_D - b_1)dv_D + \frac{1}{100} \int_{b_P^{\star\star\star(1+20\%)}}^{100} (v_D - b_2)dv_D$$

$$= \frac{182621946611}{49249080770688}v_P^2 - \frac{31438465780}{42750938169}v_P + \frac{15250297080150}{394258652003}$$

where $b_P^{\star\star\star}$ and $b_P^{\star\star\star}$ are the third-period equilibrium strategies, while b_1 and b_2 are the corresponding transaction prices:

$$b_1 = \frac{b_P^{\star\star\star} + b_D^{\star\star\star}}{2} = \frac{24175}{68921}v_P + \frac{36}{83}v_D + \frac{28800000}{5720443}$$

$$b_2 = b_P^{\star\star\star}(1 + 20\%) = \frac{58020}{68921}v_P + \frac{69120000}{5720443}$$

Therefore, the defendant's *ex ante* expected gain is given by

$$\Pi_D^{\star\star\star} = \frac{1}{100}\int\limits_0^{100} (\Pi_D^{\star\star\star}/v_P)dv_P \simeq 14.272$$

Similarly, the plaintiff's expected gain, for some value of v_P, is given by

$$\Pi_D^{\star\star\star}/v_P = \frac{1}{100}\int\limits_{b_P^{\star\star\star}}^{b_P^{\star\star\star}(1+20\%)} (b_1 - v_P)dv_D + \frac{1}{100}\int\limits_{b_P^{\star\star\star}(1+20\%)}^{100} (b_2 - v_P)dv_D$$

$$= \frac{37000321}{33366585888}v_P^2 - \frac{28084581}{115856201}v_P + \frac{102366720000}{9616064683}$$

Therefore, the plaintiff's *ex ante* expected gain is given by

$$\Pi_P^{\star\star\star} = \frac{1}{100}\int\limits_0^{100} (\Pi_P^{\star\star\star}/v_P)dv_P \simeq 2.2213$$

Using (19.11) and (19.14), we state that the Cybersettle system is 98.9% *ex post* Pareto-efficient in the last period:

$$\frac{\Pi_D^{\star\star\star} + \Pi_P^{\star\star\star}}{\Pi_D^e + \Pi_P^e} \simeq 98.9\% \tag{19.12}$$

19.5.3   Proof of Proposition 3

We proceed in three steps. We first determine the *general* equilibrium strategies in the Chatterjee-Samuelson (CS) mechanism (step 1). Next, we determine the (updated) beliefs of the parties and infer from it their per-period equilibrium strategies (step 2). Finally, we compute the total expected gains from agreement in each period and compare these gains to those in the Cybersettle process (step 3).

Step 1: The general equilibrium strategies in the CS mechanism
Following the CS bargaining rule, the payoffs to both the defendant and the plaintiff are:

$$\phi_D = \begin{cases} u_D - (b_D + b_P)/2 & \text{if } b_D \geq b_P \\ 0 & \text{if } b_D < b_P \end{cases}$$

$$\phi_P = \begin{cases} (b_D + b_P)/2 - v_P & \text{if } b_D \geq b_P \\ 0 & \text{if } b_D < b_P \end{cases}$$

Then, the maximization problems for the defendant and plaintiff are respectively:[16]

$$\max b_D \left(v_D - \left(\frac{3b_D + a_P + c_P \underline{v}_P}{4} \right) \right) \left(\frac{b_D - a_P - c_P \underline{v}_P}{c_P(\bar{v}_P - \underline{v}_P)} \right)$$

$$\max b_P \left(\frac{3b_P + a_D + c_D \bar{v}_D}{4} - v_P \right) \left(\frac{a_D + c_D \bar{v}_D - b_P}{c_D(\bar{v}_D - \underline{v}_D)} \right)$$

The first-order conditions for which yield

$$b_D = \frac{2}{3} v_D + \frac{1}{3}(a_P + c_P \underline{v}_P) \tag{19.13}$$

$$b_P = \frac{2}{3} v_P + \frac{1}{3}(a_D + c_D \bar{v}_D) \tag{19.14}$$

By manipulating (19.13) and (19.14), we obtain the following linear equilibrium strategies:

$$b_D(v_D) = \frac{2}{3} v_D + \frac{25}{3} + \frac{1}{4} \underline{v}_P \tag{19.15}$$

$$b_P(v_P) = \frac{2}{3} v_P + \frac{1}{4} \bar{v}_D \tag{19.16}$$

Step 2: The learning process
-First period-
The information structure has not evolved and each party has the same prior beliefs:

$$v_P \in [\underline{v}_P^\star, \bar{v}_P^\star]; \underline{v}_P^\star = 0; \bar{v}_P^\star = 100$$

$$v_D \in [\underline{v}_D^\star, \bar{v}_D^\star]; \underline{v}_D^\star = 0; \bar{v}_D^\star = 100$$

Using (19.15) and (19.16), the first-period equilibrium strategies of the defendant and plaintiff are

---

[16] Considering linear strategies, we know that b_D is uniformly distributed on $[a_D + c_D \underline{v}_D, a_D + c_D \bar{v}_D]$ and b_P is uniformly distributed on $[a_P + c_P \underline{v}_P, a_P + c_P \bar{v}_P]$.

$$b_D^\star(v_D) = \frac{2}{3}v_D + \frac{25}{3} \tag{19.17}$$

$$b_P^\star(v_P) = \frac{2}{3}v_P + 25 \tag{19.18}$$

-Second period-

The negotiations achieve the second period if and only if the parties fail to reach an agreement in the first period. No agreement in the first period implies that $b_D^\star(v_D) < b_P^\star(v_P)$ and, given (19.17) and (19.18), the parties' beliefs are revised as follows:

$$v_P \in [\underline{v}_P^{\star\star}, \bar{v}_P^{\star\star}]; \underline{v}_P^{\star\star} = v_D - 25; \bar{v}_P^{\star\star} = 100$$

$$v_D \in [\underline{v}_D^{\star\star}, \bar{v}_D^{\star\star}]; \underline{v}_D^{\star\star} = 0; \bar{v}_D^{\star\star} = v_P + 25$$

Using (19.15) and (19.16), the second-period equilibrium strategies of the defendant and plaintiff are

$$b_D^{\star\star}(v_D) = \frac{11}{12}v_D + \frac{25}{12}$$

$$b_P^{\star\star}(v_P) = \frac{11}{12}v_P + \frac{25}{4}$$

Step 3: The welfare analysis
-First period-

Following the first-period equilibrium strategies in (19.17) and (19.18), the parties reach an agreement if and only if $v_D \leq v_P + 25$ and the transaction price is given by the average of the two propositions $b = (v_D + v_P + 50)/3$.

Therefore, the defendant's *ex ante* expected gain is given by

$$\Pi_D^\star = \frac{1}{100} \int_0^{75} (\Pi_D^\star/v_P) dv_P \simeq 7.0313$$

where $\Pi_D^\star/v_P$ is the defendant's expected gain, for some value of v_P, and is given by

$$\Pi_D^\star/v_P = \frac{1}{100} \int_{v_P+25}^{100} (v_D - b) dv_D = \frac{75}{4} - \frac{1}{4}v_P$$

Similarly, the plaintiff's *ex ante* expected gain is given by

$$\Pi_P^\star = \frac{1}{100} \int_0^{75} (\Pi_P^\star/v_P)dv_P \simeq 7.0313$$

where $\Pi_P^\star/v_P$ is the plaintiff's expected gain, for some value of v_P, and is given by

$$\Pi_P^\star/v_P = \frac{1}{100} \int_{v_P+25}^{100} (b - v_P)dv_D = \frac{1}{200}v_P^2 - \frac{3}{4}v_P + \frac{225}{8}$$

Using (19.11), we state that the CS mechanism is 84.4% *ex post* Pareto-efficient in period 1:

$$\frac{\Pi_D^\star + \Pi_P^\star}{\Pi_D^e + \Pi_P^e} \simeq 84.4\%$$

-Second period-

Following the first-period equilibrium strategies in (19.17) and (19.18), the parties reach an agreement if and only if $v_D \geq v_P + 50/11$ and the transaction price is given by the average of the two propositions $b = (11/24)(v_P + v_D) + 25/6$.

Therefore, the defendant's *ex ante* expected gain is given by

$$\Pi_D^{\star\star} = \frac{1}{100} \int_0^{1050/11} (\Pi_D^{\star\star}/v_P)dv_P \simeq 8.2832$$

where $\Pi_D^{\star\star}/v_P$ is the defendant's expected gain, for some value of v_P, and is given by

$$\Pi_D^{\star\star}/v_P = \frac{1}{100} \int_{v_P+50/11}^{100} (v_D - b)dv_D = \frac{3}{1600}v_P^2 - \frac{37}{88}v_P + \frac{44625}{1936}$$

Similarly, the plaintiff's *ex ante* expected gain is given by

$$\Pi_P^{\star\star} = \frac{1}{100} \int_0^{1050/11} (\Pi_P^{\star\star}/v_P)dv_P \simeq 8.2832$$

where $\Pi_D^\star/v_P$ is the plaintiff's expected gain, for some value of v_P, and is given by

$$\Pi_P^{\star\star}/v_P = \frac{1}{100} \int_{v_P+50/11}^{100} (b - v_P)dv_D = \frac{1}{320}v_P^2 - \frac{51}{88}v_P + \frac{4725}{176}$$

Using (19.11), we can state that the CS mechanism is 99.4% *ex post* Pareto-efficient in period 2:

$$\frac{\Pi_D^{\star\star} + \Pi_P^{\star\star}}{\Pi_D^{e} + \Pi_P^{e}} \simeq 99.4\% \tag{19.19}$$

Following (19.12) and (19.19), we can conclude that the CS bargaining mechanism is more effective in promoting efficiency than Cybersettle since it is able to extract 99.4% of the potential group profit in the second period while Cybersettle achieves only 98.9% of this profit in the third period.

20 Payment and the Internet: issues and research perspectives in economics of banking

David Bounie and Pierre Gazé

20.1 Introduction

For a long time the question of payments on the Internet was associated with the rise of a new monetary form, electronic money, sometimes issued by non banks. This monetary trend oriented research in the field of monetary economics[1] and prompted some economists and bankers to claim that "central banks would lose their ability to implement monetary policy. The successors to Bill Gates put the successors to Alan Greenspan out of business" (King, 1999: 411) or "the 21st century will see the birth and development of a dematerialized offer of private moneys of which the services, escaping any public regulation, will compete with current fiduciary moneys" (Dorn, 1999: 45). But electronic money is not used today on the Internet (European Central Bank, 2003) and private electronic moneys have completely disappeared, since payments on the Internet are carried out by way of other electronic payment systems (EPS).

In view of this situation, the aim of this chapter is threefold. The first objective is to analyze these EPS and to propose an economic analysis of retail payment developments on the Internet. Our chapter shows that EPS form a heterogeneous group that cannot be reduced simply to the evolution of electronic money, and that information technologies in general and the Internet in particular have afforded non banks with opportunities to challenge banking prerogatives to differing degrees: securing the payment order, clearing and settlement, unit of account, etc.

The second objective of this chapter consists in discriminating between lasting developments and innovations adopted or rejected by economic

We thank Michel Gensollen, Thierry Pénard, Anne Lavigne and an anonymous referee for helpful comments and suggestions on preliminary versions.
[1] The reader is referred, for instance, to the works of Browne and Cronin (1995), Tanaka (1996), Kobrin (1997), Berentsen (1998), King (1999), Friedman (1999) and Goodhart (2000).

agents. We note that lasting developments are in part today to the benefit of non banks in the particular fields of: i) the securing of payment orders carried out with debit and credit cards; ii) the clearing and settlement of financial debts; iii) the intermediation in deposits on special-purpose accounts; and iv) the issuing of private liabilities. A key development introduced by the Internet is the possibility to organize payments by limiting or even completely bypassing the use of banks and interbank payment systems. Non banks competing for payments make it possible for contemporary banks to unhinge payment intermediation from financial intermediation. The economic impact of these developments remains limited and has not compromised the organization of the payment system as a whole but does nevertheless raise questions about the reasons for such a challenge and the economic stakes of the entry of new non banking competitors into the field of payments.

The third objective of the chapter is to explore the implications and economic consequences of the fact that non banks are competing for the production of payments. From empirical work by Radecki (1999) and Rice and Stanton (2003) in the United States, it clearly appears that income from payments is significant for the financial equilibrium of banks. But an essential and equally difficult question is whether this challenge can have an impact on financial intermediation. Following Black's (1975) theoretical argument, Mester et al. (2001) confirm that checking account information is used by banks in monitoring commercial borrowers. However, this significant result hardly resonates in contemporary banking theories in which the function of the payment remains a banking by-product, financial intermediation being the core. The production of payments can, by contrast, be seen as a banking function of prime importance that legitimates its role in financial intermediation (Bullard and Smith, 2003). From this point of view, the development of EPS, as part of a movement to dispute the banking monopoly in payments, takes a particular direction. It raises key questions for economics of banking: could the payment function historically justify the existence of banks? Could the payment function explain today's domination of banks over their competitors? In brief, is the payment function strategic for banks?

This chapter addresses these issues in four parts. In the first part we analyze the main characteristics of payment developments on the Internet. In the second part we discuss the economic implications of these developments and in the third part we present some perspectives for future research in economics of banking. In the fourth and last part we conclude this chapter.

20.2 Developments in payments on the Internet: presentation

In contemporary monetary economies, money can be defined as a claim on an issuing institution – banks – incorporated in media and generally accepted between economic agents by means of payments instruments. Money is thus incorporated in various media such as metal, paper or accounts. These media determine the monetary form and confer on money its status: fiduciary money or scriptural money. But, to exert its power of legal tender and to fulfill its role as a medium of exchanges, money requires payment instruments. These consist of means of payment and means of exchange (Goodhart, 1990). Means of payment – notes and coins – are the payment instruments of fiduciary money; they allow the immediate extinction of debts contracted during the exchange. By contrast, means of exchange (checks, credit and debit cards, etc.), the payment instruments of scriptural moneys, constitute only some vehicles and procedures for exchanging payment orders between consumers, sellers and banks that the latter settle within the framework of interbank payment systems. Payment orders can be transmitted physically between economic agents and banks (checks) or by remote means (bank card), for example via telecommunications networks. In this framework, the Internet can constitute a new "medium" for economic agents and banks to transfer payment orders. But the Internet does not merely provide new possibilities for banks and economic agents to transfer payment orders, it affords the opportunity to alter all the elements and stages of bank scriptural payment – the payment order, the clearing and the settlement – and contributes directly to the evolution of the form of money, with electronic money. In the latter case, new payment procedures, distinct from scriptural payment, could be used. Throughout the rest of the chapter we will call electronic payment systems all the vehicles and procedures which allow payment orders to be exchanged between economic agents via the Internet. The following sections describe these EPS.

20.2.1 *Securing payment orders: payment protocols with debit and credit cards*

The traditional payment with debit and credit cards is not well suited to the Internet because of security problems. To get round this shortcoming, protocols to secure payment orders are necessary. There are two rival types of protocol: low-quality protocols and high-quality protocols. The low-quality protocol such as Secure Sockets Layer (SSL), conceived by a non bank (Netscape) and standardized by the Internet Engineering

Task Force under the name of Transport Layer Security (TLS), is today marketed by banks and non banks within a competitive market.[2] The current version of this protocol in use does not ensure the complete security of payments insofar as the payer is not authenticated during the payment session. The seller is thus not guaranteed against attempted fraud by opportunistic consumers. By contrast, the high-quality protocol, conceived by banks and banking networks such as Visa, MasterCard, etc. (SET, I-Pay, Cyber-COMM, etc.), integrates a mechanism of electronic signature which authenticates with certainty the payer (digital certificates or smart card); the seller is thus guaranteed against the risks of fraud. However, this type of protocol is expensive because it requires an investment in software or hardware for consumers, which considerably increases the production costs of payments and ultimately the price and the cost of the solution.

Characteristic 1

The absence of security in Internet protocols has led to the growth of a market for the securing of payment orders characterized by: 1) competition between banks and non banks; and 2) an offer of vertically differentiated protocols.

20.2.2 The pre-clearing procedures with billing systems

Some non banks provide consumers with the possibility to buy goods and services during a determined period from sellers affiliated to the non bank (iPin, w-HA, etc.). The purchases are aggregated and paid at the end of the period, at the time of the reception of a bill, using a banking means of exchange such as the check, for instance. This system, that originally appeared with the "kiosk Minitel" in France, is not limited to the Internet. It is used to settle some debts in traditional trade (electricity, water, etc.) and is also spreading today within the framework of mobile networks in the context of the invoicing of data services: NTT DoCoMo (I-Mode), Vodafone (Live), Orange (World). Non banks such as mobile operators and Internet service providers then organize an intermediation by collecting their customers' payments, using bills and transferring to the sellers the incomes of the transactions minus a fee.[3]

---

[2] Banks market various SSL-based commercial solutions to their debit and credit cards under different brands.

[3] In the United States, some "bill consolidators" have been developed, such as Spectrum for banks and CheckFree and Transpoint for non banks. These consolidators are third parties that aggregate data from multiple billers such as Yahoo! and America Online. The non bank consolidators have taken the lead in the market with CheckFree, whose services were used by nearly 75% of the companies surveyed by a Gartner Group study (quoted by Au and Kauffman, 2001).

A pre-compensation of payer and payee positions is thus made by the non bank, which has as a direct consequence: the reduction of the number of entries in bank accounts and interbank payment systems. Instead of directly paying all the transactions to the merchants by way of banking means of exchange, the consumer settles only an aggregate of all consumptions with the non bank. The billing system is nevertheless still conceived of as a complement to the bank account insofar as the ultimate payment of the bill (aggregate of consumptions) can be made only via a banking payment.

Characteristic 2
The billing system allows a pre-clearing of payments carried out between economic agents. It is conceived of as complementary to the bank account, so that recourse to the banking structure is necessary to settle all the contracted debts.

20.2.3 The settlement procedures outside the banking industry with trusted systems

Some non banks provide consumers and sellers with the management of deposits on special-purpose accounts credited from their banking accounts. To order the payment and to mobilize the deposits, the payer has various means including scratch cards (InternetCash, EasyCode), login and password (PayPal), etc. The most famous EPS in this class is the Paypal system developed in the United States and established in some European countries.[4] PayPal is designed for any type of monetary transfer between economic agents such as auctions (eBay), gifts, etc. from special-purpose accounts. Monetary transfers are completed by e-mail. The funds received by the payee can be left in deposits on the special-purpose accounts or transferred into a bank account. PayPal takes a two-part tariff (fixed and variable) on transactions received on special-purpose accounts and also manages the float of the system. PayPal acts as a "notary" in certifying the terms of transactions from special-purpose accounts open on its books. It organizes an intermediation in payments by fulfilling all the traditional functions of the banks: it provides payment instruments, manages accounts and carries out the clearing and the settlement between accounts. PayPal's special-purpose account is thus designed to be a substitute to the bank account: any payment between special-purpose accounts no longer involves an entry in the bank

---

[4] Some banks also propose certain person-to-person payment services, but with less success (Citigroup).

account and a settlement in interbank payment systems. The only link with banks remains when special-purpose accounts are credited or debited through credit and debit card systems.

Characteristic 3

The trusted system allows the payment, clearing and settlement of financial debts between economic agents from special-purpose accounts managed by non banks. The trusted system is conceived as a substitute to the bank account: the recourse to an interbank payment system is no longer necessary. A non bank scriptural money is then exchanged between economic agents.

20.2.4 The settlement procedures outside the monetary system with trusted and loyalty systems

Some non banks propose to consumers and sellers the management of funds on special-purpose accounts. A non bank scriptural money then makes it possible to settle the payer and payee positions affiliated to the EPS. A specific characteristic of these EPS is to exchange a private monetary base whose unit of account is fictitious or backed to a metal like gold, silver, palladium, etc. (E-gold, Barter Trust, Bigvine, LassoBucks). In the E-gold system, for example, the special accounts are made up of titles of a precise weight of a metal. Starting from these special-purpose accounts, the users transfer their titles close to the seller belonging to the system. Any transaction in this case is intermediated by the non bank. In order to ensure the users' confidence, the non bank offers a full cover of the gold deposits as in theories on "narrow banking" (Greenbaum and Thakor, 1995).

Similar systems called loyalty systems have also been developed during the 2000s (Flooz, I-point, Webmiles, etc.). These EPS have allowed the aggregation of loyalty points made out in a fictitious unit of account (beenz) on special-purpose accounts. The loyalty points were bought by the sellers and issued by the non bank at a definite rate which, according to the EPS, could be converted into scriptural money by the consumers or spent at sellers adhering to the system; the goods were then numbered with the fictitious unit of account. The loyalty points collected by the sellers during these purchases were then repurchased by the non bank at a less favorable rate of exchange (Godschalk, 2001).

Characteristic 4

Non bank scriptural moneys backed to private liabilities circulate on the Internet. Non banks manage special-purpose accounts and carry out the clearing and settlement between special-purpose accounts in a "private" unit of account.

20.2.5 A new monetary form with electronic money

The electronic money is a claim on a bank or an electronic money institution[5] incorporated in the memory of a microprocessor (electronic purse (EP)) or a hard disk (virtual purse (VP)) in the economic agents' possession. EP is a microprocessor card on which monetary units are stored. EP was designed originally as a substitute to coins and notes. But the difficulties of user adoption led issuers to search for multiple applications. The payment by EP on the Internet falls under this search for added value. A dozen EPs such as Avant (Finland), GeldKarte (Germany), Minipay (Italy), Chipper (Netherlands), Visacash (Spain), etc. were launched on the basis of this principle. VP constitutes the software counterpart of EP on a hard disk with the difference that the latter is strictly dedicated to payment of information goods on the Internet. Several VPs have been designed, such as Millicent (United States), ClickPay (Denmark), Ecash (United States) and Magex (United Kingdom).

The payment procedure with EP or VP is carried out in three stages. First the payer charges his EP or VP in exchange for funds debited on his bank account. The holder (payer) then directly transfers to the seller the monetary units registered on his EP or VP. During this stage, the customer's EP or VP is debited with the amount of the transaction and the seller's device is credited with the corresponding monetary value. In the third stage, depending on the system used, the seller either keeps the electronic units on his device to re-use them directly or returns them to the issuer of electronic money in exchange for a credit on his bank account.

Characteristic 5

Electronic money constitutes a new monetary form distinct from fiduciary and scriptural moneys.

20.2.6 Comments on the developments

The entire EPS, summarized in Table 20.1,[6] has not been as successful as anticipated. In this part we distinguish the EPS which were rejected by the market or which experienced a weak development, from those that took the lead in the market or seem to be in the process of adoption.

Our first remark is that at the time of writing there is no electronic money system in operation on the Internet. Concerning the virtual

---

[5] The 2000/46/CE European directive clarified the issuing regime of electronic money in Europe by granting a monopoly to banks and electronic money institutions (a new banking actor)

[6] See Appendix.

purse, the bulletin of the European Central Bank (2003: 65) emphasizes that "most of the initiatives were closed down before they were able to operate on a wider scale". This remark seems also to apply to the electronic purse: "The Internet is not yet the panacea that creates a business case for e-purses. Anecdotal evidence with respect to the earliest Internet-enabled e-purses tells us that, by December 1999, fewer than 40 Internet sellers were accepting the Proton card. As for the Avant card in Finland, we have been assured that there is only one (!) seller accepting it on the Internet" (Böhle and Krueger, 2001: 25). Likewise, non bank scriptural moneys backed to "private" monetary bases circulate on the Internet but represent only a marginal development. This result thus contrasts with all of the economic literature that was mainly focused on the monetary implications of the electronic money and the non bank scriptural moneys backed to the private monetary base.

Conclusion 1

The developments related to trusted and loyalty systems (characteristic 4) and electronic money (characteristic 5) are real but marginal or even nil today on the Internet.

In spite of a low number of general statistics on payments carried out on the Internet, our second remark is that all the specialists and the specialized professional press agree on: 1) the success of the SSL protocol in payments, to the detriment of electronic signature-based EPS; 2) the success of trusted systems such as PayPal; and 3) the development of billing systems. The success of the SSL protocol in payments by credit and debit card seems undeniable today at international level. Gustafson, the vice-president of Visa US, estimated in 2000 that almost 90% of the websites that accepted payment by credit card used SSL. These figures seem to be confirmed by the ninth barometer of electronic commerce in France where 71.8% of the commercial sites that made it possible to carry out a transaction online as at 1 June 2001 offered an SSL securization. In terms of transactions, the Fédération des Entreprises de Vente à Distance in France reports that in 2001 payments by credit and debit cards accounted for 61% of the total of all sales on the Internet. Likewise, the success of the trusted system PayPal is seldom questioned. PayPal manages nearly 42 million accounts in 38 countries and registers a yearly average growth of 28,000 new users. In the third quarter of 2002, eBay claimed that PayPal users had generated a total of $1.79 billion in Total Payment Volume, representing a 93% increase from the $925 million generated in the third quarter of the previous year" (Gonzalez, 2003). Finally, the multiplication of the billing systems by portal sites (Yahoo!, AOL), the Internet service providers (Wanadoo, etc.) and mobile operators (Orange, Vodafone, etc.) confirms the development of such solutions. Unfortunately no statistics are available on diffusion of the billing system.

Conclusion 2

The developments related to payment protocols with bank cards (characteristic 1) and trusted systems (characteristic 3) are real and significant whereas those related to billing systems (characteristic 2) seem to be in a phase of development.

These conclusions show that the Internet offers the opportunity to non banks to challenge banks' payment function to different degrees. The object of the following section consists in assessing the implications of this challenge for banks and the banking structure.

20.3 The development of payments on the Internet: economic implications

The development of some EPS previously analyzed has had several economic and banking implications.

The first is related to the banking standardization of the payment instruments (characteristic 1). In the domain of the securization of payment orders with debit and credit cards, banks have lost their monopoly[7] and non banks have taken the lead in the market with low-quality protocol in terms of security. Several reasons can explain this situation, including the installed base and the network externalities in favor of the low-quality protocol; the legal framework that does not favor innovation; the decrease of risk aversion to fraud; the fees imposed on merchants to finance the high fixed costs of the option. A direct economic consequence of the development of a low-quality protocol for payment on the Internet is probably an increase in fraud and a decrease in online transactions for risk-averse consumers. But the development of a high-quality protocol in the framework of a bank monopoly is not necessarily more efficient because of high fees imposed on merchants and consumers. In a recent paper, Bounie and Bourreau (2004) show that even if the level of security can be higher, competition between suppliers of payment security is always 1) preferable to stimulate the development of electronic commerce, and 2) socially desirable.

---

[7] In some countries like France, the payment instruments are specified and normalized by interbank organizations in order to determine the levels of risk incurred by transfers of money in which the banks are ultimately legally responsible.

Conclusion 3

In the particular framework of secured payments by credit and debit card on the Internet, banks have lost control of the standardization of payment protocols.

The second development, concerning billing systems (characteristic 2) and trusted systems (characteristic 3), is related to the incapacity of the current scriptural payment systems to take into account electronic exchanges of low values. The reason is that banks have to clear and settle their different positions in the frame of interbank payment systems, which involves higher fixed costs for all the participants (loss of time, fees, etc.). One of the main advantages of some EPS is then to increase consumers' surplus and merchants' profits by limiting or removing the entries on bank accounts and interbanking payment systems (by means of payment aggregation and special-purpose accounts).

For consumers, first of all, the fixed costs per transaction are very low insofar as the investment costs are null, the procedures of payment are simplified (no loss of time), etc. The low fixed costs by transaction of these EPS thus explain their use for payments of informational goods of low values (micro-payments). Moreover, the variable costs by transaction (proportional to the transaction value) are also very weak because consumers either profit from the float of the system (delayed debit in billing systems) or have quasi-null risks of fraud.

Within the framework of the trusted systems, the potential loss supported by consumers in case of fraud or a dysfunction is limited to the value deposited on a special-purpose account. The risk of an uncontrolled access to the bank account is thus eliminated. The billing and trusted systems can thus be substituted for the use of credit and debit card for transactions of a certain size. For sellers, secondly, the trade-off is more tricky. With PayPal, for instance, the decision to adopt will partly depend on the sales turnover. PayPal does not charge set-up or monthly fees, unlike banks with bank accounts. Nevertheless, the transaction fees are slightly higher so that PayPal can become more expensive for certain types of trade whose volumes and transaction values are significant. In the case of billing systems, the trade-off will also depend on the number and the value of the transactions. A solution such as w-HA in France, for example, takes a fee that amounts to around 30% on the sellers' turnover, whereas the banking commission lies between 1% and 2%. Billing systems do not take any fixed fee on transactions and so could interest retailers oriented towards online micro-content distribution.

All in all, the decrease of fixed costs for some EPS has a direct consequence: they are taking the lead in the market of small-value payments and of information goods, and are competing with banks in some market segments. However, price and cost advantages for consumers and sellers are obtained at the expense of non-interoperability with other EPS, which would involve the setting up of a non banking organization and would imply interchange fees related to clearing and settlement procedures. A key variable in the adoption of such systems thus lies in network externalities (Kuttner and McAndrews, 2001), a classical problem of "two-sided markets" (Rochet and Tirole, 2002).

Conclusion 4

The inefficiency of banking payment instruments has led to the emergence of EPS adapted to new forms of online commerce. By limiting entries in bank accounts and interbank payment systems, EPS make it possible to lower the fixed and variable fees by transaction. But the savings in costs are obtained at the price of a non-interoperability between EPS

The third development summarized by conclusions 2 and 4 shows that billing and trusted systems can compete with credit and debit cards on the Internet for transactions of some sizes and can be used as a substitute for banking payment instruments. But EPS may also find a domain of transaction in traditional commerce and become substitutes for coins and notes, checks, credit and debit cards, etc.[8] On the whole, banks could be challenged for a part of the income generated by transaction fees. But banking revenues derived from payment activities should not be underestimated. For instance, Rice and Stanton (2003) suggest that, on average, 16% of the operating revenue of the top 40 American bank holding companies is derived from payment-related activities.[9]

This ratio can be placed in the more general context of financial deregulation which has concerned the majority of economies since the 1980s. Deregulation was at the origin of increasing competition between the sources of financing whose direct consequence has been a structural fall in the margins of intermediation and where the corollary is a constant rise in the shares of commissions in the net banking product (Allen et al., 2002). The trend towards decreasing incomes related to intermediation could contribute to making the loss of payment market shares less bearable.

Conclusion 5

A significant challenge for banking intermediation in payments could in the long term reduce banking profitability.

---

[8] We have in mind the numerous solutions implemented on mobile phones, at the initiative of mobile operators.

[9] A first analysis by Radecki (1999) estimated that payment-related business could be estimated between one-third and two-fifths of the combined operating revenue of the 25 largest US banks.

The fourth development in billing systems (characteristic 2) and trusted systems (characteristic 3) enabled us to show that the quantity of information available on bank accounts could be reduced in the long term because of payment aggregation and special-purpose accounts.[10] One of the comparative advantages of banks in financial intermediation is their access to borrower accounts (provided that borrowers use the bank as their exclusive depository). The bank account then can become a formidable tool to monitor an existing loan insofar as it provides a stream of borrower data. A check cancellation, for instance, can inform the bank on the nature of the difficulties encountered by borrowers. Consequently, when borrowers are also depositors, banks have an advantage of cost to proceed to the monitoring of the granted loans. This theoretical argument developed by Black (1975) has recently been tested by Mester et al. (2001). Their empirical study aims at testing the usefulness of checking account information in monitoring commercial borrowers. According to the authors, the main characteristic of the information contained in the movements of check accounts is its continuity. Banks enjoy free access to continuous borrower data on the most timely basis possible and have an advantage compared with other institutions which lend but do not manage checking accounts. A firm that lends capital without jointly distributing payment instruments can obtain economic and financial information to assess the quality of borrowers but it can do so only on a discrete basis and cannot use it as a cheap form of monitoring. The management of a checking account and the resulting distribution of payment instruments allow the conditions under which financial intermediation is carried out to be improved. Consequently, a significant decrease of information on bank accounts in the long term could raise the costs of financial intermediation (due to detection and control of moral hazards associated with a rising probability of borrower bankruptcies).

Conclusion 6

A significant challenge for banking intermediation in payments and deposits could in the long term increase the cost of financial intermediation.

All these conclusions show that EPS provided by non banks can emerge because of the inefficiency of bank payment instruments. We showed

---

[10] Obviously, for this prediction to be correct, the fraction of transactions being conducted online by non bank EPS and the market share of non bank EPS must be high enough and experience a significant increase to generate a significant loss of information for banks. Furthermore, such a prediction assumes that banks do not react to the competitive pressure exerted by non bank EPS.

that competition for the banking payment function was not without consequences from an economic point of view because: i) payment contribution to banking revenues is significant; ii) payment information is useful for monitoring borrowers; and iii) non banks collect deposits on special-purpose accounts. However, even if the payment function can appear strategic for banks, its role in modern theories on banking intermediation tends to be minimized. The last part of this chapter aims to specify some research perspectives related to the integration of the payment function in modern banking theories.

20.4   The payment function in economics of banking: research perspectives

Modern banking theories justify the role and existence of banks because of information imperfections in financial markets (Bhattacharya et al., 1998). The bank is then an intermediary that makes it possible to solve these imperfections more efficiently than non-intermediated markets. Four complementary sets of banking theories are traditionally proposed to explain the role of banks in the resolution of these imperfections (Freixas and Santomero, 2003). The first focuses on the mandate given to banks by depositors to screen potential clients ex ante either because banks are better than the average investor or because there are economies of scale in the resolution of problems of information asymmetries. A second group of theories concentrates on the ex post role of banks in controlling the actions and efforts of borrowers (Diamond, 1984). A third series of works concerns the service of insurance against risks of liquidity, provided by banks to depositors (Diamond and Dybvig, 1983). Lastly, a fourth set of contributions considers that banks have the duty to create a safe asset (Gorton and Pennacchi, 1990).

Within this framework, the essential economic role of banks is to be a financial intermediary whose main functions consist in servicing loans and ensuring depositors. Paradoxically, the role of banking liabilities in payments as well as the procedures by which payments will be fulfilled are absent from theoretical works even when these are related to liquidities and bank deposits. For example, in Diamond and Dybvig's theory on banking intermediation, economic agents prefer to contract with a bank to have liquidities held in the form of bank deposits, and thus face random risks in their consumption plan, rather than investing in illiquid assets subject to risk depreciation. The bank then justifies its existence vis-à-vis the financial markets by guaranteeing a deposit contract that protects depositors against the risks of liquidity. Within this model, only the levels of consumption that will be obtained by economic agents are taken into account in the event of an investment liquidation. But, even though the formal framework proposed by the authors allows us to better understand the role of deposit contracts in the supply of liquidities, it does not allow us to explain why: i) banking liabilities will also be useful in payments; and ii) banks will offer procedures to organize the transfer of liabilities between economic agents via payment instruments.

Conclusion 7

The role of bank liabilities in payments as well as the procedures to organize the transfer of payments via payment instruments do not play any specific role in financial intermediation theories.

It is only recently that a link between payment intermediation and financial intermediation has been established, by Bullard and Smith (2003). These authors consider a pure exchange economy with overlapping generations of agents who live for three periods. More precisely, there are three types of agent: lenders, borrowers and intermediaries. Lenders and borrowers try to form financial relations because each of them is endowed at a given period and wants to consume at another period.[11] This situation would not be complicated if people lived in the same location and could easily communicate, but that is not the case. Borrowing or lending is complex precisely because each agent is operating in an economy consisting of different locations.[12] In consequence, in the presence of spatial separation and limited communication, lenders and borrowers encounter difficulties in communicating, which complicates borrowing and lending of the direct finance type. Consequently, Bullard and Smith maintain that if there were no other agents, "credit transactions would not be feasible".

One of the interesting contributions of these authors is then to introduce the services of intermediaries who never change location. Considering the specific patterns of meeting and communication among agents throughout the different periods, the authors demonstrate three essential results:

---

[11] Lenders want to consume in middle age, are endowed when young and change location after the first period; borrowers want to consume when young, are endowed in middle age and change location after the second period.

[12] The economy consists in two locations. Between the first and second periods, lenders move to a different location while borrowers remain in their original location and between the second and third periods borrowers also change location. In consequence, borrowers who are endowed in their second period are not able to make loan repayments to lenders and the latter who want to consume in their second period are not reunited with the agents to whom they made loans.

- One, the only way to organize credit transactions among agents in the two economies relies on preexisting circulating liabilities provided by intermediaries.
- Two, it is only because intermediaries issue circulating liabilities that they are able to make loans. Consequently, "in contrast to the existing literature on banking, which emphasizes how banks can help overcome informational asymmetries in lending or can help insure depositors, we build a model of banks based on their role in issuing media of exchange" (Bullard and Smith, 2003: 195).
- Three, while it is always feasible for borrowers to issue their own liabilities, it is socially desirable for the whole economy to use the intermediaries' liabilities because it is the solution which minimizes the number of costly transactions between agents.

Conclusion 8
Circulating liabilities in payments constitutes one of the bases of financial intermediation for banks.

In the previous analysis, however, the payment instrument function of the intermediary is ignored. We understand why borrowers may find it beneficial to use the intermediary circulating liabilities in payments (less costly), but the formal framework does not take into account the payment instrument problem. In other words, intermediaries issue liabilities that have face values and economic agents can accept or refuse them, but the model is silent on the sphere of acceptance of liabilities allowed by the payment instrument technology. In brief, everything happens as if payment instruments that ensured the circulation of the liabilities were identical between intermediaries (one technology, absence of competition), commonly accepted (any problems of networks, acceptance between agents), adapted to all sizes of transaction ("micro" and "macro" payments) and to all types of transaction, functioning in any location in the economy, etc. But payment instruments produced by intermediaries such as banks are expensive and sometimes little used (network externalities) or hardly adapted to certain transactions (on the Internet, for example). The economic agents can certainly hold liabilities that are potentially accepted by all the economic agents, but the maladjustment of the payment instrument to some transactions can prevent them from effectively using their liabilities. Banks can thus appear as a bad intermediary in providing payment technologies. Now, insofar as the ultimate goal of the economic agents is to mobilize liabilities to face various and random payments, they simultaneously need an ex ante contract ensuring that they have liquid liabilities and an efficient payment technology to mobilize those liabilities. What would be the point of liabilities potentially accepted by all the economic agents if payment instruments that allowed their circulation were unsuited to payments?

In this context, several stakes arise in terms of future researches. The first consists in better distinguishing two essential and distinct services provided by banks: the production of liquidity and the production of payment services. Up to now, modern theories on financial intermediation[13] did not dissociate payment services from liquidity services. This was, however, natural insofar as historically the two functions were provided by the same economic agent, the bank. The advantage of conceptualizing the distinction between payment services and liquidity services is its usefulness. But the organization of payment on the Internet shows that it is becoming necessary to distinguish these two functions more carefully insofar as they can be provided by two distinct economic actors. To carry out an interesting economic distinction, it would be advisable to define the liquidity concept independently of that of the payment. Liquidity is the capacity of an asset to be generally accepted in trade with speed, little uncertainty on the value and low transaction costs. In our monetary economy, liquidity thus indicates the facility (speed, cost and uncertainty) with which an asset is transformed into fiduciary or scriptural money. The payment service indicates the means by which the asset circulates among debtors and creditors. Schematically, the bank produces liquidity in its role of financial intermediation (by converting some illiquid assets into liquid ones, thanks to the law) and produces payment services in its payment intermediation role.

The second challenge for future research would consist in prior investigation of the role and impact of the efficiency of payment instruments on the sphere of acceptance of banking liabilities. Within the framework of the PayPal-type system, for example, which offers a high degree of liquidity (a claim on banking liabilities), the efficiency of the payment procedures allows PayPal to take the lead in a specific market and to collect resources on special-purpose accounts. An interesting extension of current research would then consist in studying how the quality of the payment instruments allows banks and non banks to impose their liabilities in payment and how the efficiency of the payment technology would offer, *in fine*, the opportunity for banks and non banks to provide credits.[14] In this case, financial intermediation would be contingent on the sphere of acceptance of the payment technology.

---

[13] Such as that of Diamond and Dybvig (1983)

[14] For several months at the time of writing, PayPal has been offering US users the option of opening a line of credit to fund purchases over the Internet.

Finally, a third challenge would consist in integrating into financial intermediation models the costs and benefits of payment production. At the equilibrium within the framework of a competitive game between banks and non banks, these probably have an impact on market share distribution in deposits and ultimately on the allocation of capital resources in financial markets.

Conclusion 9

The sphere of liability acceptance is contingent on the payment instrument efficiency. In an economy where payment production can potentially be unhinged from financial intermediation activities, it is important to distinguish liquidity services from payment services and to assess their economic effects.

20.5 Conclusion

The economic weight of the retail payment systems is considerable. In a recent paper, Humphrey et al. (2003: 172) claimed that "an electronic payment costs only from one third to one half as much as a paper-based payment. If a country moves from a wholly paper-based payment system to close to an all electronic system, it may save 1% or more of its GDP annually once the transition costs are absorbed." From an economic point of view, the Internet, which contributes to payment electronification, could constitute a strong lever to accomplish this goal.

However, our analysis shows that even if the Internet can reduce the social cost of payments, it is also at the origin of a transformation in banking organization with the upsurge of non banks in all payment domains: payment order, clearing and settlement, collection of resources on private accounts and issuing of private liabilities. In fact, because payment is at the core of coordination of commercial activities, it requires constant adaptation to commercial trends, to the transformation of economic activities. This adaptation generally involves a transformation of payment instruments whose function is to ensure the transmission of the monetary values in economic exchanges. However, changes are generally attended by the appearance of new actors who control technological progress and seek to legitimately extract a part of the rents. In this case, payment instruments become the instruments of domination of new non banking powers in the payment domain. Our analysis shows that competition for the banks' payment function is not without consequences from an economic point of view. First, payment contribution to bank revenues is significant. Second, payment information participates in the monitoring of borrowers and so impacts on the financial intermediation function of contemporary banks. Third, payment technology efficiency enables non banks to collect resources on special-purpose accounts. In this context, the payment function appears to be a strategic variable for contemporary banks.

Yet the role of payments in modern theories on financial intermediation tends to be minimized, as the core of bank activities consists in financial intermediation. In the last section we attempted to provide some future research perspectives in economics of banking, articulated around the payment function. In particular, we stressed the need to distinguish more clearly between the production of liquidity and that of payment services. Up to now, modern theories on financial intermediation have not dissociated these two services. But the changes introduced by payments on the Internet show that it is becoming necessary to distinguish these two functions more carefully insofar as they can be provided by banks and non banks. This dissociation would be all the more relevant since the sphere of acceptance of banks' and non banks' liquidities strongly depends on payment technology efficiency.

20.6 Appendix

Table 20.1. *Typology and characteristics of electronic payment systems*

Type of EPS	Example	Origin of standardization	Market structure	Monetary form	Keeping of accounts	Monetary base	Integration with the banking system	Type of transaction
Secured payment order protocols with bank card	SSL	Non-bank	Competitive	Scriptural	Bank	Institutional	Complement	B2C
	SET	Bank	Oligopoly	Scriptural	Bank	Institutional	Complement	B2C
Trusted systems	PayPal	Non-bank	Oligopoly	Scriptural	Non-bank	Institutional	Substitute	B2C / C2C
	E-gold	Non-bank	Monopoly	Scriptural	Non-bank	Private	Substitute	B2C / C2C
Loyalty systems	Beenz	Non-bank	Competitive	Scriptural	Non-bank	Private	Substitute	B2C
Billing systems	I-pin	Non-bank	Oligopoly	Scriptural	Non-bank	Institutional	Complement*	B2C
Electronic purse	Proton, Mondex	Bank	Oligopoly	Electronic (hardware)	Bank	Institutional	Complement	B2C / C2C
Virtual purse	Ecash, Millicent	Non-bank	—	Electronic (software)	Bank	Institutional	Complement	B2C**

*"Substitute" with order payment and clearing procedures but "complement" with the settlement.
**Some C2C protocols were theoretically conceived of but not commercially implemented (Schneier, 1996).

21 Electronization of Nasdaq: will market makers survive?

Delphine Sabourin and Thomas Serval

21.1 Introduction

During the last decades, stock markets have been witnessing the emergence and the development of new electronic trading systems all around the world. Because the traditional and historical stock market for electronic trading platforms has been Nasdaq, we concentrate on this marketplace. Created in 1971, the National Association of Securities Dealers Automated Quotation system was designed as a dealer market whose purpose was to enhance the efficiency of over-the-counter (OTC) markets. In 30 years, technological innovations that enabled Internet-based trading systems have dramatically changed the structure of the Nasdaq marketplace. Originally designed as financial information networks, new electronic trading systems now bypass the market makers[1] on the stock markets and allow investors to directly compensate and execute their orders with more discretion. They offer the promise of lower trading costs, trader anonymity and faster executions. It is worth stressing that financial networks have always been ahead of most technological changes because efficiency of the system is easy to monetarize.

Electronization of trading has made competition between alternative trading venues greater than before. The rapid growth of electronic trading platforms raises several questions of interest for academics, regulators and investors: is the co-existence of traditional dealers and electronic trading systems sustainable? Will technology drive the convergence towards a pure trading mechanism or can we expect a stable hybrid market architecture?

In view of these issues, the aim of this chapter is twofold. The first objective is to examine the exact nature of the competition between dealers and electronic trading systems in order to understand the reasons

We thank Eric Brousseau, Nicolas Curien, Virginie Lethiais and an anonymous referee, as well as seminar participants at GREQAM, University of Aix-Marseille II and CNAM, for insightful comments and suggestions.
[1] The terms "dealers" and "market makers" will be used interchangeably in this chapter.

for each trading venue's current success and the rapid growth in the use of automated trade execution. The Internet technology is shown to have played a big role in the development of electronic trading systems over the past few years since it has enabled the business model of financial networks to change from a closed system with proprietary standard to a more open system. But network economics underlines that the current success of electronic trading systems does not guarantee their long-term viability. The second objective of this chapter then consists in investigating the possible outcomes of the competition between dealers and electronic trading venues. Using a microstructure model, our analysis provides insights about the viability of hybrid market designs.

This chapter proceeds as follows. In Section 21.2, we stress the key variables that drive competition between automated trading mechanisms and Nasdaq market makers. Besides, the current structure of Nasdaq is shown to be the result of technological and regulatory changes. Empirical evidence and theoretical studies of the impact of Nasdaq's electronization on market performance are reviewed in Section 21.3. In Section 21.4, using a synthetic microstructure model, we provide insights about the possible co-existence of competing trading mechanisms. Section 21.5 concludes. Proofs are collected in the appendix.

21.2 The evolution of Nasdaq: from a dealer market to a hybrid market design

In the current hybrid Nasdaq's structure, automated trading systems named as alternative trading systems (ATSs) compete for order flow with dealers. In this section, we first stress the key differences between ATSs and dealer markets, before underlining the main reasons for ATSs' success. The global organization of Nasdaq and issues of interest are then examined.

21.2.1 Dealer markets versus ATSs

Key differences between dealer markets and ATSs
Dealer markets (DMs) and ATSs differ along many dimensions.

The nature of intermediation
In a DM, market makers are the only suppliers of liquidity. They are a counterparty in all transactions and quote two prices: the bid price, at which they are willing to buy securities, and the ask price, at which they will sell. The difference between those two prices is the market maker's spread. Market makers' bid and ask prices typically depend on the size of

the order, thus dealers quote price-quantity schedules. Dealers stand ready to trade at those prices, thus creating an environment of immediate and continuous trading. By contrast, ATSs offer market participants the possibility to meet directly without the intervention of an intermediary, thus often implying lower trading costs. An ATS is an electronic matching system which displays buy and sell orders. When the latter match, a deal is made and reported to the quoting system.

Anonymity

Second, contrary to DMs, trading on electronic platforms is anonymous. Therefore, investors whose trading motivation is information-based may prefer to trade on an ATS rather than on a DM. ATSs are indeed popular among buy-side firms since they enable them to trade large volumes of orders anonymously, thus decreasing the chance that other market participants find out and cause the market to move against them.

Transaction fees

Third, an important feature of DMs is that dealers act as principals, committing their own capital and generating profits from the bid-ask spread. By contrast, ATSs do not take proprietary positions but act as agents for other counterparties, by displaying their orders. This key difference implies that *for-profit* ATSs charge a fee per transaction, unlike market makers, who are not allowed to charge fees. The level of transaction fees may play an important role in the outcome of competition between market makers and ATSs.

After-hours trading

Interestingly, there is another consequence to the ATSs' working process. By providing electronic access and acting as a middleman, ATSs have been able to offer after-hours trading capacities enabling traders to better manage their positions, though liquidity is generally lower when the primary market is closed.[2]

Varieties of ATSs

Furthermore, we distinguish two categories within ATSs: electronic communication networks (ECNs), which work as electronic limit-order books (ELOBs), and crossing networks (CNs). These two varieties of

---

[2] We recognize that ATSs and DMs differ along other dimensions not mentioned here (tick size, pre-trade transparency, post-trade reporting, regulatory status, etc.). However, the nature of intermediation, anonymity, transaction fees and after-hours trading are, in our view, the key variables that will drive future competition.

Table 21.1. *ELOB illustration: ECN Island (http://www.island.com)*

Buy limit-orders		Sell limit-orders	
Shares	Price	Shares	Price
1,000	35.66	1,000	35.80
500	35.37	400	35.95
100	35.34	300	35.98
240	35.30	600	36.00
60	35.28	250	36.04

Let us assume that the limit-order book is given by Table 21.1. An incoming buy market order of size 1,550 would be executed at the total price
$P = 1000{*}35.80 + 400{*}35.98 + 150{*}35.98 = 55577.$

networks differ in the types of orders permitted and in the times at which trading can occur. The US Securities and Exchange Commission (SEC) defines ECNs as "electronic trading systems that automatically match buy and sell orders at specified prices" (http://www.sec.gov/answers/ecn.htm). Therefore, ECNs allow participants to enter the prices at which they wish to trade, i.e. to submit limit orders. More precisely, a limit order specifies a quantity, a limit price and a trade direction. It is a commitment to trade up to the specified quantity of the asset at prices at least as favorable as the specified *limit price*.[3] Limit orders that do not execute immediately after order submission are gathered in a limit-order book for other subscribers to view. Traders can also submit market orders that specify only a quantity and a trade direction. Incoming market orders are matched with limit orders standing in the book. Thus, *limit orders supply liquidity* while *market orders demand it* (Table 21.1 illustrates the ELOB's working process). Hereafter, the terms "limit-order traders" (resp. "dealers" or "market makers") and "liquidity providers" are used interchangeably within the ELOB (resp. DM). Like DMs, ECNs provide a continuous trading facility. Contrary to ECNs, CNs match *unpriced* buying and selling interests only at scheduled cross times. The price at which the trades execute is derived from another market, which is typically the midpoint of the bid-ask spread in the primary market. Therefore, the advantage of a CN is that it minimizes price impact.[4] Besides, an important role of financial markets is to

---

[3] A sell (resp. buy) limit order of size q and limit price p indicates that the trader is willing to sell (resp. buy) q shares at a price higher (resp. lower) than or equal to p.
[4] A trade has a large price impact when it causes adverse price changes, i.e. large buy orders drive up ask prices while sell orders push prices down.

discover the prices at which buyers and sellers can trade. But, since traders enter unpriced buy and sell orders, CNs do not contribute to price discovery. As a consequence, CNs cannot exist independently of the primary price-setting mechanism. By contrast, because ECNs provide a price-discovery mechanism, they can exist and grow independently. When analyzing the outcome of competition between ATSs and DMs, we will therefore focus on ECNs. ATSs and DMs may cater to different clienteles, who weight the potential benefits of trading on an ATS against the costs. In particular, ATSs may cater to institutional investors placing large-sized orders. This is illustrated by the success of Instinet, the largest ECN by its market share, which has institutional and market-making users.

21.2.2 Why the hybridization of Nasdaq?

The Nasdaq market, originally designed as a pure DM, has now turned into a hybrid market structure where both ECNs (or ELOBs) and market makers co-exist.[5] The same stocks can now be traded within either the DM or ECNs, implying order flow fragmentation. Although private trading networks have existed since 1969, the growth of ECNs is a very recent phenomenon. Accounting for 30% of Nasdaq share volume by 1999, these new players were attracting nearly half of the order flow by the end of 2002 (source: Nasdaq Economic Research – see Table 21.2). At the time of writing, there were nine private ECNs registered by the SEC.[6] The growing importance of ECNs' market share has deterred Nasdaq officials from providing detailed statistics about individual ECN market share. However, Instinet and Island, the two largest ECNs, accounted for 29% of all Nasdaq volume in November 2003 (source: Instinet Group). While Instinet is used by market makers and institutions, the Island ECN is popular among smaller traders since it is easy to use and relatively inexpensive relative to other ECNs. Another phenomenon is the growing number of ECNs registered as exchanges that compete both inside and outside Nasdaq.

A regulatory change

Two causes can be discerned for this substantial growth pattern. First, the changing SEC regulations introduced in 1997 enabled existing

---

[5] Since CNs cannot exist without the DM, we focus hereafter on the competition between ECNs and market makers.

[6] ECNs which have completed alliance with stock exchanges (e.g. Archipelago) are included in the ECN category. When a merger between a pair of ECNs has occurred, we here account for two such entities.

Table 21.2. *Market share by venue in December 2002*

Market makers	ECNs	Other participants in Nasdaq-listed stocks
48.7%	49.9%	1.4%

ECNs include Instinet, Island, Archipelago, RediBook, Brut, Attain, B-Trade, Track and Nex Trade. Other participants include Amex and the Chicago Stock Exchange.
Source: Nasdaq Economic Research.

networks to compete directly with Nasdaq dealers. Before the reform, competition from limit orders on Nasdaq was thought unnecessary since reasonable spreads were assumed to result from price competition for order flow among dealers (Bertrand competition). The empirical study of Klock and McCormick (1999) tried to persuade the research community that the number of market makers had a negative and highly significant impact on spreads. However, the authors did not take into account structural changes of Nasdaq which were likely to result in lower spreads. Furthermore, the seminal work of Christie and Schultz (1994) proved empirically that Nasdaq dealers implicitly colluded before 1994 in order to maintain wide spreads. They found that odd-eighth quotes at that time were virtually non existent for many securities. Subsequent regulatory investigations led the SEC to adopt in January 1997 the Order Handling Rules (OHR) whose main aspects are the following:

- *Limit order display*: this rule enabled investors to compete directly with Nasdaq dealers by allowing them to submit binding limit orders. Prior to 1997, market makers could disregard public limit orders. Under the new SEC rule, dealers have four options when receiving a customer limit order: (i) execute the order against their own inventory, (ii) incorporate the new price into their quotes on the Nasdaq quote montage with the corresponding quote size, (iii) forward the order to another market maker who would comply with the rule or (iv) dump the limit order into an ECN for immediate execution.
- *Display of ECNs' quotes posted by market maker*: under this new rule, market makers posting orders on ECNs must make those orders available for the public as well. Prior to the reform, the presence of alternative pricing systems enabled dealers to quote one set of prices for retail customers on Nasdaq while offering more favorable prices to other market makers or institutions on an ECN. Indeed, when ECNs like Instinet first developed, they served primarily as trading vehicles for institutional investors and broker-dealers. This rule forced

dealers who place limit orders on ECNs to display their ECNs' quotes in the Nasdaq market.

By enabling ECNs to compete with the traditional Nasdaq market, the "OHR" regulation has favored the emergence and the development of ECNs. The reform has also mitigated the negative effects of the suspected imperfect competition among Nasdaq dealers. Several empirical studies reported that quoted and effective Nasdaq spreads have narrowed by approximately 30% due to the reform (Barclay et al. (1999), Weston (2000)).

The Internet technology

While the growth of ECNs has benefited from SEC regulations, the force of competition from these new trading platforms has been driven by technological advances. The advent of the Internet technology has indeed brought about a dramatic reduction in the cost of transmitting and exchanging information rapidly among a large number of people. This has made it possible to design more open and transparent market mechanisms, based on widely disseminated information.

Building a new network generally entails a lot of fixed costs, thus leading to a natural monopoly. However, technology can lower the fixed costs and allow an oligopolistic market structure to emerge. Today, technology allows the creation of private networks like ECNs on public networks like the Internet. Thanks to the open interface, the *new* ATSs have access to a huge basis of potential customers through the Internet. For instance, Instinet, the oldest ECN, is based on proprietary terminals and protocol, but recent networks like Island are based on open interfaces. Hence, using the Internet as a means of communication significantly reduced the fixed cost of developing an alternative network and enabled ATSs to grow fast at a low cost.

The recent proliferation of ATSs and their success in gaining market shares led the SEC to consider how to better integrate these trading venues into the National Market System. In December 1998, the SEC adopted the regulation ATS whose main goal was twofold. First, prior to the reform, ECNs were registered by the SEC as broker-dealers. The new regulation has opened the way for ECNs to become registered as exchanges. The SEC has also broadened the notion of "exchange" to allow for private for-profit firms to become exchanges when their business involves the consolidation of orders of multiple parties and setting up facilities for trading. Besides, for ECNs to be properly integrated into the national market system, regulation ATS requires that *not only* ECNs' quotes posted by market makers but *all* ECNs' best-priced orders must be displayed into the Nasdaq Montage. The hybridization of Nasdaq is thus the resulting combination of technological innovations and new regulations.

21.2.3 Nasdaq's current organization and future changes

The organization of Nasdaq

Figure 21.1 gives a summarized view of the organization of Nasdaq. Orders come from either individual or institutional investors. They are routed through several communication systems (public phone network, private network or the Internet) to an order entry firm. Order entry firms have to make a reasonable effort to obtain the best execution price for their clients. They are supposed to choose the best market participants to execute the order. However, because of preferencing arrangements or vertical integration between order entry firms and market participants, they do not always choose the best prices. Large investors can bypass the order entry firms by dealing directly with market participants. Importantly, in October 2002 Nasdaq launched the order-display and execution network SuperMontage as a way to attract order flow by increasing liquidity. Since then, market participants allowed to enter and revise multiple quotes on the order-display facility of SuperMontage include market makers, ATSs and UTP (unlisted trading privileges) exchanges.[7] SuperMontage provides the best quotes and orders of all market makers, ECNs and UTP exchanges which trade Nasdaq securities to order entry firms and some online brokers. The order is then routed to one or several market participants for execution. Orders can be directed to a particular market center or not. In the latter case, the order will be matched automatically with the best quotes available on the opposite side of the market.

It is worth stressing that transactions in Nasdaq-listed securities can be delivered not only through the Nasdaq trading system but also through other methods. Orders can indeed be directly routed to ECNs, market makers or UTP exchanges for execution, without using the Nasdaq SuperMontage facility. A large part of transactions which take place outside Nasdaq SuperMontage is due to preferencing arrangements between brokers and market participants.[8]

---

[7] UTP exchanges are permitted to participate in Nasdaq stocks' markets pursuant to unlisted trading privileges granted by the SEC. They include in particular Amex and the Chicago Stock Exchange.

[8] It is also noteworthy that Island and Instinet, the two largest ECNs, do not participate in SuperMontage. Hence, its introduction did not reduce the competition between the Nasdaq DM and both ECNs.

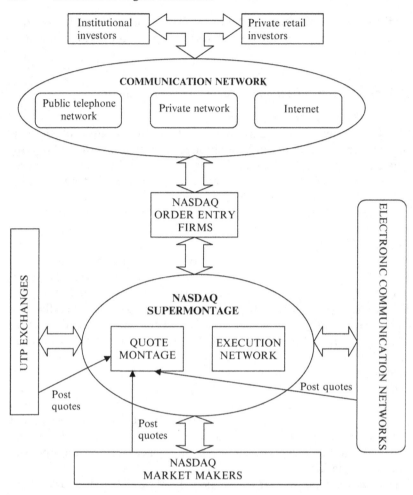

Figure 21.1. The organization of Nasdaq.

The future of the marketplace

The previous developments have underlined the rapid growth of ATSs. However, their future remains quite uncertain. Using network theory insights, Benhamou and Serval (2000) conjectured that ECNs will either merge or disappear. In network economics, the issue of critical mass is indeed of fundamental importance. A network needs to reach a critical mass in order to experience positive externalities. A network externality appears when a good is more valuable as more people use it. Regarding financial networks, ATSs attract more traders when orders easily find a match and execute without adverse price changes, i.e. when the market is sufficiently liquid. Therefore, ATSs are more valuable to customers as more customers engage in trading at that location. The critical-mass effect and the positive liquidity externality explain why the number of ATSs is evolving rapidly. A way to deal with critical mass is to establish alliances or mergers to benefit from network interconnections. Most illustrative of these network effects, Instinet and Island, the two largest ECNs, merged in September 2002 into one electronic marketplace branded INET in order to provide their customers with deeper liquidity. Similarly, the ECN Archipelago completed the merger of Archipelago ECN and REDIBook ECN platforms. Some ECNs (e.g. Instinet) also provide transaction services at several exchanges. In addition, some ECNs have applied to become exchanges. Such a strategy has been chosen by Archipelago whose alliance with the Pacific stock exchange in July 2002 enabled it to create the all-electronic, totally open Archipelago Exchange (ArcaEx). This status change allows an ECN to become a destination for listed shares, thereby diversifying its businesses.

In light of these observations, a natural question to ask is whether the co-existence of ATSs and market makers is sustainable. Is the current architecture simply a transition to a single trading mechanism? Will technology drive the convergence towards a pure electronic market architecture? Or can competing market structures continue to co-exist? In order to investigate the outcome of competition between a DM and an ELOB, we first model both structures as separate entities. The under-standing of the exact nature of each market design and the comparison of their specific features are then used to provide insights about the viability of hybrid market structures. The model presented in Section 21.4 builds on market microstructure theory. Since the way trading is organized affects the prices at which investors trade, market microstructure is indeed a major determinant of each market structure's future success and of the industrial structure of the trading services industry.

21.3   A review of the literature

In this section, we review the empirical literature on the hybridization of Nasdaq and its impact on market quality. In addition, the analysis conducted in Section 21.4 contributes to theoretical research on compe-tition between different trading locations, which we then examine.

21.3.1   A growing empirical literature

There is by now a substantial amount of empirical papers looking at the impact of automation of trading on market liquidity and trading costs.[9] Most notably, Domowitz (2002) and Domowitz and Steil (1999) study the relationship between trading costs, technology and the nature of intermediation in financial markets. They find that the adoption of automated market structures contributes to trading costs reduction, where total trading costs are the sum of explicit (fees and commissions) and implicit costs (price impact costs, including bid-ask spreads). This is in particular the case when comparing executions via ATSs and Nasdaq dealers. Further, Domowitz (2002) is the first to investigate the connection between the automation of market structure and the realization of implicit cost savings. The author argues that the presence of an ELOB that characterizes automated markets affects traders' incentives and abilities to monitor the market. The existence and dissemination of order book information[10] enable traders to continuously monitor the market liquidity. This allows traders to strategically execute their transactions when the market is sufficiently liquid, implying a reduction of implicit trading costs.

Other papers examine the growth of ECNs and their competitive impact on Nasdaq (Weston (2001), Barclay et al. (2003)). Their results suggest that ECNs provide a significant source of competition to market makers. Weston (2001) shows that the increased market share of ECNs leads to tighter Nasdaq bid-ask spreads. Barclay et al. (2003) find that ECN trades are more prevalent in stocks that have high trading volume, high stock-return volatility and fewer market makers.[11]

Biais et al. (2003) focus on the relationship between the reduction in the costs of accessing markets brought by the Internet technology and the intensity of competition between strategic liquidity providers. Using data from the ECN Island, they test the hypothesis that Internet-based markets increase competition and lead to a perfectly competitive market situation. They find that before April 2001, Island limit-order traders earned oligopoly rents. By contrast, a regulatory change intensified the competition between Nasdaq dealers and Island liquidity suppliers after April 2001. As a consequence, the hypothesis that Island liquidity providers do not earn rents cannot be rejected.

Previous results suggest that the wide dissemination of information and the reduction in the costs of providing liquidity on Internet-based

---

[9] See also Conrad et al. (2003) and Jain (2002).
[10] The ELOB continuously provides investors with quotes and number of shares at both sides of the market (see the example in Figure 21.1).
[11] The relative contributions of Nasdaq dealers and ECNs to price discovery are investigated in Huang (2002) and Barclay et al. (2003). Other empirical works include Gresse (2002), who studies the impact of the POSIT crossing network on the dealer market segment of the London Stock Exchange.

trading platforms have decreased trading costs incurred by traders and increased the competitiveness of the market for liquidity supply. However, the Internet technology by itself is not sufficient to eliminate market power in the supply of liquidity on financial markets. Competition between different trading mechanisms also plays an important role.

21.3.2 Theoretical studies

Several papers have examined the ability of markets to co-exist. Glosten (1994) addresses the question of the ability of markets to co-exist with an idealized ELOB. He shows that the latter does not invite competition from other markets while other markets do: the ELOB is competition-proof. However, the analysis that leads to this prediction assumes that there is an infinite number of limit-order traders supplying liquidity on the ELOB: the market for liquidity supply is perfectly competitive. Parlour and Seppi (2003) present a model of competition for order flow between different pairings of pure competitive limit-order markets and hybrid specialist/limit-order markets (like the NYSE). Investors are assumed to incur transaction costs per share when submitting orders to the ELOB. The authors find that neither a pure ELOB nor a hybrid specialist/ELOB is competition-proof for all market parameterizations. Besides, they show that competing exchanges may well co-exist.[12]

Related to the interaction between ATSs and a DM, Hendershott and Mendelson (2000) and Dönges and Heinemann (2001)[13] focus on the case of a CN operating next to a DM. Both papers show that, when investors assign the same value to trading, it is very unlikely that both markets co-exist. Conversely, when the value assigned to trading differs across traders, multimarket structures can co-exist. Hendershott and Mendelson (2000) find that the CN is characterized by two effects. The first is a positive "liquidity effect" whereby an increase in CN trading attracts additional traders on the CN. The second is a negative "crowding" effect, whereby low-liquidity preference trades compete for execution with high-liquidity preference trades and may therefore "crowd out" high-liquidity preference trades.

The work most closely related to the issues discussed in this paper is Viswanathan and Wang (2002). They study the customer's choice with respect to an ELOB, a DM and an *exogenous* hybrid version of the two. A finite number of risk-averse liquidity providers supplies liquidity on each market structure. Some assumptions may play a key role, however,

---

[12] See also Pagano (1989) and Chowdhry and Nanda (1991).
[13] See also Degryse et al. (2003).

when examining the optimality of the hybrid structure. The latter is analyzed by assuming that orders smaller than an exogenous size are executed on the ELOB while orders larger than this cutoff point are routed to the DM. Therefore, the segmentation of traders is driven by exogeneity assumptions. Furthermore, when considering the hybrid structure, traders are not allowed to split their orders across the DM and the ELOB. Differently, we conjecture that these assumptions affect the properties of the equilibrium in the hybrid market. Therefore, when investigating the possible equilibria in the hybrid structure in the next section, we allow rational traders to opt for one of four possible strategies: no trading, trading exclusively on the DM, trading exclusively on the ELOB or optimally splitting their orders across both market venues. Our approach differs from Viswanathan and Wang (2002) in other important ways. First, we consider *for-profit* ELOBs. A key feature of electronic trading platforms is thus that they charge fees to investors using their trading facility. Second, only market makers can provide liquidity on DMs. This is not the case on ELOBs since not only market makers but also brokers and investors can subscribe to ELOBs. Thus, we assume that the number of liquidity providers on ELOBs can be greater than the number of market makers on DMs.

Besides, static equilibrium models of limit-order books include Glosten (1994), Biais et al. (2000) and Viswanathan and Wang (2002). Biais et al. (2000) extend the work of Glosten (1994) to the case of *imperfect competition* between risk-neutral liquidity providers in the presence of informational asymmetries. As in Glosten (1994), they show that the ELOB exhibits a small-trade bid-ask spread whereby the ask price demanded by limit-order traders for the sale of a very small quantity is strictly larger than the bid price quoted for the purchase of a very small quantity. As in Biais et al. (2000), Viswanathan and Wang (2002) obtain a general characterization of equilibrium in the ELOB and focus on the linear equilibrium case. Differently, they consider risk-averse limit-order traders and do not model informational asymmetries.

21.4   The model

We study the interaction between a DM and an ELOB using the fact that these trading mechanisms differ along two dimensions:

- the existence of transaction fees on the ELOB only
- the pricing rules.

On the ELOB, each transaction is charged with fees. Therefore, the trader incurs both explicit (fees) and implicit (spreads) trading costs in the ELOB, while only implicit costs in the DM. We assume hereafter that a transaction of size q is charged with a proportional transaction fee cq ($c > 0$) in the ELOB. Note that both the trader[14] and liquidity providers incur transaction fees when their orders get executed. The difference in pricing rules refers to the "discriminatory" nature of the ELOB's price auction. An incoming market order is matched with limit orders standing in the book. Since it can possibly hit multiple limit orders, the market order can thus be executed at multiple prices.[15] This feature of ELOBs implies that the equilibrium strategy of limit-order traders depends on the distribution of incoming orders,[16] which in turn is endogenous. By contrast, a uniform-like auction takes place in a DM. When all dealers are identical, a trader's order is executed at a single unit price. It follows that dealers set price-quantity schedules that do not depend on the distribution of order flow.

At a first step, the setup of the model is presented. Then, we describe some features of the equilibria in the DM and the pure ELOB before turning to the hybrid market structure. Comparison of equilibria in pure market designs is used to provide insights about the possible co-existence of both competing trading mechanisms.

21.4.1 The framework

We consider a financial market for a risky asset with a stochastic liquidation value denoted by u. We assume that u is normally distributed with $E[v] = \bar{v}$ and $Var[v] = \sigma_v^2$. Two types of agents participate in the market: liquidity providers (limit-order traders within the ELOB and market makers within the DM) and a trader. Since we consider continuous trading mechanisms, there exists only one trader in the market at each trading round. All agents are rational and risk averse. In order to simplify the computation, we assume that liquidity providers and the trader have the same risk aversion parameter ρ. There are N market makers on the DM and M limit-order traders on the ELOB, where $M \geq N \geq 3$. Indeed, only market makers can provide liquidity on DMs, while market makers, brokers and investors can place orders on ELOBs.

Preferences
The trader chooses a trading strategy that maximizes his expected utility and desires to trade the risky asset before the realization of its final value.

---

[14] Hereafter, the terms "trader" and "investor" are used interchangeably.
[15] See the example provided in Figure 21.1.
[16] For more details, see Viswanathan and Wang (2002).

His trading strategy consists of the vector of his trades with liquidity providers. He is assumed to have a CARA utility and demands liquidity for hedging reasons. The trader's private information then consists of his initial endowment I in the risky asset with $Var[I] = \sigma_I^2$.

Hereafter, we assume without loss of generality that the trader buys shares. The case of a seller can be analyzed symmetrically. When the trader buys the total quantity $q \geq 0$, his final wealth is

$$w = (q+1)v - P(q)$$

where $P(q)$ is the investor's total trading costs. Since the trader's utility is CARA, his objective function writes[17]

$$U(\theta, q) = \theta q - \frac{\rho \sigma_v^2}{2} q^2 - P(q) \qquad (21.1)$$

where θ is defined as

$$\theta = \bar{v} - \rho \sigma_v^2 I$$

The parameter θ reflects the trader's private liquidity shock, since the initial risky endowment I can also be viewed as a liquidity shock for the trader's portfolio. Intuitively, a large buy order is due to a large and negative liquidity shock I. The quantity purchased by the trader is therefore expected to increase with θ. Hereafter, the trader will be identified by his private valuation for the asset θ. Since a trader buys shares when he faces a *negative* liquidity shock I, we assume that the random variable θ is uniformly distributed[18] on $[\bar{v}, \bar{\theta}]$. The density and cumulative functions of θ are respectively denoted by f and F.

The first and third terms on the right-hand side of eq. 21.1 interpret easily. For a given purchase of size $q > 0$, the trader's gains from trade are higher when his private value for the asset θ is larger while they decrease with his total payment $P(q)$. The second term on the right-hand side of eq. 21.1 represents the costs incurred by the trader due to uncertainty over the future value of the asset. The value of the asset may indeed adversely change after transactions take place.

Since the trader buys shares, his optimal trade sizes to each liquidity provider belong to the trades that maximize $U(\theta, q)$ so long as these quantities are positive. When the trader θ buys the optimal total quantity $q(\theta)$, we denote by $V(\theta)$ his corresponding welfare, such that

$$V(\theta) = U\left(\theta, q(\theta)\right)$$

---

[17] The trader's objective function is derived as in Biais et al. (2000).
[18] This assumption is made for tractability. In particular, it allows for linear equilibria in the ELOB.

Each of N (resp. M) risk-averse liquidity providers within the DM (resp. the ELOB), indexed by $i = 1, \ldots, N$ (resp. M), competes for the trader's buy order by setting ask price-quantity schedules. Therefore, these price-quantity schedules $p_i(z)$ or equivalently their inverse functions $z_i(p)$ represent the liquidity providers' trading strategies. We assume that each liquidity provider, say for instance liquidity provider i, chooses his optimal demand curve $z_i(.)$ so that for each marginal market-clearing price p, he maximizes the following mean-variance derived utility of profits:[19]

$$E_\theta\left[T_i\Big(z_i(p)\Big) - \bar{v}z_i(p) - \frac{\rho\sigma_v^2}{2}z_i(p)^2\right]$$

where $T_i(z_i(p))$ is the total payment received by liquidity provider i minus possible explicit transaction fees charged to him.[20] The third term of this profit function measures inventory costs borne by risk-averse liquidity providers due to uncertainty over the future value of their portfolios. The riskiness of inventories increases with the risk of the asset measured by its public volatility σ_v^2, the liquidity providers' risk aversion parameter ρ and the size of the transaction.

We assume that the trader can split his order among liquidity providers of each trading mechanism and across the DM and the ELOB in the hybrid structure. When the trader splits his order between liquidity providers, we denote by $q_i \geq 0$ the quantity purchased and $P_i(q_i)$ his total trading cost to liquidity provider i, where $q = \Sigma_i q_i$ and $P(q) = \Sigma_i P_i(q_i)$.

Timing and equilibrium concept

In every market design, the timing of the game is the following:

- First, nature chooses the initial endowment I. The trader then knows his private valuation for the asset θ.
- Second, liquidity providers simultaneously set ask price schedules $p_i(.)$ or equivalently demand curves $z_i(.)$.
- Third, the trader θ selects his orders q_i for all i given the liquidity providers' price-quantity schedules, so as to maximize his objective function $U(\theta, q)$ where $q = \Sigma_i q_i$.
- Finally, the final value of the asset v is realized.

---

[19] This assumption implies that the model belongs to the "inventory paradigm" where the *ex ante* inventory is null for all liquidity providers.

[20] Explicit transaction fees do not exist on the DM and are thus incurred only by ELOB liquidity providers.

We then stress the main features of symmetric linear Nash equilibria in the pure DM, the pure ELOB and the hybrid market structure. In every market structure, the Nash equilibrium is such that (i) each agent maximizes his objective function given the trading strategies of other market participants and (ii) the market-clearing condition is verified:

$$q(\theta) = \sum_i z_i(p)$$

We focus on symmetric linear equilibria in the pure DM and the pure ELOB such that all liquidity providers post the same linear equilibrium price-quantity schedules. In the hybrid market, since the investor is allowed to split up across the DM and ELOB, two situations may emerge for DM (resp. ELOB) liquidity providers, depending on whether they are the only liquidity suppliers to the investor (no splitting) or are competing with ELOB (resp. DM) liquidity suppliers (splitting). Thus, we extend the linear framework to the hybrid market structure by assuming that liquidity providers are bound to post linear by blocks schedules, where each block corresponds to one of these two possible situations. As suggested in Madhavan (1992), one may argue that these linear equilibria are "the most natural equilibria given the computational burden facing agents in the economy".[21]

21.4.2 Pure dealer market versus pure electronic limit-order book

The pure dealer market

N risk-averse market makers enter in competition to supply liquidity to the agent with $N \geq 3$.[22] An important feature of the DM stems from the fact that the pricing function of dealers exhibits no spread for infinitesimal trades. The unit price charged by dealers for infinitesimal sales $p_d(z = 0)$ is indeed equal to their common reservation value $\bar{v}$ and is therefore identical for infinitesimal purchases and sales.[23] This property stems from the uniform nature of the auction that takes place in the DM and is consistent with existing literature.

---

[21] The linear hypothesis also facilitates the comparisons across different trading mechanisms.

[22] Due to uniform pricing, marginal prices are also unit prices on the DM.

[23] Since we assume in this chapter that the incoming trader is a buyer while liquidity providers are sellers, the equilibrium ask price schedule enables only the measurement of half spreads. For instance, the zero-quantity half spread within the pure DM is the difference between $p_d(z = 0)$ and $\bar{v}$. However, since the case of a trader-seller can be analyzed symmetrically, the spread is merely equal to twice the half spread.

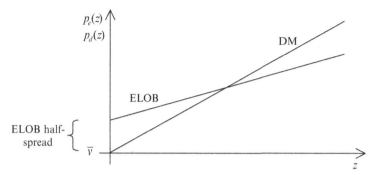

Figure 21.2. Comparison of ask price-quantity schedules within the pure DM and the pure ELOB.

Result 1 In the pure DM, the dealers' equilibrium price schedule exhibits no spread for infinitesimal trades.

Therefore, no trader is rationed, i.e. there is no range of private-value traders where neither a buyer nor a seller submits an order. The set of private-value traders who participate in the pure DM is then $\Theta_d = (\underline{v}, \bar{\theta})$. See Figure 21.2.

The pure electronic limit-order book

In the ELOB, the trader's order is matched with limit orders standing in the book. M liquidity providers compete to supply liquidity to the trader with $M \geq 3$.[24] Consistent with current regulations, we assume that a strict price priority rule holds in the ELOB, i.e. a limit-order trader cannot sell the $(z - 1)$th share at a higher price than the zth one. Therefore, ask price-quantity schedules $\{p_i(z)\}_{i=1,\ldots,M}$ must be increasing within the ELOB.

Contrary to the pure DM, a strictly positive measure of private-value traders is excluded from the ELOB. The set of private-value traders who participate to the pure ELOB is indeed $\Theta_e = (\theta_e, \bar{\theta})$, where the private value θ_e is strictly higher than the average public value of the asset $\bar{v}$ (see Figure 21.3, (1) and (2)). This feature stems from the fact that, contrary to the DM, the equilibrium price-quantity schedule exhibits a zero-quantity spread within the ELOB (see Figure 21.2). Since a discriminatory auction takes place within the ELOB, limit-order traders charge a positive mark-up to investors even for very small order sizes. The ask

---

[24] Since a discriminatory auction takes place within the ELOB, for a given $z > 0$, $p_i(z)$ is the marginal ask price at which liquidity provider i sells the zth unit. Equivalently, $z_i(p)$ is the total quantity liquidity provider i is willing to sell when the last unit is sold at the marginal ask price p.

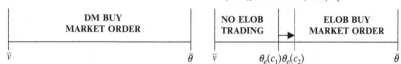

Figure 21.3. Private-value buyer segmentation within the pure DM and the pure ELOB for different values of c and M.

price charged by limit-order traders for infinitesimal sales $p_e(z = 0)$ is indeed strictly greater than their common reservation value $\bar{v}$. It results from discriminatory pricing that some small private-value investors $\theta \in (\bar{v}, \theta_e)$ are made better off not trading on the ELOB.

Result 2 In the pure ELOB, the equilibrium price schedule set by limit-order traders exhibits a zero-quantity spread.

In addition, there is a positive relationship between the level of the transaction fee and ELOB spreads. This illustrates the fact that the ELOB trading mechanism, where the ELOB acts as an agent for subscribers, affects implicit costs incurred by traders. Further, since spreads move up when c increases, the trader faces both higher implicit and explicit trading costs when the transaction fee goes up. An increase in c thus induces some traders to exit the market (see Figure 21.3 (4)), thereby possibly questioning the ELOB viability. This effect leads us to examine the condition under which the pure ELOB is viable, i.e. when it is non empty.

Result 3 If the transaction fee is higher than a threshold value c_{max}, then the electronic limit-order book is not viable.

Contrary to the DM, this condition reveals that the ELOB may not exist. If the transaction fee is too high, the ELOB fails to attract any trader. Once the fee is low enough, however, the ELOB starts to attract trading volume and as more limit-order traders provide liquidity, new private-value traders find it profitable to trade on the ELOB (see Figure 21.3 (3)).

21.4.3 The hybrid market

In the hybrid market architecture, both the DM and the ELOB may co-exist and interact. N market makers and M limit-order traders enter in competition to supply liquidity to the agent with $M \geq N \geq 3$. Since the risky asset can now be traded on two different trading venues, the trader θ has four trading options: (i) no trading, (ii) trading exclusively on the DM, (iii) trading exclusively on the ELOB or (iv) splitting his order across the DM and the ELOB.[25]

One may wonder which private-value traders prefer to split their order across both trading mechanisms rather than to trade exclusively on the DM or exclusively on ELOB. The analysis of the functioning of each trading mechanism in isolation allows us to gain intuition about the operation of the hybrid market design. Price-quantity curves set by liquidity suppliers differ in two important ways across the pure DM and the pure ELOB due to the difference in the nature of auctions. There is a zero-quantity spread in the pure ELOB only, while price-quantity schedules are flatter in the pure ELOB than in the pure DM (see Figure 21.2). These specific features characterizing the ELOB and the DM when operating as separate entities also prevail in the hybrid market design. In particular, there is a small-trade spread on the ELOB, thereby forcing some small-order traders to exit the ELOB. Then intuitively, small-order traders will rationally opt for the DM either because they are excluded from the ELOB or because DM prices are more attractive than ELOB ones, while large-order traders will be attracted by the ELOB. Furthermore, since traders are allowed to split their orders across both trading mechanisms, traders not excluded from the ELOB optimally split their orders across both trading mechanisms as a way to minimize their total trading costs. Thus, no trader finds it optimal to trade exclusively on the ELOB.

Result 4 In the hybrid market design, the optimal segmentation of traders is such that a trader with a low private value θ trades exclusively on the DM while a high-value trader splits his order across the DM and the ELOB.

The ELOB attracts traders whose private valuation for the asset is high enough, that is, traders with high liquidity shocks. This conjecture appears consistent with the evolution of Nasdaq. Instinet, the first ECN by its market share competing with Nasdaq market makers, has a clientele composed of institutional investors. It was also the first ECN to

---

[25] The proofs of the following results are available on request.

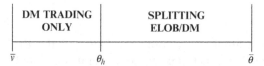

Figure 21.4. Illustration of Result 4 when the trader buys shares.

appear in 1969 in order to allow for institutional investors to rebalance their portfolios once the traditional markets were closed.

As in the pure ELOB, an increase in the transaction fee induces some investors to exit the ELOB, possibly making the ELOB unattractive for all private-value traders. Then, if the transaction fee charged by the ELOB is too high, the DM and the ELOB are not able to co-exist and the hybrid market structure consists only of a DM. Moreover, since there exists an alternative to ELOB trading in the hybrid market design, this condition is harder to fulfill in the hybrid market than in the pure ELOB. Further, the ELOB viability condition is harder to verify when the DM becomes more competitive. When the number N of dealers increases, the ELOB indeed faces increasing difficulty in capturing some trades. Thus, it may be the case that the ELOB must charge a lower transaction fee to attract some traders. This result is consistent with the empirical study in Barclay et al. (2003), who find that ECNs trades are more prevalent in stocks that have fewer Nasdaq market makers. See Figure 21.4.

> *Result 5 If the transaction fee charged by the ELOB is too high, the DM and the ELOB are not able to co-exist. In such a case, the ELOB fails to attract any order and the hybrid market design consists only of a DM. Moreover, the ELOB viability condition is harder to verify when the DM becomes more competitive.*

21.5   Conclusion

In this chapter we have analyzed an important feature of Internet economics: the recent growth of Internet-based financial marketplaces. Using market microstructure theory, the analysis conducted suggests that, if the ELOB is viable and traders do not assign the same value to trading, trading volume does not concentrate on a single trading venue. The co-existence of an ELOB and a DM may not be sustainable, however, since the ELOB may fail to attract any order. This is indeed the case when the fee charged to cover the ELOB's costs exceeds a threshold level, thus deterring entry on the ELOB. This negative link between the ELOB viability and the level of fees may contribute to explaining the wave of mergers and alliances between ECNs within the

Nasdaq marketplace. Under the reasonable assumption that ELOBs' average costs decrease with trading volume, the aggregation of order flows following a merger may reduce ELOBs' average costs, thus giving them room to lower the fees they charge to traders. Mergers and alliances then may make it easier for ELOBs to meet their viability constraints.

While we have concentrated in this chapter on the Nasdaq market-place, our analysis may also shed light on the decision of the European Commission in April 2004 to allow internalization of customer orders by investment institutions in Europe. This regulatory change may soon change the Euronext ELOB into a hybrid market design where orders may be executed by dealers through internalization as well as within the existing central ELOB, thereby possibly enhancing the stock market performance in Europe.

Finally, other issues connected to the ECNs' future have not been debated in this chapter. Thus, there is room for extensions. In particular, the existence of explicit transactions fees on ELOBs appears to be critical to the outcome of competition between a DM and an ELOB. One may then wonder if there exists an optimal ELOB business model. Moreover, the introduction of the Nasdaq SuperMontage has led to changes in the competition between Nasdaq dealers and ECNs. Another research per-spective thus involves the analysis of these evolutions and their impact on market performance.

21.6   Appendix

21.6.1   Proof of Result 1

The proof solves for the Nash equilibrium within the pure DM given by the dealers' demand curves $\{z_i \ (.)\}_{i=1,...,N}$ (or equivalently their price schedules) and the investor's total trade size $q_d(\theta)$. A uniform-like auction takes place in the DM. Therefore, the equilibrium strategy of market makers is independant of the distribution of incoming orders. This result is due to Viswanathan and Wang (2002) and has two impli-cations. First, the objective function of dealer i rewrites

$$\pi_i(p) = pz_i(p) - \bar{v}z_i(p) - \frac{\rho\sigma_v^2}{2}z_i(p)^2 \qquad (21.2)$$

for a possible market-clearing price p where dealer i's trading strategy is represented by his demand function $z_i(p)$. Second, the trader's and dealers' equilibrium strategies need not be determined jointly. We first determine the dealers' optimal strategies before solving for the trader's best response to the dealers' schedules.

Step 1: Dealers' best price-quantity schedules

The proof constructs the Nash equilibrium for the DM by solving for a dealer's best response to the conjectured strategies adopted by other dealers and then shows the conjectures are consistent. Equilibrium in the pure DM is here derived as in Madhavan (1992). In this part of the proof, we represent the market maker i's strategy by his demand schedule $z_i(p)$, the inverse function of $p_i(z)$. For a given total order size $q(\theta)$, the market maker i's residual supply curve writes:

$$z_i = q(\theta) - \sum_{j \neq i, \, j=1}^{N} z_j(p) \tag{21.3}$$

where p is the market-clearing price. Since we focus on symmetric linear equilibria, we suppose dealer i conjectures that other dealers adopt strategy functions of the form: for $j \neq i$

$$z_j(p) = \alpha_d + \beta_d p$$

It follows from eq. 21.3 that for dealer i the price functional is given by

$$p = \frac{1}{(N-1)\beta_d}[q(\theta) - z_i - (N-1)\alpha_d] \tag{21.4}$$

The objective function of dealer i is given by

$$\pi_i = p z_i - \bar{v} z_i - \frac{\rho \sigma_v^2}{2} z_i^2 \tag{21.5}$$

Substituting eq. 21.4 into eq. 21.5 and solving for the optimal demand, we obtain

$$z_i\Big(q(\theta)\Big) = \frac{[q(\theta) - (N-1)(\alpha_d + \beta_d \bar{v})]}{[2 + \rho \sigma_v^2 (N-1)\beta_d]} \tag{21.6}$$

Using the market-clearing condition

$$q(\theta) = z_i(p) + (N-1)(\alpha_d + \beta_d p) \tag{21.7}$$

and substituting eq. 21.7 into eq. 21.6 yields the best response of dealer i:

$$z_i(p) = \frac{(N-1)\beta_d}{[1 + \rho \sigma_v^2 (N-1)\beta_d]}(p - \bar{v}) \tag{21.8}$$

The symmetry assumption then implies that the unique symmetric linear equilibrium is such that

$$z_i(p) = \alpha_d + \beta_d p \tag{21.9}$$

It follows from eq. 21.8 and eq. 21.9 that

$$\beta_d = \frac{(N-2)}{(N-1)\rho \sigma_v^2} \tag{21.10}$$

$$\alpha_d = -\beta_d \bar{v} \tag{21.11}$$

Therefore, the only symmetric equilibrium price-quantity schedule is given by

$$p_d(z) = \bar{v} + \frac{(N-1)}{(N-2)}\rho\sigma_v^2 z$$

for every $z > 0$.

Step 2: The trader's optimal order size
For a market-clearing price p, the trader's objective function when he purchases a total quantity $q \geq 0$ is

$$U(\theta,q) = \theta q - \frac{\rho\sigma_v^2}{2}q^2 - pq$$

The trader's first-order optimality condition then writes:

$$0 = \theta - \rho\sigma_v^2 q_d - p - q_d\frac{\partial p}{\partial q_d} \qquad (21.12)$$

Given that dealers use the strategies $z_i(p) = \alpha_d + \beta_d p$ for all $i = 1, \ldots, N$, the market-clearing condition is

$$q_d = N(\alpha_d + \beta_d p)$$

Using the market-clearing condition, the first-order condition given by eq. 21.13 rewrites

$$0 = \theta + \frac{\alpha_d}{\beta_d} - q_d\left(\rho\sigma_v^2 + \frac{2}{N\beta_d}\right) \qquad (21.13)$$

Since β_d is strictly positive, the second-order condition is satisfied. Then, using eq. 21.10, 21.11 and 21.13, the trader's total optimal strategy writes:

$$q_d(\theta) = \frac{N(N-2)(\theta - \bar{v})}{(N^2-2)\rho\sigma_v^2}$$

for $\theta \in [\bar{v}, \bar{\theta}]$.

21.6.2 Proof of Result 2

The proof solves for the Nash equilibrium within the pure DM given by the dealer's demand curves $\{z_i(.)\}_{i=1,\ldots,M}$ (or equivalently their price schedules) and the investor's total trade size $q_e(\theta)$. The derivation of the Nash equilibrium in the pure ELOB is based on Viswanathan and Wang (2002). A discriminatory auction takes place in the ELOB. Therefore, the equilibrium strategy of liquidity providers depends on the distribution of incoming orders, which in turn is endogenous. Hence, the trader's and liquidity providers' equilibrium strategies need to be determined jointly.

Step 1: The trader's optimal total strategy $q_e(p, \theta)$ for a marginal market-clearing price p

Given that liquidity providers use the strategies $z_i(p)$ for $i = 1, \ldots, M$, the trader's objective function when he purchases a total quantity $q \geq 0$ is

$$U(\theta, q) = \theta q - \frac{\rho \sigma_v^2}{2} q^2 - pq + \sum_{i=1}^{M} \int_{p_0^i}^{p} z_i(u) du - cq$$

where p_0^i is the intercept of liquidity provider i's demand schedule with the ask price axis. The trader's first-order optimality condition then writes:

$$0 = \theta - \rho \sigma_v^2 q_e - p - q_e \frac{\partial p}{\partial q_e} + \frac{\partial p}{\partial q_e} \sum_{i=1}^{M} z_i(p) - c$$

Using the market-clearing condition $q_e = \sum_{i=1}^{M} z_i(p)$, the first-order condition rewrites

$$0 = \theta - \rho \sigma_v^2 q_e - p - c \qquad (21.14)$$

The second-order condition for the trader is then given by

$$-\rho \sigma_v^2 - \frac{\partial p}{\partial q_e} < 0$$

Derivation of the market-clearing condition over q_e yields $\frac{\partial p}{\partial q_e} = \frac{1}{\sum_{i=1}^{M} \frac{\partial z_i}{\partial p}(p)}$. Because strict price priority holds on the ELOB, the trader will face increasing demand schedules $z_i(p)$, implying that the second-order condition is satisfied.

The first-order condition given by eq. 21.14 yields that the trader's total optimal strategy writes:

$$q_e(p, \theta) = \frac{(\theta - p - c)}{\rho \sigma_v^2} \qquad (21.15)$$

so long as this quantity is strictly positive and is equal to zero elsewhere. We denote by Θ_e the set of private-value traders who buy a strictly positive quantity on the ELOB, that is:

$$\Theta_e \triangleq \{\theta \in [\bar{v}, \bar{\theta}], q_e(\theta) > 0\}$$

Using the optimality condition in eq. 21.14, the trade size q_e verifies

$$0 = 1 - \left(\rho \sigma_v^2 + \frac{\partial p}{\partial q_e}\right) \frac{dq_e}{d\theta}$$

Since $\frac{\partial p}{\partial q_e} > 0$, it follows that q_e increases with θ. Hence, the set Θ_e of private-value traders such that q_e is strictly positive is then an interval of the form $(\theta_e, \bar{\theta})$. We then show that there is a unique $\theta_e > \bar{v}$ such that $q_e(\theta) > 0$ for $\theta \in (\theta_e, \bar{\theta})$ and $q_e(\theta) = 0$ for $\theta \in [\bar{v}, \theta_e]$.

Step 2: Necessary condition characterizing liquidity providers' optimal trading strategies

The Nash equilibrium is such that each liquidity supplier maximizes $E_{\theta \in \Theta_e} \left[P_i \big(z_i(p) \big) - (\bar{v} + c) z_i(p) - \frac{\rho \sigma_v^2}{2} z_i(p)^2 \right]$ given the trading strategies of other market participants. The liquidity providers' objective function accounts for the *ex post* participation constraint of the trader, since the expected profit of each liquidity provider is maximized over the set Θ_e. The residual supply curve faced by liquidity provider i is defined by

$$z_i(p) = q_e(p, \theta) - \sum_{j \neq i, j=1}^{M} z_j(p)$$

for all $i = 1, \ldots, M$. We can view the bidding process as an auction in which one of the bidders (labeled the 0th bidder) uses the strategy $z_0(p) \triangleq \frac{\theta}{\rho \sigma_v^2} - q_e(p, \theta)$. Using eq. 21.15 and rewriting the liquidity provider i's residual supply curve gives

$$z_i(p) = \frac{\theta}{\rho \sigma_v^2} - \sum_{j \neq i, j=0}^{M} z_j(p)$$

Besides, the payment received by liquidity provider i can be written as

$$P_i \big(z_i(p) \big) = \int_0^{z_i(p)} p(u) du = A(\theta) - B(p)$$

where

$$A(\theta) = \sum_{k=0}^{M} \int_0^{z_k(p)} p(u) du$$

$$B(p) = \sum_{j=0, j \neq i}^{M} \int_0^{z_j(p)} p(u) du$$

We note that

$$\frac{\partial A}{\partial \theta} = \sum_{k=0}^{M} p \frac{\partial z_k}{\partial \theta} = \frac{p}{\rho \sigma_v^2}$$

$$\frac{\partial B}{\partial p} = \sum_{j=0, j \neq i}^{M} p \frac{\partial z_j p}{\partial p} = -p \frac{\partial z_i(p)}{\partial p}$$

Considering $A(\theta)$ as the state variable and $p(\theta)$ as the control variable, we define the problem's Lagrangian by

$$L = f(\theta | \theta \geq \theta_e) \left[A(\theta) - B(p) - (\bar{v} + c) z_i(p) - \frac{\rho \sigma_v^2}{2} z_i(p)^2 \right] + \lambda \frac{p}{\rho \sigma_v^2}$$

where $f(\theta | \theta \geq \theta_e)$ is the density function of the random variable θ for the trader's private value being larger than θ_e. The first-order optimality conditions give

$$0 = \frac{\partial L}{\partial p} = f(\theta|\theta \geq \theta_e)\frac{\partial z_{ie}(p)}{\partial p}[p - \bar{v} - c - \rho\sigma_v^2 z_{ie}(p)] + \frac{\lambda}{\rho\sigma_v^2} \quad (21.16)$$

and

$$\frac{\partial L}{\partial A} = -\frac{\partial \lambda}{\partial \theta} = f(\theta|\theta \geq \theta_e) \quad (21.17)$$

Using the transversality condition $\lambda(\bar{\theta}) = 0$, eq. 21.17 leads to $\lambda(\theta) = 1 - F(\theta|\theta \geq \theta_e)$ where $F(\theta|\theta \geq \theta_e)$ is the cdf for the trader's private value being larger than θ_e. Then, rewriting eq. 21.16 gives the following characterization of liquidity supplier i's optimal trading strategy:

$$\frac{\partial z_{ie}(p)}{\partial p} = -\frac{g(\theta)}{\rho\sigma_v^2[p - \bar{v} - c - \rho\sigma_v^2 z_{ie}(p)]}$$

which rewrites as

$$\sum_{j=0, j\neq i}^{M} \frac{\partial z_{je}(p)}{\partial p} = \frac{g(\theta)}{\rho\sigma_v^2[p - \bar{v} - c - \rho\sigma_v^2 z_{ie}(p)]} \quad (21.18)$$

where g is defined by $g(\theta) \triangleq \frac{1-F(\theta|\theta\geq\theta_e)}{f(\theta|\theta\geq\theta_e)}$.

Step 3: Characterization of the linear symmetric equilibrium

We here look for liquidity suppliers' trading strategies of the form $z_{je}(p) = \alpha + \beta p$ for all $j = 1, \ldots, M$. The market-clearing condition $q(p, \theta) = \sum_{j=1}^{M} z_{je}(p)$ implies

$$\theta = \rho\sigma_v^2[z_0(p) + M(\alpha + \beta p)] \quad (21.19)$$

where $z_0(p) = \frac{(p+c)}{\rho\sigma_v^2}$. Besides, since θ is uniformly distributed on $[\bar{v}, \bar{\theta}]$, $g(\theta) = \bar{\theta} - \theta$. Due to the assumption made on the distribution of the random variable θ, the function $g(\theta)$ does not depend on the conjectured threshold private value θ_e. Plugging eq. 21.19 into eq. 21.18, we obtain

$$\rho\sigma_v^2(M - 1)\beta + 1 = \frac{[\bar{\theta} - p - c - \rho\sigma_v^2 M(\alpha + \beta p)]}{[p - \bar{v} - c - \rho\sigma_v^2 z_{ie}(p)]}$$

or

$$\rho\sigma_v^2 z_{ie}(p) = p - \bar{v} - c - \frac{[\bar{\theta} - p - c - \rho\sigma_v^2 M(\alpha + \beta p)]}{[\rho\sigma_v^2(M - 1)\beta + 1]}$$

From the above relation, we can solve for

$$\beta = \frac{1}{\rho\sigma_v^2}\left[1 + \frac{[\rho\sigma_v^2 M\beta + 1]}{[\rho\sigma_v^2(M - 1)\beta + 1]}\right]$$

$$\alpha = -\beta(\bar{v} + c) - \frac{[\bar{\theta} - \bar{v} - 2c]}{\rho\sigma_v^2[\rho\sigma_v^2(M - 1)\beta + 1 - M]}$$

Due to strict price priority on the ELOB, we are looking for linear solutions $z_{ie}(p)$ such that β is strictly positive. Therefore, the only solutions of the above equation are

$$\beta_e = \frac{1}{\rho\sigma_v^2}\left[1 + \sqrt{\frac{(M+1)}{(M-1)}}\right] \tag{21.20}$$

and

$$\alpha_e = -\beta_e\left[\bar{v} + c + \frac{[\bar{\theta} - \bar{v} - 2c]}{\Phi_e}\right] \tag{21.21}$$

with

$$\Phi_e = \sqrt{(M+1)}\left[\sqrt{(M+1)} + \sqrt{(M-1)}\right] \tag{21.22}$$

The equilibrium ask price-quantity schedule $p_e(.)$ is the inverse of the demand function $z_e(.)$ and then writes:

$$p_e(z) = \frac{(z - \alpha_e)}{\beta_e}$$

for all $z > 0$.

Step 4: Equilibrium market-clearing price $p_e(\theta)$
For $\theta \in \Theta_e$, the equilibrium market-clearing price satisfies the market-clearing condition $q_e(p_e(\theta), \theta) = M(\alpha_e + \beta_e p)$. Eq. 21.15 yields that

$$p_e(\theta) = \frac{[\theta - c - \rho\sigma_v^2 M\alpha_e]}{[1 + \rho\sigma_v^2 M\beta_e]} \tag{21.23}$$

where α_e and β_e are given by eq. 21.21 and 21.20.

*Step 5: Sufficient condition characterizing liquidity providers'
optimal trading strategies*
Sufficiency of the solutions of the necessary condition 21.18 is guaranteed if the Lagrangian is concave in the control variable p, that is, if

$$f(\theta)\frac{\partial^2 z_{ie}(p)}{\partial p^2}[p - \bar{v} - \rho\sigma_v^2 z_{ie}(p)] + f(\theta)\frac{\partial z_{ie}(p)}{\partial p}\left[1 - \rho\sigma_v^2\frac{\partial z_{ie}(p)}{\partial p}\right] < 0$$

The linear symmetric equilibrium such that strict price priority holds on the ELOB is characterized by $\frac{\partial^2 z_{ie}(p)}{\partial p^2} = 0$ and $\frac{\partial z_{ie}(p)}{\partial p} > 0$. Therefore, a sufficient condition is

$$\frac{\partial z_{ie}(p)}{\partial p} > \frac{1}{\rho\sigma_v^2} \tag{21.24}$$

or $\beta_e > \frac{1}{\rho\sigma_v^2}$. Eq. 21.20 yields that this inequality holds for all $M \geq 2$.

Step 6: The trader's optimal total quantity purchased
The trader θ's optimal trade size $q_e(\theta)$ is given by

$$q_e(\theta) = q_e\left(p_e(\theta), \theta\right)$$

so long as $q_e(\theta, p_e(\theta))$ is positive. Plugging eq. 21.23 into eq. 21.15, we obtain

$$q_e(\theta) = \frac{(\theta - \theta_e)}{\left(\rho\sigma_v^2 + \frac{1}{M\beta_e}\right)} \tag{21.25}$$

where the threshold private value θ_e is defined by

$$\theta_e \triangleq c - \frac{\alpha_e}{\beta_e}$$

or

$$\theta_e \triangleq \bar{v} + 2c + \frac{[\bar{\theta} - \bar{v} - 2c]}{\Phi_e} > \bar{v} \tag{21.26}$$

Since α_e and β_e are uniquely defined, we verify the existence of a unique private value θ_e such that $q_e(\theta) > 0$ and is given by eq. 21.1 for $\theta > \theta_e$ and $q_e(\theta) = 0$ for $\theta \in [\bar{v}, \theta_e]$.

21.6.3   Proof of Result 3

The pure ELOB is viable if and only if the measure of traders willing to trade within the ELOB is strictly positive. This condition then writes $\bar{\theta} > \theta_e$. Using eq. 21.26, this condition is equivalent to

$$[\bar{\theta} - \bar{v} - 2c]\left[1 - \frac{1}{\Phi_e}\right] > 0 \tag{21.27}$$

From eq. 21.22, we observe that $\Phi_e > 1$ for all $M \geq 2$. Thus, the ELOB viability condition 21.27 rewrites

$$c < c_{\max} \triangleq \frac{(\bar{\theta} - \bar{v})}{2}$$

22 Multi-level governance of the digital space: does a "second rank" institutional framework exist?

Eric Brousseau

22.1 Property rights as a way to think regulations

In any economic space, a set of fundamental rules delineates the rights to use economic resources and allocates these rights to interacting agents. The activity of settling these "rules of the game" played by agents can be qualified as regulation. This broad definition of regulation is useful for at least two purposes. First, it creates a common framework for thinking both so-called "self-regulation" and "State regulation", since it does not refer to the entity responsible for setting up the "rules of the game" for the "players". Indeed, it can either be some exogenous third party – such as the State – or the players themselves that (consciously or not) interact and set collective rules. Second, in the spirit of Coase (1960), this definition makes it clear that the management of externalities, public goods and other sources of "market failures" is an aspect of the greater activity of organizing the framework in which agents interact and exchange[1] and corresponds to the notion of a property rights (PRs) system as stated by Barzel (1989) and North (1990). By delineating and allocating rights of uses to economic agents, a PRs system establishes the way they can individually or collectively make decisions about the uses of resources.

A grant provided by the CNRS Interdisciplinary Research Program on the Information Society supported the initial research. This chapter benefited from fruitful discussions and useful suggestions made by participants to the workshop "Governance, Regulations, Powers on the Internet" held in Paris in May 2005 and organized by Meryem Marzouki (LIP6/PolyTIC, CNRS), Cecile Meadel (CSI, Ecole National Supérieure des Mines de Paris) and myself. Comments by Niva Elkin-Koren (University of Haifa and New York University), Willam J. Drake (International Centre for Trade and Sustainable Development) and Yves Schemeil (University of Grenoble and IUF) were especially helpful. The paper was also discussed during the workshops organized to prepare this book. I warmly thank participants. Usual caveats apply.

[1] Indeed, "public regulation" refers to the setting of limits in the use of resources (or obligations to use them in a specific way). A "regulation" – in the traditional understanding – consists therefore in setting more precisely the user rights actually granted to the owner of a given asset (such as an infrastructure).

617

In that general understanding, setting a PRs system implies four major activities: setting rules; supervising their enforcement and punishing infringements; settling conflicts, since there are always ambiguities in rules and therefore different interpretations; and implementing decision mechanisms when rules do not apply, since there is always some incompleteness in a system of rules.

A property rights approach to regulation is useful to analyze the way the Internet is governed, because the cyber-world is increasingly considered as a model for a new regulatory regime based on decentralized and State-free regulation often qualified as self-regulation.[2] At first sight, the Internet and Internet-based activities have been developing on the basis of governance mechanisms based on contractual agreements or communities' self-regulations. This is due both to the global connectivity provided by the Internet's (end-to-end) architecture and (open) standards – which allow traditional State norms to be easily bypassed – and to the coding and tracking capabilities provided by digital technologies – that allow self-enforceable property rights and rules to be implemented at a (relatively) low cost (see below).

This chapter is an attempt to analyze the principles of an institutional framework which could be adapted to the regulation of the Internet and related activities. This will lead to an analysis of why some aspects of the coordination of activities should be centrally managed, and why hierarchical principles should be implemented to organize the relationships among regulatory bodies. We will first review the reasons why technology challenges the traditional institutional framework (22.2). We will then review the contributions of the economics and multi-level governance and of federalism in setting up the principles that should inspire the institutional design behind the regulation of the digital world (22.3). This will lead us to analyze the specificities of the problems raised by the governance of the Internet, highlighting the principle that should inspire an ideal governance architecture (22.4). Actual governance mechanisms and the design of new ones seem, however, to drive the system away from this ideal type (22.5). We will then analyze the available mechanisms that would favor a more satisfying path of evolution (22.6).

---

[2] However, careful observation of the facts leads one to qualify this simplifying view. The establishment of technical standards and above all the management of the addressing system are centralized (cf. note 3). States also play an essential role. The US government is the main inventor in the Internet, and remains the owner of the addressing system, even though its management is delegated to non-governmental organizations (see Brousseau, 2001, 2004a).

22.2   What is new with the Internet?

In the following pages, we will deal with the regulation of both networks (infrastructures and services) and contents.[3] While Internet technologies enable the separation of the management of network services from the management of information services, the strong technical and economic interdependencies between the two call for a simultaneous analysis of their regulation. Today the Internet is de facto co-regulated by national governments – that intervene however without strongly co-coordinating among themselves – by professional entities – whose competencies overlap and which are not always legitimate – and authorities responsible for the technical standardization and management of the system – in particular the ICANN (Internet Corporation for Assigned Names and Numbers; http://www.icann.com/), the IETF (Internet Engineering Task Force; http://www.ietf.org/) and the W3C (World Wide Web Consortium; http://www.w3.org/) that are very dynamic but lack strong institutional roots (see the introductory chapter and Section 22.4 below; see also Brousseau (2001, 2004)). These various entities contribute to designing rights of use over information flows or network components.

The fuzzy set that regulates the Internet draws from a recent, but rich, history during which computer scientists working within US governmental agencies progressively established the technical principles that govern the management of a decentralized network. This effort was then transferred to private initiatives when the Internet became commercial and open to private investments (Leiner et al., 2000). Earlier and later, regulation initiatives bypassed the traditional intergovernmental mechanisms of international standardization and regulation (Brousseau, 2001, 2004). Four main reasons explain this. First, the velocity of innovation

---

[3] According to the Working Group on Internet Governance working in the frame of the World Summit of the Information Society (WSIS), "Internet governance is the development and application by Governments, the private sector and civil society, in their respective roles, of shared principles, norms, rules, decision-making procedures, and programmes that shape the evolution and use of the Internet." It encompasses therefore the management of infrastructure and of critical Internet resources (addressing system, communication protocol, standards, etc.), issues related to the management of priority, reliability and security over the Internet (including spam, network security, cybercrime, consumer protection, privacy, etc.) and issues that are relevant to the Internet, but with impact much wider than the Internet, which include competition policy, regulation of e-commerce and e-business, intellectual property rights (IPRs) and also freedom of expression, freedom of the press, multi-linguism and multi-culturalism; these latter dimensions being highlighted in particular by many of the stakeholders involved in the WSIS process. It proves, nevertheless, that it is quite impossible to disentangle the management of content and container since the regulation of the latter aspects determine how agents can be empowered or not to manage contents.

in both digital networks and multi-media technologies was quite incompatible with the slowness of these international or intergovernmental agencies. Second, until 1998, the Internet was essentially a US network, and it is still dominated by US players. Third, the liberal ideology of, respectively, the inventors and the entrepreneurs of the Internet explains their mistrust in international or intergovernmental bureaucracies. Fourth, technology enabled regulatory principles to be implemented on a decentralized basis.

The present institutional framework is problematic for at least two reasons. First, it is partly inefficient in the sense that there is incompleteness, conflicts and defaults in enforcement in the set of implemented rules. Second, the current processes used to establish these rules do not guarantee that the interests of all the stakeholders are fairly taken into account. It is therefore necessary to investigate what the basic principles of the regulation of the cyber-world should be. Indeed, many specialists advocate that, beyond a common minimal technical regulation – the publication of open standards and a transparent management of the addressing system – the Internet and its uses should be decentrally self-regulated. The combination of an abundance of essential resources, strong competition among information and network service providers, and the ability to decentrally configure the services supported by the network according to the preferences of the users is supposed to allow adaptation to each and everybody's preferences, without fear of conflicting uses and capture (as summed up by Frischmann, 2001 and Elkin-Koren and Salzberger, 2000).

Before discussing this view, let us remind the reader why the Internet and digital technologies profoundly change the economics of regulation and more generally the economics of institutional frameworks. Following a New Institutional approach, it is indeed useful to consider institutional frameworks as "social technologies" which impact on economic efficiency, both because they have to be considered as a production means and because they are costly to produce. A cost/benefit analysis has therefore to be applied to institutional frameworks.

According to Barzel (1989) and North (1990), any institutional framework can be analyzed as a property rights system, the latter notion referring to a set of rules and mechanisms that delineates rights of use over economic resources and allocates them to decision makers so as to enable them to take economic actions.[4] A PRs system is based, first, on a

---

[4] This fundamental understanding of property rights clearly differs from the legal notion of property rights, but the latter is included in the former. Barzel and North's analysis aims at synthesizing how an institutional framework results in economic properties through

delineation (measure) of these rights of use – consisting in establishing the frontiers between different ways of using resources and among regimes for appropriating the output of these uses – and on a process of allocation of these rights – that are granted to individuals or groups – which together generate measurement costs. Second, enforcement mechanisms implement these rights of use by excluding every unentitled agent from access to the protected resources or from capturing the output of its use. This refers to controlling access, supervising uses, granting authorization for uses and punishing unauthorized uses (either to get damages or to dissuade potential infringers) and generates enforcement costs.

Digital technologies and the Internet architecture have an essential impact on both measurement and enforcement operations. Indeed, due to the decreasing cost of information processing and to the increasing capabilities of information and communication technologies (ICTs) and to the decentralized management of the Internet, individual agents have access to capabilities that allow them to individually implement property rights (22.2.1) and to set up self-enforcing collective rules (22.2.2) at much lower costs than before. Moreover, the efficiency and the credibility of traditional regulatory frames are challenged by digital technologies (22.2.3).

22.2.1 Coding and tracking as a way to decentrally design and enforce property rights

Digital technologies allow a self-enforcing system of property rights over information goods and services to be implemented (Lessig, 1999). Indeed any set of information that is codifiable in a computer can be either encrypted to control *ex ante* its uses (code of access) or easily, instantaneously and cheaply tracked to control *ex post* how it has been used. Moreover, digital technologies allow the implementation, at very low cost, of customized conditions of exchanges over contents, since contracts governing information exchanges are made self-enforceable through digital codes. Consequently, agents can tailor the conditions of exchanges of intangibles to the specificities of the exchange and of the parties. This results in a more "decentralized" setting of property rights

the allocation of decision rights to agents and through their ability to be exchanged (to achieve a more efficient use of resources). Their definition of property rights encompasses what we usually call property rights, but also the regulations that bound economic agents' decision rights, the law that establishes boundaries to the free will of agents, and the informal rules (such as social customs) that mitigate and frame individual freedom of decision, and contracts since they allow agents to delineate the rights of use transferred to other agents.

as could be deduced from the frameworks of Barzel (1989) and North (1990).

As analyzed in Brousseau (2001, 2004a, b), digital technologies provide content creators and network operators with means to de facto self-claim and implement property rights by enabling them to control access to their resources. They also make it possible to finely tune at reasonable costs the transfer of these rights of access and of uses among economic agents. Decentralization creates a more efficient property rights system, since any centrally settled rules never perfectly fit to the local individual needs and constraints, resulting in maladaptation costs borne by the users of the rule (see Section 22.3, and the analyses of Barzel, 1989; North, 1990; and Brousseau and Raynaud, 2006).

22.2.2 Information spaces as a way of implementing self-regulations

Not only can individual property rights be individually measured and enforced, but collective regulations can also be more decentrally designed and enforced. Digital networks relying on the end-to-end principle allow "information spaces" to be created and access to them to be controlled. These information spaces can be of very different natures: mailing lists, secured websites, forums, intra- and extranets, etc. In each case, some individual or entity is in charge of managing the list of subscribers who can access the common space. This entity therefore controls in/exclusions in/from the resulting on-line community aimed at sharing resources or at interacting within the closed space. Control of access allows implementation of a collective regulation since those who do not comply are denied access to the information space. It is essential to point out that the collective regulation can of course concern the use of the network or access to contents. However, it can also organize more broadly the interactions among the members of the on-line community. If threatened with exclusion from the information space, individuals are likely to comply to on-line set regulations, even if their interactions are performed partly off-line (such as in the case of the transaction of a tangible good).

Thanks to this ability, information technologies considerably reduce the costs of implementing self-regulations. Well known by historians and anthropologists (e.g. Bernstein, 1992, 1996; Cooter, 1994, 1996; Granovetter, 1985), self-designed and self-enforced regulations allow communities to implement collective order either to organize collective action or to solve coordination difficulties. However, the efficiency of self-regulations decreases when communities become larger and more diverse. Indeed, each infringer is less visible because information circulates less efficiently. Moreover, each member of the community has fewer incentives to practice retaliations since they are costly and since a member's individual action is less visible (Milgrom et al., 1990). Digital technologies facilitate the implementation of collective rules because they enable individual behavior more easily to be tracked, because rules can be implemented into the code and because the ultimate retaliation – exclusion from the community – is technically easy and cheap to manage.

22.2.3 How ICTs challenge traditional institutional frameworks

While digital technologies favor the implementation of self-regulation, digital networks make traditional institutional frameworks less effective. The Internet is a-territorial by nature, while traditional public regulations are implemented on a territorial basis. The Internet's interconnectivity is the basis of its ability to support the sharing of communication functions and contents. Its decentralization guarantees its reliability, its efficiency and its ability to develop. The Internet is therefore the medium of a worldwide connectivity that overcomes existing regulations based on territorial jurisdiction and government legitimacy. Two evolutions come into play. First, digital networks allow the bypassing of nation-state-based regulatory frameworks. Second, the legitimacy (and the efficiency) of these previous frameworks is called into question due to the properties of the new technological infrastructure. These evolutions concern both the rights to access and use information and networks, and the norms used by agents to coordinate many dimensions of social interactions, and in particular those that organize the use and exchange of economic resources.

First, any legislation can be bypassed through the Internet because no governmental agency would be able to efficiently supervise the exchanges of information among Internet users under their jurisdiction and between them and foreign third parties to guarantee the enforcement of existing laws. Moreover, these exchanges can be faked and the potential infringers of the law can use a wide set of technical means to perform operations that would be forbidden by some technical means operated by the State.[5] The generalized interconnectivity as well as the possibility to break codes and reciprocally to strongly encrypt limits the ability of governments to control network-based activities.[6] In practice,

---

[5] Individually set-up property rights and private regulations based on codes can also be cracked by hackers and bypassed – this is discussed in the next section.

[6] The governments could try to control information flows by creating a "national Internet". It would, however, result in wide losses of positive network externalities.

this ability to bypass traditional public regulations does not result in massive development of illegal activities in all domains, even if cyber-crime is developing, and if some practices like file sharing raise major concerns in some domains, such as cultural industries. However, it grants many stakeholders a bargaining power that enables them to claim for the reshaping of a lot of legislation either because they consider the existing legislation as no longer tailored to the problems they are supposed to solve or because existing national orders create a handicap in the global competition taking place in the digital space. It results in a direct confrontation and unchecked competition among norms in many domains, which is reinforced by the ability of services providers and contents providers to locate their information-processing devices in territories where the norms that are the most in accordance with their preferences apply.[7]

Second, the legitimacy and the efficiency of traditional regulations are also in question. Some features of traditional institutional frameworks are no longer justified because the new technological infrastructure renews the economics of information and many of the optimal tradeoffs behind the current regulatory framework. In some cases it is the principle of State regulation which is challenged per se, in others it is the way public intervention was designed that is no longer relevant because the problems it addressed have changed with the new technologies. Let us quote two sets of examples.

First, the traditional governmental intervention in the design of intellectual property rights systems was largely justified because physical constraint was, in the last resort, the only way to really prevent unen-titled agents from accessing and using information. Producers of know-ledge and information had to rely on public authorities acting as their agents to guarantee the effectiveness of their exclusive rights of use. The

Moreover, it would necessitate the ability to effectively forbid any uncontrolled intercon-nection with a foreign network to avoid creating a gateway. Moreover, having the government scanning the details of private uses of information might violate citizens' privacy and might be a threat toward civil liberties. That said, since 11 September 2001, governments have been relying on Internet service providers (ISPs) to more efficiently track end-users or deny access to some servers. There is, however, an irreducible diffi-culty in controlling end-to-end networks.

[7] This destabilizes existing legal frameworks, despite the fact that international conven-tions could be set up to implement common legal principles. On the one hand, intergov-ernmental regulations are subjected to a prisoner's dilemma. To stimulate their national economies some States can decide not to ratify these conventions, thus bounding their impact (digital paradises). On the other hand, the possibility of agreeing on common norms is quite limited because the various legal systems result from contrasted historical and philosophical traditions, which bring us back to divergent ideologies about human nature, social logic or economic activity.

resulting design of a unified regime of IPRs, whatever the technical domain and the industry, had, however, strong maladaptation costs (Brousseau and Raynaud, 2006; Brousseau and Bessy, 2006). Indeed, to be implemented by a central government, a rule – for instance, of duration and scope of protection – has to be generic to be applied to a wide set of situations, resulting in lack of effectiveness or efficiency in many specific situations (the optimal delay of disclosure being, for instance, different in a rapidly evolving and in stable technological domains). Thanks to the ability to implement self-enforced IPRs, digital technologies allow content creators and innovators to decide on the optimal rules of diffusion/protection to be applied given the specificity of what they produce, the technological and competitive context and the business model they want to implement.

In addition, IPRs were designed at the national level because for a long time it was the relevant economic space and because an authority of last resort was available at this level only. Today the economic space is increasingly global and the same is true for the information space. In many respects it is meaningless to guarantee exclusive rights of use over information in some territories and not in others. Since digital technologies enable effective exclusive rights of uses wherever the information is used, the usefulness of national IPRs systems decreases.

Second, the new technological context affects the logic of the design of former rules. For instance, many regulations concerning the diffusion of information (e.g. restrictions or banning of certain contents, organization of specific distribution channels, etc.) were justified because traditional broadcasting technologies – in particular hertzian analog radio and TV – made it impossible to control access to information. Because they allow controlling access to contents on a customized basis (i.e. user by user), digital technologies turn many traditional regulations restricting publication rights and channeling contents into obsolete tools.

In the same spirit, digital networks overcome the traditional boundaries and the implementability of communication (one-to-one) versus broadcasting (one-to-many) regulations. Most information services are hybrids between these two extremes, even inventing new logics for sharing and exchanging information.

The former national regulations are no longer relevant because agents now have the possibility of decentrally implementing more efficient orders established within communities characterized by common practices or preferences rather than by location or jurisdiction. Is a new institutional framework needed then? Some authors argue that information and digital resources are almost pure indivisible and non-rival goods that render the implementation of common rules useless since these rules will be spontaneously and decentrally produced by agents and communities implementing self-enforcing property rights and rules. If a resource does not cause conflicting claims among its potential users, scarcity does not arise and there are no economic problems. There are, however, generic (Section 22.3) and specific (Section 22.4) arguments to justify some central coordination of the rule-making and enforcement process in the digital world.

22.3   The economics of multi-level governance

To better understand how rule setting can be optimally organized, it is useful to rely on the economics of constitutional design and multi-level governance which seeks to clarify at what "level" of coordination different types of coordination problems should be solved, so as to understand the optimal way of organizing an institutional framework.[8]

The New-Institutional Approach to Property Rights provided by Barzel (1989) and North (1990) is a useful framework to deal with this issue. In a given group – let us say a nation – the measure and the enforcement of property rights can be performed either centrally by an authority of last resort – generally the State, that benefits from the monopoly of the legitimate violence – or decentrally by the agents. In the former case, the government defines for each set of economic resources the rights that can be associated to them (e.g. *usus, fructus* and *abusus*) and maintains a cadastre in which each of these rights over any resource is recognized for individuals or groups. Then the government sets up and operates an enforcement mechanism to expel any unentitled agents from the protected use of these resources. It can be an *ex ante* mechanism – e.g. a guard or an encryption mechanism that forbids access – or an *ex post* mechanism that assesses violation and punishes infringers. The alternative is to have the property rights self-delineated and self-enforced by agents. In the latter case, individuals (or groups)

---

[8] As Hooghe and Marks (2001) point out, the notion of multi-level governance – together with others such as multi-tiered governance, polycentric governance, multi-perspectival governance, FOCJ (functional, overlapping, competing jurisdictions) – seeks to describe how governance has been changing in western societies. All refer to the dispersion of authority away from central government, upwards to the supranational level, downwards to subnational jurisdictions, and sideways to public/private networks. Two bodies of economics literature have investigated these notions in particular. Neoclassical political economists and public choice theorists (e.g. Ostrom and Walker, 1997; Rosenau, 2001) insist on the idea that governance results from the setting of dispersed self-rule on the part of diverse voluntary groups that overlap and interact in a complex way among each other and with imperfect markets and imperfect public-interest-seeking institutions. Theorists of (fiscal) federalism have gone from studies focused primarily on formal constitutional federations to a costs/benefits analysis of centralization vs. decentralization of authority (e.g. Oates, 1972, 1999).

claim for exclusiveness of usage, and they use available means (and in the last resort, violence) to have their claims enforced by third parties. The New Institutional Economics (NIE) approach to property rights analyzes the advantages and disadvantages of centralization and decentralization (Barzel, 1989; North, 1990; Brousseau and Fares, 2000; Brousseau and Raynaud, 2006; see also Brousseau, 2004a and Brousseau and Bessy, 2006, in the specific case of IPRs). It leads to the idea that establishing a PRs system, either fully centrally or fully decentrally, would be inefficient in the sense that the costs of setting up a complete PRs system[9] would be too high compared with the benefit agents would get in being able to use resources, invest in the genesis of production capabilities and organize trade. Any property rights system results therefore from a tradeoff between the advantages of centralization and decentralization.

In a recent paper Brousseau and Raynaud (2006) point out the main "factors" playing a role in the tradeoff enabling the identification of the optimal level/mode of coordination to solve a given coordination problem in a specific context. On the one hand, centralization provides agents with (i) scale and scope effects, (ii) learning and specialization benefits and (iii) means to reduce losses of collective welfare (by allowing an increased consistency among local rules, an internalization of externalities, the genesis of positive network effects due to the use of common standards of interactions). Indeed, the entity in charge of centrally designing a rule for a community will take into account the interdependencies among agents and the net benefit of alternative rules at the collective level, while decentralized negotiations could fail to consider these elements if transaction costs are not zero, if information asymmetries arise, if property rights are incomplete, etc. On the other hand, centralization generates inefficiencies due to (i) static maladaptation[10] (linked to

[9] Completeness of property rights corresponds to an ideal. It would indeed mean that any potential use of any resources would be identified and associated to a right granted to either an individual or a group. A complete PRs system would enable almost costless transactions since agents would only have to bear the cost of meeting and agreeing on the terms of the exchange. Transaction would not be free, however, because the costs of the property rights system would have to be covered, but once established, variable transaction costs would be extremely low (limited to information and negotiation costs).

[10] Maladaptation costs refer to the opportunity costs borne by an agent when, to coordinate with others, he relies on a rule that is not the one that would result in the best net outcome for him compared with the most advantageous available solutions. Agents might be led to accept coordination solutions that do not minimize their private transaction costs because when interacting with other agents and in particular with communities, collective constraints and/or asymmetries in bargaining power can lead a single agent to accept rules that do not fit perfectly to its particular needs and individual preferences.

the increasing heterogeneity of individual preferences); (ii) dynamic maladaptation (due to the reduced renegotiability of collective rules and therefore the difficulty in adapting compromises to new circumstances); (iii) the increasing enforcement requirements (since there are increasing incentives to free-ride due to the rising maladaptation costs inherent in a larger, less homogeneous, community; and (iv) the rising private capture of coordination. Indeed, when an order is both general and centrally designed, the interests that can influence the design of the order have strong incentives to distort collective governance in their favor. First, it is profitable, since the order applies to a wide set of agents. Second, it is rational because it is difficult for agents to escape from this rent extraction (since the order is general, agents have few exit options).

This tradeoff that is inherent to the solving of any coordination problem makes it clear that there is no "optimal" rule-making solution/level that cancels the cost of coordinating the use of economic resources. Agents therefore play on complementarities between levels/modes of coordination to try to minimize the coordination costs they bear (and maximize their efficiency in using and exchanging economic resources).

First, agents have to organize a "division of labor" among the various tools they can rely on to coordinate: general institutions, community ones and contracts. To do so, they divide actual coordination problems into several smaller ones to be solved by the level/mode of coordination that minimizes their private costs. Here a principle of "subsidiarity" applies. The relevant level of coordination has to fit with the "generality" of the addressed issue that can concern a pair of agents, a subset of the population or the whole population. Agents build complementary contractual arrangements, self-regulations and general institutions to solve the various dimensions of their coordination problems in relation to the optimal centralization/decentralization tradeoff for each of these dimensions.

Second, each level/mode of governance potentially generates inefficiencies. Complementarities among them should also be considered in terms of interactions. A "check and balance" principle has to be managed between the various levels of governance and in particular between general and mandatory institutions and local (or specialized) and voluntary ones.[11] The former – qualified as public institutions in

---

[11] In our framework, public institutions are the results of an evolutionary process of extension of the scope and rigidification of contractual arrangements, then collective self-regulations, that start by being applied to small groups and specific coordination issues to expand to wider groups and to the solving of more generic coordination problems. By reference to the notion of Institutional Framework defined by Yoram Barzel (1989) and Douglass North (1990), public institutions are mandatory – agents

our framework – should (i) control for monopoly capture by the latter – qualified as private institutions – and (ii) be used to reinforce the bounded enforcing capabilities of private institutions since the latter are sometimes unable to implement and enforce an efficient private order (which, usually, cannot rely on violence to incite agents to comply). Private institutions and governance mechanisms are useful in (i) allowing innovation in the institutional framework, and (ii) limiting the discretionary power of those in control of public institutions. Their ability to bypass and even overcome the public order constrains public institutions not to be overly inefficient.

These elements call for a multi-level governance of any coordination problem, which should apply in the digital world as well. One of the characteristics of any multi-level governance is that a last-resort regulating entity should overhang all the norm-setting entities; just as a supreme court does in a constitutional State. The role of such a last-resort entity is to enhance the efficiency of the global order resulting from the decentralized production of norms. It is in charge of avoiding incompatibilities among norms and maximizing positive network externalities among them, as well as avoiding the capture of norms by individuals or groups seeking to exercise dominance. It is also responsible for guaranteeing the enforcement of locally set orders as long as they contribute to collective efficiency.[12] At the national level, the (federal) State, and in particular the supreme court, are these last-resort regulators placed above local government orders and private order setters. At the international level, due to the increasing globalization of the economy but also because of many other aspects of collective problems – in particular environmental and security ones – there is a necessity for the emergence of such last-resort regulating entities responsible for harmonizing and controlling the interacting orders resulting from the decentralized initiatives of national public systems (i.e. national States) and private entities that set international orders in many domains: business, technology, culture and politics.

---

do not choose to enforce the related rules – and general – the associated rules apply to wide and heterogeneous sets of situations and agents. Private institutions are voluntary and specialized.

[12] There is therefore convergence of interests between central and local norm setters. The central norm setter can facilitate the role of local norm setters in strengthening their ability to implement their norms. The local norm setters can, in turn, accept the constraints imposed by the last-resort regulator in exchange for this support. Such potential bargaining allows both levels of regulation to reinforce each other, since the local regulators recognize the legitimacy of the (collective) constraints imposed by the last-order regulator, while the latter recognizes the contribution of the local norm setters to the implementation of an efficient general order.

22.4   Institutional stakes in the digital sphere

While strong arguments call for a decentralized settlement of IPRs and collective rules in the digital world (Section 22.2), we have just reviewed the general arguments mitigating this initial view (Section 22.3). A certain degree of centralization is useful. This general statement is reinforced in the digital world because digital networks and digital activities impact on the provision of two categories of essential resources. First, the IPRs regime and the collective rules organizing access and use of information goods have a direct influence on the efficiency with which information and knowledge can be used, shared and produced. Second, digital networks are *per se* resources allowing coordination among agents. There are two levels of understanding for this assertion. Digital networks are communication tools allowing agents to contact each other, exchange information, etc. In addition, end-to-end networks provide agents with the capability of creating private orders to manage access to and use of information and coordination resources. Thus, the regulation of digital networks affects both the ability to collectively produce and use information and knowledge and the capability to produce/use relevant and efficient inter-individual coordination platforms.[13] It is essential to assess whether a fully decentralized production of the institutional frameworks regulating the access to and use of these essential resources would be efficient.

We will start by pointing out that the efficiency of measurement (22.4.1) and enforcement (22.4.2) operations could be enhanced thanks to some centralization, whereas full decentralization would lead to inefficiencies. Then we will show that these arguments are reinforced by the sustainability of monopolies in the digital world (22.4.3).

22.4.1   Can measurement operations be totally decentralized?

The way according to which property rights and collective rules are set on digital networks affects the efficiency of the use of rival resources and non-rival resources. Brousseau (2004a) details why, in both cases, full decentralization generates inefficiencies.[14] We will concentrate here

---

[13] We give a very broad understanding of the notion of coordination platform. It stands for a coordination solution provided to a community by a system of common rules. It is not restricted therefore to a technical digital platform.

[14] As far as measurement operation resources are concerned, the main problem with rival resources is the way the initial endowment of property rights is performed. It can generate non-neutral wealth distribution effects. It can also lead to illegitimate capture when the rights granted on digital networks impact on rights that were granted

and in the following section on the most strategic issue: non-rival resources. Concerning non-rival resources, the limit to the decentralized setting of property rights is an excessive protection of these resources, forbidding access to many potential users while the resource is non-rival. On the one hand, it is possible today to claim for exclusive right of use over digitized information and knowledge (e.g. embedded in software) simply by encrypting it. It is also possible to control access to information spaces providing coordination resources. On the other hand, both types of resources are non-rival (if there is no congestion effect within the information space in the latter case) and there are important collective benefits to be gained from organizing free access to these resources.

In the case of information and knowledge, there are spillovers. Maximizing diffusion enables the production of new information and new knowledge to be maximized because of the possible recombination of the existing stock and because the ability to use a specific set of information or knowledge often depends upon the access to complementary information. A central system guaranteeing some fundamental rights of access to information should be able to guarantee the exploitation of these externalities.

In the case of coordination platforms, the ability to create customized and efficient coordination means relies on access to an open platform on which tools to create those means are available. Moreover, the openness of coordination platforms maximizes for each member the number of potential counterparts in the exchange (whether exchange is of a market type or not). It then reinforces the chances of any transactor to get in touch with the right counterpart. It reduces also the ability of those participating in a platform to capture monopoly rents on other members and incites them to enhance efficiency, as well as reinforcing the division of labor. Again, a central system guaranteeing the openness of (generic and more specific)[15] coordination platforms is essential to maximize the likelihood of exploiting these externalities.

---

outside of them. As far as it concerns enforcement, full decentralization means a loss of benefit from potential efficiency gains linked to centralization; in particular the ability to manage externalities and the ability to benefit from economies of scale and scope (see Brousseau, 2004b; and also Brousseau and Raynaud, 2006 or the previous section in this chapter that recalls the general tradeoff between the two ways of setting orders).

[15] There are indeed two issues at stake. First, the openness of the network infrastructure and services in which these platforms are grounded is essential. Put another way, the Internet infrastructure, architecture and essential resources should remain open. Second, the platforms built by communities of all kinds on the Internet should remain open. More precisely, access to them should be guaranteed in fair conditions to avoid the development of oligopolies or oligopsonies aimed purely at capturing rents. In relation to the first point, see the note on Internet transparency. RFC-2775: ftp://ftp.rfc-editor.org/in-notes/rfc2775.txt/ M. S. Blumenthal and D. D. Clark "Rethinking the design of the Internet: The end-to-end arguments vs. the brave new world", in B. Compaine and S. Greenstein

It has to be pointed out that in the former institutional frameworks organized at the national level, the government often acted to limit private capture of resources considered as essential facilities. Think, for instance, of the IPRs system with the obligation of disclosure and with the process of transferring private property to the public domain with the passing of time. Think also of the competition policies aimed at guaranteeing access to exchange platforms.

These arguments call for some centrality, both to select the collectively optimal system and to compensate those who are harmed by a system in which PRs are bounded compared with what they would get if a system of unlimited rights to control access and uses prevailed.

22.4.2   The limits to a fully decentralized enforcement

Assuming that the above-mentioned measurement problems have been solved, a too decentralized enforcement of PRs and self-regulation could lead to an inefficient protection of non-rival resources and generally speaking to an overly weak enforcement of private orders, depriving agents respectively of an efficient protection of their exclusive rights of use (or of remuneration) and of the benefits of relying on decentrally set-up coordination means.

Self-enforcement in the digital world relies on two pillars: code and control of access to information spaces. However, none of these methods guarantees a perfect enforcement. First, no cryptographic system is inviolable. Code-based protection is therefore imperfect. Second, the enforceability of norms founding virtual communities is also in question. The power of coordinators of virtual communities is obviously bounded by the ability of Internet users to access alternative communities providing them with the same type of service (or an alternative one they prefer) and by the ability of the providers of means of access to identify the users (because the only identity that is certain over the Internet is that of the computers). This calls for an entity able to guarantee enforcement in the last resort by being able to punish infringers. In this case, centralization of enforcement is justified for two reasons.[16] There is obviously a need

---

(eds.), *Communications Policy in Transition: The Internet and Beyond*, MIT Press, Sept. 2001 (http://www.ana.lcs.mit.edu/anaweb/PDF/Rethinking_2001.pdf).

[16] Central enforcement, in turn, calls for some centralization of measurement. Indeed, central supervision of uses implies at least a mechanism that will register claims of exclusive rights of uses over information – implying a categorization of the various types of material eligible for protection – and that will check for the legitimacy and the absence of overlap among these claims.

for some exercise of constraint in the last resort. Indeed, even if a self- or local regulatory mechanism can rely on its ability to exclude infringers, its credibility is bounded by the cost borne by the infringers in case of exclusion. If this cost is inferior to the benefit an agent can earn by violating the local regulation, the self-enforcement mechanism will be unable to prevent (major) infringements. A last-resort enforcement device able to increase the costs of violating the local regulation by implementing additional retaliation would reinforce the enforceability of local regulation (see Milgrom et al., 1990; Lemley, 1999; Brousseau and Fares, 2000; Brousseau and Raynaud, 2006). In addition, a central mechanism granted with power of constraint could guarantee a minimum transparency to control how the closed information spaces are actually used. Indeed, a virtual community can be organized to infringe the rights or break the rules established by another on-line community. More generally, if agents agree on principles that allow them at a collective level to maximize efficiency – e.g. by optimally dealing with the protection/diffusion dilemma (see Besen and Raskind, 1991) – some of them could use ITs and digital networks to create sub-spaces where these common rules would be violated. These sub-spaces could be of very different types: peer-to-peer (P2P) communities to bypass the right of remuneration of creators of content, marketplaces to bypass regulations of market exchanges, private networks built on the digital infrastructure to manage communication flow a different way (e.g. to manage priority for voice or video streams). Bypassing collective rules can ruin their sustainability. This is true for whatever the type of rules ensuring the provision of a public good to a community and whatever this public good is: an open access platform, open access information or knowledge. For instance, collective agreement on remuneration rights to be allocated to the creators or inventors could be hindered by the development of communities faking their sharing of contents.[17] In other cases, the sharing of information within OSS communities could be discouraged by private capture of knowledge and the associated wealth and reputation by some free-riders. The possibility of having collective rules enforced in the last resort is therefore necessary to avoid phenomena comparable to the tragedy of the commons, the commons being in that case the

---

[17] Two scenarios could then arise. One, the creator of contents will reduce their investments in creation. Two, since investors in the creation of digital sequences could fear not getting any return if disclosing them, and since they can cheaply control access to them, it could give rise to a private over-protection, in the sense that the collectivity will be deprived of the potential positive externalities of open access (externalities of diffusion, spillovers, etc.).

collective rules that "optimally" solve the protection/open access dilemma in the provision of public goods.

22.4.3   Sustainable monopolies in the digital era

The problems raised by a full decentralization of the settlement of property rights and regulation are reinforced by the long-term sustainability of monopolies in the digital world. First, fixed costs make monopolies stable and viable in the digital world (Shapiro and Varian, 1999; Noe and Parker, 2000). Second, network externalities are also strong drivers of monopoly dominance through the possible privatization of (interface and interoperation) standards. Network effects push for interoperability among the different components of the digital sphere. Players are incited to take control of the interface and interoperability standards because they are essential means of controlling access to various markets. They therefore play on increasing returns of adoption and viral contagion to reinforce their ability to control the long-term evolution of standards and therefore of market structures.[18] The combination of the two allows some players or some coalitions to gain control over the ability to settle the basis of property rights systems and collective coordination means, so as to have their interests prevailing without really allowing alternative interests to compete on a fair basis, thus harming collective welfare.

We explained above that a PRs system based on self-claims and self-enforcement could lead to an excessive private capture of non-rival resources as information and knowledge or as coordination platforms. Producers of these public goods will indeed be incited to fully and endlessly restrict access, while collective efficiency calls for limited exclusion in the short run and full openness in the long run, to allow creators/producers to be remunerated while maximizing diffusion and access. The impact of digital technologies on market structure makes this over-restriction of access to information, knowledge and coordination means sustainable in the long run, leading to an under-optimal availability of these public goods both in the short and long run. Never-ending restricted access to public goods would have strong redistribution effects since some players would be able to endlessly capture rents. Second, it can have a strong negative collective effect such as hindering

---

[18] Digital goods are composite goods made of the assembling of several components (Economides and Salop, 1992; Economides, 1996; Brousseau and Pénard, 2007). In such a context, if standards are not fully open, agents are bounded in their ability to assemble and lock into a specific relationship with a restricted set of suppliers, who play on switching costs to be able to capture rents in the long run.

innovation (because of restricted entry and because of reduced spillover effects) and fragmenting the open platform of coordination, resulting in making valuable deals impossible.

These threats lead to the necessity of binding economic agents' ability to restrict access to contents and coordination platforms. This induces the limiting of agents' encryption capacities (e.g. mandatory registration of code keys to trustworthy third parties) to maintain a minimal level of transparency aimed at enabling supervision by some antitrust authority. Moreover, reducing encryption capabilities limits de facto the levels of barriers to entry and therefore the strength of monopoly power. More generally, self-enforcement has to be supervised by some last-resort authority to ensure that encryption and self-regulation are not combined to develop and exercise monopoly power, and to guarantee open competition in the long run.[19] Indeed, competition is the best solution to provide agents and communities with incentives to implement efficient solutions.

The openness of coordination platforms should also be maintained. We mentioned above that the end-to-end connectivity provides the agents with the ability to implement self-regulations in the digital world. For instance, it grants ISPs the ability to manage their network the way they want, such as by implementing specific standards, specific addressing systems, etc. Depending on whether or not the ISP complies with Internet standards and with Internet management principles, the ISP makes the network part of the Internet or a specific network, connected to the Internet by a gateway controlled by the ISP. The latter solution aimed at increasing (local) quality – e.g. by managing priorities within digital flows or by reducing the scarcities of IP addresses – strongly decreases the transparency and the reliability of the network (because communication protocols become partly incompatible, because the addressing system is then composed of various non-transparent layers, etc.). Moreover, it gives a wide power of control to ISPs because the network is no longer of an end-to-end type. In the case of the generalization of such a behavior, the automatic interoperability among networks

---

[19] In that respect, it has to be pointed out that there is a strong transparency–security dilemma over the Internet. On the one hand, the long-term sustainability of the competitive process in information networks calls for a minimum level of transparency. This is essential to enable users to compare alternative supply conditions. This is also crucial for supervising potential anti-competitive behavior. On the other hand, the protection of contents (both the privacy of information exchanges and property rights) leads to encryption. This raises complex problems, because even if it is not justified to broadcast publicly the content of all information exchanges, it is necessary to verify that information exchanges are not harmful for the collectivity as could be the case if they were aimed at settling collusive agreements, infringing intellectual property rights or performing criminal activities.

would disappear and ISPs would have to negotiate interconnection agreements and manage gateways among their networks. This would lead them to define what their users can do when they are interacting with users of other networks (by authorizing or forbidding various practices). Put another way, with the collapse of the end-to-end principle, network operators would become able to control the information service provision on their networks. They would therefore be tempted to adopt strategies aimed at decreasing the competitive advantages of their competitors (either by forbidding access and downgrading the quality/price ratio of competitors' services or by providing exclusive services on their own network). Such strategies would lead in the long run to the emergence of uncontestable monopolies, but they would also lead in the short term into a decreasing ability among information and coordination service providers to market their services on the global infrastructure (with unavoidable consequences on the diversity and on the price benefiting the final users, since providers will have to write off the fixed cost of the service provision on a reduced audience). This would have strong distribution effects and would harm innovation. Thus, without constitutional principles guaranteeing the protection of some fundamental rights to the users of the Internet and without antitrust policies aimed at maintaining a sufficient level of contestability, public goods that are provided on an open basis may simply disappear, which is a fundamental concern when the public goods result in the infrastructure on which additional public goods are provided (together with private goods).

Through this example, it is clear that it is essential to guarantee in the digital economy the end-to-end character of the Internet that is at the heart of its reliability and flexibility. More generally, there is a tension between the individual ability to implement local specialized orders and the necessity to preserve some common coordination means. It is therefore obvious that the latter calls for the binding of the abilities of local regulators to implement their preferred orders.

22.5   Optimal vs. actual governance mechanisms

To sum up, digital technologies challenge the efficiency of the existing institutional framework, based on interactions among public and private norm setters under the control of public national authorities. ICTs empower all kind of communities by providing them with tools allowing the implementation, at relatively low cost, of collective orders which can be built behind, beside or above the existing public orders built by national States. One of the interests of the Internet is precisely its ability to structure communities emancipated from previous institutional frameworks or geographical constraints. (However, it does not mean that communities defined on pre-existing jurisdictional or geographical bases are not relevant when it comes to regulating located practices and problems.) The decrease in enforcement costs allows self-enforceable regulations to be built on a larger scale than before, their sole boundary being the minimal consistency of communities (whose members should share values and preferences). The second main advantage of the Internet and related technologies is that codes allow a strong customization of the management of rights of access and use, reducing maladaptation costs borne by agents in the pre-existing institutional frameworks. Finally, yet importantly, the ability of individuals and communities to self-organize and to design innovating coordination processes is a strong source of technical, organizational and institutional innovation. A coordination of these practices is nevertheless unavoidable to guarantee the efficiency, consistency and sustainability of this ability to implement innovative coordination solutions adapted to economic agents' needs.

A full decentralization of the design of the regulatory framework would lead to an excessive privatization of information and coordination platforms that would be detrimental to collective welfare because it would deprive society of access to non-rival resources. In addition, the fragmentation of the Internet and of the information space would reduce opportunities to coordinate efficiently. This calls for a last-resort authority with the purpose of bounding the power of norm setters to force them to provide access to their resources (disclosure rules, open access obligations, bounded encryption capabilities, etc.). At the same time, the last-resort enforcer should guarantee the norm setters a reinforced enforceability of the rules they set (as long as they do not infringe any superior constitutional principles). Digital enforcement mechanisms being subject to bypass, especially if encryption capabilities are bounded, local norms could be subject to an excessively high violation rate, ruining communities' abilities to implement efficient collective orders adapted to various specific situations and preferences.

It should be pointed out that the questions raised by the Internet are not only linked to the fact that digital technologies upset the traditional trade-off between self-implemented orders and the State's authority-based orders. They also have to do with the global nature of the end-to-end network, which means that there is no last-resort arbitrator. What is at stake is not only fixing the problems raised by the proliferation of self-regulations. More generally, it means dealing with the proliferation of orders. While the technology is empowering private norm setters, the orders built by national States are still in force. First, as long as the interactions that are regulated on digital networks still have a material and therefore a located dimension, national States can affect them. Second, even for fully digitized operations, national States can try to force the users of the Internet to enforce their legislation. They try to do so in particular by threatening to sue ISPs if the latter do not make national legislation enforceable for the local users. Moreover, for many citizens, national States remain essential legitimate regulators, expected to provide them with security and protection of some fundamental rights (and at least defense against economic dominance). In addition, while national governments often fail to coordinate because they have conflicting interests, convergences may exist. In such cases – like network security – national States really have an ability to impose an order.[20] Consequently, while the initiators of private orders can bypass the traditional providers of public orders, the former still have the ability to implement some orders and to influence the private orders that eventually attempt to bypass them. It remains true, however, that this ability is bounded. The current situation is therefore characterized neither by the disappearance of public regulations nor by the perpetuation of the traditional State regulation organized at the national level and associated to intergovernmental coordination at the international level, but by the proliferations of orders implemented either by State or non-State actors both at the infra- and supranational levels. Indeed, private institutions, either local or global, settle various types of self-regulations in parallel with efforts made by local and national governments together with intergovernmental organizations. The noticeable characteristic of the current situation is that there is no established hierarchy among these orders. None of them is able to impose itself on the others in the sense that the norms of the "hierarchically inferior" orders would have to comply with those of a "supreme" one.

The need for central coordination results neither in the need for traditional direct State intervention[21] nor in the need for centrally designed regulations. The economics of multi-level governance calls for a federal institutional model enforcing a subsidiarity principle. A central and last-resort device should overhang the decentralized, multi-level and multi-type process of norms implementation. Its role

---

[20] In practice, a coalition of the most powerful national governments is sufficient. G8 members, backed by the leading emerging countries (China, India, Brazil), have enough influence to convince most national governments to follow them. Regional unions or alliances are also used to leverage the bargaining power of these nation-states dominating the international scene.

[21] In any case, there is neither global government nor an adequate intergovernmental agency.

would not be to set up norms but rather to settle conflicts among norms decentrally implemented in order to guarantee, in particular, a minimum level of consistency among orders and their conformity with basic constitutional principles aimed at implementing most efficient solutions by taking into account interdependencies and the interests of the wider possible set of stakeholders as well as guaranteeing access to essential public goods.

Beyond its logical justification, the implementation of a regulator of last resort is made possible by the necessity to centrally manage the addressing system of the Internet. The mastering of the management of the addressing system by the entity that would be responsible for the regulation in the last resort will allow this entity to possess the means of its assignment. Indeed, it would enable it to exert a credible threat of excluding agents from the access to the cyber-world that it could use to have its decisions and regulations respected. In turn, only a well-designed entity should be allowed to control the system of inclusion/expulsion from the Internet.

There are, however, problems raised by the above conclusion drawn from theory, namely how this last-resort authority should be constituted and implemented. In a sense, it should be at the same time: the constituent assembly and the supreme court of a global "cyber republic", since it should set up the constitutional principles and implement them. However, can such a body be instituted in the absence of an entity like a global government, or of a recognized concept of global citizenship, or of accepted processes to elect global representatives? In any case, the way the present regulation of the Internet is designed and implemented does not fit at all with these principles.

Presently, embryos of several alternative regulatory frameworks are developing in parallel with the development of an international debate on the institutional framework required to govern and regulate digital networks (and the information- and knowledge-based society). To a certain extent, the developing solutions are complementary since they do not address exactly the same issues. Several organizations emerged in the 1990s to oversee the technical regulation of the Internet, while more recently international forums have been established to discuss the economic, political and social aspects of the regulation of the Internet. On the one hand, the former organizations could become the technical administrators of the Internet in charge of implementing the principles resulting from the "political" debates. On the other hand, these organizations and forums can be considered as resulting from alternative visions of the way the Internet and information activities should be regulated: namely, on a unilateral or multi-lateral basis. The Internet being the result of the efforts of the US federal government, the latter decided to delegate the technical governance of what was becoming a global network to a new type of agency, whose model had to be invented, but which should be neither an intergovernmental organization nor an agency emanating from the United Nations. This led to the foundation of ICANN in 1998. The same year, the UN and its agencies, in particular the ITU,[22] launched a process aimed at implementing a multi-lateral system to govern the Internet grounded in international treaties.

ICANN, the organization in charge of "governing" the addressing system of the Internet, is the core of the US unilateral strategy. It already plays a central role. By being responsible for distributing IP numbers and domain names, ICANN controls de facto inclusion and exclusion from the Internet. ICANN draws from a tumultuous process of creation[23] and evolution. With the development of the commercial Internet and its internationalization, numerous groups of interests pushed for the emergence of an organization that would involve all the stakeholders of the Internet. ICANN managed to include most of them. ICANN's members can therefore be either public or private organizations involved in the development or the uses of the Internet, government and public agencies, and individuals ("netizens"). Ad hoc committees group these various communities and there are complex processes of election and nomination in a wide number of committees responsible for the various domains dealt with by ICANN. In addition, ICANN coordinates with

---

[22] Headquartered in Geneva, the International Telecommunication Union (www.itu.int) is an international organization within the United Nations system. It was established in 1865 to facilitate the international interconnection of telegraphy and is a unique partnership of industry – formerly the national telecommunications monopolies – and governments. The ITU develops mutually agreed non-binding recommendations aimed at enabling interconnection and interoperability among telecommunication networks, which are based on rules of interoperation (and numbering) and common standards (formerly performed by the CCITT, now called ITU-T).

[23] Taking into account the enlargement of the Internet, the scientists who greatly contributed to its design and development – especially Vint Cerf and Robert Kahn – funded the Internet Society (ISOC) in 1992. This non-profit organization aimed at managing the Internet by taking into account the interests of all its stakeholders. The IETF and the IAB thus became components of ISOC. Initially ISOC was supposed to manage both the standards and the addressing system of the Internet. However, policy makers and industry lobbies denied the legitimacy of this new organization to manage the domain name system (DNS). Because ISOC was supposed to be controlled by US computer scientists, these groups estimated that it was not able to take into account the interests of non-US citizens, foreign governments and those of the industry, especially the owners of intellectual title deeds (especially trademarks and brands). This led to the foundation of ICANN in 1998 as a compromise between the historical Internet community and new stakeholders (governments, business community). An MoU signed with the US government established its mandate.

several other organizations in charge of related issues, such as the World Intellectual Property Organization (WIPO) or the Internet Engineering Task Force (IETF). Figure 22.1 synthesizes the complex web of committees and cooperative relationships.

The main weaknesses of ICANN in its present form are as follows. First, the legitimacy of each member is not at all guaranteed by any accreditation process. Moreover, the relationships (and the hierarchy) among the various types of members are unclear. This results in an organization that does not guarantee that the interests of the various stakeholders are taken into account and sorted into a hierarchy, nor that its decisions will be consistent, nor that it can even make decisions. Figure 22.1 illustrates well the highly complex organization of ICANN at the time of writing. Among other things, it shows clearly that the various categories of stakeholders are not considered equally in the decision process. Commercial interests, and in particular those of the dominant corporations in the digital industries, are clearly overweighed compared with those of citizens and even of the (non-US) governments.

Second, it is not autonomous since ICANN is a contractor of the US government. Moreover, the contract between the US government and ICANN is only transitory, and the technical implementation of the DNS (and therefore ICANN's decisions) is ensured by another contractor of the US government: Verisign. As a result, ICANN is neither an independent organization nor a strong one. It is presently not autonomous and the institutions responsible for the enforcement of ICANN's rules in the last resort (the US courts and the US government) cannot be considered as fully legitimate – since their purpose is to protect the interests of US citizens and people, they cannot impartially protect the interests of all the stakeholders of the Internet.[24]

Given its dependence on the US government, its lack of actual authority and its fuzzy way of taking into account and balancing the various interests of the stakeholders, ICANN's legitimacy is often challenged when it comes to transforming it into the authority responsible in the last resort for the regulation of the Internet. Because of the US government's lack of desire to let it become a multilateral entity, a coalition of the UN, of many national governments and of many non-governmental organizations (NGOs) agreed to launch an initiative aimed at (re)founding

---

[24] The US Department of Commerce holds a lot of power. It remains the owner of the addressing system. Thanks to the contracts with Verisign, it is able to de facto veto ICANN's decisions, since Verisign implements these decisions only after approval by the US DoC. Third, the US DoC continues to directly control several top-level domain names. Fourth, the DoC owns 10 of the world's 13 root servers, the computers that store files of the domain names. That said, the US influence is not only due to the power of the government, but draws also from the involvement – which requires significant dedicated means – and from the technical expertise of the individuals who act on behalf of their agency or company in the various ICANN (and related organizations) committees and conferences.

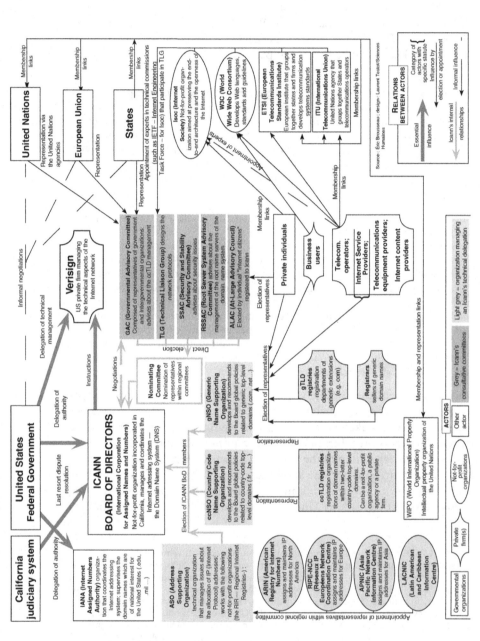

Figure 22.1. Internet governance: the current institutional framework.

the principles of the governance of the information society. This led to the World Summit on the Information Society (WSIS),[25] responsible for establishing the basis of a global governance of digital activities. However, this initiative features three strong weaknesses:

First, the objectives of the process are rather unclear. Because the various governments – and especially the US government – did not agree on a precise agenda before launching the process, the WSIS covers all the aspects of the regulation of the information society.[26] This excessively broad agenda makes it impossible to concentrate on a specific set of fundamental questions on which agreements and compromise could be discussed. In addition, all the possible lobbies are playing a complex game in this process.

Second, the decision mechanisms are unclear. On the one hand, the WSIS is an intergovernmental conference organized by the UN. On the other hand, NGOs, corporations and many other categories of stakeholders are invited to contribute in the frame of a fuzzy process of consultation/contribution.

Third, this process was launched without the agreement and is run without the effective participation of the authorities that are currently in control of the essential resources and of the technical regulatory tools that command the governance of the Internet. In particular, the US government does not support the process, meaning that what will come out of it will most probably not be implemented.[27]

---

[25] The UN General Assembly Resolution 56/183 (21 December 2001) endorsed the holding of the World Summit on the Information Society (http://www.itu.int/wsis/index.html) in two phases, hosted in Geneva in December 2003 and in Tunis in November 2005. The goal of a UN summit is fundamentally to settle a plan of action that could include intergovernmental conferences and the settling of a new international organization. More generally, it aims at reaching consensus. The ITU was at the origin of the Summit and is in charge of organizing it. While recommending representation from governments at the highest level, the Summit also invited participation of all relevant UN bodies and other international organizations, non-governmental organizations, private sector, civil society and media to establish a multi-stakeholder process. Several preparatory conferences, working groups and on-line consultations were run to prepare the two phases of the Summit.

[26] According to the official declaration resulting from the Geneva Summit in 2003, the goals of the WSIS embrace techno-economic regulation of digital activities (provision of universal, accessible, equitable and affordable infrastructure and services; solutions aimed at guaranteeing information and network security; consumer protection; transparent, pro-competitive, technologically neutral and predictable public economic regulations), socio-political regulation of information and knowledge-based activities (in particular the guarantee of privacy, pluralism and media diversity, optimal intellectual property regimes encouraging creativity and the need to share knowledge, education and the reduction of the digital divide) and the promotion of political and philosophical principles such as the rule of law, human rights and fundamental freedoms, the respect for cultural and linguistic diversity as well as traditions, religions, etc.

[27] From the US and ICANN points of view, the WSIS is seen as an attempt by, respectively, the UN and the ITU to gain control over the regulation of the Internet. While there is consensus over the idea that new authorities placed above the bodies in charge of the technical regulation should take charge of the social regulation necessary for the

Thus, the authorities and the processes that are currently at the heart of the regulation of the Internet do not guarantee at all that the first best institutional architecture to regulate the digital world could be designed and implemented.

This is well illustrated by the report of the Working Group on Internet Governance (WGIG) released in July 2005 to prepare the conclusion of the WSIS. The report (www.wgig.org) was prepared by a 40-member UN panel gathered from around the world and including representatives from business, academia and government. It benefited from multiple inputs provided by all kind of stakeholders. The working group was unable to agree on a single alternative. Instead, it presents four options. These range from a maximal option of a global Internet council – based on three components, one to address policy issues, one for oversight and one for global coordination – within the UN system that would take over supervision of ICANN and set international Internet policy, to a "status quo plus" arrangement that would enhance the role of ICANN's existing governmental advisory committee (GAC). Intermediate solutions are the creation of a world body to address public policy issues stemming from the work of ICANN, or the creation of a body to address a broader range of public policy issues. In a context in which the US Department of Commerce continues to claim that it has no intention of giving up its historic role as overseer of the Internet domain name and addressing system run by ICANN (stressing the need to ensure stability and security), it is likely that the WSIS will result in the setting up of several forums to coordinate efforts in favor of on-line security (from the control of spam to tracking and management of identity) to combat Internet-related crime, to harmonize business-related legislation, to manage issues related to freedom of expression and human rights, etc., but will fail to implement authorities able to really govern the Internet.

development of the information- and knowledge-based economy and society, there is clearly a remaining fundamental opposition between multilateralism and an alternative vision. The leader of the alternative vision is clearly the US government. However, it is supported by a set of other stakeholders – from non-US governments to commercial interests and including NGOs – that fear a regulatory framework in which multilateralism would mean capture by governments, and especially non-democratic governments, of the regulation of the digital space. The forces opposed to the multilateral approach have legitimacy, since up to now they have developed a technical system that remains open and reliable. Moreover, they benefit from a strong position, since the US government remains the owner of the essential resources of the Internet and is able, through a policy of bilateral agreements (with other governments or with private organizations) and potential retaliations against commercial interests (in particular ISPs and hardware and software makers), to incite enforcement of the fundamental principles it promotes.

22.6 Toward a step-by-step approach to the design of regulatory frameworks

Could a relevant order emerge from the complex process occurring today in which a wide number of individuals and organizations is acting and interacting in non-hierarchical ways either by decentrally creating (private) orders or by lobbying in the various arenas creating orders (from standardization committees to intergovernmental negotiations and including national law-making processes or the design of self-regulation mechanisms)? The reply could be yes if a relevant arena to harmonize these initiatives could be organized.

Before analyzing how it could be possible, it is useful to consider the current situation. On the one hand, it could be considered as chaotic. On the other hand, there are several enabling conditions for a harmonization.

While there is a proliferation of regulating entities with different status, there is no hierarchy among them. More precisely, none of these entities is able to definitively impose its order on the others (even if some entities have more "bargaining" power than others). This is due to the self-implementation capabilities provided by the digital technologies to the various norm setters. More precisely, on the one hand, private norm setters can bypass public authorities to implement faked or trans-territorial orders, but on the other hand, public authorities or social communities still benefit from their traditional means to set collective orders. Thus, whatever the nature of the institutions currently involved in the settlement of rules that play a role in the regulation of the Internet, they have to "negotiate", since no norm setter is able to impose its order on other norm setters. This permanent "bargaining" is well illustrated by what is happening today in relation to file sharing in the music industry among the P2P "communities", the governments and the lobbies of the authors, artists and recording companies.

Second, "negotiation" among the various producers of collective orders is possible and necessary because most of these orders are not complete. They do not seek to measure and enforce a complete set of property rights, rather to delineate rights of use only for a limited number of uses and for a limited number of resources. In concrete terms, some private orders implement technical standards to organize on-line sharing of information, other orders design rules to be applied to the encryption of information, while others organize auction mechanisms on specific markets, etc. While there is sometimes direct competition between two orders, much of the competition among norm setters is at the fringe of their domain of competence. There are therefore many cases in which the various orders are complementary and the promoters of these orders have incentives to negotiate (or to adopt some open meta-standards) to guarantee compatibility among their orders.

In addition to these two enabling conditions, there is a strong driving force for harmonization: the needs of users. Two phenomena are combining. First, the globalization of many activities, and in particular of the economy, makes it worthwhile for many players, especially businesses, to benefit from a seamless global information and coordination space. They have therefore a strong interest in the reduction of the trans-territorial heterogeneity of formal and informal public norms. Second, most communities behind private norms are not exclusive. They are fuzzy sets (in the sense of the fuzzy sets theory), meaning that a given individual often belongs to several communities. Individuals and organizations are also pushing for a harmonization of the norms established by private digital/on-line norm setters since it would simplify and make less costly the activities they perform in the various on-line communities to which they belong.[28]

While there is competition among norm setters to establish and widen the scope of their coordination solutions (Brousseau and Raynaud, 2005), there are creating conditions and impetus leading them to harmonize the institutional framework they are building. Indeed, since the digital space is the locus where many norms interact, it is permanently revealing conflicts among private orders, among public orders and among public and private orders. Public and private norm setters cannot ignore these conflicts of norms because they reduce the value of use of their norms and their potential adoption. Moreover, they cannot rely only on the selection process among norms, because selection takes time and is uncertain.

To satisfy the adopters of their norms or potential ones and therefore their sustainability, norm setters – whether they are public authorities, professional organizations, on-line self-organized communities, market organizers, etc. – have incentives to cooperate to solve conflict either *ex ante* or *ex post*.

Ex ante, multiple decentralized negotiations already exist. Two types of negotiations occur. First, at the national level, public authorities negotiate with the private order setters, often by involving them in the processes of adapting the legal order to the opportunities and constraints raised by digital technologies and by the development of the knowledge-based economy. Second, at the global level, there is minimal coordination among the various private entities, where responsibilities overlap or

---

[28] Even if in some cases one of the advantages of on-line activities is that they allow individuals to live several parallel lives.

interact. When one considers the "technical" regulation of the Internet, there are, for instance, various formats of coordination among the IETF, the W3C, ICANN and many other standards-setting committees. In addition, weak coordination exists among public orders through the management of international treaties and intergovernmental organizations responsible for designing common rules to be applied to information resources and networks (WIPO, ITU, etc.). Negotiations take place also within non-specialized intergovernmental organizations such as the UN, the OECD or the European Union. Negotiations do occur then, but their decentralization does not by any means guarantee convergence. Moreover, targeted and local negotiations may end up in incompatible agreements, transforming only the "level" of discrepancies among decentrally set norms. It would therefore be useful to implement an international forum in which these decentralized negotiations could be coordinated, even weakly. A minimal way to do so would simply be to share information and knowledge about the properties of alternative regulations. To a certain extent, a common "blackboard", such as those which characterize many on-line communities (Gensollen, Chapter 5, this volume), would be a useful tool to allow sharing of experience and knowledge and to incite the adoption of more efficient practices. Of course, such *ex ante* coordination could be further developed, especially under the pressure of users/citizens, who would value more universal platforms of coordination (to manage the production/distribution/sharing of information and knowledge, and to support inter-agent coordination).

One of the main drivers of the evolution of rules toward common rules is the (judicial) resolution of conflict. Indeed, when there are gains to be made by trading or cooperating, when exchanges are hindered by discrepancies among property rights systems and among collective regulations, parties have strong incentives to have the system of rules evolving. They can bypass the existing institutional framework, but it comes with a cost (either because they have to settle on alternative orders or because the existing framework being mandatory – e.g. the law – bypassing it could be costly). The alternative strategy is to try to have the conflict resolved by a mechanism responsible in the last resort for solving conflicts between the two orders. In addition to the (local) conflict resolution, such a solution has a strong advantage. It allows those who are in charge of setting collective orders to learn about the inefficiencies of the solution they implement. In addition, the way the conflict is solved can provide the two norm setters with solutions to avoid future conflicts. Put another way, conflict resolution is a powerful tool not only enabling an *ex post* solving of problems due to conflicts among norms, but also making it possible to benefit from learning capabilities and innovation efforts aimed at identifying discrepancies among norms and satisfying solutions to harmonize them. Again, this call for a common arena to solve conflicts is related to the proliferation of regulations in the cyber-world. To a certain extent, the cooperation between WIPO and ICANN played this role in the case of property rights over commercial names (trademarks and domain names; Méadel and Marzouki, 2004).

Implementing a framework, comparable in its functioning but not in its constituency to that of the World Trade Organization (WTO), in which the various norm setters would be able to explicitly negotiate *ex ante* and to solve *ex post* conflicts would therefore be the second-rank solution to the current problem raised by the proliferation of public and private orders on the Internet. It would be a second-rank solution because it would be less satisfactory than the management of an *ex ante* coordination based on the settling of basic constitutional rights of the global cyber-citizens and the implementation of an authority of last resorts to guarantee them. Indeed, it would take time to reach a global agreement on a set of fundamental basic rights, and the negotiations being organized among unequal norm setters, the optimality of the solution would not be guaranteed. However, an organized negotiation has two advantages over fully decentralized negotiation. Centralization is a necessary (not sufficient) condition for designing consistent "local" solutions. In addition, centralization creates the possibility of benefits from learning and knowledge-sharing effects.

Part VII

The impacts of the Internet at the macro level

23 Mobile telephony and Internet growth: impacts on consumer welfare

Gary Madden, Michael Schipp and Joachim Tan

23.1 Introduction

Since the early 1990s, mobile telephony and Internet network subscription sustained rapid growth in Europe (Welfens and Jungmittag, 2003). Pricing, technical innovation and regulatory framework change are seen as important to continued network growth. In March 2002, the European Union adopted a package of Directives that significantly revised the 1998 regulatory framework for electronic communications networks and services in Europe. In particular, the new regulatory approach seeks to be responsive to technological and market developments by being more neutral in its treatment of similar services provided via alternative technical means (such as narrowband, broadband and mobile) and by allowing regulation to be withdrawn as effective competition develops (Cawley, 2004). However, as mobile telephony and the Internet are network-delivered services, positive demand externality effects may also be important in explaining such network growth. That is, when network externalities are important, consumers' valuation of network subscription is increased with network size – or equivalently, subscription can expand independently of any change to market conditions. Should network effects be shown to be empirically important in explaining network evolution, they should also be considered in future regulatory framework changes.

This study develops a procedure to determine the importance of network effects. Model estimates provide an annual measure of consumer welfare change for the representative OECD region subscriber. Following Hausman (1981), our model is based on the compensating variation (CV) approach, which consists in assessing welfare improvement due to a price fall as the extra income the consumer would be willing to accept in place of the price fall. Further, the study indicates the welfare gain, as measured by CV, decreases with network size.

The chapter is organised as follows. Section 23.2 states the methodology and shows how Hausman's CV formula may be adapted to the context of a dynamic demand model incorporating network effects, as specified by Madden et al. (2004). The demand system is such that current network size depends on the past size of the network and expectations for future size. This specification reflects the dynamic optimizing behavior by a representative consumer whose subscription choice is influenced by a telecommunications service network effect. Section 23.3 reports model parameter estimates based on annual OECD data for 30 member states for the period 1996 through 2000. CV values are constructed from the parameter estimates and discussed. The services considered are fixed-line and mobile telephony, and the Internet. Section 23.4 concludes.

23.2   Methodology

A feature of electronic communication networks is that consumers receive more utility the larger is the subscriber base. That is, a consumer's welfare increases monotonically with the network size (Squire, 1973; Rohlfs, 1974). Accordingly, the presence of a network effect impacts on both current subscriber and marginal non-subscriber welfare. That is, for subscribers, network subscription growth provides greater consumer welfare. Further, marginal non-subscribers are more likely to subscribe, at current prices, the larger is network subscription. To identify the increase in consumer welfare due to a price fall then requires the separation of any consumer welfare gain due to a movement along the subscription demand curve (direct price effect), from any indirect welfare gain originating from network expansion (network externality effect).

Hausman (1981) uses the CV method to measure consumer welfare rise in response to a price fall for a non-network good. The change in consumer welfare induced by a network effect is obtained by adapting Hausman's (1997) measure of the change in consumer welfare caused by the introduction of a new good. The consumer welfare change is obtained by treating the prevailing subscription price, before the price change, as the reservation price of a new subscriber, i.e. the price at which she will decide to subscribe. As such, the network's growth leads to a change in the current reservation price. With the reservation price change identified, the variation to consumer welfare is then calculated.

23.2.1   Compensating variation and Hausman's approach

A price fall impacts on the demand for any given good in two different ways. First, the price fall has an effect which is equivalent to an income increase, stimulating demand for the good considered and for all other goods (income effect). Second, it makes the consumer demand less for

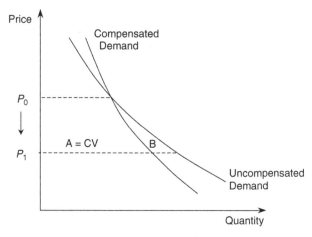

Figure 23.1. Compensating variation CV.

other goods and more for the good considered, the relative price of which is lowered (substitution effect). In order to separate the income effect from the substitution effect, consider a two-step process. In the first step (substitution effect), price is lowered from its initial to its final level, while the income effect is controlled by lowering income simultaneously with price, so as to hold utility constant. In the second step (income effect), price remains unchanged whereas the initial level of income is restored. By definition, the income removed in the first step, and then restored in the second step, is the compensating variation, CV. The CV is interpreted as the amount that the consumer should be compensated if he were not to benefit from the price fall, i.e. CV is the exact measure of the change in consumer welfare caused by a price fall.

Defining the compensated demand function as the hypothetical demand that would prevail under compensating income variation (during the first step), CV measure is simply the area A in Figure 23.1, viz., the area lying to the left of the compensated demand curve, between the initial and the final price lines, P_0 and P_1. The difficulty is that compensated demand functions are not readily obtainable from market data. Only uncompensated demand functions are observed, indicating equilibrium demand at given prices and income. Now, using the uncompensated demand curve instead of the compensated demand curve leads to an inexact measure of welfare change. In particular, this measure includes the income effect, and based on consumer surplus variation SV, results in the area $A + B$ in Figure 23.1, rather than on the compensating variation CV. A sufficient condition for CV and SV to be equivalent is that the marginal utility of income is constant, which is not generally consistent with observed behavior.[1] The measurement of CV, not SV, is thus required in order to obtain a proper assessment of welfare change.

Hausman (1981) employed the microeconomic theory of consumer behavior to derive the unobserved compensated demand curve from the observed uncompensated demand curve. From the observed demand function, and Roy's identity (see Appendix), the expenditure function[2] is first derived, i.e. the variable income the consumer must be allocated when price varies in order to keep her utility constant. Then, the compensated demand function is obtained as the derivative of the expenditure function with respect to price. Finally, CV, i.e. the exact measure of welfare variation due to a price change, is calculated.

23.2.2 The case of network goods

Next, Hausman's approach must be adapted to the context of network goods. Following Madden et al. (2004), an uncompensated network demand equation system is first specified as:

$$
\begin{aligned}
N_{i,t} = {} & \theta_{i0} + \theta_{ii}(N_{i,t-1} + \beta N_{i,t+1}) \\
& + \sum_{i \neq j} \theta^1_{ij} N_{j,t-1} + \sum_{i \neq j} \theta^2_{ij} N_{j,t} + \sum_{i \neq j} \theta^3_{ij} N_{j,t+1} + \theta_{iP} P_{i,t} + \gamma Y_t
\end{aligned} \tag{23.1}
$$

where $N_{i,t}$ is the demand for service i at time t (defined in terms of the size of network i), $P_{i,t}$ is the price of subscription to network i and Y_t is the real per capita income. The response of demand to a price fall is indicated by parameter θ_{iP} (for a normal good $\theta_{iP} < 0$). Besides the price effect, increasing network size at time $t-1$ leads to another impact on demand at time t, i.e. a network effect indicated by parameter θ_{ii} ($0 < \theta_{ii} < 1$). Also, as the current size $N_{i,t}$ of network i is a function of network size $N_{i,t+1}$ in the next period, an anticipated fall in future price $P_{i,t+1}$ for network i yields an increase in current subscription if $\beta > 0$. Moreover, $\theta^3_{ij} > 0$ implies the anticipated fall in the price of network j induces a current period increase in subscription for network i. A permanent price fall implies a larger increase in current subscription than for a temporary

---

[1] This condition requires that indifference curves are collinear. Decreasing marginal utility of income produces a compensated demand curve steeper than the corresponding uncompensated demand curve and results in SV being an inexact measure of welfare.

[2] The prime approach to the analysis of consumer behavior involves the maximization of a strictly quasi-concave utility function, subject to some budget constraint. The dual approach considers the minimization of the expenditure function, subject to utility being set at or greater than some prescribed level. When the indirect utility function is monotonically increasing in income, and the expenditure function is monotonically increasing in utility, either function can be inverted to derive the other corresponding function.

price fall, since the permanent price fall combines a fall in current and all future prices.

Following Hausman's approach (see Appendix), the exact measure, $CV_{i,t}$, of change in consumer welfare due to a price change from $P_{i,t}$ to $P_{i,t+1}$ is then calculated as:

$$CV_{i,t} = \frac{1}{\gamma}\left(N_{i,t+1} + \frac{\theta_{iP}}{\gamma}\right) - \frac{1}{\gamma}\left(N_{i,t} + \frac{\theta_{iP}}{\gamma}\right)e^{\gamma(P_{i,t+1} - P_{i,t})} \qquad (23.2)$$

The compensating variation $CV_{i,t}$ reflects a movement along the compensated demand curve and reflects the direct price effect on welfare.

In order to assess the network effect from (23.2), one has to determine the change $P_{i,t+1} - P_{i,t}$ in reservation subscription price which produces a one-unit increase in network size, $N_{i,t+1} - N_{i,t} = 1$. For new subscribers, the size of the network is just large enough to induce them to join at the prevailing subscription price. Assuming network size is perfectly observable, and subscribers are able to join at any time, the prevailing network subscription price is equal to new subscriber's reservation price P_i^*.[3] Then, calculating the change in the reservation price P_i^* with respect to a network subscription N_i increase gives $\partial P_i^*/\partial N_i = (1 - \theta_{ii})/\theta_{iP}$, which being negative reveals the reservation price decreases in network subscription. The change in consumer welfare induced by a unit increase in network size (from $N_{i,t} = N_i$ to $N_{i,t+1} = N_i + 1$) and a fall in reservation price $P_{i,t+1} - P_{i,t} = \partial P_i^*/\partial N_i = (1 - \theta_{ii})/\theta_{iP}$, (23.2) becomes

$$CV_{i,t}^{NE} = \frac{1}{\gamma}\left(N_{i,t} + 1 + \frac{\theta_{iP}}{\gamma}\right) - \frac{1}{\gamma}\left(N_{i,t} + \frac{\theta_{iP}}{\gamma}\right)e^{\gamma(1 - \theta_{ii})/\theta_{iP}}. \qquad (23.3)$$

Equation (23.3) measures the change in welfare at time t due to the price adjustment caused by a unitary network increase.

23.3 OECD consumer surplus change

Biannual rental price data are required to estimate (23.2) and (23.3). These data are collected for 30 OECD member country markets for 1996, 1998 and 2000 from the OECD *Communications Outlook* (1997, 1999, 2001, 2003). Annual quantity (network size) and income data for

---

[3] Within a representative consumer framework, for a new subscriber over time, demand is zero until the market price falls to a level below the subscriber's reservation price. To measure the change in consumer welfare for a marginal increase in network size then appears quite similar to measuring a change in consumer welfare with the introduction of a new service, as Hausman (1997) asserts the correct price for a new good in the pre-introduction period is the reservation price, i.e. the virtual price which sets demand equal to zero.

1996 to 2000 are obtained from the International Telecommunication Union *World Telecommunications Indicators Database* (2003).[4] Fixed-line price data are the fixed component of the OECD's basket of residential telephony charges. Mobile telephony price is the fixed component of the OECD's basket of consumer mobile telephony charges. Internet price is the OECD's Internet access basket for 20 hours using discounted public switched telecommunication network (PSTN) rates. Income (GDP per capita) and price data are denominated in United States dollars according to OECD purchasing power parity. Both income and prices are deflated by the US consumer price index (CPI) to allow comparison through time. Fixed-line telephony quantity is the number of main telephone lines. Mobile telephony quantity is mobile telephone subscribers, while Internet quantity is the number of Internet users. Quantity variables are per 100 persons. The resulting index data is comprised of 79 observations.

The demand function specification (23.1) is from Madden et al. (2004), a perfect foresight model that holds the marginal utility of wealth constant for each individual, but allows variation across individuals. Thus, in the present context, the intercepts (θ_{i0}) in the cross-country model capture, in part, country-specific variation of the marginal utility of wealth. The specification is relaxed further by allowing time-specific effects to capture unanticipated growth in wealth. Deviations in country- and time-specific means are captured by adding an argument for per capita income to the demand function, which is associated with changes in marginal wealth across countries and through time. The resulting augmentation is a two-way (country and time) effects model. In addition, given there is a possibility for simultaneity between network effects, the regression model is specified as a standard form vector autoregressive model. Estimates of the network, price and income coefficients for fixed-line and mobile telephony and Internet service are from Madden et al. (2004).[5]

Table 23.1 presents estimates of network, price and income coefficients for fixed-line and mobile telephony and Internet services, respectively.

---

[4] An implicit assumption in using these data, following Becker et al. (1994), is that per capita telecommunications consumption reflects the behavior of a representative consumer.

[5] The presence of unobserved components means that two-stage instrumental variables estimation is required. Past network size is an endogenous variable because of the dependence of network size on the unobserved components. However, caution is required when implementing instrumental variables since, as Nelson and Startz (1990) warn, the use of lagged values as instruments when estimating stochastic Euler equations can lead to bias. Thus, instruments for network size are restricted to future access and use prices. Particular care is taken to ensure instruments are good predictors of network size. The resulting equations are estimated in Limdep 8.0 using the unbalanced panel data set described above.

Table 23.1. *Network, price and income coefficients estimates*

	Fixed line	Mobile	Internet
θ_{ii}	0.96240	0.86260	0.96510
θ_{iP}	−0.00256	−0.00497	−0.02889
γ	0.00015	0.00045	0.00025

Source: Madden et al. (2004)

Table 23.2. *Direct welfare gain by telecommunications service*

Service	Year	Subscription per 100 persons	CV (US$)	CV/income
Fixed line	1996	50	28	0.001
	1998	52	31	0.001
	2000	54	33	0.001
Mobile	1996	13	13	0.001
	1998	26	26	0.001
	2000	56	56	0.002
Internet	1996	6	6	0.001
	1998	15	15	0.001
	2000	29	28	0.001

Benchmark is actual annual demand

All coefficient estimates are correctly signed and significant. Table 23.2 reports estimates of the change in welfare resulting from a fall in price. As shown, a price fall has an immediate impact on CV of 0.1–0.2% of income. From Table 23.2, a fall in mobile telephone subscription price provides the most direct benefit to consumers after 2000, followed by that for fixed-line service. Table 23.3 shows the indirect (or network externality) effect on welfare in fixed-line and mobile telephony and Internet service, respectively. CV estimates indicate that the benefit derived from a small increase in network size is large relative to that for the direct price effect.

Table 23.3 reveals the relative welfare benefit (relative increase in CV) at 2000 from a network effect for fixed-line telephony subscribers is almost six times larger than that for mobile telephony subscribers. This finding is in part explained by the relatively large fall in reservation price, $(1 - \theta_{ii})/\theta_{iP}$, for mobile telephony (−27.7) compared with that for fixed-line telephony (−14.7). Adding to the difference in magnitude is the negative scale factor θ_{iP}/γ, which is −17.1, −11.0 and −115.6 for

Table 23.3. *Indirect welfare gain by telecommunications service*

Service	Year	Subscription per 100 persons	CV (US$)	CV/income
Fixed line	1996	50	58	0.003
	1998	52	58	0.003
	2000	54	57	0.002
Mobile	1996	13	22	0.001
	1998	26	18	0.001
	2000	56	10	0.000
Internet	1996	6	41	0.002
	1998	15	41	0.002
	2000	29	41	0.002

Benchmark is actual annual demand

Table 23.4. *Mobile and fixed-line service price ratio*

Year	Mean	Standard deviation	Minimum	Maximum
1996	2.64	1.89	0.64	9.95
1998	2.43	1.74	0.25	6.92
2000	1.29	1.23	0.01	6.60

fixed-line and mobile telephony demand and Internet demand, respectively. The ratio indicates the relative importance of price-to-income effects on network growth. The greater the magnitude of the ratio, the greater the impact on CV. While differences in scale explain some of the difference in CV for 1996, the scale effect has a negligible impact by 2000. Thus, the difference in valuation is due mainly to relative access prices between fixed-line and mobile telephone service. Table 23.3 also reveals that the welfare gain, as measured by annual CV, decreases with network size. Namely, an 8% growth in the fixed-line network accords with an inelastic fall in annual CV of 2% for the period. The substantial growth in mobile and Internet networks (330% and 380%, respectively) also corresponds with a decline in annual CV for the mobile and Internet networks of 54% and less than 1%, respectively.

Further, Table 23.4 provides an overview of changes to the mobile and fixed-line service price ratio. Mean values for 1996 and 1998 indicate annual mobile telephone subscription price is almost double that for fixed-line subscription. Sample standard deviations indicate substantial cross-country variation. For example, in 1996, highest price mobile subscription (France) is higher than fixed-line telephony by a factor of ten. In 2000, the subscription price of mobile telephony in Korea (the highest in the sample) is almost seven times higher than that for fixed-line telephony. Thus, the increase in consumer welfare induced due to an expansion in mobile telephony subscription is constrained by the relatively high subscription price.[6]

Finally, Internet service expenditure is a relatively small proportion of communications expenditure compared with that for mobile telephony. Accordingly, the network effect induced by increased network size is less constrained than that for mobile telephony. However, since the subscription price includes the fixed-line subscription charge, it too is relatively constrained when compared with fixed-line access. These findings suggest that concentrating solely on the welfare impact of price falls yields an underestimate of consumer benefit. That is, while the direct effect from a price fall in telecommunications networks matters, indirect benefit from subsequent network expansion is also important. This finding has important consequences for the conduct of universal service policy.

23.4 Conclusion

This study uses Hausman's (1981) CV approach to measure the direct consumer welfare change from a price fall and an indirect network externality effect. The study demonstrates a method to obtain exact estimates of welfare change. Once econometric price and income parameter estimates are obtained, the corresponding change in consumer welfare is calculated. Additionally, this study demonstrates the importance of controlling for the network effect to obtain an accurate assessment of the total impact on consumer welfare. Estimates indicate a direct increase in welfare from a subscription price fall is at most 0.2% of income. However, larger indirect welfare increases occur via a network effect. Surprisingly, mobile telephony welfare increases appear to provide the smallest improvement. However, this result is explained by a high mobile subscription price when compared with fixed-line telephony and Internet service prices. That is, the relatively high mobile subscription price constrains the network effect. Finally, study findings support competition policy designed to place downward pressure on subscription prices. The study provides indirect justification for the continuation of universal service policy.

---

[6] The economic constraint is reflected in the size of the price and income coefficients across services.

While the empirical estimates of CV for telephony and Internet networks contained in this study are revealing, it is important to note that the underlying source of welfare gains differs by network. That is, the network effects linked to (fixed-line and mobile) point-to-point communication services differ from that due primarily to information services. Conversely, information service growth is related to the installed base of terminals, in particular connected PCs. Accordingly, fixed and mobile telephones mostly generate communications network effects and, so far, few information service effects (which could change with the emergence of the third-generation mobile telephony and growth in mobile data markets). Additionally, the Internet generates mostly information service network effects, typically through e-mail, the dominant but not exclusive use. This latter network externality is very important because the quantity and quality of data available on the Web is highly correlated with the size of network subscriber base. Further, it is reasonable to expect that this Internet communications externality will become increasingly important. Finally, as the model cannot distinguish these effects, the results are likely to underestimate the true impact of Internet network growth on CV.

23.5   Appendix: Hausman's approach and proof of equation (23.2)

Consider the dynamic and deterministic demand system specified by Madden et al. (2004),

$$N_{i,t} = \theta_{i0} + \theta_{iP}P_{i,t} + \gamma Y_t + F_{i,t} + G_{-i,t} \tag{23.4}$$

$$F_{i,t} = \theta_{ii}(N_{i,t-1} + \beta N_{i,t+1}) \tag{23.5}$$

$$G_{-i,t} = \sum_{j \neq i} \theta_{ij}^1 N_{j,t-1} + \sum_{j \neq i} \theta_{ij}^2 N_{j,t} + \sum_{j \neq i} \theta_{ij}^3 N_{j,t+1}, \tag{23.6}$$

where $N_{i,t}$ is consumer demand for network i at time t, under price level $P_{i,t}$, and Y_t is consumer's income at time t. Terms $F_{i,t}$ and $G_{-i,t}$ reflect the own-network and cross-network externalities, respectively.

Allowing price P_i and income Y to vary at time t from their observed levels $P_{i,t}$ and Y_t, the uncompensated demand function $N_{i,t}(P_i, Y)$ is defined:

$$N_{i,t}(P_i, Y) = \theta_{i0} + \theta_{iP}P_i + \gamma Y + F_{i,t} + G_{-i,t} \tag{23.7}$$

The linear uncompensated demand function, $N_{i,t}(P_i, Y)$, derives from its generating quadratic indirect utility function, $U_t(P_i, Y)$, through

Roy's identity:

$$N_{i,t}(P_i, Y) = -\frac{\partial U_t(P_i, Y)/\partial P_i}{\partial U_t(P_i, Y)/\partial Y} = \left(\frac{\partial Y}{\partial P_i}\right)_{U_t} \tag{23.8}$$

Following Hausman (1981), to enable a valid welfare comparison to be made, before and after a price change, requires that the consumer remains at constant utility U_t, i.e. on a same indifference curve. If price of service i departs from $P_{i,t}$ at time t, to remain on the same indifference curve requires that, simultaneously, income departs from Y_t. Denoting $Y_t(P_i)$ the expenditure function, i.e. the current income associated with current price P_i along a constant utility path, Roy's identity implies:

$$\frac{dY_t(P_i)}{dP_i} = N_{i,t}(P_i, Y_t(P_i)) = \gamma Y_t(P_i) + \theta_{iP}P_i + \theta_{i0} + F_{i,t} + G_{-i,t} \tag{23.9}$$

The solution to differential equation (23.7) is:

$$Y_t(P_i) = -\frac{1}{\gamma}\left(\theta_{iP}(P_i + 1/\gamma) + \theta_{i0} + F_{i,t} + G_{-i,t}\right) + U_{i,t}e^{\gamma P_i}$$

$$= Y_t - \frac{1}{\gamma}\left(N_{i,t} + \theta_{iP}/\gamma + \theta_{iP}(P_i - P_{i,t})\right) + U_{i,t}e^{\gamma P_i}, \tag{23.10}$$

in which the constant of integration $U_{i,t}$ (reflecting the invariance of utility) derives from the initial condition $Y_t(P_{i,t}) = Y_t$:

$$U_{i,t} = \frac{1}{\gamma}(N_{i,t} + \theta_{iP}/\gamma)e^{-\gamma P_{i,t}} \tag{23.11}$$

Hence, finally:

$$Y_t(P_i) = Y_t - \frac{1}{\gamma}(N_{i,t} + \theta_{iP}/\gamma)(1 - e^{\gamma(P_i - P_{i,t})}) - \frac{\theta_{iP}}{\gamma}(P_i - P_{i,t}) \tag{23.12}$$

From the expenditure function $Y_t(P_i)$, the compensated demand function $N_{i,t}^C(P_i)$ is derived as:

$$N_{i,t}^C(P_i) = N_{i,t}[P_i, Y_t(P_i)] = \frac{dY_t(P_i)}{dP_i} = \left(N_{i,t} + \frac{\theta_{iP}}{\gamma}\right)e^{\gamma(P_{i,t+1} - P_{i,t})} - \frac{\theta_{iP}}{\gamma} \tag{23.13}$$

Now consider a virtual transition from time t to time $t+1$, in which the price falls from $P_{i,t}$ to $P_{i,t+1} < P_{i,t}$ and income is simultaneously lowered from Y_t to $Y_t(P_{i,t+1}) < Y_t$, in order to make the consumer insensitive to the price fall. The difference, or "compensating variation", $CV_{i,t} = Y_t - Y_t(P_{i,t+1})$, is the income reduction which offsets the price fall benefit to the consumer. Conversely, $CV_{i,t}$ is a measure of the consumer's welfare gain due to the price reduction from $P_{i,t}$ to $P_{i,t+1}$.

The explicit expression of $CV_{i,t}$, as in equation (23.2), then derives from (23.10) and (23.11), i.e.:

$$CV_{i,t} = Y_t - Y_t(P_{i,t+1}) = \int_{P_{i,t}}^{P_{i,t+1}} N_{it}^C(P_i)dP_i$$

$$= \frac{1}{\gamma}\left(N_{i,t} + \theta_{iP}(P_{i,t+1} - P_{i,t}) + \frac{\theta_{iP}}{\gamma}\right) - \frac{1}{\gamma}\left(N_{i,t} + \frac{\theta_{iP}}{\gamma}\right)e^{\gamma(P_{i,t+1} - P_{i,t})}$$

$$= \frac{1}{\gamma}\left(N_{i,t+1} + \frac{\theta_{iP}}{\gamma}\right) - \frac{1}{\gamma}\left(N_{i,t} + \frac{\theta_{iP}}{\gamma}\right)e^{\gamma(P_{i,t+1} - P_{i,t})} \qquad (23.14)$$

24 Globalization, the Internet and e-business: convergence or divergence in cross-country trends?

Kenneth L. Kraemer and Jason Dedrick

24.1 Introduction

Globalization has become the subject of heated debate in recent years, a debate that is being intensified by the spread of low-cost information and communications technologies (ICTs), particularly the Internet. There is excitement about the Internet's potential for linking people and organizations across great distances and national borders, opening new markets for business and providing greater choice for consumers. Yet there is concern in many countries that the Internet is accelerating a globalization process that is causing serious economic dislocation as competition intensifies, trade imbalances grow and jobs disappear.

The United States has led the world in adopting the Internet and creating new models of e-business. The environment for e-business in the United States has generally been positive, supported by a large consumer market, favorable government policies, a deregulated telecommunications market, a dynamic venture capital market and positive business and consumer attitudes toward information technology. U.S. companies have used the Internet to create new businesses, transform old ones and coordinate their supply chains. Outside the U.S., consumers have tapped the Internet to buy products that might be unavailable or expensive locally. Businesses are using the Internet to reach new markets and coordinate with global production networks.

However, many countries worry about the U.S.-centric technology, language and culture of the Internet, and fear being left behind if they

This research is part of the Globalization and E-Commerce Project of the Center for Research on Information Technology and Organizations (CRITO) at the University of California, Irvine. The material is based on work supported by a grant from the National Science Foundation under grant #0085852 (CISE/IIS/DST). Any opinions, findings and conclusions or recommendations expressed in this material are those of the author(s) and do not necessarily reflect the views of the National Science Foundation.

fail to adopt new technologies and business practices. Developing countries and international organizations want to ensure that the spread of e-business takes place in such a way as to promote development and not increase the gap between rich and poor countries.

Given the potential opportunities and perceived threats of globalization and e-business diffusion, there needs to be better knowledge of the global forces driving its diffusion, how national environments and policies influence Internet and e-business use and the economic impacts of Internet-based e-business. We define e-business as the use of the Internet by a firm to buy, sell or provide support for its products or services. This is a broad definition, with e-commerce or "online sales" being only one of seven e-business activities that might be conducted on the Internet. The others are advertising and marketing, making purchases online, after-sales customer service and support, exchanging operational data with suppliers, exchanging operational data with business customers and formally integrating the same businesses processes with suppliers or other business partners.

This chapter reports findings from a major research effort to develop knowledge about e-business. In conjunction with twenty colleagues from ten economies, we developed a four-year study of globalization and e-commerce,[1] which analyzed the use and impacts of e-business at the global, national and industry levels using quantitative and qualitative methods. We examined the overall diffusion of Internet-enabled commerce in forty countries and focused on case studies in ten economies in order to identify differences and similarities in drivers and barriers, diffusion and impacts of e-business. We used secondary data and collected our own data through a common survey of 2,100 firms across the ten national economies in order to enrich our understanding of how e-business was unfolding broadly and within each economy.

The remainder of this chapter describes the theory and conceptual framework of the study and the major findings regarding the driving forces, diffusion and impacts of e-business across the countries and firms in the study.

24.2   Theory and conceptual framework

We adopted the theory and framework of Berger and Dore (1996), as well as much innovation research, which asks what environmental and policy variations influence innovation outcomes in different national

---

[1] Although labeled Globalization and E-Commerce, the study was actually about the broader concept of e-business as defined above.

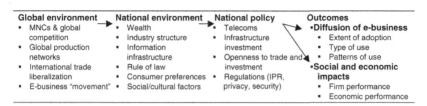

Global environment	National environment	National policy	Outcomes
• MNCs & global competition	• Wealth	• Telecoms	• **Diffusion of e-business**
• Global production networks	• Industry structure	• Infrastructure investment	• Extent of adoption
• International trade liberalization	• Information infrastructure	• Openness to trade and investment	• Type of use
• E-business "movement"	• Rule of law	• Regulations (IPR, privacy, security)	• Patterns of use
	• Consumer preferences		• **Social and economic impacts**
	• Social/cultural factors		• Firm performance
			• Economic performance

Figure 24.1. Conceptual framework.

contexts. One view is that global flows of goods, capital, people and technology are leading to convergence across countries in the organization of economic activities (Bell, 1973; Ohmae, 1990; Womach et al., 1991). Another view is that the impact of these forces on individual countries will vary according to the economic, political and social context of the country, and as a result, there will remain significant national differences in economic organization (Boyer, 1996; Wade, 1996; Dedrick and Kraemer, 1998).

In order to examine these views, the research looked specifically at the globalization of the Internet and e-business, and posited that the *diffusion and impacts of e-business* are driven by forces in the *global environment* which are intermediated by *national environmental factors* and *national policy* (Figure 24.1).

At the *global environment* level, processes such as globalization of production and markets, multinational corporation (MNC) strategies and technical innovation are driving all countries and industry sectors toward the adoption of Internet and e-business innovations. In addition, there is a global flow of information about "best practices" or effective e-business models produced by the IT industry, consultancies, academics and the business press. We refer to this as the global e-business movement.

The intermediating factors between the global environment and outcomes refer to national factors which constrain or enhance innovation outcomes. The first is the *national environment*, including wealth, industry structure, information infrastructure, financial systems, human resources, social and cultural factors, and consumer preferences. The second is *national policy*, including liberalization of telecommunications and IT markets, government investment in information infrastructure, and regulations such as consumer protection and intellectual property rights protection.

Outcomes refer to the *diffusion of e-business use* and to particular *social and economic outcomes*. E-business diffusion refers to the extent of adoption by firms and consumers, volume of transactions and services done online, and patterns of e-business use. Pattern refers to the sectors/ activities where e-business is used in a country, what companies are involved and how services are delivered. Social and economic outcomes include the effects of e-business on firm and economic performance.

As suggested earlier, it is commonly assumed that e-business is a globalizing force moving all countries and industries toward greater convergence. This is supported by the fact that much e-business is driven by global production networks and multinational corporations, and in turn is facilitated by open trade regimes, global competition and global telecommunications networks. However, both theory and prior research suggest there might be greater diversity among countries. Several studies have shown that great diversity exists even among East Asian economies following the so-called "East Asian model of economic development" (Boyer, 1996; Wade, 1996; Dedrick and Kraemer, 1998). Studies at the firm level suggest that there might be more convergence in upstream activities in the value chain and more divergence in activities that are downstream (Porter, 1986; Bartlett and Ghoshal, 1989; Globerman et al., 2001).

Indeed, we found from our various studies that all countries are converging toward greater use of Internet-based e-business and the standard practices this implies. However, we also found that the countries diverge considerably in the extent and character of use and impacts, and that these differences stem mainly from differences in the national environment, such as wealth, industry structure, information infrastructure and rule of law.

At the firm level, we found more convergence in e-business that involves upstream activities in the value chain, such as design and manufacturing, as well as in business-to-business (B2B) transactions, both of which are defined by common business processes and standards for integration. By contrast, we found greater divergence in downstream sales and marketing activities, and in business-to-consumer (B2C) transactions, as these activities must be tailored to local consumer preferences, business practices, and different languages and cultures. We further found that global firms are more advanced in using e-business for coordination and B2B sales than local firms, whereas local firms are equally advanced in using the Internet for B2C sales, services and marketing.

In short, there is broad global convergence toward greater e-business use, but considerable divergence in the pattern of use across countries and firms, depending on national environment and firm characteristics.

24.2.1 Methodology

The research was carried out using multiple methods. These included analysis of secondary data, historical case studies, a cross-country firm-level

Table 24.1. *GEC survey sample*

	Manufacturing	Wholesale/retail	Banking/insurance	Total
Small (25–249 employees)	364	357	365	1,086
Large (250+ employees)	379	344	330	1,053
Total	743	701	695	2,139

Source: GEC survey, CRITO

survey and annual workshops among the twenty participating research-ers. For each country, an individual expert or team prepared (1) a historical case study, (2) a qualitative analysis of the environmental and policy factors influencing e-business adoption and (3) a quantitative study of the nature of e-business use, and the impacts of e-business. These studies provided rich historical and qualitative background for understanding country-level data from secondary sources and firm-level data from the survey. Three annual workshops were held to review and discuss findings at each stage.

To have a broad representation of both developed and developing economies, the firm-level survey was conducted in the United States and nine other economies (Brazil, China, Denmark, France, Germany, Japan, Mexico, Singapore and Taiwan) during the period of February–April 2002 (Table 24.1). The survey instrument was designed on the basis of literature review, interviews with IT managers and discussions with country managers from the International Data Corporation (IDC), which cooperated in the survey effort. The sample consisted of large and small firms within each country, with specific establishments for each randomly selected firm within each size cell. Establishments were equally distributed across three industry sectors that are leading users of the Internet for e-business – finance, manufacturing and wholesale/ retail distribution. The sample frame was obtained from a list source representative of the entire local market, except in China where the sample focused on the more economically dynamic regions of Beijing, Shanghai, Guangzhou and Chengdu. About 200 establishments were surveyed in each country, except in the U.S., where 300 were surveyed.

It is important to note that survey respondents were screened by the question "Do you use the Internet to buy, sell or support products or services?" So, the final sample represents firms actually using the Internet for e-business, rather than the full population of firms in each country. This is an important distinction as it means that the firms are among the lead users in a country.

The final dataset contains 2,139 valid cases. Table 24.1 shows the sample by firm size and industry sector. Most respondents were the people most involved in key decisions about e-business adoption and use: CEOs, business unit managers, CIOs and IS directors.

24.3   Forces driving and shaping e-business

24.3.1   Globalization

The global diffusion of e-business is a process driven by a variety of forces. These include the strategies of multinational corporations and the related growth of global competition, the development of global production networks, international trade liberalization regimes such as the World Trade Organization, the creation of a low-cost global information and communications infrastructure, and an "e-business movement" driven by the IT industry and various opinion leaders (Figure 24.1). These forces are felt by all countries to varying degrees, but are more prominent in shaping diffusion in countries that have open trade and investment regimes, have more firms that are part of global productions networks and have more firms engaged in global competition.

MNCs are powerful global institutions that drive the diffusion of new technologies and business practices in two ways. First, they bring resources, including capital, knowledge and their own IT-based business practices, wherever they operate and diffuse these resources to their employees and to local firms with which they do business. Second, MNCs bring competition to local markets, creating pressure for local firms to adopt these technologies and business practices in order to survive.

These corporations also drive e-business diffusion through their coordination of global production networks. Production in manufacturing industries such as autos, electronics, textiles and toys has extended across national borders and become increasingly globalized or regionalized. During the last two decades, global production networks have expanded into developing regions such as Asia, Latin America and Eastern Europe. Many service industries have also begun to globalize in recent years, with call centers, IT services, software production and business process outsourcing (BPO) moving to diverse places such as India, Ireland, Israel, Russia, the Caribbean and the Philippines (Dossani and Kenney, 2004).

Participation in global networks is an important driver of e-business, as they rely heavily on telecommunications and IT-enabled processes for coordination and collaboration. Some economies have domestic firms that participate in these global networks as suppliers or subcontractors (e.g. Taiwan) or serve as production platforms for subsidiaries of MNCs (e.g. Singapore, China), while others such as the U.S., Germany and Japan are coordinators of such networks. Although the roles differ, the integration of countries into global production networks often involves the adoption of e-business as a condition for participation.

Institutions such as the World Trade Organization (WTO), the International Telecommunication Union (ITU) and the World Intellectual Property Organization (WIPO) have been instrumental in creating more open rules and effective regulations for trade, investment, telecommunications and intellectual property. The WTO has extended global trade rules to include services, such as financial services and telecommunications, helping to provide a better technical and financial infrastructure to support e-business. Liberalization of other IT-related services might provide more impetus to the globalization of e-business, but WTO negotiations on services have been unsuccessful in recent years.

The ITU has promoted telecommunications liberalization and the expansion of low-cost telecommunications, wireless and Internet services to developing countries. Lower costs and greater diffusion of telecommunications and the Internet have facilitated the global expansion of e-business and also supported IT-enabled business strategies such as offshore outsourcing of business operations.

Under the WTO, agreements on the trade-related aspects of intellectual property rights (TRIPS) set common international rules for intellectual property protection. These are important in building the necessary confidence for intellectual property holders to provide more content online, and encourage greater production of intellectual property worldwide.

A phenomenon that we call the e-business movement is another significant driver of e-business. This movement got an early impetus from the information superhighway strategy promoted by the Clinton-Gore administration as a new driver of economic growth, and was picked up by a number of other countries in the form of national information infrastructure plans. For example, all ten economies in our study developed such plans (see Kahin and Wilson, 1997 for other examples). In reality, the rapid growth of the Internet made parts of these plans obsolete, but their emphasis on deregulation and private-sector leadership remained. Within the private sector, the IT industry saw new market opportunities and began proselytizing to their customers about the benefits of e-business. The movement has been fostered by venture capitalists, business media, industry associations, academics and governments. The movement was hyped beyond reality during the dot.com boom, then widely discredited in the ensuing bust. However, in the aftermath of the boom and bust, there has been strong evidence of an

IT-driven surge in productivity for many firms and countries. Also, the excess physical capacity (e.g. fiber optic networks) installed during the boom years has left in place a high-quality, low-cost infrastructure even after many of its builders have disappeared.

The global forces described here tend to drive convergence across countries. MNCs try to standardize internal practices worldwide and push their suppliers and partners to align processes and technologies with those of the MNC. Countries that sign WTO and other agreements are forced to accept global norms that reduce differences in national policies. Global production networks rely on ICTs to improve coordination, shorten time-to-market, cut inventory and reduce errors. In many industries there is convergence to common or compatible software tools, communication protocols and business practices.

24.3.2 National environments

Just as global competition is a key factor driving countries toward adoption of e-business, national market forces are the key determinant of e-business diffusion within countries and, along with national policy, tend to create diversity among countries in e-business adoption and use. It is generally the case that new technologies are adopted first and most intensively by richer countries, which have the financial resources to invest in these technologies, the human resources and infrastructure to support their use and higher wage rates that make it worthwhile to introduce labor-saving technologies (Caselli and Coleman, 2001).

Figure 24.2 illustrates this point, showing the relationship between online sales as a percent of GDP (diffusion) and GDP per capita (wealth) for forty countries, including the GEC survey countries. It shows a positive and significant relationship between wealth and diffusion, and that there is a large gap in online sales activity between developed and developing countries. However, it also shows that there is considerable variance even among countries at similar income levels, which suggests that other factors besides wealth must explain country differences. We use online sales as an indicator of e-business to compare countries, as it is the only measure for which comparable national data are available. Also, while e-business is much broader than online sales, our research suggests that online sales is one indicator that is a clear differentiator across countries.

One of these key factors identified in the country cases is industry structure – particularly the degree of globalization of firms in a country (Gibbs et al., 2003). We define firm globalization in terms of organization structures (establishments in multiple countries, headquarters abroad), percentages of sales and procurement abroad, and pressure

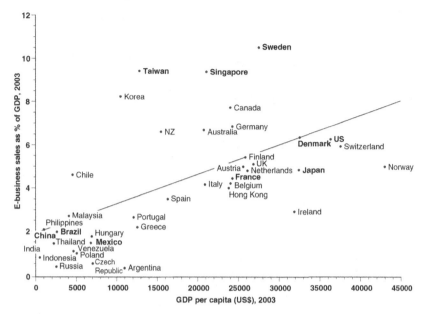

Figure 24.2. E-business diffusion and wealth.
Source: GEC secondary database, CRITO.

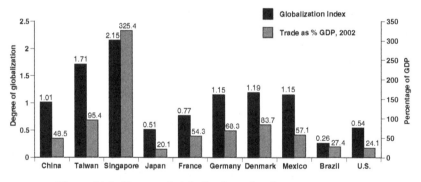

Figure 24.3. Degree of globalization of each economy.
Source: GEC survey, CRITO; World Bank, 2004.

from international competition. Empirical analysis indicates that more highly global firms engage more extensively in e-business (Gibbs et al., 2004; Kraemer et al., 2005).

Among the participants in our survey, those rated highest on our index of globalization are Taiwan and Singapore, whose small economies are highly integrated into global production networks (Figure 24.3). Singapore is a production platform and business hub for global MNCs, whereas Taiwan is a global supplier to MNCs. These two countries also have the highest volume of trade as a percent of GDP (Figure 24.3) and the highest ratio of online sales to GDP (Figure 24.2). Although Japan, the U.S. and to a lesser extent Brazil have large MNCs, these countries are rated lowest on the index of globalization primarily because their firms are oriented more toward their large domestic economies and international trade is a smaller percent of total GDP (Figure 24.3).

France, Germany and Denmark are in the middle on globalization and trade, which reflects their unique mix of large and small internationally oriented firms within the European market. Although China looks very similar to these countries, its rating largely reflects its position as a rapidly growing market for global MNCs as well as its export and local production requirements for access to the local market.

In an effort to identify and discriminate among other national factors, we conducted a cross-country empirical analysis of factors from the cases and prior research (Gibbs et al., 2003; Hargittai, 1999; Oxley and Yeung, 2001; North, 1986). These included investment resources, competitive pressure, information infrastructure, payment mechanisms and rule of law. The analysis showed that e-business activity has a direct relationship to measures of information infrastructure and to rule of law, and that other posited factors such as financial resources, experience with direct marketing and availability of payment facilitators are not significantly related (Shih et al., 2005). However, when we introduced rule of law as a moderator, we found significant interaction effects with several of the variables, including market capitalization, direct marketing revenue, Internet users and credit card use. These findings support the argument that rule of law is a very important national environmental factor in determining the willingness of businesses and consumers to engage in e-business. Especially interesting is the relationship between rule of law and the other factors, which shows that various potential facilitators or enablers of e-business matter only when the rule of law is strong. When the rule of law is weak, investors are not likely to invest in e-business, consumers are not willing to use their credit cards online, Internet users are not likely to take the leap from web surfing to online buying, and people who buy from direct marketers will prefer shopping by phone or mail to buying online.

In summary, the country-level data show that wealth, industry structure, a more advanced information infrastructure and the rule of law are important environmental facilitators of e-business use. Other national environmental factors such as competitive pressure and investment resources were found to be important in the qualitative country case studies, but not in the quantitative analyses.

24.3.3 National policy

The global diffusion of the Internet and e-business has been driven mainly by market forces and the private sector rather than by national policy. However, policy initiatives have played an important role in paving the way for e-business, accelerating the process and shaping its impacts in different countries. Some of these initiatives occurred during the late 1980s and early 1990s whereas others were coincident with the commercialization of the Internet in 1995 and the ensuing development of Internet-based e-business.

Liberalization of telecommunications, financial services and transportation services in many countries has been an important driver of Internet diffusion and e-business. In fact, the OECD found a strong link between the degree of competition in telecommunications and Internet diffusion across its member countries (OECD, 1996). These findings are supported by our finding that telecommunications infrastructure, rule of law and greater use of credit cards (associated with greater competition in financial services) are associated with higher levels of e-business (Shih et al., 2005). Likewise, deregulation of the trucking and airlines industries in the U.S. and elsewhere was a precursor to the rapid growth of cargo and courier services that are critical to supporting e-business (Fomin et al., 2003).

In addition, the governments of all ten economies in our study have developed national plans for encouraging Internet and e-business use (Gibbs et al., 2003). They have exempted Internet purchases from taxes, implemented online government procurement, enacted enabling e-business legislation (such as digital signatures) and in some cases offered incentives or subsidies to help smaller firms go online. However, both our case studies and survey results suggest that the impacts of targeted e-business promotion have been quite limited.

24.3.4 Firm-level drivers

Moving to the firm level, the GEC survey asked executives what factors influenced their decision to go online. We found that the strongest drivers of e-business adoption were the desire to expand markets for existing products and services, to improve coordination with customers and suppliers, and to enter new markets. These motivations were consistent with the messages of the "e-business movement" which claimed that the Internet allowed firms to tap into new markets without having to make costly investments in physical facilities, and to create a seamless supply chain that could respond quickly to changes in supply and demand conditions (Table 24.2).

Table 24.2. *Firm drivers of e-business adoption*

Percent indicating driver is a significant factor	Global	Rated # 1 by
To expand market for existing product or services	47.9	U.S., Germany
To improve coordination with customers and suppliers	43.7	France, Singapore, Brazil, Mexico
To enter new businesses or markets	42.0	Taiwan
Customers demanded it	36.9	Japan, China
To reduce costs	35.7	Denmark
Major competitors were online	31.3	
Suppliers required it	22.3	
Required for government procurement	15.2	
Government provided incentives	8.3	

Source: GEC survey, CRITO

The survey shows that firms are more likely to respond to customer pressure (36.9%) than to supplier pressure (22.3%), suggesting that e-business adoption is pulled rather than pushed through the value chain. In the case of manufacturers as well as distributors, "customers" are other businesses, whether other manufacturers, distributors or retailers. In global value chains, small and medium-sized businesses frequently are suppliers to larger domestic manufacturers, which in turn are suppliers to large international customers. In industries such as computers, electronics and automobiles, large MNCs have pushed suppliers to adopt e-commerce technologies as a requirement for doing business (Chen, 2003). For retailers and many financial services companies, the customer is the final consumer, who may desire the convenience of online sales and services in addition to existing channels.

Among other external factors, competitive pressure was a relatively important driver of demand, cited by 31%. Government promotion and incentives had little impact, suggesting again that e-business is mainly driven by market forces. However, the impacts of government policy were greater for developing countries, where there may be fewer resources or market incentives to go online.

Different drivers are more important in some countries than others, as Table 24.2 shows. But at the broader level, there was a consistent focus on either market expansion or coordination in all countries, which reflects the nature of the Internet as a widely available open network that can be used either to reach new customers at a relatively low cost, or as a flexible underlying platform that can support a variety of value chain configurations.

Table 24.3. *Firm barriers to e-business adoption*

Percent indicating driver is a significant factor	All firms	Rated # 1 by
Concern about privacy of data or security issues	44.2	All others
Inadequate legal protection for Internet purchases	34.1	
Need for face-to-face customer interaction to sell our products	33.8	Denmark, France
Costs of implementing an e-commerce site	33.6	
Customers do not use this technology	31.4	
Finding staff with e-commerce expertise	26.5	Germany
Our ability to use the Internet as part of our business strategy	24.8	
Business laws do not support e-commerce	24.2	
Making needed organizational changes	23.9	
Prevalence of credit card use in the country	20.3	
Taxation of Internet sales	16.5	
Cost of Internet access	15.1	

Source: GEC survey, CRITO

24.3.5 Firm-level barriers

The GEC survey also asked respondents what they saw as barriers to e-business adoption. Here, a somewhat surprising response was that the biggest barriers were concerns over privacy and security of data, as well as inadequate legal protection for Internet purchases (Table 24.3). This may be due in part to the newness of e-commerce and the fact that both businesses and consumers were still getting comfortable with the relatively anonymous online transactions involved. But it also clearly reflected the need for an effective legal and regulatory environment, reinforcing the country-level findings regarding the rule of law (Shih et al., 2005). Among the three industries studied, concern about privacy and security was ranked number one by all industries, but was highest in the financial sector, where this barrier was cited by 62% of firms.

Interestingly, privacy and security concerns were rated the number one barrier in all countries except the three European ones, where stronger privacy protections have been enacted. Such protections were once criticized in the U.S. as inhibiting e-commerce by creating unnecessary burdens on business, but now it appears that they may actually create a more conducive environment for online business.

The number three barrier was the need for face-to-face customer interaction. This reflects firms' perceptions of customer preferences and the fact that the Internet is not a replacement for personal interaction in many cases. Even in the U.S., where mail order and other direct marketing businesses are well established, the need for face-to-face interaction was cited by 42% of respondents as a significant barrier.

In summary, our survey results show that the biggest drivers of e-business adoption are the desire for market expansion and improved value chain coordination. The most important barrier was concern about privacy and security issues, followed by inadequate legal protection for Internet purchases. This reinforces the national-level findings that e-business drivers are economic and structural in nature, while barriers are more institutional and legal. We would expect these factors to influence the extent and patterns of e-business diffusion and use.

24.4   Diffusion of e-business

A general finding from the research is that the Internet and e-business use have spread to both developed and developing countries. There is a broad acceptance that the technology is valuable and that both firms and countries cannot afford to be left behind or left out. Even a country such as China, which has a strong desire to control the flow of information, seeks only to place limits on how the Internet is used, not to prevent its use. Singapore, which still bans satellite TV dishes, places only limited controls on Internet use. The point is that everyone is aware of the economic importance of being connected.

24.4.1   Extent of e-business diffusion

E-business on the Internet is still in its early stages. However, it is growing rapidly, as online sales are equivalent to nearly 10% of GDP in some countries.[2] Secondary data indicate that B2B online sales are much larger than B2C sales both globally and at the country level (IDC, 2004).

While the U.S. leads in total online sales, it is no longer the leader relative to GDP (Figure 24.4). Instead, the small trading economies of Singapore and Taiwan have the highest revenues as a percent of GDP, due in large part to their roles in the global production networks of the computer and electronics industries. In addition, these are two places where aggressive government promotion of e-business may be having an impact (Wong and Ho, 2004; Chen, 2003).

---

[2] These figures should be interpreted cautiously, as e-business revenues are based on sales and can involve double counting, while GDP is based on value added.

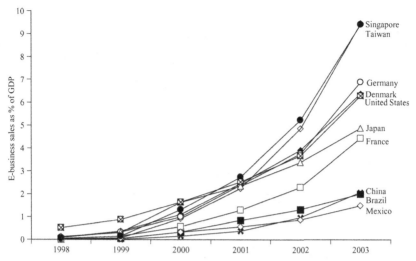

Figure 24.4. Internet-based e-business diffusion, 1998–2003.
Source: IDC, 2004.

The next group of countries includes Germany, Denmark and the U.S. Germany is a central hub for banking, manufacturing and distribution businesses in the European Union and both its large and *middlestand* companies are intensively engaged in international trade (Koenig et al., 2003). Denmark is a small open economy actively trading within the European Union (Andersen et al., 2003) and has a relatively high proportion of large internationally oriented businesses.

Lagging behind the developed countries are Japan and France. Both of these countries have more domestically oriented firms and both were relatively late to adopt Internet-based e-commerce. In the case of France, consumers and firms were slow to adopt the Internet due to the high cost of PCs and the high price and low quality of Internet connections.[3] Some also argue that the existence of the Minitel system made France slow to adopt the Internet because it performed functions similar to the Internet (Brousseau, 2003; Brousseau and Kraemer, 2003). In both France and Japan, large businesses in manufacturing and distribution had already made substantial investments in EDI systems for their value chains and were slower to adopt B2B technologies.[4]

---

[3] We are grateful to an anonymous reviewer for this important clarification.

[4] In a related analysis, we found that EDI users generally tend to view switching costs as a significant barrier to adoption of the Internet for e-business. This suggests that firms have developed deeper understanding about the benefits as well as the costs of

The final group includes the developing countries of Brazil, Mexico and China. In these cases, the leading firms are actually quite aggressive in adopting the Internet, according to our survey, but there remain large segments of the economy in which IT is barely used (Tigre and Dedrick, 2003; Palacios and Kraemer, 2003; Tan and Wu, 2003).

24.4.2 Patterns of e-business use among firms

Moving to the firm level, the character of e-business diffusion is indicated by the percentage of firms using the Internet for different purposes (Figure 24.5). The GEC survey indicates that firms make multiple uses of the Internet for business, but surprisingly, online sales are the lowest use (30% of all firms). The largest number of firms uses the Internet for communication with customers, including advertising, marketing and customer services (44–58%). In addition, many firms use the Internet for coordination, including exchanging operational data (48–51%) and integrating business processes (34%) with suppliers and business customers.

The low percent of firms using the Internet for sales is surprising given that "expanding markets" and "entering new markets" are major drivers of e-business adoption (Table 24.2). The findings indicate that e-business is more than just sales. E-business includes activities internal to the firm and beyond, extending to suppliers, business partners and customers. The relatively large proportion of firms engaged in these other activities indicates that they are complements if not prerequisites to online selling. Also, firms can use the Internet as a marketing tool to attract more customers to their existing sales channels.

The GEC survey also indicates that the pattern of e-business use is different for highly global firms than for more local firms (Figure 24.5). The two groups' use of the Internet for customer-oriented activities, such as advertising, marketing and online sales, is similar. However, highly global firms use the Internet more for supply chain coordination through information sharing with suppliers and business customers than do highly local firms. They also are more likely to use the Internet to formally integrate some of their business processes (e.g. procurement, sales, operations) with these partners.[5] All of this suggests that the key

---

interorganizational information systems through their EDI experience and thus tend to be more cautious in switching to the Internet (Zhu et al., 2006). These findings illustrate the subtle role of *path dependency* in standards migration in different country environments.

[5] Formal analysis further shows that these differences are statistically significant (Gibbs et al., 2004; Kraemer et al., 2005).

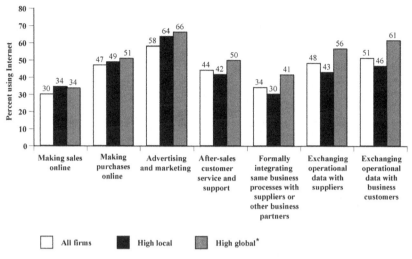

Figure 24.5. Firm uses of e-business.
Source: GEC survey, CRITO.
*Note: High global is top 25% of firms in degree of firm internationalization. Low global is bottom 25%.

difference between global and local firms is that global firms are using the Internet and e-business more actively to integrate their upstream and downstream operations with their suppliers and business partners.

Global firms are also more likely to use the Internet for after-sales customer service and support. This suggests that global firms add value to their products through use of the Internet for service enhancements such as order tracking, online customer support and various user tools (Chen, 2003). These differences reflect the fact that global firms operate internationally in production chains where the Internet can reduce geographic and time boundaries and enable better coordination, integration and efficiency in response to global competition. In contrast, local firms operate within a country or region and focus mainly on local markets where they have a physical presence through which to provide this particular form of customer service, which may involve product returns or repairs.

24.4.3 B2B and B2C e-business among firms

While the level of e-business is increasing over time, direct selling on the Internet is still low among individual firms. The GEC survey indicates that about 35% of the firms engage in online sales over the Internet

Table 24.4. *B2B and B2C sales and services*

Firms doing online sales	
Percent B2B only	12.9
Percent B2C only	7.1
Percent both B2B and B2C	15.0
Total	35.0
Firm online sales as % of total sales (among firms selling online)	
B2B	15.2
B2C	18.6
Total	33.8
Firms doing online services	
Percent B2B only	23.1
Percent B2C only	12.9
Percent both B2B and B2C	33.3
Total	69.3

Source: GEC survey, CRITO

(Table 24.4). About twice as many firms engage in B2B sales (12.9%) compared with B2C sales (7.1%) and a substantial proportion engage in both (15%). Among firms selling online, the percent of total sales conducted on the Internet is just 15.2% for B2B and 18.6% for B2C.

In contrast to online sales, online services are provided by twice as many firms (69.3%). These services range from catalogs to product reviews, product specifications, product configuration, technical support, customer service, bill paying, account information and research/ planning tools. This variety of services reinforces the point made earlier that communication with customers is a key use of e-business and that e-business is about much more than simply online sales. The higher level of online service provision may reflect the fact that many services can be provided entirely online and do not require a payment mechanism or physical delivery.

Given differences in the nature of B2B and B2C transactions, we would expect to find considerably more local variation in B2C than in B2B e-business. B2B transactions involve two firms, both of which are attempting to achieve some kind of performance goals such as increasing sales and profits, reducing costs or improving coordination. In this case, there is presumably a willingness to adopt common technologies and business practices to achieve such results, even within the context of different national business practices. B2C transactions, by contrast, involve selling products or services to consumers, who may have much more varied utility functions and less willingness to change their

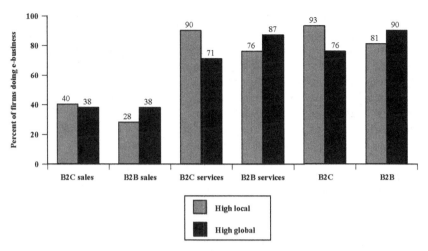

Figure 24.6. B2B and B2C e-business in highly local and highly global firms.
Source: GEC survey, CRITO.

purchasing behavior just to reduce transaction costs. Local cultural differences such as preference for face-to-face transactions and the buying experience would also lead to greater variation in B2C.

The findings from the case studies and the GEC survey confirm the expectation. The GEC survey found that highly global firms are more likely to engage in B2B, including both B2B sales and B2B services (Figure 24.6). Highly local firms, meanwhile, are more likely to engage in B2C, especially in terms of providing services to consumers online. The two groups were equally likely to engage in B2C sales, which implies that any advantages or greater motivation local firms have in the consumer market do not make a difference in terms of actually selling online. Instead, the big difference is in B2C services, where local firms were significantly more likely to conduct business online.

The reasons could have to do with better ties to local supply chain partners. Two examples are product availability information and order tracking, both of which are common services offered on B2C websites. Providing these services online requires integration with warehouses, distribution centers and shipping companies to track inventory and shipment information. This may be easier for local firms that have well-established relationships with local partners.

Global firms might also see less payoff or competitive advantage in providing online services to consumers. Knowledge of consumer markets is less transferable from country to country, and it is expensive for firms to gain local knowledge. Global firms may be deterred from providing B2C services by challenges due to national differences in language, culture, consumer behavior and government regulations, which may be especially important in the often highly regulated financial sector.

These survey findings are reinforced by the country case studies showing heavy use of B2B technologies such as EDI, extranets and supply chain management applications by globally oriented firms in industries such as automobiles and electronics (Chen, 2003; Tachiki et al., 2004). Meanwhile, local retailers and financial services firms are leaders in many countries in providing a wide range of services to consumers, taking advantage of their knowledge of the local market and existing distribution infrastructures. All of this suggests that there is a contrasting pattern of digitization of business: rationalization of the coordination of business partners by global firms, especially in manufacturing, and extension of markets by local firms, especially in services.

In summary, countries are using the Internet for business and the use is growing rapidly. B2B transactions considerably exceed B2C transactions, both globally and in all countries. Survey data show similar results at the firm level. They also show that the most common applications of e-business are for communication with customers (marketing, advertising and customer service) and value chain coordination (exchanging data with business customers and suppliers), while online selling is the least common use.

An important differentiator among firms in both intensity and nature of e-business use is their level of globalization. Highly global firms do more business online overall than more local firms. However, there was no significant difference in terms of selling, buying or marketing. The biggest difference was in activities related to value chain coordination. It appears that global firms face more pressure to coordinate their geographically dispersed value chains and support global customers. Local firms are just as likely to buy and sell online, and actually provide more services to consumers online. We expect these differences in the use of e-business between global and local firms to have implications for the nature and extent of e-business impacts between the firms.

24.4.4 Patterns of e-business use among economies

The use of e-business for different activities varies by country, but the pattern is not a simple divide between developed and less developed economies (Figure 24.7). Rather, it is related to endogenous features of these economies and their global linkages. Firms in the developed countries of Germany, Denmark and the U.S. are nearly equally engaged in

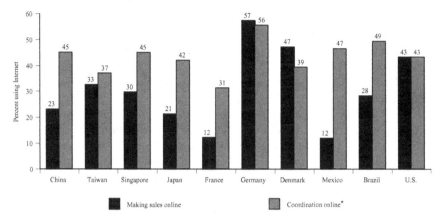

Figure 24.7. E-business uses across economies.
Source: GEC survey, CRITO.
*Note: Coordination online is a composite measure, which included information exchange (exchanging operational data with suppliers, exchanging operational data with business customers) and business process integration (formally integrating same business processes with suppliers or other business partners).

online sales and online coordination with their suppliers and business partners. This reflects their large market areas (Germany and especially Denmark sell to other European countries) and the substantial participation in national and international value chains by both large and small firms.

All of the other economies show a markedly greater uptake of the Internet for coordination than online sales, although the difference is less in Taiwan than elsewhere. However, the explanation for this pattern differs by country and lies in deep structural differences between the countries. For example, the high online coordination in Singapore reflects its position as a production platform for foreign multinationals, while lower online sales reflects its small domestic market and lack of a substantial regional market.

The high online coordination relative to online sales in the developed economies of Japan and France reflects the industry structures in those countries, which are marked by industrial groups led by large leading firms that can capture the benefits of improved coordination. Both Japan and France, however, have dense networks of neighborhood retail establishments and cultural preferences for face-to-face purchases, which discourage online sales. Both countries also are heavy users of EDI and may be continuing to use that technology for electronic transactions, while employing the more flexible Internet technologies for coordination purposes. In addition, Japan has been slow to adopt online sales because "it is not always clear to Japanese managers that e-commerce represents a better business model" (Tachiki et al., 2004). Finally, France's particularly low level of online sales reflects its slow overall adoption of the Internet.

The developing economies of China, Mexico and Brazil show a large difference between these two uses, with coordination far exceeding online sales. The case studies indicated that in all of these countries, use of the Internet for business is driven more by the manufacturing sectors where participation in global production networks pushes them toward greater use of the Internet, primarily as a coordination tool. Brazil's higher level of online sales is driven by the financial sector, which has long been a leading user of IT, even for consumer services. In all of these countries, the unequal distribution of income, lack of credit card use and poor delivery infrastructure limits the market potential of B2C e-business. These variations in e-business for sales and coordination reinforce our earlier conclusions that there is considerable national divergence in e-business use and that it is driven by differences in the structural features of the various economies.

24.5   Impacts of e-business

24.5.1   Firm-level impacts

Firms in the survey report a wide range of impacts from going online. Intangible benefits such as improvements in customer service, internal efficiency, coordination, sales area coverage and competitive position are reported more frequently than more tangible benefits such as staff productivity gains, increased sales and cost reductions (Figure 24.8). This may reflect the difficulty of measuring impacts and linking them directly to Internet use.

While firms do report benefits from going online, in some cases consumers may have gained at the expense of firms, as they have the ability to gather information and search for lower prices online, even if they end up buying in a store. For instance, car shoppers can gather extensive data about new cars, including dealer invoice prices, which improves their bargaining position and reduces the information advantage previously enjoyed by dealers.

Firms that operate more globally achieve more benefits than firms that operate locally on every dimension surveyed (Figure 24.8). This may be because they can amortize their investments in e-business over a wider

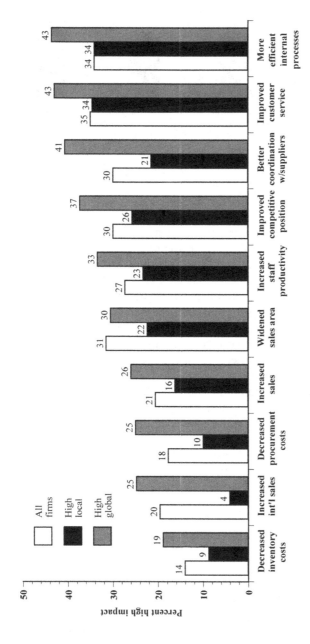

Figure 24.8. Firm impacts from e-business.
Source: GEC survey, CRITO.

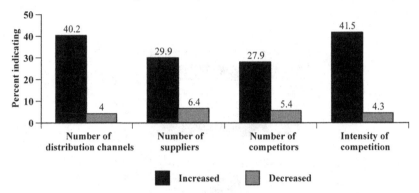

Figure 24.9. Competitive impacts of e-business.

Source: GEC survey, CRITO.

customer base, or because their global experience gives them an advantage in using the technology to a greater effect. One of the biggest differences between global and local firms is that global firms are much more likely to report increased international sales. This suggests that the Internet can help international firms to expand their international business, but is rarely a means for non-international firms to go global. It also refutes the notion that the Internet removes barriers to entry to foreign markets or that most firms can sell globally without developing a physical presence in those markets.

Adoption of the Internet for business also has significant impacts on firms' competitive environment and range of value chain partners. Far more respondents reported increased numbers of distribution channels and suppliers than those who reported a decrease (Figure 24.9). The same is true for intensity of competition and for the number of competitors that businesses face. Taken together, these findings indicate that firms are operating in increasingly complex environments, with more competition and more value chain partners. The Internet and e-business may be driving some of this increased complexity, but conversely, adopting e-business may be a response to greater complexity arising from factors such as deregulation and globalization.

24.5.2 Country-level impacts

There are marked differences across the countries in terms of reported impacts. For instance, Figure 24.8 shows the number of firms reporting that sales increased was 20.5%. However, Figure 24.10 shows that this figure ranges from 36% in Mexico to just 1% in Japan. Likewise, the

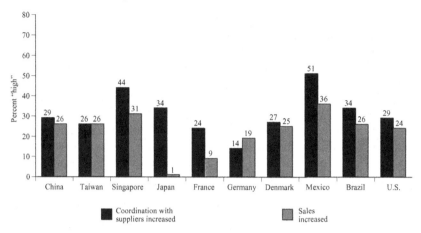

Figure 24.10. Performance impacts of e-business in different economies. Source: GEC survey, CRITO.

number of firms reporting improved coordination with suppliers ranged from 14% in Germany to 51% in Mexico.

One interpretation of these differences is that the impact of e-business is related to the nature of use. The most vivid case is Japan, where 34% reported better coordination with suppliers, but only 1% reported higher sales. This reflects the fact that Japanese firms have concentrated on improving supply chain efficiency more than online selling, a fact that Tachiki et al. (2004) attribute to the nature of Japan's industry structure with its keiretsu industry groups and its complex distribution channels. The pattern is reversed in Germany, which had already applied EDI through the supply chain, even down to mid-sized firms. German firms were aggressive in using the Internet for coordination, yet given their earlier investment in EDI, they may have had less room for improvement in supplier coordination.

24.6 Discussion and conclusions

24.6.1 Global trends

Based on both the qualitative and quantitative findings of the GEC project, we can identify several important trends in the development of e-business technologies and practices. These include the factors that influence adoption and diffusion, the nature of use and impacts on firm performance.

Common factors that influence diffusion and adoption of e-business can be found at the global, national and firm level. At the global level these include trade liberalization, which has steadily advanced in past decades via the GATT, WTO, regional trade agreements and other efforts to expand trade and investment flows. The impacts of trade liberalization are most visible in countries such as Mexico, Brazil and China, which have dramatically opened up to trade and investment. Each of these countries now boasts major industry sectors that are globally competitive and that also are national leaders in e-business adoption. Global forces also include the "e-business movement", an intellectual movement that has carried both faith in technology and knowledge of its use around the world. In talking with business people, academics and policy makers in both developed and developing countries, it is clear that they are convinced of the promise of e-business and quite well versed in its use.

The other major force behind diffusion of e-business is the continuing expansion of multinational corporations and the global production networks they coordinate. These firms rely heavily on IT and e-business to coordinate their own far-flung operations as well as their production and distribution networks. They employ advanced technologies wherever they go and require their business partners to adopt technologies and business practices as a price of doing business. They also put pressure on local companies to adopt e-business to compete with them.

At the national level, we identified several common economic and technological factors that influence adoption, including wealth, industry structure (more global firms), information infrastructure and the rule of law. We also found that other factors, such as credit card use, are strongly moderated by the rule of law, which is apparently critical to the willingness of firms and individuals to engage in online transactions. Case studies confirm that the absence of a strong rule of law is a significant barrier to e-business adoption. However, both case studies and survey results show that government e-business promotion has a limited impact on adoption.

At the firm level, our survey results show that the biggest drivers of e-business adoption are desire for market expansion and improved value chain coordination. The most important barrier is concern about privacy and security issues, followed by inadequate legal protection for Internet purchases. This reinforces the national-level findings that e-business drivers are economic in nature, while barriers are more institutional or legal.

As for how firms are actually using the Internet for business, secondary data show that B2B transactions dwarf B2C, both globally and in all countries. The GEC survey data show similar results at the firm level. They also show that the most common applications of e-business are for communication with customers and value chain coordination, while online selling is the least common use.

An important differentiator among firms in both intensity and nature of e-business use is their level of globalization. Overall, highly global firms do more business online than more local firms. However, there is no significant difference in terms of selling, buying or marketing. The biggest difference is in activities related to value chain coordination. It appears that global firms face more pressure to coordinate their geographically dispersed value chains and support global customers. Local firms are as likely to buy and sell online and actually provide more services to consumers online.

The impacts of e-business on firm performance are generally consistent with the ways in which it is used. The biggest impacts are improvement in customer service, coordination with suppliers, internal processes and expansion of firms' sales area. In the area of impacts, the global/local split is most dramatic. Highly global firms report greater benefits on every indicator of sales, efficiency and coordination, perhaps because they are able to achieve economies of scale from their e-business investments or because their broader experience with IT enables them to utilize the Internet more effectively.

24.6.2 National diversity in e-business

While there is a good deal of convergence across countries in terms of drivers, barriers, uses and impacts of e-business, we also found evidence of national divergence and diversity in the survey, and especially in the country cases. To generalize, we found that upstream activities in the value chain tended toward global convergence, while downstream activities showed more national and even local diversity.

For instance, case studies show that firms in almost all countries tend to use older technologies such as EFT and EDI in support of upstream business processes such as financial transaction clearing, supply chain management and just-in-time inventory systems. These firms are adopting newer Internet-based technologies to lower costs and increase flexibility in such processes. Internet technologies also allow smaller upstream firms with limited resources to be linked to the electronic networks of their larger customers.

For downstream activities such as retailing and consumer financial services, there are real differences across national economies in how much e-business is used and the form that it takes. These differences can be explained by differences in consumer behavior, social norms or industry structure. For instance, shoppers in places such as France, Taiwan and Japan have been less willing to buy products sight unseen, or to pay for them in advance with credit cards. They also are used to making daily shopping trips to local stores. So in those countries, online buying has been slower to catch on and transactions often are handled through local convenience or department stores and paid for with cash on delivery. In the U.S., consumers are more familiar with long-distance shopping over the phone and as a result, online purchases are generally paid for by credit card and delivered by courier to the customer's home.

Other examples of national diversity in consumer-oriented e-business include the success of the i-mode and other mobile Internet services in Japan (Tachiki et al., 2004) and the emergence of strong local content suppliers in Brazil to satisfy demand for local language and cultural content (Tigre, 2003; Tigre and Dedrick, 2003). From Europe to Asia, use of mobile data communications such as short messaging service (SMS) has run well ahead of the U.S. In fact, it has been reported that the simple business of downloading ring tones reached $2.5 billion worldwide in 2003, mostly outside the U.S. (Schoenberger, 2004). These examples reflect differences in consumer preferences, regulatory environment and industry structure.

24.6.3 American hegemony in e-business

Many countries have been concerned about U.S. influence over the Internet, fearing that globalization will bring a loss of national economic control and the invasion of U.S. culture. The Internet was invented in the U.S., built on the English language and in its earlier days had an individualistic frontier culture that was very American. Some U.S. firms saw e-business as a way to lower barriers to entry and compete in new international markets, a possibility that was not so attractive to incumbent national firms in those markets.

After all the hype and fear, the evidence shows that the Internet and e-business have become dominated less over time by U.S. companies and business practices. The dot.com boom and bust in the U.S. did have echoes in a number of other countries, but within the context of their own entrepreneurial traditions and supported mainly by domestic investors. In addition, other nations have not been content merely to imitate U.S. approaches to e-business, but have developed strategies suited to their own economic and social context.

24.7   Conclusions

The mantra often heard in the dot.com bubble years was "the Internet changes everything." After the crash, a more common sentiment was that the Internet had not changed much of anything. Many new e-tailers were founded but only a few such as Amazon and eBay survived, while traditional retail firms learned to use the Internet as an additional channel. While B2B e-business involves large volumes of transactions, the highly touted B2B exchanges disappointed investors, as both buyers and sellers were hesitant to join. Finally, many technology suppliers crashed, along with their plans to become rich by selling the picks and shovels of the Internet gold rush. For example, Commerce One, a company that developed software for B2B exchanges, had a market capitalization of over $20 billion in 2000, but was on the verge of bankruptcy by 2004 (San Jose Mercury News, 2004).

Yet, while it appears the revolution did not quite happen as expected, the rapid growth of e-commerce transactions continued throughout the dot.com crash, reaching over $1.6 trillion worldwide in 2003 (IDC, 2004). Meanwhile, the Internet is becoming firmly entrenched in consumers' buying habits, at least as a source of information, and increasingly for actual purchases. For businesses, it is becoming inconceivable not to have a website, and most firms are moving to use the Internet to improve internal efficiency and coordinate with customers and suppliers, as well as to buy and sell online. In many cases, the result is a reinforcement of existing business relationships, but at the same time there are examples of more transformational effects. For instance, eBay claims that over 430,000 individuals are using its platform to earn a significant share of their income, creating a national and even international marketplace for craftspeople, artists, collectors and entrepreneurs (Kampert, 2004).

Another example of more dramatic change is the role that e-business technologies have played in enabling the global relocation of knowledge activities such as R&D, software development, call centers, product design and back-office financial and legal work. The dramatic reduction in international telecommunications costs and growth of the Internet have made it economically feasible to take advantage of low-cost skilled labor in places such as India, Ireland, Israel, China and the Philippines.

To summarize, e-business has been driven by a combination of broad global forces tempered by national environments and firm-level business imperatives. Adoption has been quite rapid in developed countries, while the more globally oriented sectors in developing countries have been quick to follow. The technology has been used more for coordination than for transactions, but transaction volumes have been growing steadily. The impacts of e-business so far have been more incremental than revolutionary. The impact has been to support, rather than transform, existing patterns of business activity, and to reinforce the advantages of more global firms, particularly in B2B commerce, while allowing local firms greater opportunities in the B2C domain. But it must be remembered that commercial use of the Internet is less than a decade old and we may be seeing just the beginning of the types of transformations that will be apparent in coming years.

25 ICTs and inequalities: the digital divide

Alain Rallet and Fabrice Rochelandet

25.1 Introduction

At the beginning of the 1990s, authors argued that globalization went hand in hand with the "end of geography", implying the declining relevance of spatial considerations in shaping patterns of industry organization, owing to the development of information and communication technologies (ICTs) and the Internet (O'Brien, 1992). Virtual space was supposed to act as a substitute for physical space. This naïve thesis was quickly criticized insofar as the Internet is a virtual network strongly rooted in the physical space of geography. But how does space matter in analyzing a network such as the Internet and its economic impacts?

There are several ways to deal with this question. Some papers have emphasized the logistical constraints of the virtual world, more precisely the dialectics induced by the use of ICTs between "de-territorialization" and "re-territorialization" of economic activities. The Internet allows the virtualization of certain aspects of economic activities (online orders for e-commerce, for instance) but implies that other aspects should be embedded in physical space (after-sales service or repair service must be close to customers). Other papers have looked into the geographic impacts of the Internet: are Internet uses biased in favor of agglomeration or dispersion trends? Models of economic geography (Fujita and Thisse, 2000) show that the decline of communication costs through geographical space, as transport costs, tends to polarize more and more economic activities because distance is no longer an obstacle for agglomeration factors such as economies of scale, indivisibilities, social interactions, etc.

More recently, attention has been focused on inequalities of access to the information society pushed by uneven geographical diffusion of ICTs and the Internet. This is the well-known topic of the digital divide. The digital divide has not only a geographical dimension but also an important social side (DiMaggio et al., 2004). Yet the geographical dimension has been at the center of the public debate, boosted by international institutions such as the UN, the World Bank and the OECD.

Nothing could be more justified than the question raised by the digital divide debate: What are the socio-economic or socio-geographic disparities linked to the current technological revolution based on ICTs and the Internet? But the debate is rather confused because the digital divide is a vague and extensive notion (from telecommunication infrastructures to training programs) applied to very different situations (nations, regions, organizations, communities). As Yu (2002) points out, the notion is so wide and ambiguous that it can be used to support public investments in broadband networks or/and to promote the liberalization of telecommunication markets. As a matter of fact, it is clear only that the digital divide notion belongs to the rhetoric of institutions which, as Colby (2001) underlines, have a strong inclination to choose the solution before determining the possible issue. This leads scholars to define how a legitimate but rhetorical question could be turned into academic research. This is the aim of this chapter.

In the first section, the origin, definitions, measures and policies related to the digital divide notion are briefly examined. The second section suggests going beyond an ill-defined notion by distinguishing problems according to different geographical scales and then two different fields (production and use of ICTs). The last section is focused on three major questions to reduce the digital divide: market versus public policies, the respective role of infrastructures, uses and contents, and the substitution of the traditional delay approach for an evolutionary and contextual approach to rethink geographical inequalities linked to ICTs and the Internet.

25.2   A confused and geometry-variable notion

The analyses on the digital divide have given rise to significant data production. But, the notion proves insufficiently defined regarding the conceptual aspect and then remains uncertain and not very operational considering the effects of policies inspired by one or another conception. We will first recall the origins of the notion before examining its definitions and suggested measures. Recommended policies and their stakes will conclude this section.

25.2.1   The notion and its origins

The speech on the digital divide started in the early 1990s with the distinction between *Information haves* and *Information have-nots*. The debate in the field of telecommunications is not a new one as it takes root in the problem of universal service in the USA and the *telephone gap*.[1] It has then been extended to gaps in computer equipment rates, Internet access inequalities and more recently to broadband networks inequalities. In addition, the debate which was initially restricted to OECD countries, now involves all countries by adding a new dimension to international inequalities as far as economic development is concerned.

From the early 1990s, American studies on the digital divide emphasize the risks linked to the exclusion of some social groups from ICTs.[2] But the digital divide phrase itself would have been evoked in 1995 by Long-Scott (1995), who showed the risks of excluding the poorest people and minorities from communication technologies with regard to the participation in democratic life. The following year, the digital divide phrase became popular through the debate on the regulatory framework in the telecommunication sector in the USA further to the Telecommunication Act 1996. Fitting into the more general issue of universal access, discussions are therefore focused on Internet access inequalities in this country and the role of education to fill the divide.

European countries, then, intended to take up the digital divide message, firstly for emphasizing their delay compared with the USA and then for setting up the huge project of building a European information society, a project which was initiated by the Bangemann report (1994) and relayed by the "eEurope" ambitious plan in 1999 in which appear many projects on the fields of e-democracy, e-commerce, e-learning, e-health, Internet access for disabled people and so on. The purpose was to enable Europe to take advantage of Internet opportunities and New Economy promises. Moreover, for each European country, it was the question of filling up the gaps between regions, towns/cities, organizations, social groups and individuals following the US initiatives.

Lastly, the digital divide debate was extended to peripheral economies. Taking into account the contribution of ICTs to the economic growth in the USA and Europe, these economies aimed to increase their hardware equipment rates and connection rates to the Internet, as well as to liberalize their telecommunication markets and educate their

---

[1] In the early 1990s, 6% of the population in the USA did not have a telephone line, essentially the elderly, poor minorities and single women with children. See Schement (1994).

[2] In particular, the Rand Corporation studies in 1995, on the universal email opportunity, and in 1998, on the necessity of educating citizens and workers about ICTs, as well as the one of American Minister/Secretary of Education on the importance of connecting schools to the Internet.

populations to use these new technologies. The UN continues to work actively on this issue.

25.2.2 Which definition?

Whatever its application field may be, the digital divide refers to the idea of a potential irreversible division between two groups: on the one hand, those who benefit from the digital economy, called *the Haves*, and on the other hand, those who are excluded, called *the Have-nots*. But this definition can be studied at different levels.

First, the digital divide was initially conceived as a kind of exclusion of those who do not have access to ICTs. In this analysis, access to computer equipment appears to be the central issue and moreover this technological view presupposes ICTs access as the foremost condition for wealth. These technologies are likely to generate productivity gains in whichever economic, institutional and cultural environment they are diffused.

A more elaborate perspective focuses on the actual uses of ICTs. It relies on the hypothesis of technological neutrality. The important thing is not to increase the equipment stocks and Internet connections but to make use of them. The digital divide is therefore defined as the separation between those (individuals, social groups, regions, countries) who use ICTs in an efficient way and those who do not use them or use them inefficiently. The analysis relies not much on equipment and access but on the conditions of effective use, appropriation and ICTs promotion beside excluded people.[3]

A third perspective relies upon the contents (information, knowledge, services, entertainment) which provides Internet access. Having access to equipment and networks and knowing how to use them are necessary conditions to benefit from contents, but the contents should exist and consequently, they may have been produced. For example, a worker may have a computer connected to his company's intranet web server. He may also have acquired the know-how for using and surfing through the firm's internal network. But the data and knowledge bases needed for efficient use of the information system are not already elaborated. This aspect of the digital divide is often neglected, but contents are as important as access and uses.

---

[3] For example, Hargittai (2002) distinguishes a divide in the digital divide – a second-degree divide – between connected individuals who have required competences, skills and know-how to accomplish rapid and efficient researches on the Internet and the other "connected" individuals.

To summarize, according to Baker (2001), the digital divide can be defined as a sub-optimal situation from the point of view of (1) the access to equipment (initial conception), (2) the uses and (3) the availability of contents and services. The OECD definition, to which most of the studies refer,[4] particularly emphasizes the first two levels: "The gap between individuals, households, businesses and geographic areas at different socio-economic levels with regard both to their opportunities to access information and communication technologies (ICTs) and to their use of the Internet for a wide variety of activities. The digital divide reflects various differences among and within countries. The ability of individuals and businesses to take advantage of the Internet varies significantly across the OECD area as well as between OECD and non-member countries. Access to basic telecommunications infrastructures is fundamental to any consideration of the issue, as it precedes and is more widely available than access to and use of the Internet" (OECD, 2001).

Several features are emphasized:

- the application of the digital divide notion would be universal: individuals, households, organizations, regions, countries;
- this notion refers to different geographical scales: international (within the OECD countries, between the industrialized countries and the less developed ones) and intra-national (disparities within regions, rural and urban areas);
- access to ICTs and uses of ICTs are two specific and distinct issues;
- the digital divide is primarily conditioned by the access to basic telecommunications infrastructures.

---

[4] See Montagnier, Muller and Vickery (2002), Johnston (2001). See in particular the analogy with automobiles made by the latter: "Uneven penetration of information and communication technologies in countries both within the OECD and beyond . . . gap between people who have the opportunity for regular access to the Internet and people who have irregular or no opportunity to access the Internet . . . The automobile analogy is quite good in this context. The arrival of the combustion engine and the automobile transformed our societies. But an automobile or any number of them are of little use without roads to run on. And their efficient use depends on good access to those roads in all communities. As the roads link to highways and super highways, the system becomes even more efficient by being faster and able to handle greater volumes of traffic. But the vehicles carrying people and produce must have capable drivers. And those drivers must be well trained by competent instructors. So, we need highways, access to highways, vehicles, trained drivers, and instructors. And we also need the rules of the road consistently applied. As applied to ICT and the Internet, the absence of any one of these elements creates a digital divide."

25.2.3   Which measures?

According to the definition, several types of indicators are taken in consideration to evaluate the digital divide.[5] Considering the notion in a wide context – disparities in ICTs access and uses – the elaboration of relevant, precise and comprehensive indicators requires significant available data on:

- infrastructures: density of electric networks, telecommunications and Internet penetration rates, etc.;
- the level of education within the population: literacy and school attendance; familiarity with computers; number of schools, universities, training programs in computerizing; second language learning and practice (English in particular);
- equipment: number of terminals and hosts, equipment rates;
- skills and know-how: value-to-weight ratio of ICT sectors, number of computer science engineers, national network operators, foreign partners, skilled labor;
- the potential access to these infrastructures and equipments: geographical density of hardware equipments and access to telecommunication networks, location of equipments, proportion of collective equipments (tele-centres, cybercafes), possibility to connect, freedom of expression, etc.;
- the actual access and uses of equipment: nature and volume of information flows (texts, video, sound, B2B), practices of professional and non-professional users, nature and economic weight of activities using ICTs.

These criteria are unstable as the digital divide notion is changing with the technology: it was initially necessary to measure the gaps in computer equipment rates, then in Internet connection rates and nowadays in access rates to broadband networks.

The measures of gaps bring out methodological issues and problems in interpreting results. Data are not available everywhere; series are often incomplete; variables are heterogeneous; the comparison of one geographic area with another one or from a period to another one proves problematical; ICTs producers and users (individuals, firms, associations, non-profit organizations) are very different and change according to periods, geographical areas, cultures and institutional environments.

---

[5] For a survey of the indicators used, see Montagnier, Muller and Vickery (2002).

Nevertheless, in spite of these important drawbacks, more elaborate indicators were suggested by the Canadian Agency for International Development and ORBICOM (Sciadas, 2002) in order to assess the degree of ICTs diffusion in a given economy (the degree of a country's "ICT-ization"). To do that, a synthetic indicator ("info-state") combines two others, info-density and info-use. "Info-density" refers to the ICT-based productive capabilities of a country. It combines network indicators (main lines, Internet sites, mobile users per 1,000 inhabitants) and indicators of skills and competences (literacy and schooling rates). "Info-use" assesses the ICTs' appropriation by households, firms and administration (Internet, radio and PC users, proportion of households with TV and cable-television network per 1,000 inhabitants) as well as their effective propensity to use ICTs (ICTs expenses in the gross domestic product, international telecommunications per inhabitant). The digital divide is therefore quantified by the disparities of "info-state" indicators between the different countries at a given point in time and by their evolution over time.

This study aims to set up a more complex measure of the digital divide that proves different from the recurrent accumulative data arrays. But few elements are communicated on the methodology. More generally, this kind of analysis integrates a controversial distinction between "traditional" capital and ICT capital. In fact, with the diffusion of ICTs inside most equipment, it becomes difficult to see differences between traditional capital and ICT capital. This difficulty also extends to consumption goods: one can watch a movie on a TV as well as on a mobile phone or a computer. It can thus be asked whether measuring the digital part of the economy is not a blind alley when considering the general-purpose nature of ICTs (Rallet, 2003).

25.2.4 A controversial institutional view

As we have already pointed it out, the digital divide topic particularly aims at settling public policies.

Generally, there is a consensus to make ICTs the driving force of the new industrial revolution ("informational") boosting economic growth and social welfare. They are supposed to bring productivity gains to all economic activities, to stimulate the development of new processes and products, to increase wages and favor the careers of workers who use them, to increase the accessibility to public services (health, education, etc.) and their efficiency, to enable individuals or organizations to extend their possibilities thanks to easier access to information, and even to democratize political life.

Besides, no one denies the fact that there are many strong inequalities in the diffusion of ICTs even within industrialized regions and countries. The debate is focused on the possible ways of reducing the divide and thus overcoming the risks of marginalizing activities, people or geographic areas because of their "exclusion" from informational revolution.

On the one hand, there are those who think that the current inequalities in ICTs diffusion are a major problem which requires public intervention. The digital divide may add another inequality to existing socio-economic inequalities between countries, regions, workers and social groups. Specific help policies would therefore be needed to correct observed gaps. Many authors and institutions (Dertouzos, 1997; ONU, 1999; Sachs, 2000) recommend such policies in order to favor the technological adjustment of those excluded compared with those who already benefit from digital revolution.

On the other hand, there are those who argue that the digital divide is only a consequence of existing socio-economic inequalities and as such must be demystified. In this approach, it might be advisable to firstly reduce the socio-economic gaps by encouraging the economic development of the peripheral areas and countries. These economic adjustments will act as the starting point for technological needs and uses similar to central regions and countries. In this approach, the digital divide is solved by itself and does not need specific policies any more.[6]

Moreover, existing inequalities represent an obstacle only if they become permanent. Yet, most of the supporters of public intervention presuppose it but they do not show the real demonstration of it – except for the question of basic infrastructures. At this point, there is confusion between (1) the *effects* induced by the ICTs unequal diffusion, and (2) the *factors of evolution* of this unequal diffusion. There cannot be any incidence for increasing inequalities of ICT diffusion because these inequalities have negative effects on growth and social welfare. Rather, there are links that must be established. Otherwise public policies would be justified by the negative effects of inequalities in which factors are not analyzed but presupposed.

The advocates of market self-regulation give an answer to this last issue. With the partisans of public intervention, they go along with the idea that unequal diffusion of ICTs tends to widen development gaps as pointed out by Montagnier, Muller and Vickery (2002):

---

[6] According to supporters of public policies, however, economic development does require ICTs access and uses.

"Because of the network effects associated with ICTs, society as a whole would fail to gain the full benefits from wider use." But they deny the fact that current inequalities of diffusion might become permanent, as markets will enable the sharing out of the technological resources according to actual needs. It will be all the more feasible since ICT markets rely upon dynamic network externalities which ignore social and geographical frontiers. Any public intervention is therefore perceived as a source of mistaken signals sent to economic agents except if it aims to prevent monopoly induced by increasing returns.

The position of market supporters relies on a dual belief. The first one (shared with the opposing position) is that ICTs do have positive impact on growth and welfare, and the second one is the idea of a generalized and convergent diffusion of ICTs. From our viewpoint, it seems important to question these two beliefs.

25.3 Different problems according to the level of development and geographical scale

The digital divide term is used to point out regional inequalities as well as inequalities within nations, social groups and categories of firms. These inequalities and their criteria are cumulative: the personal computer penetration and Internet access rates are lower for poor people living in poor regions or countries than for poor people living in wealthy countries. But mechanisms and problems are not the same from one social group, category of enterprise, region or country to another one. And the solutions too: what is good for a region or a country is not necessarily useful for a social group, and inversely. For instance, reducing the digital divide within regions may increase it within social groups. The probability is very high because the wealthiest social groups in poor territories are far more able to capture benefits coming from public policies supposed to help these territories. The issue of whether public policies may target geographical areas or individuals ("place prosperity" versus "people prosperity", see Hoover, 1971) is a traditional debate in regional economics.

We are focusing here on the geographical dimensions of the digital divide. We distinguish the divide within industrialized countries, between industrialized and less developed countries, between regions within the same country, between rural and urban spaces. Two major problems occur but in different ways, with more or less intensity according to the geographic scale.

25.3.1   Different kinds of digital divide

Between developed countries

As there are significant available data, this dimension of the digital divide has led to a lot of statistical works concerning OECD countries (OECD, 2001; Montagnier, Muller and Vickery, 2002; Schmitt and Wadsworth, 2002). Two different aspects are considered: on the one hand, the importance of the ICT sector in the economy of those countries, on the other hand, the uses of ICTs by firms, government departments and households.

Due to the fact that the ICT sector experienced high rates of growth in the 1990s, it was supposed to become the new driving force of economic growth. By cumulating many indicators (relative shares of ICTs in employment, value added, R&D expenditure and international trade), the OECD has classified its member countries in several classes: the highest ICT-intensive countries (Finland, Hungary, the Irish Republic, South Korea, Sweden, the UK, the USA), the average ICT-intensive countries (Canada, Denmark, France, Greece, Italy, Japan, Mexico, Netherlands, Norway, Switzerland) and the lowest ICT-intensive countries (Australia, Belgium, Czech Republic, Poland, Portugal, Spain, Turkey).

The word "backwardness" is more often used than "divide" to qualify the unequal diffusion of digital revolution within OECD countries. But there are still considerable gaps and the significant advance of the USA in the relative importance of the ICT sector and the diffusion of ICT uses has led to the question of its reversible or irreversible nature. Considering the fact that these inequalities have macroeconomic impacts, European authorities have encouraged ICT diffusion so as to increase the efficiency of organizations (firms and government departments) and to ensure better coordination within European Union markets (Pohjola, 2002).

Between developed and developing countries

In the developing countries, the access to computers and infrastructures is the main problem, due to the hardware costs and the weak development of telecommunications networks. Most studies are based on the data produced by the International Telecommunication Union (www.itu.int/ITU-D/ict/statistics). They show that the lowest rates of access to PCs and the Internet in these countries are essentially explained through socio-economic variables of development level (Chinn and Fairlie, 2004; Norris, 2002; Hargittai, 1999; Kiiski and Pohjola, 2002).

Between regions within a country

On a regional context, the debate on the digital divide essentially deals with the unequal deployment of telecommunication networks in national territories. In OECD countries, it is focused on broadband networks (DSL, cable, optical fiber, wireless technologies), taking account of the good coverage of national territories by previous networks (fixed telephony, cellular phone). Initially launched by the Al Gore program on information highways, the debate has been renewed with the development of the DSL market. The problem is well known: in a variable way according to the technology which is used (cable, optical fiber, DSL, radio local loop, 3G mobile, Wi-Fi, Wi-Max, satellite), the diffusion of broadband networks is limited to the more dense and less distant areas for both economic reasons – sufficient market size is required to take advantage from investments – and technical reasons, in particular the distance from the local central office to home for DSL technology.

In this respect, there are three different types of territories:

• towns in which size and density justify private financing in specific broadband infrastructures (cable, optical fibers, radio local loop) or which have broadband access via telephone network (DSL technology) through competitive operators;
• "grey" areas which have broadband access via only one operator, more often the incumbent operator. Their size and density are not sufficient enough to recoup private investments in alternative networks.[7] Access is not really the problem but rather the cost of this access due to lack of competition;
• rural areas which are served neither by DSL technologies due to distance or lack of equipment nor by alternative technologies for lack of profitability. At present, 90% of households and firms may have DSL access in France (ART, 2004).

Between rural and urban spaces

On the population side, the differences between rural and urban spaces are all the more important since the development level of the country is low because of a lack of telecommunication infrastructures in rural areas or due to archaic networks in these countries. This is especially the case in Africa (see Chéneau-Loquay, 2002 and the studies carried out by the Africanti network, www.africanti.org). When this variable is neutralized, especially in the OECD countries, the observed gaps between rural and

---

[7] Grey areas represented 40% of residential and business lines in France at the end of 2004 (source: ART, 2004).

urban access rates exist but they are not so relevant.[8] In the USA, Internet connection rates in urban and rural populations were mostly equivalent in 2001 (51% versus 48.7%, source: Montagnier, Muller and Vickery, 2002). In the developed countries, the differences between rural and urban areas come mainly from social disparities in terms of households' income, education level and so on. That is clearly seen at a lower scale (suburbs/city centre). Thus, in the USA, Internet connection rates in central urban areas are lower than in other urban areas and seem to get close to the rates prevailing in rural areas. The digital divide reflects the "inner city problem" of American cities. In the same way, a study carried out by the Foundation Getulio Vargas in 2003 and based on micro-data highlights a strong correlation between income and digital inclusion factor within municipal district maps of Rio de Janeiro. The smaller the geographical scale, the higher the social matter behind the digital divide.

As for firms, ICTs adoption rates at the outset have been lower in rural areas than in urban areas even if variables such as size and sector are controlled. However, in the recent period, adoption rates tend to converge. The inequalities are now observed through the usages or the "second-level" divide (Galliano and Roux, 2003, 2004).

25.3.2   Two major problems with variable intensity according to level of development

As already mentioned, the geographical dimension of the digital divide has two aspects. The first is related to the geographical concentration of the ICT sector in some countries or regions. The second is the territorial discrimination induced by the unequal deployment of telecommunication networks.

Inequalities linked to ICTs production

Let us reiterate that ICTs have two different impacts on growth. Varying from one country to another, the relative importance of the ICT sector and its growth rate lead to disparities in economic growth. But insofar as they are used as equipment goods in all sectors, ICTs also impact the whole economy (Colecchia and Schreyer, 2001).

The importance of barriers to entry (significant fixed costs, especially R&D expenditures), the presence of increasing returns and the localization of most innovations in the more ICT-intensive countries show that

---

[8] International comparisons are difficult in fact because statistical definitions of urban and rural areas are different according to countries.

it is quite utopian to catch up with those industrialized regions and countries that took the lead. It is especially the case with the USA (Silicon Valley), even if there are some niche market strategies (mobile phones in Europe and Japan, video games in France) and complementary strategies (software coproduction in India and more generally, the necessary relocation of this sector in order to reduce costs and follow decreasing prices strategies which enable higher growth rates in software markets to be maintained).

Therefore, the foremost question is to know whether a country which does not produce ICTs may be as efficient in ICTs uses as a country which produces them. If yes, the divide would not be extended to the most important impact of ICTs in the economy, i.e. their use as inputs in all activities. In the case of a perfectly competitive economy, productivity gains in the ICT sectors are rapidly transferred to users' sectors through the decline of equipment prices (with constant quality).

But:

- There is no perfect competitive economy, particularly in the ICT sectors which are characterized by increasing returns. Thus, the transmission of productivity gains can be done unequally as far as countries are concerned. In the 1990s, firms in the USA acquired their ICT equipment 10% cheaper than in Canada and 30–75% cheaper than in other countries (Montagnier, Muller and Vickery, 2002).

- In the case of an economy characterized by a rapid technological obsolescence, the delay in accessing new products and processes plays a major role. This delay is very short in countries which produce these technologies.

- The impact of the two variables mentioned above – price of technologies and delay in diffusion – on the digital divide depends on how intellectual property rights (IPRs) are defined and experienced. The debates on online piracy or open source software are part of the digital divide issue (CNUCED, 2004). The non-respect of IPRs favors a rapid diffusion of ICTs in the short term. But that could turn against developing countries if contents provided by these countries are not protected. That is why the actual driving force for reducing the digital divide is not piracy in the long run but the race between the open source model which gains ground in developing countries and leading firms in the computer industry which are forced to find adapted solutions to these countries (PC discount, specific licenses for second-hand PCs, easing of anti-piracy control). The reduction of the digital divide will benefit from externalities associated with the worldwide battle to connect more and more consumers.

- Linkages between production of ICTs and ICTs uses rely on technological externalities (transfer of know-how, information exchanges,
"industrial atmosphere") which are more strongly dependent upon
territorial context than pecuniary externalities. Due to informational
localized exchanges and local users–producers interactions, a stronger
and more innovative dynamics of ICTs uses will take place in ICTs
producer countries than in those which only use ICTs.
- The position of Europe in comparison with the USA is often used to
demonstrate this issue (Cohen and Debonneuil, 2000) but it also affects
the relationship between industrialized and less developed countries.

It raises the problem of channels able to transmit productivity gains,
innovations of products and know-how between producer areas and user
areas. These channels depend on two types of proximities: a geographical proximity and a relational proximity (Rallet and Torre, 2005). The
geographical proximity favors informational externalities between producers and users of technologies because of the ease of daily contacts. It
is a factor of geographical concentration. But economic agents are also
close due to their belonging to the same professional community or the
same organization without being necessarily co-located (relational proximity). That is the case in the Internet world where professional communities or innovative users are organized on a large, often worldwide,
geographic scale. The members of these communities are generally
located in metropolises so that the transmission of ideas and know-
how is done from metropolis to metropolis, even within global cities
(Sassen, 1991). The combined game of the two proximities (physical
and relational) explains why the dynamic interactions between production and uses are made in the framework of positive informational
externalities provided by the global network of metropolises. This
"archipelago economy" may result in strong inequalities with geographic
areas located out of the archipelago.

*Territorial discrimination produced by the unequal deployment of
telecommunication networks*

The digital divide begins with unequal access to infrastructure networks,
though it cannot be reduced to this. As in the field of transport means,
digital infrastructures are a necessary condition (but non-sufficient) for
local and regional development. By digital infrastructures, we mean
anything that gives access to networks (i.e. computer equipment and
connection to telecommunication networks).

The problem is mostly related to developing countries and peripheral
regions because for developed countries and central regions, the

liberalization of telecommunication markets has led to a competitive race to connect as many customers as possible, which tends to homogenize the conditions of accessing telecommunication networks.[9] Price gaps remain but they may gradually disappear owing to the convergence of the regulatory framework in this sector within the OECD countries (OECD, 2002). In fact, these regions and countries begin to be concerned with excessive infrastructures, except for the last mile connectivity. The matter is not so much to develop infrastructures but knowing what they can be used for. For the moment, the development of broadband networks is mainly drawn by uses such as entertainment (TV, music online, video on demand, etc.) and peer-to-peer file exchanges.

Network access remains a problem for developing countries and peripheral areas because it cannot be solved purely by market forces. The race to connections based on network externalities is a strong instrument to reduce geographical inequalities, but it faces the problems of insolvency and insufficient market size in less densely populated or poor areas. In industrialized countries, nearly all the population and firms have access to advanced broadband networks. Of course, the coverage is not equal among areas, but the needs are also unequal. In developing countries or regions, the territorial discrimination by advanced networks is stronger because facilities are very likely to be concentrated in the biggest cities.

The evolution of the digital divide based on infrastructure coverage depends upon two types of factors: technological and regulatory. The impact of technological change on the digital divide is contradictory. On the one hand, there is an increase in the number of alternative technologies (DSL, cable, fixed and mobile lines, radio, Wi-Fi, satellite) which diversify network access and, consequently, ways of reducing "dead areas". On the other hand, technological innovation tends to reproduce geographical inequalities continuously by creating new infrastructure needs (mobile phone followed by DSL technology, then Wi-Fi, Wi-Max, satellite) and leading to faster and faster broadband networks. The continuous and rapid rate of technological change left many areas in a constant state of "catch-up". But now, firms take their location decisions according to the current state of the network coverage instead of the future one. If access to the broadband network becomes a competitive norm for firms, they may need access not in two years but immediately. The unceasing development of network technologies reproduces inequalities of access continuously.

---

[9] This phenomenon has already been observed in the development of the telephone network in the USA at the beginning of the twentieth century (Mueller, 1996).

Regulation has two main aspects as well. Firstly, the liberalization of telecommunication markets is seen as a tool for bridging the digital divide as it is argued by international institutions such as the OECD (OECD, 2004). In this respect, these institutions underline the correlation between the liberalization of telecommunication markets and the geographical extension of networks as well as the decreasing access costs and the increasing quality of services. (Monopolies which still prevail in some countries are not likely to expand networks but to practice higher prices and provide services with lower quality or old-fashioned attitudes regarding technological change.) Such a trend is effectively observed within the OECD countries and even in metropolitan areas of non-OECD countries where competition may effectively be more efficient than regulated monopoly to develop networks due to the potential market of these areas. But it leaves unsolved the problem of remote or less densely populated areas and even the problem of poor areas in rich regions.

It follows the second regulatory aspect, that is authorizing local public authorities to remedy market failures by becoming operators of telecommunication networks. In most countries, they were allowed to build passive infrastructure that they could rent out to private operators. The problem may not be necessarily solved insofar as initial market size in these areas does not enable private operators to recoup their investments. When becoming an operator of active infrastructures (or more often an operator of operators because this task is generally delegated to a third party), local public authorities intend not only to provide facilities instead of private failing operators but also to stimulate local demand for services. However, these public initiatives, which are looking complementary to the market – public networks are created where there is no market – are ambiguous because they often consist in subsidizing alternative operators on the market. Their aim is often less giving access to broadband network where it does not exist than building networks in competition with the incumbent operator which initially acted as a local monopoly.

25.4   Three research issues

The digital divide cannot be boiled down to a rhetorical or institutional notion. From our viewpoint, it reflects three main analytical questions. In the first section, we wonder about the respective roles of the market and public intervention so that the divides could be reduced. The second one aims to go beyond the approach of inequalities in terms of access or uses so as to link access, uses and contents. In the third section, we suggest substituting a path-dependency approach for the traditional digital divide approach based on the notion of "backwardness" which assumes a universal model of diffusion.

25.4.1 Market or public intervention?

At the beginning, the digital divide as a notion was developed by partisans of public intervention. This was thought to be the only way to prevent the threat for excluded geographic areas or individuals in the information society. Then, by contrast, some authors argued that the market was efficient enough to reduce the divide.

As Piazolo (2001) says, "the digital divide will diminish with time until the gap in the density of computers and Internet hosts just reflects the different economic development stages during the catch-up process". In this perspective, many recommend the "laissez-faire" attitude (Wallsten, 2002; Dasgupta, et al., 2002; Compaine, 2000; Quah, 1999) so that public policies should not interfere. Thus, Quah (1999) suggests favoring the liberalization of telecommunication markets in order to decrease Internet access costs and accelerate the diffusion of ICTs. To achieve this purpose, financial markets should be developed in order to facilitate financing projects aiming to settle networks and improve their running. In the same way, Becchetti and Adriani (2003) show that economic growth is affected by the quality of the telephone network, hardware and telecommunication equipment whose role consists in diffusing knowledge.[10] So, competition is the condition for the development of networks.

Furthermore, according to the "leapfrogging" argument, efficient computer and telecommunication markets may potentially enable each country or region to leapfrog some stages which were previously followed by ICT producer countries and ensure a catch-up process often

---

[10] Becchetti and Adriani (2003) analyze the digital divide from the perspective of endogenous growth theory and the incidence of technological progress on gaps between wealthy and poor countries. According to them, the studies in this field make the mistake of considering the knowledge merely as a non-rival good which can be reproduced and diffused on a wide scale through informational devices such as software and databases. As a consequence, knowledge is implicitly considered as integrated to methods of production which are freely accessed in all countries. However, the diffusion and access to this reproduced knowledge with low costs are governed by the lifting of technical constraints such as network ability to transmit rapidly the highest volume of knowledge, network access to individuals and the use of performing computers and terminals connected to networks. Under this hypothesis, they test the relation between ICT diffusion and gross domestic product per inhabitant for 115 countries and show that ICT diffusion is a condition for economic growth.

with better conditions thanks to more recent equipment, more adapted training and so on.

These propositions have given rise to many critics. Thus, Steinmueller (2002) argues against each way of universalizing any digital model to catch up. The benefits of catching-up strategies based on the liberalization of telecommunication markets are limited to some geographic areas and to some economic agents considering their strict conditions of application.[11] These strategies are unlikely to be followed by positive effects in countries where telecommunication and electric infrastructures are poor, scientific and technical knowledge required for local/national industries is not available locally, and skilled labor is sadly lacking. According to Johnston (2001), the liberalization of telecommunication markets has enabled and will enable a reduction in the digital divide in developed countries by decreasing Internet access costs, but it is not the same for the North/South divide because infrastructures do not exist or are insufficient in most less developed countries and peripheral regions. Several conditions are required for developing countries to increase access to ICTs, in particular by giving private investors the confidence they need to make sustainable investments in fixed and mobile telecommunication networks: previous stabilization of the institutional framework, elimination of corruption, implementation of independent regulation agencies with significant power, and national training programs.

From our point of view, it seems important:

- *Not to underestimate market ability to diffuse ICTs because of the very economic nature of these markets*. Due to the presence of high fixed costs and network externalities, they are characterized by an exponential growth (Shapiro and Varian, 1998). Technologies such as mobile phones have been rapidly diffused in all geographic areas and social categories and not only in the OECD countries (see the current Chinese case). This trend will go on. In fact, the ICT industry has faced severe slowdown in its growth since the year 2000. Apart from the bursting of the Internet bubble, this has been caused by the slowness in the design of new contents and services, as well as prices for computer hardware and network access for a large part of the population being too high, especially

---

[11] According to Steinmueller (2001), four conditions must be met for effective implementation of these types of strategies: (1) acquisition of specific competences and adaptation of existing equipment, (2) some initial market conditions for equipment and knowledge exchanges, (3) the necessity of acquiring technologies and complementary abilities and (4) downstream integrated requirements.

in developing countries. This industry is forced to reduce its costs so that it will continue to base its growth on an enlarged dynamics supplied by strong network externalities.

A possible solution would be the relocation of computer and telecommunication industries – so far limited to hardware – such as developing software in India and locating R&D centres for mobile phones in China. It would mean that some developing countries and peripheral regions might attract some industry segments and contribute to a less concentrated geography of ICTs production.

• *To determine the nature of the current limits of the market.* The market expansion faces the insolvency of one part of the potential demand, i.e. insufficient levels of incomes, distance and low density of some geographical areas. To get round the income constraint, the industry has to decrease its costs. But the model of ICTs diffusion which is spread in developing countries through manufacturers and operators (one private computer per individual/household, one private access to the Internet) limits the ability to increase the demand of ICT products in these countries. The reduction of the divide relies on the adoption of other models of diffusion (cheaper terminals as in the network computer configuration, renting instead of purchasing, collective access rather than private, use of open source software). "Market boundaries" are not so much those of the ICTs market in general but rather those of the diffusion model initiated in the USA. Other models of diffusion may solve the problem. But they may go against the current economic interests of leading manufacturers.

In the case where market size is not enough due to low density in rural and distant areas, public initiative is needed. But there are three risks: (1) the opposition of private operators (as noted above), (2) a waste of public funds in case of wrong technological choices (high level of sunk costs associated with rapid technological change) and (3) excessive technological investment regarding the actual or anticipated needs.

• *To extend the market/public intervention debate to other stages of the digital divide instead of the mere question of access to infrastructure.* As mentioned above, the current debate is focused on access. Of course, it proves a necessary condition for reducing the divide. And having access to equipment and networks is now the dominant issue for developing countries and regions. But even if the access issue were solved, the digital divide would still exist at other levels, i.e. those of usage and content. It is obviously more difficult to overcome the divide at these other levels.

25.4.2   Access, uses and contents

Having access to computer equipment and network infrastructures is often considered as an end in itself. But the impact of access on economic performances and social welfare depends on actual uses and particularly on the availability of contents. The relation between ICTs and growth relies on two linkages, which are not spontaneously ensured.

From access to usages

Having a computer or Internet access does not mean using it. Ultimately, usage matters. Unlike computer equipment and network connection, usages are not acquired because of a mere decision to purchase them. They require time and learning process.

To focus on usages rather than access is now topical for public institutions. This shift of emphasis is also supported by scholars. As new competences are required to be able to use ICTs, the recommended solution is to increase investments in human capital – which are often neglected in favor of equipment investments – and to overcome illiteracy. But moving from access to usages is not sufficient. Why are these technologies used? What are they used for? Are there available services?

From usages to services and contents

Behind the digital divide topic, there is a fear of an increasing divergence in economic performances resulting from regions' and countries' uneven capacity to innovate through new products or processes by using ICTs. The expected performances are mainly related to the improvement of organizational efficiency and the development of new markets. It implies not only using technologies but also creating new services and contents.

The relation between ICTs and economic performances has been largely discussed and analyzed in the "productivity paradox" debate. Whichever result may come out (refutation or confirmation of the productivity paradox, see Mairesse, 2002), the great merit of this debate has been to attract attention on the very conditions for ICTs to give rise to economic performance.

In fact, two conditions must be met:

1. As an output, the use of ICTs must lead to new products or services, i.e. the development of new markets. But it takes time.
2. As an input, an efficient use of ICTs requires organizational changes (Brousseau and Rallet, 1999; Brynjolfsson and Hitt, 2000). At the stage of networks, ICTs turn out to be coordination technologies that improve the efficiency of organizations by reducing internal running

costs, improving inter-relations among firms and customer relationships or strengthening ties between public services and citizens, hospitals and patients, universities and students as well. It implies the implementation of new intra- or interorganizational services (intranets, ERP, extranets, CRM, electronic marketplaces) and the production of new contents such as databases, knowledge bases and informational services.

The process has just started because innovation has so far been mainly focused on hardware and network infrastructures. Final services are still not really well developed by comparison with the importance of infrastructures, although in future they might be a source of significant divergence of growth between geographic areas. Regions and countries will differ not only due to uneven capabilities in using ICTs but in making efficient use of ICTs leading to new products and organizational innovations.

To address this issue, relations between access, uses and contents should be stated precisely. In the traditional case of telephone, network access, usage and contents are one and the same thing. Having access to network and benefit from voice service are similar because there is one access, one terminal and one service. The duplication of network accesses, as well as the diversification of terminals and the development of different services on the Internet, lead to more complex links between access, uses and contents.

Literature on the digital divide is grounded in a "push" linear relationship between access, contents and services. The easier the access, the more intense the uses. And the more intense the uses, the greater the number of new services which come out. In these conditions, it proves rational to bear efforts on access. The current policies focused on access might limit disparities. This thesis is partially justified: easy access to technologies and intensive uses are in favor of the emergence of new services and contents. The justification relies on the fact that ICTs are general-purpose technologies whose applications are not defined *ex ante*. Taking advantage of easy access to ICTs and getting accustomed to their use creates a favorable environment for the emergence of value-added services and new contents.

However, there is no mechanical link, especially between usages and contents. Developed uses may not necessarily lead to new contents. For instance, having a DVD player and knowing how to use it does not imply that there are contents ready to be read on this player. The production of contents and services requires (i) complementary investments, and ii) some conditions favorable to the emergence of a market. Services and contents may be considered as complementary goods to access and uses. A large installed base favors the production of contents but does not resolve the famous "chicken and egg" problem induced by the existence of indirect network externalities (Rohlfs, 2001). In the digital divide debate, these problems are neglected because everything is done as if the only services which can be developed on the Internet are communication services. For these services, having a terminal is a sufficient condition for their existence, because they are self-produced by network users (direct externalities). All you have to do is to plug in. That is not the same for informational or transactional services and for contents which must be produced.

However, the production of services (except communication services) and contents strongly depends on the institutional and economic environment. The development of intra-organizational or business-to-business services and contents depends on the very nature of firms and the specific features of industrial organization of their sector. A country or sector in which bureaucratic organizations are dominant and business practices are weakly organized will face difficulties in bringing out new services and digital contents to improve the competitiveness of these firms. The ability to produce services and digital contents for final market depends on a country or region's specialization in competences and know-how required for their implementation. It is easier to produce audiovisual digital contents in regions specialized in cultural industries, e-health services in towns which have important medical competences, e-learning where there is already a concentration of educational institutions, online games where there are video games industries and so on.

The capacity to produce services and digital contents is not only *pushed* by access to infrastructures, it is also *pulled* by existing competences and resources required for services as well as the ability to increase their value through their digitalization. Bigger towns and areas specialized in digitalized services turn out to be mostly favored by taking advantage of complementary competences and an environment suitable for innovation such as "creative atmosphere" (Florida, 2002), venture capital, etc. In this perspective, the digital divide comes from an unequal ability of geographical areas to benefit from network access, i.e. transforming competences and resources into value-added services and digital contents.

The digital divide will be all the more important when the development in wealthy regions is simultaneously pushed by easier access to network infrastructures and pulled by a supply of services and digital contents which lies on specific competences and favorable environment. By contrast, providing easier access in a peripheral region will not be sufficient to reduce it.

25.4.3 Different paths of diffusion

The digital divide debate implicitly sets up the American model of ICTs and Internet diffusion as the reference model against which the level of diffusion in other countries and regions should be evaluated. It is thus dominated by the issue of "backwardness" which measures the delay between the adoption of a technology by the leading country/region and its adoption or diffusion in a given country or region.

Benchmarking methods support this issue, which explicitly aims to line up less advanced experiences on characteristics of the most advanced experience. At a first stage, the purpose is to compare the different access levels with the levels prevailing in the USA (proportion of households having a computer, Internet access, etc.). Secondly, this aim is extended to contents: e-commerce, e-learning, e-health. It is thus observed that some developing countries adopt policies to promote e-commerce under the influence of international institutions (CNUCED, 2004), though their retail trade is still dominated by traditional methods and logistical networks do not exist or are in an embryonic state. In the same way, countries launch themselves into e-learning projects despite the fact that their school system is inadequate. The reproduction of experiences inspired by the most advanced countries can thus lead to inefficient uses. Antonelli (2003) argues that the development of ICTs reflects the specific conditions of the US economy in the earlier 1990s, which was characterized by a great number of skilled workers. The use of these technologies in other countries or regions with different local factors and relative prices cannot lead to the same economic perform-ances. From this point of view, the digital divide could be redefined as the application of technologies initially built and implemented in a particular economic environment to different environments.

The idea of a universal model which would permit all experiences to be assessed and classified comes down to accepting technological deter-minism: ICTs may generate determined models of organization and business-boosting competitiveness. However, ICTs are compatible with very different organizational models (Brousseau and Rallet, 1999). The impact of ICTs depends upon the organizational, institutional, social and cultural environments in which they are implemented. So it proves difficult to anticipate a priori their future effects. Because they are general-purpose technologies, ICTs do not have generic but contingent effects. Even within OECD countries, the models of ICTs diffusion are diversified despite similar levels of development. Scandinavia and Europe are advanced in mobile phones, Japan in some contents and i-mode, the USA in network technologies and some contents and services such as e-commerce. This corresponds to the trajectories taken by the ICT industry in these countries as well as previous economic specializations, urban organization and ways of life.

It is more interesting to show the diversified paths of diffusion from explanatory variables concerning access, usages and provided services and then to redefine the inequalities of diffusion into these paths. It seems clear, for example, that individual computer equipment and access to the Internet cannot constitute a model of reference enabling the evaluation of the digital divide which separates the USA from Africa. Considering the lack of infrastructure and lower incomes, access in Africa is provided via privately or publicly owned collective access points (Chéneau-Loquay, 2002). By contrast, it is meaningful to compare regions or countries whose access relies upon collective solutions.

To simply characterize these various trajectories, let us give two possible values to each part of our three-layer model (access, uses and services):

- Access can be private/individual or public/collective.
- Usages can be sophisticated or simple. This depends essentially on the nature of the terminal. If the terminal is a computer, uses are rather sophisticated because they are based on the "do it yourself" model which characterizes computer products. By contrast, there is the "ready for use" model based on the electronic consumer goods industry. Terminals such as mobile phones and TV are easier to use and usages are simplified due to the ergonomic know-how of the industry.
- Services may result from a commercial supply or a cooperative model based on the role of communities in an economy grounded on non-rival informational goods (see Gensollen in this book).

Therefore, some combinations can be distinguished as many access/uses/service possible trajectories. The "occidental" path, prevailing in the USA and Europe, combines private and individual accesses with "do it yourself" uses and with informational services which are mainly co-operative given the current difficulty of selling informational goods on the Internet. The "Asian" path is quite different because it tends to substitute the "ready to use" usages for computer usages model. From this model emerges an economy of informational commercial services and online transactions (mainly on mobile phone networks). The "Asian" path is mixing "individual private access/simplified uses/online commercial services". The third path concerns developing countries. It is built from collective and public accesses when it takes the way of "do it yourself" uses, but this way seems hopeless. The future is rather on the side of private access/simplified uses from mobile phones/commercial services which are basic, cheaper or subsidized.

25.5 Conclusion

This chapter has sketched the different ways of switching the digital divide issue into a research topic. Beyond its legitimate nature – which inequalities are linked to ICTs and Internet diffusion? – this issue should be analyzed thoroughly so as to elaborate more appropriate policies orientated against the digital divide.

We have first observed that there are different problems according to the level of development and geographical scales (industrialized countries, developing countries, regions, rural/urban). Two major problems are underlined but with unequal intensity according to geographical environment: the concentration of ICTs production and its linkages to ICTs uses, and territorial discrimination by network infrastructures. We have then defined three main research issues: to clarify the "market versus public intervention" debate, to analyze the interdependences between access, uses and contents into a three-layer model, and to define diversified paths of diffusion in order to give sense to the notion of the digital divide.

References

Abreu, Dilip. 1988. "On the Theory of Infinitely Repeated Games with Discounting," *Econometrica*, 56, pp. 383–96.

Adams, Stephen B. and Orville R. Butler. 1999. *Manufacturing the Future: A History of Western Electric*. Cambridge: Cambridge University Press.

Adams, William James and Janet L. Yellen. 1976. "Commodity Bundling and the Burden of Monopoly," *Quarterly Journal of Economics*, 90, August, pp. 475–98.

Adar, Eyta and Bernardo A. Huberman. 2000. "Free Riding on Gnutella," *First Monday*, 5:10, http://www.firstmonday.dk/issues/issue5_10/adar/index.html

Affleck, John. 2000. "IBM shareholders reject return to traditional pension plan," *Associated Press Newswires*, 25 April.

Agence de Régulation des Télécommunications (ART). 2004. *L'intervention des collectivités locales dans les télécommunications*. http://www.art-telecom.fr

Aghion, P. and J. Tirole. 1997. "Formal and Real Authority in Organizations," *Journal of Political Economy*, 105, pp. 1–29.

Akerloff, George. 1970. "The Market for 'Lemons': Quality Uncertainty and the Market Mechanism," *Quarterly Journal of Economics*, 4:3, pp. 488–500.

Albano Gian Luigi and Alessandro Lizzeri, "Strategic Certification and Provision of Quality," *International Economic Review*, 44:1, pp. 267–83, 201.

Alchian, Armen A. 1963. "Reliability of Progress Curves i, Airframe Production," *Econometrica*, 31:4 (Oct.), pp. 679–93.

Allen, Franklin and Anthony M. Santomero. 2001. "What Does Financial Intermediation Do?," *Journal of Banking Finance*, 25, pp. 271–94.

Allen, Franklin, Philip E. Strahan and James McAndrews. 2002. "E-Finance: An Introduction," *Journal of Financial Services Research*, 22:1–2, August/October.

Allen, Robert. 1983. "Collective Invention," *Journal of Economic Behavior and Organization*, 4, pp. 1–24.

Anand, Vineeta. 1999. "Big Blues: IBM's Conversion Draws Watchdogs: Switch to cash balance plan raises concern from lawmakers about age discrimination," *Pensions and Investments*, 6 September, 1.

Andersen, Kim Viborg, Niels Bjorn-Andersen, and Helle Zinner Henriksen. 2003. "Globalization and E-Commerce: Environment and Policy in Denmark," *Communications of the Association for Information Systems*, 12, pp. 218–75.

Anderson, Simon P., André De Palma and Jacques-François Thisse. 1992. *Discrete Choice Theory of Product Differentiation*. Cambridge, MA: MIT Press.

Anderson, Mark C., Rajiv D. Banker, and Sury Ravindran. 2000. "Executive Compensation in the Information Technology Industry," *Management Science*, 46:4, pp. 530–47.

Anderson, Simon P. and Stephen Coate. 2000. "Market Provision of Public Goods: The Case of Broadcasting," NBER Working Paper 7513.

Andreoni, James. 1989. "Giving with Impure Altruism: Applications to Charity and Ricardian Equivalence," *Journal of Political Economy*, 97:6, pp. 1447–58.

Andrews, Dorine C., Jenny Preece, and Murray Turoff. 2001. "A Conceptual Framework for Demographic Groups Resistant to Online Community Interaction," *Proceedings of the 34th International Conference on System Sciences*.

Antonelli, Cristiano. 2003. "The Digital Divide: Understanding the Economics of New Information and Communication Technology in the Global Economy," *Info. Econ. Pol.*, 15, pp. 173–99.

Aoki, Masahiko. 2001. *Towards a Comparative Institutional Analysis*. Cambridge, MA: MIT Press.

Aoyama, Yuko and Manuel Castells. 1994. "Path Towards the Information Society: Employment Structure in the G7 Countries," *International Labour Review*, 133:1, pp. 5–33.

Arditi, Lynn. 2004. "Angry Shareholders, Workers, Retirees Speak Out at IBM's Annual Meeting," *Providence Journal* (RI), 28 April.

Ariely, Dan, Axel Ockenfels, and Alvin Roth. 2003. "An Experimental Analysis of Ending Rules in Internet Auctions," *RAND Journal of Economics*.

Armstrong, Mark. 2002. "Competition in Two-Sided Markets," Oxford University.

Armstrong, Mark, Simon Cowan, and John Vickers. 1994. *Regulatory Reform – Economic Analysis and British Experience*. Cambridge, MA: MIT Press.

Armstrong, Mark and Chris Doyle. 1994. "Interconnection and the Effects of Entry," mimeo.

Arthur, Brian W. 1996. "Increasing Returns and the New World of Business," *Harvard Business Review*, July–August, pp. 100–09.

———. 1989. "Competing Technologies, Increasing Returns, and Lock-In by Historical Events," *Econ. J.*, 99:394, pp. 116–31.

———. 1988. "Competing Technologies: An Overview," in *Technical Change and Economic Theory*, Giovanni Dosi, Chris Freeman, Ryan Nelson, Gerald Silverberg, and Luc Soete, eds. London: Pinter Publishers, pp. 590–607.

———. 1988. "Self-Reinforcing Mechanisms in Economics," in P. W. Anderson, K. J. Arrow, and D. Pines, eds., *The Economy as an Evolving Complex System*. Addison-Wesley.

Artus, Patrick. 2001. *La nouvelle économie*. Paris: La Découverte, Coll. Repères.

Asvanund, Atip, Karen Clay, Ramayya Krishnan, and Michael D. Smith. 2004. "An Empirical Analysis of Network Externalities in Peer-to-Peer Music-Sharing Networks," *Information Systems Research*, 15:2, pp. 155–74.

———. 2003. "Intelligent Club Management in Peer-to-Peer Network," Working Paper, Carnegie Mellon University, Pittsburgh, PA.

Athey, Susan and Philip Haile. 2002. "Identification in Standard Auction Models," *Econometrica*, 70:6, pp. 2107–40.

Au, Yoris A. and Robert J. Kauffman. 2001. "Should We Wait? Network Externalities and Electronic Billing Adoption," *Proceedings of the 34th Hawaii International Conference on System Sciences*.

Aumann, Robert J. 1976. "Agreeing to Disagree," *Annals of Statistics*, 4:6, pp. 1236–39.

Auriol Emmanuelle and Steven Schilizzi. 2003. "Quality Signalling Through Certification Theory and an Application to Agricultural Seed Markets," University of Toulouse.

Axelrod, Robert. 1984. *The Evolution of Cooperation*. New York: Basic Books.

Axelrod, Robert and William D. Hamilton. 1981. "The Evolution of Cooperation," *Science*, 211, pp. 1390–96.

Ba, Sulin and Paul Pavlou. 2002. "Evidence of the Effect of Trust Building Technology in Electronic Markets: Price Premiums and Buyer Behavior," *MIS Quarterly*, 26:3, pp. 243–68.

Bacharach, Michael and Oliver Board. 2002. "The Quality of Information in Electronic Groups," *Netnomics*, 4, pp. 73–97.

Bailey, Joseph. P. 1998. "Electronic Commerce: Prices and Consumer Issues for Three Products: Books, Compact Discs, and Software," Organization for Economic Co-operation and Development, OCDE/GD, (98)4.

——— 1997. "The Economics of Internet Interconnection Agreements," *Internet Economics*, L. McKnight and J. P. Bailey, eds. Cambridge, MA: MIT Press, pp. 155–68.

Bailey, Joseph P. and Yannis Bakos. 1997. "An Exploratory Study of the Emerging Role of Electronic Intermediaries," *International Journal of Electronic Commerce*, 1:3, pp. 7–20.

Bajari, Patrick and Ali Hortaçsu. 2003. "The Winner's Curse, Reserve Prices and Endogenous Entry: Empirical Insights from eBay Auctions," *RAND Journal of Economics*, 3:2, pp. 329–55.

Baker, Malcolm and Jeffrey Wurgler. 2002. "Market Timing and Capital Structure," *J. Finance*, 57:1, pp. 1–32.

Baker, Paul M. A. 2001. "Policy Bridges for the Digital Divide: Assessing the Landscape and Gauging the Dimensions," *First Monday*, 6:5, firstmonday.org.

Bakos, Yannis. 2001. "The Emerging Landscape for Retail E-Commerce," *Journal of Economic Perspectives*, Winter, 15:1, pp. 69–80.

——— 1998. "The Emerging Role of Electronic Marketplaces on the Internet," *Communications of the ACM*, August, 41:8, pp. 35–42.

——— 1997. "Reducing Buyer Search Costs: Implications for Electronic Market Places," *Management Science*, 43:12, pp. 1676–92.

Bakos, Yannis and Erik Brynjolfsson. 2000. "Bundling and Competition on the Internet", Working Paper, New York University – General and Massachusetts Institute of Technology (MIT) – Sloan School of Management.

——— 1999a. "Bundling Information Goods: Pricing, Profits and Efficiency," *Management Science*, December.

——— 1999b. "Aggregation and Disaggregation of Information Goods: Implications for Bundling, Site Licensing and Subscriptions," in *Internet Publishing and Beyond: The Economics of Digital Information and Intellectual Property*, D. Hurley, B. Kahin, and H. Varian, eds. MIT Press.

Bakos, Yannis, Erik Brynjolfsson, and Douglas Lichtman. 1999. "Shared Information Goods," *Journal of Law and Economics*, April.

Bakos, Yannis and Chrysanthos Dellarocas. 2003. "Cooperation Without Enforcement? A Comparative Analysis of Litigation and Online Reputation

as Quality Assurance Mechanisms," Working Paper, New York University –
General and Massachusetts Institute of Technology (MIT) – Sloan School of
Management.

Baldwin, Carliss Y. and Kim B. Clark. 2000. *Design Rules*: Vol.1. *The Power of
Modularity*. Cambridge, MA: MIT Press.

Bank, David. 2004. "New code: After 18-month battle, Oracle finally wins over
PeopleSoft," *Wall Street Journal*, 14 December.

Barbieri, Allen. 1999. CFO of Buy.com, personal communication with Erik
Brynjolfsson, 26 April 2004, in Aliso Viejo, California.

Barclay, Michael J., William G. Christie, Jeffrey H. Harris, Eugene Kandel, and
Paul H. Schultz. 1999. "The Effects of Market Reform on the Trading
Costs and Depths of Nasdaq Stocks," *Journal of Finance*, 54:1, pp. 1–34.

Barclay, Michael J., Terrence Hendershott, and D. Timothy McCormick. 2003.
"Competition among Trading Venues: Information and Trading on Electronic
Communications Networks," *Journal of Finance*, 58:6, pp. 2637–65.

Barley, Steve R. 1986. "Technology as an Occasion for Structuring: Evidence
from Observations of CT Scanners and the Social Order of Radiology
Departments," *Administrative Science Quarterly*, 31, pp. 78–108.

Barlow, John. 2000. "The Next Economy of Ideas. Will copyright survive the
Napster bomb? Nope, but creativity will," *Wired*, October.

1994. "The Economy of Ideas. A framework for rethinking patents and
copyrights in the Digital Age," *Wired*, March.

Baron, David P. 2002. "Private Ordering on the Internet: The eBay Community
of Traders," *Business and Politics*, Nov., 4:3, pp. 245, 30p.

Baron, David and David Besanko. 1984. "Regulation, Asymmetric Information,
and Auditing," *RAND Journal of Economics*, 15:4, pp. 447–70.

Barr, Joe. 1999. "Interview with Richard Stallman *Linux World Today*," 15
August, http://www.linuxworldtoday/f_lwt-indepth7.html

Barrey, S., F. Cochoy, and S. Dubuisson-Quellier. 2000. "Designer, packager et
merchandiser: trois professionnels pour une même scène marchande,"
Sociologie du travail, 42, pp. 457–82.

Barros, Pedro, Hans J. Kind, Tore Nilssen, and Lars Sørgard. 2002. "Media
Competition when the Audience Dislikes Advertising: A Theory of Vertical
Alliances on the Internet," Working Paper, http://www.nhh.no/sam/cv/
paper/barros-kind-nilssen-sorgard-mediaportals.pdf

Bartlett, Chris and Sumantra Ghoshal. 1989. "Managing Across Borders: New
Strategic Requirements," *Sloan Management Review*, 28, pp. 7–17.

Barzel, Yoram. 1989. *Economic Analysis of Property Rights*. Cambridge: Cambridge
University Press.

Bass, Len J., Paul Clements, and Rick Kazman. 1998. *Software Architecture in
Practice*. Addison-Wesley.

Bassett, Ross Knox, 2002. *To the Digital Age: Research Labs, Start-Up Companies,
and the Rise of MOS Technology*. Johns Hopkins University Press.

Baumol, William J., John C. Panzar, and Robert D. Willig. 1982. *Contestable
Markets and the Theory of Industry Structure*. San Diego: Harcourt Brace
Jovanovich.

Baumol, William J. and J. Gregory Sidak, 1994a. "The Pricing of Inputs Sold to
Competitors," *Yale Journal of Regulation*, 11:1, pp. 171–202.

1994b. *Toward Competition in Local Telephony.* MIT Press and the American Enterprise Institute, Washington DC.

Baye, Michael R. and John Morgan. 2001. "Information Gatekeepers on the Internet and the Competitiveness of Homogeneous Product Markets," *Amer. Econ. Rev.*, 91:3, June, pp. 454–74.

2000. "A Simple Model of Advertising and Subscription Fees," *Econ. Letters*, 69, pp. 345–51.

Bayers, Chip. 2000. "Capitalist Econstruction," *Wired*, March.

1996. "The Great Web Wipeout," *Wired*, April.

Beaudouin, V., S. Fleury, M. Pasquier, B. Habert, and C. Licoppe. 2002. "Décrire la toile pour mieux comprendre les parcours." *Réseaux*, 116, pp. 19–51.

Becchetti, Leonardo and Fabrizio Adriani. 2003. "Does the Digital Divide Matter? The Role of ICT in Cross-Country Level and Growth Estimates," CEIS Tor Vergata Research Paper 4, http://www.ssrn.com

Beck, U. 2001. *La société du risque. Sur la voie d'une autre modernité.* Paris: Aubier.

Becker, Gary Stanley, Michael Grossman, and Kevin Murphy. 1994. "An Empirical Analysis of Cigarette Addiction," *American Economic Review*, 84, pp. 396–418.

Bell, Daniel. 1973. *The Coming of Post-Industrial Society.* New York: Basic Books.

Belleflamme, P. 2004. "Versioning in the Information Economy: Theory and Applications," Working Paper.

Bellinger, Bob. 1989. "The Spark of Silicon Valley," *Electronic Engineering Times*, 13 March.

Bender, Christian J. 2003. "Tradable Music Certificates – The Protection of Music as a Global Commons," Working Paper, University of Muenster – International Business.

Benghozi, Pierre-Jean. 2001. "Relations interentreprises et nouveaux modèles d'affaires," *Revue Economique*, Special Issue "Economie de l'Internet," 52, pp. 167–90.

Benghozi, Pierre-Jean and Alberto Bono. 2003. *TICs et nouvelles formes d'organisation dans le secteur de la distribution industrielle européenne*, PREDIT ACISE-TIC proceedings, 199p. http://www.predit.prd.fr/predit3/documentFo.fo?cmd=visualize&inCde=17331

Benghozi, Pierre-Jean and Thomas Paris. 2006. "The Economics and Business Models of Prescription in the Internet," this volume.

2003. "De l'intermédiation à la prescription: le cas de la télévision," *Revue Française de Gestion*, janv.-fév., 142, pp. 205–27.

Benhamou, Eric and Thomas Serval. 2000. "On the Competition Between ECNs, Stock Markets and Market Makers," Financial Market Group Working Papers, no. 345, London School of Economics.

Benkler, Yochai. 2002. "Coase's Penguin, or Linux and the Nature of the Firm." *Yale Law Journal*, 112, pp. 369–446.

2000. "Net Regulation: Taking Stock and Looking Forward," *University of Colorado Law Review*, 203, p. 1233.

Bental, Benjamin and Menahem Spiegel. 1995. "Network Competition, Product Quality and Market Coverage in the Presence of Network Externalities," *Journal of Industrial Economics*, 43:2, pp. 197–208.

Berentsen, Alexander. 1998. "Monetary Policy Implications of Digital Money," *Kyklos*, 51:1, pp. 89–117.

Berg, Joyce, John Dickhaut, and Kevin McCabe. 1995. "Trust, Reciprocity, and Social History," *Games Econ. Behav.*, 10:1, pp. 122–42.

Berg, Sanford V. 1988. "Duopoly Compatibility Standards with Partial Cooperation and Standards Leadership," *Information Economics and Policy*, 3, pp. 35–53.

Berger, Susan and Ronald Dore, eds. 1996. *National Diversity and Global Capitalism*. Ithaca: Cornell University Press.

Bergstrom, Ted, Lawrence E. Blume, and Hal Varian. 1986. "On the Private Provision of Public Goods," *Journal of Public Economics*, 29, pp. 25–49.

Berle, Adolph A. and Gardiner C. Means. 1932. *The Modern Corporation and Private Property*. New York: Macmillan.

Berlin, Leslie. 2001. "Robert Noyce and Fairchild Semiconductor, 1957–1968," *Business History Review*, 75:1, pp. 63–102.

Bernstein, Lisa. 1996. "Merchant Law in a Merchant Court: Rethinking the Code's Search for Immanent Business Norms," *University Pennsylvania. Law Review*, 144(5), pp. 1765–821.

——— 1992. "Opting Out of the Legal System: Extra Legal Contractual Relations in the Diamond Industry," *Journal of Legal Studies*, 21, pp. 115–57.

Bernstein, Peter. 1998. "Are Networks Driving the New Economy?" *Harvard Business Review*, Nov.–Dec., pp. 159–66.

Besen, Stanley M. and Leo J. Raskind. 1991. "An Introduction to the Law and Economics of Intellectual Property," *Journal of Economic Perspectives*, 5, pp. 3–27.

Bessen, James. 2001. "Open Source Software: Free Provision of Complex Public Goods," Working Paper, Research on Innovation.

Bessy, C. and F. Chateauraynaud. 1995. *Experts et faussaires. Pour une sociologie de la perception*. Paris: Metailié.

Best, Michael H. 2001. *The New Competitive Advantage: The Renewal of American Industry*. Oxford University Press.

Betz, David and Jon Edwards. 1986. "Interview with Richard Stallman," *Byte*, july http://www.gnu.org/gnu/byte-interview.html

Bezroukov, Nicolai. 1999. "Open Source Development Software as a Special Type of Academic Research (Critique of Vulgar Raymondism)," First Monday, http://www.firstmonday.dk/issues/issue4_10/bezroukov/index.html

Bhargava Hermant and Juan Feng. 2002. "Paid placement strategies for Internet search engines," eleventh international conference on World Wide Web, Association for Computing Machinery, Honolulu, Hawaii, USA, Session on Auctions and E-commerce.

Bhattacharya, Sudipto, Arnoud W. A. Boot, and Anjan V. Thakor. 1998. "The Economics of Bank Regulation," *J. Money, Credit, Banking*, 30:4, pp. 745–70.

Biais, Bruno, Christophe Bisière, and Chester Spatt. 2003. "Imperfect Competition in Financial Markets: Island versus Nasdaq," IDEI Working Paper.

Biais, Bruno, David Martimort, and Jean-Charles Rochet. 2000. "Competing Mechanisms in a Common Value Environment," *Econometrica*, 68:4, pp. 799–837.

Biglaiser, Gary. 1993. "Middlemen as Experts," *RAND Journal of Economics*, 24, pp. 212–24.

Bisin, Alberto and Danilo Guaitoli. 1998. "Moral Hazard and Non-Exclusive Contracts," CEPR Discussion Papers 1987.

Black, Bernard S. and Ronald J. Gilson. 1998. "Venture Capital and the Structure of Capital Markets: Banks versus Stock Markets," *J. Finan. Econ.*, 47:3, pp. 243–77.

Black, Edwin. 2001. *IBM and the Holocaust: The Strategic Alliance Between Nazi Germany and America's Most Powerful Corporation.* Little, Brown and Company.

Black, Fisher. 1975. "Banks Funds Management in an Efficient Market," *J. Finan. Econ.*, 2, pp. 323–39.

Blass, Asher and Yishay Yafeh. 2001. "Vagabond Shoes Longing to Stray: Why Foreign Firms List in the United States," *J. Banking Finance*, 25:3, pp. 555–72.

Bogenrieder, Irma and Bart Nooteboom. 2003. "Social Structures for Learning," Erasmus University Rotterdam – Erasmus Research Institute of Management (ERIM) and Erasmus University Rotterdam – Faculteit der Bedrijfskunde (FBK).

Böhle, Knud and Malte Krueger. 2001. "Payment Culture Matters: A Comparative EU-US Perspective on the Internet Payments," Institute for Prospective Technological Studies, Background Paper 4.

Boltanski, L. and Thévenot, L. 1991. *De la justification. Les économies de la grandeur.* Paris: Gallimard.

Bolton, Gary E., Elena Katok, and Axel Ockenfels. 2004. "How Effective Are Electronic Reputation Mechanisms? An Experimental Investigation," *Management Science*, 50:11, pp. 1587–602.

Bolton, Patrick and David S. Scharfstein. 1996. "Optimal Debt Structure and the Number of Creditors," *J. Polit. Economy*, 104:1, pp. 1–25.

Bonaccorsi, Andrea and Cristina Rossi. 2003a. "Altruistic Individuals, Selfish Firms? The Structure of Motivation in Open Source Software," Working Paper, Sant'Anna School of Advanced Studies – Laboratory of Economics and Management (L.E.M.).

2003b. "Comparing Motivations of Individual Programmers and Firms to Take Part in the Open Source Movement. From Community to Business," Working Paper, Sant'Anna School of Advanced Studies – Laboratory of Economics and Management (L.E.M.), http://opensource.mit.edu/papers/bnaccorsirossimotivationlong.pdf

2003c. "Contributing to the Common Pool Resources in Open Source Software. A Comparison Between Individuals and Firms," Working Paper, Sant'Anna School of Advanced Studies – Laboratory of Economics and Management (L.E.M.).

2003d. "Licensing Schemes in the Production and Distribution of Open Source Software: An Empirical Investigation," Working Paper, Sant'Anna School of Advanced Studies – Laboratory of Economics and Management (L.E.M.).

2003e. "Why Open Source Software Can Succeed," *Research Policy*, July, 32:7, pp. 1243–58.

Bonanno, Giacomo and John Vickers. 1988. "Vertical Separation," *Journal of Industrial Economics*, 36:3, pp. 257–65.

Boorstin, Eric. 2004. "Music Sales in the Age of File Sharing," Ph Dissertation, Princeton, http://www.princeton.edu/~eboorsti/thesis/

Bork, R. 1978. *The Antitrust Paradox*. New York: Basic Books.

Borrus, Michael and John Zysman. 1997. "Wintelism and the Changing Terms of Global Competition: Prototype of the Future?," BRIE Working Paper 96B, Feb.

Boston Consulting Group. 2002. Survey of free software/open source developers conducted by the Boston Consulting Group. See <http://www.osdn.com/bcg>

Bounie, David and Marc Bourreau. 2004. "Sécurité des paiements et développement du commerce électronique," *Revue Econ.*, 4:55, pp. 689–714.

Boutet, J. 2001. "Le travail devient-il intellectuel?," *Travailler*, 6, pp. 55–70

Bowles, Samuel, Robert Boyd, Ernst Fehr, and Herbert Gintis. 1997. "Homo Reciprocans: A Research Initiative on the Origins, Dimensions, and Policy Implications of Reciprocal Fairness," Working Paper, http://www-unix.oit.umass.edu/~gintis

Boyer, Robert. 1996. "The Convergence Hypothesis Revisited: Globalization but Still the Century of Nations?," in *National Diversity and Global Capitalism*. S. Berger and R. Dore, eds. Ithaca: Cornell University Press.

Braunstein, Yale and Lawrence J. White. 1985. "Setting Technical Compatibility Standards: An Economic Analysis," *The Antitrust Bulletin*, 30, pp. 337–55.

Breton, P. and Proulx, S. 2002. *L'explosion de la communication à l'aube du XXIème siècle*. Paris: La Découverte.

Breu, Karin and Christopher Hemingway. 2002. "Collaborative Processes and Knowledge Creation in Communities-of-Practice," *Creativity and Innovation Management*, 11:3, pp. 147–53.

Brousseau, Eric. 2004a. "Property Rights in the Digital Space," in Enrico Colombatto (ed.), *Companion to Economics of Property Rights*. Cheltenham, UK and Northampton, MA, USA: Edward Elgar Pub., pp. 438–72.

2004b. "Property Rights on the Internet: Is a Specific Institutional Frame Needed?," *Economics of Innovation and New Technology*, 13(5), July, pp. 489–507.

2003. "E-Commerce in France: Did Early Adoption Prevent Its Development?," *The Information Society*, 16:1, pp. 45–57.

2002. "The Governance of Transaction by Commercial Intermediaries: An Analysis of the Re-Engineering of Intermediation by Electronic Commerce," *International Journal of the Economics of Business*, 9:3, Nov., pp. 353–74.

2001. "Régulation de l'Internet: l'autorégulation nécessité-t-elle un cadre institutionnel?," *Revue Economique*, Special Issue, "Economie de l'Internet," ed. by Eric Brousseau and Nicolas Curien, Oct., 52, pp. 349–77.

2000. "Commerce électronique: Ce que disent les chiffres et ce qu'il faudrait savoir," *Economie et Statistiques*, pp. 339–40, 2000–9/10, pp. 147–70 (English translation at http://www.insee.fr/en/ffc/docs_ffc/Is53_339-340.pdf – [Accessed May 2005]).

Brousseau, Eric and Christian Bessy. 2006. "Public and Private Institutions in the Governance of Intellectual Property Rights," in B. Andersen (ed.),

Intellectual Property Rights: Innovation, Governance and the Institutional Environment. Cheltenham, UK and Northampton, MA, USA: Edward Elgar Pub.

Brousseau, Eric and Mhand Fares. 2000. "The Incomplete Contract Theory and the New-Institutional Economics Approaches to Contracts: Substitutes or Complements?," in Claude Ménard (ed.), *Institutions, Contracts, Organizations, Perspectives from New-Institutional Economics.* Cheltenham: Edward Elgar Pub., pp. 399–421.

Brousseau, Eric and Kenneth L. Kraemer. 2003. "Globalization and E-Commerce: The French Environment and Policy," *Communications of the Association for Information Systems,* 10, pp. 73–127.

Brousseau, Eric and Thierry Pénard. 2007. "The Economics of Digital Business Models: A Framework to Analyze the Economics of Assembling," *Review of Network Economics,* vol. 6.

Brousseau, Eric and Alain Rallet (eds.). 1999. *Technologies de l'information et de la communication, organisation et performances économiques,* Paris: Commissariat Général du Plan.

Brousseau, Eric and Raynaud, Emmanuel. 2006. "The Economics of Private Institutions: An Introduction to the Dynamics of Institutional Frameworks and to the Analysis of Multilevel Multi-Type Governance" (18 July, 2006). Available at SSRN: http://ssrn.com/abstract=920225

Brown, Jeffrey R. and Austan Goolsbee. 2002. "Does the Internet Make Markets More Competitive? Evidence from the Life Insurance Industry," *Journal of Political Economy,* 110:3, pp. 481–507.

Browne, Frank X. and David Cronin. 1995. "Payments Technologies, Financial Innovation, Laissez-Faire Banking," *Cato J.,* 15:1.

Browning, John and Spencer Reiss. 1998. "Encyclopedia of New Economy," *Wired,* March, April, and May.

Browning, Larry D. and Judy C. Shetler. 2000. *Sematech: Saving the U.S. Semiconductor Industry.* Texas: A&M Press.

Brynjolfsson, Erik and Lorin M. Hitt. 2000. "Beyond Computation: Information Technology, Organizational Transformation and Business Performance," *J. Econ. Perspect.,* 14:4, pp. 24–48.

Brynjolfsson, Erik and Brian Kahin, eds. 2000. *Understanding the Digital Economy: Data, Tools, and Research.* Cambridge, MA and London: MIT Press, pp. vi, 401.

Brynjolfsson, Erik and Michael Smith. 2000. "Frictionless Commerce? A Comparison of Internet and Conventional Retailers," *Management Science,* 46:4, pp. 563–85.

Bucklin, Louis P. 1966. *A Theory of Distribution Channel Structure.* Berkeley: Institute of Business and Economic Research, University of California.

Bughin, Jacques and John Hagel III. 2000. "The Operational Performance of Virtual Communities – Towards a Successful Business Model?," *Electronic Markets,* Oct., 10:4, pp. 237, 7p.

Bughin, Jacques and Michael Zeisser. 2001. "The Marketing Scale Effectiveness of Virtual Communities," *Electronic Markets,* Dec., 11:4, pp. 258, 5p.

Bullard, James and Bruce D. Smith. 2003. "Intermediaries and Payments Instruments," *J. of Econ. Theory,* 109:2, pp. 172–97.

Bulow, Jeremy and John Roberts. 1989. "The Simple Economics of Optimal Auctions," *Journal of Political Economy*, 97:5, pp. 1060–90.

Burdett, Kenneth and Kenneth L. Judd. 1983. "Equilibrium Price Dispersion," *Econometrica*, 51:4, pp. 955–69.

Burgelman, Robert A. 1994. "Fading Memories: A Process Theory of Strategic Exit in Dynamic Environments," *Administrative Science Quarterly*, 39:1, pp. 24–56.

Burns, Judith. 2000. "SEC tells IBM it can't stop vote on pension plan," *Dow Jones News Service*, 16 Feb.

Burstein, Meyer L. 1960. "The Economics of Tie-In Sales," *Review of Economics and Statistics*, 42:1 (Feb.), pp. 68–73.

Buscatto. 2002. "Les centres d'appels, usines modernes? Les rationalisations paradoxales de la relation téléphonique," *Sociologie du travail*, 44, pp. 99–117

Buzzel, Robert D. 1985. *Marketing in the Electronic Age*. Boston, MA: Harvard Business School Press.

Cabral, Luis. 1990. "On the Adoption of Innovations with 'Network' Externalities," *Mathematical Social Sciences*, 19, pp. 229–308.

Cabral, Luis and Ali Hortaçsu. 2003. "Dynamics of Seller Reputation: Theory and Evidence from eBay," mimeo, University of Chicago.

Cachard, Olivier. 2002. *La régulation internationale du marché électronique*. Paris: LGDJ.

Caillaud, Bernard and Bruno Jullien. 2003. "Chicken and Egg: Competition among Intermediation Service Providers," *RAND Journal of Economics*, Summer, 34:2, pp. 309–28.

2001. "Competing Cybermediaries," *European Economic Review*, May, 45:4–6, pp. 797–808.

Callon, M. 1998. *The Embeddedness of Economic Markets in Economics. The Laws of the Markets*. Oxford: Blackwell, pp. 1–57.

Camerer, Colin. 1998. "Can Asset Markets Be Manipulated? A Field Experiment with Racetrack Betting," *Journal of Political Economy*, 106:3, pp. 457–82.

Camp, Jean. 2001. "Sustainable Open Source Software Business Models," *Creative Destruction: Business Survival Strategies in the Global Internet Economy*. Cambridge, MA and London: MIT Press, pp. 213–28.

Canadian Agency for International Development/ORBICOM. 2002. *Monitoring the Digital Divide*, ITU-Council Working Group on the World Summit on the Information Society, document WG-WSIS/6-E, 21 Sept.

Canter, Laurence and Siegel Martha. 1994. *How to Make a Fortune on the Information Superhighway*. New York: HarperCollins.

Carayol, Nicolas and Jean-Michel Dalle. 2000. "Science wells: Modelling the 'problem of problem choice' within scientific communities," presented at the 5th WEHIA Conference, GREQAM, Marseille, June.

Carbone, James. 2004. "Targeting design," *Purchasing*, 21 Oct.

2002. "Electronics outsourcing: design moves into EMS spotlight," *Purchasing*, 17 Jan.

2000. "Growth means more consolidation, more services," *Purchasing*, 19 Oct.

Cardon, Dominique. 2003. "Cooperation électronique et changement organisationnel," (Electronic Cooperation in Organisational Change. With English summary), *Travail et Emploi*, April, 0:94, pp. 45–50.

Carnoy, Martin, Manuel Castells, Stephen S. Cohen, and Fernando Henrique Cardoso. 1993. *The New Global Economy in the Information Age.* Penn State University Press.

Carpenter, Marie, William Lazonick, and Mary O'Sullivan. 2003. "The Stock Market and Innovative Capability in the New Economy: The Optical Networking Industry," *Industrial and Corporate Change*, 12:5, pp. 963–1034.

Casadesus-Masanell, Ramón and Pankaj Ghemawat. 2003. "Dynamic Mixed Duopoly: A Model Motivated by Linux vs. Windows," Working Paper, Harvard University – Competition and Strategy Unit and Harvard University – Competition and Strategy Unit.

Caselli, Francesco and Wilbur John Coleman II. 2001. "Cross-Country Technology Diffusion: The Case of Computers," *The American Economic Review*, 91:2, pp. 328–35.

Cassidy, John. 2002. *dot.con: The Greatest Story Ever Sold.* Penguin.

Castro, Janice. 1995. "Just Click to Buy. Madison Avenue meets the online world and neither will be the same again," *Time*, special issue *Welcome to Cyberspace*, March.

Cawley, Richard. 2004. "The New Approach to Economic Regulation in the Electronic Communications Sector in Europe: The Application of Regulatory Remedies," *Journal of Network Industries*, 9, pp. 3–22.

Chan, Calvin M. L., Mamata Bandhar, Lih-Bin Oh, and Hock-Chuan Chan. 2004. "Recognition and Participation in a Virtual Community," *Proceedings of the 37th International Conference on System Sciences*, pp. 1–10.

Chandler Jr., Alfred D. 2001. *Inventing the Electronic Century: The Epic Story of the Consumer Electronic and Computer Industries.* Free Press.

1990. *Scale and Scope: The Dynamics of Industrial Capitalism.* Belknap Press.

1977. *The Visible Hand: The Managerial Revolution in American Business.* Harvard University Press.

1962. *Strategy and Structure: Chapters in the History of the American Industrial Enterprise.* MIT Press.

Chase, Marilyn. 1983. "The chip race," *Wall Street Journal*, 4 Feb.

Chatterjee, Kalyan and William Samuelson. 1983. "Bargaining Under Incomplete Information," *Operations Research*, 31:5, pp. 835–51.

Che, Yeon-Koo. 1996. "Customer Return Policies for Experience Goods," *J. Ind. Econ.*, 44, pp. 17–24.

Chemmanur, Thomas J. and Paolo Fulghieri. 1999. "A Theory of the Going Public Decision," *Rev. Finan. Stud.*, 12:2, pp. 249–79.

Chen, Tain-Jy. 2003. "Globalization of E-Commerce: Environment and Policy of Taiwan," *Communications of the Association for Information Systems*, 12, pp. 326–53.

Chen, Yubo, Scott Fay, and Qi Wang. 2003. "Marketing Implications of Online Consumer Product Reviews," University of Florida Working Paper.

Chen, Yuxin, Ganesh Iyer, and V. Paddy Padmanabhan. 2002. "Referral Infomediaries and Retail Competition," Working Paper, New York University – Department of Marketing, University of California,

Berkeley – Marketing Group, and Washington University, St. Louis – John M. Olin School of Business.

Chéneau-Loquay, Annie. 2002. "Modes d'accès et d'utilisation d'Internet en Afrique: les grandes tendances," *Africa e Mediterraneo*, 41, pp. 12–5.

Chesbrough, Henry and Richard S. Rosenbloom. 2002. "The Role of the Business Model in Capturing Value from Innovation: Evidence from Xerox Corporation's Technology Spin-Off Companies," Working Paper, Industrial and Corporate Change, Entrepreneurial Management Unit and Harvard Business School.

Chevalier, Judith A. and Dina Mayzlyn. 2006. "The Effect of Word of Mouth on Sales: Online Book Reviews," *Journal of Marketing Research*, 43:3, pp. 345–54.

Chinn, Menzie David and Robert W. Fairlie. 2004. "The Determinants of the Global Digital Divide: A Cross-Country Analysis of Computer and Internet Penetration," NBER Working Paper W10686, http://www.econ.yale.edu/~egcenter

Chircu, Alina M. and Robert J. Kauffman. 1999. "Strategies for Internet Middlemen in the Intermediation/Disintermediation/Reintermediation Cycle," *Electronic Markets*, 9:2, pp. 109–17.

Cho, In-Koo and David M. Kreps. 1987. "Signaling Games and Stable Equilibria," *Quart. J. Econ.*, 102, pp. 179–221.

Choi, Jay Pil. 1998. "Tying and Innovation: A Dynamic Analysis of Tying Arrangements," Columbia University Working Paper.

Chou, Chien-fu and Oz Shy. 1990a. "Do Consumers Always Gain when More People Buy the Same Brand?," mimeo.

1990b. "Supporting Services and the Choice of Compatibility," mimeo.

1990c. "Partially Compatible Brands and Consumer Welfare," mimeo.

Chowdhry, Bhagwan and Vikram Nanda. 1991. "Multimarket Trading and Market Liquidity," *Review of Financial Studies*, 4:3, pp. 483–511.

Christie, William G. and Paul H. Schultz. 1994. "Why Do Nasdaq Market Makers Avoid Odd-Eighth Quotes?," *Journal of Finance*, 49:4, pp. 1813–40.

Church, Jeffrey and Niel Gandal. 1992a. "Integration, Complementary Products, and Variety," *Journal of Economics and Management Strategy*, 1:4, pp. 653–75.

1992b. "Network Effects, Software Provision and Standardization," *Journal of Industrial Economics*, 40:1, pp. 85–104.

1990. "Complementary Network Externalities and Technological Adoption," *International Journal of Industrial Organization*, 11, pp. 239–60.

Clay, Karen, Ramayya Krishnan, and Eric Wolff. 2001. "Prices and Price Dispersion on the Web: Evidence from the Online Book Industry," NBER Working Paper 8271.

Clay, Karen, Ramayya Krishnan, Eric Wolff, and Danny Fernandes. 2001. "Retail Strategies on the Web: Price and Non-Price Competition in the Online Book Industry," *Journal of Industrial Economics*, 50:3, pp. 351–67.

Clemons, Eric, Il-Horn Hann, and Lorin M. Hitt. 2002. "Price Dispersion and Differentiation in Online Trave: An Empirical Investigation," *Management Science*, 48:4, pp. 534–49.

1998. "The Nature of Competition in Electronic Markets: An Empirical Investigation of Online Travel Agent Offerings," Working Paper, the Wharton School of the University of Pennsylvania, June.

Clemons, Eric K., Lorin M. Hitt, Bin Gu, Matt E. Thatcher, and Bruce W. Weber. 2002. "Impacts of E-Commerce and Enhanced Information Endowments on Financial Services: A Quantitative Analysis of Transparency, Differential Pricing, and Disintermediation," *Journal of Financial Services Research*, 22:1–2, Aug./Oct.

Coase, Ronald H. 1960. "The Problem of Social Cost," *J. Law Econ.*, 3, pp. 1–44.

1937. "The Nature of the Firm," *Economica*, 4, pp. 386–405.

Cochoy, F. 2002. *Une sociologie du packaging, ou l'âne de Buridan face au marché.* Paris: Presses Universitaires de France.

1999. *Une histoire du marketing. Discipliner l'économie de marché.* Paris: La Découverte.

Cochrane, John H. 2005. "The Risk and Return of Venture Capital," *Journal of Financial Economics*, 75:1, pp. 3–52.

Coffee, John C. 2002. "Understanding Enron: It's about the Gatekeepers, Stupid," Columbia Law School, Working Paper no. 207.

Cohen, Adam. 2002. *The Perfect Store: Inside eBay.* Little Brown & Company, p.1.

Cohen, Daniel and Michèle Debonneuil. 2000. *Nouvelle économie*, Rapport du Conseil d'Analyse Economique. Paris: La Documentation Française.

Cohen, Stephen S. and Gary Fields. 1999. "Social Capital and Capital Gains in Silicon Valley," *California Management Review*, 41:2, pp. 108–30.

Colby, Dean. 2001. "Conceptualizing the 'Digital Divide': Closing the 'Gap' by Creating a Postmodern Network that Distributes the Productive Power of Speech," *Communication, Law and Policy*, 6, pp. 123–4.

Colecchia, Alessandra and Paul Schreyer. 2001. "ICT Investment and Economic Growth in the 1990s: Is the United States a Unique Case? A Comparative Study of Nine OECD Countries," STI Working Paper 2001/7, OECD.

Compaine, Benjamin. 2000. "Re-Examining the Digital Divide," Working Paper, Internet and Telecoms Convergence Consortium, MIT, http://itel. mit.edu/itel/docs/jun00/digdivide.pdf

Conrad, Jennifer, Kevin M. Johnson, and Sunil Wahal. 2003. "Institutional Trading and Alternative Trading Systems," *Journal of Financial Economics*, 70:1, pp. 99–134.

Constant, David, Sara Kiesler, and Lee Sproull. 1994. "What's Mine Is Ours, or Is It? A Study of Attitudes about Information Sharing," *Information Systems Research*, 5:4, pp. 400–21.

Cooke, Sandra D. 2003. "Information Technology Workers in the Digital Economy," in US Department of Commerce, *The Digital Economy 2003*, Chapter 2, online at https://www.esa.doc.gov/2003.cfm

Cooper, Michael J., Orlin Dimitrov, and P. Raghavendra Rau. 2001. "A Rose. Com by Any Other Name," *J. Finance*, 56, pp. 2371–88.

Cooter, Robert D. 1996. "Decentralized Law for a Complex Economy: The Structural Approach to Adjudicating for the New Law Merchant," *University of Pennsylvania Law Review*, pp. 1643–96.

1994. "Structural Adjudication and the New Law Merchant: A Model of Decentralized Law," *International Review of Law and Economics*, 14, pp. 215–31.

Copeland, Tom, Tim Koller, and Jack Murrin. 2000. *Valuation. Measuring and Managing the Value of Companies*. New York: Wiley, 3rd edition.

Coppinger, Vicki, Vernon Smith, and Jon Titus. 1980. "Incentives and Behavior in English, Dutch and Sealed-Bid Auctions," *Economic Inquiry*, 43, pp. 1–22.

Corbett, Charles and Uday Karmakar. 1999. "Optimal Pricing Strategies for an Information Intermediary," technical report, UCLA Andersen Graduate School of Management, Working Paper, pp. 99–101.

Cornelli, Francesca and Oved Yosha. 2003. "Stage Financing and the Role of Convertible Securities," *Rev. Econ. Stud.*, 70:1, pp. 1–32.

Cortese, Amy. 1997. "A Way Out of the Web Maze," *Business Week*, 24 Feb.

Cournot, Augustin. 1927. *Researches into the Mathematical Principles of the Theory of Wealth*, N. T. Bacon trans., original work published 1838. New York: Macmillan.

Cousin, O. 2002. "Les ambivalences du travail. Les salariés peu qualifiés dans les centres d'appel," *Sociologie du travail*, 44, pp. 499–520.

Cox, Howard and Simon Mowatt. 2004. "Consumer-Driven Innovation Networks and E-Business Management Systems", *Qualitative Market Research: An International Journal*, 7:1, pp. 9–11.

Cox, James C. 2000. "Implications of Game Triads for Observations of Trust and Reciprocity," Working Paper.

Cox, James C., Bruce Roberson and Vernon Smith. 1982. "Theory and Behavior of Single Object Auctions," in *Research in Experimental Economics*, Vernon L. Smith, ed. JAI Press.

Coy, Peter. 2002. "Going, Going, Gone . . . Sucker!," *Business Week*, 20 March.

Crawford, Vincent and Joel Sobel. 1982. "Strategic Information Transmission," *Econometrica*, 50:6, pp. 1431–51.

Crémer, Jacques. 1984. "On the Economics of Repeat Buying," *RAND J. Econ.*, 15, pp. 396–403.

Crémer, Jacques, Patrick Rey, and Jean Tirole. 2000. "Connectivity in the Commercial Internet," *Journal of Industrial Economics*, 48, pp. 433–72.

Cronin, Charles. 2002. "Music Copyright Infringement Online Archive," Working Paper, Columbia University – Columbia Law School.

Crystal, Graef. 1991. *In Search of Excess: The Overcompensation of American Executives*. W. W. Norton.

1978. *Executive Compensation*. American Management Association.

Curien, Nicolas. 2004. "Auto-organisation de la demande: apprentissage par infomédiation," *Revue d'Economie Politique*, 113, pp. 43–60.

Curien, Nicolas and Emmanuelle Fauchart. 2003. "Reseaux d'infomediation et auto-organisation de la demande" (with English summary), *Revue d'Economie Industrielle*, Special Issue 2nd–3rd Trimesters, 0:103, pp. 131–53.

Curien, Nicolas, Emmanuelle Fauchart, Gilbert Laffond, Jean Lainé, Jacques Lesourne, and François Moreau. 2001. "Forums de consommation sur Internet: un modèle évolutionniste," *Revue Econ.* "Economie de l'Internet", Oct., 52, pp. 119–35.

2000. "Surfing on the Net as a Source of Market Segmentation: A Self-Organization Approach," *Communications and Strategies*, 40, pp. 125–37.

Curien, Nicolas and Michel Gensollen. 1992. *Economie des télécommunications: ouverture et réglementation.* Paris: Economica.

Curien, Nicolas, Gilbert Laffond, Jean Lainé, and François Moreau. 2004. "To Contribute or Not to Contribute in Online Communities," Working Paper, CNAM.

Curran, Lawrence J. 1997. "An expanding universe (growth of electronics contract manufacturers)," *Electronic Business Today*, 1 Aug.

D'Adderio, Luciana. 2003. "Configuring Software, Reconfiguring Memories: The Influence of Integrated Systems on the Reproduction of Knowledge and Routines," *Industrial and Corporate Change*, April, 12:2, pp. 321–50.

Dai, Qizhi and Robert J. Kauffman. 2002. "B2B E-Commerce Revisited: Leading Perspectives on the Key Issues and Research Directions," *Electronic Markets*, Mar., 12:2, pp. 67–83.

Dalcher, Darren. 2003. "Beyond Normal Failures: Dynamic Management of Software Projects," *Technology Analysis and Strategic Management*, Special Issue Dec., 15:4, pp. 421–39.

Dale, Arden. 2004a. "Judge rules IBM must make back payments in pension case," *Dow Jones Newswires*, 18 Feb.

2004b. "Update: IBM pension settlement leaves unresolved issues," *Dow Jones News Service*, 30 Sept.

Dalle, Jean-Michel. 1997. "Heterogeneity vs. Externalities: A Tale of Possible Technological Landscapes," *Journal of Evolutionary Economics*, 7, pp. 395–413.

Dalle, Jean-Michel and Paul A. David. 2001. "On Open Source Software and the Organization of Cathedral-Building: Metaphors and Realities," Working Paper, SIEPR-NOSTRA Project on the Economics of Open Source Software, December, revised version submitted to *First Monday*.

Dalle, Jean-Michel and Paul A. David. 2003/2005. "The Allocation of Software Development Resources in 'Open Source' Production Mode," Ch. 16, in *Perspectives on Free and Open Source and Free Software*, J. Feller, et al., eds., Cambridge MA: MIT Press. [2003 preprint available at: http://siepr. stanford.edu/papers/pdf/02-27.pdf]

Dalle, Jean-Michel, Paul A. David, Rishab Aiyer Ghosh, and W. Edward Steinmueller. 2005. "Advancing Economic Research on the Free and Open Source Software Mode of Production" (in *Building Our Digital Future: Future Economic, Social and Cultural Scenarios Based on Open Standards*, Marleen Wynants and Jan Cornelis, eds. Brussels: Vrije Universiteit Brussels (VUB)). [Pre-print as SIEPR Discussion Paper (December 2004) available at: http://siepr.stanford.edu/programs/ OpenSoftware_David/NSFOSF_Publications.html]

Dalle, Jean-Michel, Paul A. David, Rishab Aiyer Ghosh, and Frank Wolak. 2004. "Free and Open Source Software Developers and the Economy of 'Regard': A Quantitative Analysis of Code-Signing Patterns Within the Linux Kernel," paper presented to the EPIP3 Seminar, Schuola Superiore Sant'Anna, Pisa, April, and to the Oxford Workshop on Libre Software (OWLS), Oxford Internet Institute, June.

Dalle, Jean-Michel, Paul A. David, Rishab Aiyer Ghosh and W. Edward Steinmueller. 2005. "Advancing Economic Research on the Free and

Open Source Software Mode of Production" (in *How Open Will the Future Be? Social and Cultural Scenarios Based on Open Standards and Open-Source Software*, eds. M. Wynants and J. Cornelis, Brussels: VUB Press. [Previous version available at: http://siepr.stanford.edu/papers/pdf/04-03.html]

Dalle, Jean-Michel and Nicolas Jullien. 2003. "'Libre' Software: Turning Fads into Institutions?," *Research Policy*, Jan., 32(1), pp. 1–11.

———. 2000. "NT vs. Linux, or Some Explorations into the Economics of Free Software," in *Application of Simulation to Social Sciences*, G. Ballot and G. Weisbuch, eds. Paris, France: Hermès, pp. 399–416.

Dang-Nguyen, Godefroy and Thierry Pénard. 2007. "Network Cooperation and Incentives Within Online Communities," This volume.

———. 2001. "Interaction et coopération en réseau: un modèle de gratuité" (Interaction and Cooperation Inside Internet Communities. With English summary), *Revue Economique*, Special Issue "Economie de l'Internet," Oct., 52, pp. 57–76.

Darbi Michael and Edi Karni. 1973. "Free Competition and the Optimal Amount of Fraud," *Journal of Law and Economics*, 16, pp. 67–88.

Dasgupta, Partha and Paul A. David. 1994. "Toward a New Economics of Science," *Research Policy*, 23:5, pp. 487–521.

———. 1987. "Information Disclosure and the Economics of Science and Technology," ch. 16 in *Arrow and the Ascent of Modern Economic Theory*, G. Feiwel, ed. New York: New York University Press, pp. 519–42.

Dasgupta, Susmita, Somik Lall, and David Wheeler. 2002. "Policy Reform, Economic Growth, and the Digital Divide: An Econometric Analysis," World Bank Working Paper 2567, http://econ.worldbank.org

D'Aspremont, Claude, Jean Jaskold Gabszewicz, and Jean-François Thisse. 1979. "On Hotelling's Stability in Competition," *Econometrica*, 47, pp. 1145–50.

David, Paul A. 2004. "Understanding the Emergence of Open Science Institutions: Functionalist Economics in Historical Context," *Industrial and Corporate Change*, 13:1, Aug.

———. 2003. "The Economic Logic of 'Open Science' and the Balance Between Private Property Rights and the Public Domain in Scientific Data and Information: A Primer," in National Research Council, *The Role of the Public Domain in Scientific Data and Information*. Washington, DC: National Academy Press.

———. 2002a. "La coopération, la créativité et la culture des débats dans les sciences," in *Institutions et innovation: de la recherche aux systèmes sociaux d'innovation*" (sous la direction de Jean-Phillipe Touffut). Paris: Bibliothèque Albin Michel Economie, pp. 67–104.

———. 2002b. "Cooperation, Creativity and Closure in Scientific Research Networks: Modeling the Simpler Dynamics of Invisible Colleges," SIEPR/CEEG-Social Science and Technology Seminar Series Paper (4 December). [Available at: http://siepr.stanford.edu/programs/SST_Seminars/David_All.pdf]

———. 2001a. "Tragedy of the Public Knowledge 'Commons'? Global Science, Intellectual Property and the Digital Technology Boomerang," Research Memoranda 003, Maastricht: MERIT, Maastricht Economic Research Institute on Innovation and Technology.

2001b. "Path Dependence, Its Critics and the Quest for 'Historical Economics,'" in *Evolution and Path Dependence in Economic Ideas: Past and Present*, eds. P. Garrouste and S. Ioannidies. Cheltenham, Glos.: Edward Elgar.

2000. "Patronage, Reputation, and Common Agency Contracting in the Scientific Revolution: From Keeping 'Nature's Secrets' to the Institutionalization of 'Open Science,'" (unpublished; under review at *Journal of Economic History*).

2000. "Understanding Digital Technology's Evolution and the Path of Measured Productivity Growth: Present and Future in the Mirror of the Past," in Eric Brynjolfsson and Brian Kahin (eds.), *Understanding the Digital Economy*. MIT Press, pp. 49–95.

1998a. "Communication Norms and the Collective Cognitive Performance of Invisible Colleges," in *Creation and Transfer of Knowledge: Institutions and Incentives*, Physica-Verlag series Contributions to Economics, G. Barba Navaretii et al., eds. Berlin, Heidelberg, New York: Springer-Verlag.

1998b. "Common Agency Contracting and the Emergence of 'Open Science' Institutions," *American Economic Review*, May, 88(2), pp. 15–21.

1990. "The Dynamo and the Computer: An Historical Perspective on the Modern Productivity Paradox," *American Economic Review* (Papers and Proceedings), 80:2, pp. 355–61.

1985, "Clio and the Economics of QWERTY," *American Economic Review*, 75(2), pp. 332–37.

David, Paul A., Andrew H. Waterman, and Seema Arora. 2003. "FLOSS-US: The Free/Libre Open Source Software Developer Survey for 2003: A First Report," September. [Available at: http://www.stanford.edu/group/floss-us/report/ FLOSS-US-Report.pdf]

De Bijl, Paul W.J. and Sanjeev Goyal. 1995. "Technological Change in Markets with Network Externalities," *International Journal of Industrial Organization* 13(3), pp. 307–25.

De Fornel, M. 1994. "Le cadre interactionnel de l'échange visiophonique," *Réseaux*, 64.

De La Pradelle, M. 1996. *Les Vendredis de Carpentras. Faire son marché à Paris ou ailleurs*. Paris: Fayard.

DeBare, Ilana. 1997. "Intel options go companywide," *San Francisco Chronicle*, 12 Feb.

Dedrick, Jason and Kenneth. L. Kraemer. 1998. *Asia's Computer Challenge: Threat or Opportunity for the United States and the World?* New York: Oxford University Press.

Deffains, Bruno and Philippe Fenoglio. 2001. "Economie et ordre juridique de l'espace virtuel," *Revue Economique*, 52, pp. 331–47.

Degeratu, Alexandru, Arvind Rangaswamy, and Jianan Wu. 1998. "Consumer Choice Behavior in Online and Regular Stores: The Effects of Brand Name, Price, and Other Search Attributes," presented at Marketing Science and the Internet, MIT/INFORMS College on Marketing Mini-Conference. Cambridge, MA, 6–8 March.

Degryse, Hans, Mark Van Achter, and Gunther Wuyts. 2003. "Dynamic Order Submission Strategies with Competition Between a Dealer Market and a Crossing Network," Working Paper, K. U. Leuven.

Dellarocas, Chrysanthos N. 2004. "Strategic Manipulation of Internet Opinion Forums: Implications for Consumers and Firms," MIT Sloan Working Paper no. 4501–04, http://ccs.mit.edu/dell/papers/onlineopinionforums.pdf

2003. "The Digitization of Word-of-Mouth: Promise and Challenges of Online Reputation Mechanisms," *Management Science*, 49:10, pp. 1407–24.

2003. "Efficiency and Robustness of Binary Feedback Mechanisms in Trading Environments with Moral Hazard," Working Paper, Massachusetts Institute of Technology (MIT) – Sloan School of Management.

2001. "Building Trust On-Line: The Design of Reliable Reputation Reporting: Mechanisms for Online Trading Communities," Working Paper 4180–01, Massachusetts Institute of Technology (MIT) – Sloan School of Management, http://papers.ssrn.com/ sol3/papers.cfm?abstract_id=289967

Dellarocas, Chrysanthos, Ming Fan, and Charles A. Wood. 2004. "Self-Interest, Reciprocity, and Participation in Online Reputation Systems," MIT Sloan Working Paper 4500–04, http://ssrn.com/abstract=585402

Delong, Bradford. 2003. "Don't Worry about Deflation," *Wired*, Aug.

Demers, Elizabeth and Katharina Lewellen. 2003. "The Marketing Role of IPOs: Evidence from Internet Stocks," *J. Finan. Econ.*, 68:3, pp. 413–37.

Dempsey, Bert J., Debra Weiss, Paul Jones, and Jane Greenberg. 2002. "Who Is an Open Source Software Developer?," *Communications of the ACM*, 45:2, pp. 67–72.

1999. "A Quantitative Profile of a Community of Open Source Linux Developers," SILS Tech. Rep. TR-1999–05, School of Information and Library Science, University of North Carolina at Chapel Hill, October. [Available at: www.metalab.unc.edu/osrt/].

Deneckere, Raymond, and Carl Davidson. 1985. "Incentives to Form Coalitions with Bertrand Competition," *RAND J. Econ.*, 16, pp. 473–86.

Dennis, Reid. 2000. "Institutional Venture Partners," in Udayan Gupta, ed., *Done Deals: Venture Capitalists Tell Their Stories.* Harvard Business School Press, pp. 179–90.

Dertouzos, Michael L. 1997. *What Will Be: How the New World of Information Will Change our Lives.* New York: HarperEdge.

DeSanctis, Gerardine, Matthew Wright, and Lu Jiang. 2001. "Building a Global Learning Community," *Communications of the ACM*, Dec., 44:12, pp. 80–3.

Dewan, Rajiv, Bing Jing, and Abraham Seidmann. 2001. "Product Customization and Price Competition on the Internet," Working Paper, New York University – Information Systems and Simon School, University of Rochester.

Dewan, Sanjeev and Vernon Hsu. 2001. "Trust in Electronic Markets: Price Discovery in Generalist Versus Specialty Online Auctions," mimeo, University of Washington Business School.

Dewatripont, Mathias and Eric Maskin. 1995. "Credit and Efficiency in Centralized and Decentralized Economies," *Rev. Econ. Stud.*, 62:4, pp. 541–65.

DeYoung, Robert. 2003. "The Performance of Internet-Based Business Models: Evidence from the Banking Industry," *Journal of Business*, 21 April.

Diamond, Douglas W. and Phillip H. Dybvig. 1983. "Bank Runs, Deposit Insurance, and Liquidity," *J. Polit. Economy*, 91:3, pp. 401–9.

Diamond, Peter. 1984. *A Search-Equilibrium Approach to the Micro Foundations of Macroeconomics*. Cambridge, MA: MIT Press.

——. 1982. "Aggregate Demand Management in Search Equilibrium," *Journal of Political Economy*, 90, pp. 881–94.

DiCarlo, Lisa. 1999. "IBM cashes in: Wielding a massive arsenal of patents Big Blue shakes up the high-tech industry," *PCWeek*, 20 September.

DiBona, Chris, Sam Ockman and Mark Stone, eds. 1999. *Open Sources: Voices from the open source revolution*. Sebastopol: O'Reilly.

DiMaggio Paul et al. 2004. "Digital Inequality: From Unequal Access to Differentiated Use," in *Social Inequality*, Kathryn Neckerman, ed. New York: Russell Sage Foundation, pp. 355–400.

Dixit, Avinash K. and Robert S. Pyndick R. 1994. *Investment under Uncertainty*. Princeton: Princeton University Press.

Dodier, N. 2003. *Leçons politiques de l'épidémie de sida*. Paris: Editions de l'EHESS.

Domis, Olaf de Senerpont. 2003. "Latitude for change," *Daily Deal*, 1 Dec. 2003.

Domowitz, Ian. 2002. "Liquidity, Transaction Costs, and Reintermediation in Electronic Markets," *Journal of Financial Services Research*, 22:1–2, Aug./ Oct., pp. 141–57.

Domowitz, Ian and Benn Steil. 1999. "Automation, Trading Costs, and the Structure of the Trading Services Industry," *Brookings-Wharton Papers on Financial Services*, R. E. Litan and A. M. Santomero, eds.

Donath, Judith S. 1999. "Identity and Deception in the Virtual Community," in *Communities in Cyberspace*, Marc Smith and Peter Kollock, eds. London: Routledge Press.

Dönges, Jutta and Frank Heinemann. 2001. "Competition for Order Flow as a Coordination Game," Finance and Accounting Working Paper, no. 64, Goethe-University Frankfurt.

Donlan, Thomas. 2000. "Cisco's bids," *Barron's*, 8 May, pp. 31–4.

Dorn, James. 1999. "L'avènement des monnaies privées," in Henri Lepage and Patrick Wajsman (eds.), *Vingt économistes face à la crise*. Paris: Editions Odile Jacob.

Dossani, Rafiq and Martin Kenney. 2004. "The Next Wave of Globalization: Exploring the Relocation of Service Provision to India," Palo Alto: Asia/ Pacific Research Center, Stanford University, Working Paper.

Dudey, Marc. 1990. "Competition by Choice: The Effect of Consumer Search on Firm Location Decisions," *American Economic Review*, 80(5), pp. 1092–104.

Dukes Anthony and Esther Gal-Or, "Negotiations and exclusivity contracts for advertising," 12th Southeast Economic Theory and International Economics Meetings, 2001.

Durett, Richard and Simon A. Levin. 1994. "The Importance of Being Discrete and Spatial," *Theor. Popul. Biol.*, 46, pp. 363–94.

Dybvig, Philip H. and Chester S. Spatt. 1983. "Adoption Externalities as Public Goods," *Journal of Public Economics*, 20, pp. 231–47.

Dyson, Esther. 1996. "Netscape's Secret Weapon," interview with Jim Barksdale, *Wired*, March.

——. 1995. "Intellectual Value," *Wired*, July.

Eaton, B. Curtis. 1982. "An Economic Theory of Central Places," *Econ. J.*, 92, pp. 56–72.

1976. "Free Entry in One-Dimensional Models: Pure Profits and Multiple Equilibria," *J. Reg. Sci.*, 16, pp. 21–33.

Eaton, David H. 2002. "Valuing Information: Evidence from Guitar Auction on eBay," mimeo, Murray State University.

Economides, Nicholas. 2005a. "The Economics of the Internet Backbone," in Ingo Vogelsang (ed.) *Handbook of Telecommunications*. Amsterdam: Elsevier Publishers. [Pre-publication copy at http://www.stern.nyu.edu/networks/ Economides_ECONOMICS_OF_THE_INTERNET_BACKBONE.pdf]

2005b. "Telecommunications Regulation: An Introduction," in Richard R. Nelson, ed., *The Limits and Complexity of Organizations*, Russell Sage Foundation Press, New York. [Pre-publication copy at http://www.stern. nyu.edu/networks/Economides_Telecommunications_Regulation.pdf]

1996. "The Economics of Networks," *International Journal of Industrial Organization*, 14:2, March, pp. 673–99.

1996a. "Network Externalities, Complementarities, and Invitations to Enter," *European Journal of Political Economy*, 12, pp. 211–32.

1996b. "Vertical Integration and Compatibility of Complementary Components," mimeo.

1996c. "The Economics of Networks," *International Journal of Industrial Organization*, Oct., 14:6, pp. 673–99.

1994a. "How to Enhance Market Liquidity," in R. A. Schwartz, ed., *Global Equity Markets*. New York: Irwin Professional.

1994b. "Quality Choice and Vertical Integration," Discussion Paper EC-94-22, Stern School of Business, N.Y.U.

1993a. "Network Economics with Application to Finance," *Financial Markets, Institutions and Instruments*, 2(5), pp. 89–97.

1993b. "A Monopolist's Incentive to Invite Competitors to Enter in Telecommunications Services," in G. Pogorel, ed., *Global Telecommunications Services and Technological Changes*. Amsterdam: Elsevier.

1993c. "Mixed Bundling in Duopoly," Discussion Paper EC-93-29, Stern School of Business, N.Y.U.

1992. "Liquidity and Markets," in *New Palgrave Dictionary of Finance*.

1991a. "Compatibility and the Creation of Shared Networks," in M. Guerin-Calvert and S. Wildman (eds.), *Electronic Services Networks: A Business and Public Policy Challenge*. New York: Praeger Publishing Inc.

1991b. "Compatibility and Market Structure," Discussion Paper EC-91-16, Stern School of Business, N.Y.U.

1989a. "Desirability of Compatibility in the Absence of Network Externalities," *American Economic Review*, 78(1), pp. 108–21.

1989b. "Symmetric Equilibrium Existence and Optimality in Differentiated Product Markets," *J. Econ. Theory*, 47, pp. 178–94.

1988. "Variable Compatibility Without Network Externalities," Discussion Paper no. 145, Studies in Industry Economics, Stanford University.

1984. "Equilibrium Coalition Structures," Discussion Paper no. 273, Columbia University, Department of Economics.

Economides, Nicholas and Fredrick Flyer. 1995. "Technical Standards Coalitions for Network Goods," Discussion Paper no. EC-95–12, Stern School of Business, N.Y.U.

Economides, Nicholas and Jeff Heisler. 1994. "Equilibrium Fee Structure in a Monopolist Call Market," Discussion Paper EC-94–15, Stern School of Business, N.Y.U.

Economides, Nicholas and Charles Himmelberg. 1995. "Critical Mass and Network Size with Application to the US Fax Market," Discussion Paper no. EC-95–11, Stern School of Business, N.Y.U. mimeo.

Economides, Nicholas and William Lehr. 1995. "The Quality of Complex Systems and Industry Structure," in W. Lehr, ed., *Quality and Reliability of Telecommunications Infrastructure*. Hillsdale, NJ: Lawrence Erlbaum.

Economides, Nicholas and Steven C. Salop. 1992. "Competition and Integration Among Complements, and Network Market Structure," *Journal of Industrial Economics*, March, 40(1), pp. 105–23.

Economides, Nicholas and Robert A. Schwartz. 1995a. "Electronic Call Market Trading," *Journal of Portfolio Management*, Spring, 21(3), pp. 10–18.

1995b. "Equity Trading Practices and Market Structure: Assessing Asset Managers' Demand for Immediacy," *Financial Markets, Institutions and Instruments*, Nov., 4(4).

Economides, Nicholas and Aloysius Siow. 1988. "The Division of Markets Is Limited by the Extent of Liquidity: Spatial Competition with Externalities," *American Economic Review*, 78(1), pp. 108–21.

Economides, Nicholas and Lawrence J. White. 1996. "One-Way Networks, Two-Way Networks, Compatibility, and Antitrust," in *Opening Networks to Competition: The Regulation and Pricing of Access*, David Gabel and David Weiman (eds.). Kluwer Academic Press.

1995. "Access and Interconnection Pricing: How Efficient is the 'Efficient Component Pricing Rule'?," *Antitrust Bulletin*, Fall, 40:3, pp. 557–79.

1994. "Networks and Compatibility: Implications for Antitrust," *European Economic Review*, 38, pp. 651–62.

Economides, Nicholas and Glenn A. Woroch. 1992. "Benefits and Pitfalls of Network Interconnection," Discussion Paper no. EC-92–31, Stern School of Business, N.Y.U.

Ederington, Louis H. and Michael Dewally. 2003. "A Comparison of Reputation, Certification, Warranties, and Information Disclosure as Remedies for Information Asymmetries: Lessons from the On-Line Comic Book Market," Working Paper, Price College of Business, University of Oklahoma.

Elfenbein Daniel, and Joshua Lerner. 2003. "Ownership and Control Rights in Internet Portal Alliances," *RAND Journal of Economics*, 34:2, pp. 356–69.

Elkin-Koren, Niva and Eli Salzberger. 2000. "The Economic Analysis of Cyberspace: Challenges Posed by Cyberspace to Legal Theory and Legal Rules," *International Review of Law and Economics*, 19, pp. 553–82.

Ellam, Andrew. 2003. "Overture and Google: Internet Pay-Per-Click (PPC) Advertising Auctions," London Business School Case Study, CS-03–022.

Elliott, Margaret S. and Walt Scacchi. 2003. "Free Software Development: A Case Study of Software Development in a Virtual Organizational Culture," April, http://opensource. mit.edu/papers/eliottscacchi.pdf

Ellison, Glenn and Sara Fisher Ellison. 2004. "Search, Obfuscation, and Price Elasticities on the Internet," mimeo, MIT.

Ellsworth, Jill and Mathew Ellsworth. 1994. *The Internet Business Book.* New York: Wiley.

Elmer-Dewitt, Philip. 1994. "Battle for the Soul of the Internet," *Time,* 25 July.

Elyakime, Bernard, Jean-Jacques Laffont, Patrice Loisel, and Quang Vuong. 1994. "First Price Sealed Bid Auctions with Secret Reservation Price," *Annales d'Economie et Statistique,* 34, pp. 115–41.

Encaoua, David, Michel Moreaux, and Anne Perrot. 1992. "Demand Side Network Effect in Airline Markets," mimeo.

Engers, Maxim and Joshua S. Gans. 1998. "Why Referees Are Not Paid (Enough)?," *American Economic Review,* 88, pp. 1341–49.

Eppen, Gary D., Ward A. Hanson, and Richard Kipp Martin. 1991. "Bundling – New Products, New Markets, Low Risk," *Sloan Management Review,* 32(4), pp. 7–14.

Epple, Dennis. 1987. "Hedonic Prices and Implicit Markets: Estimating Demand and Supply Functions for Differentiated Products," *Journal of Political Economy,* 95:1, pp. 59–80.

Epstein, Larry and Michael Peters. 1999. "A Revelation Principle for Competing Mechanisms," *Journal of Economic Theory,* 88, pp. 119–60.

Ergas, Henry and Eric Ralph. 1994. "Pricing Network Interconnection: Is the Baumol-Willig Rule the Answer?," mimeo.

Ericson, Richard and Ariel Pakes. 1995. "Markov Perfect Industry Dynamics: A Framework for Empirical Work," *Review of Economic Studies,* 62:1, pp. 53–82.

European Central Bank. 2003. "Electronification of Payments in Europe," Monthly Bulletin, May.

European Commission. 1994. *Europe and the Global Information Society,* Bangemann report.

EVCA. 2003. European Venture Capital Association, *2003 Yearbook,* Zaventem, Belgium.

Experian. 2001. "The Internet Fraud: A Growing Threat to Online Retailers," Experian White Paper.

Eymard-Duvernay, F. 1986. La qualification des produits. Le travail: marchés, règles, conventions, R. Salais and L. Thévenot. Paris: INSEE-Economica.

Fabel, Oliver and Erik E. Lehmann. 2002. "Adverse Selection and Market Substitution by Electronic Trade," *International Journal of the Economics of Business,* July, 9:2, pp. 175–93.

Faloutsos, Michalis, Petros Faloutsos, and Christos Faloutsos. 1999. "On Power-Law Relationships of the Internet Topology," *ACM SIGCOMM Computer Communication Review,* 29:4.

Fama, Eugene F. and Kenneth French. 2001. "Disappearing Dividends: Changing Firm Characteristics or Lower Propensity To Pay?," *J. Finan. Econ.,* 60:1, pp. 3–43.

Farrell, Joseph and Garth Saloner. 1992. "Converters, Compatibility, and the Control of Interfaces," *Journal of Industrial Economics,* 40(1), pp. 9–36.

1988. "Coordination Through Committees and Markets," *RAND Journal of Economics,* 19(2), 235–252.

1987. "Competition, Compatibility and Standards: The Economics of Horses, Penguins, and Lemmings," in Landis Gabel, ed., *Product Standardization and Competitive Strategy*. Amsterdam: North Holland.

1986a. "Installed Base and Compatibility: Innovation, Product Preannouncement, and Predation," *American Economic Review*, 76, pp. 940–55.

1986b. "Standardization and Variety," *Economics Letters*, 20, pp. 71–74.

1986c. "Economic Issues in Standardization," in J. Miller, ed., *Telecommunications and Equity*. Amsterdam: North Holland.

1985. "Standardization, Compatibility, and Innovation," *RAND Journal of Economics*, 16, pp. 70–83.

Farrell, Joseph and Carl Shapiro. 1990. "Horizontal Mergers: An Equilibrium Analysis," *Amer. Econ. Rev.*, 80:1, pp. 107–26.

Fehr, Ernst, Simon Gächter, and Georg Kirchsteiger. 1997. "Reciprocity as a Contract Enforcement Device: Experimental Evidence," *Econometrica*, 65:4, pp. 833–60.

Feldman, Michal, Kevin Lai, John Chuang, and Ion Stoica. 2003. "Quantifying Disincentives in Peer-to-Peer Networks," 2nd Workshop on the Economics of Peer to Peer Systems, http://www.sims.berkeley.edu/research/confer ences/p2pecon/program.html

Feller, Joe and Brian Fitzgerald. 2002. "Understanding Open Source Software Development," UK: Addison-Wesley.

Ferleger, Louis and William Lazonick. 1993. "The Managerial Revolution and the Developmental State: The Case of U.S. Agriculture," *Business and Economic History*, 22:2, pp. 67–98.

Ferrando, Jorge, Jean Gabszewicz, Didier Laussel, and Nathalie Sonnac. 2004. "Two-Sided Network Effects and Competition: An Application to Media Industries," Working Paper, http://www.crest.fr/pageperso/lei/sonnac/ FGLS.pdf

Fershtman, Chaim and Arthur Fishman. 1992. "Price Cycles and Booms: Dynamic Search Equilibrium," *American Economic Review*, 82:5, pp. 1221–33.

Fershtman, Chaim and Neil Gandal. 2004. "The Determinants of Output per Contributor in Open Source Projects: An Empirical Examination," Working Paper, Tel Aviv University – The Eitan Berglas School of Economics and Tel Aviv University, Department of Public Policy.

Flichy, Patrice. 2007. *The Internet Imaginaire*. Cambridge, MA: MIT Press.

1999. "Internet ou la communauté scientifique idéale," *Réseaux*, 97.

1995. *Dynamics of Modern Communication*. Sage.

Florida, Richard. 2002. "The Economic Geography of Talent," *Annals of the Association of American Geographers*, 92:4, pp. 743–5.

Fomin, Vladislav V., John L. King, Sean T. McGann, and Kalle J. Lyytinen, 2003. "Globalization and Electronic Commerce: Environment and Policy in the U.S.," *Communications of the Association for Information Systems*, 10, pp. 276–325.

Foray, Dominique. 2004a. *The Economics of Knowledge*. Cambridge, MA: MIT Press.

2004b. "Patents and the Dynamics of Innovation in the Software Industry: European Policy Issues in a Global Context," communication to the 4th EPIP conference in Copenhagen (March 2005).

Foray, Dominique and Jean-Benoit Zimmermann. 2001. "L'économie du logi-
ciel libre: organisation coopérative et incitation à l'innovation," *Revue Economique*, 52, pp. 77–93.

Forge, Simon. 2000. "Open Source: The Economics of Giving Away Stuff, and Software as a Political Statement," *Info*, February, 2:1, pp. 5–7.

Franke, Nikolaus and Eric von Hippel. 2003. "Satisfying Heterogeneous User Needs via Innovation Toolkits: The Case of Apache Security Software," *Research Policy*, 32(7), pp. 1199–215, Special Issue on open source software development edited by Georg von Krogh and Eric von Hippel.

——— 2003. "Finding Commercially Attractive User Innovations: A Performance Evaluation of the 'Lead User Construct'," Working Paper, Vienna University of Economics and Business Administration – General and Massachusetts Institute of Technology (MIT) – Sloan School of Management.

Freixas, Xavier and Anthony Santomero. 2003. "An Overall Perspective on Banking Regulation," Federal Reserve Bank of Philadelphia, Working Papers, 02:1.

Freund, Bob. 2002. "IBM Stockholders Reject Pension Proposal," *Post-Bulletin* (Rochester, MN), 30 April.

Freund, Jesse and Bayers Chip. 1998. "Hacker-Philosopher," *Wired*, May.

Frey, Carol. 1999. "IBM Makes Pension Plan More Attractive to Younger Workers," *News and Observer* (Raleigh, NC), 4 May, D1.

Frey, William. 1999. "The Zero Effect," Rants & Raves, *Wired*, Dec.

Friberg, Richard, Mattias Ganslandt, and Mikael Sandstrom. 2000. "E-Commerce and Prices: Theory and Evidence," SSE/EFI Working Paper Series in Economics and Finance no. 389, Stockholm School of Economics.

Friedman, Benjamin M. 1999. "The Future of Monetary Policy: The Central Bank as an Army with Only a Signal Corps," *Int. Finance*, 2:3, pp. 321–38.

Friedman, Eric and Paul Resnick. 2001. "The Social Cost of Cheap Pseudonyms," *Journal of Economics and Management Strategy*, 10(2), pp. 173–99.

Friesen, G. Bruce. 2004. "Redefining B2C From 'Business to Consumer' to 'Building Toward Community'!," *Consulting to Management – C2M*, Mar., 15:1, pp. 21–6.

Frischmann, Brett M. 2001. "Privatization and Commercialization of the Internet: Rethinking Market Intervention into Government and Government Intervention into the Market," *Columbia Science and Technology Law Review*, Volume II, 2000–2001, http://www.stlr.org/html/archive/ [accessed June 2005].

Fujita, M. and J. F. Thisse. 2000. "The Formation of Economic Agglomerations: Old Problems and New Perspectives," in J. M. Huriot and J. F. Thisse (eds.), *Economics of Cities. Theoretical Perspectives*. Cambridge: Cambridge University Press.

Fulkerson, Bill and Michael Shank. 2000. "The New Economy Electronic Commerce, and the Rise of Mass Customization," *Handbook on Electronic Commerce*, pp. 411–30, International Handbooks on Information Systems. Heidelberg and New York: Springer.

Fundação Getulio Vargas. 2003. "Mapa da Exlusão Digital," Centro de Politicas Sociais do Instituto Brasileiro de Economia da FGV, Rio de Janeiro.

Fuscaldo, Donna. 2001. "IBM Shareholders Vote on Proposal Attacking Pension Plan," *Dow Jones News Service*, 24 April.

Gabszewicz, Jean, Didier Laussel, and Nathalie Sonnac. 2004. "Network Effect in the Press and Advertising Industries," Working Paper, http://www.crest.fr/pageperso/lei/sonnac/network%20effects.pdf

Gabszewicz, Jean and Jacques-François Thisse. 1979. "Price Competition, Quality, and Income Disparities," *Journal of Economic Theory*, 20, pp. 340–59.

Gabszewicz, Jean Jaskold and Paolo Garella. 1986. "'Subjective' Price Search and Price Competition," *Int. J. Ind. Organ.*, 4, pp. 305–16.

Galambos, Louis. 1992. "Theodore N. Vail and the Role of Innovation in the Modern Bell System," *Business History Review*, 66:1, pp. 95–126.

Galbraith, John Kenneth. 1967. *The New Industrial State*. Houghton Mifflin.

Galliano, Danielle and Pascale Roux. 2004. "La fracture numérique rural/urbain: le cas des firmes industrielles françaises," *Colloque TIC et inégalités: les fractures numériques*, 18 and 19 nov., Paris, http://www.egir.u-psud.fr/digitaldivide/

2003. "Espaces, organisations et TIC: les enseignements d'une comparaison intersectorielle," *Revue Géographie, Economie et Société*, 5:3.

Gambardella, Alfonso and Bronwyn H. Hall. 2004. "Proprietary vs. Public Domain Licensing of Software and Research Products," Working Paper. Scuola Superiore Sant'Anna, Pisa. Feb. (Revised version forthcoming in *Research Policy*).

Gandal, Neil. 2001. "The Dynamics of Competition in the Internet Search Engine Market," Economics Department, University of California, Berkeley, Working Paper E01-295.

1979. "Structural Organization of Secondary Markets: Clearing Frequency, Dealer Activity and Liquidity Risk," *Journal of Finance*, 34, pp. 577–93.

1976a. "Price Dispersion in the Government Securities Market," *Journal of Political Economy*, 84.

Garbade, Kenneth and William Silber. 1976. "Technology, Communication and the Performance of Financial Markets, 1840–1975," *Journal of Finance*, 33.

Garcia, M.-F. 1986. "La construction sociale d'un marché parfait," *Actes de la recherche en sciences sociales*, 65, pp. 2–15.

Garfinkel, Simson. 1993. "Is Stallman Stalled?," *Wired*, First Issue.

Garicano, Luis and Steven N. Kaplan. 2001. "The Effects of Business-to-Business E-Commerce on Transaction Costs," *Journal of Industrial Economics*, Dec., 49:4, pp. 463–85.

Garr, Doug. 1999. *IBM Redux: Lou Gerstner and the Business Turnaround of the Decade*. HarperBusiness.

Garratt, Rod, Mark Walker, and John Wooders. 2002. "Experienced Bidders in Online Second-Price Auctions," Working Paper, University of Arizona.

Garzarelli, Giampaolo and Roberto Galoppini. 2003. "Capability Coordination in Modular Organization: Voluntary FS/OSS Production and the Case of Debian GNU/Linux," Working Paper, Universita degli Studi di Roma, "La Sapienza" and ACME Solutions s.r.l.

Gaudeul, Alexandre. 2004. "Shareware Competition: Selling an Experience," University of Toulouse Working Paper.

2003a. "Internet Intermediaries' Editorial Content Quality," University of Toulouse.

2003b. "Shareware Competition: Selling an Experience," Working Paper, http://econwpa.wustl.edu:80/eps/game/papers/0409/0409008.pdf

Gaudeul, Alexandre and Bruno Jullien. "Intermediation on the Information Markets," Internet and Digital Eds., Eric Brousseau and Nicolas Curien.

Geertz, C. 1979. "Suq. The Bazaar Economy in Sefrou," in *Meaning and Order in Moroccan Society. Three Essays in Cultural Analysis*, G. Geertz C.H., and L. Rosen, eds. Cambridge: Cambridge University Press.

Geisel, Jerry. 1999. "IBM debuts innovative health plan for retirees," *Business Insurance*, 24 May, 1.

Gensollen, Michel. 2006. "Information Goods and Online Communities," This volume.

2001. "Internet: marché électronique ou réseaux commerciaux?" (Internet: Digital Market or Commercial Networks? With English summary), *Revue Economique*, Special Issue Oct., 52:0, pp. 137–61.

2000. "Creation of Value on the Internet," *Réseaux. The French Journal of Communication*, 7:2, pp. 117–53.

1999. "La création de valeur sur Internet." *Réseaux*, 97, pp. 15–76.

Gerstner Jr., Louis V. 2002. *Who Says Elephants Can't Dance?* HarperBusiness.

Ghosh, Rishab Aiyer. 2003. "Clustering and Dependencies in Free/Open Software Development: Methodology and Preliminary Analysis," MERIT-Infonomics Institute and SIEPR-Project NOSTRA Working Paper, 15 Feb., http://open source.mit.edu/papers/

Ghosh, Rishab Aiyer and Paul A. David. 2003. "The Nature and Composition of the Linux Kernel Developer Community: A Dynamic Analysis," SIEPR-Project NOSTRA Working Paper (Feb. 21), http://opensource.mit.edu/papers/

Ghosh, Rishab Aiyer, Rudiger Glott, Bernhard Kreiger, and Gregario Robles. 2002. *The Free/Libre and Open Source Software Developers Survey and Study—FLOSS Final Report*, June, http://www.infonomics. nl/FLOSS/report/

Ghosh, Rishab Aiyer and Vipul Ved Prakash. 2000. "The Orbiten Free Software Survey," *First Monday*, 5:7, http://www.firstmonday. org/issues/issue5_7/ghosh/

Gibbons, Robert. 1992. *A Primer in Game Theory*. Harlow: Pearson Higher Education.

Gibbs, Jennifer, Kenneth L. Kraemer, and Jason Dedrick. 2004. "Firm Internationalization and E-Commerce Use: A Cross-Country Exploration," Irvine, CA: Center for Research on Information Technology and Organizations (CRITO).

2003. "Environment and Policy Factors Shaping Global E-Commerce Diffusion: A Cross-Country Comparison," *The Information Society*, 16, pp. 5–18.

Gibson, J. J. 1979. *The Ecological Approach to Visual Perception*. Boston: Houghton Mifflin.

Gille, Laurent and Philippe Mathonnet. 1994. *L'intermédiation électronique*. Paris: Sirius, Commissariat Général du Plan.

Gintis, Herbert. 2003. "Solving The Puzzle of Prosociality," *Rationality and Society*, 15:2, pp. 155–87, http://www-unix.oit.umass.edu/~gintis/

Giraud-Héraud, Eric, Abdelhakim Hammoudi, and Mahdi Mokrane. 2003. "Multiproduct Firm Behaviour in a Differentiated Market," *Can. J. Econ.*, 36:1, pp. 41–61.

Giraud-Héraud, Eric, Louis-Georges Soler, and Hervé Tanguy. 2001. "Internet et la distribution de biens physiques. Analyse de l'émergence de nouvelles structures verticales dans le secteur du vin," *Revue Econ.*, 52, pp. 213–32.

Glimstedt, Henrik and William Lazonick. 2005. "The Evolution of Stock Options at Ericsson," INSEAD Working Paper, Jan.

Globerman, Steven, Thomas W. Roehl, and Stephen Standifird. 2001. "Globalization and Electronic Commerce: Inferences from Retail Brokering," *Journal of International Business Studies*, 32:4, pp. 749–68.

Glosten, Lawrence R. 1994. "Is the Electronic Open Limit Order Book Inevitable?," *Journal of Finance*, 49(4), pp. 1127–61.

Godschalk, Hugo. 2001. "Failure of Beenz and Flooz Indicates the End of Digital Web-Currencies?," *ePSO Newsletter*, 10, Nov.

Goetz, Thomas. 2003. "Open Source Everywhere," *Wired*, Nov.

Goldberg, Michael. 1994. "The (Second Phase of the) Revolution Has Begun," interview with Jim Clark, *Wired*, Oct.

Goldstein, Harry and Ronil Hira. 2004. "Spectrum R&D 100: The World's Biggest R&D Spenders Are Putting Their Money on Software and Service," *IEEE Spectrum*, Nov.

Golle, Philippe, Kevin Leyton-Brown, and Ilya Mironov. 2001. "Incentives for Sharing in Peer-to-Peer Networks," Working Paper, Standford University, Palo Alto, CA.

Gompers, Paul and Josh Lerner. 2002. *The Venture Capital Cycle*. Cambridge, MA: MIT Press, 385p.

Gonzalez, Andrés G. 2003. "PayPal and eBay: The Legal Implications of the C2C Electronic Commerce Model," 18th BILETA Conference: Controlling Information in the Online Environment, April, QMW, London (http://www. bileta.ac. uk/03papers/Guadamuz.html).

Gonzalez-Barahona, Jesus M., Luiz Lopez, and Gregorio Robles. 2004. "The Community Structure of the Modules in the Apache Project," GSyC Working Paper, Universidad Rey Juan Carlos (Mostoles), Feb., http://open source.mit.edu/papers/

Gonzalez-Barahona, Jesus and Gregorio Robles. 2003. "Free Software Engineering: A Field to Explore," *Upgrade*, 4(4), Aug.

— 2004. "Getting the Global Picture," a presentation at the Oxford Workshop on Libre Software (OWLS), Oxford Internet Institute, 25–26 June. [Available at: http://www.oii.ox.ac.uk/fiveowlsgohoot/postevent/Barahona&Robles_OWLS-slides.pdf]

Gonzalez-Barahona, Jesus M. et al. 2002. "Counting potatoes: The size of Debian 2.2" (Version 3a: 3 Jan.), http://people.debian.org/~jgb/debian-counting/counting-potatoes/

Goodhart, Charles A. E. 2000. "Can Central Banking Survive the IT Revolution?," Future of Monetary Policy and Banking Conference, World Bank, 11 July.

— 1990. *The Evolution of Central Banks*. Cambridge, MA: MIT Press.

Gordon, Robert J. 2000. "Does the 'New Economy' Measure Up to the Great Inventions of the Past?," *Journal of Economic Perspectives*, (14)4, Fall, pp. 49–74.

Gorton, Gary and George, and G. Pennacchi. 1990. "Financial Intermediaries and Liquidity Creation," *J. Finance*, 45, pp. 49–71.

GPL (General Public License). 1991. Version 2.

Gradstein, Mark. 1994. "Efficient Provision of a Discrete Public Good," *International Economic Review*, 35(4), pp. 877–97.

Granovetter, Mark. 1985. "Economic Action and Social Structure: The Problem of Embeddedness," *American Journal of Sociology*, 91:3, Nov., pp. 481–510.

_____. 1973. "The Strength of Weak Ties," *Amer. J. Sociology*, 78:6, pp. 1360–80.

Green, Milford B. 2004. "Venture Capital Investment in the United States 1995–2002," *The Industrial Geographer*, 2:1, pp. 2–30.

Greenbaum, Stuart I. and Anjan Thakor. 1995. *Contemporary Financial Intermediation*. Dryden Press.

Gresse, Carole. 2002. "Crossing Network Trading and the Liquidity of a Dealer Market: Cream-Skimming or Risk-Sharing?," Working Paper, University of Paris X Nanterre.

Griffith, Victoria. 1999. "Tailored Marketing on the Internet: Does It Really Capture Consumers?," *Strategy and Business*, Fourth Quarter.

Grindley, Peter C. and David J. Teece. 1997. "Managing Intellectual Capital: Licensing and Cross-Licensing in Semiconductors and Electronics," *California Management Review*, 39:2, pp. 8–41.

Gross, Ben and Alessandro Acquisti. 2003. "Balance of Power on eBay: Peers or Unequals?," 2nd Workshop on the Economics of Peer to Peer Systems, http://www.sims.berkeley.edu/research/conferences/p2pecon/program.html

Grossman, Sanford J. 1981. "The Informational Role of Warranties and Private Disclosure," *Journal of Law and Economics*, 24, pp. 461–83.

Grove, Andrew S. 1996. *Only the Paranoid Survive*. Doubleday.

Gu, Bin and Sirkka Jarvenpaa. 2003. "Are Contributions to P2P Technical Forums Private or Public Goods? An Empirical Investigation," 2nd Workshop on the Economics of Peer to Peer Systems, http://www.sims. berkeley.edu/research/conferences/p2pecon/program.html

Guadagni, Peter M. and John D. C. Little. 1983. "A Logit Model of Brand Choice Calibrated on Scanner Data," *Marketing Science*, 2:3, Summer.

Guerra, Gerardo A. 2001. "Certification Disclosure and Informational Efficiency: A Case for Ordered Ranking of Levels," Discussion Paper Series, 64, January, University of Oxford, Department of Economics.

Güth, Werner and Hartmut Kliemt. 2004. "The Evolution of Trust (Worthiness) in the Net," *Analyse and Kritik*, 26:1, pp. 203–19.

Guttman, Joel M. 2000. "On the Evolutionary Stability of Preferences for Reciprocity," *Europ. J. Polit. Economy*, 16:1, pp. 31–50.

Gyourko, Joseph and Asuka Nakahara. (undated). "The Impact of New Information Technologies on the Commercial Brokerage Industry: Phase III: What Does New Information Technology Make Possible and Under What Conditions Will Changes Occur?," Working Papers, Wharton School Samuel Zell and Robert Lurie Real Estate Center, University of Pennsylvania.

Hackett, Steven C. 1992. "A Comparative Analysis of Merchant and Broker Intermediation," *Journal of Economic Behaviour and Organization*, 18:3, pp. 299–315.

Hagel, John III and Arthur G. Armstrong. 1997. *Net Gain: Expanding Markets Through Virtual Communities*. Boston, MA: Harvard Business School Press, 256p.

Haile, Philip, Han Hong, and Matthew Shum. 2003. "Nonparametric Tests for Common Values in First-Price Sealed-Bid Auctions," Working Paper, Yale University, Nov.

Hall, Brian J. and Jeffrey B. Leibman. 1998. "Are CEOs Really Paid Like Bureaucrats?," *Quarterly Journal of Economics*, 113:3, pp. 653–91.

Hand, John R. M. 2001. "Evidence on the Winner-Takes-All Business Model: The Profitability Returns-to-Scale of Expenditures on Intangibles Made by U.S. Internet Firms, 1995–2001," Working Paper, University of North Carolina at Chapel Hill – Accounting Area

2000. "Profits, Losses and the Non-Linear Pricing of Internet Stocks," mimeo, University of North Carolina, Chapel Hill.

Hansen, Robert. 1986. "Sealed Bid Versus Open Auctions: The Evidence," *Economic Inquiry*, 24, pp. 125–14.

Hanson, Ward A. and Richard Kipp Martin. 1990. "Optimal Bundle Pricing," *Management Science*, 32(2), Feb.

Hardin, Garrett. 1968. "The Tragedy of the Commons," *Science*, 162:3859, pp. 1243–8, 13 Dec.

Hargittai, Eszter. 2002. "Second-Order Digital Divide: Differences in People's Online Skills," *First Monday*, 7:4, http//firstmonday.com

1999. "Weaving the Western Web: Explaining the Difference in Internet Connectivity Among OCED Countries," *Telecommunications Policy*, 23, pp. 701–18.

Harhoff, Dietmar, Joachim Henkel, and Eric von Hippel. 2003. "Profiting from Voluntary Information Spillovers: How Users Benefit from Free Revealing Their Innovations," *Research Policy*, 32:10 (December), pp.1753–69.

Harrington Jr., Joseph E. 2001. "Comment on 'Reducing Buyer Search Costs: Implication for Electronic Marketplaces'," *Management Science*, 47:12, pp. 1727–32.

Harsanyi, John C. 1967–1968. "Games with Incomplete Information Played by Bayesian Players," *Management Science*, 14, pp. 159–82, 321–34, 486–502.

Harstad, Ronald, John Kagel, and Dan Levin. 1990. "Equilibrium Bid Functions for Auctions with an Uncertain Number of Bidders," *Economics Letters*, 33, pp. 35–40.

Hart, Oliver D. and Jean Tirole. 1990. "Vertical Integration and Market Foreclosure," in N. Baily and C. Winston, eds., *Brookings Papers on Economic Activity*.

Hartley, Bob and Brendan D'Cruz. 2001. "Making Sense of E-Business," *Global Business and Economics Review*, June, 3:1, pp. 68–83.

Haruvy, Ernan, Ashutosh Prasad, and Suresh Sethi. "Harvesting Altruism in Open Source Software Development," Working Paper, University of Texas – Department of Marketing and University of Texas – Department of Information Systems and Operations Management.

Hasker, Kevin, Raul Gonzalez, and Robin Sickles. 2003. "An Analysis of Strategic Behavior and Consumer Surplus in eBay Auctions," Working Paper, Rice University.

Hatchuel, Armand. 1995. "Les marchés à prescripteurs: crises de l'échange et genèse sociale", in *L'inscription sociale du marché*, Annie Jacob and Hélène Vérin, eds. Paris: L'Harmattan, pp. 203–25.

Hauble, G. and V. Trifts. 2000. "Consumer Decision Making in Online Shopping Environments: The Effects of Interactive Decision Aids," *Julkaisussa Marketing Science*, Winter, pp. 4–21.

Hauert, Christoph and Heinz Georg Schuster. 1997. "Effects of Increasing the Number of Players and Memory Size in the Iterated Prisoner's Dilemma; a Numerical Approach," *Proceedings of the Royal Society London B*, 264, pp. 513–19.

Hausman, Jerry. 1981. "Exact Consumer Surplus and Deadweight Loss," *American Economic Review*, 71, pp. 662–76.

1997. "Valuation of New Goods under Perfect and Imperfect Competition," in Timothy Bresnahan and Robert Gordon (eds.), *The Economics of New Goods*. Chicago: University of Chicago Press.

Hawkins, Richard W. 2002. "The Phantom of the Marketplace: Searching for New E-Commerce Business Models," *Communications and Strategies*, 2nd Quarter, 0:46, pp. 297–329.

Hayek, Friedrich. 1978. *Competition as a Discovery Procedure*, in *New Studies in Philosophy, Politics and Economics*. Chicago: University of Chicago Press.

Hays, Laurie. 1994. "Blue period: Gerstner is struggling as he tries to change ingrained IBM culture," *Wall Street Journal*, 13 May.

Hedman, Jonas and Thomas Kalling. 2001. "The Business Model: A Means to Understand the Business Context of Information and Communication Technology," Working Paper Series, Lund University, Institute of Economic Research, no. 2001/9.

Hege, Ulrich, Frédéric Palomino, and Armin Schwienbacher. 2006. "Venture Capital Performance: The Disparity Between Europe and the United States," mimeo, HEC Paris, http://campus.hec.fr/profs/hege

Heide, Jan B. 1994. "Interorganizational Governance in Marketing Channels," *Journal of Marketing*, 58, pp. 71–85.

Heilemann, John. 2000. "David Boies: The Wired Interview," *Wired*, Oct.

Heller, Michael A. 1998. "The Tragedy of the Anticommons: Property in the Transition from Marx to Markets," *Harvard Law Review*, 111, pp. 621–88.

Heller, Michael A. and Rebecca S. Eisenberg. 1998. "Can Patent Deter Innovation? The Anticommons Tragedy in Biomedical Research," *Science*, 280, pp. 698–701.

Hellmann, Thomas. 1998. "The Allocation of Control Rights in Venture Capital Contracts," *RAND J. Econ.*, 29:1, pp. 57–76.

Hendershott, Terrence and Haim Mendelson. 2000. "Crossing Networks and Dealer Markets: Competition and Performance," *Journal of Finance*, 55(5), pp. 2071–115.

Henkel, Joachim, Konrad Stahl, and Uwe Walz. 2000. "Coalition Building in a Spatial Economy," *J. Urban Econ.*, 47, pp. 136–63.

Hennion, A., S. Maisonneuve, and E. Gomart. 2000. *Figures de l'amateur. Formes, objets, pratiques de l'amour de la musique aujourd'hui.* Paris: La documentation française.

Henrich, Joseph, Robert Boyd, Samuel Bowles, Colin Camerer, Ernst Fehr, Herbert Gintis, and Richard McElreath. 2001. "In Search of Homo Economicus: Behavioral Experiments in 15 Small-Scale Societies," *Am. Econ. Rev.*, 91:2, pp. 73–8.

Henshaw, Robin. 2001. "What Next for Internet Journals?," *First Monday*, 6:9.

Hertel, Guido, Sven Niedner, and Stefanie Herrmann 2003. "Motivation of Software Developers in Open Source Projects: An Internet-Based Survey of Contributors to the Linux Kernel," *Research Policy*, July, 32:7, pp. 1159–77.

Hillman, Robert A. and Jeffrey J. Rachlinski. 2001. "Standard-Form Contracting in the Electronic Age," Working Paper, Cornell Law School.

Hiltzik, Michael A. 2000. *Dealers of Lightning: Xerox PARC and the Dawn of the Computer Age.* HarperBusiness.

Himmelberg, Charles P. and Bruce C. Petersen. 1994. "R&D and Internal Finance: A Panel Study of Small Firms in High Tech Industries," *Rev. Econ. Statist.*, 76:1, pp. 38–51.

Hirshleifer, Jack. 1983. "From Weakest-Link to Best-Shot: The Voluntary Provision of Public Goods," *Public Choice*, 41, pp. 371–86.

Hof, Robert. 1998. "The 'Click Here' Economy," Annual Report on Information Technology Doing Business in the Internet Age, *Business Week*, 22 June.

1997. "Internet communities," *Business Week*, 5 May.

Hoffman, Bryce G. 1999. "Fremont, Calif.-Based Microchip Maker Has Become One of Hottest Stocks," *Knight-Ridder Business Tribune News*, 23 July.

Hoffman, Donna L. and Thomas P. Novak. 1996. "Marketing in Hypermedia Computer-Mediated Environments: Conceptual Foundations," *Journal of Markting*, 60(3), pp. 50–68.

Holmes, Stanley. 1996. "Unionizing the Nerds," *PC Week*, 28 Oct.

Holt, Charles. 1980. "Competitive Bidding for Contracts under Alternative Auction Procedures," *Journal of Political Economy*, 88, pp. 433–45.

Hong, Harrison, José Scheinkman, and Wei Xiong. 2004. "Asset Float and Speculative Bubbles," mimeo, Princeton University.

Hooghe, Liesbet and Gary Marks. 2001. "Types of Multi-Level Governance," *European Integration online Papers* (EIoP), vol. 5, http://econpapers.hhs.se/article/erpeiopxx/p0071.htm [Accessed June 2005]

Hoover, Edgar M. 1971. *An Introduction to Regional Economics.* New York: A. Knopf.

Hopenhayn, Hugo. 1992. "Entry, Exit, and Firm Dynamics in Long Run Equilibrium," *Econometrica*, 60, pp. 1127–50.

Hotelling, Harold. 1929. "Stability in Competition," *Econ. J.*, 39, pp. 41–57.

Houser, Dan and John Wooders. 2006. "Reputation in Auctions: Theory and Evidence from eBay," *Journal of Economics and Management Strategy.*

Howitt, Peter and Preston McAfee. 1988. "Stability of Equilibria with Externalities," *Quarterly Journal of Economics*, 103, pp. 261–77.

Hsu, David H. and Martin Kenney. 2004. "Organizing Venture Capital: The Rise and Demise of American Research and Development, 1946–1973," Working Paper, 5 Sept.

Huang, Roger D. 2002. "The Quality of ECNs and Nasdaq Market Maker Quotes," *Journal of Finance*, 57(3), pp. 1285–319.

Hubbard, Richard L. 1982. "IRS Gives Some Answers on Incentive Stock Options," *Legal Times*, 11 Jan.

Huberman, Bernardo and Natalie Glance. 1994. "Beliefs and Cooperation," *Proceedings of the International Conference on Chaos and Society*, June.

1993. "The Outbreak of Cooperation," *Journal of Mathematical Sociology*, 17:4, pp. 281–302.

Hui, Kai-Lung and Ivan P. L. Png. 2003. "Piracy and the Legitimate Demand for Recorded Music," *Contributions to Economic Analysis and Policy*, 2:1, Article 11.

Humphrey, David, Magnus Willesson, Ted Lindblom, and Göran Bergendahl. 2003. "What Does it Cost to Make a Payment?," *J. of Network Economics*, 2:2, pp. 159–74.

Hunter, Lisa M., Chickery J. Kasouf, Kevin G. Celuch, and Kathryn A. Curry. 2004. "A Classification of Business-to-Business Buying Decisions: Risk Importance and Probability as a Framework for E-Business Benefits," *Industrial Marketing Management*, Feb., 33:2, p. 145, 10p.

Hutchby, I. 2000. *Conversation and Technology*. Cambridge: Polity.

Hutchins, E. 1995. *Cognition in the Wild*. Cambridge, MA: MIT Press.

Hutchins, Edwin. 1995. *Cognition in the Wild*. MIT Press.

Hvide, Hans. 2002. "Segmentation and Pricing Behavior in a Market for Certification," Norwegian School of Economics and Business.

Hyde, Alan. 2003. *Working in Silicon Valley: Economic and Legal Analysis of a High-Velocity Labor Market*. M. E. Sharpe.

IDC. 2004. Internet Commerce Market Model. Framingham, MA.

Ingold, T. 2000. *The Perception of the Environment. Essays in Livelihood, Dwelling and Skill*. London. Routledge.

iQuantic-Buck. 2002. "Stock Options: Industry Practices and International Accounting Board Proposals," Buck Consultants.

Ivanova-Stenzel, Radosveta and Tim Salmon. 2003. "Bidder Preferences Among Auction Institutions," *Economic Inquiry*.

Jackson, Tim. 1997. *Inside Intel: Andy Grove and the Rise of the World's Most Powerful Chip Company*. Dutton.

Jain, Pankaj. 2002. "Institutional Design and Liquidity at Stock Exchanges Around the World," Working Paper, Indiana University.

Janssen, Maarten C. W. and José Luis Moraga-González. 2004. "Strategic Pricing, Consumer Search and the Number of Firms," *Review of Economic Studies*, 71:4, pp. 1089–118.

2000. "Pricing, Consumer Search and the Size of Internet Markets," Tinbergen Institute Discussion Paper TI 2000–042/1.

Janssen, Maarten C. W., José Luis Moraga-González, and Matthijs R. Wildenbeest. 2004. "Consumer Search and Oligopolistic Pricing: An Empirical Investigation," Tinbergen Institute Discussion Paper TI 2004–071/1, June.

Janssen, Maarten C. W. and Rob van der Noll. 2002. "Electronic Commerce and Retail Channel Substitution," Working Paper, Erasmus University Rotterdam – Rotterdam School of Economics.

Jarvenpaa, Sirkka L., Kathleen Knoll, and Dorothy E. Leidner. 1998. "Is Anybody Out There? The Implication of Trust in Global Virtual Teams," *Journal of Management Information Systems*, 14:4, pp. 29–64.

Jeanneret, Y. 2000. *Y a-t-il (vraiment) des technologies de l'information*. Lille: Presses du Septentrion.

Jensen, Michael C. 1986. "Agency Costs of Free Cash Flow," *Amer. Econ. Rev.*, 76, pp. 323–9.

Jensen, Michael C. and William H. Meckling. 1976. "Theory of the Firm: Managerial Behavior, Agency Costs and Ownership Structure," *Journal of Financial Economics*, 3:4.

Jin, Ginger Z. and Andrew Kato. 2002. "Blind Trust Online: Experimental Evidence from Baseball Cards," Working Paper, University of Maryland.

Johnson, Eric, Wendy Moe, Peter Fader, Steven Bellman, and Gerald Lohse. 2004. "On the Depth and Dynamics of Online Search Behavior," *Management Science*, 50:3, pp. 299–308.

Johnson, Justin Pappas. 2002. "Some Economics of Open Source Software," *Journal of Economics and Management Strategy*, 11:4, pp. 637–62 .

Johnson, M. Eric and Seungjin Whang. 2003. "E-Business and Supply Chain Management: An Overview and Framework," Working Paper, Tuck School of Business at Dartmouth and Stanford University – Graduate School of Business.

Johnston, Donald J. 2001. "Reducing the International Digital Divide," *Federal Reserve Bank of Kansas City Proceedings*, pp. 193–9.

Jonscher, Charles. 1994. "An Economic Study of the Information Technology Revolution," in Thomas J. Allen and Michael S. Scott-Morton (eds.), *Information Technology and the Corporation of the 1990s. Research Studies*. Oxford, New York, Toronto and Melbourne: Oxford University Press, pp. 5–42.

————. 1983. "Information Resources and Economic Productivity," *Information Economics and Policy*, 1: pp. 13–35.

Kagel, John H., Ronald M. Harstad, and Dan Levin. 1987. "Information Impact and Allocation Rules in Auctions with Affiliated Private Values: A Laboratory Study," *Econometrica*, 55, pp. 1275–304.

Kagel, John and Alvin Roth (eds.). 1995. *The Handbook of Experimental Economics*. Princeton: Princeton University Press.

Kahin, Brian (ed). 1990. *Commercialization of the Internet*, RFC 1192.

Kahin, Brian and Hal R. Varian, eds. 2000. *Internet Publishing and Beyond: The Economics of Digital Information and Intellectual Property*, Harvard Information Infrastructure Project. Cambridge, MA and London: MIT Press, pp. vi, 243.

Kahin, Brian and Ernest Wilson, eds. 1997. *National Information Infrastructure Initiatives: Vision and Policy Design*. Cambridge, MA: MIT Press.

Kahn, Alfred and William Taylor. 1994. "The Pricing of Inputs Sold to Competitors: Comment," *Yale Journal of Regulation*, 11(1), pp. 225–40.

Kahn, Barbara E. and Leigh McAllister. 1997. *Grocery Revolution. The New Focus on the Consumer.* Reading, MA: Addison-Wesley.

Kalyanam, Kirthi and Shelby McIntyre. 2001. "Returns to Reputation in Online Auction Markets," mimeo, Leavey School of Business at Santa Clara University.

Kampert, Patrick. 2004. "eBay: Not Just a Way of Life, It's a Living," 8 Aug., *Chicago Tribune.*

Kanawattanachai, Prasert and Youngjin Yoo. 2002. "Dynamic Nature of Trust in Virtual Teams," *Journal of Strategic Information Systems*, 11:3–4, pp. 187–213.

Kannan, Pallassana K., Ai-Mei Chang, and Andrew B. Whinston. 2000. "The Internet Information Market: The Emerging Role of Intermediaries," *Handbook on Electronic Commerce*, pp. 569–90, International Handbooks on Information Systems. Heidelberg and New York: Springer.

Kantrowitz, Barbara. 1994. "Happy Birthday: Still Wired at One," *Newsweek*, 17 Jan.

Kardaras, Dimitris, Bill Karakostas, and Eleutherios Papathanassiou. 2003. "The Potential of Virtual Communities in the Insurance Industry in the UK and Greece," *International Journal of Information Management*, Feb., 23:1, p. 41, 13p.

Katkar, Rama and David Lucking-Reiley. 2000. "Public Versus Secret Reserve Prices in eBay Auctions: Results from a Pokémon Field Experiment," Working Paper, University of Arizona.

Katok, Elena and Anthony Kwasnica. 2000. "Time Is Money: The Effect of Clock Speed and Seller's Revenue in Dutch Auctions," Working Paper, Penn State University.

Katsh, Ethan and Janet Rifkin. 2001. *Online Dispute Resolution: Resolving Conflicts in Cyberspace.* San Francisco: Jossey-Bass Press.

Katz, Elihu and Paul Lazarsfeld. 1955. *Personal Influence: The Part Played by People in the Flow of Mass Communication.* New York: The Free Press.

Katz, Michael and Carl Shapiro. 1994. "Systems Competition and Network Effects," *Journal of Economic Perspectives*, 8(2), pp. 93–115.

1992. "Product Introduction with Network Externalities," *Journal of Industrial Economics*, 40(1), pp. 55–84.

1986a. "Technology Adoption in the Presence of Network Externalities," *Journal of Political Economy*, 94, pp. 822–41.

1986b. "Product Compatibility Choice in a Market with Technological Progress," *Oxford Economic Papers*, 38, pp. 146–65.

1985. "Network Externalities, Competition and Compatibility," *American Economic Review*, 75:3, pp. 424–40.

Kazumori, Eichiro and John McMillan. 2003. "Selling Online Versus Live," Working Paper, Stanford GSB, CalTech.

Kedrosky, Paul. 1995. "The More You Sell," *Wired*, Oct.

Keegan, Paul. 1995. "The Digerati! Wired Magazine Has Triumphed by Turning Mild-Mannered Computer Nerds into a Super-Desirable Consumer Niche," *New York Times Magazine*, 21 May.

Kelleher, Kevin. 2001. "Death of the New Economy, R.I.P.," *Wired*, Nov.

Kelly, Kevin. 1999a. "The Roaring Zeros," *Wired*, Sept.

1999b. "Prophets of the Boom: Harry Dent Jr," *Wired*, Sept.

1998. *New Rules for the New Economy: Ten Radical Strategies for a Connected World*. New York: Viking.

1997a. "It Takes a Village to Make a Mall. *Net Gain*'s John Hagel on the Prerequisite for Net Commerce: Community," *Wired*, Aug.

1997b. "New Rules for the New Economy," *Wired*, Sept.

1996a. "The Economics of Ideas,", *Wired*, June.

1996b."Wealth if You Want It," *Wired*, Nov.

1994. *Out of Control: The Rise of Neo-Biological Civilization*. Reading, MA: Addison-Wesley.

Kelly, Kevin and Gary Wolf. 1997. "Push," *Wired*, March.

Kelty, Christopher M. 2001. "Free Software/Free Science," *First Monday*, 6:12 (Dec.), www.firstmonday.org/issues/issue6_12/kelty/index.html

Khalil, Fahad and Jacques Lawarree. 1995. "Collusive Auditors," *The American Economic Review*, 85:2, pp. 442–6.

Kihlstrom, Richard E. and Michael H. Riordan. 1984. "Advertising as a Signal," *Journal of Political Economy*, 92:3, pp. 427–50.

Kiiski, Sampsa and Matti Pohjola. 2002. "Cross-Country Diffusion of the Internet," *Info. Econ. Pol.*, 14, pp. 297–310.

King, Mervyn. 1999. "Challenges for Monetary Policy: New and Old," *Bank of England Quarterly Bulletin*, 39:4, pp. 397–415.

Kirby, Carrie. 2000. "Sweeping proposal: Janitors look to Silicon Valley giants for help in pay dispute," *San Francisco Chronicle*, 20 May.

Kirzner, Israel M. 1985. *Discovery and the Capitalist Process*. Chicago: University of Chicago Press.

Klemperer, Paul. 1999. "Auction Theory," *Journal of Economic Surveys*, 13:3, pp. 227–86.

Klock, Mark and Timothy D. McCormick. 1999. "The Impact of Market Maker Competition on Nasdaq Spreads," *The Financial Review*, 34(4), pp. 55–75.

Kobrin, Stephen J. 1997. "Electronic Cash and the End of National Markets," *Foreign Policy*, 107, pp. 65–77.

Koch, Stefan and Georg Schneider. 2000. "Results from Software Engineering Research into Open Source Development Projects Using Public Data," Vienna University of Economics and Business Administration, http://open source.mit.edu/papers/koch-ossoftwareengineering.pdf

Koenig, Wolfgang, Rolf T. Wigand, and Roman Beck. 2003. "Globalization of E-Commerce: Environment and Policy in Germany," *Communications of the Association for Information Systems*, 11, pp. 33–72.

Kogut, Bruce. 2003. *The Global Internet Economy*. Cambridge, MA: MIT Press, p. 520.

Kogut, Bruce and Anca Metiu. 2001. "Open-Source Software Development and Distributed Innovation," *Oxford Review of Economic Policy*, Summer, 17(2), pp. 248–64.

Kollock, Peter. 1999. "The Economics of Online Cooperation: Gifts and Public Goods in Cyberspace," in *Communities in Cyberspace*, M. Smith and P. Kollock, eds. London: Routledge.

1999. "The Production of Trust in Online Markets," in *Advances in Group Processes*, Edward J. Lawler, S. Thyne, and Henry A. Walker, eds. Greenwich, CT: JAI Press.

1996. "Design Principles for Online Communities," *PC Update*, 15:5, pp. 58–60. http://www.sscnet.ucla.edu/soc/faculty/kollock/papers/design.htm

Kollock, Peter and Mark Smith. 1999. "Introduction: Communities in Cyberspace," in *Communities in Cyberspace*, Marc Smith and Peter Kollock eds. London: Routledge Press, pp. 3–25.

Kopytoff, Verne. 2001. "Searching for Profits: Amid Tech Slump, More Portals Sell Search Engine Results to Highest Bidder," June, *San Francisco Chronicle*, 18.

Kosfeld, Michael. 2004. "Economic Networks in the Laboratory: A Survey," *Review of Network Economics*, March, 3:1, pp. 20–42.

Kotowitz, Yehuda and Frank Mathewson. 1979. "Advertising, Consumer Information and Product Quality," *Bell Journal of Economics*, 10:2.

Kozberg, Anthony. 2001. "The Value Drivers of Internet Stocks: A Business Models Approach," Working Paper, City University of New York – Stan Ross Department of Accountancy.

Kraemer, Kenneth L., Jason Dedrick, and Jennifer Gibbs. 2004. "Impacts of Globalization on E-Commerce Use and Firm Performance: A Cross-Country Investigation," *The Information Society*, 21:5, pp. 323–40.

Krishna, Vijay. 2002. *Auction Theory*. San Diego: Academic Press.

Krishnamurthy, Sandeep. 2002. "Cave or Community? An Empirical Examination of 100 Mature Open Source Projects," University of Washington, Bothell (May), http://opensource.mit.edu/papers/krishnamurthy.pdf

Krishnan, Anne. 2003. "IBM shareholders reject pension choice proposal for third time," *Herald-Sun* (Durham, NC), 30 April.

Krishnan, Ramayya, Michael D. Smith, Zhulei Tang, and Rahul Telang. 2004. "The Virtual Commons: Understanding Content Provision in Peer-to-Peer File Sharing Networks," Working Paper, Carnegie Mellon University, Pittsburgh, PA.

Krishnan, Ramayya, Michael D. Smith, and Rahul Telang. 2003. "The Virtual Commons: Why Free-Riding Can Be Tolerated in File Sharing Networks," Working Paper, Carnegie Mellon University – H. John Heinz III School of Public Policy and Management and Carnegie Mellon University – Graduate School of Industrial Administration (GSIA).

2003. "The Economics of Peer-to-Peer Networks," *Journal of Information Technology Theory and Applications*, 5:3, pp. 31–44.

Ku, Gillian, Deepak Malhotra, and J. Keith Murnighan. 2003. "Competitive Arousal in Live and Internet Auctions," Working Paper, Kellogg Graduate School of Management, Northwestern University.

Kuan, Jennifer W. 2001. "Open Source Software as Consumer Integration into Production," Working Paper, Stanford University – Institute for Economic Policy Research.

Kung, H. T. and Chun-Hsin Wu. 2003. "Differentiated Admission for Peer-to-Peer Systems: Incentivizing Peers to Contribute Their Resources," Working Paper, Harvard University, Cambridge, MA.

Kuttner, Kenneth N. and James J. McAndrews. 2001. "Personal On-Line Payments," Federal Reserve Bank of New York, *Economic Policy Review*, 7:3, pp. 35–50.

Kuwabara, Ko. 2000. "Linux: A Bazaar at the Edge of Chaos," *First Monday*, 5:3, March, http://firstmondy.org/issues/issue5_3/kuwabara/index.html (last accessed June 2006).

Kwok Sai Ho, Karl R. Lang, and Kar Yan Tam. 2002. "Peer-to-Peer Technology Business and Service Models: Risks and Opportunities," *Electronic Markets*, Sep., 12:3, p. 175, 9p.

Lakhani, Karim and Robert G. Wolf. 2003. "Why Hackers Do What They Do: Understanding Motivation and Effort in Free/Open Source Software Projects," Working Paper, Massachusetts Institute of Technology (MIT) – Sloan School of Management and the Boston Consulting Group.

Lakhani, Karim R. and Eric von Hippel. 2000. "How Open Source Software Works: 'Free' User-to-User Assistance," *Res. Pol.*, 32, pp. 923–43.

Lakhani, Karim R., Bob Wolf, Jeff Bates, and Chris DiBona. 2003. "The Boston Consulting Group Hacker Survey (in cooperation with OSDN)." [Available at: <http://www.osdn.com/bcg/bcg-0.73/BCGHackerSurveyv0-73.html>]

Lal, Rajiv and Miklos Sarvary. 1999. "When and How Is the Internet Likely to Decrease Price Competition," *Marketing Science*, 18:4, pp. 485–503.

Lamberton, Don M. 1974. *The Information Revolution*, Philadelphia: Annals of the American Academy of Po.

Lampel, Joseph and Jamal Shamsie. 2003. "Capabilities in Motion: New Organizational Forms and the Reshaping of the Hollywood Movie Industry," *Journal of Management Studies*, 40, Dec., pp. 2189–210.

Lancaster, K. 1979. *Consumer Demand: A New Approach*, New York: Columbia University Press, p. 177.

Landier, Augustin and David Thesmar. 2003. "Financial Contracting with Optimistic Entrepreneurs: Theory and Evidence," mimeo, University of Chicago.

Lane, Randall. 1994. "Venture capital heaven," *Forbes*, 18 July.

Langerak, Fred, Peter C. Verhoef, Peeter W. J. Verlegh, and Kristine de Valck. 2003. "The Effect of Members' Satisfaction with a Virtual Community on Member Participation," Working Paper, Erasmus University Rotterdam – Faculteit der Bedrijfskunde (FBK), Erasmus University Rotterdam – Department of Marketing and Organization (M&O) and Erasmus University Rotterdam – Rotterdam School of Management (RSM).

Lave, J. 1988. *Cognition in Practice*. Cambridge: Cambridge University Press.

Laye, Jacques. 2003. "Price Competition and Coalition Strategy in the Presence of Search Costs," Ph.D. thesis, Ecole Polytechnique, France, chapter 1, pp. 19–53.

Laye, Jacques, Charis Lina, and Hervé Tanguy. 2004. "Consumers' Search Cost and Emerging Structure of Web-Sites Coalitions: A Multi-Agent Based Simulation of an Electronic Market," *Cahiers du Laboratoire d'Econométrie de l'Ecole Polytechnique*, 2004–017, http://www.ceco.polytechnique.fr/CAHIERS/pdf/2004-017.pdf

Lazega, Emmanuel. 2001. *The Collegial Phenomenon: The Social Mechanisms of Cooperation Among Peers in a Corporate Law Partnership*. Oxford: Oxford University Press.

Lazonick, William. 2003. "Stock Options as a Mode of High-Tech Compensation," Working Paper, INSEAD.

Lechner, Ulrike, Katarina Stanoevska-Slabeva, and Tan Yao-Hua. 2002. "Introduction to the Special Issue: Communities in the Digital Economy," *International Journal of Electronic Commerce*, Spring, 6:3, p. 5, 3p.

Lécuyer, Christophe. 2000. "Fairchild Semiconductor and Its Influence," in Chong-Moon Lee, William Miller, Marguerite Hancock, and Henry Rowen, eds., *The Silicon Valley Edge: A Habitat for Innovation and Entrepreneurship*. Stanford University Press, pp. 158–83.

Lee, C. H. Sophie, Anitesh Barua, and Andrew B. Whinston. 2000. "The Complementarity of Mass Customization and Electronic Commerce," *Economics of Innovation and New Technology*, 9:2, pp. 81–109.

Lee, Gwendolyn K. and Robert E. Cole. 2003. "From a Firm-Based to a Community-Based Model of Knowledge Creation: The Case of the Linux Kernel Development," *Organization Science: A Journal of the Institute of Management Sciences*, Nov./Dec., 14:6, p. 633, 17p.

Lee, Ho Geun. 1998. "Do Electronic Marketplaces Lower the Price of the Goods?," *Communications of the ACM*, 41:1, pp. 73–80.

Lee, Ho Geun, J. Christopher Westland, and Sewon Hong. 1999. "The Impact of Electronic Marketplaces on Product Prices: An Empirical Study of AUCNET," *International Journal of Electronic Commerce*, 4:2, pp. 45–60.

Leiner, Barry M, Vinton G. Cerf, David D. Clark, Robert, E. Kahn, Leonard Kleinrock, Daniel C. Lynch, Jon Postel, Larry G. Roberts, and Stephen Wolff. 2000. "A brief history of the Internet," http://www.isoc.org/theInternet/history/brief.html [Accessed June 2005]

Leininger, Wolfgang, P. B. Linhart, and Roy Radner. 1989. "Equilibria of the Sealed-Bid Mechanism for Bargaining with Incomplete Information," *J. Econ. Theory*, 48:1, pp. 63–106.

Lemley, Mark A. 1999. "The Law and Economics of the Internet Norms," *Working Paper*, University of California at Berkeley.

Lerner, Joshua. 2002. "Boom and Bust in the Venture Capital Industry and the Impact on Innovation," *Economic Review*, Federal Reserve Bank of Atlanta Fourth Quarter: 25–39.

Lerner, Joshua and Jean Tirole. 2004. "A Model of Forum Shopping with Special Reference to Standard Setting Organizations," NBER Working Paper no. w10664, August, NBER.

2002a. "The Scope of Open Source Licensing," Working Paper, Harvard University – Finance Unit and Université de Toulouse I – GREMAQ.

2002b. "Some Simple Economics of Open Source Software," *J. Ind. Econ.*, June, 50:2, pp. 197–234.

Leslie, Stuart W. 1993. "How the West Was Won: The Military and the Making of Silicon Valley," in William Aspray, ed., *Technological Competitiveness: Contemporary and Historical Perspectives on the Electrical, Electronics, and Computer Industries*. IEEE Press, 75–89.

Leslie, Stuart W. and Robert H. Kargon. 1996. "Selling Silicon Valley: Frederick Terman's Model for Regional Advantage," *Business History Review*, 70:4, pp. 435–72.

Lessig, Lawrence. 2001. *The Future of Ideas*. Random House.

1999. *Code and Other Laws of Cyberspace*. New York: Basic Books.

Lethiais, Virginie. 2001. "La tarification des services sur Internet: intégration verticale et gratuité," *Revue Econ.*, 52, pp. 39–56.

Levin, Dan and James L. Smith, J. L. 1994. "Equilibrium in Auctions with Entry," *American Economic Review*, 54, pp. 585–99.

Levy, Steven. 1995. "The Year of the Internet," *Newsweek*, 25 Dec.

Lewis, Anthony. 1956. "A.T.&T. Settles Antitrust Case; Shares Patents," *New York Times*, 25 Jan.

Lewis, Diane E. 1999. "Change in pension plan stirs union talk at Big Blue," *Boston Globe*, 25 July, G1.

Lewis, Tracy R. and David E. M. Sappington. 1994. "Supplying Information to Facilitate Price Discrimination," *Int. Econ. Rev.*, 35, pp. 309–27.

Li, Huagang and Goufu Tan. 2000. "Hidden Reserve Prices with Risk Averse Bidders," mimeo, Penn State University.

Li, Jinyan. 2001. "Effectiveness of the Arm's-Length Principle in the Age of E-Commerce," *Tax Notes*, 93:11, 10 Dec.

Licoppe, C., A.-S. Pharabod, and H. Assadi. 2002. "Contribution à une sociologie des échanges marchands sur Internet," *Réseaux*, 116, pp. 97–140.

Liebowitz, Stan. 2003. "Will MP3 Downloads Annihilate the Record Industry? The Evidence so Far," in *Advances in the Study of Entrepreneurship, Innovation, and Economic Growth*, Gary Libecap, ed. JAI Press.

Liebowitz, Stan. J. 2002. "Copyright, Piracy and Fair Use in the Networked Age. A Cato Policy Analysis," Working Paper, University of Texas at Dallas – Department of Finance and Managerial Economics.

Liebowitz, Stan J. and Stephen E. Margolis. 1990. "The Fable of Keys," *Journal of Law and Economics*, 33(1), pp. 1–26.

Linnemer, Laurent. 2002. "Price and Advertising as Signals of Quality when Some Consumers Are Informed," *Int. J. Ind. Organ.*, 20, pp. 931–47.

Livingston, Jeffrey. 2002. "How Valuable Is a Good Reputation? A Sample Selection Model of Internet Auctions," mimeo.

Lizzeri, Alessandro. 1999. "Information Revelation and Certification Intermediaries," *RAND Journal of Economics*, 30, pp. 214–31.

Lohr, Steve. 2004. "I.B.M. sought a China partnership, not just a sale," *New York Times*, 13 Dec.

Lohse, Gerald L., Steven Bellman, and Eric J. Johnson. 2000. "Consumer Buying Behavior on the Internet: Findings from Panel Data," *Journal of Interactive Marketing*, 14:1, pp. 15–29.

Long-Scott, Austin. 1995. "Access Denied?," *Outlook*, 8:1, http://www.maynardije.org

Looney, Clayton A. and Debabroto Chatterjee. 2002. "Web-Enabled Transformation of the Brokerage Industry," *Communications of the ACM*, Aug., 45:8, p. 75, 7p.

Lopes, Alex B. and Dennis Galletta. 2002. "Information Value in Electronic Networks: The Case of Subscription-Based Online Information Goods," *Academy of Management Proceedings*, p. D1, 6p.

Loughran, Tim and Jay Ritter. 2004. "Why Has IPO Underpricing Changed Over Time?," mimeo, University of Florida.

Lu, Qiwen. 2000. *China's Leap into the Information Age*. Oxford University Press.

Lucas Jr., Henry C. 2002. *Strategies for Electronic Commerce and the Internet.* Cambridge, MA and London: MIT Press, pp. xiv, 265.

Lucking-Reiley, David. 2000. "Auctions on the Internet: What's Being Auctioned, and How?," *Journal of Industrial Economics*, Sept., 48:3, pp. 227–52.

2000a. "Vickrey Auctions in Practice: From Nineteenth-Century Philately to Twenty-First-Century E-Commerce," *Journal of Economic Perspectives*, 14:3, pp. 183–92.

2000b. "Auctions on the Internet: What's Being Auctioned, and How?," *Journal of Industrial Economics*, 48:3, pp. 227–52.

1999a. "Using Field Experiments to Test Equivalence Between Auction Formats: Magic on the Internet," *American Economic Review*, 89:5, pp. 1063–80.

1999b. "Experimental Evidence on the Endogenous Entry of Bidders in Internet Auctions," Working Paper, University of Arizona.

Lucking-Reiley, David, Doug Bryan, Naghi Prasad, and Daniel Reeves. 2000. "Pennies from eBay: The Determinants of Price in Online Auctions," Working Paper, University of Arizona.

Lucking-Reiley, David and Daniel F. Spulber. 2001. "Business-to-Business Electronic Commerce," *Journal of Economic Perspectives*, Winter, 15:1, pp. 55–68.

Lynch, John and Dan Ariely. 2000. "Wine Online: Search Costs and Competition on Price, Quality, and Distribution," *Marketing Science*, 19:1, Winter, pp. 83–103.

Lynch, John G. and Dan Ariely. 1998. "Interactive Home Shopping: Effects of Search Cost for Price and Quality Information on Consumer Price Sensitivity Satisfaction with Merchandise and Retention," presented at Marketing Science and the Internet, MIT/INFORMS College on Marketing Mini-Conference. Cambridge, MA, 6–8 March.

Lynn, Kathleen. 1999. "For Older Workers, Cash-Balance Pension Plans Can Hurt," *The Record* (Hackensack, NJ), 20 May.

Machlup, Fritz. 1962. *The Production and Distribution of Knowledge in the United States.* Princeton: Princeton University Press.

Madden, Gary, Aniruddah Banerjee, and Grant Coble-Neal. 2004. "Measuring Telecommunication System Network Effects," in Russel Cooper and Gary Madden (eds.), *Frontiers of Broadband, Electronic and Mobile Commerce*, Contributions to Economics series. Heidelberg: Physica-Verlag.

Madhavan, Ananth. 1992. "Trading Mechanisms in Securities Markets," *Journal of Finance*, 47(2), pp. 607–42.

Mairesse, Jacques. 2002. "The Puzzling Relationships Between the Computer and the Economy: An Overview," in *Productivity, Inequality, and the Digital Economy: A Transatlantic Perspective*, Nathalie Greenan, Yannick Lhorty, and Jacques Mairesse, eds. Cambridge, MA: MIT Press.

Mallord, Alexandre. 2002. "Les nouvelles technologies dans le travail relationnel. Uers un traitement plus personnalisé de la figure du client?," *Sciences de la Société*, 56, Mai.

Malone, Michael, 1985. "Union Worries Add New Cloud to High-Tech Industry's Horizon," *Dallas Morning News*, 10 Aug.

Malone, Thomas and Robert Laubacher. 1998. "The Dawn of the E-Lance Economy," *Harvard Business Review*, Sept.–Oct.

Mandel, Michael. 1996. "The Triumph of the New Economy. A powerful payoff from globalization and the Info Revolution," *Business Week*, 30 Dec.

Mandel, Naomi and Eric J. Johnson. 1998. "Constructing Preferences Online: Can Web Pages Change What You Want?," Working Paper, University of Pennsylvania.

Manners, David. 1997. "Hero of our time," *Electronics Weekly*, 26 March.

Mansell, Robin, Ingrid Schenk, and W. Edward Steinmueller. 2000. "Net Compatible: The Economic and Social Dynamics of E-Commerce," *Communications and Strategies*, 2nd Quarter, 0:38, pp. 241–76.

Mateos-Garcia, Juan and W. Edward Steinmueller. 2003a. "The Open Source Way of Working: A New Paradigm for the Division of Labour in Software Development?," Falmer, UK, SPRU – Science and Technology Policy Research, INK Open Source Working Paper no. 1, Jan.

——— 2003b. "Dynamic Features of Open Source Development Communities and Community Processes," Brighton: SPRU – Science and Technology Policy Studies, Open Source Movement Research INK Working Paper no. 3, Feb.

Matthews, Steven. 1995. "Comparing Auctions for Risk Averse Buyers: A Buyer's Point of View," *Econometrica*, 55, pp. 633–46.

Matutes, Carmen, and Pierre Regibeau. 1992. "Compatibility and Bundling of Complementary Goods in a Duopoly," *Journal of Industrial Economics*, 40(1), pp. 37–54.

——— 1989. "Standardization Across Markets and Entry," *Journal of Industrial Economics*, 37, pp. 359–71.

——— 1988. "Mix and Match: Product Compatibility Without Network Externalities," *Rand Journal of Economics*, 19:2, pp. 219–34.

Maynard-Smith, John. 1982. *Evolution and the Theory of Games*. Cambridge: Cambridge University Press.

Mayzlyn, Dina. 2006. "Promotional Chat on the Internet," *Marketing and Science*, 25:2, pp. 155–63.

McAfee, Randolph P. 1993. "Mechanism Design by Competing Sellers," *Econometrica*, 61, pp. 1281–312.

McAfee, Randolph P. and John McMillan. 1992. "Bidding Rings," *American Economic Review*, 82, pp. 579–99.

——— 1987. "Auctions and Bidding," *Journal of Economic Literature*, 25:2, pp. 699–738.

McAfee, Randolph P., I. McMillan, and M. D. Whinston. 1989. "Multiproduct Monopoly, Commodity Bundling, and Correlation of Values," *Quarterly Journal of Economics*, 114 (May), pp. 71–84.

McAfee, Randolph P., D. Quan, and D. Vincent. 2002. "How to Set Minimum Acceptable Bids, with an Application to Real Estate Auctions," *Journal of Industrial Economics*, 50, pp. 391–416.

McCormick, D. Timothy, James P. Selway III, and Jeffrey W. Smith. 1998. "The Nasdaq Stock Market: Historical Background and Current Operation," NASD Working Paper, 98–01.

McDonald, Cynthia G. and V. Carlos Slawson. 2002. "Reputation in an Internet Auction Market," *Economic Inquiry*, 40, pp. 633–50.

McFadden, Daniel. 2001. "The Tragedy of the Commons," *Forbes ASAP*, 9 Oct.

McGill, Sandra P. and Lowell D. Yoder. 2003. "From Storefronts to Servers to Service Providers: Stretching the Permanent Establishment Definition to Accommodate New Business Models," *Taxes – The Tax Magazine*, 81:3, March.

McHugh, Timothy. 2002. "The Growth of Electronic Person-to-Person Payments," *Fed Letter*, 180, Aug.

McKelvey, Maureen. 2001. "The Economic Dynamics of Software: Three Competing Business Models Exemplified Through Microsoft, Netscape and Linux," *Economics of Innovation and New Technology*, 10:2–3, pp. 199–236.

Méadel, Cécile and Meryem Marzouki, 2004. "Quelle justice pour Internet? L'arbitrage sur les noms de domaine," in Françoise Massit-Folléa and Serge Proulx (eds.), *Internet, nouvel espace public mondialisé*. Paris: Les Canadiens en Europe.

Melnik, Mikhail I. and James Alm. 2002. "Does A Seller's eCommerce Reputation Matter? Evidence from eBay Auctions," *Journal of Industrial Economics*, 50, pp. 337–50.

Melo de Brito, Carvalho, Tereza Cristina, and Michael Siegel. 2002. "Return on Investment from Online Banking Services: An Analysis of Financial Account Aggregation," Working Paper, University of Sao Paulo – Escola Politicnica and Massachusetts Institute of Technology (MIT) – Sloan School of Management.

Mercer Human Resource Consulting. 2001. "Future of Equity – 2003 Update," June, at www.mercerhr.com

Mester, Loretta J., Leonard I. Nakamura, and Micheline Renault. 2001. "Checking Accounts and Bank Monitoring," Federal Reserve Bank of Philadelphia, Working Paper, 1:3, pp. 1–36.

Meyer, Laurence. 2000. "Digital Platforms: Definition and Strategic Value," *Communications and Strategies*, 2nd Quarter, 0:38, pp. 127–51.

Michelacci, Claudio and Javier Suarez. 2004. "Business Creation and the Stock Market," *Rev. Econ. Stud.*, 71:2, pp. 459–81.

Milgram, Stanley. 1967. "The Small World Problem," *Psychology Today*, 2, pp. 60–7.

Milgrom, Paul R. 1981. "Good News and Bad News: Representation Theorems and Applications," *Bell J. Econ.*, 12(2), pp. 380–91.

Milgrom, Paul, Douglas C. North, and Barry Weingast. 1990. "The Role of Institutions in the Revival of Trade: The Law Merchant, Private Judges, and the Champagne Fairs," *Economics and Politics*, March, 2(1), pp. 1–23.

Milgrom, Paul R. and Robert Weber. 1982. "A Theory of Auctions and Competitive Bidding," *Econometrica*, 50, pp. 1089–122.

1986. "Price and Advertising Signals of Product Quality," *J. Polit. Economy*, 94, pp. 796–821.

Miller, D. 1998. *A Theory of Shopping*. Ithaca: Cornell University Press.

Miller, Michael W. 1984. "Unions curtail organizing in high tech," *Wall Street Journal*, 13 Nov.

Miller, Nolan, Paul Resnick, and Richard Zeckhauser. 2005. "Eliciting Honest Feedback," *Management Science*, 51:9, pp. 1359–73.

Moglen, Eben 1999. "Anarchism Triumphant: Free Software and the Death of Copyright," *First Monday*, 4(8), http://www.firstmonday.dk

Molloy, Chuck. 1989. "Hitachi, Ltd. and Electronic Data Systems form Hitachi Data Systems," *Business Wire*, 1 May.

Molteni, Luca and Andrea Ordanini. 2003. "Consumption Patterns, Digital Technology and Music Downloading," *Long Range Planning*, 36, pp. 389–406.

Montagnier, Pierre, Elizabeth Muller, and Graham Vickery. 2002. "The Digital Divide: Diffusion and Use of ICTs," OECD Paper, http://www.oecd.org

Moody, Glyn. 1997. " The Greatest OS that Never Was," *Wired*, Aug.

Moore, Gordon E. 1996. "Some Personal Perspectives on Research in the Semiconductor Industry," in Richard S. Rosenbloom and William J. Spencer, eds., *Engines of Innovation: US Industrial Research at the End of an Era*. Harvard Business School Press.

Moorhouse, John C. 2001. "Property Rights, Technology, and Internet Distribution," *Journal of Technology Transfer*, Oct., 26:4, pp. 351–61.

Moraga-González, José Luis. 2000. "Quality Uncertainty and Informative Advertising," *Int. J. Ind. Organ.*, 18, pp. 615–40.

Morgan, John and Tanjim Hossain. 2003. "A Test of the Revenue Equivalence Theorem Using Field Experiments on eBay," Working Paper, Haas Business School.

Morgan, Peter and Richard Manning. 1985. "Optimal Search," *Econometrica* 53:4, pp. 923–44.

Morningstar, Chip and Farmer Randall. 1993. "The Lessons of Lucasfilm's Habitat," in Benedikt Michael (ed.), *Cyberspace First Steps*. Boston: MIT Press, pp. 273–301.

Mowery, David C. and Nathan Rosenberg. 1989. *Technology and the Pursuit of Economic Growth*. Cambridge: Cambridge University Press.

Mueller, Milton. 1996. *Universal Service: Competition, Interconnection, and Monopoly in the Making of the American Telephone System*. Cambridge, MA: MIT Press.

Mueller, Milton M. 2002. *Ruling the Root: Internet Governance and the Taming of Cyberspace*. Cambridge, MA.: MIT Press.

Mulqueen, John T., 1989a. "Industry Watch: The Data Communications 100: A year of waiting for another to begin so something significant could happen," *Data Communications*, 1 Jan.

1989b. "Industry Watch: Connecting nets, a growth business T1 Links take bridge and router sales to new, and brighter, horizons," *Data Communications*, 1 July.

Munier, Bertrand. 2000. "Strategies in the Internet Economy: Value Creation and Mirages," *Communications and Strategies*, Special Issue 4th Quarter, 0:40, pp. 91–123.

Muniesa, Fabian. 2003. "Des marchés comme algorithmes: Sociologie de la cotation électronique à la Bourse de Paris," PhD dissertation. Paris: Ecole Nationale des Mines, Centre de Sociologie de L'Innovation.

Myerson, Roger. 1981. "Optimal Auction Design," *Mathematics of Operation Research*, 6, pp. 58–73.

Myerson, Roger B. and Mark A. Satterthwaite. 1983. "Efficient Mechanisms for Bilateral Trading," *J. Econ. Theory*, 29:2, pp. 265–81.

Nadel, Mark S. 2000. "The Consumer Product Selection Process in an Internet Age: Obstacles to Maximum Effectiveness and Policy Options," *Harvard Journal of Law and Technology*, 14:1, pp. 185–264.

Nalebuff, Bary J. 1999. "Bundling," Working Paper, School of Management, Yale University, July.

NASDAQ Economic Research. 2003. "Results on the Introduction of NASDAQ's SuperMontage," Working Paper.

Nash, John F. 1951. "Noncooperative Games," *Annals of Mathematics*, 54:2, pp. 286–95.

Nelson, Charles and Richard Startz. 1990. "The Distribution of the Instrumental Variables Estimator and Its t-Ratio when the Instrument Is a Poor One," *Journal of Business*, 61, pp. S125–40.

Nelson, Phillip. 1974. "Advertising as Information," *J. Polit. Economy*, 81, pp. 729–54.

1970. "Information and Consumer Behaviour," *J. Polit. Economy*, 78, pp. 311–29.

Netanel, Neil Weinstock. 2003. "Impose a Noncommercial Use Levy to Allow Free Peer-to-Peer File Sharing," *Harvard Journal of Law and Technology*, 17, Dec.

Niland, Powell. 1976. "Reforming Private Pension Plan Administration," *Business Horizons*, Feb., pp. 25–35.

Noble, David. 1977. *America by Design: Science, Technology, and the Rise of Corporate Capitalism*. Knopf.

Noe, Thomas H. and Geoffrey Parker. 2000. "Winner Take All: Competition, Strategy, and the Structure of Returns in the Internet Economy," (12 November), http://ssrn.com/abstract=250371 [Accessed June 2005]

Norman, D. A. 1993. *Les artefacts cognitifs. Raisons Pratiques no 4: Les objets dans l'action. De la maison au laboratoire*. Paris: EHESS, pp. 15–35.

Norris, Pippa. 2002. "The Global Divide: Information Poverty and Internet Access Worldwide," Working Paper, John F. Kennedy School of Government, Harvard University.

North, Douglass C. 2005. *Understanding the Process of Economic Change*. Princeton Univeristy Press.

1990. *Institutions, Institutional Change and Economic Performance*. Cambridge: Cambridge University Press.

1986. "The New Institutional Economics," *Journal of Institutional and Theoretical Economics*, 142, pp. 230–7.

Novak, Thomas P., Donna L. Hoffman, and Yiu-Fai Yung. 1999. "Measuring the Flow Construct in Online Environments: A Structural Modeling Approach," Working Paper, April.

Novshek, William. 1980. "Equilibrium in Simple Spatial (or Differentiated Product) Models," *J. Econ. Theory*, 22, pp. 313–26.

Nowak, Martin A. and Robert M. May. 1992. "Evolutionary Games and Spatial Chaos," *Nature*, 359, pp. 826–9.

NVP (Nederlandse Vereniging van Participatiemaatschappijen). 2000. "Rendementsmeting van Nederlandse Venture Capital Activeiten. Rapport NVP-onderzoek over de Periode 1989–1998," mimeo, The Hague.

Oates, Wallace E. 1999. "An Essay on Fiscal Federalism," *Journal of Economic Literature* 37, pp. 1120–1149.

1972. *Fiscal Federalism*. New York: Harcourt Brace Jovanovich.

Oberholzer, Felix and Koleman Strumpf. 2004. "The Effect of File Sharing on Record Sales: An Empirical Analysis," Working Paper, Harvard Business School and UNC Chapel Hill, http://www.unc.edu/~cigar/strumab.htm

O'Brien, Richard. 1992. *Global Financial Integration: The End of Geography*. New York: Council on Foreign Relations Press.

Ockenfels, Axel and Alvin E. Roth. 2003. "Late and Multiple Bidding in Second Price Internet Auctions: Theory and Evidence Concerning Different Rules for Ending an Auction," *Games and Economic Behavior.*

OECD (Organisation for Economic Cooperation and Development). 2004. *Regulatory Reform as a Tool for Bridging the Digital Divide*, www.oecd.org/dataoecd/40/11/34487084.pdf

2002. *Information Technology Outlook*, http://www.oecd.org

2001. *Understanding the Digital Divide*, http://www.oecd.org

1996. *Information Infrastructure Convergence and Pricing: The Internet*. Paris: Committee for Information, Computer and Communications Policy.

OECD Report. 1999. "The Economic and Social Impacts of Electronic Commerce: Preliminary Findings and Research Agenda," OECD Publications, France.

Offer, Avner. 1997. "Between the Gift and the Market: The Economy of Regard," *Economic History Review*, Aug., 50:3, pp. 450–76.

Ohmae, Kenichi. 1990. *The Borderless World: Power and Strategy in the Interlinked Economy*. New York: Harper Perennial.

Okimoto, Daniel I. and Yoshio Nishi. 1994. "R&D Organization in Japanese and American Semiconductor Firms," in Masahiko Aoki and Ronald Dore, eds., *The Japanese Firm: The Sources of Competitive Strength*. Oxford University Press, pp. 178–208.

Okuno-Fujiwara, Masahiro, Andrew Postlewaite, and Kotaro Suzumura. 1990. "Strategic Information Revelation," *Rev. Econ. Stud.*, 57(1), pp. 25–47.

Olson, Mancur. 1965. *The Logic of Collective Action*, Cambridge, MA: Harvard University Press.

Olsson, Ola and Bruno S. Frey. 2002. "Entrepreneurship as Recombinant Growth," *Small Business Economics*, 19(2), pp. 69–80.

O'Mahony, Siobhan. 2003. "Guarding the Commons: How Community Managed Software Projects Protect Their Work," *Research Policy*, July, 32:7, pp. 1179–98.

O'Mahony, Siobhan and Fabrizio Ferraro. 2004. "Managing the Boundary of an 'Open' Project," Working Paper, Harvard Business School and IESE Business School – University of Navarra.

Online Publishers Association. 2004. Online pay content: U.S. Market Spending Report, http://www.online-publishers.org/

2003. Online pay content: Demographic and Usage Report, http://www.online-publishers.org/

Oren, Shmuel, and Stephen Smith. 1981. "Critical Mass and Tariff Structure in Electronic Communications Markets," *Bell Journal of Economics*, 12(2), pp. 467–87.

Organisation for Economic Co-operation and Development. 1997. 1999. 2001. 2003. *Communication Outlook*. Paris: OECD.

Ostrom, Elinor. 1990. *Governing the Commons: The Evolution of Institutions for Collective Action*. New York: Cambridge University Press.

Ostrom, Elinor and James Walker. 1997. "Neither Markets Nor States: Linking Transformation Processes in Collective Action Arenas," in *Perspectives on Public Choice: A Handbook*, edited by Dennis C. Mueller. Cambridge: Cambridge University Press, pp. 35–72.

Oudshoff, Sandra, Ivor Bosloper, Tomas B. Klos, and Ben Spaanenburg. 2003. "Knowledge Discovery in Virtual Community Texts: Clustering Virtual Communities," *Journal of Intelligent and Fuzzy Systems*, 14:1, p. 13, 12p.

Oxley, Joanne E. and Bernard Yeung, 2001. "E-Commerce Readiness: Institutional Environment and International Competitiveness," *Journal of International Business Studies*, 32:4, pp. 705–23.

Paarsch, Harry. 1992. "Deciding Between the Common and Private Value Paradigms in Empirical Models of Auctions," *Journal of Econometrics*, 51, pp. 191–215.

Pagano, Marco. 1989. "Trading Volume and Asset Liquidity," *The Quarterly Journal of Economics*, 104(2), pp. 255–74.

Pagano, Marco and Ailsa Roell. 1998. "The Choice of Stock Ownership Structure: Agency Costs, Monitoring and the Decision to Go Public," *Quart. J. Econ.*, 113:1, pp. 187–225.

Palacios, Juan J. and Kenneth L. Kraemer. 2003. "Globalization and E-Commerce: Environment and Policy in Mexico," *Communications of the Association for Information Systems*, 11, pp. 129–85.

Pallatto, John. 2004. "Time for PeopleSoft Customers, Workers to Cut Best Deal," *eWeek*, 20 Dec.

Paris, Thomas (ed.). 2004. *La libération audiovisuelle – enjeux technologiques, économiques et réglementaires*. Paris: Dalloz.

Park, Sangin. 2002. "Website Usage and Seller's Listing in Internet Auctions," Working Paper, SUNY Stony Brook.

Parlour, Christine A. and Duane J. Seppi. 2003. "Liquidity-Based Competition for Order Flow," *Review of Financial Studies*, 16(2), pp. 301–43.

Patterson, William Pat. 1982. "It's semiconductors, turn to fight the Japanese," *Industry Week*, 22 Feb.

1981. "Gathering storm clouds for semiconductors," *Industry Week*, 26 Jan.

PaymentOne. 2003. Online Payments Strategies and Preferences Poll.

Pearl Meyer & Partners. 2001. "Trends 2001: Looking Forward and Back," at http://www.execpay.com/trends2001.htm

Peitz, Martin and Patrick Waelbroeck. 2004. "The Effect of Internet Piracy on CD Sales: Cross-Section Evidence," *Review of Economics on Copyright Issues*, 1:2, pp. 71–9.

2003. "Piracy of Digital Products: A Critical Review of the Economics Literature," Working Paper, University of Mannheim – Department of Economics and Free University of Brussels – European Center for Advanced Research in Economics and Statistics (ECARES).

Pénin, Julien. 2003. "Patents versus ex-post rewards : a new look," *Cahiers de recherche du Département des sciences économiques.* Université du Québec à Montréal, Département des sciences économiques, no. 20–19.

Penrose, Edith T. 1959. *The Theory of the Growth of the Firm.* Blackwell.

Peppers, Don and Martha Rogers. 1994. "Let's Make A Deal," *Wired,* Feb.

1993. *The One to One Future: Building Relationships. One Customer at a Time,* New York: Currency Doubleday.

Pereira, Pedro. 2002. "Search and Destroy: Competition Between Search Engines and Consumer Prices," Working Paper.

Perkins, Anthony B. 1996. "Electronic Communities," *Harvard Business Review,* Jul./Aug., 74:4, p. 164, 5/6p.

1994. "Venture pioneers," *Red Herring,* 1 Feb.

Perrot, Anne. 1993. "Compatibility, Networks, and Competition: A Review of Recent Advances," *Transportation Science.*

Perry, Martin K. and Robert H. Porter. 1985. "Oligopoly and the Incentives for Horizontal Mergers," *Amer. Econ. Rev.,* 75:1, pp. 219–27.

Peters, Michael. "Surplus Extraction and Competition," *Review of Economic Studies,* 3, pp. 613–31.

Peters, Michael and Sergei Severinov. 2001. "Internet Auctions with Many Traders," Working Paper, University of Wisconsin.

1997. "Competition Among Sellers Who Offer Auctions Instead of Prices," *Journal of Economic Theory,* 75, pp. 141–79.

Petroshius, Susan M. and Kent B. Monroe. 1987. "The Effect of Product Line Pricing Characteristics on Product Evaluations," *Journal of Consumer Research,* 13, pp. 511–19.

Peypoch, Ramon J. 1998. "The Case for Electronic Business Communities," *Business Horizons,* Sep./Oct., 41:5, p. 17, 4p.

Peyrache, Eloic and Lucia Quesada. 2004. "Strategic Certification," HEC Paris and University of Wisconsin-Madison.

2003. "Reputation of a Potentially Collusive Auditor," HEC Paris and University of Wisconsin-Madison.

2002. "Monopoly Intermediary and Information Transmission," University of Toulouse Working Paper.

Piazolo, Daniel. 2001. "The Digital Divide," *CESifo Forum,* 2:3, pp. 29–34, http://www.ssrn.com

Pierson, John. 1978. "Trend of higher levies on capital gains is reversed as President signs tax bill," *Wall Street Journal,* 9 Nov.

Pimentel, Benjamin. 2002. "As tech jobs decrease, interest in unions is up," *San Francisco Chronicle,* 18 July.

Platt, Charles. 2001. "The Future Will Be Fast but Not Free," *Wired,* May.

Pohjola, Matti. 2002. "New Economy in Growth and Development," *Oxford Rev. of Eco. Pol.,* 18:3, pp. 380–96.

2002. "The New Economy: Facts, Impacts and Policies," *Info. Econ. Pol.,* 14:2, pp. 133–44.

Pollock, Gregory B. and Lee Alan Dugatkin. 1992. "Reciprocity and the Evolution of Reputation," *Journal of Theoretical Biology,* 159, pp. 25–37.

Porat, Marc Uri. 1977. *The Information Economy: Definition and Measurement.* Washington: US Dept. of Commerce Office of Telecommunications.

Porter, Michael E., ed. 1986. *Competition in Global Industries*. Boston: Harvard Business School Press.

Potter, Joseph C. 1953. "Good 'human relations' keep employees happy and put IBM at the top of its field," *Wall Street Journal*, 11 Feb.

Pouloudi, Athanasia, Jochem Paarlberg, and Eric van Heck. 2003. "Web Auctions in Europe," Working Paper, Athens University of Economics and Business, Erasmus University Rotterdam – Department of Decision and Information Sciences.

PricewaterhouseCoopers. 2004. *Money Tree US Report. Q4 2003 Results*. Available at http://www.pwcmoneytree.com

Quah, Danny. 2003. "Digital Goods and the New Economy," CEP Discussion Papers from Centre for Economic Performance, LSE.

1999. "Technology and Growth, The Weightless Economy in Economic Development," LSE Discussion Paper 417.

Radecki, Lawrence J. 1999. "Bank's Payments-Driven Revenues," Federal Reserve Bank of New York, *Economic Policy Review*, July.

Radner, Roy and Andrew Schotter. 1989. "The Sealed-Bid Mechanism: An Experimental Study," *J. Econ. Theory*, 48:1, pp. 179–220.

Rallet, Alain. 2003. "Nouvelle économie et commerce électronique: mesure et démesure," *Annales des Télécommunications*, 58:1–2, pp. 147–66.

2001. "Commerce électronique ou électronisation du commerce," *Réseaux*, 106.

Rallet, Alain and André Torre. 2005. "Proximity and Localization," *Reg. Stud.*, 39:1, pp. 37–59.

Ramil, Juan F. and Neil Smith. 2004. "Qualitative Simulation of Models of Software Evolution," *Journal of Software Process – Improvement and Practice.*

Rasmusen, Eric. 2001. "Strategic Implications of Uncertainty over One's Own Private Value in Auctions," Working Paper, Indiana University.

Ratchford, Brian T., Xing Pan, and Venkatesh Shankar. 2003. "On the Efficiency of Internet Markets for Consumer Goods," Working Paper, University of Maryland – Robert H. Smith School of Business, Indiana University Bloomington – Department of Marketing and University of Maryland – Robert H. Smith School of Business.

Raymond, Eric. S. 1999. *The Magic Cauldron*. [http://www.tuxedo.org/]

1998a. "The Cathedral and the Bazaar," *First Monday*, 3:3 [http://www.first monday.dk], § 4, firstmonday.org/issues/issue3_3/raymond/index.html and www.tuxedo.org/~esr/writings/cathedral-bazaar

1998b. "Homesteading the Noosphere," *First Monday*, 3:10 (Oct.). [Available at: http://firstmonday.org/issues/issue3_10/raymond/index.html and www. tuxedo.org/~esr/writings/homesteading]

Rensberger, Boyce. 1972. "Where science grows miracles," *New York Times*, 20 Feb.

Resnick, Paul and Richard Zeckhauser. 2002. "Trust Among Strangers in Internet Transactions: Empirical Analysis of eBay's Reputation System," in *The Economics of the Internet and E-Commerce*, Michael R. Baye, editor. Volume 11 of *Advances in Applied Microeconomics*. Amsterdam: Elsevier Science.

Resnick, Paul, Richard Zeckhauser, Eric Friedman, and Ko Kuwabara. 2000. "Reputation Systems: Facilitating Trust in Internet Interactions," *Communications of the ACM*, 43:12, pp. 45–8.

Resnick, Paul, Richard Zeckhauser, John Swanson, and Kate Lockwood. 2006. "The Value of Reputation on eBay: A Controlled Experiment," *Experimental Economics*, 9:2, pp. 79–101.

Rezende, Leonardo. 2003. "Auction Econometrics by Least Squares," mimeo, University of Illinois Urbana-Champeign.

Rheingold, Howard. 1993. *The Virtual Community – Homesteading on the Electronic Frontier*. New York: Addison-Wesley.

Rice, Tara and Kristin Stanton. 2003. "Estimating the Volume of Payments-Driven Revenues," Emerging Payments Occasional Papers Series, 2003–1C, Federal Reserve Bank of Chicago.

Ridings, Catherine, David Gefen, and Bay Arinze. 2002. "Some Antecedents and Effects of Trust in Virtual Communities," *Journal of Strategic Information Systems*, 11:3–4, pp. 271–95.

Riley, John and William Samuelson. 1981. "Optimal Auctions," *American Economic Review*, 71, pp. 381–92.

Riordan, Michael and Lillian Hoddeson. 1997. *Crystal Fire: The Invention of the Transistor and the Birth of the Information Age*. Norton.

Ritter, Jay R. 2004. "Some Factoids about the 2003 IPO Market," mimeo, University of Florida, http://bear.cba.ufl.edu/ritter

Ritter, Jay R. and Ivo Welch. 2003. "A Review of IPO Activity, Pricing and Allocations," *J. Finance*, 57:4, pp. 1795–828.

Robinson, Marc. 1985. "Collusion and the Choice of Auction," *RAND Journal of Economics*, 16, pp. 141–5.

Robles, Gregorio, Stefan Koch, and Jesus Gonzalez-Barahona. 2004. "Remote Analysis and Measurement by Means of the CVSAnalY Tool," Working Paper, Informatics Department, Universidad Rey Juan Carlos, June. [Available at: http://opensource.mit.edu/papers/robles-koch-barahona_cvsa nely.pdf]

Rochet, Jean-Charles and Jean Tirole. 2004. "Defining Two-Sided Markets," mimeo, IDEI and GREMAQ, University of Toulouse.

      2003. "Platform Competition in Two-Sided Markets," *J. of the European Economic Association*, 1:4, pp. 990–1029.

      2002. "Cooperation among Competitors: The Economics of Payment Card Associations," *RAND Journal of Economics*, 33:4, pp.1–22.

Rock, Arthur. 2000. "Arthur Rock & Co.," in Udayan Gupta, ed., *Done Deals: Venture Capitalists Tell their Stories*. Harvard Business School Press, pp. 139–48.

Rohlfs, Jeffrey H. 2001. *Bandwagon Effects in High-Technology Industries*. Cambridge, MA: MIT Press.

      1974. "A Theory of Interdependent Demand for a Communications Service," *Bell Journal of Economics and Management Science*, 5(1), pp. 16–37.

Rose, Frank. 1999. "The Economics, Concept, and Design of Information Intermediaries: A Theoretic Approach," Information Age Economy series, Heidelberg: Physica, pp. xvi, 266.

Rosegrant, Susan and David R. Lampe. 1992. *Route 128: Lessons from Boston's High-Tech Community*. Basic Books.

Rosen, Sherwin. 1981. "The Economics of Superstars," *Amer. Econ. Rev.*, 71:5, pp. 845–58.

1974. "Hedonic Prices and Implicit Markets: Product Differentiation in Pure Competition," *Journal of Political Economy*, 82:1, pp. 34–55.

Rosenau, James N. 2001. "Strong Demand, Huge Supply: Governance in an Emerging Epoch," paper prepared for the Conference on Multi-Level Governance: Interdisciplinary Perspectives, sponsored by the Political Economy Center of the University of Sheffield, in I. Bache and M. Flinders (eds.), *Multi-Level Governance*. Oxford: Oxford University Press, 2004.

Rosenberg, Nathan and Richard Nelson. 1994. "American Universities and Technical Advance in Industry," *Research Policy*, 23:3, pp. 323–48.

Ross, Sheldon M. 2003. *Introduction to Probability Models*, 8th edition. Academic Press.

Roth, Alvin E. and Axel Ockenfels. 2002. "Last-Minute Bidding and the Rules for Ending Second-Price Auctions: Evidence from eBay and Amazon Auctions on the Internet," *American Economic Review*, 92:4, pp. 1093–103.

Rothkopf, Michael H. (Reviewer). 2003. "Review of The Future of eMarkets: Multi-Dimensional Market Mechanisms" by Martin Bichler. Cambridge, New York and Melbourne: Cambridge University Press, *Journal of Economic Literature*, March, 41:1, pp. 214–15.

Rowley, Jennifer. 2001. "Online Communities: Stabilising E-Business," *Global Business and Economics Review*, June, 3:1, pp. 84–93.

Rule, Colin. 2002. *Online Dispute Resolution for Business*. San Francisco: Jossey-Bass Press.

Rust, John and George Hall. 2003. "Middlemen versus Market Makers: A Theory of Competitive Exchange," *Journal of Political Economy*, April, 111:2, pp. 353–403.

Sabourin, Delphine. 2005. "Competition Between Dealer Markets and Electronic Limit-Order Books," Working Paper, University of Paris IX Dauphine.

Sabow, Steven and Erin Milligan. 2000. "Trends in Broad-Based Stock Option Plans," *Journal of Employee Ownership, Law, and Finance*, 12:2, pp. 99–105.

Sachs, Jeffrey. 2000. "Today's World Is Divided Not by Ideology but by Technology," *The Economist*, London, 26 July.

Sahlman, William A. 1990. "The Structure and Governance of Venture Capital Organizations," *Journal of Financial Economics*, 27:2, pp. 473–521.

Salant, Stephen W., Sheldon Switzer, and Robert J. Reynolds. 1983. "Losses from Horizontal Mergers: The Effect of an Exogenous Change in Industry Structure on Cournot-Nash Equilibria," *Quart. J. Econ.*, 98, pp. 185–99.

Salinger, Michael A. 1995. "A Graphical Analysis of Bundling," *Journal of Business*, 68(1), pp. 85–98.

Salop, Steven C. 1979. "Monopolistic Competition with Outside Goods," *Bell J. Econ.*, 10, pp. 141–56.

Samuelson, Pamela and Randall Davis. 2000. "The Digital Dilemma: A Perspective on Intellectual Property in the Information Age," Working Paper presented at the TPRC (Telecommunications Policy Research Conference).

San Jose Mercury News. 2004. "Former dot-com Darling Commerce One Down to Last Gasp," 23 Sept., http://www.siliconvalley.com/mld/siliconvalley/9741285.htm

Santos, Liuz Fernando F. and Moisés Ari Zilber. 2001. "Interactive Television: Perspectives and Expansion of the Electronic Commerce," Working Paper, Universidade Presbiteriana Mackenzie and Universidade Presbiteriana Mackenzie.

Santos, Tano and Joséa Scheinkman. 2001. "Competition among exchanges," *Quarterly Journal of Economics*, 116:3, pp. 1027–61.

Sassen, Saskia. 1991. *The Global City: New York, London, Tokyo*. Princeton, NJ: Princeton University Press.

Sawhney, M., E. Prandelli and G. Verona, 2003. "The Power of Infomediation," *MIT Sloan Management Review*, Winter, 44:2, p. 77, 6p.

Sawyer, Kathy. 1984. "Unions striking out in high-tech firms," *Washington Post*, 18 Mar.

Saxenian, Anna Lee. 1994. *Regional Advantage: Culture and Competition in Silicon Valley and Route 128*. Harvard University Press.

Scheinkman, José A. and Wei Xiong. 2003. "Overconfidence and Speculative Bubbles," *J. Polit. Economy*, 111:6, pp. 1183–219.

Schement, Jorge Reina. 1994. *Beyond Universal Service: Characteristics of Americans Without Telephones, 1980–1993*. Benton Foundation (www.benton.org).

Scherer, Frederic M. and David Ross. 1990. *Industrial Market Structure and Economic Performance*. Boston: Houghton Mifflin.

Schiff, Aaron. 2002. "The Economics of Open Source Software: A Survey of the Early Literature," *Review of Network Economics*, 1, March.

Schiff, Frederick. 2003. "Business Models of News Web Sites: A Survey of Empirical Trends and Expert Opinion," *First Monday*, 8:6.

Schindler, Julia. 2003. "Late Bidding on the Internet," mimeo, Vienna University of Economics and Business Administration.

Schmalensee, Richard. 1984. "Gaussian Demand and Commodity Bundling," *Journal of Business*, Jan., 57, pp. 5211–30.

Schmitt, John and Jonathan Wadsworth. 2002. "Give PC's a Chance: Personal Computer Ownership and the Digital Divide in the United States and Great Britain," Centre for Economic Performance London School of Economics and Political Science, Discussion Paper 26.

Schneidman, Jeffrey and David C. Parkes. 2003. "Rationality and Self Interest in Peer to Peer Networks," 2nd International Workshop on Peer-to-Peer Systems (IPTPS '03), Berkeley, CA, USA.

Schneier, Bruce. 1996. *Applied Cryptography*. John Wiley and Sons.

Schoenberger, Chana R. 2004. "Cell Phone Rings Equal Bling Bling," 17 February. Forbes.com http://www.forbes.com/2004/02/17/cz_cs_0217ringtones_print.html

Schrage, Michael. 1994. "Is Advertising Finally Dead?," *Wired*, Feb.

Schubert, Petra and Mark Ginsburg. 2000. "Virtual Communities of Transaction: The Role of Personalization in Electronic Commerce," *Electronic Markets*, Jan., 10:1, p. 45, 11p.

Schultz, Ellen. 2000. "Pension Cuts 101: Companies find subtle ways to pare retirement benefits," *Wall Street Journal*, 27 July.

Schulz, Norbert and Konrad Stahl. 1996. "Do Consumers Search for the Highest Price? Oligopoly Equilibrium and Monopoly Optimum in Differentiated-Products Markets," *RAND J. Econ.*, 27:3, pp. 542–62.

Schumpeter, Joseph A. 1942. *Capitalism, Socialism, and Democracy.* Harper and Bros.

Schuyten, Peter J. 1979. "To clone a computer: neophyte National Semiconductor has jolted the industry," *New York Times,* 4 Feb.

Schwartz, Eduardo S. and Mark Moon. 2000. "Rational Pricing of Internet Companies," *Financial Analysts Journal,* pp. 62–75.

Schwartz, Evan. 1997. *Webonomics: Nine Essential Principles for Growing Your Business on the World Wide Web.* New York: Broadway Books.

1996. "Advertising Webonomics 101," *Wired,* Feb.

Schwartz, Peter. 2000. "The Future of the Newconomy," *Red Herring,* July.

1999. "Long Live the Long Boom," *Wired,* Sept.

Schwienbacher, Armin. 2005. "Venture Capital Investment, Product Innovation, and Exit Decision," mimeo, University of Amsterdam.

Sciadas, George. 2002. *Unveiling The Digital Divide.* Statistics Canada: Science, Innovation and Electronic Information Division, http://www.statcan.ca

Sciardet, Hervé. 2003. *Les marchands de l'aube. Ethnographie et théorie du commerce aux Puces de Saint-Ouen.* Paris: Economica.

Scott Morton, Fiona, Florian Zettelmeyer, and Jorge Silva-Risso. 2000. "Internet Car Retailing," Working Paper, Yale School of Management, University of California, Berkeley – Marketing Group and University of California, Los Angeles – Anderson School of Management.

Seppi, Duane J. 1997. "Liquidity Provision with Limit Orders and a Strategic Specialist," *Review of Financial Studies,* 10(1), pp. 103–50.

Serval, Thomas 2001. "Lorsque les réseaux d'information deviendront des bourses," *Revue Economique,* 52, pp. 249–66.

Sethi, Rajiv and E. Somanathan. 2002. "Understanding Reciprocity," *J. Econ. Behav. Organ.,* 50:1, pp. 1–27.

Shah, Rajiv and Jay P. Kesan. 2004. "Nurturing Software: How Societal Institutions Shape the Development of Software," *Communications of the ACM.*

Shaked, Avner and John Sutton. 1982. "Relaxing Price Competition Through Product Differentiation," *Review of Economic Studies,* 49, pp. 3–13.

Shapiro, Carl and Hal R. Varian. 1999. *Information and Rules,* Cambridge, MA: Harvard Business School Press.

1998. *Information Rules: A Strategic Guide to the Network Economy.* Boston: Harvard Business School Press (http://www.inforules.com/).

Sharkey, William W. 1993. "Network Models in Economics," mimeo.

Sharma, Sandeshika. 2003. "Collective Action, Network Externalities and Free Riding: An Evolutionary Model," University of California Irvine Working Paper.

Shelton, Jay. 2004. "The Global Fabless Model," PowerPoint presentation, Fabless Semiconductor Association (FSA).

Shepard, Stephen. 1997. "The New Economy: What It Really Means," *Business Week,* 17 Nov.

Shih, Chuan-Fong, Jason Dedrick, and Kenneth L. Kraemer. 2005. "Rule of Law and the International Diffusion of E-Commerce," *Communications of the ACM.* 48:11, pp. 57–62.

Shih, Raymond and Ray Ku. 2001. "The Creative Destruction of Copyright: Napster and the New Economics of Digital Technology," *University of Chicago Law Review.*

Sigmund, Karl. 1992. "Complex Adaptive Systems and the Evolution of Reciprocation," IIASA Interim Report, IR-98–100.

Silk, Alvin, Lisa Klein, and Ernst Berndt. 2001. "The Emerging Position of the Internet as an Advertising Medium," *Netnomics,* 3, pp. 129–48.

Simon, H. 1969. *The Sciences of the Artificial.* Cambridge, MA: MIT Press.

Simon, Herbert A. 1962. "The Architecture of Complexity," *Proceedings of the American Philosophical Society,* 106 (Dec.), pp. 467–82.

Smets-Solanes, Jean-Paul and Benoît Faucon. 1999. *Logiciels libres – Liberté, égalité, business.* Paris: Edispher.

Smith, Marc. 1999. "Invisible Crowds in Cyberspace: Measuring and Mapping the Social Structure of USENET," in *Communities in Cyberspace,* Marc Smith and Peter Kollock, eds. London: Routledge Press.

Smith, Marc, Jonathan J. Cadiz, and Byron Burkhalter. 2000. "Conversation Trees and Threaded Chats," in *Proceedings of Computer Supported Cooperative Work.* ACM Press, pp. 97–105.

Smith, Michael, Joseph Bailey, and Eric Brynjolfsson. 2000. "Understanding Digital Markets: Review and Assessment," in Eric Brynjolfsson and Brian Kahin, eds., *Understanding the Digital Economy. Data, Tools and Research.* MIT Press.

Smith, Michael and Erik Brynjolffson. 2001. "Consumer Decision-Making at an Internet Shopbot: Brand Still Matters," *Journal of Industrial Economics,* 49:4 pp. 541–58.

Smith, Randall. 1986. "IBM's $300 million sale of Eurobonds is seen as move to loosen ties to Intel," *Wall Street Journal,* 10 Feb.

Sobel, Lon S. 2003. "DRM as an Enabler of Business Models: ISPs as Digital Retailers," *Berkeley Technology Law Journal,* Spring, 18:2, p. 667, 29p.

Sorensen, Alan T. 2000. "Equilibrium Price Dispersion in Retail Markets for Prescription Drugs," *Journal of Political Economy,* 108:4, pp. 833–50.

Sorenson, Olav, Jan Rivkin, and Lee Fleming. 2002. "Complexity, Networks and Knowledge Flow," University of California, Los Angeles – Policy Area, Harvard University – Competition and Strategy Unit and Harvard University – Technology and Operations Management Unit.

Spence, A. Michael. 1981. "The Learning Curve and Competition," *Bell Journal of Economics,* Spring, 12, pp. 49–70.

——— 1980. "Multi-Product Quantity-Dependent Prices and Profitability Constraints," *Review of Economic Studies,* Oct., 47:5, pp. 821–41.

Sporck, Charles. 2001. *Spinoff: A Personal history of the Industry that Changed the World.* Saranac Lake Publishing.

Spulber, Daniel F. 2003. "The Intermediation Theory of the Firm: Integrating Economic and Management Approaches to Strategy," *Managerial and Decision Economics,* June-July, 24:4, pp. 253–66.

——— 1999. *Market Microstructure: Intermediaries and the Theory of the Firm.* New York: Cambridge University Press.

——— 1996. "Market Microstructure and Intermediation," *Journal of Economic Perspectives,* Summer, 10:3, pp. 135–52.

Squire, Lyn. 1973. "Some Aspects of Optimal Pricing for Telecommunications," *Bell Journal of Economics and Management Science*, 4, pp. 515–25.

Srinivasan, Seenu, Rolph Anderson, and Kishore Ponnavolu. 2002. "Customer Loyalty in E-Commerce: An Exploration of Its Antecedents and Consequences," *Journal of Retailing*, Spring, 78:1, p. 5, 1/2p.

Stahl, Dale O. 1996. "Oligopolistic Pricing with Heterogeneous Consumer Search," *International Journal of Industrial Organization*, 14, pp. 243–68.

———. 1989. "Oligopolistic Pricing with Sequential Consumer Search," *American Economic Review*, 79:4, pp. 700–12.

Stahl, Konrad. 1982. "Differentiated Products, Consumers Search, and Locational Oligopoly," *J. Ind. Econ.*, 31, pp. 97–113.

Stallman, Richard. 1998. "The GNU Project," http://www.gnu.org/gnu/the-gnu-project.html

———. 1993. "Copywrong," *Wired*, July.

———. 1985. "The GNU Manifesto," *Dr Dobb's Journal*, March.

———. 1983. "Original announcement of the GNU Project," http://www.gnu.org/gnu/initial-announcement.html

Stanley, Ann, Dan Ashlock, and Leigh Tesfatsion. 1994. "Iterated Prisoner's Dilemma with Choice and Refusal of Partners," in *Artificial Life III*, C. G. Langton, ed. Redwood City: Addison-Wesley.

Stehman, J. Warren. 1925. *The Financial History of the American Telephone and Telegraph Company*. Houghton Mifflin.

Steinmueller, Edward W. 2001. "ICTS and the Possibilities of Leapfrogging by Developing Countries," *Int. Lab. Rev.*, 140:2, pp. 193–210.

———. 2000. "Virtual Communities and the New Economy," in *Inside the Communication Revolution*, Robin Mansell, ed. New York: Oxford University Press.

Stern, Louis W. and Frederick D. Sturdivant. 1987. "Customer-Driven Distribution Channels," *Harvard Business Review*, 65:4, pp. 34–41.

Stigler, Georges J. 1961. "The Economics of Information," *J. Polit. Economy*, 69, pp. 213–25.

Stiglitz, Joseph E. 1989. "Imperfect Information in the Product Market," in R. Schmalensee and R. D. Willig, eds., *Handbook of Industrial Organization*. New York: North-Holland, pp. 769–847.

Stoughton, Neal, Kit Pong Wong, and Josef Zechner. 2001 "IPOs and Product Quality," *J. Bus.*, 74:3, pp. 375–408.

Strahilevitz, Lior. 2003. "Charismatic Code, Social Norms, and the Emergence of Cooperation on the File-Swapping Networks," *Virginia Law Review*, 89.

Strausz, Roland. 2003. "Honest Certification and the Threat of Capture," Free University of Berlin.

———. 2003. "Honest Certification and the Threat of Capture," Departmental Working Papers, Freie Universitat, Fachbereich Wirtschaftswissenschaften.

Stromberg, David. 2002. "Mass Media Competition, Political Competition, and Public Policy," *Review of Economic Studies*, 71:1, pp. 265–84.

Stuart, Charles. 1979. "Search and the Spatial Organization of Trading," in *Studies in the Economics of Search*, S. Lippeman and J. J. McCall, eds. Amsterdam: North Holland.

Sturgeon, Timothy J. 2002. "Modular Production Networks: A New American Model of Industrial Organization," *Industrial and Corporate Change*, 11:3, pp. 451–96.

Sundararajan, Arun. 2004. "Managing Digital Piracy: Pricing and Protection," *Information Systems Research*, 15(3), pp. 287–304.

Surowiecki, James. 2002. "The New Economy Was a Myth, Right ?," *Wired*, July.

Syam, Niladri B. and Benedict G. C. Dellaert. 2002. "Consumer-Producer Interaction: A Strategic Analysis of the Market for Customized Products," Working Paper, University of Houston – C. T. Bauer College of Business and University of Maastricht (formerly University of Limburg) – Department of Marketing.

Tachiki, Dennis; Satoshi Hamaya, and Koh Yukawa, 2004. "Diffusion and Impacts of the Internet and E-Commerce in Japan," Irvine, CA: CRITO. http://crito.uci.edu/pubs/2004/GEC3Japan.pdf

Tan, Zixiang (Alex) and Ouyang Wu. 2003. "Globalization and E-Commerce I: Factors Affecting E-Commerce Diffusion in China," *Communications of the Association for Information Systems*, 10, pp. 4–32.

Tanaka, Tatsuo. 1996. "Possible Consequences of Digital Cash," *First Monday*, 1:2, August, http://www.firstmonday.org/issues/issue2/index.html (last accessed June 2006).

Tehranian, J. 2003. "Optimizing Piracy: The Uses and Limits of Intellectual Property Law Enforcement in the Cyberage," Working Paper, University of Utah.

The Economist. 2003. "Online advertising: Prime clicking time," 29 May.

The Economist. 2000. "Survey on E-Commerce," 24 Feb., http://www.economist.com/surveys/showsurvey.cfm?issue=20000226}, month Feb.

Thévenot, Laurent. 1998. *Pragmatiques de la connaissance*. In Anni Borzeix, Alban Bouvier and Patrick Pharo, eds., *Sociologie et connaissance. Nouvelles approches cognitives*. Paris: CNRS Editions, pp. 101–139.

Tigre, Paulo Bastos, 2003. "Brazil in the Age of Electronic Commerce," *Information Society*, 19:1, pp. 33–43.

Tigre, Paulo Bastos and Jason Dedrick. 2003. "Globalization and E-Commerce: Environment and Policy in Brazil," *Communications of the Association for Information Systems*, 10, pp. 189–217.

Tilton, John E. 1971. *International Diffusion of Technology: The Case of Semiconductors*. Brookings Institution.

Tirole, Jean. 1988. *The Theory of Industrial Organization*. MIT Press.

Trivers, Robert. 1971. "The Evolution of Reciprocal Altruism," *Quarterly Review of Biology*, 46, pp. 35–57.

Tumulty, Brian. 2003a. "Age bias claim tested in IBM pension conversion case," *Gannett News Service*, 5 June.

2003b. "Documents reveal IBM's reason for pension-plan change: saving money," *Gannett News Service*, 5 June.

Tung, Lai Lai, Puay Leng, Jennifer Tan, Pei Jin, Tartrice Chia, Yeow Leng Koh, and Hwee Lee Yeo. 2001. "An Empirical Investigation of Virtual Communities and Trust," *Proceedings of the 22nd International Conference on Information Systems*, pp. 307–20.

Tuomi, Ilka. 2001. "Internet, Innovation, and Open Source: Actors in the Network," *First Monday*, 6(1), 8 Jan.

2000. "Learning from Linux: Internet Innovation and the New Economy," Working Paper (Feb.). [Available at: http://www.jrc.es/~tuomiil/articles/LearningFromLinux.pdf]

Turowski, Klaus. 2002. "Agent-Based E-Commerce in Case of Mass Customization," *International Journal of Production Economics*, January, 75:1-2, pp. 69–8.

Uchitelle, Louis. 1990. "Unequal pay widespread in US," *New York Times*, 14 Aug.

Ueda, Masako. 2002. "Banks versus Venture Capital," CEPR Discussion Paper 3411.

2004. "Banks versus Venture Capital: Project Evaluation, Screening, and Expropriation," *J. Finance*, 59:2, pp. 601–21.

UNCTAD. 2004. *E-Commerce and Development Report*, http://www.unctad.org/

UNO. 1999. *Human Development Report*, chapter 2, "New Technologies and the Global Race for Knowledge," United Nations Development Program, http://www.undp.org

US Census Bureau. 2003. *Statistical Abstract of the United States: 2003.* Government Printing Office.

US Department of Commerce, Economics and Statistics Administration. 2003. *The Digital Economy 2003*, online at https://www.esa.doc.gov/2003.cfm

US Securities and Exchange Commission. 2000. "Electronic Communications Networks and After-Hours Trading".

Varian, Hal R. 2004. "System Reliability and Free Riding," University of California Berkeley Working Paper.

1997. "Buying, Sharing and Renting Information Goods," Working Paper, School of Information Management and Systems, University of California at Berkeley, May.

1994. "Sequential Provision of Public Goods," *Journal of Public Economics*, 53, pp. 165–86.

1980. "A Model of Sales," *American Economic Review*, 70:4, pp. 651–9.

Velkovska, Julia. 2002. "L'intimité anonyme dans les conversations électroniques sur les webchats," *Sociologie du travail*, 44:2.

Verity, John. 1994. "Truck Lanes for the Info Highway. CommerceNet, a bazaar for Silicon Valley, may help shape a far larger business infrastructure," *Business Week*, 18 April.

Verity, John and Hof Robert. 1994. "The Internet: How it will change the way you do business," *Business Week*, 14 Nov.

Vickrey, William. 1961. "Counterspeculation, Auctions and Competitive Sealed Tenders," *Journal of Finance*, 16, pp. 8–37.

Vincent, Daniel. 1995. "Bidding Off the Wall: Why Reserve Prices May Be Kept Secret," *Journal of Economic Theory*, 65, pp. 75–84.

Viswanathan, Suresh and James J. D. Wang. 2002. "Market Architecture: Limit-Order Books versus Dealership Markets," *Journal of Financial Markets*, 5, pp. 127–67.

Vivant, Michel. 1993. "Une épreuve de vérité pour les droits de propriété intellectuelle: le développement de l'informatique," in *L'avenir de la propriété intellectuelle*. Paris: Librairies Techniques, collection le Droit des Affaires.

Voigt, Stephan (ed). 2003. *Constitutional Political Economy*, Cheltenham: Edward Elgar Pub., The International Library of Critical Writings in Economics series, vol. 166.

von Hippel, Eric A. 2004. *Open, Distributed Innovation*. Cambridge, MA: MIT Press.

——— 2002. "Open Source Projects as Horizontal Innovation Networks – by and for Users," Working Paper, Massachusetts Institute of Technology (MIT) – Sloan School of Management.

——— 2002. "Horizontal Innovation Networks – by and for Users," Cambridge, MA, Massachussetts Institute of Technology, Sloan School of Management, Working Paper no. 4366–02, June.

——— 2001. "Learning from Open-Source Software," *MIT Sloan Management Review*, Summer.

——— 1988. *The Sources of Innovation*. New York: Oxford University Press.

von Hippel, Eric A. and Karim Lakhani. 2001. "How Open Source Software Works: 'Free' User-to-User Assistance?," Working Paper, Massachusetts Institute of Technology (MIT) – Sloan School of Management.

von Hippel, Eric A. and Georg von Krogh. 2003. "Open Source Software and the 'Private-Collective' Innovation Model: Issues for Organization Science," *Organization Science*, 14:2.

von Krogh, Georg, Sebastian Spaeth, and Karim R. Lakhani. 2003. "Community, Joining, and Specialization in Open Source Software Innovation: A Case Study," *Research Policy*, 32(7), pp. 1217–41.

von Krogh, Georg and Eric A. von Hippel. 2003. "Special Issue on Open Source Software Development," *Research Policy*, Jul., 32:7, p. 1149, 9p.

Vrechopoulos, Adam P. 2004. "Mass Customisation Challenges in Internet Retailing Through Information Management," *International Journal of Information Management*, Feb., 24:1, p. 59, 13p.

Vulkan, Nir. 1999. "Economic Implications of Agent Technology and E-Commerce," *Economic Journal*, Feb., 109:453, pp. F67–E90.

Wade, Robert. 1996. "Globalization and Its Limits: Reports of the Death of the National Economy Are Greatly Exaggerated," in *National Diversity and Global Capitalism*, S. Berger and R. Dore, eds. Ithaca: Cornell University Press.

Wallsten, Scott J. 2002. "Regulation and Internet Use in Developing Countries," World Bank Policy Research Group Working Paper 2979.

Wang, Joseph. 2003. "Is Last Minute Bidding Bad?" Working Paper, UCLA.

Ward, Michael R. 2001. "Will Online Shopping Compete More with Traditional Retailing or Catalog Shopping?," *Netnomics*, Sept., 3:2, pp. 103–17.

Wasko, Molly McLure and Robin Teigland. 2002. "The Provision of Online Public Goods: Examining Social Structures in a Network of Practice," *Proceedings of the 23rd International Conference on Information Systems*, pp. 163–71.

Watson, Jr., Thomas J. and Peter Petre. 1990. *Father, Son & Co.: My Life at IBM and Beyond*. Bantam.

Weise, Elizabeth. 2001. "Web sites pay to propel search engines," http://www.usatoday.com/tech/columnist/cceli026.htm, USA Today.

Welfens, Paul and Andre Jungmittag. 2003. "Telecommunications, Internet and Transatlantic Growth," in Claude Barfield, Gunter Heiduk, and Paul Welfens (eds.), *Internet, Economic Growth and Globalization*. Berlin: Springer.

Wellman, Barry and Milena Gulia. 1999. "Net Surfers Don't Ride Alone: Virtual Community as Community," in *Networks in the Global Village*, Barry Wellman, ed. Boulder, CO: Westview Press; also in *Communities in Cyberspace*, Peter Kollock and Marc Smith, eds. London: Routledge, pp. 167–94.

Wells, Rob, 2004. "US House Backs Court Cash Balance Pension Plan Decision," *Dow Jones International News*, 22 Sept.

Wessen, Richard. 1994. "Canter & Siegel: Stop Them Before They Spam Again!," *Netsurfer*, 24 June, http://earthsci.unimelb.edu.au/~awatkins//CandS.html

Weston, James P. 2001. "Competition on the Nasdaq and the Growth of Electronic Communication Networks," Working Paper, Jones Graduate School of Management, Houston.

——— 2000. "Competition on the Nasdaq and the Impact of Recent Market Reforms," *Journal of Finance*, 55(5), 2565–98.

Wharton, John. 1990. "Top 10 List: Intel's technological detours en route to success," *InfoWorld*, 9 April.

Whelan, David. 2001. "A Tale of Two Consumers," *American Demographics*, 23, pp. 54–7.

Whinston, Michael D. 1990. "Tying, Foreclosure, and Exclusion," *American Economic Review*, Sept., 80:4, pp. 837–59.

Whyte, William H. 1956. *The Organization Man*. Simon & Schuster.

Wilcox, Ronald T. 2000. "Experts and Amateurs: The Role of Experience in Internet Auctions," *Marketing Letters*, 11:4, pp. 363–74.

Wilson, John W. 1986. *The New Venturers: Inside the High-Stakes World of Venture Capital*. Addison-Wesley.

Wilson, Robert. 1977. "A Bidding Model of Perfect Competition," *Review of Economic Studies*, 44, pp. 511–8.

Wimmer, Bradley S., Anthony M. Townsend, and Brian Chezum. 2000. "Information Technologies and the Middleman: The Changing Role of Information Intermediaries in an Information-Rich Economy," *Journal of Labor Research*, Summer, 21:3, pp. 407–18.

Wolinsky, Asher. 1993. "Competition in a Market for Informed Experts' Services," *RAND Journal of Economics*, 24:3, pp. 380–98.

Wolverton, Troy. 1999. "eBay Users Miffed by New Fees," CNET News.com, 20 Aug.

Womach, James P., Daniel T. Jones, and Daniel Roos. 1991. *The Machine that Changed the World: How Japan's Secret Weapon in the Global Auto Wars Will Revolutionize Western Industry*. New York: Harper Perennial.

Wong, Poh-Kam and Ho Yuen-Ping. 2004. "E-Commerce in Singapore: Impetus and Impact of Globalization," Irvine, CA: CRITO. http://crito. uci.edu/pubs/2004/Singapore_GECIII.pdf

World Bank. 2004. World Development Indicators Database Online. Washington, DC. http://publications.worldbank.org/ecommerce/catalog/product?item_id& =631625

Xiaoquan, Zhang M. 2003. "A Review of Economic Properties of Music Distribution," Working Paper, Massachusetts Institute of Technology (MIT) – Sloan School of Management.

Yi, Sang-Seung and Hyukseung Shin. 1992a. "Endogenous Formation of Coalitions Part I: Theory," mimeo.

1992b. "Endogenous Formation of Coalitions Part II: Applications to Cooperative Research and Development," mimeo.

Yin, Pai-Ling. 2003. "Information Dispersion and Auction Prices," Working Paper, Harvard Business School.

Yu, Peter K. 2002. "Bridging the Digital Divide: Equality in the Information Age," *Cardozo Arts and Entertainment Law Journal*, 20:1, pp. 1–52.

Zerega, Blaise. 1999. "Real men hire fabs: Chip companies are cutting costs by outsourcing," *Red Herring*, 1 Mar.

Zettelmeyer, Florian, Fiona M. Scott Morton, and Jorge Silva-Risso. 2001. "Cowboys or Cowards: Why Are Internet Car Prices Lower?," Working Paper, University of California, Berkeley – Marketing Group, Yale School of Management and University of California, Los Angeles – Anderson School of Management.

Zhu, Kevin, Kenneth L. Kraemer, Vijay Gurbaxani, and Sean Xu. 2006. "Migration to Open-Standard Interorganizational Systems: Network Effects, Switching Costs and Path Dependency," *MIS Quarterly*, 30, pp. 515–39.

Zingales, Luigi. 2000. "In Search of New Foundations," *J. Finance*, 55:4, pp. 1623–54.

Zysman, John. 2002. "Production in the Digital Era: Commodity or Strategic Weapon?," Berkeley Roundtable on the International Economy (1 Oct.), Paper BRIEWP147. http://repositories.cdlib.org/brie/BRIEWP147

Index

Printed in the United States
By Bookmasters